PHILIP'S

STREET ATLAS
East Kent

First published in 1989 by

Philip's, a division of
Octopus Publishing Group Ltd
2–4 Heron Quays, London E14 4JP

Second colour edition 2001
Third impression 2004

ISBN 0-540-07977-4 (hardback)
ISBN 0-540-07978-2 (spiral)

© Philip's 2002

Ordnance Survey

This product includes mapping data licensed
from Ordnance Survey® with the permission of
the Controller of Her Majesty's Stationery Office.
© Crown copyright 2002. All rights reserved.
Licence number 100011710.

Printed and bound in Spain
by Cayfosa-Quebecor

Contents

III   **Key to map symbols**

IV   **Key to map pages**

VI   **Route planning**

VIII   **Administrative and Postcode boundaries**

1   **Street maps** at 3½ inches to 1 mile

206   **Town maps** of Bromley, Dartford, Gravesend, Royal Tunbridge Wells, Sevenoaks and Tonbridge

209   **Index** of towns and villages

210   **Index** of streets, hospitals, industrial estates, railway stations, schools, shopping centres and universities

Digital Data

The exceptionally high-quality mapping found in this atlas is available as digital data in TIFF format, which is easily convertible to other bitmapped (raster) image formats.

The index is also available in digital form as a standard database table. It contains all the details found in the printed index together with the National Grid reference for the map square in which each entry is named.

For further information and to discuss your requirements, please contact Philip's on 020 7644 6932 or james.mann@philips-maps.co.uk

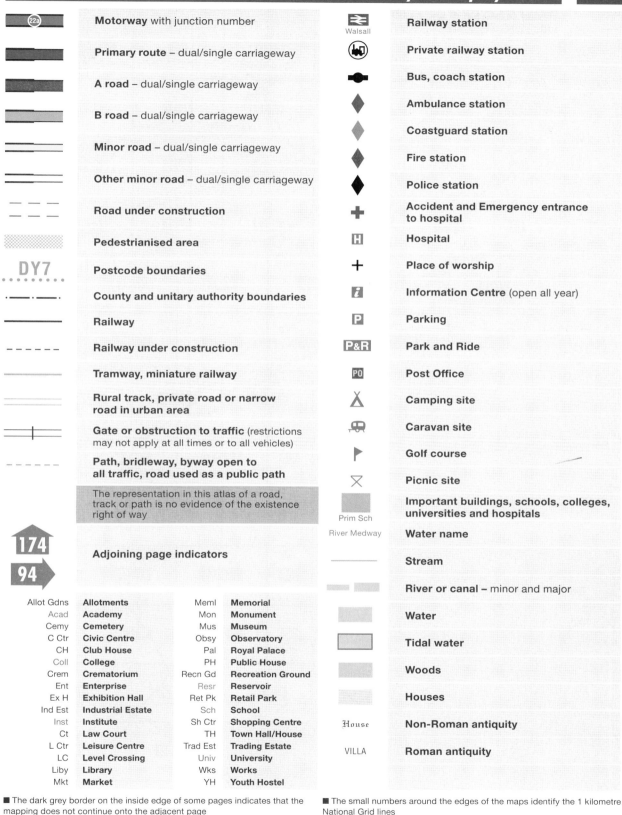

Motorway with junction number	
Primary route – dual/single carriageway	
A road – dual/single carriageway	
B road – dual/single carriageway	
Minor road – dual/single carriageway	
Other minor road – dual/single carriageway	
Road under construction	
Pedestrianised area	
DY7 **Postcode boundaries**	
County and unitary authority boundaries	
Railway	
Railway under construction	
Tramway, miniature railway	
Rural track, private road or narrow road in urban area	
Gate or obstruction to traffic (restrictions may not apply at all times or to all vehicles)	
Path, bridleway, byway open to all traffic, road used as a public path	

The representation in this atlas of a road, track or path is no evidence of the existence right of way

Adjoining page indicators

174

94

Allot Gdns	**Allotments**	Meml	**Memorial**
Acad	**Academy**	Mon	**Monument**
Cemy	**Cemetery**	Mus	**Museum**
C Ctr	**Civic Centre**	Obsy	**Observatory**
CH	**Club House**	Pal	**Royal Palace**
Coll	**College**	PH	**Public House**
Crem	**Crematorium**	Recn Gd	**Recreation Ground**
Ent	**Enterprise**	Resr	**Reservoir**
Ex H	**Exhibition Hall**	Ret Pk	**Retail Park**
Ind Est	**Industrial Estate**	Sch	**School**
Inst	**Institute**	Sh Ctr	**Shopping Centre**
Ct	**Law Court**	TH	**Town Hall/House**
L Ctr	**Leisure Centre**	Trad Est	**Trading Estate**
LC	**Level Crossing**	Univ	**University**
Liby	**Library**	Wks	**Works**
Mkt	**Market**	YH	**Youth Hostel**

Walsall	**Railway station**
	Private railway station
	Bus, coach station
	Ambulance station
	Coastguard station
	Fire station
	Police station
	Accident and Emergency entrance to hospital
H	**Hospital**
	Place of worship
i	**Information Centre** (open all year)
P	**Parking**
P&R	**Park and Ride**
PO	**Post Office**
	Camping site
	Caravan site
	Golf course
	Picnic site
Prim Sch	**Important buildings, schools, colleges, universities and hospitals**
River Medway	**Water name**
	Stream
	River or canal – minor and major
	Water
	Tidal water
	Woods
	Houses
House	**Non-Roman antiquity**
VILLA	**Roman antiquity**

■ The dark grey border on the inside edge of some pages indicates that the mapping does not continue onto the adjacent page

■ The small numbers around the edges of the maps identify the 1 kilometre National Grid lines

The scale of the maps is 5.52 cm to 1 km
3½ inches to 1 mile 1: 18103

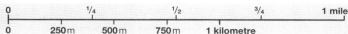

0	¼	½	¾	1 mile
0	250m 500m 750m	1 kilometre		

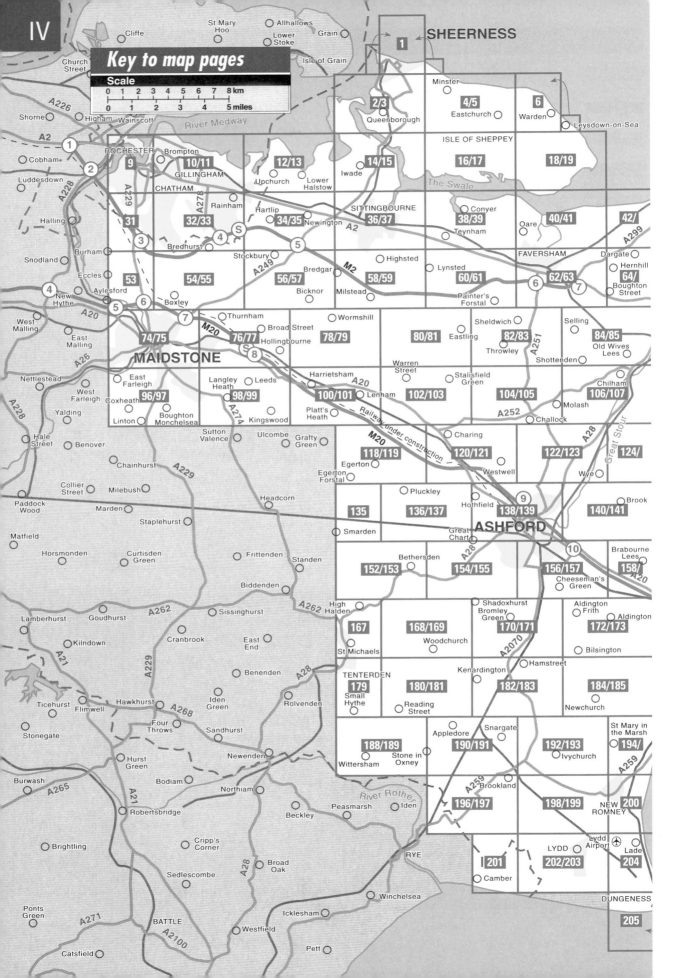

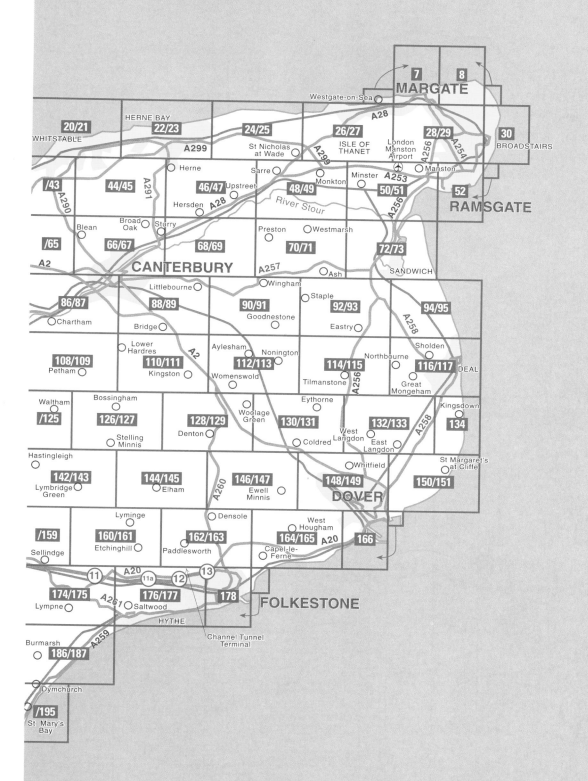

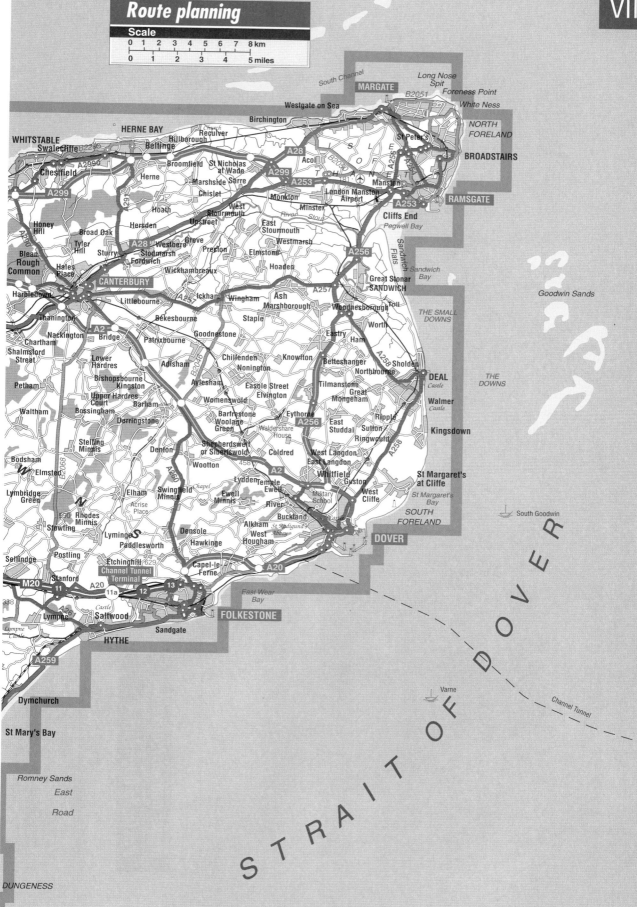

Route planning

Scale

0 1 2 3 4 5 6 7 8 km
0 1 2 3 4 5 miles

MARGATE

South Channel

Long Nose Spit
Foreness Point
White Ness

Westgate on Sea
B2051

Birchington

NORTH FORELAND

HERNE BAY

Church
Reculver

St Peter's

BROADSTAIRS

WHITSTABLE
Swalecliffe B2205
Chestfield
A2990

Hillborough
Beltinge

A28

Acol
B2050

Broomfield
St Nicholas at Wade
Herne
Marshside
Sarre
A299

I S L E
O F
T H A N E T

A256

A253

RAMSGATE

A299

Honey Hill
Broad Oak
Tyler Hill
Sturry
Blean
Rough Common
Hales Place

Chislet
Hoath
Hersden
A28
Westbere
Grove
Stodmarsh
Fordwich

Monkton
West Stourmouth
Upstreet
Preston

Minster

London Manston Airport
Manston

A253

Cliffs End

River Stour

East Stourmouth
Westmarsh

Pegwell Bay

Sandwich Flats

Goodwin Sands

HARBLEDOWN

CANTERBURY

Wickhambreaux
Elmstone
Hoaden

A256

Sandwich Bay

Great Stonar
SANDWICH

Thaninglon
Nackington
Bridge

Littlebourne
A257
Ickham
Wingham

Ash
Marshborough

Woodnesborough
Toll

THE SMALL DOWNS

Chartham
Shalmsford Street

Bekesbourne
Patrixbourne

Staple

Worth

A257

A2

Lower Hardres
Adisham

Goodnestone

Eastry
Ham

Betteshanger
Northbourne

A258
Sholden

DEAL
Castle

THE DOWNS

Petham

Bishopsbourne
Kingston
Upper Hardres Court
Barham
Bossingham
Derringstone

B2046

Aylesham
Womenswold
Easole Street
Elvington

Chillenden
Nonington

Knowlton

Tilmanstone
Great Mongeham

Ripple
Sutton
Ringwould

Walmer
Castle

Kingsdown

Waltham

Stelling Minnis

A256

East Studdal

St Margaret's at Cliffe

Bodsham
Elmsted

Denton

Barfrestone
Woolage Green

Waldershare House

Eythorne

West Langdon
East Langdon

St Margaret's Bay

Lymbridge Green

Rhodes Minnis

Shepherdswell or Sibertswold

Coldred

Whitfield
Guston

West Cliffe

SOUTH FORELAND

South Goodwin

Stowting

Wootton

458

A2

Military School

Elham

Chapel

Lydden
Temple Ewell

River

West Cliffe

DOVER

Swingfield Minnis
Acrise Place

Ewell Minnis

Bifrons

Buckland

St Radigund's Abbey

Settindge
Postling

Lyminge
Paddlesworth

Densole
Hawkinge

Alkham
West Hougham

A20

Etchinghill
Channel Tunnel Terminal

629

Capel-le-Ferne

East Wear Bay

Stanford

A20

M20
11

11a

12

13

FOLKESTONE

A23
Lympne

Castle
Saltwood

Sandgate

HYTHE

A259

Lympne Castle

Dymchurch

St Mary's Bay

Varne

Channel Tunnel

Romney Sands

East

Road

S T R A I T   O F   D O V E R

DUNGENESS

STRAIT OF DOVER

Greater London

Essex

Southend-on-Sea

Thurrock

Surrey

West Sussex

East Sussex

Major administrative and Postcode boundaries

Broadstairs
CT10
CT11
Margate
CT9
Ramsgate
Thanet
CT8
Minster CT12
Sandwich
Deal
CT14
Birchington
CT7
St Margaret's at Cliffe
Wingham
CT13
Dover
CT16
CT17
CT15
Herne Bay
CT6
Aylesham
Whitstable
CT5
CT2
CT3
Canterbury
CT1
Canterbury
CT4
Petham
Folkestone
CT19
Hawkinge
CT18
CT21
CT20
Shepway
Hythe
Faversham
ME13
Chilham
TN25
Wye
TN24
TN
28
Queenborough
ME12
ME11
Swale
ME9
Ashford
TN23
New Romney
TN29
Lydd
Sittingbourne
Ashford
TN26
Hamstreet
Grain
Newington
ME10
Kent
Bethersden
TN31
Medway
ME3
Maidstone
Lenham
Tenterden
TN30
Cliffe Woods
Gillingham
ME8
Chatham
ME7
Headcorn
TN27
Rochester
ME1
ME4
ME14
Maidstone
Staplehurst
Cranbrook
TN17
Tilbury
DA10
Meopham
DA12
Gravesend
DA11
DA13
ME2
ME20
Snodland
Aylesford
ME
16
ME15
Loose
Wateringbury
ME17
TN12
Tunbridge Wells
Hawkhurst
TN18
TN32
Dartford
DA2
Wrotham ME19
ME18
Hadlow
TN11
Tonbridge
TN3
Wadhurst
TN19
Hartley
DA3
Addington
Tonbridge & Malling
TN10
TN9
Royal Tunbridge Wells
TN2
TN4
Groombridge
TN6
Swanley DA4
DA1
DA6
DA9
Eynsford
DA
15
Sevenoaks
TN15
Otford
TN13
Sevenoaks
BR8
Dartford
DA14
DA8
DA7
DA16
Woolwich
SE18
DA17
DA18
SE28
SE2
Eltham
SE9
DA5
BR5
BR7
Orpington
BR6
Westerham
TN16
Edenbridge
TN8
TN14
TN7
Lewisham
SE12
SE3
SE7
Bromley
BR2
BR1

Scale

| 0 | 5 | 10 | 15 km |
| 0 | 5 | 10 miles |

County and unitary authority boundaries

District boundaries

Postcode boundaries

Area covered by this atlas

TQ TR

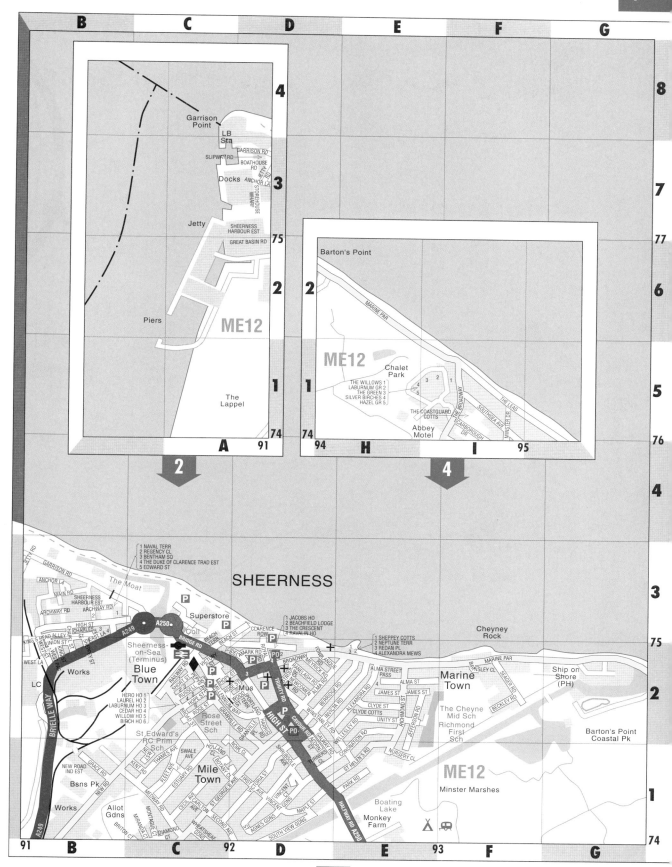

B　　　C　　　D　　　E　　　F　　　G

8

4

Garrison
Point

LB
Sta

GARRISON RD
SLIPWAY RD
BOATHOUSE
RD
FLEET LA

Docks

ANCHOR LA
STOREHOUSE
WHARF

3

7

Jetty

SHEERNESS
HARBOUR EST

75

GREAT BASIN RD

77

2

2

Piers

ME12

6

Barton's Point

MARINE PAR

ME12

2

1

Chalet
Park

THE WILLOWS 1
LABURNUM GR 2
THE GREEN 3
SILVER BIRCHES 4
HAZEL GR 5

3　2　1
4
5

1

5

The
Lappel

1

THE COASTGUARD
COTTS

THE BROADWAY
SOUTHSEA AVE
MINSTER DR
THE LEAS

74

Abbey
Motel

SCARBOROUGH
DR

A　　91

74

94

H

I　　95

76

2

4

4

1 NAVAL TERR
2 REGENCY CL
3 BENTHAM SQ
4 THE DUKE OF CLARENCE TRAD EST
5 EDWARD ST

SHEERNESS

3

JETTY RD
GARRISON RD

The Moat

ANCHOR LA
MAIN RD
SHEERNESS
HARBOUR EST
ARCHWAY RD
ARCHWAY RD

HIGH ST
CHAPEL ST
CHARLES ST
EAST LA
ROSE ST

Superstore

Cheyney
Rock

75

BREAD ALLEY
UNION ST
KING'S RD

A249
A250
Golf
BRIDGE RD
BEACH ST
BEACH ST

Clarence
Row

CLARENCE
ROW

1 JACOBS HO
2 BEACHFIELD LODGE
3 THE CRESCENT
4 RAVALIN HO

WEST LA

Sheerness-
on-Sea
(Terminus)

RAILWAY RD
SHORT ST
RUSSELL ST
ROSE ST

VICTORY ST
DELAMARK RD

ROYAL
BROADWAY

MEYRICK RD
FIELD
ANCHOR

1 SHEPPEY COTTS
2 NEPTUNE TERR
3 REDAN PL
4 ALEXANDRA MEWS

**Marine
Town**

Ship on
Shore
(PH)

LC

**Blue
Town**

HOPE ST
DENMARK RD

ALMA STREET
PASS
ALMA ST
ALMA ST

BARNSLEY CL

SEAGER RD
BECKLEY RD

2

Works

HERO HO 1
LAUREL HO 2
LABURNUM HO 3
CEDAR HO 4
WILLOW HO 5
BIRCH HO 6

Mus

HALFPENNY WAY
GRANVILLE RD
BROAD ST
RICHMOND ST
PORT ST
MILL ST

TRINITY RD
PO
HIGH ST
CAPOUR RD

PANELGATH RD
ROWMEN
ALMA RD

CLYDE ST
CLYDE COTTS
UNITY ST

BERRIDGE RD

ALEXANDRA RD
RICHMOND RD
JEFFERSON RD

JAMES ST
JAMES ST

The Cheyne
Mid Sch
Richmond
First
Sch

Barton's Point
Coastal Pk

Rose Street
Sch

St Edward's
RC Prim
Sch

ROSE ST

NEW
RD

SWALE
AVE

KENT RD
HOLLAND
RD
ALANY CL
MORE CL

INVICTA RD
WELLESLEY RD

WINSTANLEY RD

NURSERY CL

COWSTEAD RD

ST HELEN'S RD

ME12

NEW ROAD
IND EST
GRACE RD
NICY RD

THAMES AVE
FLEET AVE
ESTUARY RD

FIRST AVE
CECIL AVE
CARLTON
AVE
ST GEORGE'S AVE
SECOND AVE

VINCENT RD
VINCENT
GDNS
MAPLE ST

PARK RD

Minster Marshes

1

Bsns Pk

MEDWAY RD
MONTAGUE RD
MIRANDA RD

Mile
Town

AGNES GDNS

Boating
Lake

Works

Allot
Gdns

DIAMOND
CT
BRITON CT

WHEATSHEAF
GDNS

SOUTH VIEW GDNS

HALFPENNY RD
A250

Monkey
Farm

⛺ 🚐

91　　**B**　　**C**　　92　　**D**　　**E**　　93　　**F**　　**G**

74

3

A249
BRIELLE WAY

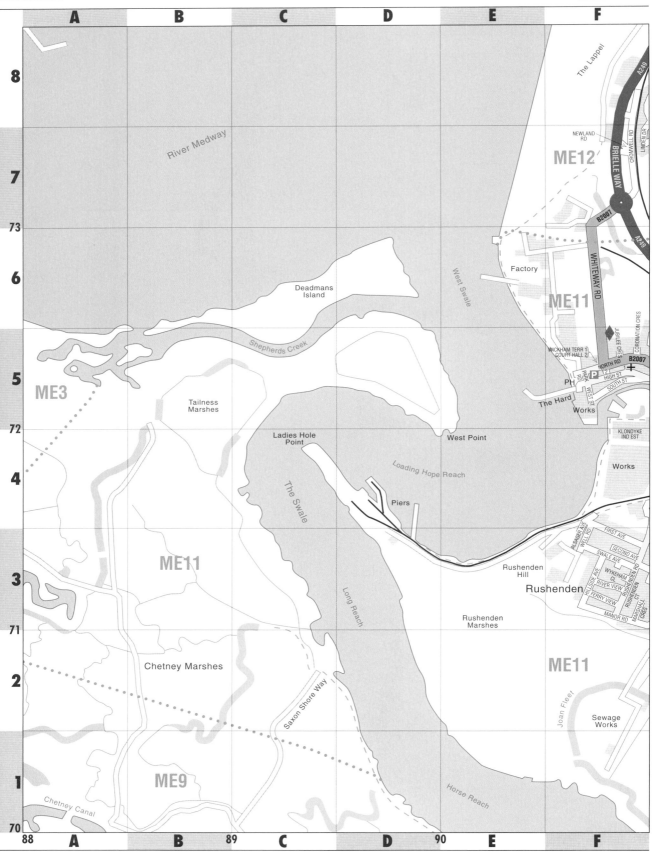

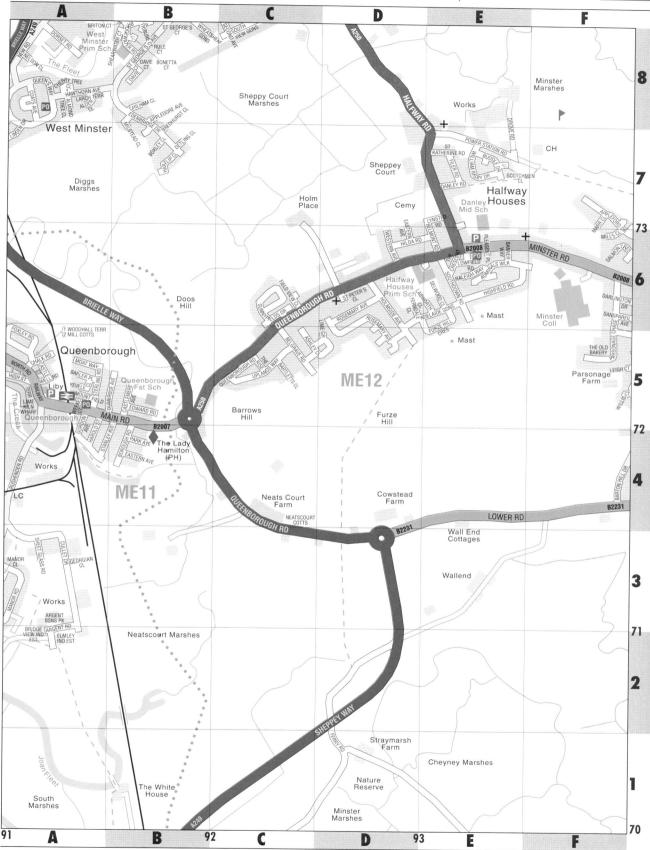

A   B   C   D   E   F

8

West Minster Prim Sch
BRIELLE WAY A249
Dorset Rd
New Rd
Nelson Cl
The Fleet
Cherry Tree
Queen's Way
Coats Ave
Linden Dr
Almond
Larch Terr
Hawthorn Ave
Alder Cl
PO
West Minster

Briton Ct
St George's Ct
Tribune Ct
Shearwater Ct
David Ave
Davie Ct
Bonetta Ct
Rule Ct
Wheatsheaf Gdns
Second Ave
South View Gdns

Sheppy Court Marshes

Minster Marshes

Works
CH

Diggs Marshes

Chilham Cl
Appledore Ave
Edenbridge Dr
Millstead Dr
Boxley Cl
Deling Cl
Hartlip Cl
Bredhurst Cl

HALFWAY RD
A250

St Katherine Rd
Power Station Rd
Drove Rd
St
Filer Rd
William Rigby Dr
Budds Dr
Danley Rd
Scotchmen Cl

7

Holm Place
Sheppey Court
Cemy
Danley Mid Sch
Halfway Houses

73

Doos Hill

St Peter's Cl
Field View Cl
Sunny Bank Dr
Eastern Ave
Western Ave
Hilda Rd
Belmont Rd
Lynsted Rd
Marg Cl
Mills Cl
Appleford Dr
P PO
B2008
Lowfield Rd
Banner Way
Raleigh Way
Southdown Way
Admirals Wlk
MINSTER RD
Salmon Cres
B2008

6

BRIELLE WAY
QUEENBOROUGH RD
Halfway Houses Prim Sch
Lime Gr
Rosemary Ave
Holmside Ave
Adelaide Gdns
Furze Hill Cres
Fernhill
Highfield Rd
Labworth Cl
Selwood Cl
Sellwood Cl
Mast
Minster Coll
Darlington Dr
Sanspareil Ave
Parsonage Chase
The Old Bakery

ME12

Foxley Rd
1 Woodhall Terr
2 Mill Cotts
Queenborough
North Rd
Chalk St
High St
Castle St
Well Rd
Yevele Cl
Moat Way
Barler Pl
Stirling Rd
Quarterpost Rd
Edward Rd
Park Ave
Eastern Ave
Borough Rd
Harold St
Stanley Ave
Gordon Rd
Castlemere Ave
Mount Pleasant Rd
Queenborough Fst Sch
Ashley Cl
Belgrave Rd
Uplands Way
Bartlett's Cl
The
Rosemary Ave
Mast

Parsonage Farm
Leigh Ct
Willis Cl

5

Liby
P
PO
RAILWAY
LIME KILN WHARF
The Creek
Queenborough
MAIN RD
B2007
A250
The Lady Hamilton (PH)
Barrows Hill
Furze Hill

72

Works
Rushenden Rd
LC
ME11

Neats Court Farm
Neatscourt Cotts
Cowstead Farm
LOWER RD
B2231
Barton Hill Dr

4

QUEENBOROUGH RD
B2231
Wall End Cottages

Manor Cl
Manor Rd
Sheet Glass Rd
Cullet Dr
Georgian Cl
Works
Argent Bsns Pk
Argent Rd
Bridge View Ind Est
Elmley Ind Est

Wallend

3

Neatscourt Marshes

71

2

Joan Fleet
South Marshes
The White House
A249
SHEPPEY WAY
Ferry Rd
Straymarsh Farm
Nature Reserve
Minster Marshes
Cheyney Marshes

1

70

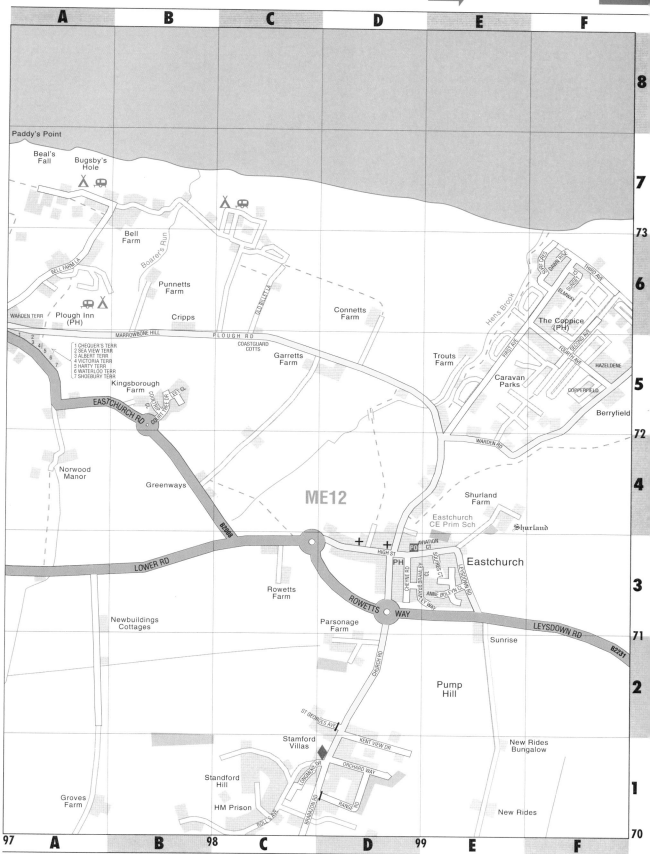

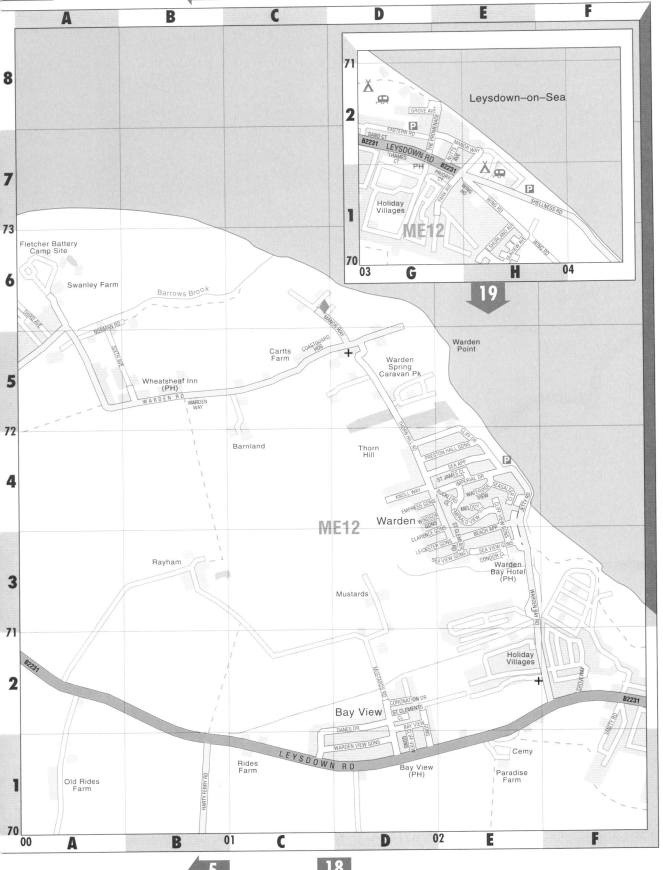

A B C D E F

8

7

73

6

5

72

4

71

2

70

00 A B 01 C D 02 E F

Inset map (top right):

71

Leysdown-on-Sea

2

GROVE AVE.
EASTERN RD
SAND CT
B2231 LEYSDOWN RD
THAMES CT
PH
B2231
PRIORY CT
PARK AVE
MANOR WAY
WING HO
WING RD
SHELLNESS RD

1

Holiday Villages

ME12

SHURLAND AVE
SEAVIEW AVE
WING RD

70
03 G H 04

19

Main map labels:

Fletcher Battery Camp Site
Swanley Farm
Barrows Brook
THIRD AVE
NORMAN RD
SIXTH AVE
Wheatsheaf Inn (PH)
WARDEN RD
WARDEN WAY
Cartts Farm
COASTGUARD HOS
MANOR WAY
Warden Spring Caravan Pk
Warden Point
Barnland
Thorn Hill
THORN HILL RD
CLIFF DR
Preston Hall Gdns
SEA APP
St James Cl
IMPERIAL DR
KNOLL WAY
WATERSIDE
SEASALTER CL
JETTY RD
BUCKLERS CL
EMPRESS GDNS
MELODY
EMERALD VIEW
WINDSOR GDNS
CLIFF VIEW GDNS
Warden
CLARENCE GDNS
ST CLEMENTS RD
BEACH APP
LEICESTER GDNS
SEA VIEW GDNS
CONDOR CL
SEA VIEW GDNS
ME12
Warden Bay Hotel (PH)
Rayham
Mustards
WARDEN BAY RD
Holiday Villages
71
B2231
2
CORONATION DR
ST CLEMENTS CL
Bay View
MUSTARDS RD
GROVE WAY
VANITY RD
B2231
DANES DR
BAY VIEW GDNS
WARDEN VIEW GDNS
LEYSDOWN RD
Cemy
Old Rides Farm
HARTY FERRY RD
Rides Farm
Bay View (PH)
Paradise Farm
1
70

E F G H I J

Westgate-on-Sea   Ledge Point   St Mildred's Bay   CT9

71

2

1 COURTLANDS WAY
2 BEACH HOUSE MEWS
3 ADRIAN MEWS
4 CONIFER CT
5 WATERSIDE DR
6 SUSSEX MANSIONS
7 BEACH RISE

PALM CT 1
ST MAWES 2
ALMARINA 3
IVYSIDE 4
SAN REMO 5
KIMBERLEY CT 6
BARCLAY CT 7
DANEHURST 8
RANDOLPH CT 9
SHERWOOD CT 10
FODBURY CT 11
ETHELBERT TERR 12

Westgate Bay

ST MILDRED'S GDNS
ST CLEMENT'S RD
THE SCHOOL

31   A   B   32   C   D   70

27

South Channel

RANDOLPH SQ 1
WELLINGTON GDNS 2
CAROLINE SQ 3
CLIFTON PL 4
CLIFTON GDNS 5

SANDPIPER CT 1
MANSION ST 2
HOMEFERN HO 3
COBB CT 4
WHITE HART MANSIONS 5
BROAD ST 6
FOUNTAIN INN CT 7
MARKET PL 8

Winter
Gardens

LB
Sta

FORT CRES

Pier

The
Harbour

Margate
Caves

NORTHDOWN RD

Tudor
Ho

The Bay

MARGATE

NEW CROSS ST 1
ALBERT TERR 2
THE CENTRE 3
GROSVENOR HILL 4
CHURCHFIELD PL 5
GATE QUAYS 6

Grotto

SHAKESPEARE PAS 1
BUENOS AYRES 2

Westbrook Bay

Dreamland
Fun Park

Royal Sch
for Deaf
Children

CT9

Margate

ALL SAINTS' AVE

ALL SAINTS
IND EST

Westbrook

Hartsdown
Park

ST PETER'S RD

33   E   F   34   G   H   35   I   J   70

J1
1 GEORGE WARREN CT
2 CHARLOTTE PL
3 SPARROW CASTLE
4 MILTON SQ
5 ARNOLD RD
6 OXFORD ST
7 HOMESTEAD CL
8 VICARAGE CRES
9 CONNAUGHT GDNS

10 THE ST JOHN BSNS CTR
J2
1 PUMP LA
2 COLLEGE SQ
3 COLLEGE WLK
4 ANCHOR HILL
5 GROTTO RD
6 GROTTO GDNS
7 ST JOHN'S ST

8 CHARLOTTE SQ
9 WINDSOR MEWS
10 PRINCES CRES
11 LAUSANNE TERR
12 VENTNOR LA

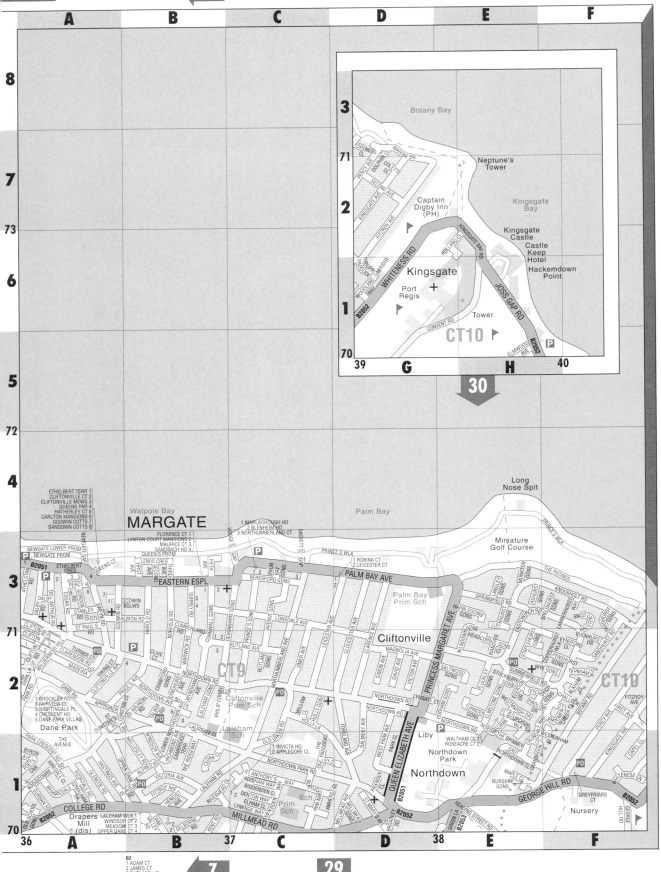

B2
1 ADAM CT
2 JAMES CT
3 RUTLAND HO
4 WESTMOUNT HO
5 HIGHFIELD CT
6 REBECCA CT
7 RICHARD CT
8 LEONA CT

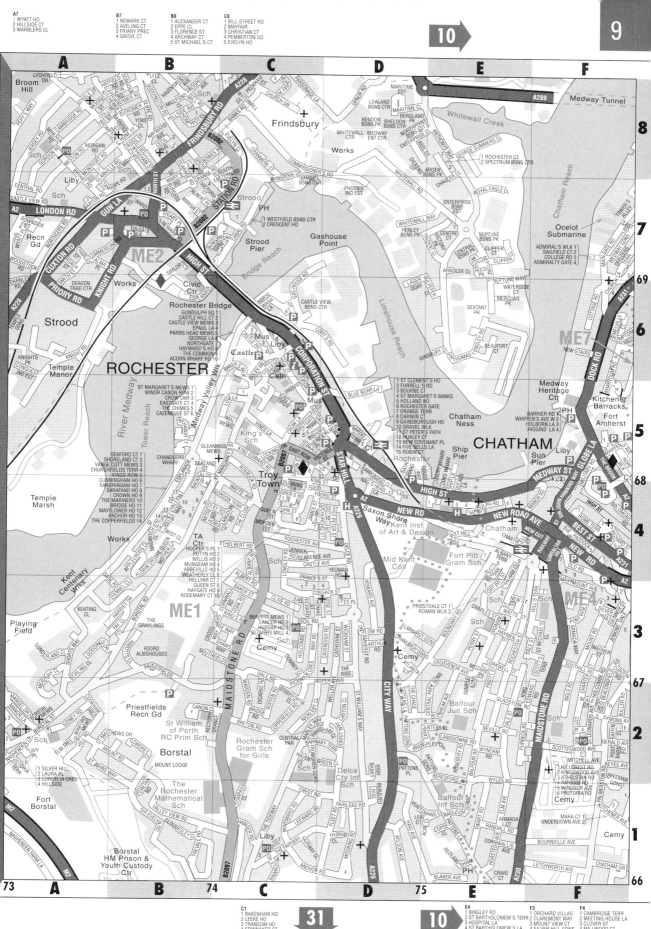

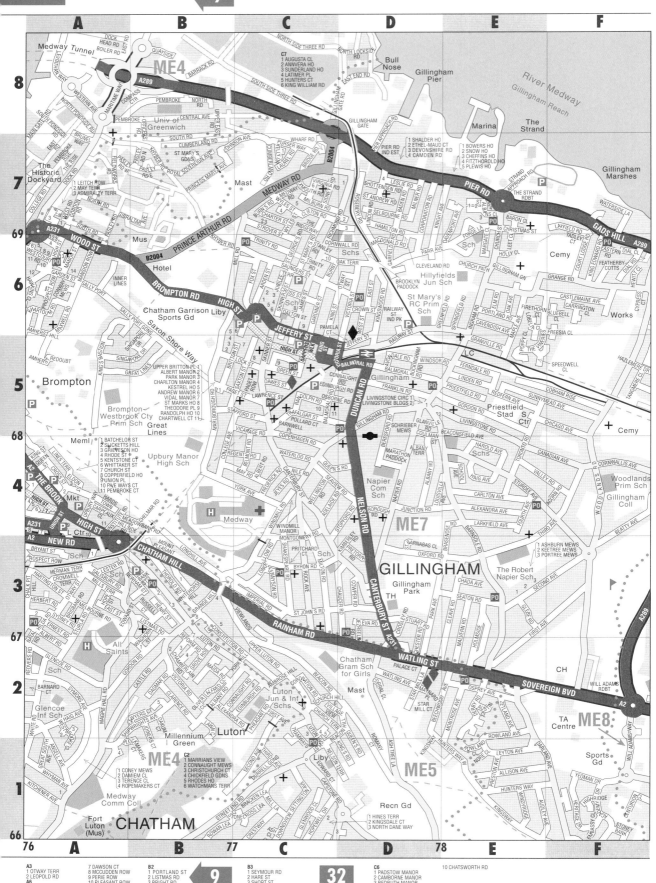

A3
1 OTWAY TERR
2 LEOPOLD RD
A6
1 VICTORY MANOR
2 TEMERAIRE MANOR
3 BARFLEUR MANOR
4 MIDDLE ST
5 CAMPERDOWN MANOR
6 RIVER ST

7 DAWSON CT
8 MCCUDDEN ROW
9 PERIE ROW
10 PLEASANT ROW
11 LENDRIM CL
12 MELVILLE CT
13 FLAXMANS CT
14 MANOR HO

B2
1 PORTLAND ST
2 LISTMAS RD
3 BRIGHT RD
4 COBDEN RD
5 SAILMAKERS CT

B3
1 SEYMOUR RD
2 HARE ST
3 SHORT ST
4 THE PICCADILLY
5 WEALDEN CT
6 OCELOT CT
7 LEONARD RD
8 CONSTITUTION HILL

C5
1 PADSTOW MANOR
2 CAMBORNE MANOR
3 REDRUTH MANOR
4 PENRYN MANOR
5 AUSTELL MANOR
6 TINTAGEL MANOR
7 GRAND CT
8 DEANE CT
9 WILL ADAMS CT

10 CHATSWORTH RD

A B C D E F

8
7
69
6
5
68
4
3
67
2
1
66

River Medway
Gillingham Reach

Copperhouse Marshes

Nor Marsh

Ferol Peak

Cinque Port Marshes

Horrid Hill

Walnut Tree Farm

Saxon Shore Way

OWE'S WAY
LOWER WOODLANDS RD
DANES HILL
GROVE
PLANTATION RD
GRANGE RD
COLYTON CL
B2004
A289
PH
GRANGE RDBT
Grange

Mill Hill

THE SPIERS
ME7
Lower Twydall

Sharp's Green

SHARP'S GN
LOWER RAINHAM RD
Visitor Ctr
Riverside Country Park

BUTTERMERE CL
HAZLEMERE DR
WINDERMERE DR
THIRL
Grench Manor
Allot Gdns

FENCHURCH RD
GRANGE RD
EASTCOURT LA

LADDS CNR

Mariners Farm

Cemy
Sports Field
CORNWALLIS AVE
CORNWALLIS RDBT
GREENVIEW WLK

Little London Farm

LOWER TWYDALL LA
MANOR CT

Three Mariners (PH)

BLOORS WHARF RD
Bloors Wharf

68

BREDGAR RD
BEECHINGS WAY IND CTR
NORTHBOURNE
1 BISHOPBOURNE GN
2 HEADCORN RD
TWYDALL ENT CTR
LITTLEBOURNE AVE
KENNINGTON
1

Pump Farm

Bloors Place

B2004

4

TEYNHAM GN
APPLEDORE
MEREWORTH
HARRIETSHAM
AYLESFORD CRES
ALLINGTON RD
N
WESTERHAM CL
LYNSTED RD
HARBLEDOWN MANOR
LEEDS SQ
GOUDHURST
BENENDEN MANOR
ASH CL
STAPLEHURST GN
MINSTER
PLUCKLEY
RUCKINGE
TON CL
CRANBROOK
BRADBURNE AVE
GIFFORD CL
HORSHAM RD
LAVENDER
KINGSNORTH RD

1 FORDWICH GN
2 BONNINGTON GN
3 SELLINGE GN

PUMP LA

Lower Rainham

3

Featherby Inf & Jun Schs
FEATHERBY RD
BROADWAY
SANCTUARY RD
CHILHAM RD
LENHAM WAY
ELMFIELD
EASTCOURT LA
LAMBERHURST GN
BRENCHLEY RD
LEWIS AVE
P
Liby
PO
SANDHURST
OUNDALE RD
WINGHAM
BEECHINGS WAY
WALTHAM
BROOM
WRIGHT CL
FRINSTED
HOLLINGBOURNE RD
DODDINGTON RD
BEECHING CL
EASTLING
RIVER VIEW
WOOTTON GN
THIRD AVE
AVON CL
LOWER BLOORS CL
67

Twydall
Twydall Schs
PIKEFIELDS
1 WOODCHURCH HO 2
TWYDALL
GREENVALE
CT
GNS
MEADOW
KING GEORGE'S MEMORIAL HO
BEGONIA AVE
PERHAM DN
NEWNHAM CL
STURRY WAY
ABSALOM CT
WOODCHURCH CRES
HAWTHORNE AVE
ROMANY RD
ASHLEY RD
Rainham Mark Gram Sch
LICHFIELD RD
HEREFORD
MONMOUTH CL
BLOORS LA
PEMBURY
ELY CT
CHESTFIELD CL
BEECHINGS CL
Thames View Inf & Jun Schs
ME8
2

Priory Sch
ABBEY RD
HALFWAY
THE CHASE
CECIL AVE
LOCARNO AVE
GENEVA AVE
SOUTH AVE
PRIM Sch
PHILLIPS CT
WILMINGTON
FRANKS
SELSTED RD
BLEAN
PATRIXBOURNE AVK
ELIZABETH CT
CALDEW
NORFOLK CL
CORSET
BEDFORD RD
DENBIGH AVE
ANSDALE RD
THE WILLOWS
MAYFIELD
PENFIELD
RENHURST
HIGH HOLMS
HIGH ELMS
CHILTON CL
Cozenton Park
BERENGRAVE LA
HARTPIECE
WERGATE CT
WOOLLEY'S CL
RUSHMEADOW CL
CHILDSCROFT RD
CHALKY BANK RD

SOVEREIGN BVD
1 TATSFIELD CL
2 KESTON CT

A2
PO
SUPERSTORE
LONDON RD
GUARDIAN CT

The Ice Bowl
GROSVENOR CT
BAILEY DR
VALENTINE CL
CENTURION CL
SCIMITAR CL
SARACEN CL
A278 HOATH WAY
COURTENAY RD
SHERMAN CL
GRANT CL
CHIEFTAIN CL
Works
EDWIN RD
MARSHALL RD
HUDSON CL
CHARLOTT
BOSTON GNS
VANCOUVER DR
JACKSON CT
JEFFERSON
A2 LONDON RD
CADEW
Playing Fields
SALISBURY RD
CENTURY RD
ROBERTS
DENBIGH AVE
BEDFORD RD
CRANFORD CL
BIRLING AVE
BLOORS LA
Liby
P
CENTURY RD
Rainham ⌖
QUINNELL'S RD
BROWN ST
SUFFOLK CL
LONGLEY RD
HOLDING ST
STATION RD
WEBSTER RD
DEVON
CUMBERLAND AVE
SOLOMON
TUFTON RD
GRANAR
HOTFIELD RD
B2004
SOMERFIELD
CAVERSHAM
PARKFIELD RD
STREETFIELD
STREETFIELD RD
PO
LC
HIGH ST A2
66

79 A B 80 C 81 D E F

F1
1 CREVEQUER CHAMBERS
2 RAINHAM SH CTR
3 GRESHAM CL
4 HARRISON CT
5 MAPLINS CL

11

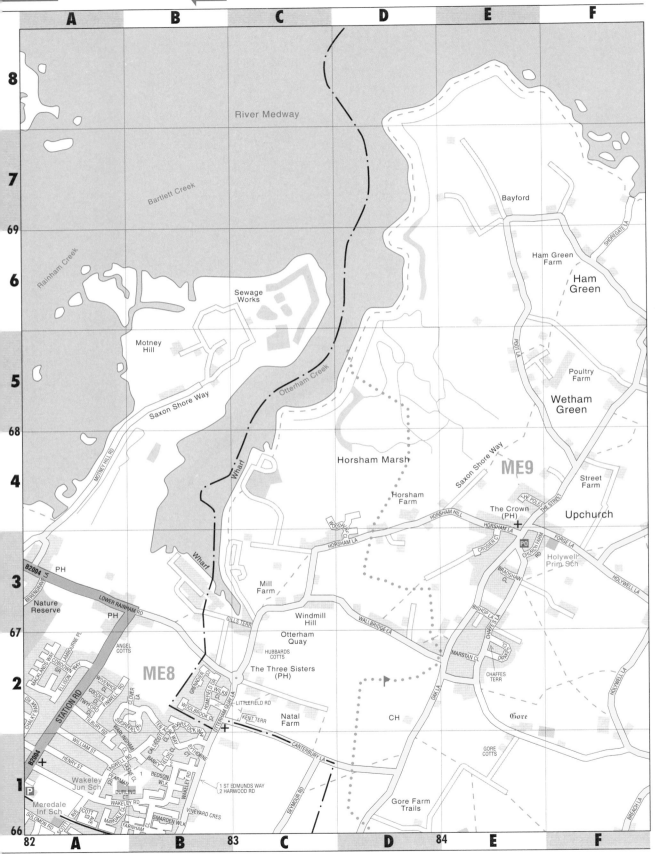

11 34

14

Greenborough Marshes

Milfordhope Creek

Slaughterhouse Point

The Shade

Stangate Creek

Milfordhope Marsh

Twinney Creek

Barksore Marshes

River Medway

Callows House

Halstow Creek

Funton Creek

Twinney Wharf

Twinney Acre

Frog Farm Cotts

Saxon Shore Way

Frog Farm

Funton Brickworks

Funton

Sewage Works

Great Barksore Farm

Saxon Shore Way

Greenways

Stray Farm

Little Barksore

Tiptree Hill

Bell Cotts

PO

THE STREET

CURLEW AVE

HEATH DR

SPWND DR

CHURCH PATH

CROUCH HILL

VICARAGE LA

THE CRESCENT

Holywell

Green Farm

PH

LANDRAIL RD

BURNTWICK DR

WESTMORLAND DR

CUMBERLAND DR

Lower Halstow

ME9

SEA VIEW COTTS

SCHOOL LA

Tiptree

WESTFIELD COTTS

Lower Halstow Sch

Elm Farm

BREACH LA

The Laurels

WARDWELL LA

Callum Hill

STICKFAST LA

Boxted Farm

BOXTED LA

HIGH OAK HILL

BELMOR AVE

Hawes Wood

Great Norwood

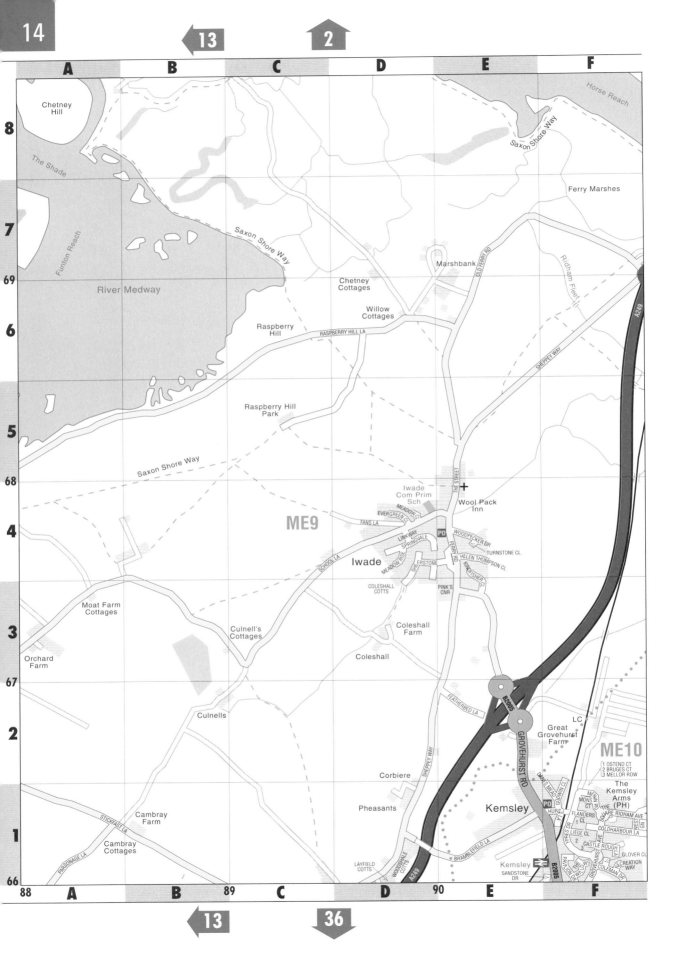

A B C D E F

8

Chetney
Hill

The Shade

7

69

Funton Reach

River Medway

Saxon Shore Way

Marshbank

Chetney
Cottages

Old Ferry Rd

Ferry Marshes

Horse Reach

Saxon Shore Way

6

Raspberry
Hill

Raspberry Hill La

Willow
Cottages

Ridham Fleet

Sheppey Way

A249

5

68

Raspberry Hill
Park

Saxon Shore Way

The Street

Iwade
Com Prim
Sch

Wool Pack
Inn

4

ME9

Fans La

Evergreen Cl

Meadow Cl

Linkway

Springvale

Meadow Rise

Sherstone

School La

Iwade

Woodpecker Dr

PO

Turnstone Cl

Ferry Rd

Helen Thompson Cl

Kingfisher Cl

Pink's
Cnr

Coleshall
Cotts

3

Moat Farm
Cottages

Culnell's
Cottages

Coleshall
Farm

Coleshall

Orchard
Farm

67

2

Culnells

Featherbed La

Sheppey Way

B2005

Grovehurst Rd

B2005

Great
Grovehurst
Farm

LC

ME10

1 OSTEND CT
2 BRUGES CT
3 MELLOR ROW

The
Kemsley
Arms
(PH)

Corbiere

Dane's Meadow

Kemsley

PO

Ware

Ridham Ave

Coldharbour La

Mons Cl

Flanders Cl

The Hurst

1

Stickfast La

Cambray
Farm

Pheasants

Liege Cl

Castle Rough

Glover Cl

Recreation Way

Coleman Dr

Grovehurst Rd

Pavilion Way

B2005

Parsonage La

Cambray
Cottages

Layfield
Cotts

Woodside Cotts

A249

Bramblefield La

Kemsley
Sandstone
Dr

66

88 A B 89 C D 90 E F

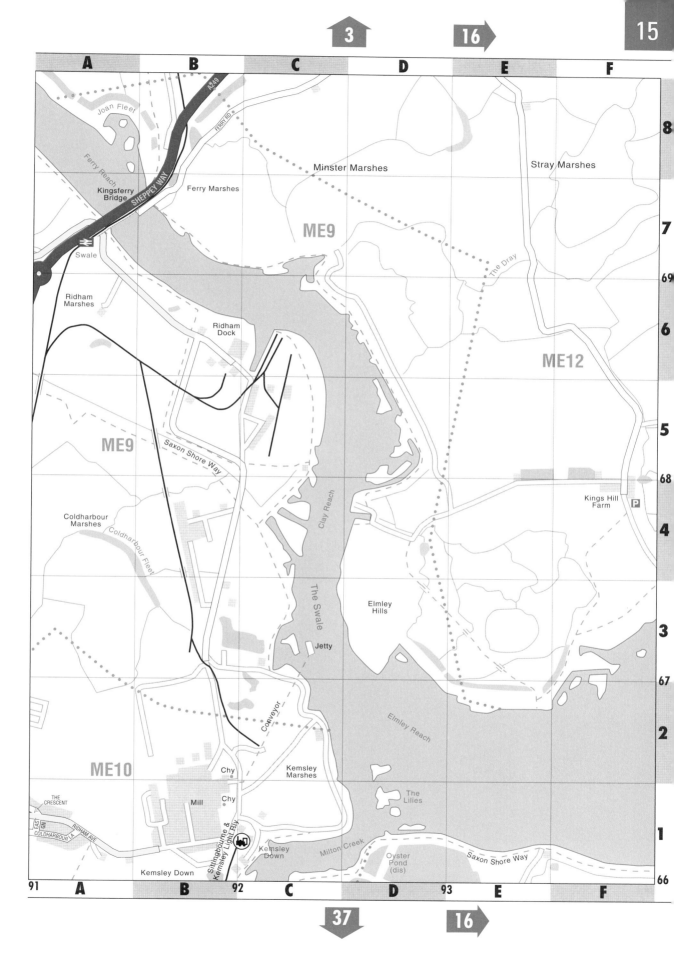

A   B   C   D   E   F

8

Joan Fleet

Ferry Reach

Minster Marshes

Stray Marshes

Kingsferry Bridge

SHEPPEY WAY

A249

FERRY RD

Ferry Marshes

7

Swale

ME9

The Dray

69

Ridham Marshes

6

Ridham Dock

ME12

5

Saxon Shore Way

ME9

68

Clay Reach

Kings Hill Farm

Coldharbour Marshes

Coldharbour Fleet

4

The Swale

Elmley Hills

3

Jetty

67

Conveyor

Elmley Reach

2

ME10

Kemsley Marshes

Chy

Mill

Chy

The Lilies

THE CRESCENT

EAST GW

RIDHAM AVE

COLDHARBOUR LA

Sittingbourne & Kemsley Light Rly

Kemsley Down

Milton Creek

Oyster Pond (dis)

Saxon Shore Way

1

Kemsley Down

66

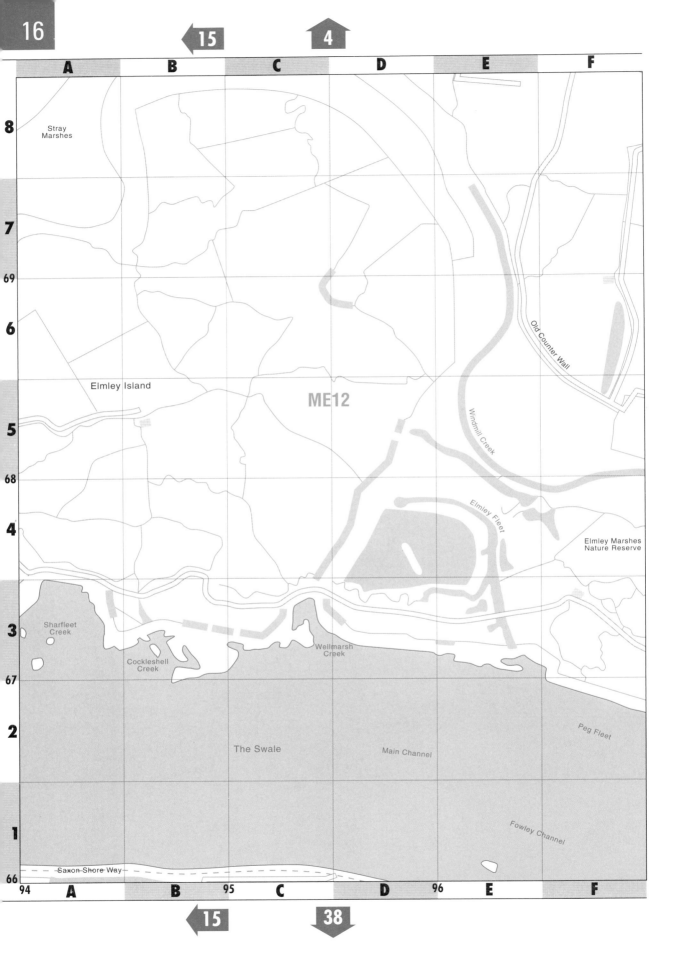

A   B   C   D   E   F

8

Stray
Marshes

7

69

6

Elmley Island

ME12

Old Counter Wall

5

Windmill Creek

68

Elmley Fleet

4

Elmley Marshes
Nature Reserve

3

Sharfleet
Creek

Cockleshell
Creek

Wellmarsh
Creek

67

2

The Swale

Main Channel

Peg Fleet

1

Fowley Channel

66

Saxon Shore Way

94   A   B   95   C   D   96   E   F

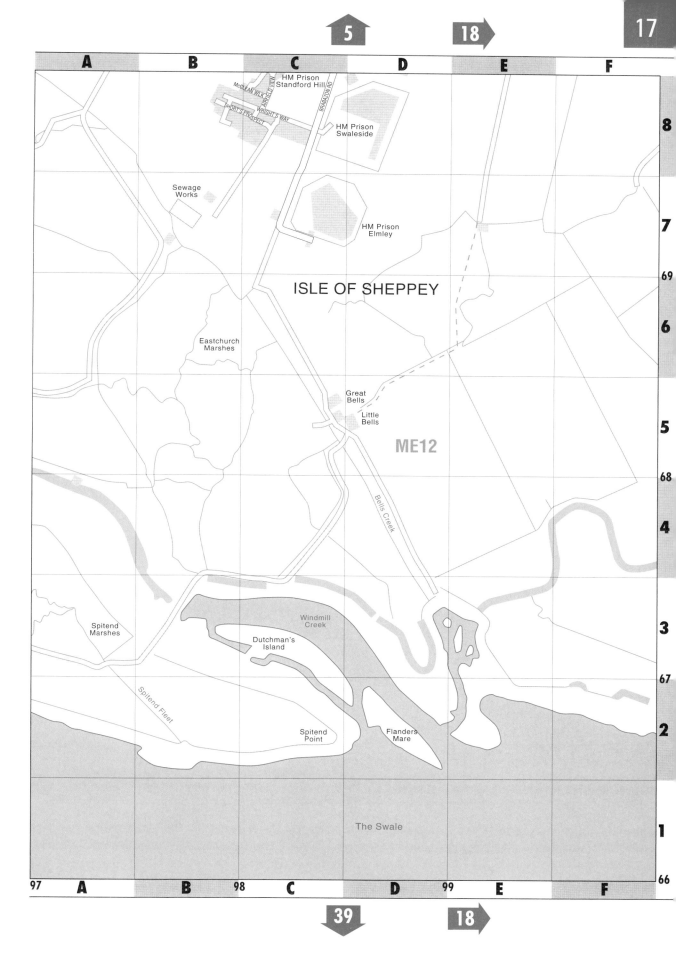

HM Prison
Standford Hill

McCLEAN WLK

FAIRFIELD VIEW

WRIGHT'S WAY

SHORT'S PROSPECT

BRABAZON RD

HM Prison
Swaleside

Sewage
Works

HM Prison
Elmley

ISLE OF SHEPPEY

Eastchurch
Marshes

Great
Bells

Little
Bells

ME12

Bells Creek

Spitend
Marshes

Windmill
Creek

Dutchman's
Island

Spitend Fleet

Spitend
Point

Flanders
Mare

The Swale

8
7
69
6
5
68
4
3
67
2
1
66

A   B   C   D   E   F

8

7

69

6

5

68

4

3

67

2

1

66

Capel Hill
Farm

Newhouse

Newhouse
Farm
Cottage

Leysdown
Marshes

Capel
Gate

Capel Fleet

ME12

Pump
Hill

HARTY FERRY RD

Harty
Marshes

Isle of Harty

Elliotts

Mocketts

Mocketts
Cottages

Sayes
Court

Park
Farm

Sayes
Court
Cottages

The
Swale

Lily
Banks

00   A   B   01   C   D   02   E   F

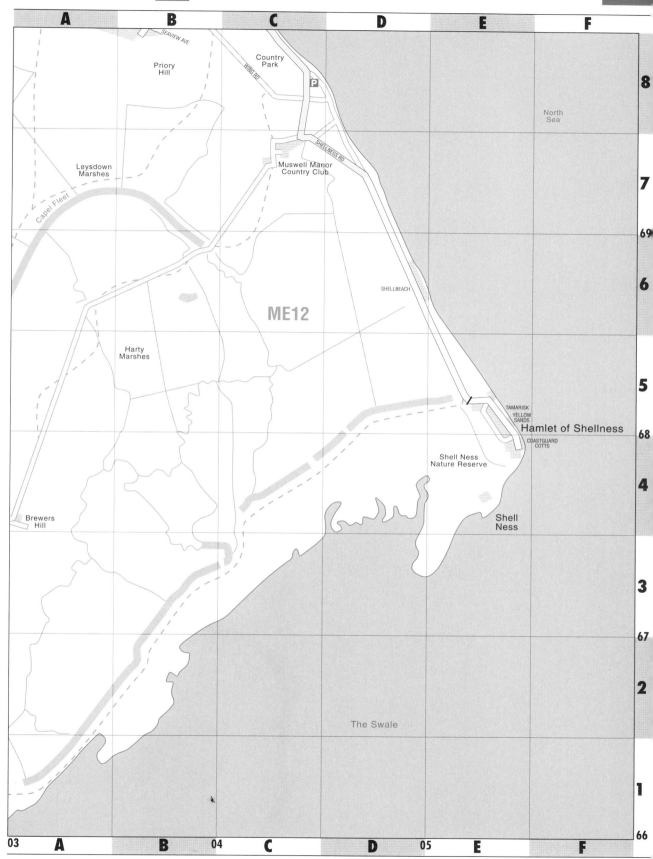

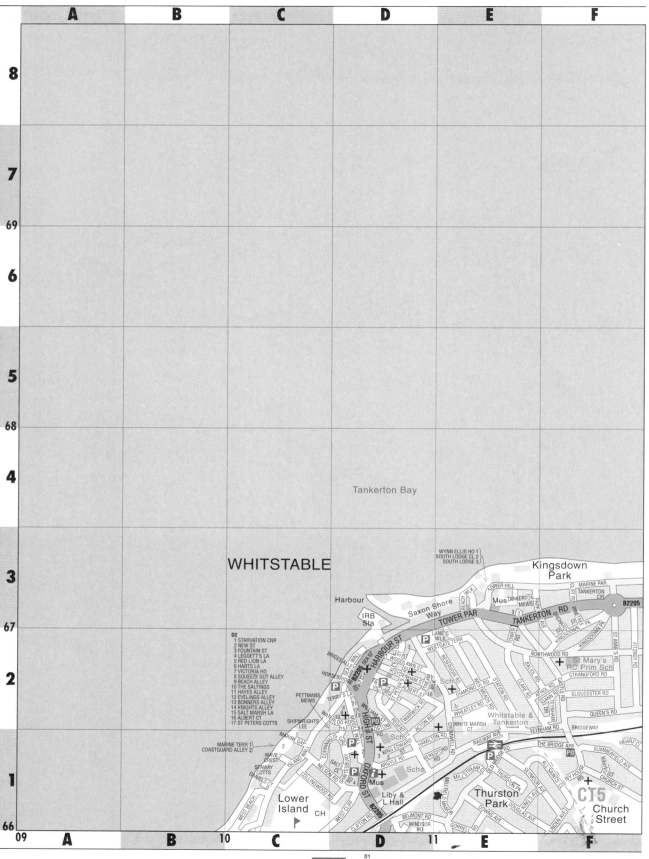

	A	B	C	D	E	F
8						
7						
69						
6						
5						
68						
4						

Tankerton Bay

WHITSTABLE

WYNN ELLIS HO 1
SOUTH LODGE CL 2
SOUTH LODGE 3

Kingsdown Park

Harbour

IRB Sta

Saxon Shore Way

TOWER PAR

TANKERTON RD

B2205

Mus Tankerton Mews

TANKERTON CIR

D2
1 STARVATION CNR
2 NEW ST
3 FOUNTAIN ST
4 LEGGETT'S LA
5 RED LION LA
6 HARTS LA
7 VICTORIA HO
8 SQUEEZE GUT ALLEY
9 BEACH ALLEY
10 THE SALTINGS
11 HAYES ALLEY
12 EVELINGS ALLEY
13 BONNERS ALLEY
14 KNIGHTS ALLEY
15 SALT MARSH LA
16 ALBERT CT
17 ST PETERS COTTS

HARBOUR ST

HIGH ST

St Mary's RC Prim Sch

Whitstable & Tankerton

MARINE TERR 1
COASTGUARD ALLEY 2

WAVE CREST

SEAWAY COTTS

DANIELS CT

COLLINGWOOD RD

OXFORD ST

Lower Island

CH

WEST BEACH

WEST CLIFF

Liby & L Hall

Mus

Thurston Park

CT5

Church Street

D1
1 REEVES ALLEY
2 KEMP ALLEY
3 SKINNER'S ALLEY
4 OXFORD MANS
5 OXFORD CL

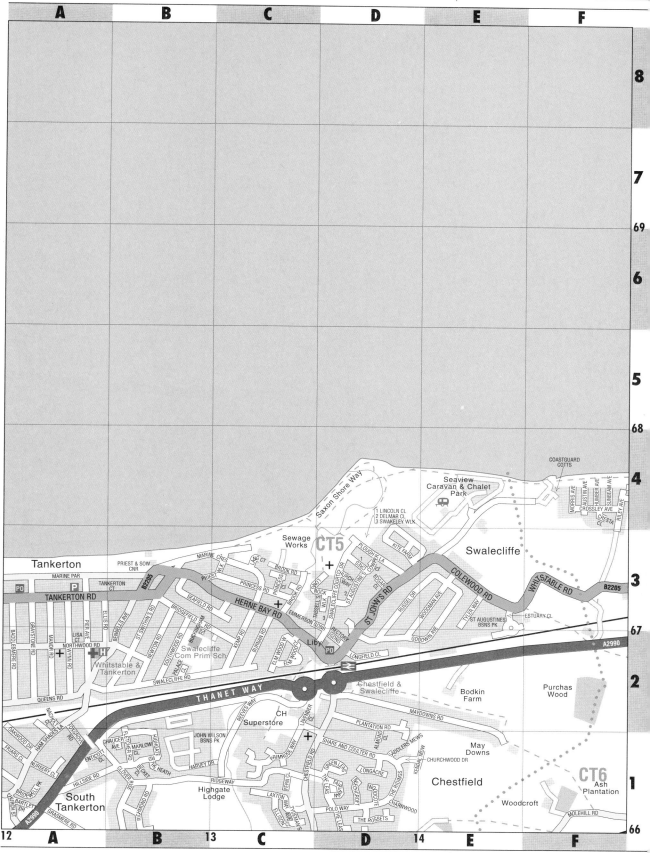

Grid references across top: A B C D E F

Grid references down right side: 8 7 69 6 5 68 4 3 67 2 1 66

COASTGUARD COTTS

Seaview Caravan & Chalet Park

Saxon Shore Way

Sewage Works

CT5

1 LINCOLN CL
2 DELMAR CL
3 SWAKELEY WLK

Swalecliffe

MORRIS AVE
AUSTIN AVE
HUMBER AVE
SUNBEAM AVE
CROSSLEY AVE
CRESTA CL
RILEY AVE

Tankerton

PRIEST & SOW CNR

MARINE PAR

TANKERTON RD
TANKERTON CT

Marine Cres

PLOUGH LA
KITE FARM

PRIEST WLK
PRINCESS RD

BROOK RD

SWAKELEY WLK
CHURCH WAY
ST AUGUSTINES RD
EDGAR RD

COLEWOOD RD

WHITSTABLE RD

B2205

HERNE BAY RD

SEAFIELD RD

PRINCESS RD
BROOK RD

RUSSELS WLK

SWALECLIFFE COURT DR
ST JOHN'S RD

RUSSEL DR
WOODMAN AVE

TYLER WAY

ST AUGUSTINES BSNS PK

ESTUARY CL

PO
PO

B2206

BRIDGEFIELD RD
BUCKINGHAM RD

KEMP RD

BURNIN RD

EMMERSON GDNS

RECTORY GDNS

GOODWIN AVE

A2990

ELLIS RD
PIER AVE
LISA CT
NORTHWOOD RD

BENNELLS AVE
ST SWITHIN'S RD
NEWTON RD
SOUTHWOOD RD

ELM WOOD V
ELM WOODS

Liby
PO

LONGFIELD CL

67

GRAYSTONE RD
MANOR RD
WYNN RD

H
Whitstable & Tankerton

Swalecliffe Com Prim Sch

PALACE CL

SWALECLIFFE RD

THANET WAY

Chestfield & Swalecliffe

Bodkin Farm

Purchas Wood

2

BADLESMERE RD

QUEENS RD

MAGDALA RD
FOXGROVE RD

REEVES WAY

CH
Superstore

LANCENDER

MAYDOWNS RD

OAKWOOD DR
FRIARS CL
NURSERY CL

HAM SHADES LA

ENTICOTT CL
CHAUCER AVE
FLETCHER RD
MARLOW RD
HIGHGATE

JOHN WILSON BSNS PK

PLANTATION RD

ALMOND CL

SADDLERS MEWS

KENDAL MDW
CHURCHWOOD DR

May Downs

BRIDEWELL PK
BARTLETT DR
CHURCH ST
A2990
GRASMERE RD

HILLSIDE RD
CLOVER RISE
BECKET RD
RICHARDSON RD

PYE HEATH

HARVEY DR
RIDGEWAY

PRIMROSE WAY

CHESTFIELD RD

SHARE AND COULTER RD

GREEN LEAS
FERN CL
FARMAN

LONGACRE

WOODCOTE
BEECHCROFT
THE RIDINGS

Chestfield

CT6
Ash Plantation

South Tankerton

Highgate Lodge

LAXTON WAY
ELLISON CL
YEOMAN'S

POLO WAY
CHARNWOOD

THE RUSSETS

Woodcroft

MOLEHILL RD

21

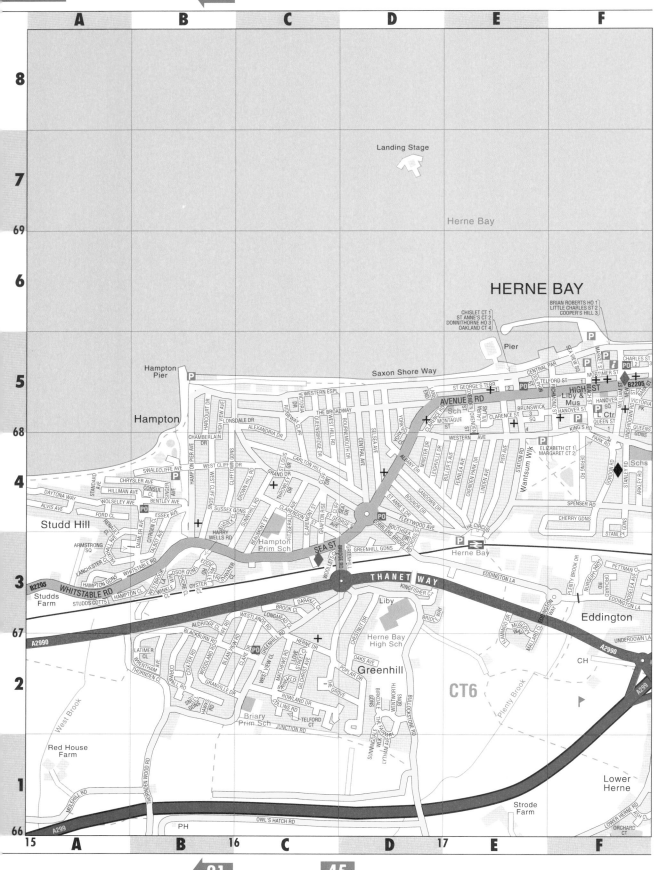

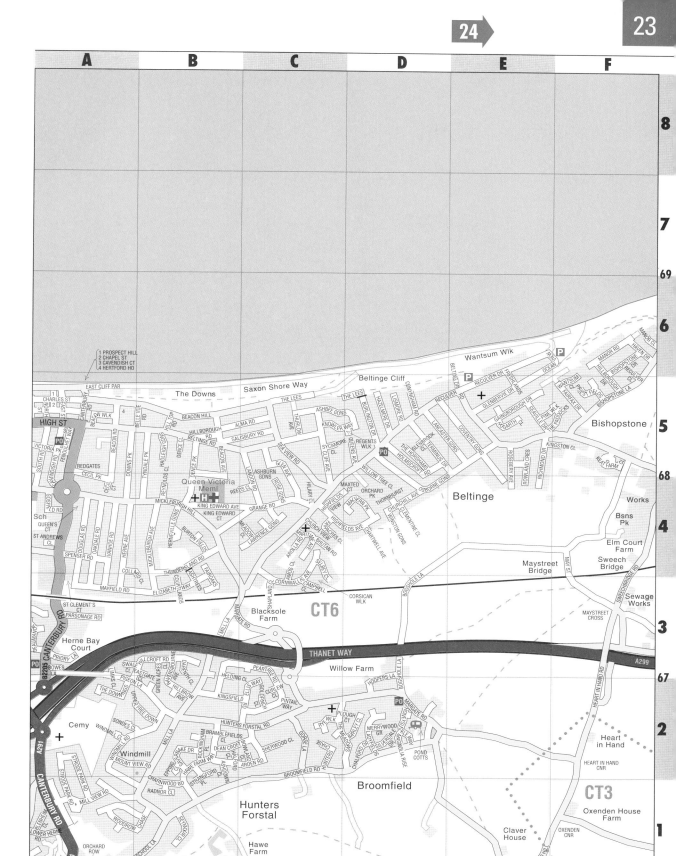

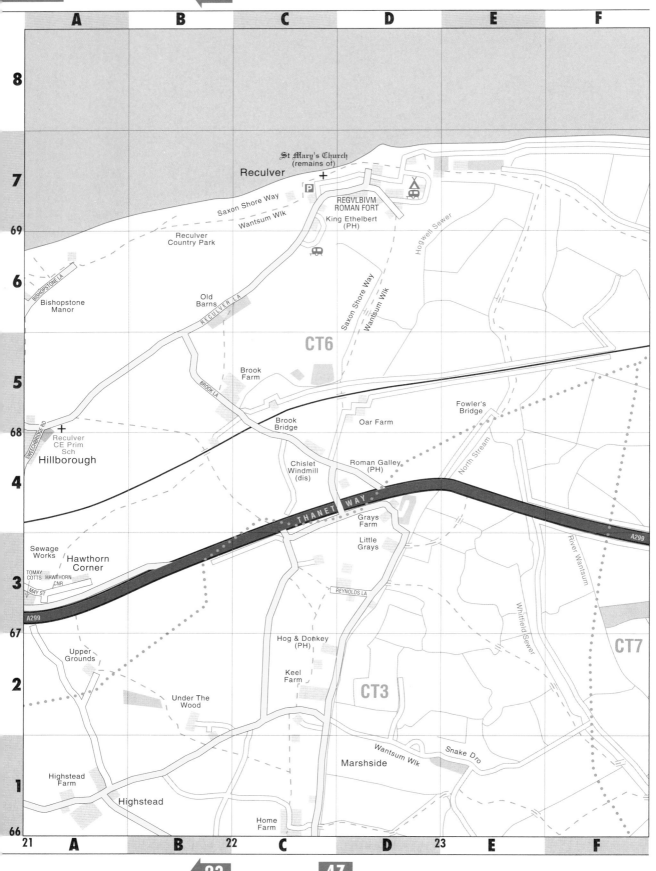

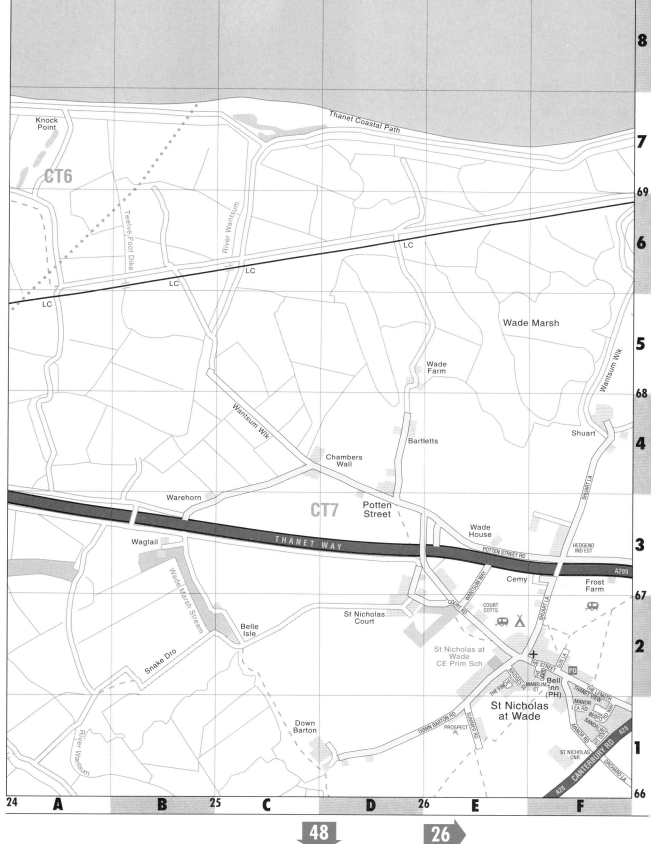

A　B　C　D　E　F

8

7

69

6

Knock Point

CT6

Twelve Foot Dike

River Wantsum

Thanet Coastal Path

LC

LC

LC

LC

Wade Marsh

Wantsum Wlk

5

68

Wade Farm

4

Wantsum Wlk

Shuart

Bartletts

Chambers Wall

Warehorn

CT7

Potten Street

SHUART LA

Wade House

POTTEN STREET RD

HEDGEND IND EST

3

67

Wagtail

THANET WAY

A299

Frost Farm

Cemy

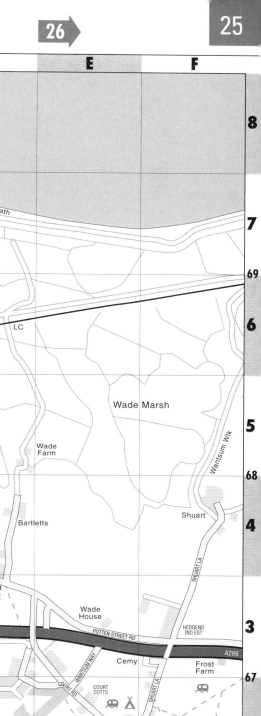

Wade Marsh Stream

Belle Isle

Snake Dro

St Nicholas Court

COURT RD

WANTSUM WAY

COURT COTTS

SHUART LA

2

St Nicholas at Wade CE Prim Sch

THE STREET

THE OAKS

SUN LA

PO

Bell Inn (PH)

THE LENGTH

MANSUM CT

THANET VIEW

BRIDGES CL

THE FINCHES CL

St Nicholas at Wade

MANOR LEA RD

BEDFORD RD

SANDALWD

MANOR RD

BELFORD

SIDE WAY

Down Barton

DOWN BARTON RD

PROSPECT PL

SUMMER RD

St Nicholas CNR

CANTERBURY RD

ORCHARD LA

A28

A28

1

66

River Wantsum

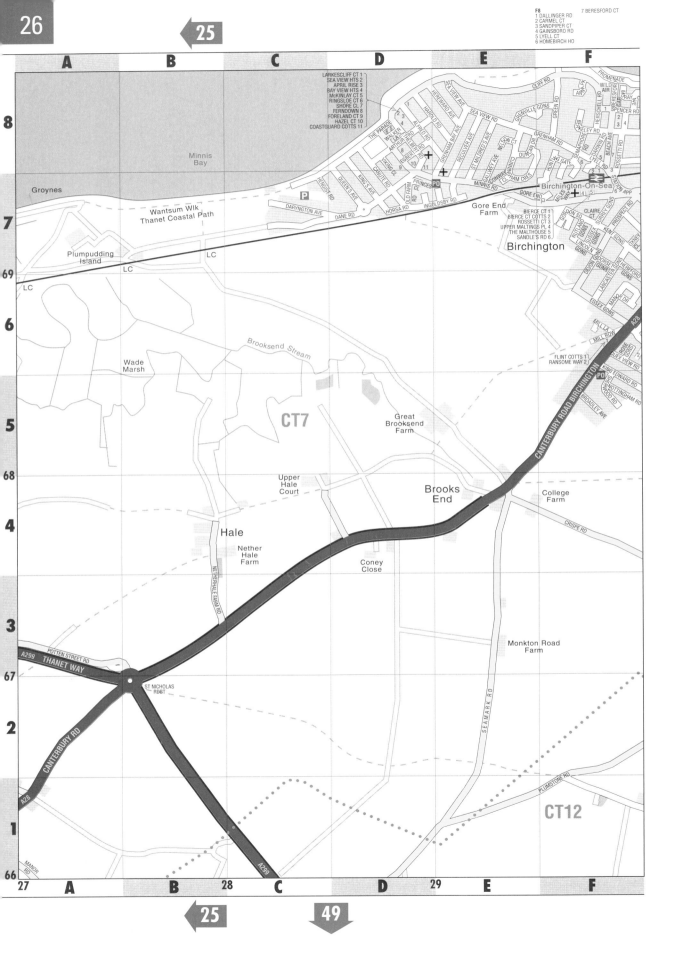

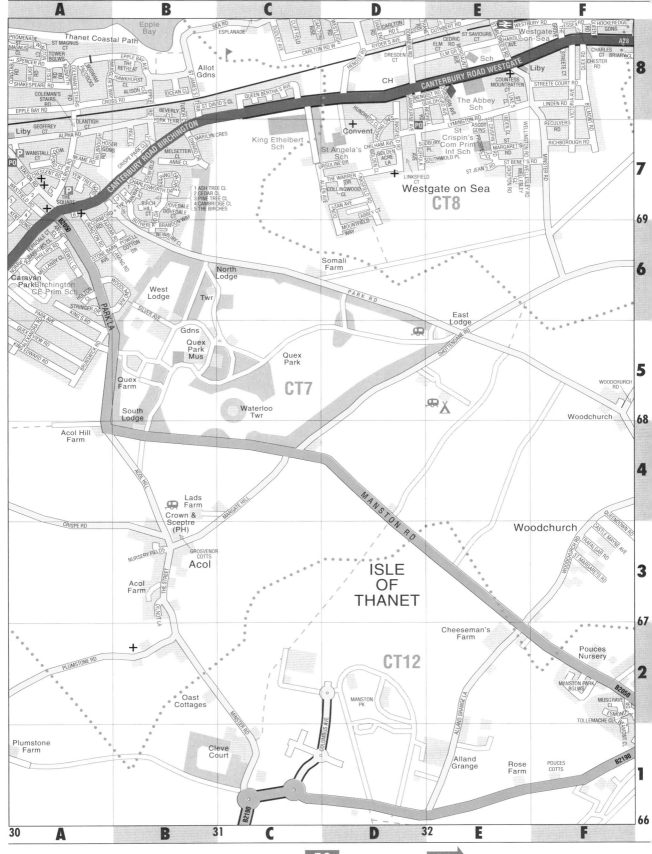

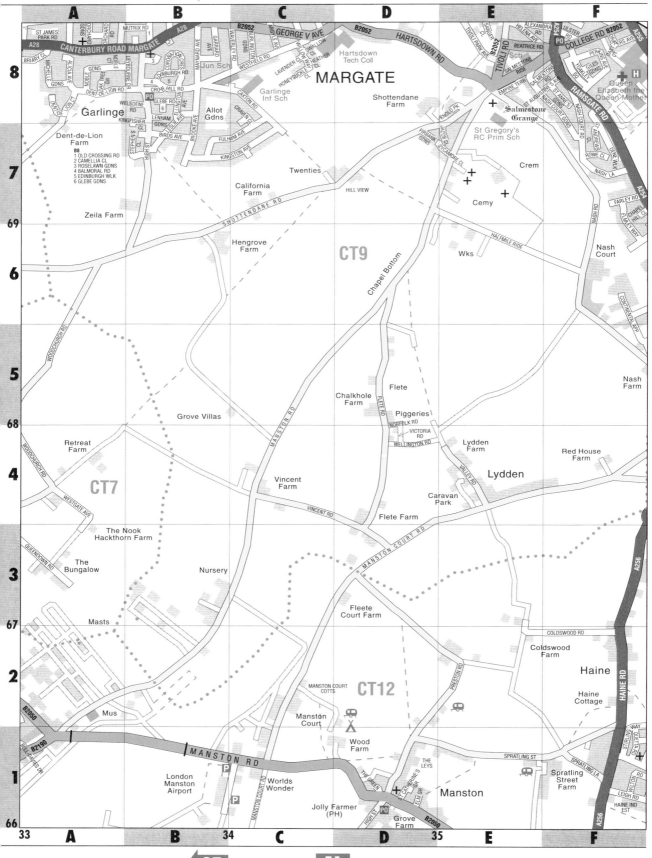

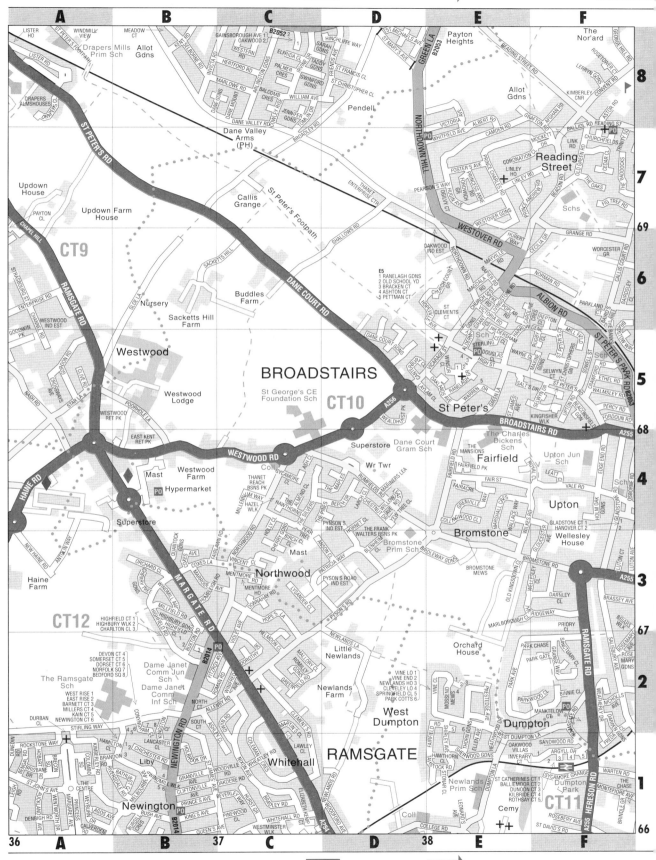

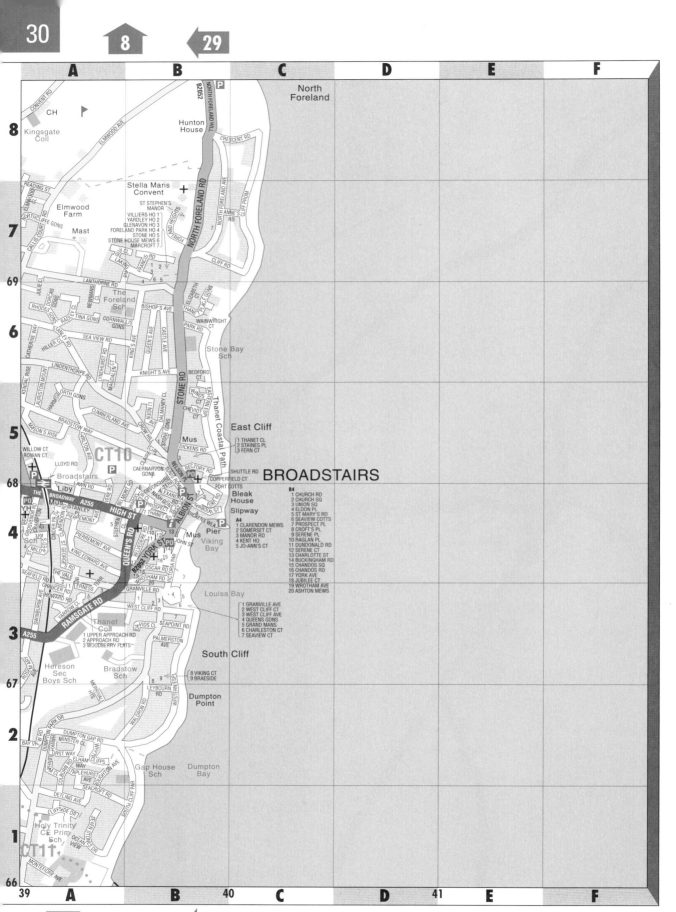

BROADSTAIRS

North Foreland

Hunton House

Stella Maris Convent

St Stephen's Manor
VILLIERS HO 1
YARDLEY HO 2
GLENAVON HO 3
FORELAND PARK HO 4
STONE HO 5
STONE HOUSE MEWS 6
MARCROFT 7

Elmwood Farm

Mast

Kingsgate Coll

The Foreland Sch

Bishop's Ave

Stone Bay Sch

East Cliff

Mus
1 THANET CL
2 STAINES PL
3 FERN CT

Broadstairs

CT10

Liby

Mus

Bleak House

Slipway

Pier

Mus

Viking Bay

B4
1 CHURCH RD
2 CHURCH SQ
3 UNION SQ
4 ELDON PL
5 ST MARY'S RD
6 SEAVIEW COTTS
7 PROSPECT PL
8 CROFT'S PL
9 SERENE PL
10 RAGLAN PL
11 DUNDONALD RD
12 SERENE CT
13 CHARLOTTE ST
14 BUCKINGHAM RD
15 CHANDOS SQ
16 CHANDOS RD
17 YORK AVE
18 JUBILEE CT
19 WROTHAM AVE
20 ASHTON MEWS

A4
1 CLARENDON MEWS
2 SOMERSET CT
3 MANOR RD
4 KENT HO
5 JO-ANN'S CT

Louisa Bay

1 GRANVILLE AVE
2 WEST CLIFF CT
3 WEST CLIFF AVE
4 QUEENS GDNS
5 GRAND MANS
6 CHARLESTON CT
7 SEAVIEW CT

South Cliff

8 VIKING CT
9 BRAESIDE

Thanet Coll
1 UPPER APPROACH RD
2 APPROACH RD
3 WOODBERRY FLATS

Hereson Sec Boys Sch

Bradstow Sch

Dumpton Point

Dumpton Bay

Gap House Sch

Holy Trinity CE Prim Sch

CT11

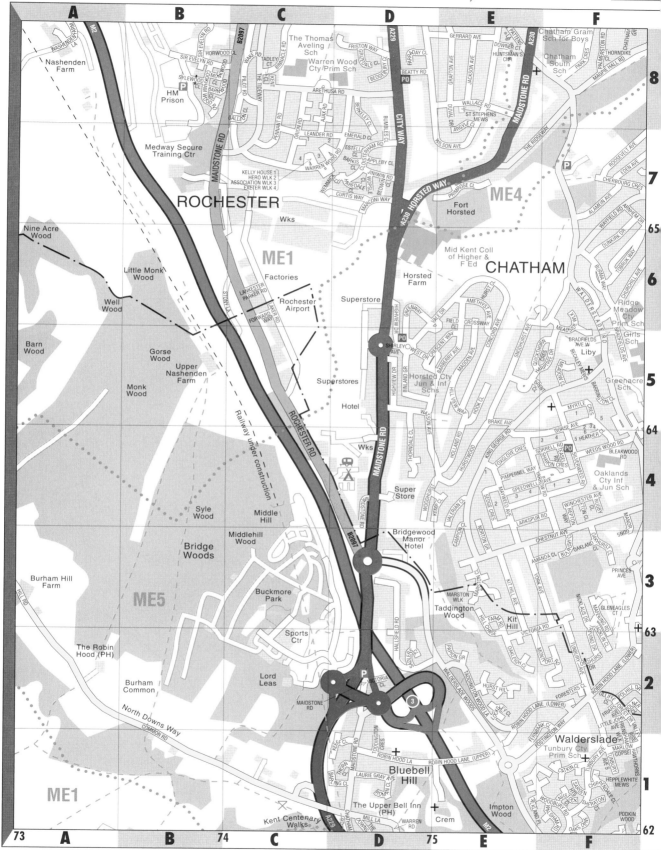

9
32

A · B · C · D · E · F

8
7
65
6
5
64
4
3
63
2
1
62

73 · A · B · 74 · C · D · 75 · E · F

32

E4
1 LAVENDER CL
2 ASPEN WAY
3 HONEYSUCKLE CL
4 GENTIAN CL

F4
1 MALLOW WAY
2 JASMINE CL
3 HAREBELL CL
4 ROSEMARY CL
5 LINDEN HOUSE
6 OAK HOUSE

F5
1 SAFFRON WAY
2 WILLOW HO
3 PINE HO
4 ROWAN HO
5 HAWTHORN HO

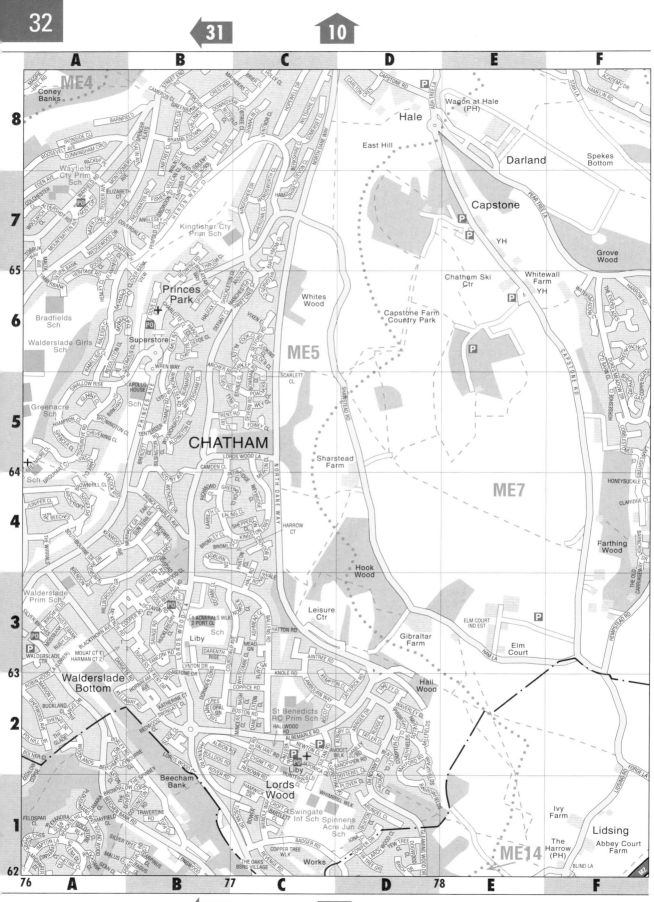

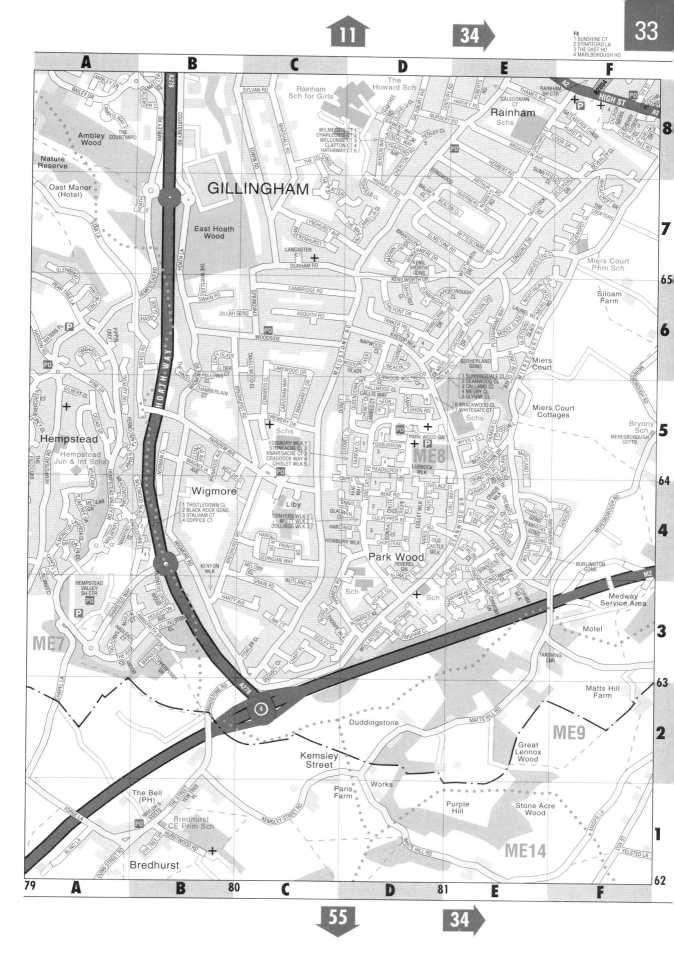

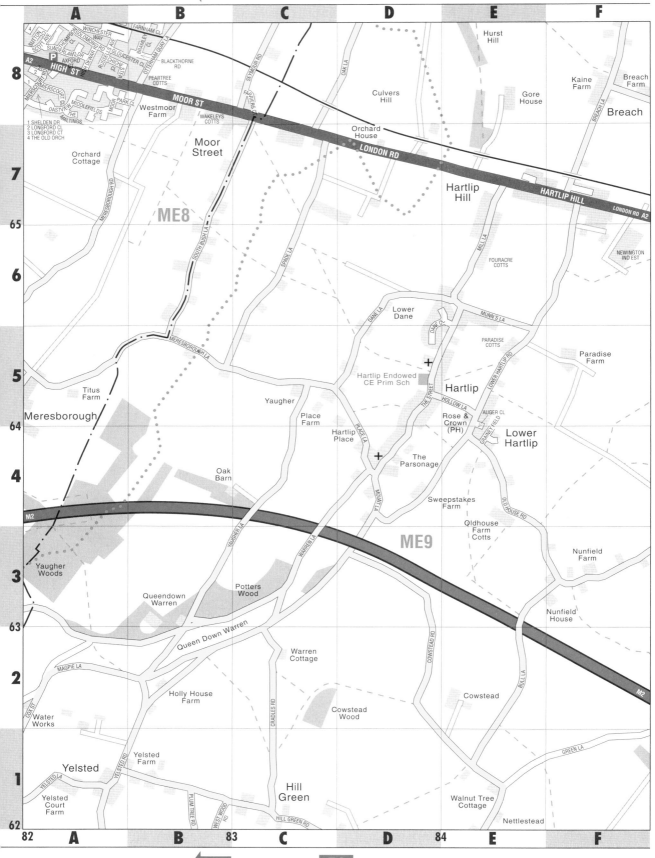

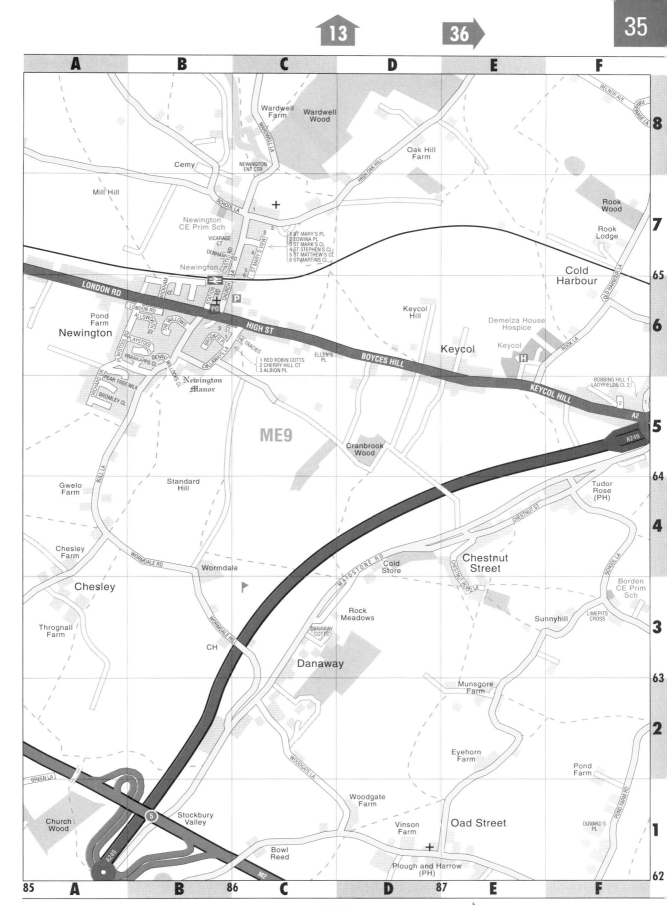

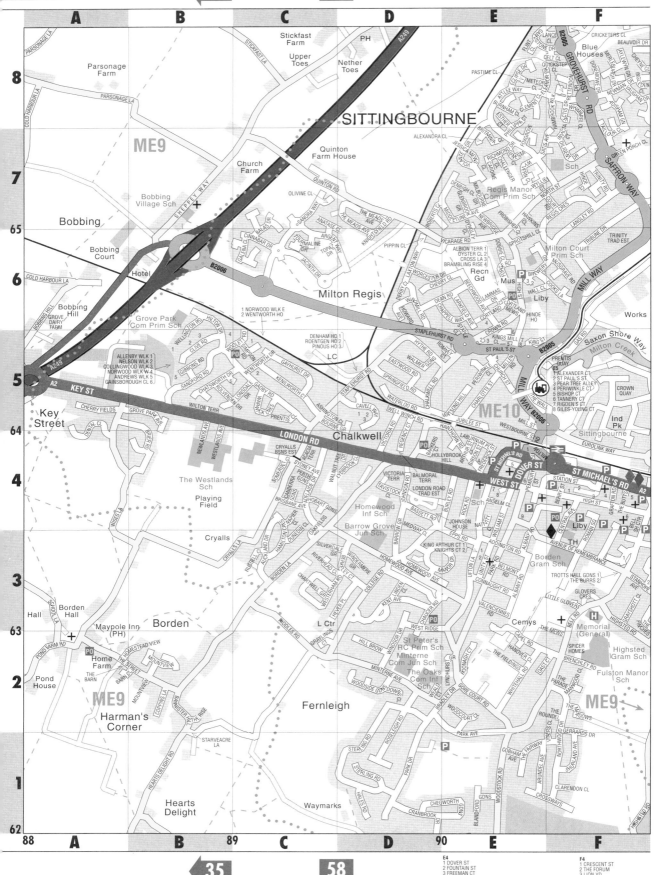

SITTINGBOURNE

ME9

Bobbing

Bobbing Court

Bobbing Hill

Grove Dairy Farm

Cold Harbour La

Hotel

Grove Park Com Prim Sch

Key Street

Borden

Maypole Inn (PH)

Home Farm

Pond House

ME9

Harman's Corner

Hearts Delight

Stickfast Farm

Upper Toes

Nether Toes

PH

Church Farm

Quinton Farm House

Bobbing Village Sch

Milton Regis

1 NORWOOD WLK E
2 WENTWORTH HO

DENHAM HO 1
ROENTGEN HO 2
PINOUS HO 3

The Westlands Sch

Playing Field

Cryalls

CRYALLS BSNS EST

LONDON RD

Chalkwell

1 ALLENBY WLK 1
  NELSON WLK 2
  COLLINGWOOD WLK 3
  NORWOOD WLK W 4
  ANDREWS WLK 5
  GAINSBOROUGH CL 6

Regis Manor Com Prim Sch

Recn Gd

Mus

Liby

Works

Milton Court Prim Sch

TRINITY TRAD EST

Saxon Shore Way

Milton Creek

Prentis Quay

ALBION TERR 1
OYSTER CL 2
CROSS LA 3
BRAMBLING RISE 4

1 ALEXANDER CT
2 ST PAUL'S ST
3 PEAR TREE ALLEY
4 PERIWINKLE CT
5 BISHOP CT
6 TANNERY CT
7 RIGDEN'S CT
8 GILES-YOUNG CT

CROWN QUAY

ME10

Ind Pk

Sittingbourne

EUROLINK WAY

Homewood Inf Sch

Barrow Grove Jun Sch

KING ARTHUR CT 1
KNIGHTS CT 2

London Road Trad Est

Johnson House

Borden Gram Sch

TROTTS HALL GDNS 1
THE BURRS 2

GLOVERS CRES

TH

Liby

Memorial (General)

Highsted Gram Sch

Fulston Manor Sch

Cemys

Spicer Homes

St Peter's RC Prim Sch
Minterne Com Jun Sch

The Oaks Com Inf Sch

L Ctr

WEST RIDGE

Fernleigh

ME9

Waymarks

E4
1 DOVER ST
2 FOUNTAIN ST
3 FREEMAN CT
4 MOCKETT CT
5 CHURCH ST
6 PEMBURY CT
7 WINGATE CT
8 THE CLOISTERS
9 MIDDLETON CT

F4
1 CRESCENT ST
2 THE FORUM
3 LION YD
4 DOES ALLEY
5 ST MICHAEL'S CL
6 BANKS YD

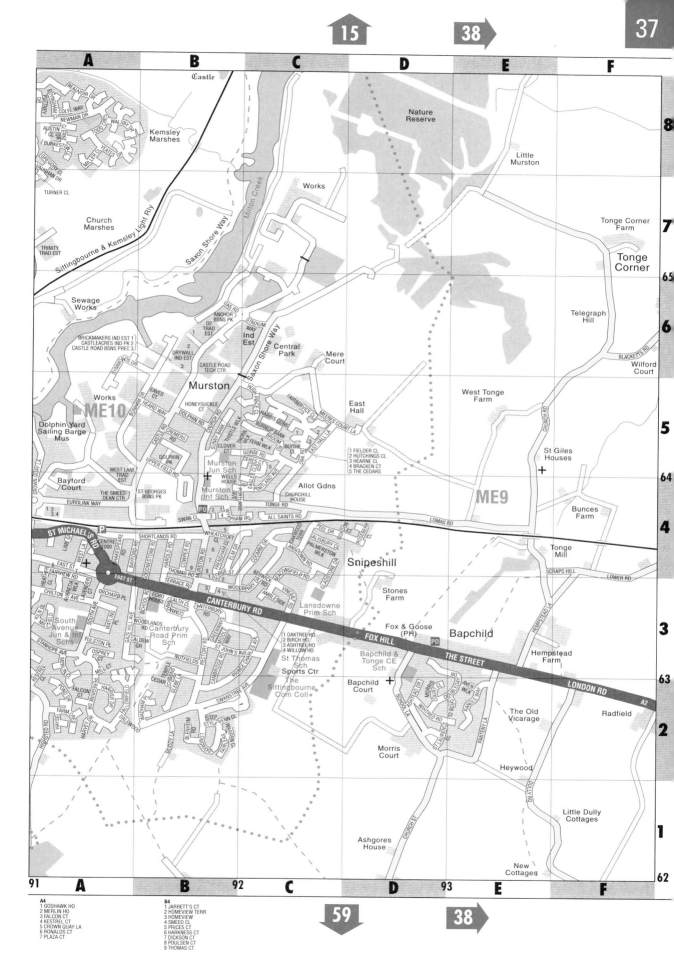

A B C D E F

8 7 65 6 5 64 4 3 63 2 1 62

Castle
Kemsley Marshes
Nature Reserve
Little Murston
Tonge Corner Farm
Tonge Corner
Church Marshes
Saxon Shore Way
Sittingbourne & Kemsley Light Rly
Milton Creek
Works
Telegraph Hill
BLACKETTS RD
Wilford Court
TRINITY TRAD EST
Sewage Works
GAS RD
ANCHOR BSNS PK
D2 TRAD EST
STADIUM WAY IND EST
Central Park
Mere Court
West Tonge Farm
CHURCH RD
BRICKMAKERS IND EST 1
CASTLEACRES IND PK 2
CASTLE ROAD BSNS PREC 3
DRYWALL IND EST
CASTLE ROAD TECH CTR
Saxon Shore Way
Murston
East Hall
St Giles Houses
ME9
Works
ME10
EAVES CT
HEARD WAY
HONEYSUCKLE CT
DOLPHIN RD
SUNNY BANK
THISTLE WLK
CHURCH RD
HIGH PRICE CL
FERN WLK
EAGLE RD
HARRIS GDNS
BURNUP BANK
BROOM
BLYTHE CL
FAIRSERVICE CL
MEERES COURT LA
OAK RD
EAST HALL LA
1 FIELDER CL
2 HUTCHINGS CL
3 HEARNE CL
4 BRACKEN CT
5 THE CEDARS
Bunces Farm
Dolphin Yard Sailing Barge Mus
SYMONDS DR
BOWMAN DR
CASTLE RD
CREMERS RD
DOLPHIN PK
UPPER FIELD RD
WEST LANE TRAD EST
ST GEORGES BSNS PK
CLOVER CT
GORSE CT
CERES CT
KILN CL
EAGLE RD
Murston Jun Sch
WELLS HOUSE
Murston Inf Sch
PORTLAND AVE
Allot Gdns
Churchill House
Tonge Mill
Bayford Court
THE SMEED DEAN CTR
EUROLINK WAY
PO
Tonge Rd
ALL SAINTS RD
WYNTHAM AVE
SWAN CL
LOMAS RD
ME9
CROWN QUAY LA
1 2 3 4
ST MICHAEL'S RD
P
LIME GR
WEST LA
EAST ST
SHORTLANDS RD
BATSFORD RD
SHAKESPEARE RD
HAROLD RD
MURSTON RD
COWPER RD
WHEATCROFT CL
PEEL DR
GORDON RD
OAKWOOD RD
PALMERSTON WLK
SALISBURY CL
LANSDOWN RD
ROSEBERY CL
Snipeshill
Tonge Mill
SCRAPS HILL
LOWER RD
CENTRE 2000
FAIRVIEW RD
HEATHER RD
ALBERTA RD
LAVENDER RD
CHILTON AVE
ORCHARD PL
SOUTH AVE
FULSTON PL
THOMAS RD
TERRACE RD
PERSHAM CT
ELM GR
FEREST
KESWICK RD
WOODBERRY RD
BEACONSFIELD RD
COOMBE DR
VINCAT RD
AMBLESIDE
GLADSTONE RD
Stones Farm
Fox & Goose (PH)
PO
Bapchild
Hempstead Farm
Hempstead La
South Avenue Jun & Inf Schs
STANHOPE AVE
MERLIN CL
KESTREL CL
POND LA
KILN CL
MILL FIELD
MILL CT
SCHOOL RD
ECHO HOUSE
HEALTH CTR
CANTERBURY RD
WOODLANDS RD
GACE HILL RD
CALDEW GR
ST JOHN'S AVE
GREENWAYS
RECTORY RD
CAMBRIDGE RD
PRINCE CHARLES AVE
MIDDLE WAY
Lansdowne Prim Sch
1 OAKTREE HO
2 BIRCH HO
3 ASHTREE HO
4 WILLOW HO
St Thomas Sch
Sports Ctr
Canterbury Road Prim Sch
Bapchild & Tonge CE Sch
FOX HILL
THE STREET
LONDON RD
A2
Bapchild Court
SCHOOL LA
ASHTEAD DR
MORRIS CT
COURT CL
WHITRED RD
AVENEY WLK
RANDOLF WAY
Hempstead Farm
Radfield
HARVEY DR
FALCON CT
TEMPLE GDNS
CEDAR CL
GLEBE LA
NUTFIELDS
SWANSTREE AVE
STEP STYLE
PENN CL
WARREN CL
FARLEYS
The Sittingbourne Com Coll
ST ALBAN'S RD
ST LAWRENCE CT
Morris Court
The Old Vicarage
HOMESTEAD RD
HAZEL RD
FARM CRES
MUDDY LA
BLENHEIM RD
SOUTHDOWNS
PANTENY LA
DOLLY RD
CHURCH ST
Heywood
Little Dully Cottages
Ashgores House
New Cottages
DALEWOOD
FALLOWFIELD
WADHAM PL

A4
1 GOSHAWK HO
2 MERLIN HO
3 FALCON CT
4 KESTREL CT
5 CROWN QUAY LA
6 RONALDS CT
7 PLAZA CT

B4
1 JARRETT'S CT
2 HOMEVIEW TERR
3 HOMEVIEW
4 SMEED CL
5 PRICES CT
6 HARKNESS CT
7 DICKSON CT
8 POULSEN CT
9 THOMAS CT

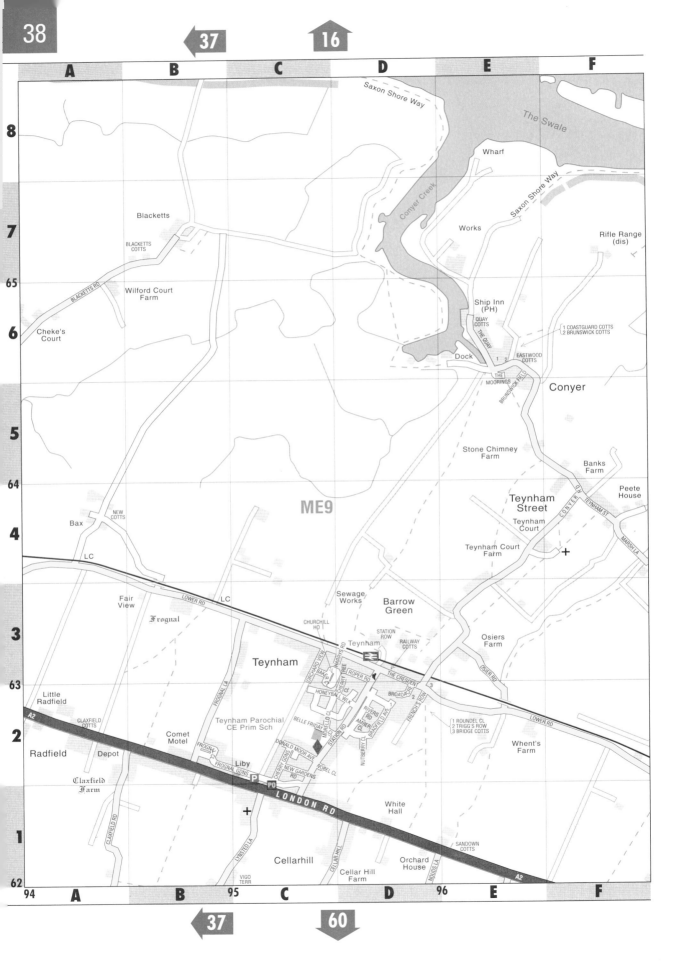

A   B   C   D   E   F

Saxon Shore Way

The Swale

8

Wharf

Conyer Creek

Works

Saxon Shore Way

Blacketts

7

BLACKETTS COTTS

Rifle Range (dis)

65

Wilford Court Farm

BLACKETTS RD

Ship Inn (PH)

6

Cheke's Court

QUAY COTTS

THE QUAY

Dock

1 COASTGUARD COTTS
2 BRUNSWICK COTTS

EASTWOOD COTTS

THE MOORINGS

Conyer

BRUNSWICK FIELD

5

Stone Chimney Farm

Banks Farm

Peete House

64

NEW COTTS

Teynham Street

CONYER RD

TEYNHAM ST

MARSH LA

ME9

4

Bax

Teynham Court

LC

Teynham Court Farm

✛

Fair View

LOWER RD

LC

Sewage Works

Barrow Green

Frognal

CHURCHILL HO

STATION ROW

Osiers Farm

3

Teynham

Teynham

RAILWAY COTTS

ORCHARD VIEW

MABRS RD

CHERRY TREE

ROPER RD

THE CRESCENT

OSIER RD

63

Little Radfield

FROGNAL LA

HONEYBALL WLK

BROAD ACRE

3

1 ROUNDEL CL
2 TRIGG'S ROW
3 BRIDGE COTTS

CLAXFIELD COTTS

Teynham Parochial CE Prim Sch

BELLE FRIDAY

MORELLO CL

RIVERS RD

AMBER CL

BRADFIELD AVE

FRENCH'S ROW

2

A2

Radfield

Comet Motel

Depot

FROGNAL

Donald Moor Ave

STATION RD

NUTBERRY CL

Whent's Farm

Liby

FROGNAL GDNS

CHERRY GDNS

NEW GARDENS RD

NOBEL CL

White Hall

Claxfield Farm

P

PO

LONDON RD

✛

1

CLAXFIELD RD

LYNSTED LA

CELLAR HILL

Sandown Cotts

NOUDS LA

Cellarhill

Cellar Hill Farm

Orchard House

62

VIGO TERR

A2

94

A   B   95   C   D   96   E   F

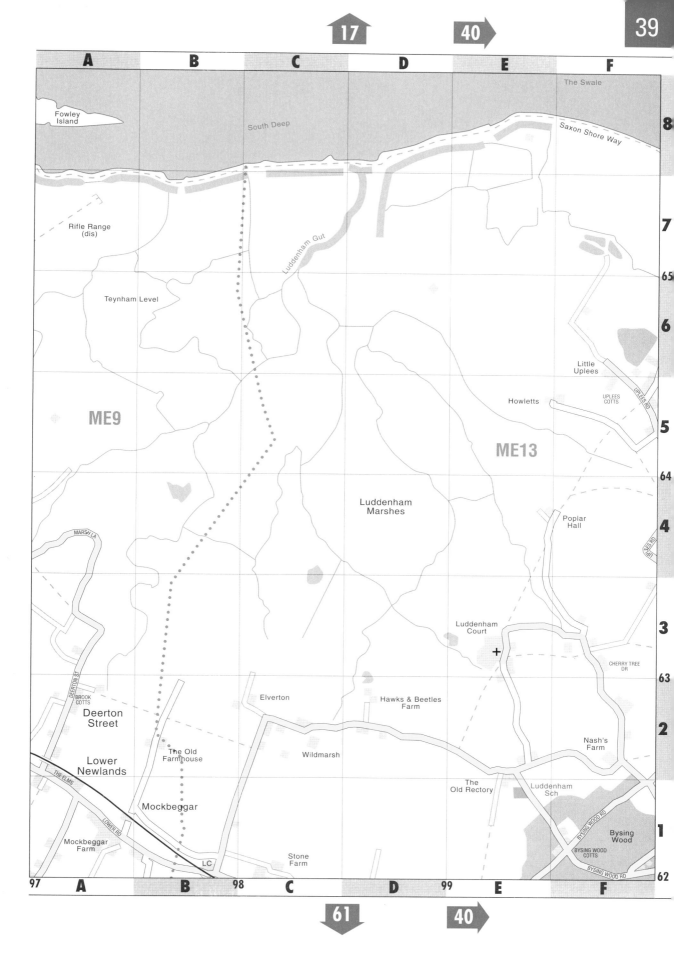

A B C D E F

The Swale

Fowley
Island

South Deep

Saxon Shore Way

8

Rifle Range
(dis)

Luddenham Gut

7

65

Teynham Level

6

Little
Uplees

ME9

Howletts

UPLEES
COTTS

UPLEES RD

5

ME13

64

Luddenham
Marshes

Poplar
Hall

UPLEES RD

4

Luddenham
Court

+

3

CHERRY TREE
DR

63

MARSH LA

Elverton

Hawks & Beetles
Farm

Nash's
Farm

2

BROOK
COTTS

DEERTON ST

Deerton
Street

The Old
Farmhouse

Wildmarsh

The
Old Rectory

Luddenham
Sch

Lower
Newlands

THE ELMS

Mockbeggar

BYSING WOOD RD

Bysing
Wood

1

LOWER RD

Mockbeggar
Farm

LC

Stone
Farm

BYSING WOOD
COTTS

BYSING WOOD RD

62

97 A B 98 C D 99 E F

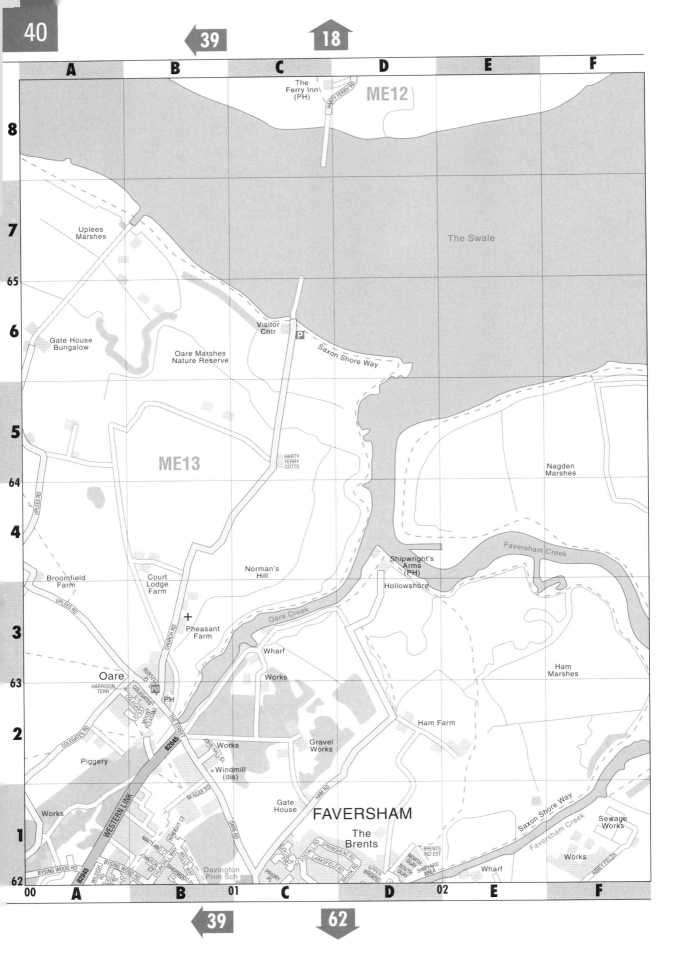

The Swale

Whitstable Bay

Groynes

Saxon Shore Way

CT5

South Bank of Swale
Nature Reserve

Cleve
Marshes

Cleve
Hill

Crown
Cottages

Graveney
Hill

Graveney
Marshes

ME13

Saxon Shore Way

Nagden

Nagden
Cottages

Warm
House

Coney
Banks

Denley Hill
Farm

SEASALTER RD

Brook
Bridge

MONKSHILL RD

Graveney
Crossing

Sandbanks
Cottages

SANDBANKS RD

Broom
Street

ALL SAINTS VIEW

Graveney

Sandbanks
Farm

The Old
Vicarage

Sandbanks

Murtons
Farm

MURTON
PL

JINSOM CL

PO

Plantation
House

Graveney
Prim Sch

HEAD HILL RD

CULMERS TERR

Culmers

PH

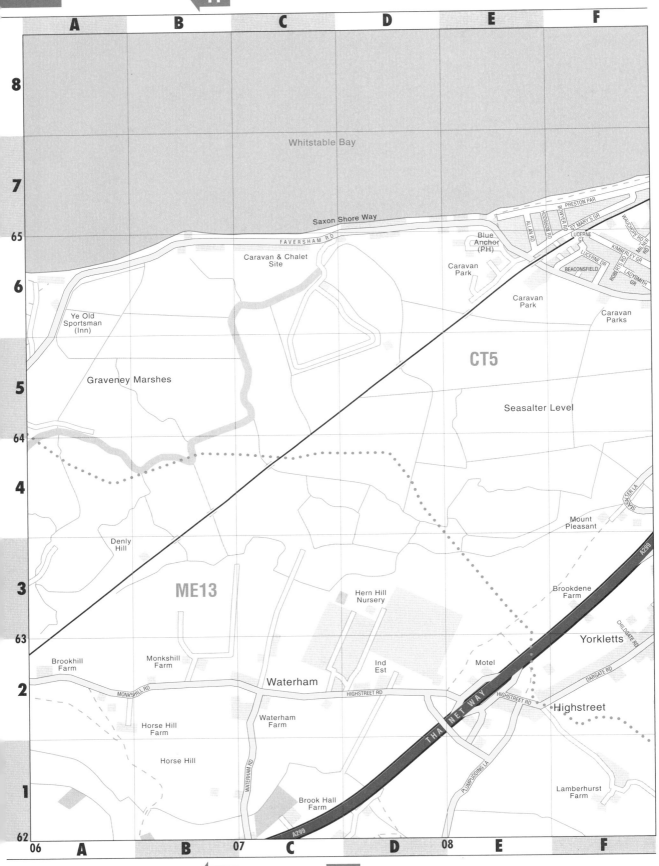

41

A B C D E F

8

Whitstable Bay

7

Saxon Shore Way

65

FAVERSHAM RD

Blue
Anchor
(PH)

PRESTON PAR

HODGSON RD
BOWYER RD
ST MARY'S GR
ALLAN RD
LUCERNE
WALDCROFT RD
MILL RD

Caravan & Chalet
Site

Caravan
Park

LUCERNE DR
ROBERTS RD
KIMBERLEY GR
BEACONSFIELD
LADYSMITH
GR

6

Ye Old
Sportsman
(Inn)

Caravan
Park

Caravan
Parks

CT5

Graveney Marshes

5

Seasalter Level

64

4

Mount
Pleasant

SEASALTER LA

A299

Denly
Hill

3

ME13

Hern Hill
Nursery

Brookdene
Farm

Yorkletts

CHILDGATE RD

63

Brookhill
Farm

Monkshill
Farm

Ind
Est

Motel

DARGATE RD

Waterham

Highstreet

MONKSHILL RD

HIGHSTREET RD

HIGHSTREET RD

THANET WAY

Horse Hill
Farm

Waterham
Farm

WATERHAM RD

2

Horse Hill

1

PLUMPUDDING LA

Lamberhurst
Farm

Brook Hall
Farm

A299

62

06 A B 07 C D 08 E F

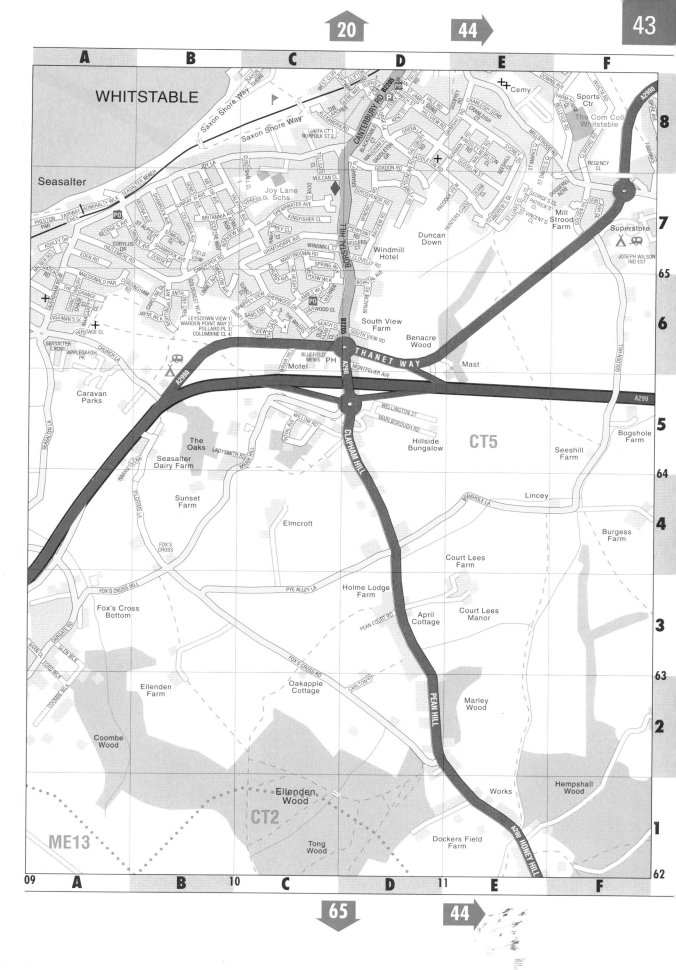

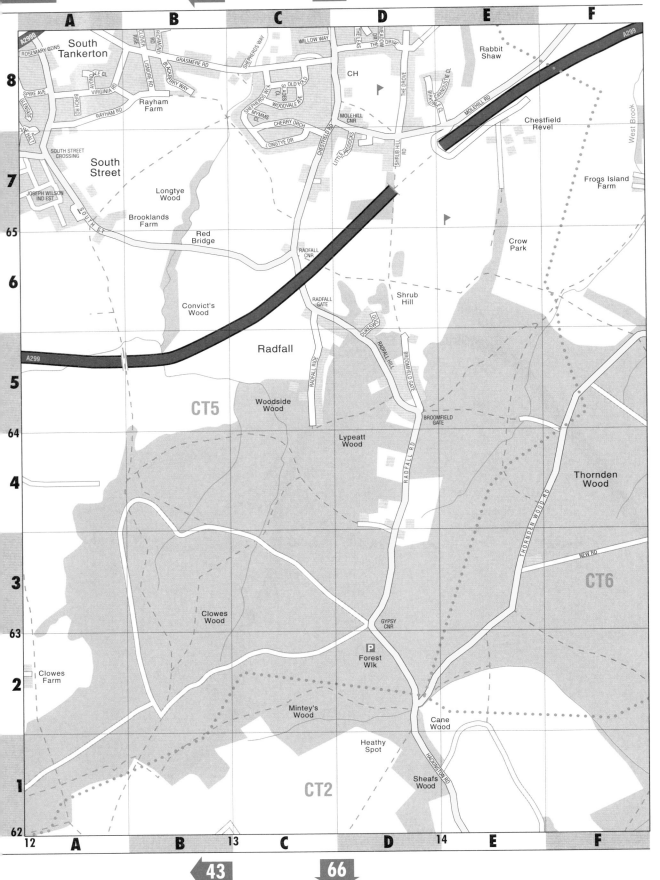

South Tankerton

ROSEMARY GDNS
A2990
CLOVER RISE
RICHMOND RD
GRASMERE RD
SHEPHERDS WAY
WILLOW WAY
THE LEAS
MEADOW DR
THE DRIVE
Rabbit Shaw
A299

VALE CL
LISMORE RD
BLACKBERRY WAY
SLADES
OLD FOLD
WOODVALE PL
CH
BIRCH RD
CARNOUSTIE CL
MOLEHILL RD
Chestfield Revel

SPIRE AVE
BIRCH RD
VIRGINIA RD
SHEPHERDS WLK
MYMMS CL
CHERRY ORCH
MOLEHILL CNR

GLENSIDE
VALE HILL
Rayham Farm
RAYHAM RD
LONGTYE DR
CHESTFIELD RD
LITTLE PADDOCKS
SHRUB HILL RD
Frogs Island Farm

West Brook

SOUTH STREET CROSSING
South Street
Longtye Wood

JOSEPH WILSON IND EST
SOUTH ST
Brooklands Farm
Red Bridge
RADFALL CNR
Crow Park

Convict's Wood
RADFALL GATE
Shrub Hill

A299
Radfall
DUKES WK
RADFALL RIDE
RADFALL HILL
BROOMFIELD GATE

CT5
Woodside Wood
BROOMFIELD GATE

Lypeatt Wood
RADFALL RD
Thornden Wood

Clowes Wood
THORNDEN WOOD RD
NEW RD
CT6

GYPSY CNR

Clowes Farm
P
Forest Wlk

Mintey's Wood
Cane Wood

Heathy Spot
HACKINGTON RD
CT2
Sheafs Wood

A   B   C   D   E   F

8

RIDLEY CL
PO
P
SCHOOL LA
ST MARTIN'S
STREET
FIELD
PALMER
Hawe
Shave
Ford
Ford Manor Farm
HERNE ST
CANTERBURY RD
A291
CHAPEL ROW
ALBION CL
NORTON
FORGEFIELDS
COLBOURN CL
Herne CE Inf & Jun Schs
Ford Manor House (rems of)
FORD HILL

NORTON AVE
STEED CL
VINTEN
Herne
Crowdown Wood
Millbank

SHEPHERDSGATE
CURTIS WAY DRI
RIDGEWAY WLK
ALBION LA
INCHROAD CL

7

RIDGEWAY RD
Ridgeway Farm
CT6
Beacon Wood
OLDHAWE HILL
Corner Farm

65
Maypole

6
Prince of Wales (PH)
Maypole Farm
MAYPOLE RD
MAYPOLE LA
BRISTLES CNR
Old Tree House
OLD TREE RD

East Blean Wood (Nature Reserve)
Mount Pleasant
SCHOOL LA
Hoath Prim Sch
MILL RD
Hoath
WOOD VIEW

5
P
Nursery
Hoath Court
Knaves Ash
CHURCH RD
HEATH HO
BARN CL
PO
Hoath
MARLEY LA

64
Hicks Forstal Farm
HICKS FORSTAL RD
Sewage Works

4
Hicks Forstal
Calfs Wood
Rushbourne Farm
Rushbourne Manor
CT3

Buckwell Wood

3
Buckwell Farm
HOATH RD
Buckwell

63
Clangate Wood
Park Rough
Chislet Park

2
Clangate

Tile Lodge Farm

1
Joiner's Farm
Hersden
CHISLET PARK COTTS
BREEZANDS LA
Hersden Com Prim Sch
ST ALBAN'S RD
SUTTON RD
PO
THE AVENUE
THE ELMS
THE OAKS
POPLARS
EAST VIEW
NORTH VIEW
ISLAND RD
CT2

62
CT2
Hoades Court
CT2
THE FIRS
ASH CRES
SHAFTESBURY RD
A28
PH
SOUTH VIEW
CANTERBURY IND PK

18   A   B   19   C   D   20   E   F

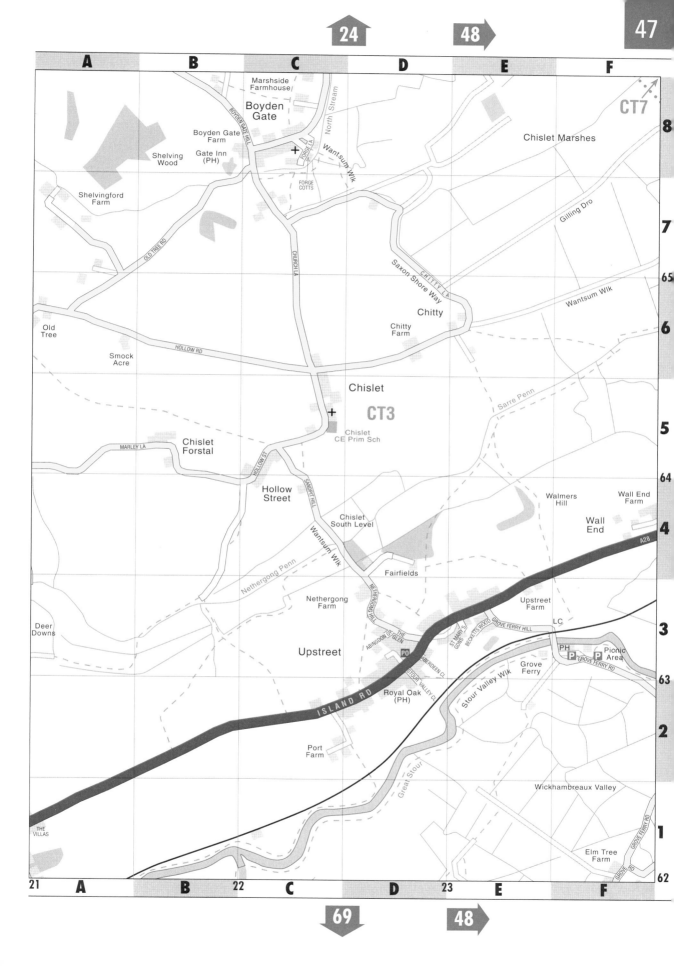

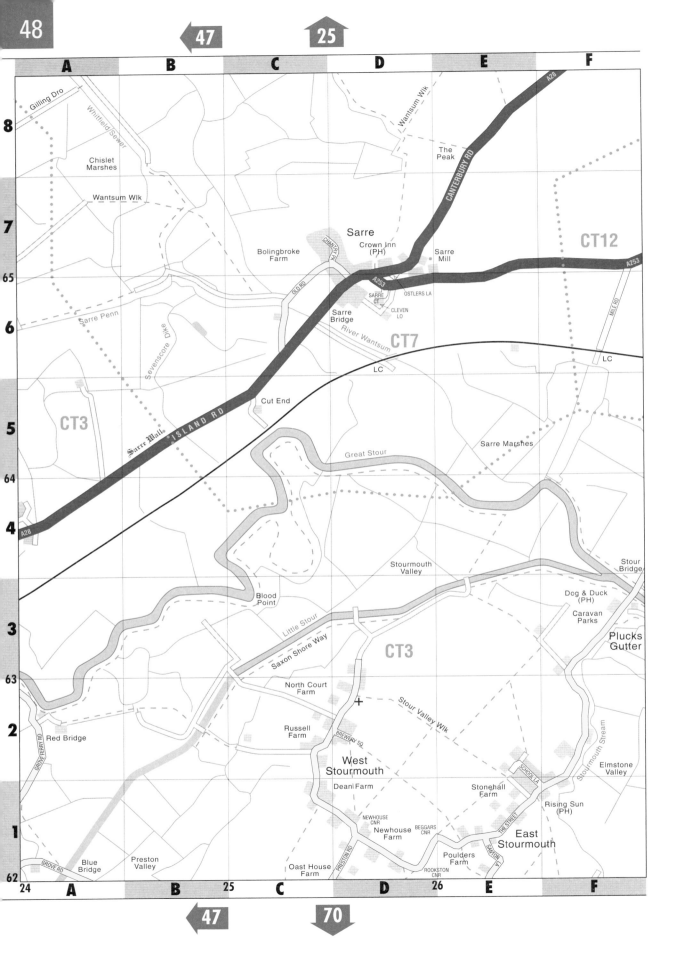

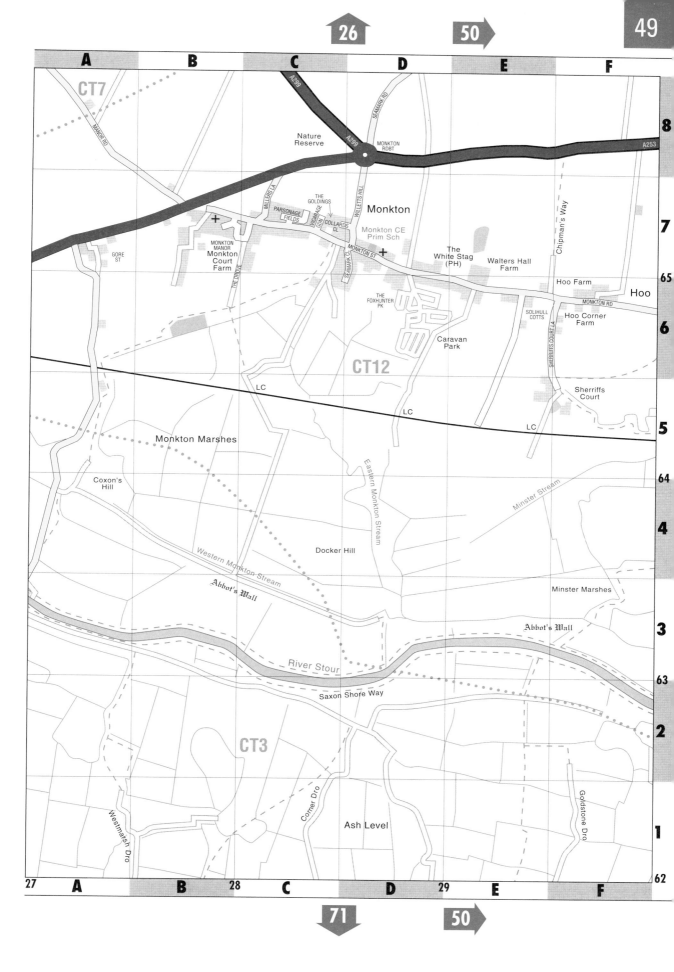

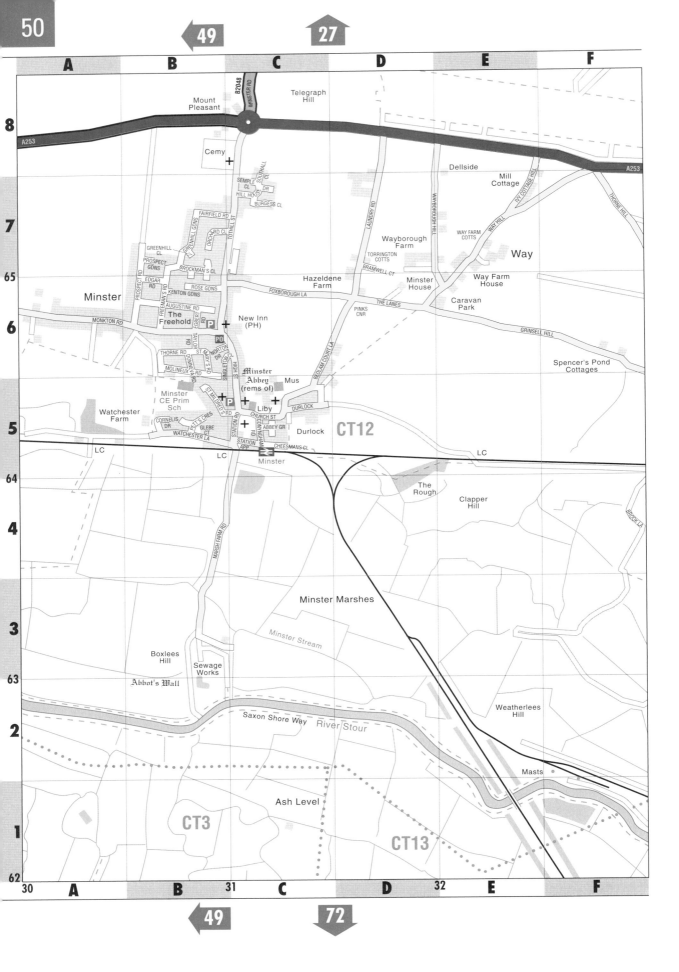

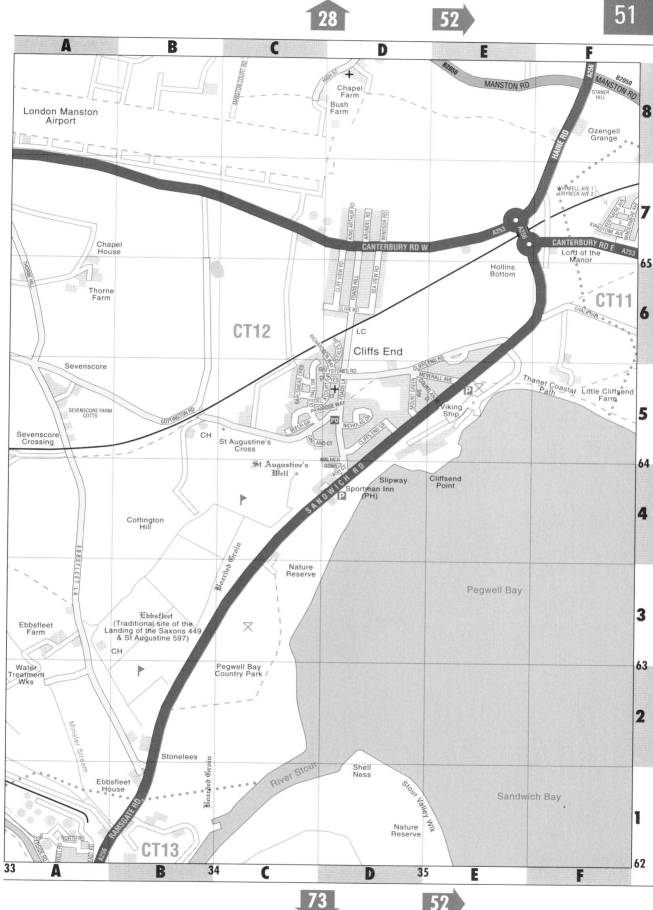

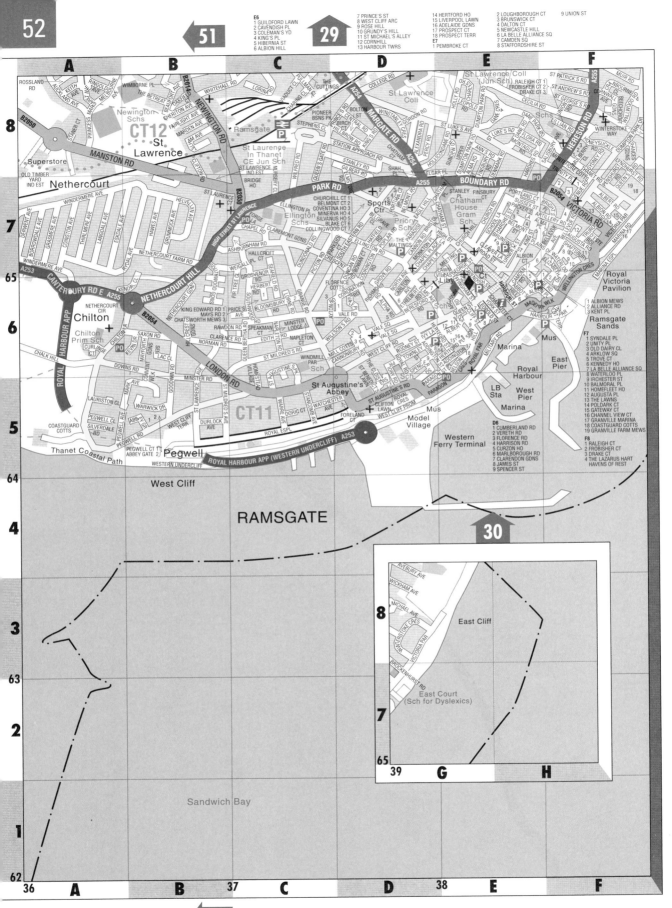

51

29

E6
1 GUILDFORD LAWN
2 CAVENDISH PL
3 COLEMAN'S YD
4 KING'S PL
5 HIBERNIA ST
6 ALBION HILL

7 PRINCE'S ST
8 WEST CLIFF ARC
9 ROSE HILL
10 GRUNDY'S HILL
11 ST MICHAEL'S ALLEY
12 CORNHILL
13 HARBOUR TWRS

14 HERTFORD HO
15 LIVERPOOL LAWN
16 ADELAIDE GDNS
17 PROSPECT CT
18 PROSPECT TERR
E7
1 PEMBROKE CT

2 LOUGHBOROUGH CT
3 BRUNSWICK CT
4 DALTON CT
5 NEWCASTLE HILL
6 LA BELLE ALLIANCE SQ
7 CAMDEN SQ
8 STAFFORDSHIRE ST

9 UNION ST

RAMSGATE

30

51

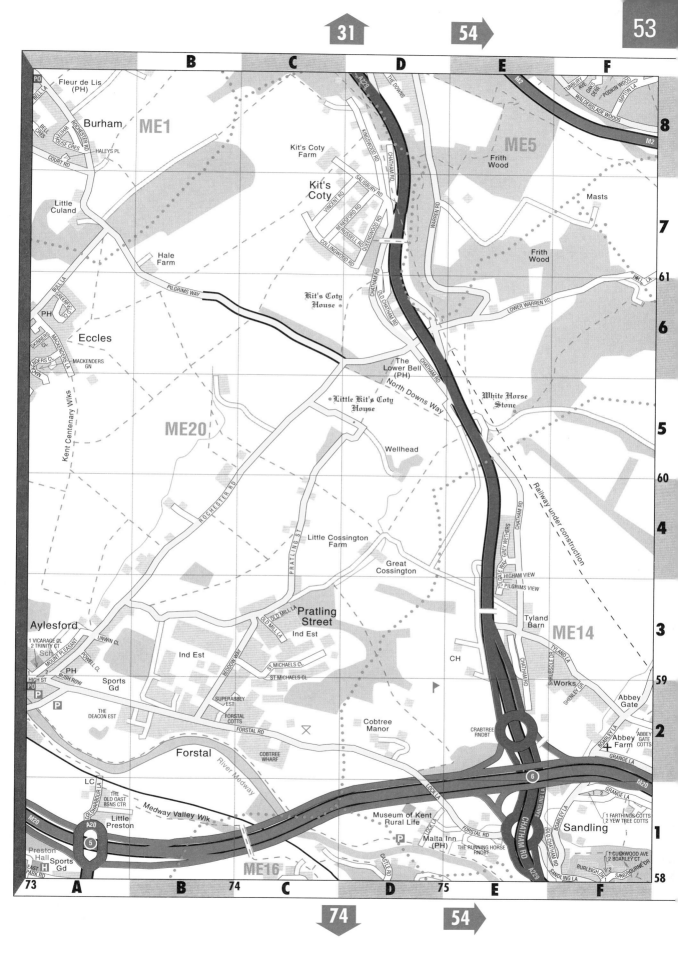

53
32

A B C D E F

8

ME5

ME7

The Alexandra
H
Round Wood
Longwood
Chequers
GEAN CL
PYRUS CL
TROTWOOD
ORBIT CL
SYLVAN GLADE
IMPTON LA
OLIVINE CL
VIOLET CL
IRIS CL
ASTRAL RD
ARBUTUS CL
1 SPENLOW DR
2 QUINION CL
3 BELLGROVE CT
SARACEN FIELD
SANDSTONE RISE
GREEN SANDS
WILDFELL CL
BOXLEY RD
LORDSWOOD LA
REVENGE RD
LORDS WOOD LA
REVENGE RD
GOLDEN WOOD CL
BADGERS RD
AUTUMN GLADE
PINEWOOD
TIMBER TOPS
GLEAMING WOOD DR
WESTFIELD SOLE RD

1 BALLARD IND EST
2 THE ENTERPRISE CTR
3 ALTBARN IND EST
4 LORDSWOOD IND EST

Cowbeck Wood

WALDERSLADE WOODS
M2

Masts

Radio Sta

Cossington Fields

Malling Wood

Mast

Westfield Sole

Westfield Sole Farm

Little Halstead Farm

YELSTED LA

DUNN STREET RD

BELL LA

7

61

Friends Wood

Monkdown Wood

ME20

6

North Downs Way

HARP FARM RD

LLOSING RD

Black Cottages

Boxley Grange

5

Kent Centenary Wlks

Harp Farm

Harp Farm

ME14

60

Boarley Warren

PILGRIMS WAY

4

Boarley Farm

Boxley Wood

North Downs Way

Downs View Farm

BOARLEY LA

Boxley House Hotel

PILGRIMS WAY

3

Curlews

GREENFIELD COTTS

THE STREET

FORGE LA

Warren Farm

59

King's Arms (PH)

+ Boxley

The Larches

Boxley Abbey (rems of)

Donkey Shaws

Street Farm

2

Park Wood

Park House

BOXLEY RD

Railway under construction

Harpole

M20

Cookes Cottage

GRANGE LA

SANDY LA

Yewtree Shaw

HARP LA

SITTINGBOURNE RD A249

1

58

Harbourlands Farm

76 A B 77 C D 78 E F

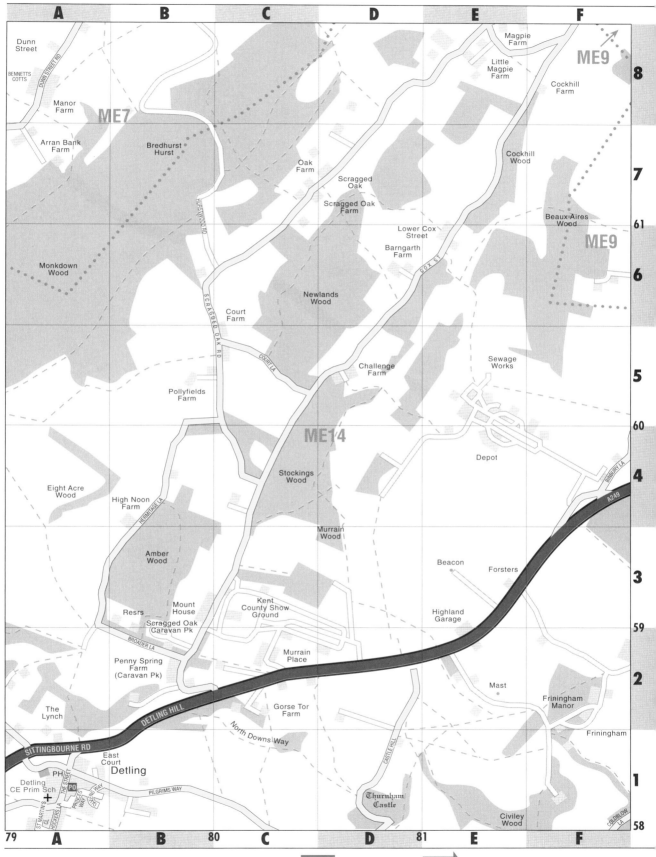

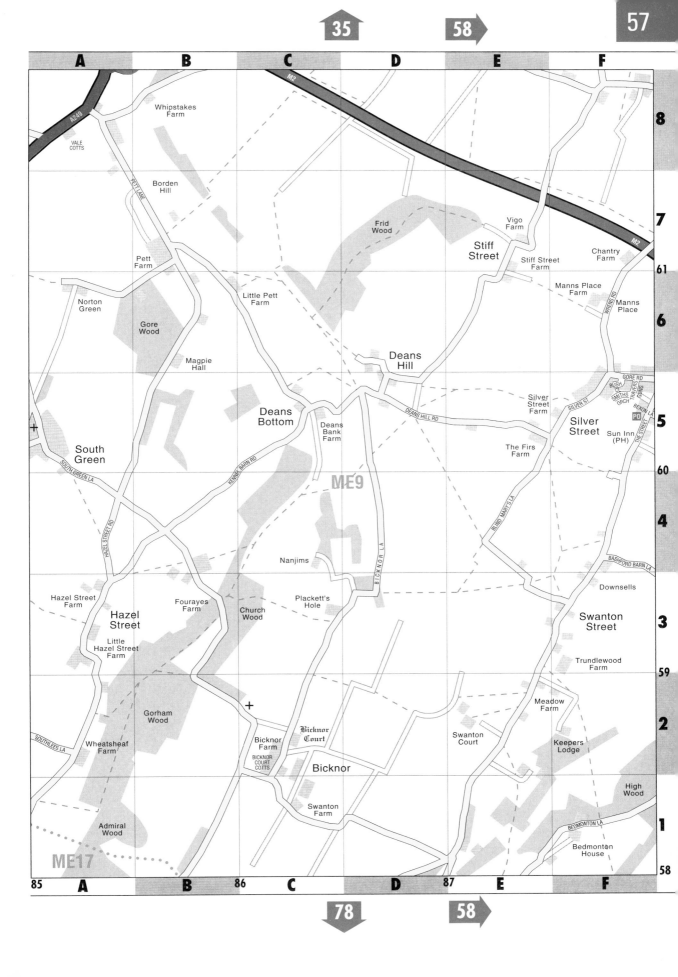

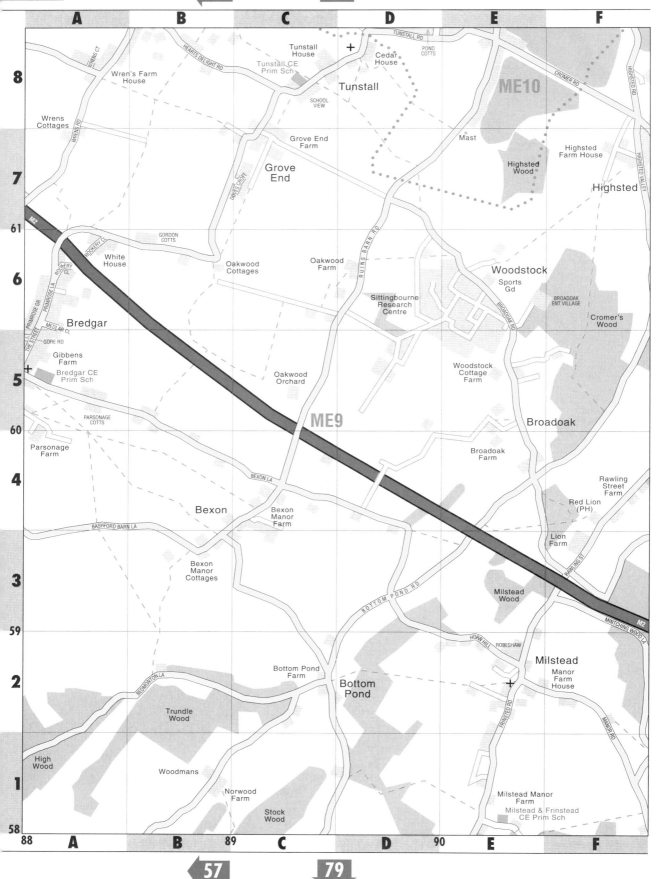

A B C D E F

8

7

61

6

5

60

4

59

3

2

1

58

WRENS CT

Wren's Farm House

Wrens Cottages

WRENS RD

HEARTS DELIGHT RD

Tunstall House

Tunstall CE Prim Sch

SCHOOL VIEW

Cedar House

TUNSTALL RD

POND COTTS

ME10

CROMER RD

HIGHSTED RD

Tunstall

Grove End Farm

Grove End

DIPES CROFT

Mast

Highsted Wood

Highsted Farm House

HIGHSTED VALLEY

Highsted

M2

GORDON COTTS

White House

ROOKERY CL

Oakwood Cottages

Oakwood Farm

RUINS BARN RD

Woodstock

Sports Gd

BROADOAK ENT VILLAGE

PRIMROSE GR

ROOKERY CL

PRIMROSE LA

Bredgar

MEDLAR CL

GORE RD

THE STREET

Sittingbourne Research Centre

Cromer's Wood

Gibbens Farm

Bredgar CE Prim Sch

Oakwood Orchard

ME9

Woodstock Cottage Farm

BROADOAK RD

Broadoak

PARSONAGE COTTS

Parsonage Farm

Broadoak Farm

Rawling Street Farm

BEXON LA

Bexon

Bexon Manor Farm

Red Lion (PH)

Lion Farm

BASHFORD BARN LA

Bexon Manor Cottages

BOTTOM POND RD

Milstead Wood

RAWLING ST

MINTCHING WOOD LA

M2

REDMONTON LA

Bottom Pond Farm

Bottom Pond

HORN HILL

ROBESHAW

Milstead

Manor Farm House

Trundle Wood

MANOR RD

High Wood

Woodmans

Norwood Farm

Stock Wood

FRINSTED RD

Milstead Manor Farm

Milstead & Frinstead CE Prim Sch

A B C D E F

8

Rodmersham
CHURCH
COTTS
Dully
House
WOOD ST
Woodstreet
House
Rodmersham
Court
Farm
Rodmersham
House
CHURCH ST
Upper Dully
Cottages

STOCKERS HILL
FRUITERER'S CL
PO
RODMERSHAM GN
Rodmersham
Green
7
STOCKERS BROW
Browning's PH
Farm
BROWNINGS ORCH
Rodmersham
Sch
GREEN LA
Scuttington
Manor
Cheney
Hill
Oak Tree
Farm
Browning's Farm
Cottage
Hill
Farm
61
BOTTLES LA
Upper
Rodmersham
Orchard
Farm
DULLY RD
6
Cheneyhill
House
Bargains Hill
Farm
CHENEY HILL
Bargains
Hill
5
PITSTOCK RD
Little
Newbury
Ludgate
LUDGATE RD
Pitstock
Farm
ME9
60
RAWLINS ST
PENFIELD LA
Penfield
House
Pinks
Farm
Newbury
Kingsdown
4
SLOUGH RD
KINGSDOWN RD
KINGSDOWN
HOUSES
Dungate
Hole Street
Farm
Erriottwood
3
M2
59
SANDPIT RD
Mintching
Wood
Erriot
Wood
2
Old
Rectory
BREWSTER
COTTS
Kingsdown
Wood
Bistock
MINTCHING WOOD LA
Bluetown
DOWN COURT RD
Pinetrees
Farm
1

58

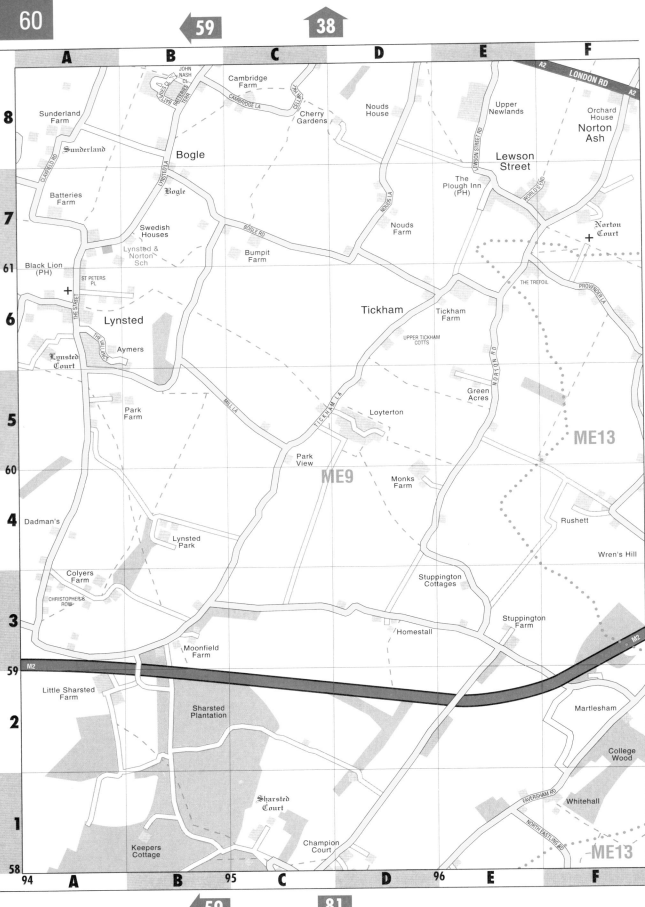

A B C D E F

8
Sunderland Farm
Sunderland
Bogle
JOHN NASH CL
BATTERIES TERR
BRISLEY CL
LYNSTED LA
CAMBRIDGE LA
Cambridge Farm
CELLAR HL
Cherry Gardens
Nouds House
Upper Newlands
LONDON RD
A2
Orchard House
Norton Ash

Bogle
Batteries Farm
Swedish Houses
BOGLE RD
Lewson Street
The Plough Inn (PH)
LEWSON STREET RD
WORLD'S END
Norton Court

7

61
Black Lion (PH)
St Peters Pl
Lynsted & Norton Sch
THE STREET
Bumpit Farm
Nouds Farm
NOUDS LA
THE TREFOIL
PROVENDER LA

6
Lynsted
THE VALLANCE
Aymers
Lynsted Court
Tickham
Tickham Farm
UPPER TICKHAM COTTS
NORTON RD

Park Farm
MILL LA
TICKHAM LA
Loyterton
Green Acres
5

60
Park View
ME9
Monks Farm
ME13

4
Dadman's
Lynsted Park
Rushett
Wren's Hill

Colyers Farm
CHRISTOPHER'S ROW
Stuppington Cottages

3
Moonfield Farm
Homestall
Stuppington Farm
M2

59
M2
Little Sharsted Farm
Martlesham

2
Sharsted Plantation
College Wood

1
Sharsted Court
FAVERSHAM RD
Whitehall
NORTH EASTLING RD
ME13

58
Keepers Cottage
Champion Court

94 A B 95 C D 96 E F

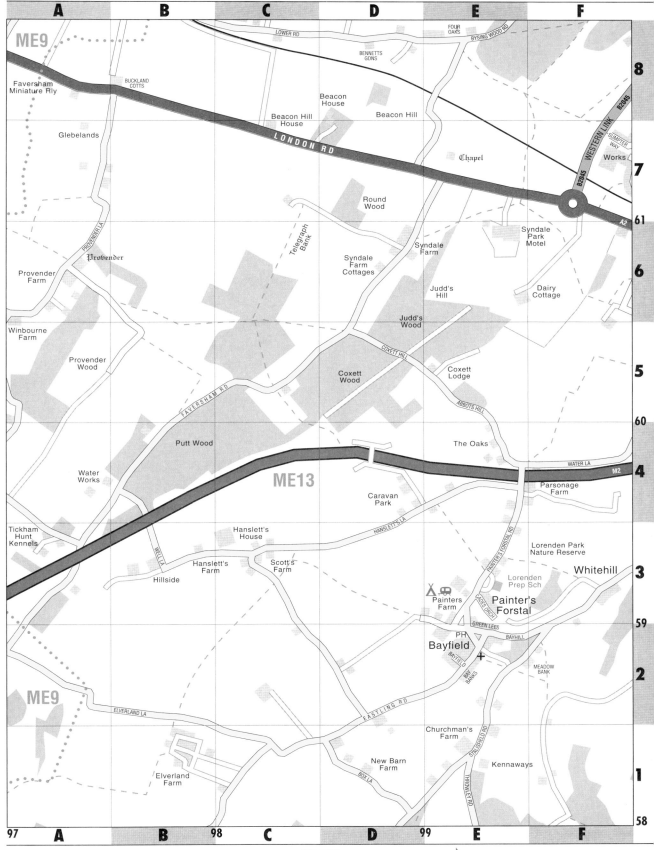

ME9

Faversham Miniature Rly

Glebelands

BUCKLAND COTTS

LOWER RD

BENNETTS GDNS

FOUR OAKS

BYSING WOOD RD

Beacon House

Beacon Hill House

Beacon Hill

LONDON RD

WESTERN LINK

B2045

SUMPTER WAY

Works

Chapel

Round Wood

Syndale Park Motel

A2

Telegraph Bank

PROVENDER LA

Provender

Provender Farm

Syndale Farm

Syndale Farm Cottages

Judd's Hill

Dairy Cottage

Winbourne Farm

FAVERSHAM RD

Provender Wood

Judd's Wood

COXETT HILL

Coxett Wood

Coxett Lodge

ABBOTS HILL

Putt Wood

The Oaks

WATER LA

M2

Water Works

ME13

Caravan Park

Parsonage Farm

Tickham Hunt Kennels

WELL LA

Hanslett's House

HANSLETT'S LA

PAINTER'S FORSTAL RD

Lorenden Park Nature Reserve

Whitehill

Hanslett's Farm

Hillside

Scott's Farm

Painters Farm

CATES ORCH

Lorenden Prep Sch

Painter's Forstal

GREEN LEES

BAYHILL

ME9

ELVERLAND LA

PH

Bayfield

BAYFIELD

BAY BANKS

MEADOW BANK

EASTLING RD

Churchman's Farm

STALISFIELD RD

Elverland Farm

BOX LA

New Barn Farm

Kennaways

THORNLEY RD

8 7 61 6 5 60 4 3 59 2 1 58

A B C D E F

C7
1 CURTIS WAY
2 CASLOCKE ST
3 HATCH ST
4 BECKETT ST
5 MENDFIELD ST
6 WATER LA

C7
7 REEVES PAS
8 WESTBROOK WLK

D7
1 MARKET PL
2 MIDDLE ROW
3 GANGE MEWS
4 GARFIELD PL
5 HUGH PL
6 BACK LA

7 CROSS LA
8 JACOB YD
9 GATEFIELD LA
10 HERBERT DANE CT
11 JOHN ANDERSON CT
12 QUEENS PAR

13 ST MARY CT
14 WILLIAM GIBBS CT
15 LIMES PL

61
40

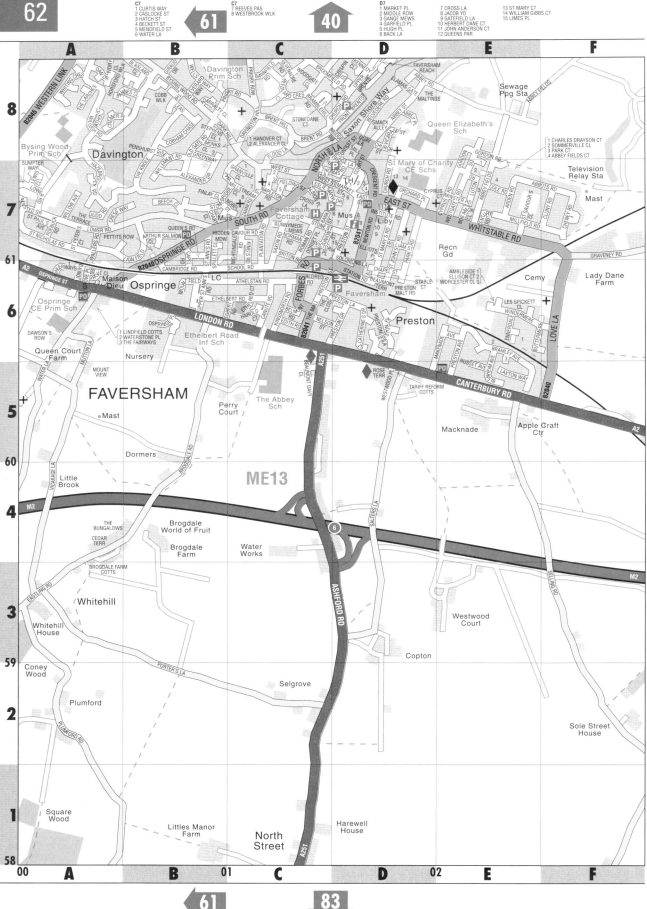

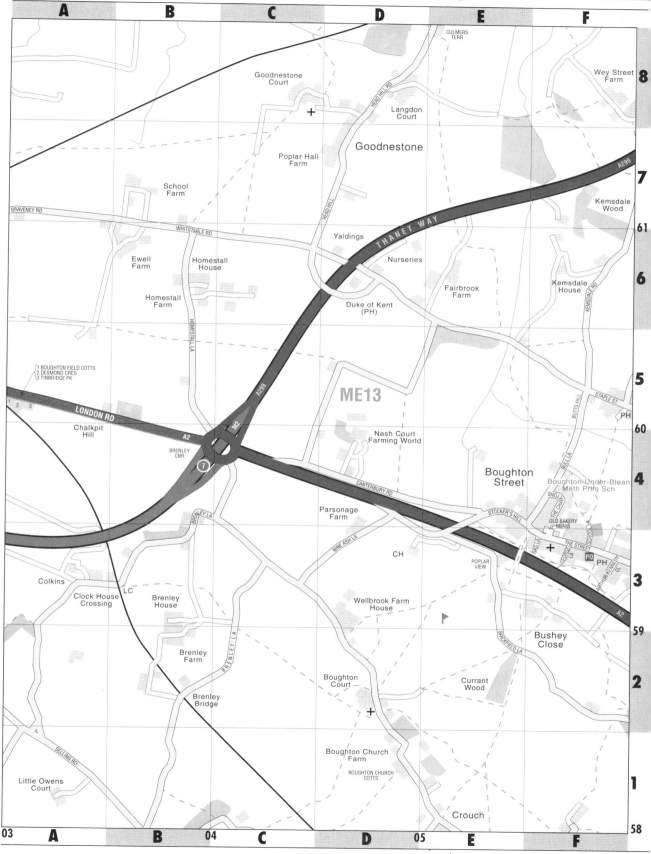

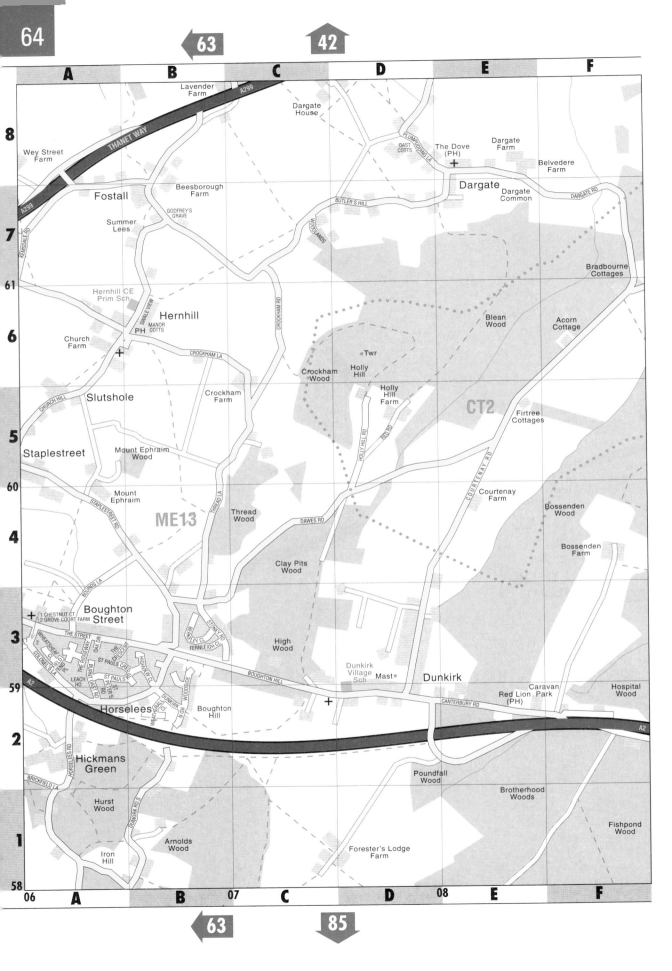

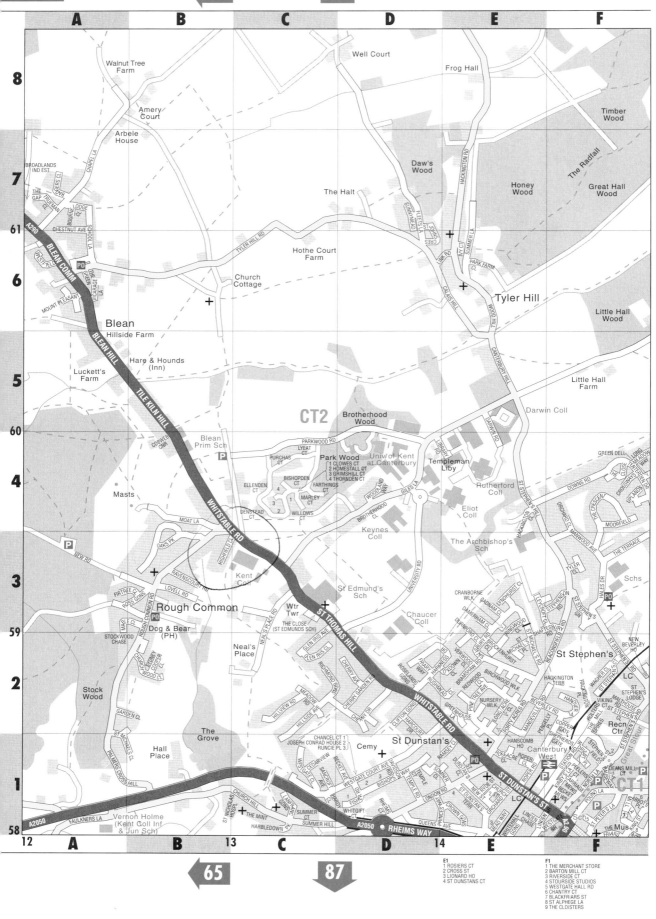

A B C D E F

8

Walnut Tree Farm

Well Court

Frog Hall

Timber Wood

Amery Court

Arbele House

The Radfall

7

BROADLANDS IND EST

Daw's Wood

Honey Wood

Great Hall Wood

THE GAP

61

A290

The Halt

Hothe Court Farm

Tyler Hill

Little Hall Wood

6

PO

Blean

Church Cottage

Little Hall Farm

Hillside Farm

5

Hare & Hounds (Inn)

Luckett's Farm

TILE KILN HILL

Darwin Coll

Little Hall Farm

60

CT2

Brotherhood Wood

GREEN DELL

Blean Prim Sch

PARKWOOD RD

Park Wood
1 CLOWES CT
2 HOMESTALL CT
3 GRIMSHILL CT
4 THORNDEN CT

Univ of Kent at Canterbury

Templeman Liby

4

Masts

ELLENDEN CT

BISHOPDEN CT

FARTHINGS

Rutherford Coll

MARLEY CT

WILLOWS CT

Eliot Coll

MOAT LA

DENSTEAD CT

Keynes Coll

The Archbishop's Sch

P NEW RD

Kent Coll

The Archbishop's Sch

Schs

3

RAVENSCOURT RD

St Edmund's Sch

Chaucer Coll

PO

LOVELL RD

ST THOMAS HILL

Rough Common

Wtr Twr

59

Dog & Bear (PH)

THE CLOSE (ST EDMUNDS SCH)

St Stephen's

STOCKWOOD CHASE

Neal's Place

NEW BEVERLEY HO

2

Stock Wood

WHITSTABLE RD

GARDEN CL

Recn Ctr

1

The Grove

St Dunstan's

Canterbury West

CT1

Hall Place

Cemy

PO

ST DUNSTAN'S ST

A2050

Vernon Holme (Kent Coll Inf & Jun Sch)

THE MINT

RHEIMS WAY

58

FAULKNERS LA

HARBLEDOWN

SUMMER HILL

A2050

THE MUS

12 A B 13 C D 14 E F

E1
1 ROSIERS CT
2 CROSS ST
3 LIONARD HO
4 ST DUNSTANS CT

F1
1 THE MERCHANT STORE
2 BARTON MILL CT
3 RIVERSIDE CT
4 STOURSIDE STUDIOS
5 WESTGATE HALL RD
6 CHANTRY CT
7 BLACKFRIARS ST
8 ST ALPHEGE LA
9 THE CLOISTERS

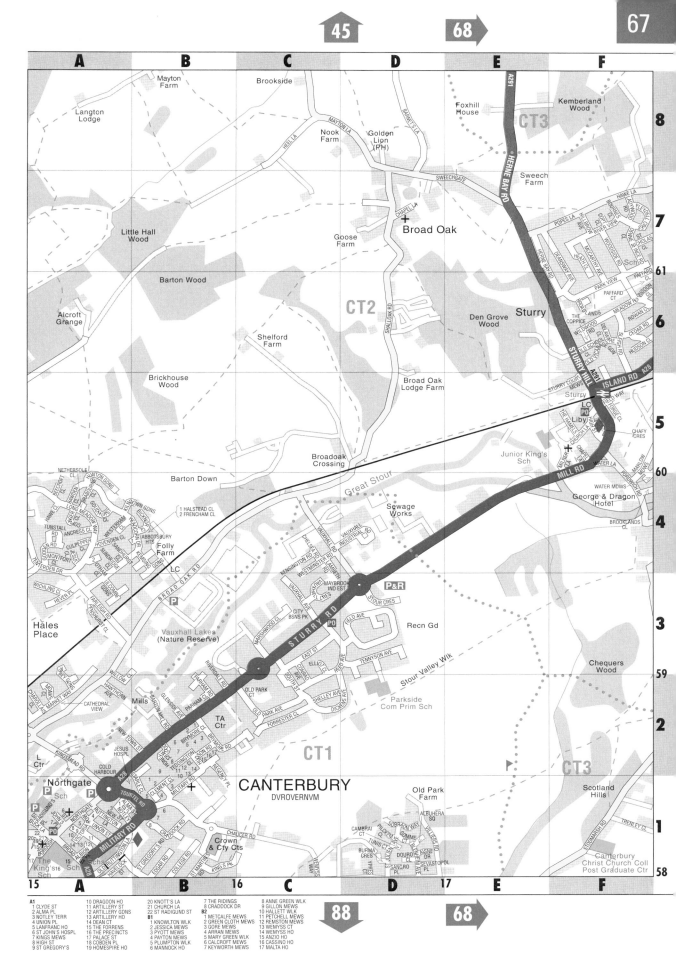

A1
1 CLYDE ST
2 ALMA PL
3 NOTLEY TERR
4 UNION PL
5 LANFRANC HO
6 ST JOHN'S HOSPL
7 KINGS MEWS
8 HIGH ST
9 ST GREGORY'S

10 DRAGOON HO
11 ARTILLERY ST
12 ARTILLERY GDNS
13 ARTILLERY HO
14 DEAN CT
15 THE FORRENS
16 THE PRECINCTS
17 PALACE ST
18 COBDEN PL
19 HOMESPIRE HO

20 KNOTT'S LA
21 CHURCH LA
22 ST RADIGUND ST
B1
1 KNOWLTON WLK
2 JESSICA MEWS
3 PYOTT MEWS
4 PAYTON MEWS
5 PLUMPTON WLK
6 MANNOCK HO

7 THE RIDINGS
8 CRADDOCK DR
B2
1 METCALFE MEWS
2 GREEN CLOTH MEWS
3 GORE MEWS
4 ARRAN MEWS
5 MARY GREEN WLK
6 CALCROFT MEWS
7 KEYWORTH MEWS

8 ANNE GREEN WLK
9 GILLON MEWS
10 HALLETT WLK
11 PETCHELL MEWS
12 REMSTON MEWS
13 WEMYSS CT
14 WEMYSS HO
15 ANZIO HO
16 CASSINO HO
17 MALTA HO

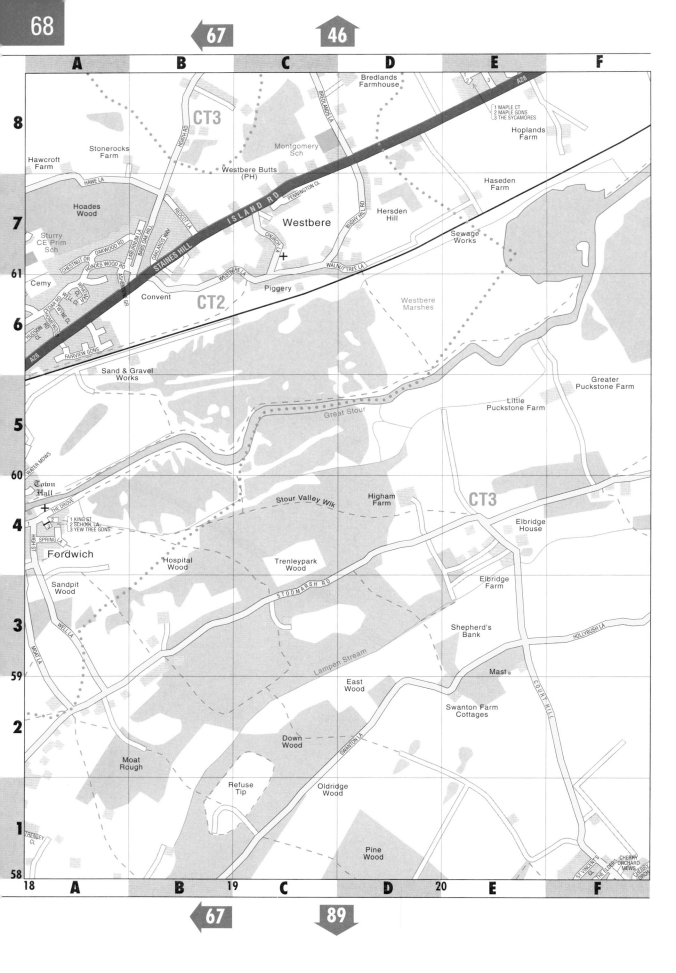

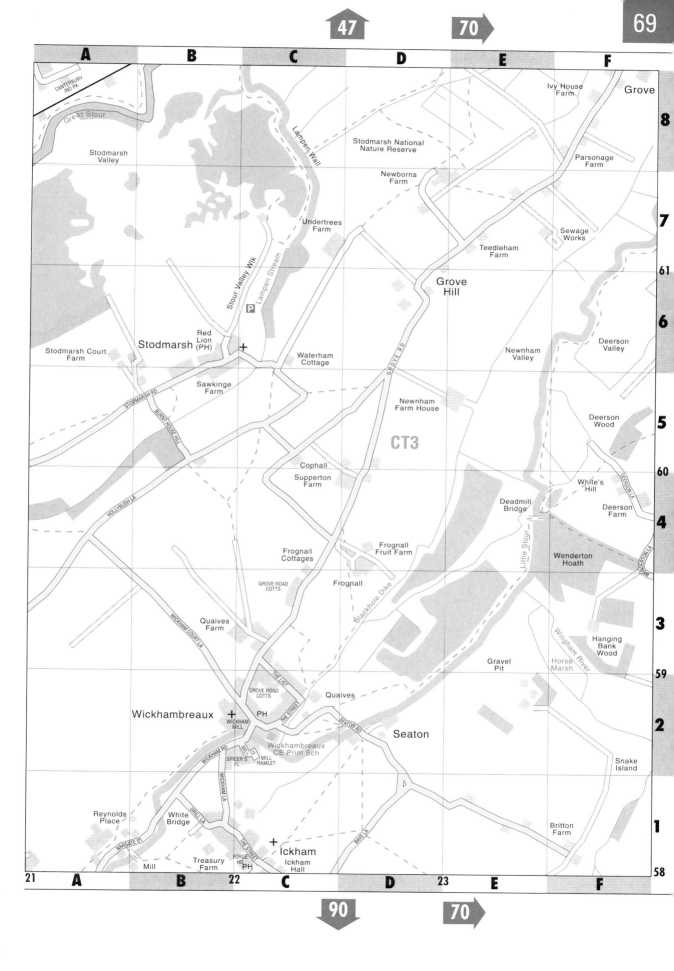

A B C D E F

8

7

61

6

5

60

4

3

59

2

1

58

Little Stour

Marleybrooks Farm

GROVE RD

Depot

Preston Valley

GROVE WAY

PRESTON RD

STOURMOUTH RD

The Gables

Hatchers Farm Nursery

Half Moon & Seven Stars (PH)

PO

BISHOP JENNER CT

Preston

THE STREET

THE DOWNS

SHOTFIELD CL

THE FORSTAL

Preston Prim Sch

LOWER SANTON LA

SANTON LA

Santon Farm

Little Santon Farm

PARK RD

MILL LA

CT3

Lodge Farm

PADBROOK LA

Sheerwater

Preston Court

COURT LA

LANGTON COTTS

Ladydown Farm

LONGMETE RD

Rookery Farm

Sheerwater Rd

SHEERWATER RD

Elmstone

Preston Lane Farm

Sweech Farm

PRESTON LA

Little Court Farm

DEERSON LA

Wyborne's Charity

Carpenter's Farmhouse

PRESTON RD

Deaconland Farm

Hoaden Farm

Hoaden

Church Hill Farm

Perry Farm

Little Perry Farm

Walmestone

PERRY LA

Heart's Delight Kennels

Boundary Farm

HEART'S DELIGHT LA

Perry

Little Walmestone

Walmestone Nursery

Herons Hall

Nash Farm

Nash Court Farm

FOUR TURNINGS

NASH RD

Little Nash Farm

Nash

Wenderton Farm

WENDERTON LA

Cretan Court

Preston Hill Farm

Lower Shatterling Farm

Green Man Boarding Kennels

ASHEN TREE COTTS

Shatterling Court Farmhouse

Shatterling

Little Shatterling Farm

The Frog & Orange PH

Wingham Bird Pk

Great Rusham Farm

RUSHAM RD

Moorhills Nurseries

A257 PEDDING HILL

PEDDING LA

Broom Hill

PRESTON HILL

Stone Down

Broomhill

A257 GOBERY HILL

PETTS LA

Beaute Farm

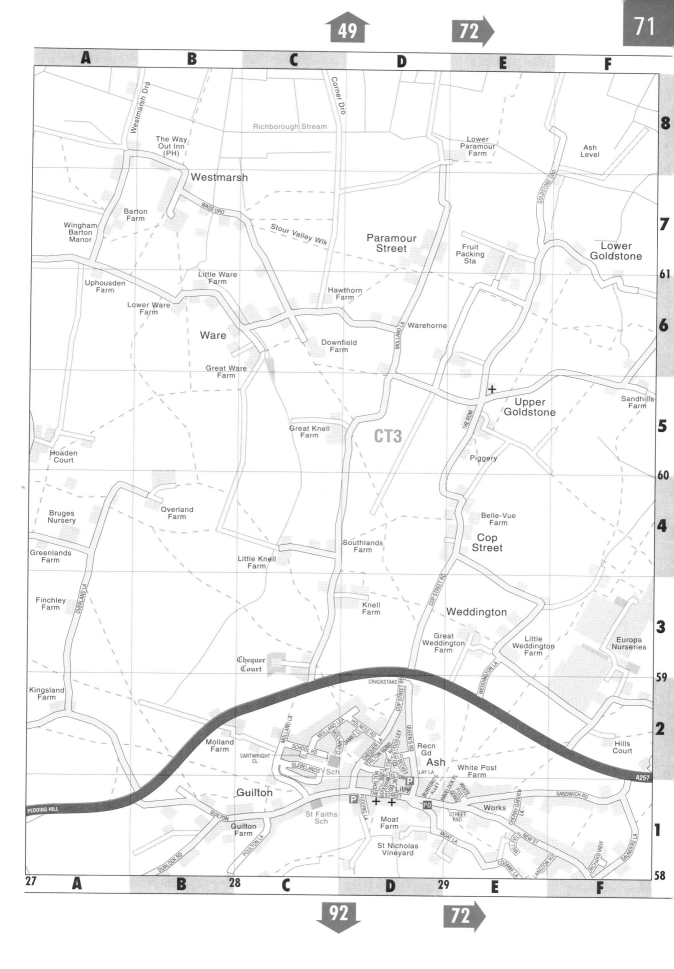

49
72
92
72

A B C D E F

8
7
61
6
5
60
4
3
59
2
1
58

27 A B 28 C D 29 E F

Westmarsh Dro
The Way Out Inn (PH)
Westmarsh
Richborough Stream
Corner Dro
Lower Paramour Farm
Ash Level
Barton Farm
Wingham Barton Manor
Wass Dro
Stour Valley Wlk
Paramour Street
Fruit Packing Sta
Lower Goldstone
Goldstone Dro
Little Ware Farm
Uphousden Farm
Lower Ware Farm
Hawthorn Farm
Molland La
Warehorne
Ware
Downfield Farm
Great Ware Farm
Upper Goldstone
The Row
Sandhills Farm
Hoaden Court
Great Knell Farm
Great Knell Farm
CT3
Piggery
Bruges Nursery
Overland Farm
Belle-Vue Farm
Cop Street
Greenlands Farm
Overland La
Little Knell Farm
Southlands Farm
Finchley Farm
Knell Farm
Weddington
Great Weddington Farm
Little Weddington Farm
Cop Street Rd
Europa Nurseries
Chequer Court
Crackstake
Cop Street Rd
Weddington La
Kingsland Farm
Molland La
Molland Lea
School Rd
Holness Rd
James Cl
Midland Ct
Chequer La
Field
Woods Ley
Woods Ley
Queen's Rd
Recn Gd
Hills Court
Molland Farm
Cartwright Cl
Glebelands
Sch
Guilton Gdns
Chilton La
Chilton Pl
Becks
Ash
White Post Farm
A257
Pedding Hill
Liby
Chilton
The Goldings
Chilton Street
Burfro's Alley
Lay La
Have Dick Pl
White Post Gdns
Street End
Works
Sandwich Rd
Guilton
St Faiths Sch
Pudding La
Moat Farm
PO
New St
Cherry Garden La
Guilton La
Guilton Farm
Poulton La
St Nicholas Vineyard
Moat La
Church Field
Langdon Ave
Orchard View
Coombe La
Saunders La
Durlock Rd

A B C D E F

8

7

61

6

5

60

4

3

59

2

1

58

30 A B 31 C D 32 E F

Potts Farm Dro

Ash Level

Richborough Stream

White House

WHITEHOUSE DRO

Bride Farm

Guston Farm

RUBERY DRO

Sparrow Castle

Richborough Farm

Fleet Farm

Castle Farm

Richborough Castle
ROMAN FORT
(remains of)

CT3

CT13

CASTLE COTTS

Cooper Street Farmhouse

Mus

Sewage Works

A256

Swallows Brook Farm

COOPER STREET DRO

Cooper Street

Stour Valley Wlk

Goshall Valley

Goshall Stream

River Stour

Brookestreet Farmyard

LC

The Monks' Wall

RICHBOROUGH RD

Little East Street Farm

Saxon Shore Way

North Poulders Stream

East Street

East Street Farm

WANTSUME LEES

Nature Reserve

North Poulders

White Mill Mus

Ind Est

MILL CL

GOSS HALL LA

Goss Hall

A257

THE CAUSEWAY

ASH RD

LC

STRAND

P

SANDWICH RD

Each End

South Poulders

Sandwich Inf Sch

The Butts

Mus

P

Each End House

MOAT SOLE

ST THOMAS'S HOSP

LC

Each Manor Farm

Mary-le-bone Hill

F1
1 GUESTLING MILL CT
2 CRAIGHTON FLATS
3 CHURCH STREET ST MARY'S
4 VICARAGE LA
5 GUILDCOUNT LA
6 HARNET ST
7 WANTSUM MEWS
8 STOUR CT
9 LOOP COURT MEWS
10 TANNERY LA
11 ST JOHN'S COTTS
12 WATTS YD
13 WHITEFRIARS WAY

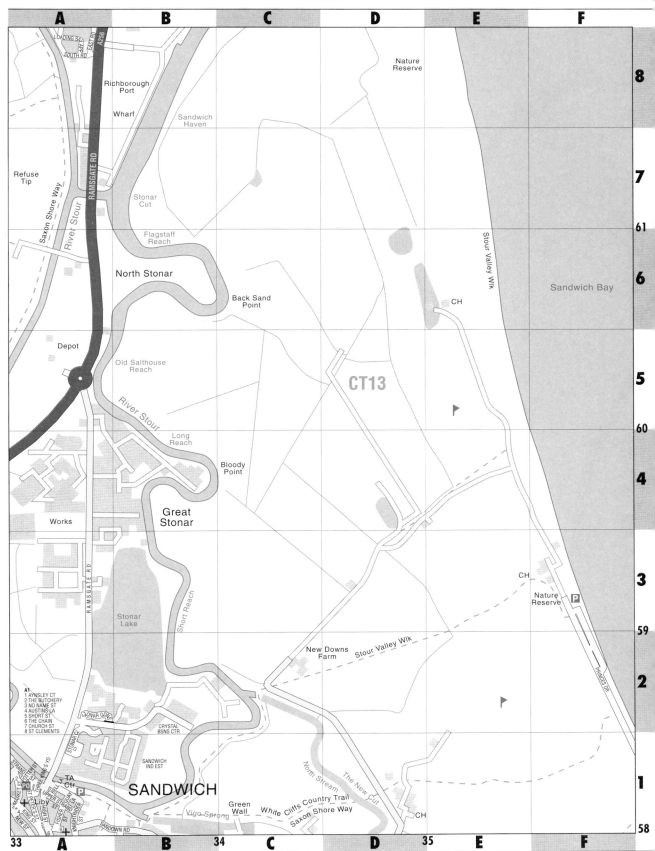

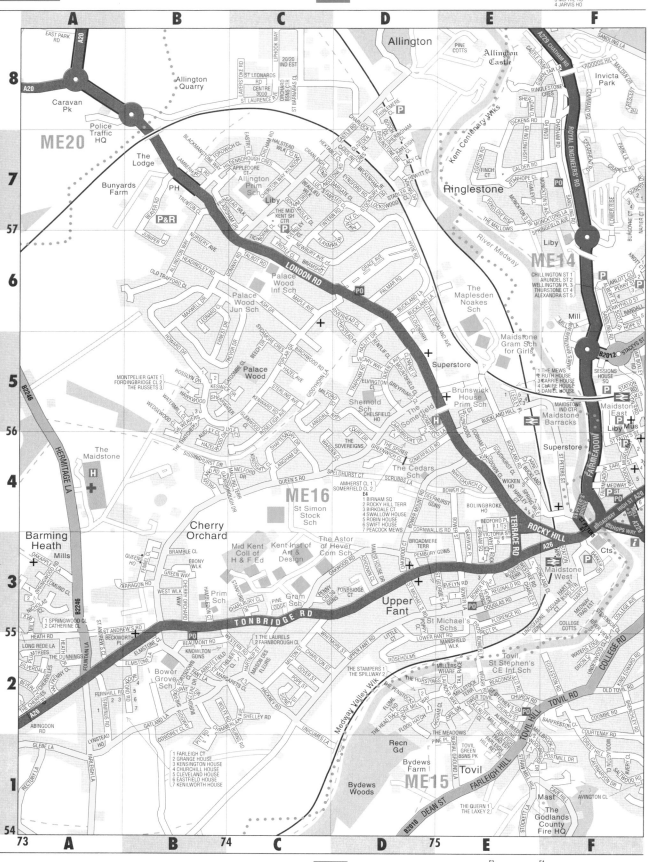

F7
1 GAGETOWN TERR
2 GILBERT TERR
3 McPHIE HO
4 JARVIS HO

E3
1 NEWTON CL
2 ORCHARD PL
3 OLDCHURCH CT
4 RYECAULT CL
5 WHITE ROCK PL
6 VICTORIA CT
7 WESTREE CT

F4
1 HAVOCK LA
2 MARKET ST
3 MARKET COLONNADE
4 MARKET BLDGS
5 ROYAL STAR ARC
6 MIDDLE ROW

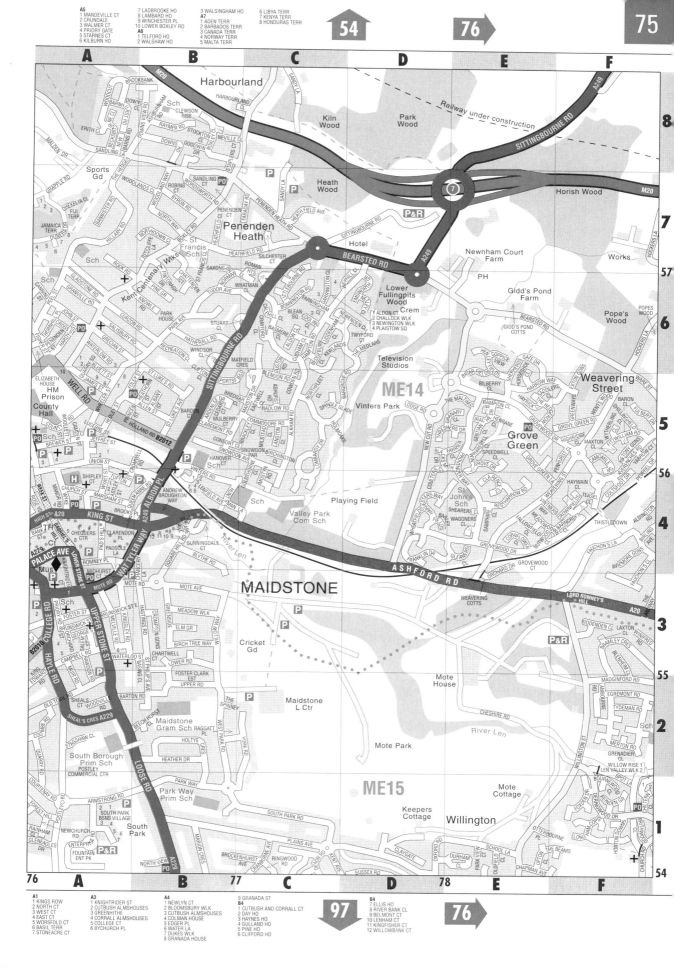

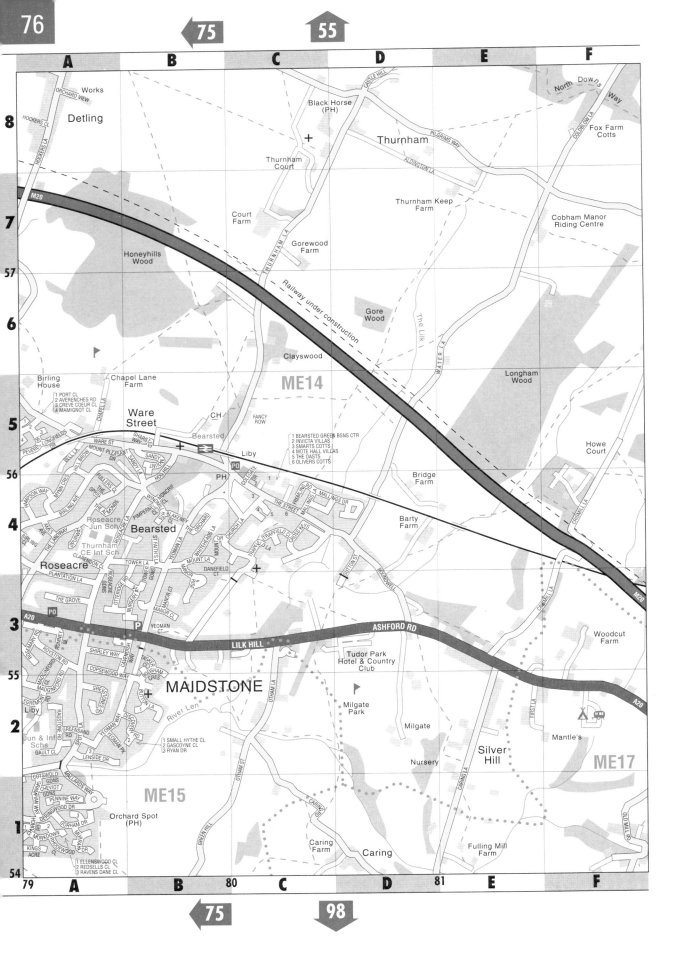

75
55

A B C D E F

8

Works
ORCHARD VIEW
Detling
HOCKERS CL

Castle Hill
North Downs Way

Black Horse
(PH)
Thurnham

Fox Farm
Cotts
COLDBLOW LA

PILGRIMS WAY

7

M20

Thurnham
Court
Thurnham Keep
Farm

ALDINGTON LA

Cobham Manor
Riding Centre

57

Court
Farm

THURNHAM LA

Gorewood
Farm

Honeyhills
Wood

Railway under construction

6

Gore
Wood

THE LILK

WATER LA

Longham
Wood

Clayswood

ME14

Birling
House
1 PORT CL
2 AVERENCHES RD
3 CREVE COEUR CL
4 MAMIGNOT CL

Chapel Lane
Farm

5

Ware
Street

CH

Bearsted

FANCY
ROW

1 BEARSTED GREEN BSNS CTR
2 INVICTA VILLAS
3 SMARTS COTTS
4 MOTE HALL VILLAS
5 THE OASTS
6 OLIVERS COTTS

Howe
Court

WARE ST

PEVERE

LONGFIELDS

SHARS
WAY

SANDY
CL

Liby
PO

HILL BROW

WYNN CRES

BELLI
THE ALMONDS

MOUNT PLEASANT
DR

OXENGATE

THE STREET

FREMLINS

MALLINGS DR

Bridge
Farm

56

HAMPSON WAY

FULLERS CA

THE SPRIG

SANDY LA

HOG HILL

PH

MALLINGS LA

4

Roseacre
Jun Sch

Bearsted

Thurnham
CE Inf Sch

BIRLING AVE
ARLES
THE LANDWAY

PIMPERNEL CL

WINDMILL
CL

BLAKENEY
CL

THE ORCHARD

WHITEHEADS LA

CHURCH LA

TRAPFIELD CL

CROSS KEYS

Barty
Farm

Roseacre

CLARENDON CL

ROSEACRE LA

ST FAITH'S LA

MANOR DR

MOUNT LA

TRAPFIELD LA

SUTTON ST

ROUNDWELL

PLANTATION LA

TOWER LA

DANEFIELD
CT

OTTERIDGE RD

ROSEACRE
GDNS

TOWER
GDNS

MANOR CT

MANOR RISE

3

A20
PO

P

YEOMAN
CT

LILK HILL

ASHFORD RD

CRISMILL LA

M20

Woodcut
Farm

SHIRLEY WAY

CAVERSHAM

CROSHAM
CRES

Tudor Park
Hotel & Country
Club

FIRST LA

ROYSTON RD
ROSEMARY RD
ROMNEY CL

COPSEWOOD WAY
GREYSTONES RD
SUTTON LA

55

MADGINFORD RD
MADGINFORD CL
EGREMONT RD

YEOMAN WAY
DISCOVERY
RD

OTHAM LA

Milgate
Park

Milgate

Mantle's

ME17

2

Liby
Jun & Inf
Schs
GAULT CL

RAGSTONE RD
GREENSAND RD

YEOMAN PK
LENSIDE DR

River Len

OTHAM ST

1 SMALL HYTHE CL
2 GASCOYNE CL
3 RYAN DR

Nursery

Silver
Hill

CARING LA

MAIDSTONE

MALLARDS WAY

ME15

COTSWOLD
GDNS
CHEVIOT
GDNS
PENNINE WAY
DERINGWOOD DR
GORHAM DR

Orchard Spot
(PH)

GREEN HILL

CARING
RD

1

KINGS
ACRE
MONKDOWN
RIDGEWOOD
DR

Caring
Farm

Caring

Fulling Mill
Farm

OLD MILL RD

1 ELLENSWOOD CL
2 REDSELLS CL
3 RAVENS DANE CL

54

79 A 80 B C 81 D E F

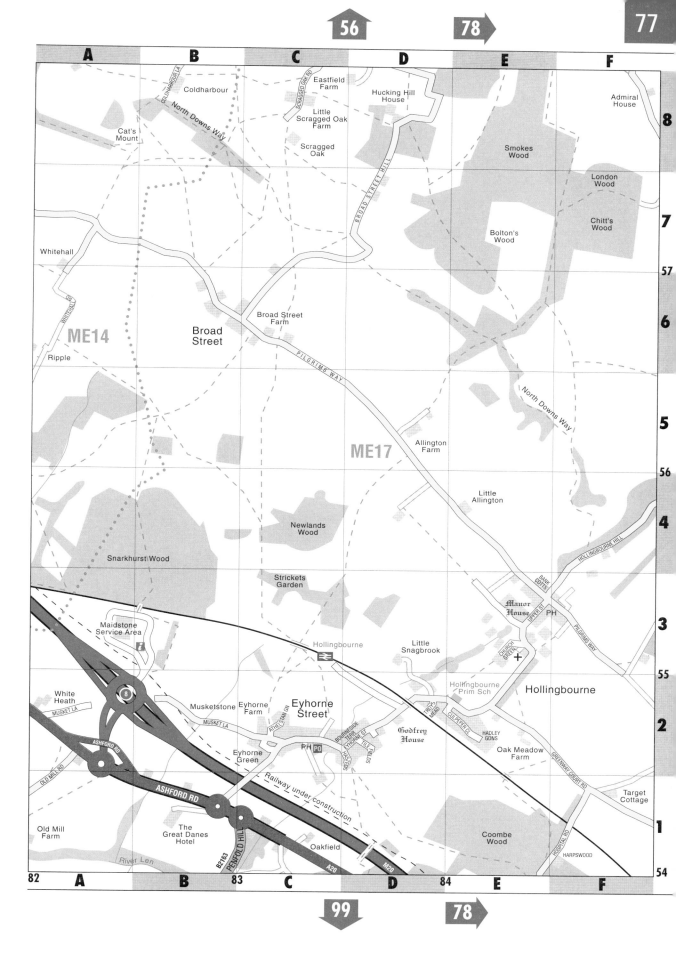

A B C D E F

8

7

57

6

5

56

4

3

55

2

1

54

Coldharbour
COLDHARBOUR LA
SCRAGGED OAK RD
Eastfield Farm
Little Scragged Oak Farm
Scragged Oak
Hucking Hill House
Admiral House

Cat's Mount
North Downs Way

Smokes Wood

London Wood

Chitt's Wood

Bolton's Wood

Whitehall
WHITEHALL RD

ME14

Ripple

Broad Street

Broad Street Farm
BROAD STREET HILL

PILGRIMS WAY

North Downs Way

Allington Farm

ME17

Little Allington

HOLLINGBOURNE HILL

Newlands Wood

Snarkhurst Wood

Strickets Garden

BANK COTTS
Manor House
UPPER ST
PH
PILGRIMS WAY

Maidstone Service Area

Hollingbourne

Little Snagbrook

CHURCH GREEN

Hollingbourne

White Heath
MUSKET LA

Musketstone
Eyhorne Farm
ATHELSTAN GDN
MUSKET LA

Eyhorne Street

BOURNESIDE TERR
EYHORNE ST
TILE FIELDS
HASTES

Godfrey House

TROYS MEAD
CULPEPER CL

Hollingbourne Prim Sch

Hollingbourne

ASHFORD RD
OLD MILL RD

Eyhorne Green
PH PO

HADLEY GDNS

Oak Meadow Farm

GREENWAY COURT RD

Target Cottage

Old Mill Farm

The Great Danes Hotel

B2163
PENFOLD HILL

ASHFORD RD

Oakfield

A20

Railway under construction

M20

Coombe Wood

HOSPITAL RD
HARPSWOOD

River Len

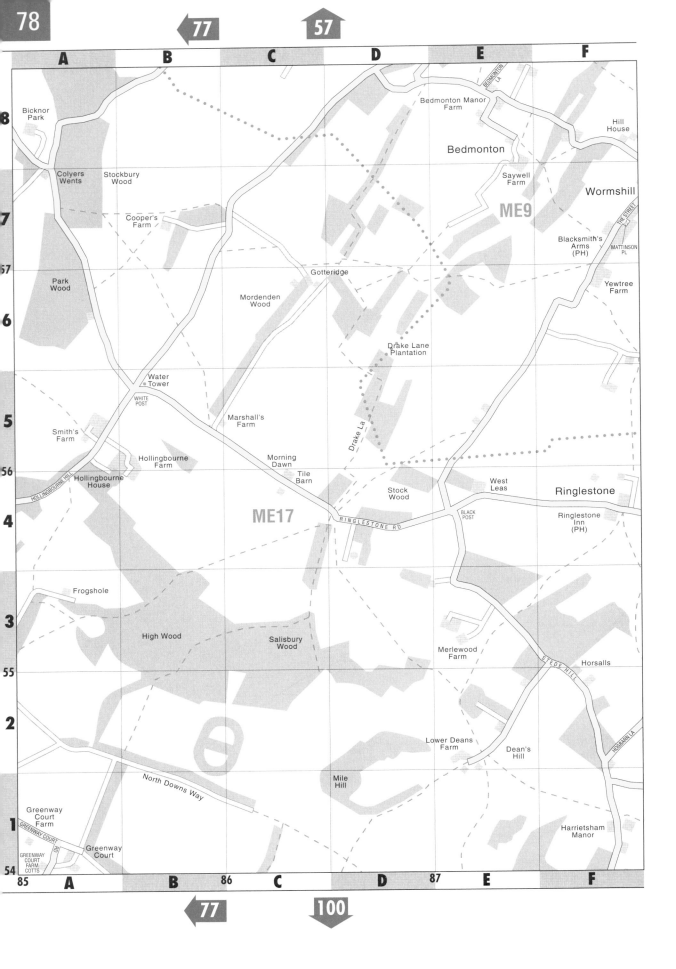

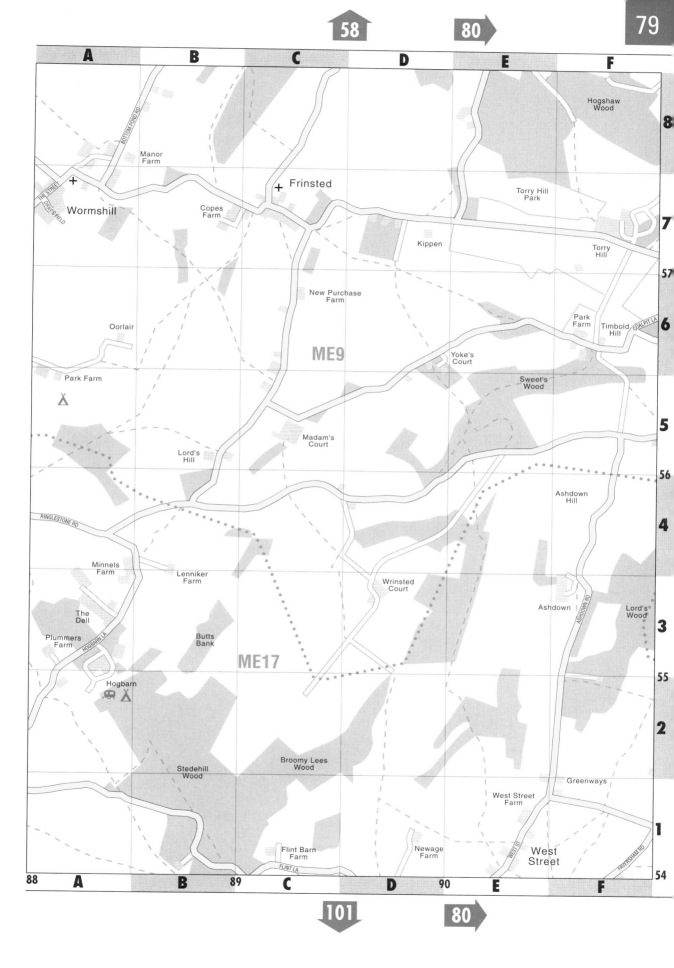

A   B   C   D   E   F

Hogshaw
Wood

8

Manor
Farm

THE STREET

BOTTOM POND RD

DRAY'S FIELD

+
Wormshill

+ Frinsted

Copes
Farm

Torry Hill
Park

7

Kippen

Torry
Hill

57

New Purchase
Farm

Park
Farm

Timbold
Hill

COALPIT LA

6

Oorlair

ME9

Yoke's
Court

Sweet's
Wood

Park Farm

5

Lord's
Hill

Madam's
Court

Ashdown
Hill

56

RINGLESTONE RD

4

Minnels
Farm

Lenniker
Farm

Wrinsted
Court

Ashdown

ASHDOWN RD

Lord's
Wood

3

The
Dell

HOGBARN LA

Butts
Bank

ME17

Plummers
Farm

Hogbarn

55

2

Stedehill
Wood

Broomy Lees
Wood

Greenways

West Street
Farm

Flint Barn
Farm

FLINT LA

Newage
Farm

WEST ST

West
Street

TAVERSHAM RD

1

88   A   B   89   C   D   90   E   F   54

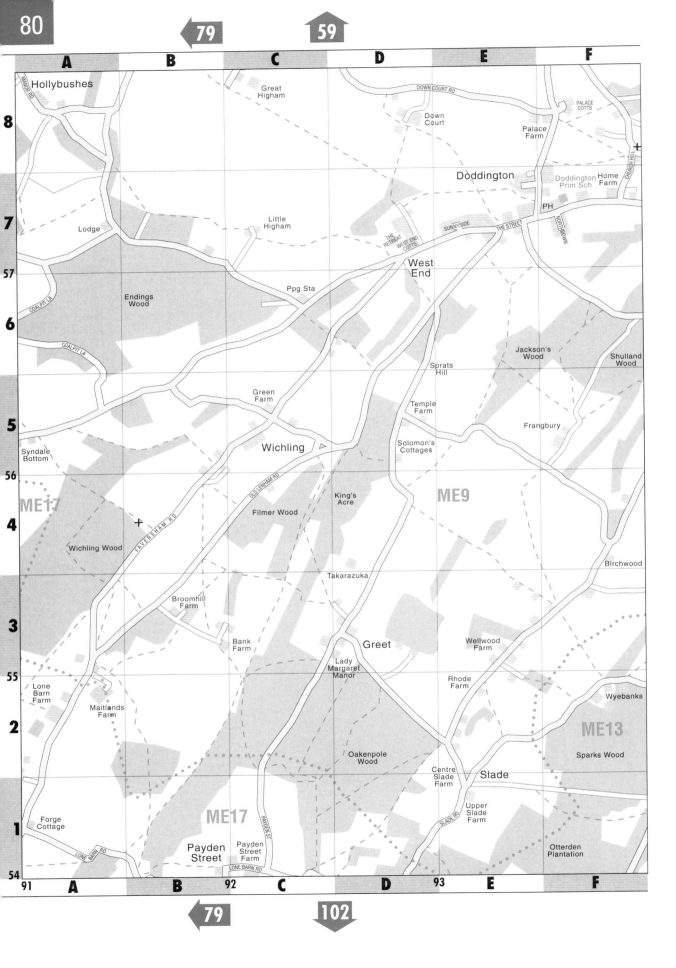

79
59

A B C D E F

Hollybushes

Great
Higham

DOWN COURT RD

Down
Court

PALACE
COTTS

Palace
Farm

8

Doddington

Doddington
Prim Sch

Home
Farm

PH

Lodge

Little
Higham

THE RETREAT

WEST END
COTTS

SUNNYSIDE

THE STREET

NORTHDOWN

7

COALPIT LA

57

West
End

Endings
Wood

Ppg Sta

Jackson's
Wood

Shulland
Wood

COALPIT LA

6

Sprats
Hill

Green
Farm

Temple
Farm

Frangbury

5

Wichling

Solomon's
Cottages

Syndale
Bottom

56

ME9

ME17

King's
Acre

OLD LENHAM RD

Filmer Wood

4

Wichling Wood

TAVERSHAM RD

Birchwood

Takarazuka

Broomhill
Farm

3

Bank
Farm

Greet

Wellwood
Farm

Lady
Margaret
Manor

Rhode
Farm

Lone
Barn
Farm

55

Wyebanks

Maitlands
Farm

ME13

2

Sparks Wood

Oakenpole
Wood

Centre
Slade
Farm

Slade

ME17

PAYDEN ST

Upper
Slade
Farm

SLADE RD

1

Forge
Cottage

Payden
Street
Farm

Payden
Street

Otterden
Plantation

LONE BARN RD

LONE BARN RD

54

91 A B 92 C D 93 E F

79
102

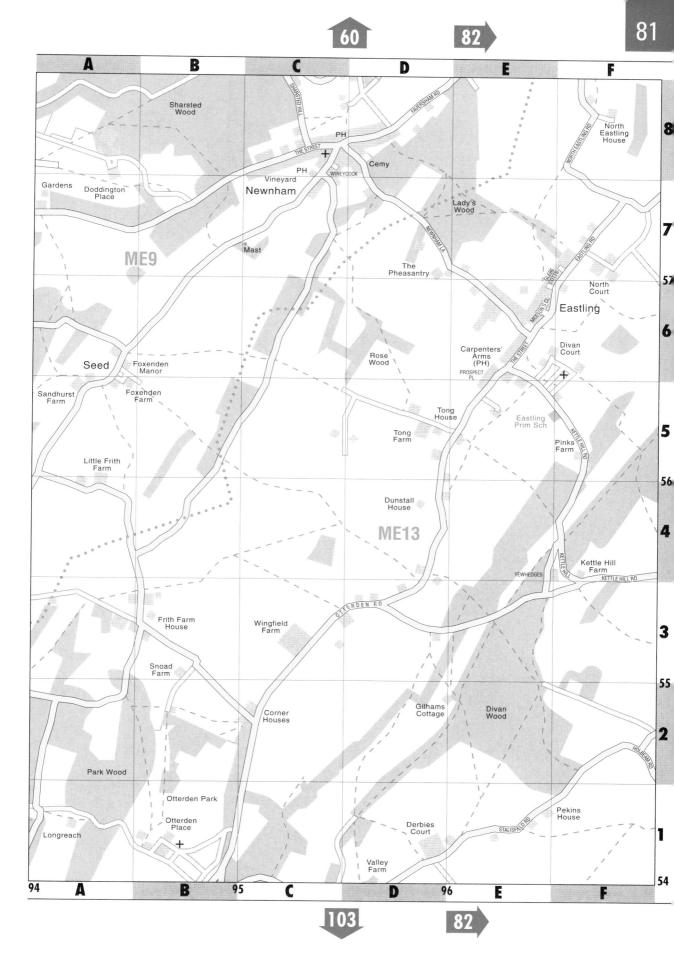

A   B   C   D   E   F

8

Sharsted
Wood

North
Eastling
House

PH

Cemy

The Street

Wineycock

PH

Vineyard

Newnham

Lady's
Wood

7

Gardens

Doddington
Place

57

ME9

Mast

The Pheasantry

North
Court

Eastling

6

Seed

Foxenden
Manor

Rose
Wood

Carpenters'
Arms
(PH)

Divan
Court

Sandhurst
Farm

Foxenden
Farm

PROSPECT
PL

Tong
House

Eastling
Prim Sch

Pinks
Farm

5

Little Frith
Farm

Tong
Farm

56

Dunstall
House

ME13

4

Kettle Hill
Farm

YEWHEDGES

Frith Farm
House

Wingfield
Farm

OTTERDEN RD

KETTLE HILL RD

3

Snoad
Farm

55

Corner
Houses

Gilhams
Cottage

Divan
Wood

2

Park Wood

HOLBEAM RD

Otterden Park

Pekins
House

Otterden
Place

Derbies
Court

STALISFIELD RD

1

Longreach

Valley
Farm

54

94   A   B   95   C   D   96   E   F

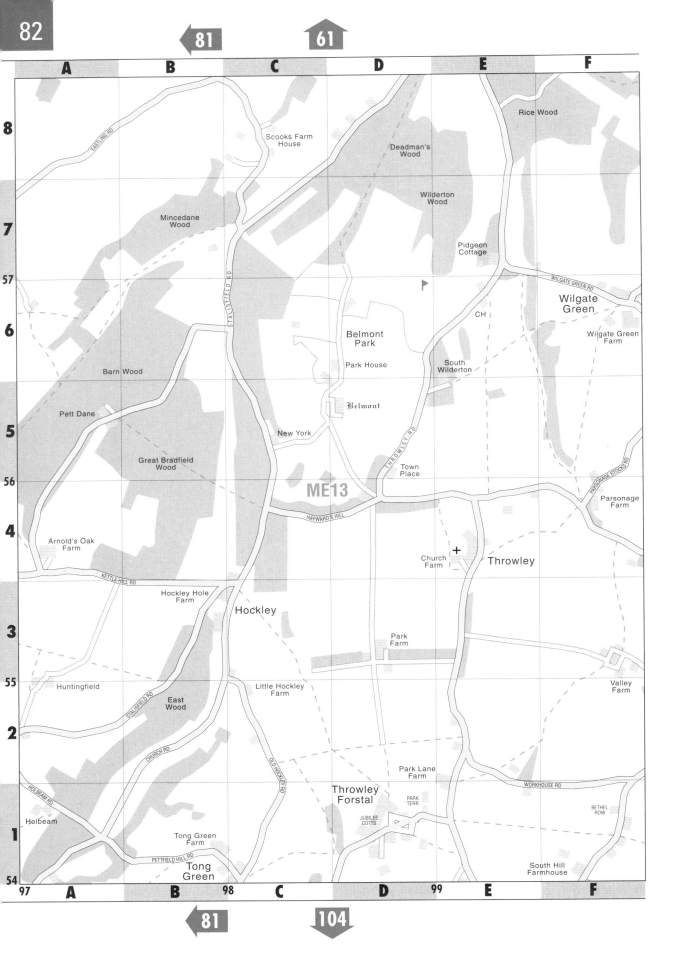

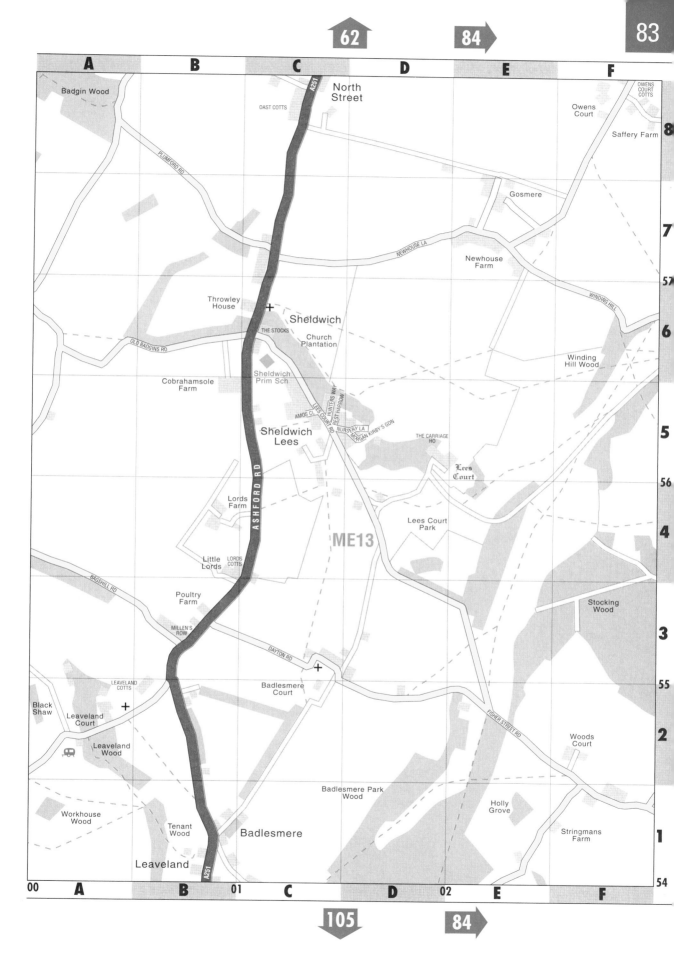

A **B** **C** **D** **E** **F**

Badgin Wood

North Street

OAST COTTS

OWENS COURT COTTS

Owens Court

Saffery Farm

8

PLUMFORD RD

A251

Gosmere

7

NEWHOUSE LA

Newhouse Farm

57

Throwley House

Sheldwich

WINDING HILL

OLD BADGINS RD

THE STOCKS

Church Plantation

Winding Hill Wood

6

Cobrahamsole Farm

Sheldwich Prim Sch

HUNTERS WAY

AMOS CL

LEES COURT RD

BEST HARROW

NURSERY LA

EGAN KIRBY'S GDN

THE CARRIAGE HO

Sheldwich Lees

5

Lees Court

Lords Farm

56

Lees Court Park

ME13

4

Little Lords

LORDS COTTS

BAGSHILL RD

ASHFORD RD

Poultry Farm

Stocking Wood

MILLEN'S ROW

DAYTON RD

3

LEAVELAND COTTS

Badlesmere Court

55

FISHER STREET RD

Black Shaw

Leaveland Court

Woods Court

2

Leaveland Wood

Badlesmere Park Wood

Holly Grove

Workhouse Wood

Tenant Wood

Badlesmere

Stringmans Farm

1

Leaveland

A251

54

00 **A** **B** **01** **C** **D** **02** **E** **F**

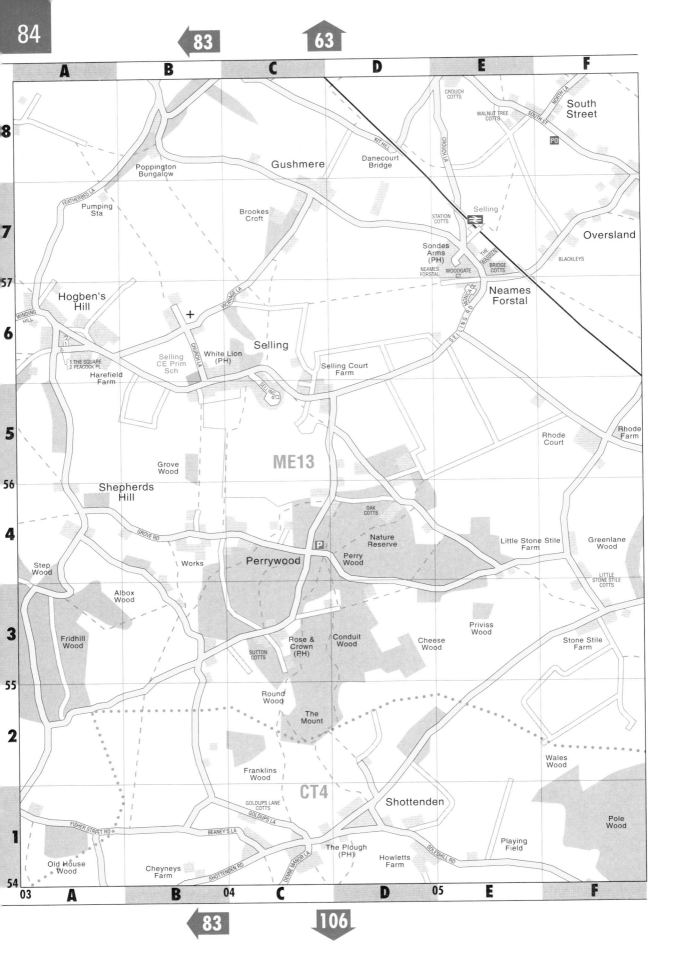

83
63

A B C D E F

8

7

57

6

5

56

4

3

55

2

1

54

03 A B 04 C D 05 E F

83
106

South Street

CROUCH COTTS

WALNUT TREE COTTS

NORTH LA

SOUTH ST

PO

Gushmere

KIT HILL

Danecourt Bridge

CROUCH LA

Overland

Poppington Bungalow

Selling

STATION COTTS

Sondes Arms (PH)

NEAMES FORSTAL

WOODGATE CT.

BRIDGE COTTS

THE WARREN

BLACKLEYS

Neames Forstal

FEATHERBED LA

Pumping Sta

Brookes Croft

VICARAGE LA

SELLING RD

MONICA PL

Hogben's Hill

WINDING HILL

+

White Lion (PH)

Selling

Selling Court Farm

Rhode Court

Rhode Farm

Selling CE Prim Sch

CHURCH LA

SELLING RD

1 THE SQUARE
2 PEACOCK PL

Harefield Farm

Grove Wood

ME13

Shepherds Hill

GROVE RD

OAK COTTS

Nature Reserve

Little Stone Stile Farm

Greenlane Wood

Step Wood

Works

P

Perrywood

Perry Wood

LITTLE STONE STILE COTTS

Albox Wood

Priviss Wood

Stone Stile Farm

Fridhill Wood

SUTTON COTTS

Rose & Crown (PH)

Conduit Wood

Cheese Wood

Round Wood

The Mount

Wales Wood

Franklins Wood

CT4

Shottenden

Pole Wood

GOLDUPS LANE COTTS

GOLDUPS LA

FISHER STREET RD

BEANEY'S LA

DRONE MANOR LA

The Plough (PH)

Howletts Farm

SOLESHILL RD

Playing Field

Old House Wood

Cheyneys Farm

SHOTTENDEN RD

A B C D E F

Meadow
Wood

Chrislocks
Wood

Winterbourne
Wood

South
Bishops Den

8

Winterbourne

ME13

Court
Wood

Denstead
Wood

7

57

Fox
Wood

Saw
Mill

Goulds
Wood

Joan Beech
Wood

Nickle
Wood

6

Rhode
Common

Bower
Wood

Upper
Ensign

5

56

Gorewell
Wood

Highfield
Springs

Lower
Ensden

LOWER ENSDEN RD

4

Shiversalls
Shaw

North Downs Way

New Forest
Farm

Chestnut
Plantation

NEW FOREST LA

Phyllis
Farm

CT4

3

SHRIMPTON CT

NEW CUT RD

Old Wives
Lees

North
Court

SELLING RD

Shalmsford
Bridge

55

NORTH DOWNS CT

OAST
HO

Lower Lees Rd

PH
THE
PADDOCK

PO

SHALMSFORD RD

A28

GREEN LA

BOWERLAND LA

Hawkin's
Rough

LEES
TERR

2

COBBS HILL

Cork
Farm

LONG HILL

Thorpe
Farm

Bowerland
Farm

PILGRIMS LA

Great Stour

MULBERRY HILL

BOWERLAND LA

WHITE HILL

CANTERBURY RD

1

A28

LC

54

06 A B 07 C D 08 E F

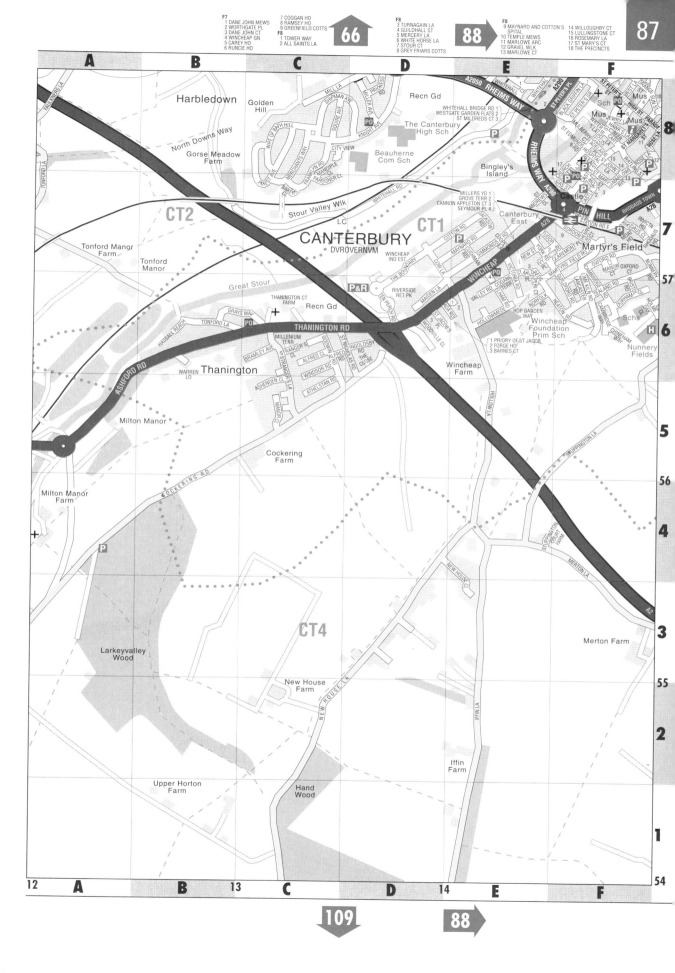

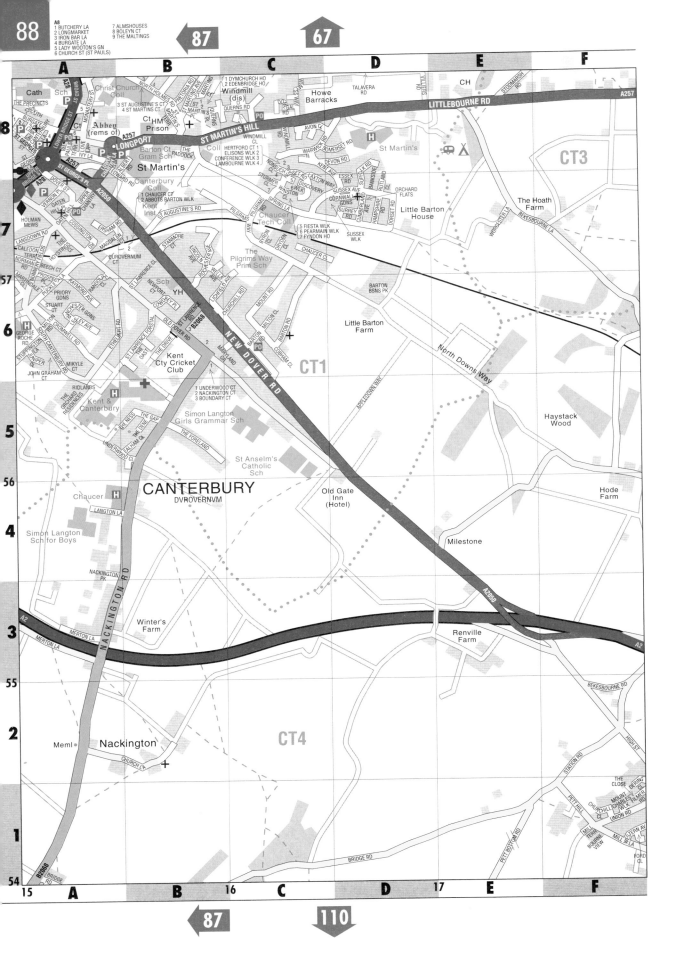

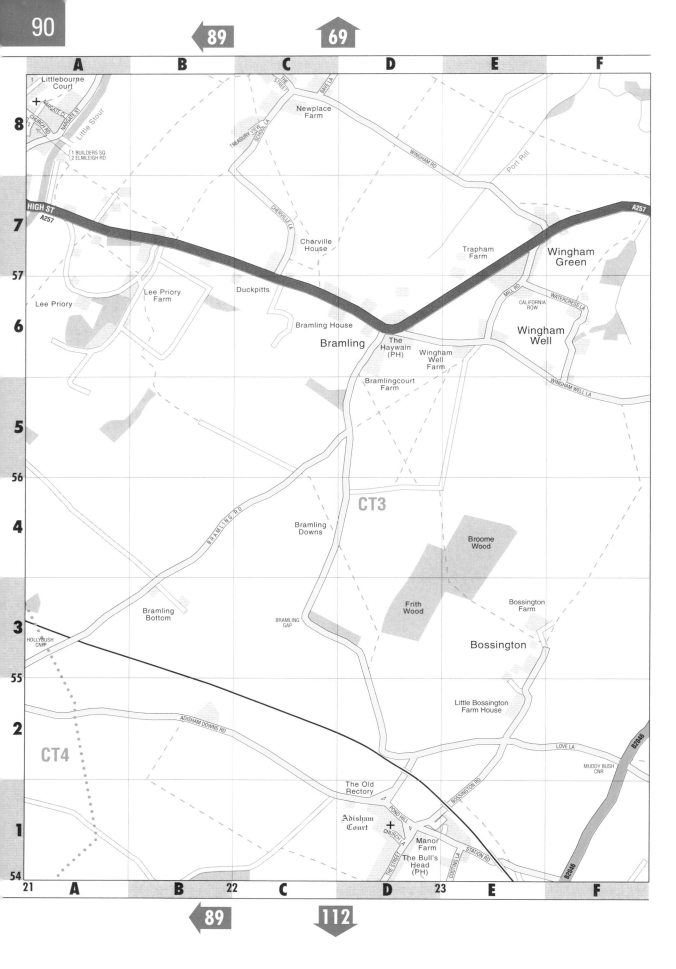

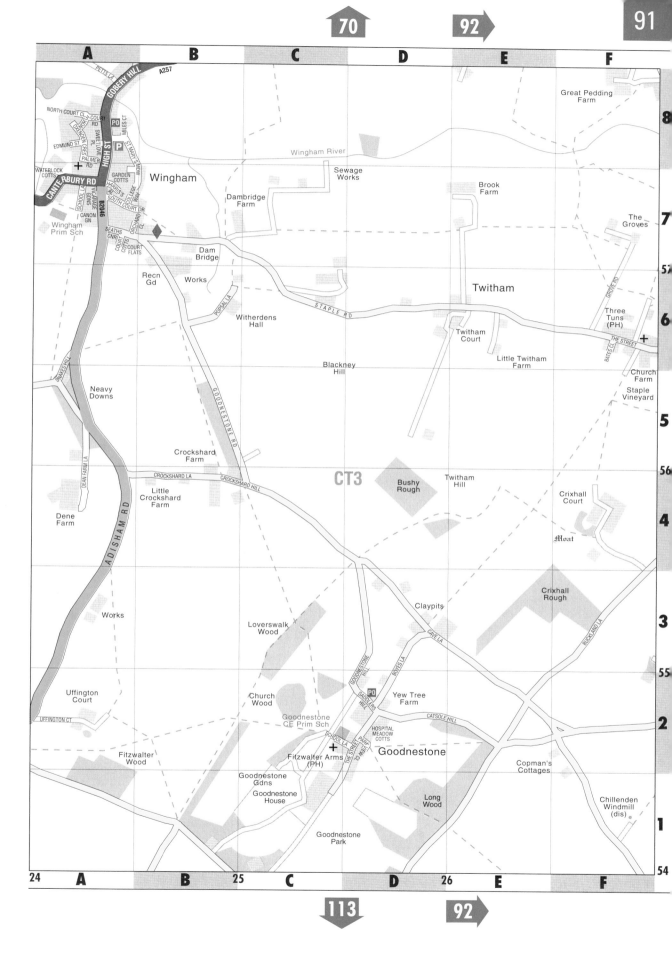

A B C D E F

8

Nursery
Durlock
Durlock Bridge
Poulton Farm
Ash Coombe Vineyard
Coombe
Coombe Farm

7
Ringleton Manor
Radar Sta
The Rookery

57
Little Flemings Farm
Black Pond Farm
Christian Court

Staple Farm
Nurseries
1 THE OAST
2 THE OAST PADDOCK
3 THE COURTYARD
Chapel Farm
FLEMING RD
Flemings
Ringlemere Farm

6
LOWER RD
Mill Road Farm
Fernleigh
Flemings House
DRAINLESS RD

THE STREET
SCHOOL LA
Barnsole
Staple
PH
Gander Court
Mushroom Farm

5
MILL RD
Nurseries
Chalk Farm Lodge
CHALK PIT LA
Onionbeds

56
BUCKLAND LA
Summerfield Farm
CT3
CT13
Denne Court Farm

4
Summerfield
Summerfield Farm Pottery
Hammill Court
The Hammill Brick Works
Dix's Farm

Hammill
Hammill Farm

3
Green La
GREEN LA

55
Lower Rowling Farm
Great Tickenhurst Farm

2
Rowling House
Upper Rowling Farm
MEADOW COTTS
Rowling Court
Tickenhurst
Middle Heronden Farm

1
Little Tickenhurst Farm
Heronden
HERONDEN RD
THORNTON LA

54
27 A B 28 C D 29 E F
Tickenhurst Shave
Heronden Farm

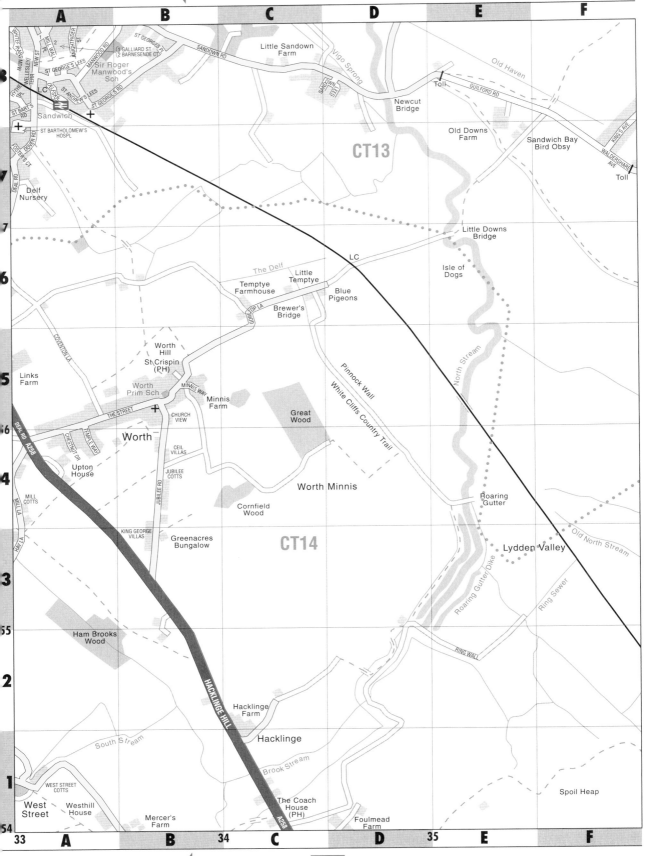

Sandwich Bay

Royal
St George's
Golf Links

Sandwich Bay
Estate

KING'S AVE
COASTGUARD
COTTS
NORTH RD
PRINCES DR

WALDERSHARE AVE

SHAWDON AVE

FRANCIS AVE

CAMBRIDGE AVE

DICKSON'S
CNR

Lyddcourt
Stile

CT13

Lydden

Mary Bax's
Stone

Old North Stream

CT14

Chequers
(PH)

White Cliffs Country Trail

Saxon Shore Way

Tenants
Hills

Walnut Tree
Farm

Sandhills

REDHOUSE WAY

CH

GOLF RD

Sandown Castle
(remains of)

CANUTE RD

SANDOWN RD

CL
PAVILIONS

1 CASTLE WLK
2 CANUTE WLK

THE MARINA

ETHELBERT RD.

GOLF CT 1
LINKS CT 2

Penfold Sewer

Spoil
Heap

A   B   C   D   E   F

8
7
57
6
5
56
4
3
55
2
1
54

36   A   B   37   C   D   38   E   F

74

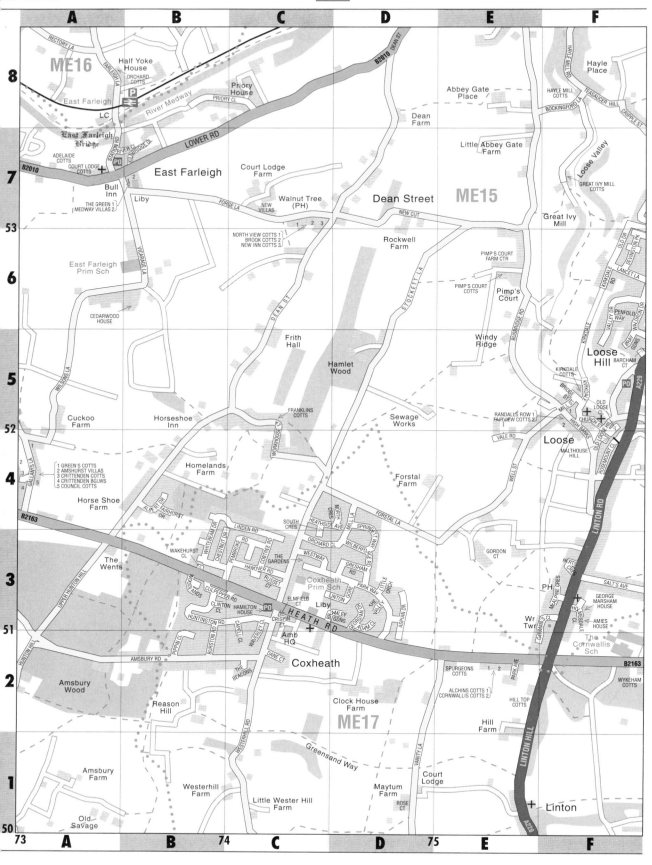

A B C D E F

8

ME16

Half Yoke House
ORCHARD COTTS
Priory House
PRIORY CL
River Medway
B2010 DEAN ST
Dean Farm
Abbey Gate Place
HAYLE MILL RD
Hayle Place
HAYLE MILL COTTS
BOCKINGFORD LA
TEASAUCER HILL
CRIPPLE ST

East Farleigh
LC
LOWER RD
Little Abbey Gate Farm
ME15
Loose Valley

7

East Farleigh Bridge
ADELAIDE COTTS
COURT LODGE COTTS
B2010
PO
Bull Inn
East Farleigh
Liby
THE GREEN 1
MEDWAY VILLAS 2
STATION RD
TURNER CL
KILNBRIDGE CL
VICARAGE LA
Court Lodge Farm
FORGE LA
Walnut Tree (PH)
NEW VILLAS
1 2 3
Dean Street
NEW CUT
Great Ivy Mill
GREAT IVY MILL COTTS
Great Ivy Mill

53

NORTH VIEW COTTS 1
BROOK COTTS 2
NEW INN COTTS 3
Rockwell Farm
STOCKETT LA
PIMP'S COURT FARM CTR
OLD LA
SEVINGTON PK
LANCET LA
KIRKDALE

6

East Farleigh Prim Sch
CEDARWOOD HOUSE
DEAN ST
Frith Hall
PIMP'S COURT COTTS
Pimp's Court
BUSBRIDGE RD
Windy Ridge
PENFOLD WAY
VALLEY DR
GRAY GDNS
WACHORN DR
KIRKDALE
Loose Hill
BARCHAM CT

5

WILSONS LA
Cuckoo Farm
Horseshoe Inn
FRANKLINS COTTS
WORKHOUSE LA
Hamlet Wood
Sewage Works
KIRKDALE COTTS
BRIDGE MILL ST
RANDALLS ROW 1
FAIRVIEW COTTS 2
HIGH BANKS
KRONE
OLD LOOSE CL
CHURCH ST
PO
A229

52

GALLANTS LA
1 GREEN'S COTTS
2 AMSHURST VILLAS
3 CRITTENDEN COTTS
4 CRITTENDEN BGLWS
5 COUNCIL COTTS
Homelands Farm
Forstal Farm
VALE RD
WELL ST
Loose
MALTHOUSE HILL
RUSSMOUNT CL
OLD LOOSE

4

1 2
3
4 5
Horse Shoe Farm
ALBERT DR
FAIRHURST
FORSTAL LA
LINTON RD

B2163

3

UPPER HUNTON HILL
The Wents
WOODLANDS
WHITEBEAM DR
CHESTNUT DR
PEMBROKE RD
LINDEN RD
COBTREE RD
WAKEHURST CL
HANOVER RD
RUSSELL CT
The Gardens
SOUTH CRES
WESTWAY
NORTH CRES
HEATHSIDE AVE
MILL LA
ORCHARD CL
SPRINGFIELD RD
WILBERFORCE RD
Park Way
GRESHAM RD
THE LITTLE ORCH
Coxheath Prim Sch
Liby
GORDON CT
HERTS CL
SALT'S AVE
MALPINE CRES
PH
GEORGE MARSHAM HOUSE
AMIES HOUSE
Wr Twr

51

HUNTON HILL
CULPEPPER RD
CLINTON CL
Hamilton House
PO
ELMFIELD CT
CRISPIN CT
HEATH RD
Liby
BRAMLEY GDNS
GEORGIAN DR
THE VALLEY
LINTON CL
ADYM CL
ASPEN DR
CARMAN'S CL
HQ AVENUE
The Cornwallis Sch

2

HUNTINGTON RD
BURSTON RD
CAPELL CL
WAVERLEY CL
PIPPIN CL
Amb HQ
AMSBURY RD
THE BEACONS
DANE CL
Coxheath
Clock House Farm
ME17
SPURGEONS COTTS
1 2
ALCHINS COTTS 1
CORNWALLIS COTTS 2
PARK AVE
HILL TOP COTTS
LINTON HILL
WYKEHAM COTTS

B2163

Amsbury Wood
Reason Hill
Greensand Way
Hill Farm

1

Amsbury Farm
WESTERHILL RD
Westerhill Farm
Little Wester Hill Farm
VANITY LA
Maytum Farm
ROSE CT
Court Lodge
Linton

50

Old Savage

73 A B 74 C D 75 E F

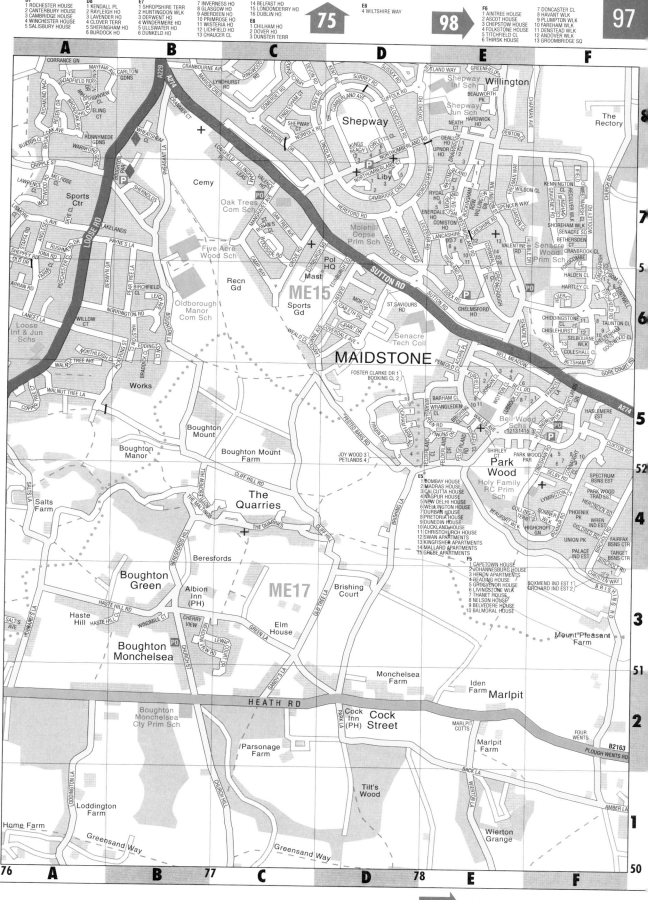

D7
1 ROCHESTER HOUSE
2 CANTERBURY HOUSE
3 CAMBRIDGE HOUSE
4 WINCHESTER HOUSE
5 SALISBURY HOUSE

D8
1 KENDALL PL
2 RAYLEIGH HO
3 LAVENDER HO
4 CLOVER TERR
5 SHERINGHAM HO
6 BURDOCK HO

E7
1 SHROPSHIRE TERR
2 HUNTINGDON WLK
3 DERWENT HO
4 WINDERMERE HO
5 ULLSWATER HO
6 DUNKELD HO
7 INVERNESS HO
8 GLASGOW HO
9 ABERDEEN HO
10 PRIMROSE HO
11 WISTERIA HO
12 LICHFIELD HO
13 CHAUCER CL
14 BELFAST HO
15 LONDONDERRY HO
16 DUBLIN HO

E8
1 CHILHAM HO
2 DOVER HO
3 DUNSTER TERR

E8
4 WILTSHIRE WAY

F6
1 AINTREE HOUSE
2 ASCOT HOUSE
3 CHEPSTOW HOUSE
4 FOLKSTONE HOUSE
5 TITCHFIELD CL
6 THIRSK HOUSE
7 DONCASTER CL
8 HAVANT WLK
9 PLUMPTON WLK
10 FAREHAM WLK
11 DENSTEAD WLK
12 ANDOVER WLK
13 GROOMBRIDGE SQ

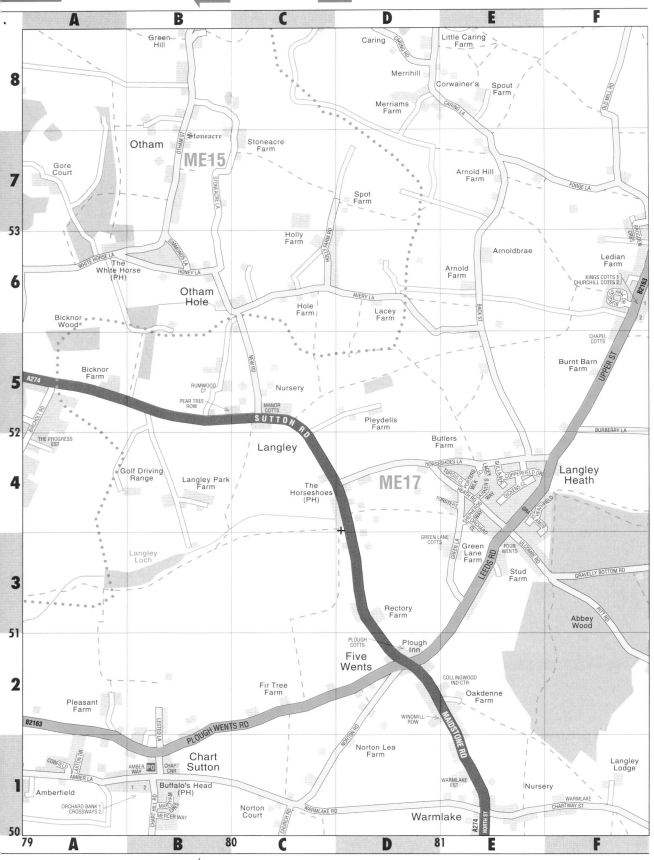

A B C D E F

8

Green Hill

Caring

Little Caring Farm

CARING RD

Merrihill

Corwainer's

Spout Farm

Merriams Farm

CARING LA

Otham

OTHAM ST

Stoneacre

ME15

Stoneacre Farm

Arnold Hill Farm

FORGE LA

7

Gore Court

STONEACRE LA

53

SIMMONDS LA

Holly Farm

HOLLY FARM RD

Spot Farm

Arnoldbrae

Ledian Farm

WHITE HORSE LA

The White Horse (PH)

HONEY LA

Arnold Farm

KINGS COTTS 1
CHURCHILL COTTS 2

B2163

6

Otham Hole

AVERY LA

BACK ST

S HALL OR
1
2

CHAPEL COTTS

Bicknor Wood

Hole Farm

Lacey Farm

UPPER ST

Burnt Barn Farm

5

A274

Bicknor Farm

NEW RD

RUMWOOD CT

PEAR TREE ROW

Nursery

MANOR COTTS

SUTTON RD

Pleydells Farm

BURBERRY LA

52

BRICKBOLT RD

THE PROGRESS EST

Langley

Butlers Farm

4

Golf Driving Range

Langley Park Farm

The Horseshoes (PH)

ME17

HORSESHOES LA

TURGIS C
CORTERS
WLK

HEATH RD

SKINNER'S
LACEY
GILLIARD
COPPERFIELD DR

Langley Heath

FORSTERS

WAY
THE ORCHARD
DICKENS CL
UNWAY
ST CL
SHEPHERDS

GRASSLANDS
HEATHFIELD

Langley Loch

GREEN LANE COTTS

GREEN LA

Green Lane Farm

FOUR WENTS

LEEDS RD

ULCOMBE RD

Stud Farm

GRAVELLY BOTTOM RD

3

51

Rectory Farm

Abbey Wood

PITT RD

PLOUGH COTTS

Plough Inn

2

Fir Tree Farm

Five Wents

COLLINGWOOD IND CTR

Oakdenne Farm

MAIDSTONE RD

Pleasant Farm

B2163

PLOUGH WENTS RD

LESTED LA

WINDMILL ROW

NORTON RD

Cobfield

LAXTON DR

AMBER WAY

PO

CHART CNR

Chart Sutton

Norton Lea Farm

WARMLAKE EST

Nursery

Langley Lodge

1

Amberfield

AMBER LA

CHART HILL RD

MARSHAM
CRES

Buffalo's Head (PH)

Norton Court

CHURCH RD

WARMLAKE RD

Warmlake

A274
NORTH ST

WARMLAKE

CHARTWAY ST

ORCHARD BANK 1
CROSSWAYS 2

MERCER WAY

50

79 A B 80 C D 81 E F

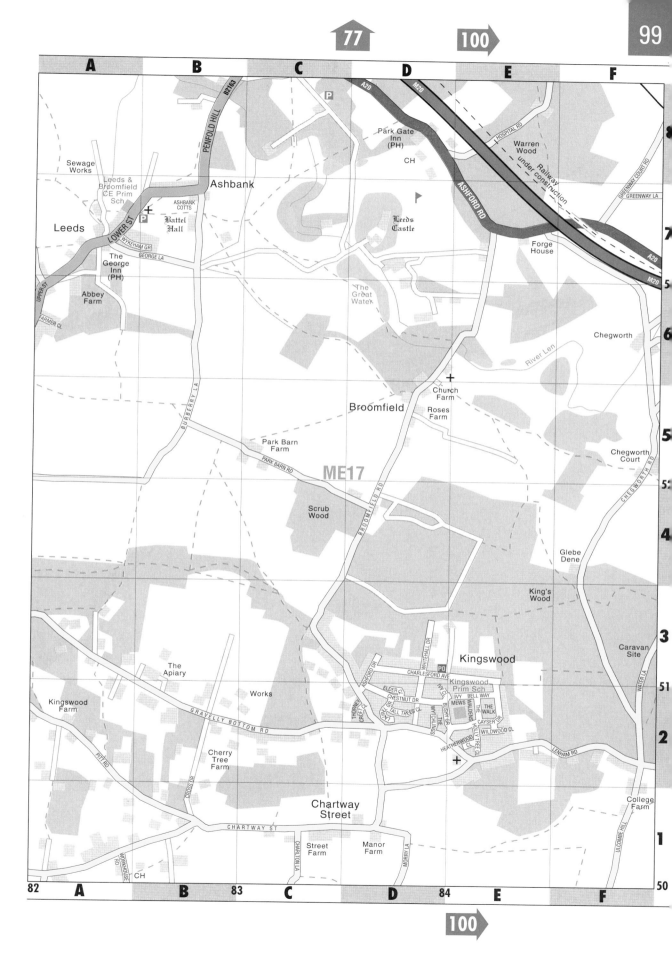

A   B   C   D   E   F

Sewage
Works

Leeds &
Broomfield
CE Prim
Sch

Ashbank

ASHBANK
COTTS

Battel
Hall

Leeds

The George
Inn
(PH)

Abbey
Farm

PENFOLD HILL

B2163

P

A20

M20

Park Gate
Inn
(PH)

CH

Leeds
Castle

HOSPITAL RD

Warren
Wood

Railway
under construction

GREENWAY COURT RD

GREENWAY LA

Forge
House

ASHFORD RD

A20

M20

The
Great
Water

Chegworth

River Len

Church
Farm

Broomfield

Roses
Farm

BURBERRY LA

Park Barn
Farm

PARK BARN RD

ME17

Scrub
Wood

BROOMFIELD RD

Chegworth
Court

CHEGWORTH RD

Glebe
Dene

King's
Wood

Caravan
Site

The
Apiary

Works

GRAVELLY BOTTOM RD

Kingswood
Farm

CROSS DR

Cherry
Tree
Farm

PITT RD

WHITEHALL DR

Kingswood

CHARLESFORD AVE

PO

ASHFORD DR

THORN

CROFT CL

ELDER CL

CHESTNUT DR

LAUREL

TALL TREES CL

WYCH ELMS

BUSH GR

Kingswood
Prim Sch

IVY
MEWS

BELL WAY

WALDENS

THE
WALK

CAYSER DR

WILDWOOD CL

HOLLY TREE CL

HEATHERWOOD

CL

LENHAM RD

WATER LA

College
Farm

ULCOMBE HILL

Chartway
Street

CHARTWAY ST

CHARLTON LA

Street
Farm

Manor
Farm

MORRY LA

WORKHOUSE RD

CH

82   83   84

8

7

6

5

4

3

2

1

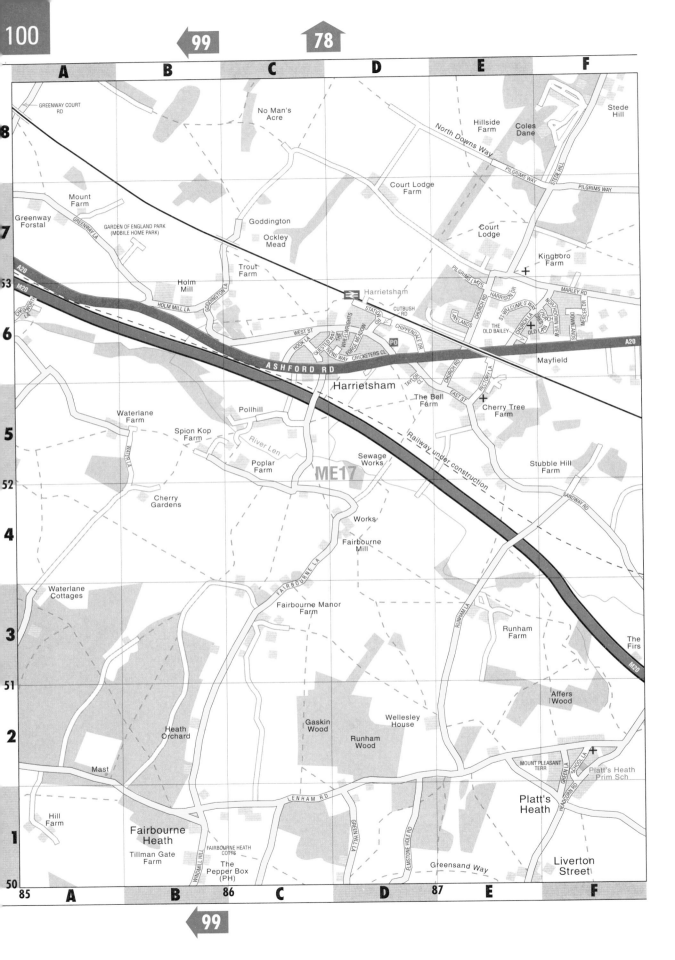

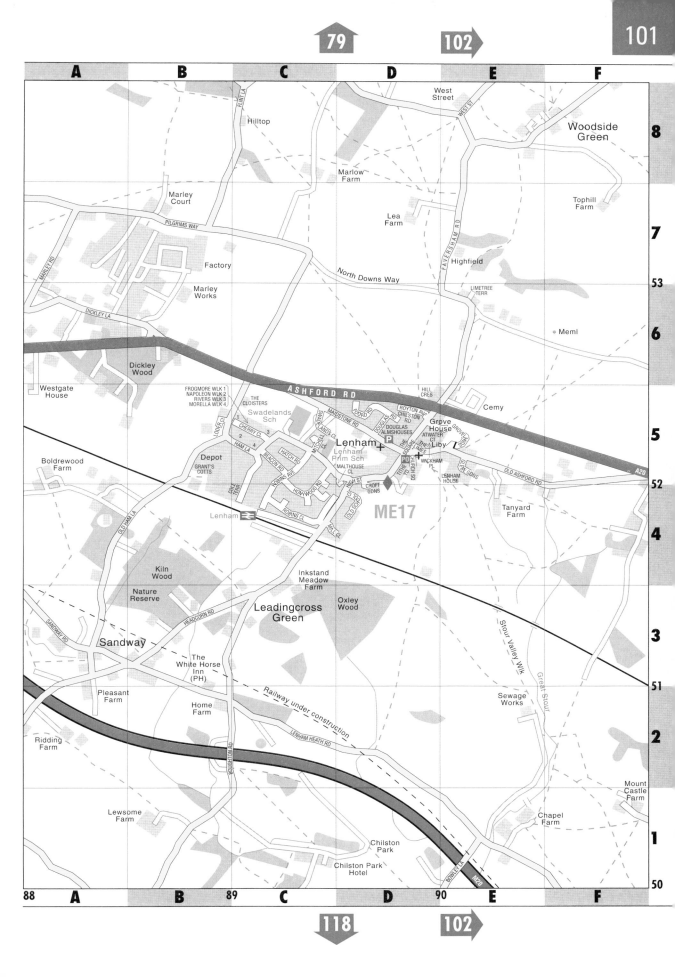

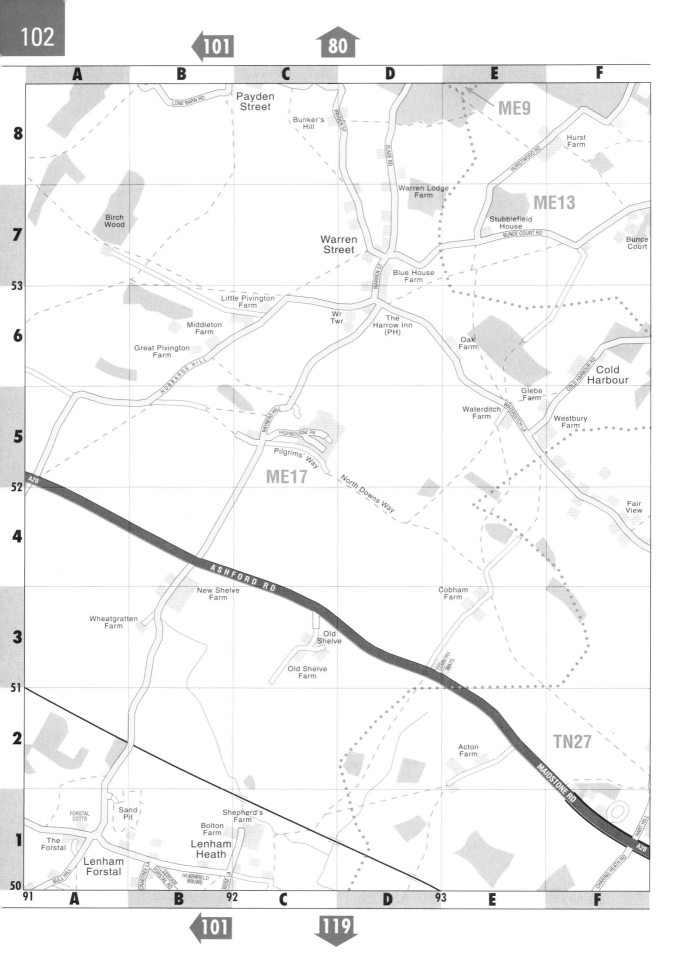

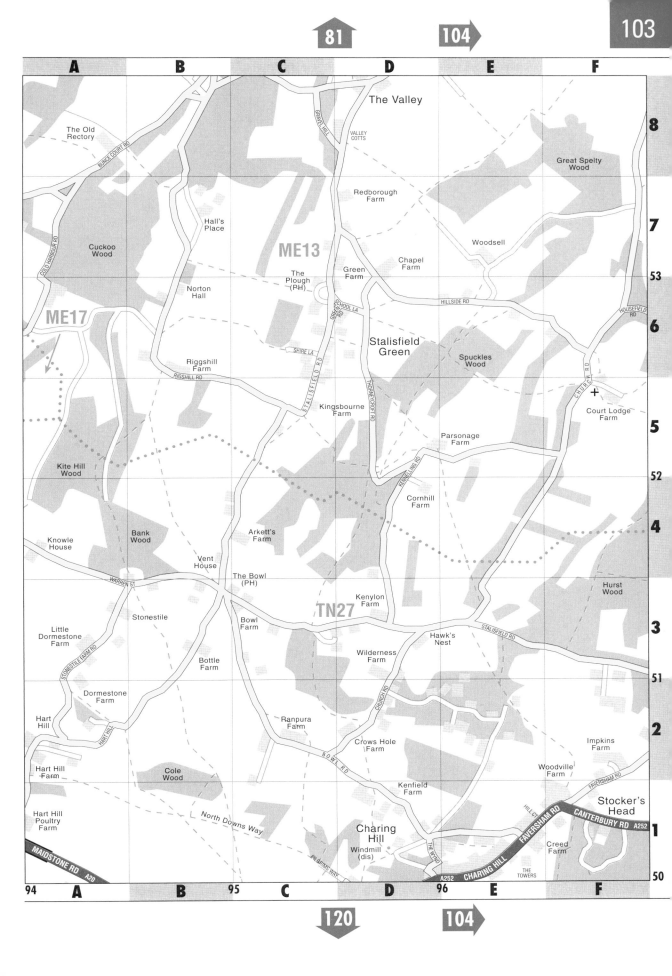

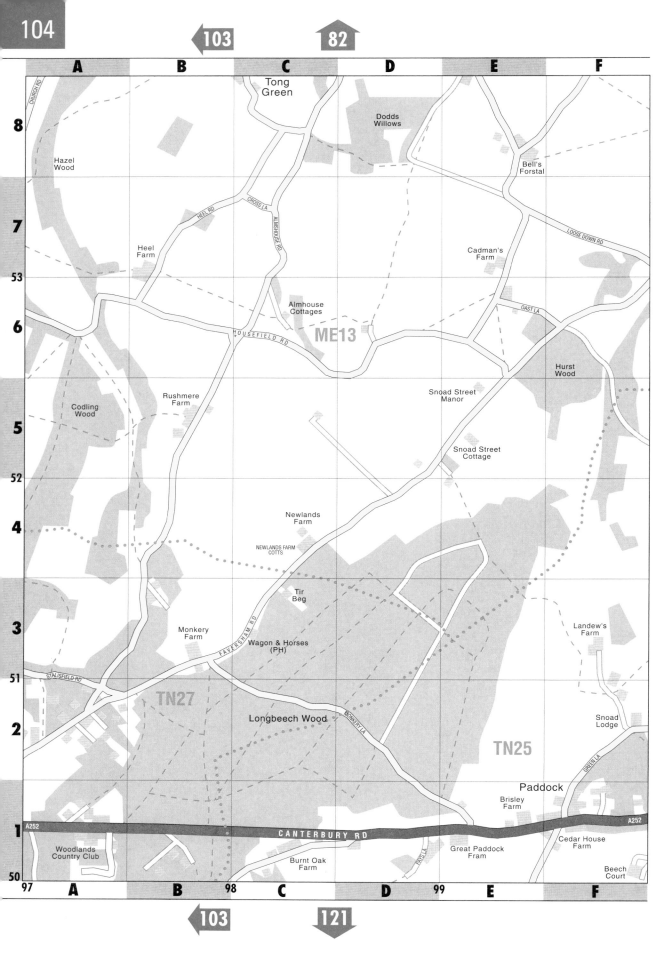

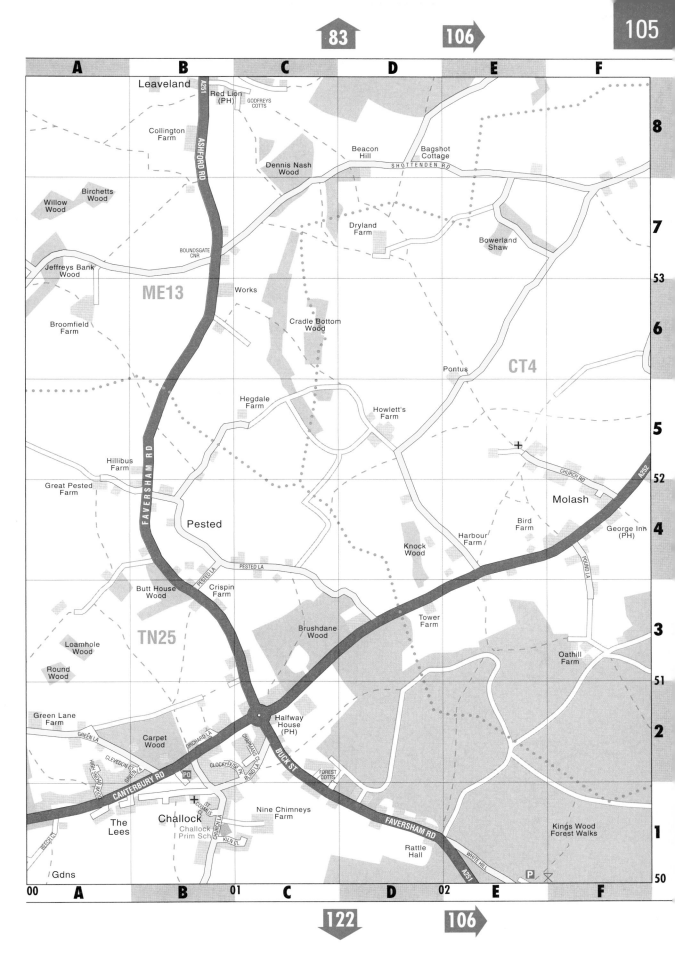

A B C D E F

Leaveland

A251

ASHFORD RD

Red Lion
(PH)

GODFREYS
COTTS

Collington
Farm

8

Dennis Nash
Wood

Beacon
Hill

Bagshot
Cottage

SHOTTENDEN RD

Willow
Wood

Birchetts
Wood

Dryland
Farm

Bowerland
Shaw

7

Jeffreys Bank
Wood

BOUNDSGATE
CNR

53

ME13

Works

6

Broomfield
Farm

Cradle Bottom
Wood

Pontus

CT4

Hegdale
Farm

Howlett's
Farm

5

Hillibus
Farm

FAVERSHAM RD

CHURCH RD

A252

52

Great Pested
Farm

Molash

Pested

Bird
Farm

George Inn
(PH)

4

Harbour
Farm

Knock
Wood

PESTED LA

PESTED LA

Crispin
Farm

Butt House
Wood

ROUND LA

TN25

Brushdane
Wood

Tower
Farm

3

Loamhole
Wood

Oathill
Farm

Round
Wood

51

Green Lane
Farm

Halfway
House
(PH)

2

GREEN LA

Carpet
Wood

ORCHARD LA

CHAPLAINS CL

BLIND LA

BUCK ST

CLEVEDON CL

GREEN LA

CANTERBURY RD

PO

CLOCKHOUSE PK

FOREST
COTTS

HIGH SNOAD WOOD

Nine Chimneys
Farm

Challock

The
Lees

COSMUS

Challock
Prim Sch

CHURCH LA

KILN CL

FAVERSHAM RD

Kings Wood
Forest Walks

1

BEECH CL

Rattle
Hall

WHITE HILL

A251

P

Gdns

50

00 A B 01 C D 02 E F

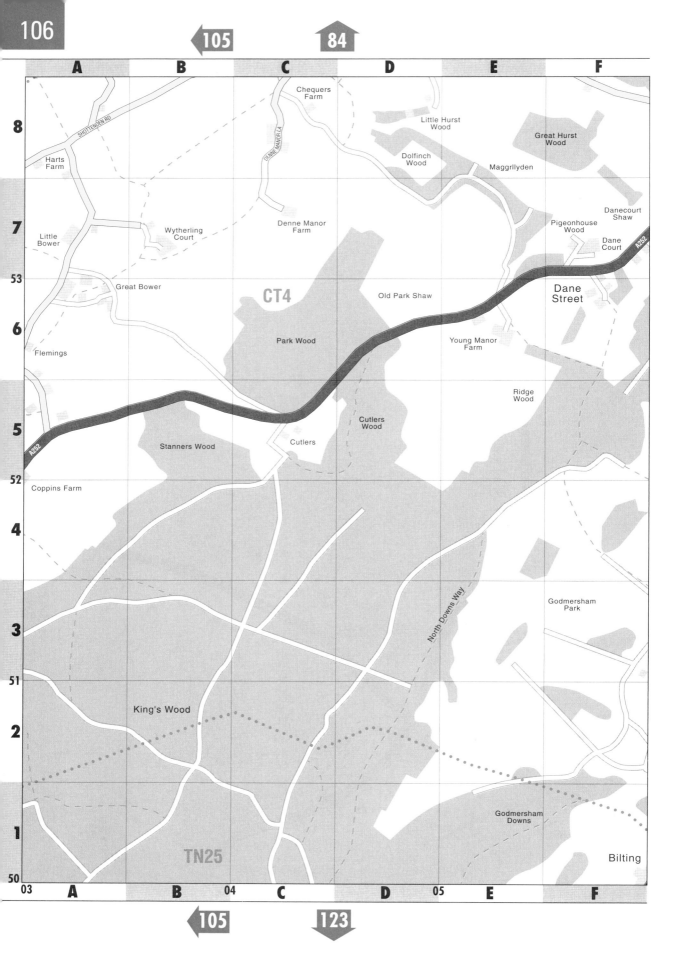

105
84

A B C D E F

8

Chequers Farm

SHOTTENDEN RD

Little Hurst Wood

Great Hurst Wood

Harts Farm

DENNE MANOR LA

Dolfinch Wood

Maggrllyden

7

Wytherling Court

Denne Manor Farm

Danecourt Shaw

Pigeonhouse Wood

Little Bower

Dane Court

A252

53

Great Bower

CT4

Old Park Shaw

Dane Street

6

Park Wood

Young Manor Farm

Flemings

Ridge Wood

5

Stanners Wood

Cutlers Wood

A252

Cutlers

52

Coppins Farm

4

Godmersham Park

3

North Downs Way

51

King's Wood

2

Godmersham Downs

1

TN25

Bilting

50

03 A B 04 C D 05 E F

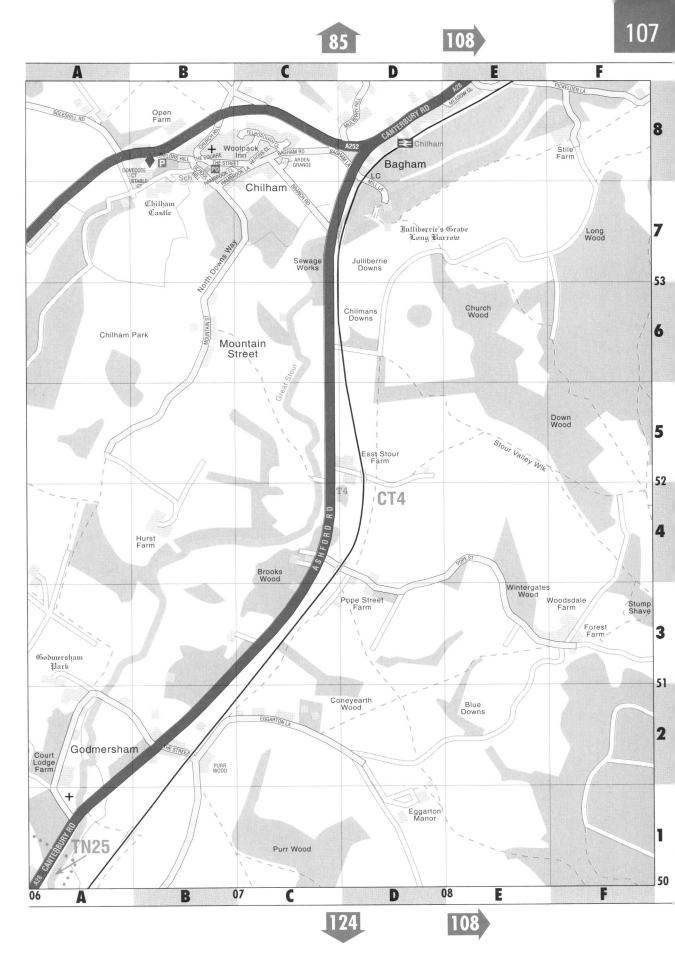

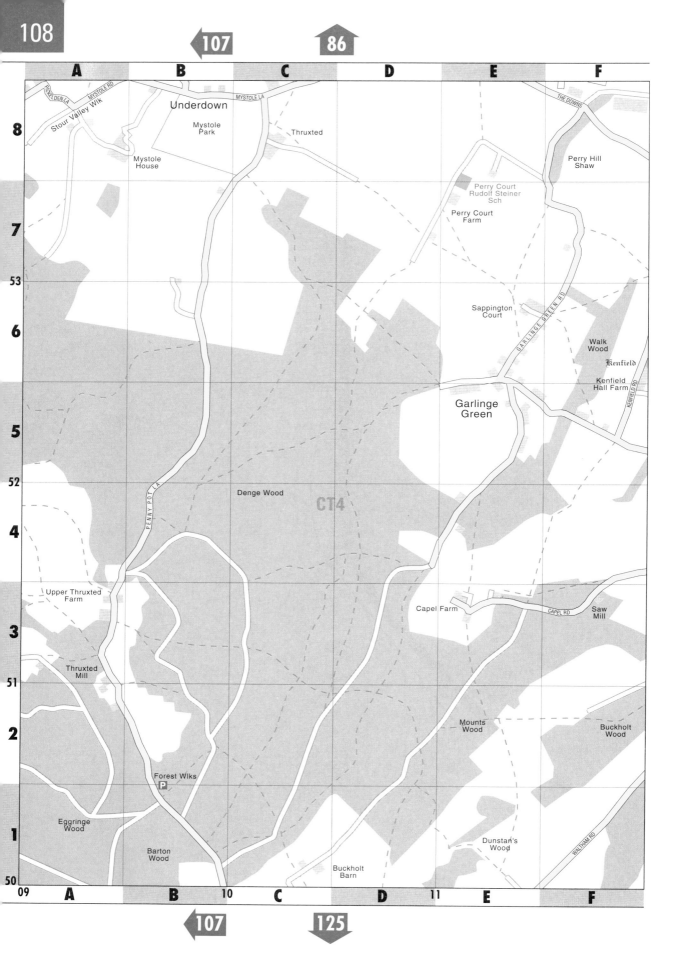

A   B   C   D   E   F

8

Underdown

Mystole La

Thruxted

Mystole Park

The Downs

Perry Hill Shaw

Mystole House

Stour Valley Wlk

Mystole Rd

Pickelden La

7

Perry Court Rudolf Steiner Sch

Perry Court Farm

53

6

Sappington Court

Garlinge Green Rd

Walk Wood

Kenfield

Kenfield Hall Farm

Kenfield Rd

Garlinge Green

5

52

Denge Wood

CT4

4

Penny Pot La

Upper Thruxted Farm

Capel Farm

Capel Rd

Saw Mill

3

Thruxted Mill

51

Mounts Wood

Buckholt Wood

2

Forest Wlks

P

1

Eggringe Wood

Dunstan's Wood

Waltham Rd

Barton Wood

Buckholt Barn

50

09   A   B   10   C   D   11   E   F

109
88

A B C D E F

8

Whitehill
Wood

Middle
Pett
Farm

7

North Court
Farm

Warren
Wood

Little
Pett
Farm

Redhill
Wood

The
Shave

53

Lower
Hardres

BUTTS CT

6

Little
Eaton
Farm

PO

BUTTS
MEADOW

Lenhall
Farm

PH

Stockfield
Wood

SCHOOL LA

PETT BOTTOM RD

Avenue
Wood

5

Pett
Bottom

The
Duck
(PH)

CT4

Cook's
Farm

TAPLEYS HILL

52

4

Gorsley
Wood

CROWS CAMP RD

Pilot's
Wood

PILOT'S FARM RD

Broxhall
Farm

3

Broxhall
Wood

BROXHALL RD

Equestrian
Centre

Langham
Park
Farm

HARDRES COURT RD

St Andrew's
Wood

WOODGATE

PHEASANTS HALL RD

51

Bursted
Manor

2

BOW HILL

Hardres
Court
Farm

BURSTED HILL

Park
Rough

Reed
Farm

Upper
Hardres
Court

Bursted
Wood

1

The
Manor
House

Westwood
Farm

Marley
Wood

50

15 A B 16 C D 17 E F

127

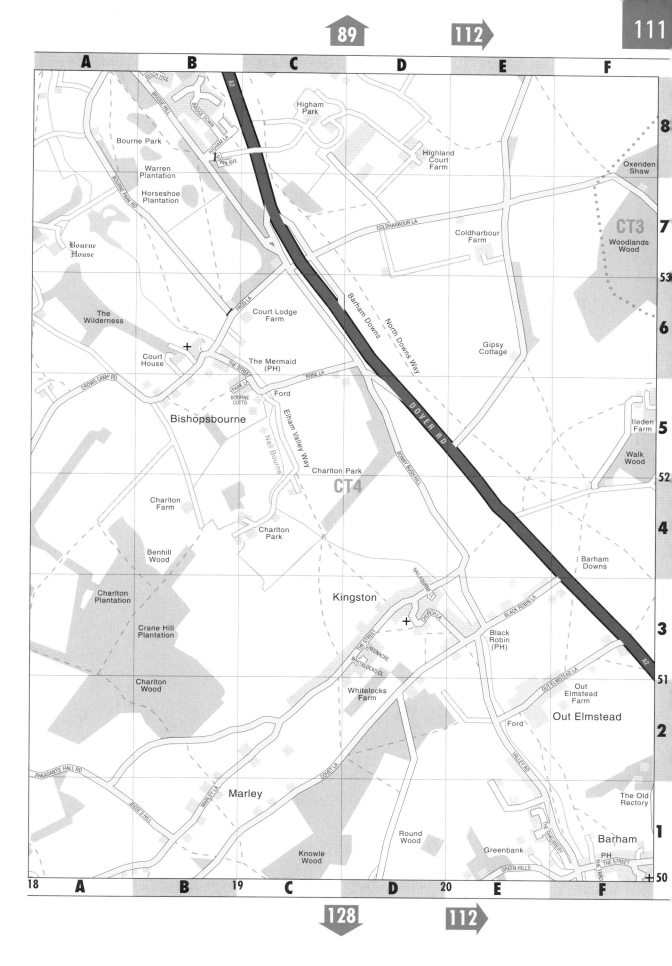

89 112

A B C D E F

8

Beech Hill

Bourne Park

Higham
Park

Highland
Court
Farm

Oxenden
Shaw

Warren
Plantation

BRIDGE HILL

HIGHAM LA

CHAPLIN AVE

7

Horseshoe
Plantation

COLDHARBOUR LA

Coldharbour
Farm

CT3
Woodlands
Wood

BOURNE PARK RD

53

Bourne
House

FROG LA

The
Wilderness

Court Lodge
Farm

Barham Downs

North Downs Way

6

Gipsy
Cottage

Court
House

THE STREET

The Mermaid
(PH)

ROSE LA

CROWS CAMP RD

PARK LA

BOURNE
COTTS

Ford

Ileden
Farm

5

Bishopsbourne

Elham Valley Way

Nail Bourne

DOVER RD

Walk
Wood

Charlton Park

BONNY BUSH HILL

52

CT4

Charlton
Farm

4

Charlton
Park

Benhill
Wood

Barham
Downs

Charlton
Plantation

Kingston

HALL BOURNE LA

CHURCH LA

BLACK ROBIN LA

3

Crane Hill
Plantation

THE STREET

THE GREENACRE

WHITELOCKS CL

Black
Robin
(PH)

OUT ELMSTEAD LA

Charlton
Wood

Whitelocks
Farm

Out
Elmstead
Farm

51

Out Elmstead

Ford

2

PHEASANTS' HALL RD

COVET LA

VALLEY RD

The Old
Rectory

JESSE'S HILL

MARLEY LA

Marley

THE SHRUBBERY

1

Round
Wood

Greenbank

Barham

Knowle
Wood

GREEN HILLS

THE STREET

THE YARD

PH

50

18 A B 19 C D 20 E F

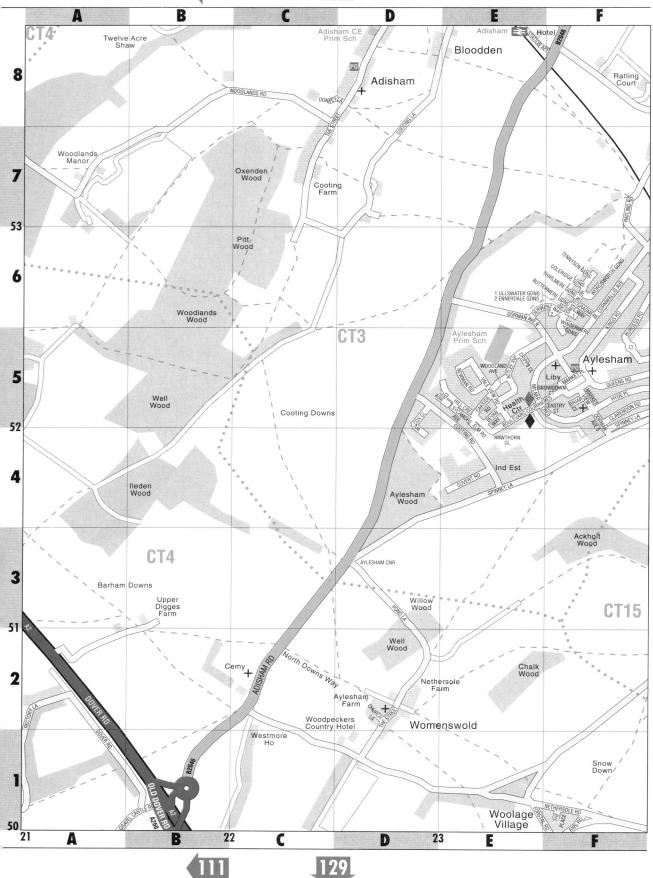

CT4

Twelve Acre Shaw

8

Woodlands Manor

Adisham CE Prim Sch

WOODLANDS RD

Bloodden

Adisham Hotel

B2046

Ratling Court

PO

Adisham

DONKEY LA

THE STREET

COOTING LA

STATION RD

7

Oxenden Wood

Cooting Farm

53

Pitt Wood

6

Woodlands Wood

CT3

TENNYSON GDNS

COLERIDGE GDNS

WORDSWORTH GDNS

THIRLMERE GDNS

BUTTERMERE GDNS

GRASMERE

CORNWALLIS AVE

RATLING RD

1 ULLSWATER GDNS
2 ENNERDALE GDNS

DERWENT WAY

DORMAN AVE N

WINDERMERE GDNS

KINGS RD

BURGESS RD

Aylesham Prim Sch

5

Well Wood

Cooting Downs

WOODLAND AVE

ATTLEE AVE

CHIPS CL

VALE VIEW RD

OAKSIDE RD

Aylesham

NEWMAN RD

HILL CRES

Liby

PO

MARKET PL

QUEENS RD

SNOWDOWN CT

MARKET VIEW

HYDE PL

ASH CL

COX CL

SYCAMORE

ELM RD

BEVAN WAY

Health Ctr

MILNER

COURTENAYS

LEASTRY CT

BRIAN VIEW CL

CLARENDON RD

52

COOTING RD

BOULEYARD

DORMAN AVE S

SPINNEY LA

HAWTHORN CL

4

Ileden Wood

COVERT RD

Ind Est

SPINNEY LA

Aylesham Wood

Ackholt Wood

3

CT4

Barham Downs

AYLESHAM CNR

CT15

Upper Digges Farm

Willow Wood

51

RECTORY LA

A2

DOVER RD

ADISHAM RD

NORTH DOWNS WAY

POND LA

Well Wood

Chalk Wood

2

Cemy

Aylesham Farm

Nethersole Farm

CHURCH LA

THE STREET

Womenswold

Woodpeckers Country Hotel

1

B2046

Westmore Ho

Snow Down

OLD DOVER RD

A2

A260

GRAVEL CASTLE RD

NETHERSOLE RD

THE FIRS RD

FORSTAL RD

THE PLACE

Woolage Village

50

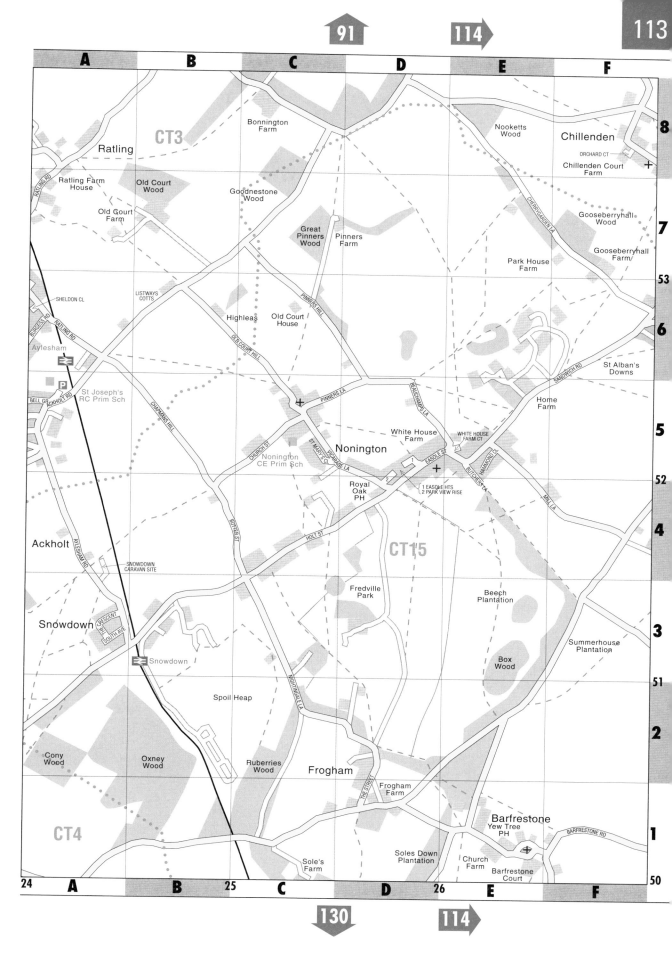

A B C D E F

8

CT3

Bonnington
Farm

Nooketts
Wood

Chillenden

Ratling

ORCHARD CT

Chillenden Court
Farm

Ratling Farm
House

Old Court
Wood

Goodnestone
Wood

7

Gooseberryhall
Wood

Old Court
Farm

Great
Pinners
Wood

Pinners
Farm

CHERRY GARDEN LA

Gooseberryhall
Farm

Park House
Farm

53

SHELDON CL

LISTWAYS
COTTS

PINNERS HILL

6

Highleas

Old Court
House

St Alban's
Downs

BURGESS RD

RATLING RD

Aylesham

OLD COURT HILL

PINNERS LA

BEAUCHAMPS LA

SANDWICH RD

Home
Farm

BELL GR

ACKHOLT RD

St Joseph's
RC Prim Sch

CHAPMANS HILL

CHURCH ST

ST MARY'S CL

VICARAGE LA

White House
Farm

WHITE HOUSE
FARM CT

5

Nonington
CE Prim Sch

Nonington

EASOLE ST

HAMMOND CL

1
2

WHITE HOUSE
FARM CT

52

Royal
Oak
PH

2

1 EASOLE HTS
2 PARK VIEW RISE

BUTCHERS LA

MILL LA

BUTTER ST

HOLT ST

CT15

4

Ackholt

AYLESHAM RD

SNOWDOWN
CARAVAN SITE

Fredville
Park

Beech
Plantation

Summerhouse
Plantation

3

Snowdown

THE CRESCENT

SOUTH AVE

Box
Wood

51

Snowdown

Spoil Heap

NIGHTINGALE LA

2

Cony
Wood

Oxney
Wood

Ruberries
Wood

Frogham

THE STREET

Frogham
Farm

Barfrestone

Yew Tree
PH

BARFRESTONE RD

1

CT4

Sole's
Farm

Soles Down
Plantation

Church
Farm

Barfrestone
Court

24 A 25 B C 26 D E F 50

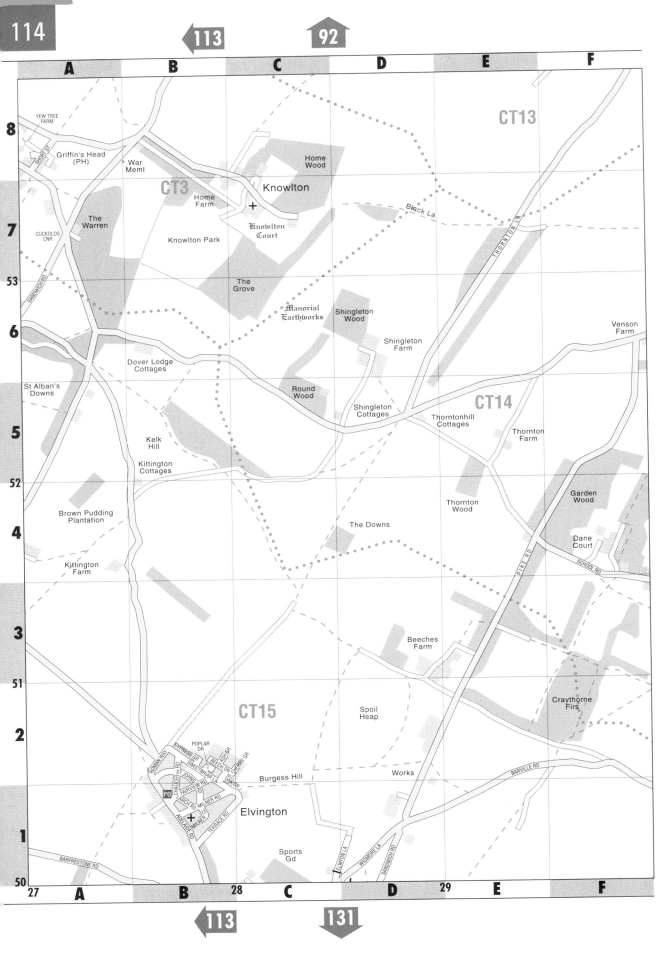

113
92

A B C D E F

8

YEW TREE
FARM

Griffin's Head
(PH)

SHORT ST

War
Meml

CT3

Home
Farm

Knowlton

Home
Wood

CT13

7

CUCKOLDS
CNR

The
Warren

SANDWICH RD

Knowlton Park

Knowlton
Court

Black La

THORNTON LA

53

The
Grove

Manorial
Earthworks

Shingleton
Wood

6

Dover Lodge
Cottages

Shingleton
Farm

Venson
Farm

St Alban's
Downs

Round
Wood

Shingleton
Cottages

Thorntonhill
Cottages

CT14

Thornton
Farm

5

Kelk
Hill

Kittington
Cottages

Thornton
Wood

Garden
Wood

52

Brown Pudding
Plantation

4

Kittington
Farm

The Downs

PIKE RD

Dane
Court

SCHOOL RD

3

Beeches
Farm

Craythorne
Firs

51

CT15

Spoil
Heap

2

ROMAN WAY

CYPRESS GR

POPLAR
DR

ASH GR

BEECH DR

CHERRY GR

SWEETBRIAR LA

OAK GR

J CHAUCER ST

LARCH RD

JOHNS
ST

FAIRVIEW RD

MILNER RD

Burgess Hill

Works

BARVILLE RD

PO

ADELAIDE RD

MILNER
CT

TERRACE RD

Elvington

1

BARFRESTONE RD

Sports
Gd

ELMFIELD LA

WIGMORE LA

SANDWICH RD

50

27 A B 28 C D 29 E F

113
131

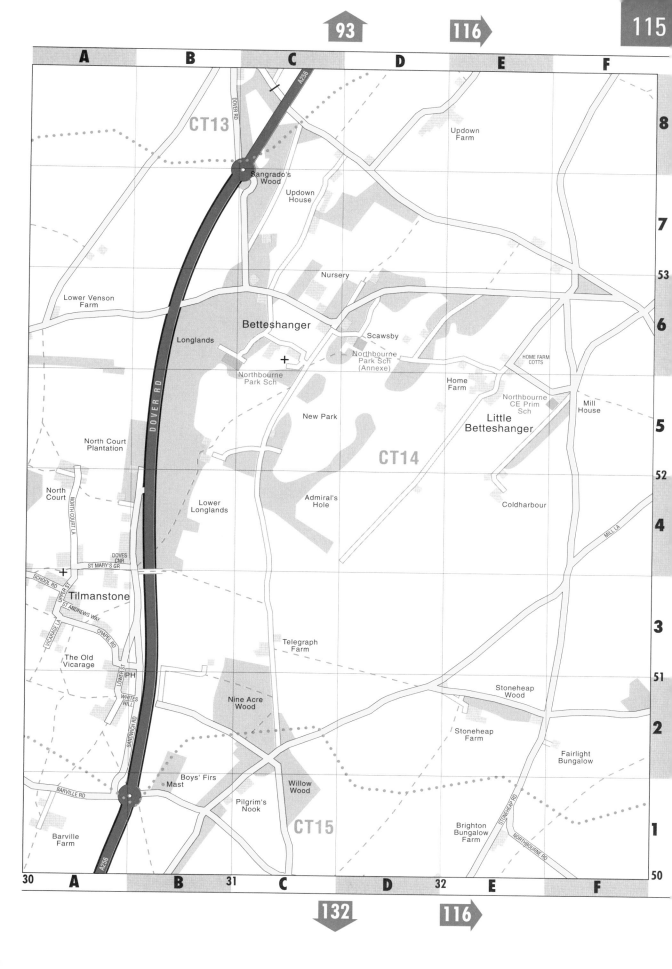

A   B   C   D   E   F

CT13

DOVER RD

A256

Sangrado's
Wood

Updown
Farm

Updown
House

8

Nursery

7

53

Lower Venson
Farm

Betteshanger

6

Longlands

Scawsby

Northbourne
Park Sch
(Annexe)

HOME FARM
COTTS

Northbourne
Park Sch

Home
Farm

Northbourne
CE Prim
Sch

Mill
House

New Park

Little
Betteshanger

5

North Court
Plantation

CT14

52

North
Court

Lower
Longlands

Admiral's
Hole

Coldharbour

MILL LA

4

NORTH COURT LA

DOVES
CNR

ST MARY'S GR

School RD

Tilmanstone

ST ANDREWS WAY

Telegraph
Farm

3

VICARAGE LA

CHAPEL RD

The Old
Vicarage

LOWER ST

Stoneheap
Wood

51

PH

WHITES
HILL

Nine Acre
Wood

Stoneheap
Farm

2

SANDWICH RD

Fairlight
Bungalow

Boys' Firs
Mast

Willow
Wood

STONEHEAP RD

BARVILLE RD

Pilgrim's
Nook

CT15

Brighton
Bungalow
Farm

NORTHBOURNE RD

1

A256

Barville
Farm

50

30   31   32

A   B   C   D   E   F

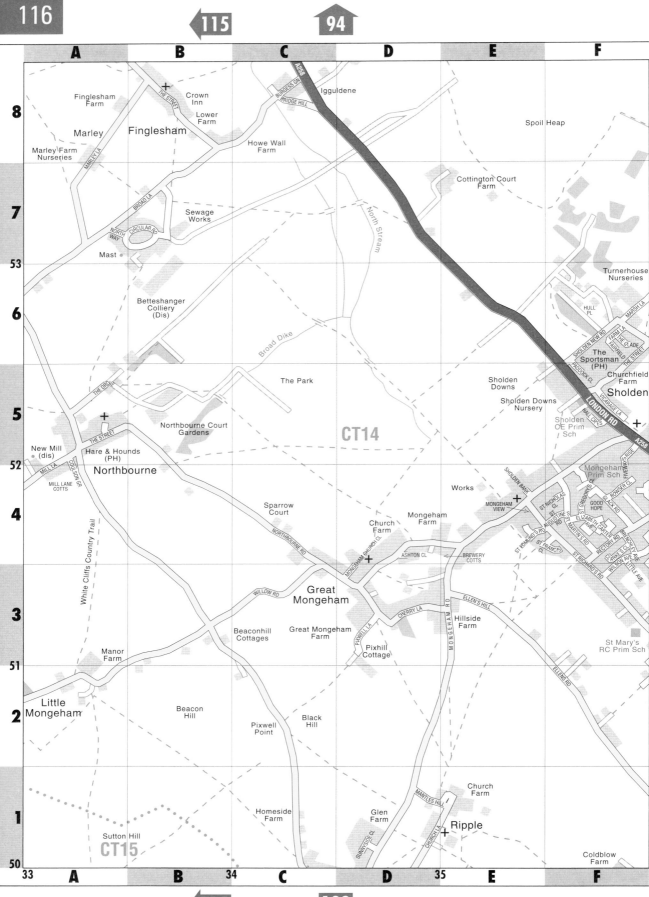

A B C D E F

8
7
53
6
5
52
4
3
51
2
1
50

Finglesham
Farm
Crown Inn
Lower Farm
THE STREET
A258
BURGESS GR
BRIDGE HILL
Igguldene
Spoil Heap
Marley
Finglesham
Howe Wall Farm
Cottington Court Farm
Marley Farm Nurseries
MARLEY LA
BROAD LA
Sewage Works
NORTH WAY
CIRCULAR RD
Mast
North Stream
Turnerhouse Nurseries
Betteshanger Colliery (Dis)
Broad Dike
SHOLDEN NEW RD
HULL PL
FARM LA
THE GLADE
FAIRFIELD
MARSH LA
THE STREET
The Sportsman (PH)
THE DROVE
The Park
Sholden Downs
Churchfield Farm
Sholden
PADDOCK CL
VICARAGE LA
LONDON RD
A258
Northbourne Court Gardens
Sholden Downs Nursery
Sholden CE Prim Sch
HALL GDNS
THE STREET
Hare & Hounds (PH)
THE STREET
New Mill (dis)
MILL LA
COLT'SON GR
CT14
Sholden Bank
Mongeham Prim Sch
SYMBOL S
Northbourne
MILL LANE COTTS
Works
Mongeham View
SHOLDEN BANK
ST NICHOLAS CL
BONKER CL
BLACK RD
Sparrow Court
Mongeham Farm
ST MARTIN'S RD
GOOD HOPE
ELIZABETH CARTER
Church Farm
MONGEHAM CHURCH CL
ST EDMUND'S RD
ST AUGUSTINE'S RD
ST GREGORY'S
ST FRANCIS CL
ST RICHARD'S RD
RECTORY RD
BRENCHLEY AVE
CLARKE'S AVE
WILSON AVE
LITTLE AVE
NORTHBOURNE RD
Ashton Cl
ASHTON CL
Brewery Cotts
White Cliffs Country Trail
WILLOW RD
Great Mongeham
CHERRY LA
Hillside Farm
ELLEN'S HILL
St Mary's RC Prim Sch
Manor Farm
Beaconhill Cottages
Great Mongeham Farm
PIXWELL LA
Pixhill Cottage
MONGEHAM RD
ELLENS RD
Little Mongeham
Beacon Hill
Pixwell Point
Black Hill
Church Farm
Homeside Farm
Glen Farm
MANTLES HILL
Ripple
Sutton Hill
CT15
SUNNYSIDE CL
CHURCH LA
Coldblow Farm

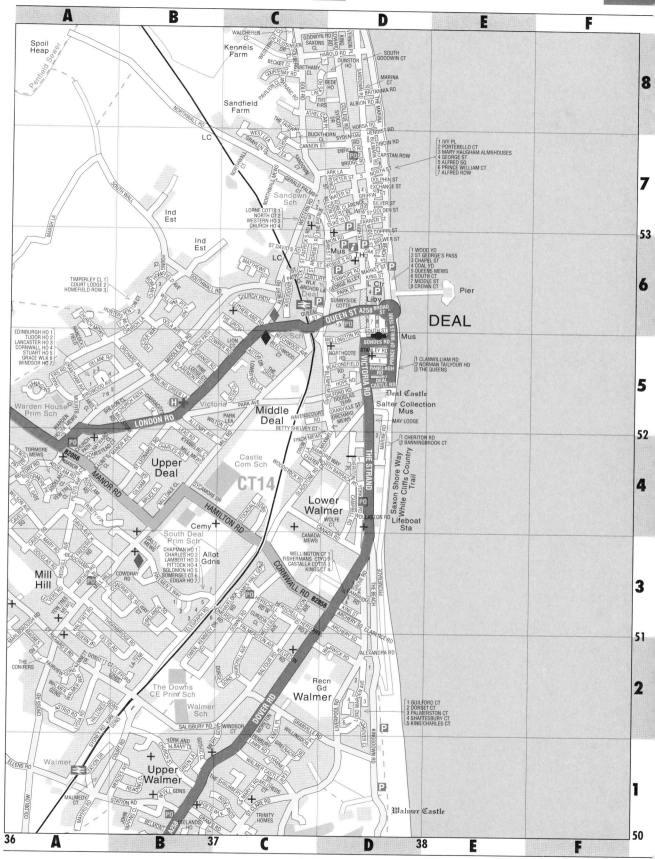

DEAL

CT14

Mill Hill

Upper Deal

Middle Deal

Lower Walmer

Walmer

Upper Walmer

Warden House Prim Sch

South Deal Prim Sch

The Downs CE Prim Sch

Walmer Sch

Walmer Castle

Pier

1 IVY PL
2 PORTEBELLO CT
3 MARY HAUGHAM ALMSHOUSES
4 GEORGE ST
5 ALFRED SQ
6 PRINCE WILLIAM CT
7 ALFRED ROW

1 WOOD YD
2 ST GEORGE'S PASS
3 CHAPEL ST
4 COAL YD
5 QUEENS MEWS
6 SOUTH CT
7 MIDDLE ST
8 CROWN CT

1 CLANWILLIAM RD
2 NORMAN TAILYOUR HO
3 THE QUEENS

1 CHERITON RD
2 BANNINGBROOK CT

1 GUILFORD CT
2 DORSET CT
3 PALMERSTON CT
4 SHAFTESBURY CT
5 KING CHARLES CT

1 CHAPMAN HO
2 CHARLES HO
3 LAMBERT HO
4 PITTOCK HO
5 SOLOMON HO
6 SOMERSET CT
7 EDGAR HO

1 WELLINGTON CT
2 FISHERMANS CTYD
3 CASTALLA COTTS
4 KINGS CT

EDINBURGH HO 1
TUDOR HO 2
LANCASTER HO 3
CORNWALL HO 4
STUART HO 5
GRACE WLK 6
WINDSOR HO 7

TIMPERLEY CL 1
COURT LODGE 2
HOMEFIELD ROW 3

LORNE COTTS 1
NORTH CT 2
WESTERN HO 3
CHURCH HO 4

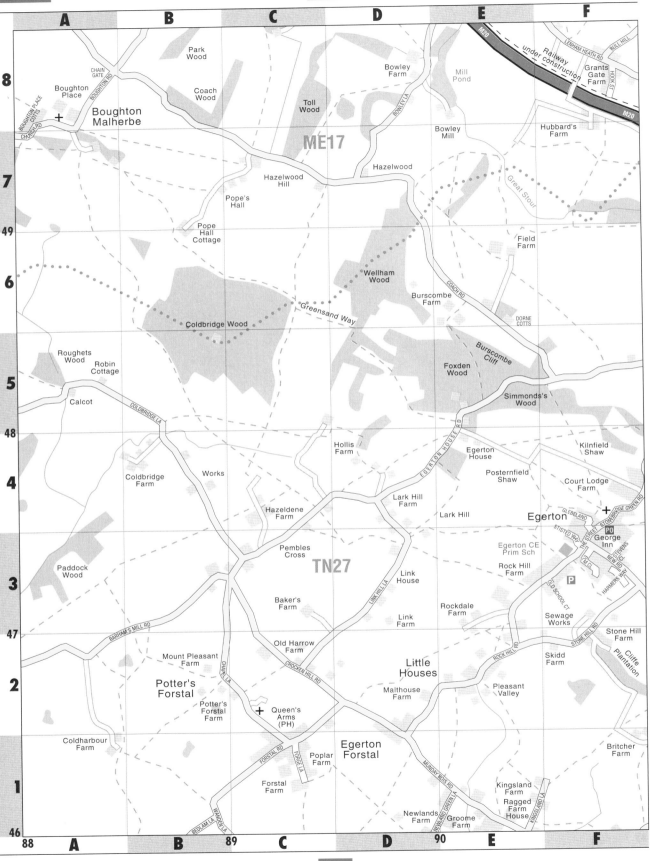

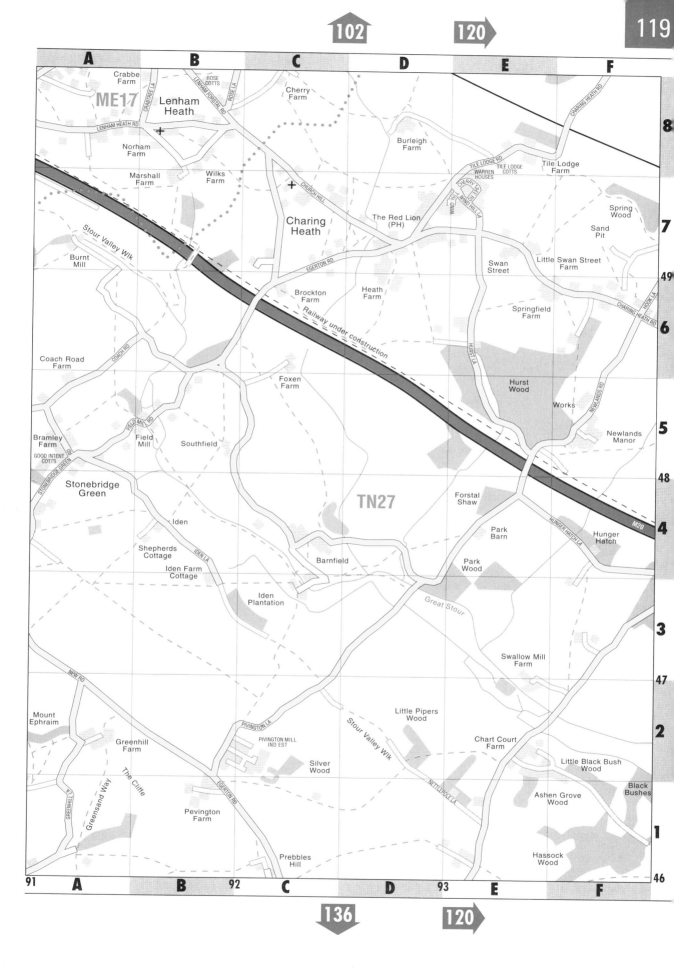

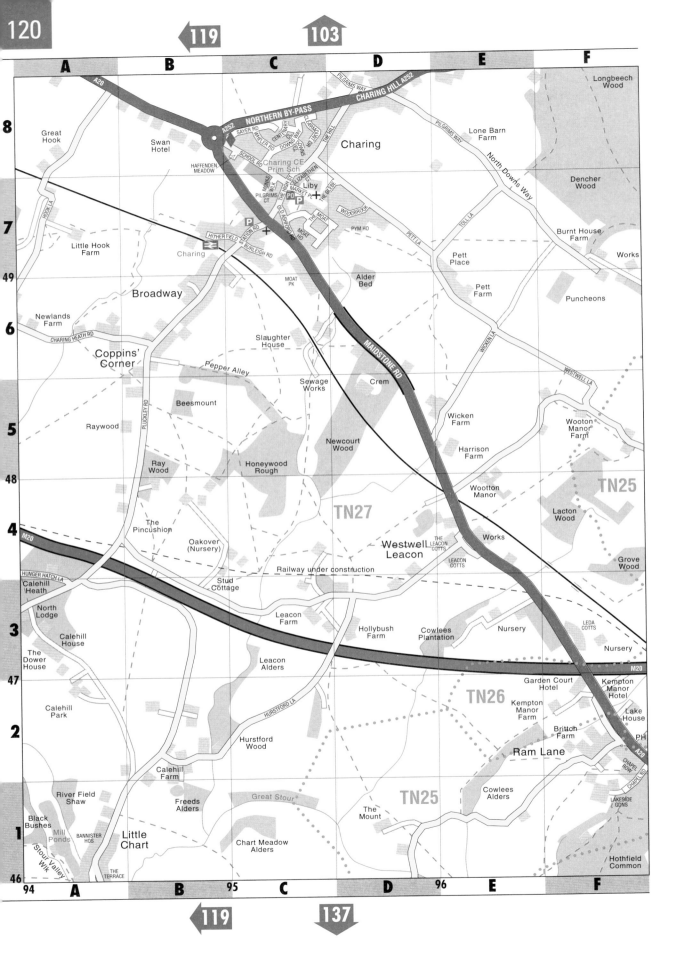

← 121

↑ 105

A   B   C   D   E   F

8

Ashes Wood

Well Wood

A251

WHITE HILL

Brabourne Hill
Plantation

CHURCH LA

Brabourne Hill
Wood

7

Church Wood

Challock Manor

Round
Wood

Prickle
Down
Wood

Crow Down

Young's Plantation

+

49

Coronation
Toll

Mount Ephraim

6

Pear Tree
Toll

Hayward's
Garden

Yewtree
Toll

Jack's Hut Wood

Old Rook
Toll

Jackdaw Toll

FAVERSHAM RD

5

Round
Wood

Browns

48

Eastwell Park **TN25**

Home Farm

Brewhouse

4

The
Beeches

Eastwell Park
(Hotel)

The
Flying Horse
Inn

PILGRIMS WAY

St Mary's Church
(rems of)

North Downs Way

SEATON
COTTS

Boughton
Lees

3

Aviary
Wood

MIDDLETON
COTTS

EASTWELL
TERR

ELM COTTS
PROSPECT
COTTS

WYE RD

+

Dogkennel
Plantation

+

47

Eastwell
Lake

Rook Toll

Tower Farm

LENACRE ST

Rectory
Wood

THE OLD
RECTORY

2

Rectory
Plantation

Eastwell Court

1

TN26

Lake
Wood

Brookies
Lodge

Park Barn
Farm

Podberry
Wood

TN24

A251

46

00   A   B   01   C   D   02   E   F

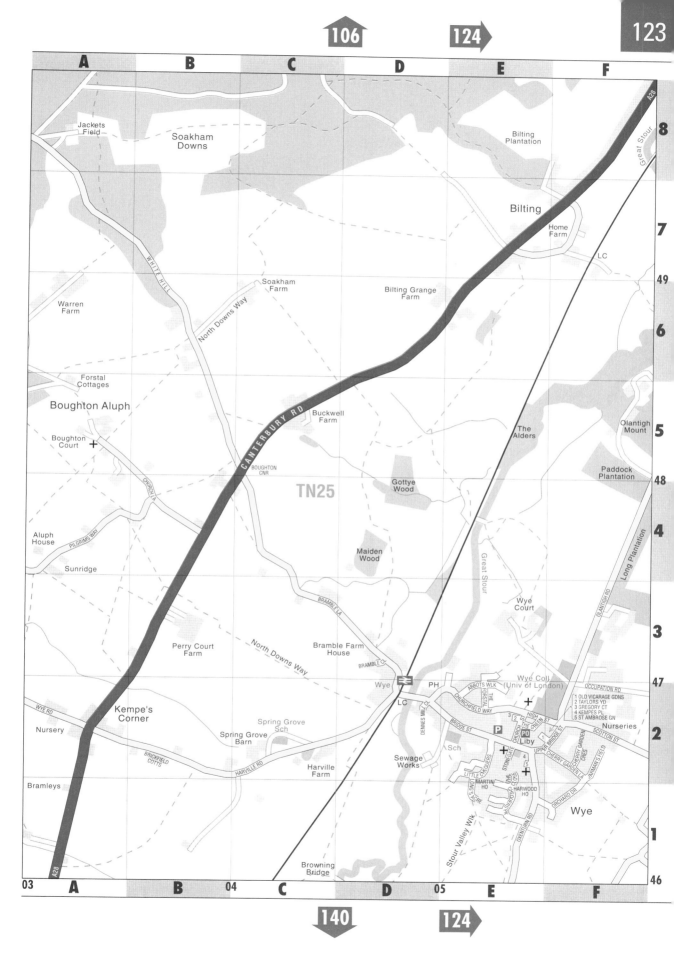

106
124
140
124

A　B　C　D　E　F

8
7
49
6
5
48
4
3
47
2
1
46

Jackets Field

Soakham Downs

Bilting Plantation

Bilting

Home Farm

LC

WHITE HILL

Warren Farm

Soakham Farm

Bilting Grange Farm

North Downs Way

Great Stour

Forstal Cottages

Boughton Aluph

CANTERBURY RD

Buckwell Farm

The Alders

Olantigh Mount

Boughton Court

BOUGHTON CNR

Paddock Plantation

CHURCH LA

TN25

Gottye Wood

Aluph House

PILGRIMS WAY

Maiden Wood

Long Plantation

Sunridge

Wye Court

OLANTIGH RD

Great Stour

BRAMBLE LA

Perry Court Farm

North Downs Way

Bramble Farm House

BRAMBLE CL

Wye

PH

Wye Coll. (Univ of London)

OCCUPATION RD

1 OLD VICARAGE GDNS
2 TAYLORS YD
3 GREGORY CT
4 KEMPES PL
5 ST AMBROSE GN

LC

ARBOTS WLK

THE FORSTAL WAY

CHURCHFIELD WAY

HIGH ST

Nurseries

SCOTTON ST

WYE RD

Kempe's Corner

Spring Grove Sch

DENNES MILL CL

BRIDGE ST

Sch

THE CREW

UPPER BRIDGE ST

P

PO

Liby

CHERRY GARDEN LA

CHERRY GARDEN CRES

JARMAN'S FIELD

Nursery

Spring Grove Barn

BRICKFIELD COTTS

HARVILLE RD

Harville Farm

Sewage Works

LITTLE CHEQUERS

CHURCH ST

STONEGATE

THE CLOSE

LONG'S ACRE

MARTIN HO

MASTERS RD

HARWOOD HO

ORCHARD DR

Wye

Bramleys

Stour Valley Wlk

OXENTURN RD

Browning Bridge

A28

03　04　05

A28

Great Stour

8 Ripple Farm

Trimworth Manor

Little Winchcombe

Works

Thornham Lodge

Winchcombe Farm

Tye Wood

7 Crundale

CT4

Glenwood Farm

Viney's Wood

Oxen Lees Wood

49 Black Edge Wood

Fairisle Farm

Church Wood

Great Stour

6 Crundale House

Crundale Downs

Little Olantigh Farm

Warren Wood

OLANTIGH RD

Nursery

5 Marriage Wood

Roughets

48 Round Wood

Kidney Clump

Marriage Hill

4 Marriage Farm

Beech Wood

Stour Valley Wlk

Sheepfold

3 Mast

Pett Street Farm

47 North Downs Way

Down Farm

Prout's Spinney

HASSELL ST

2 **TN25**

Meml (Crown)

Collyerhill Wood

Hurst Wood

SCOTTON ST

COLDHARBOUR LA

Woodmans Arms (PH)

1 WITHERSDANE COTTS
2 BERNARD SUNLEY HALL
3 THE GARDEN HALL

Withersdane Hall

Coldharbour Farm

Coombe Manor

Centre for European Agricultural Studies

AMAGE ROAD COTTS

AMAGE RD

1 Wye Downs

Little Combe

46

06 07 08

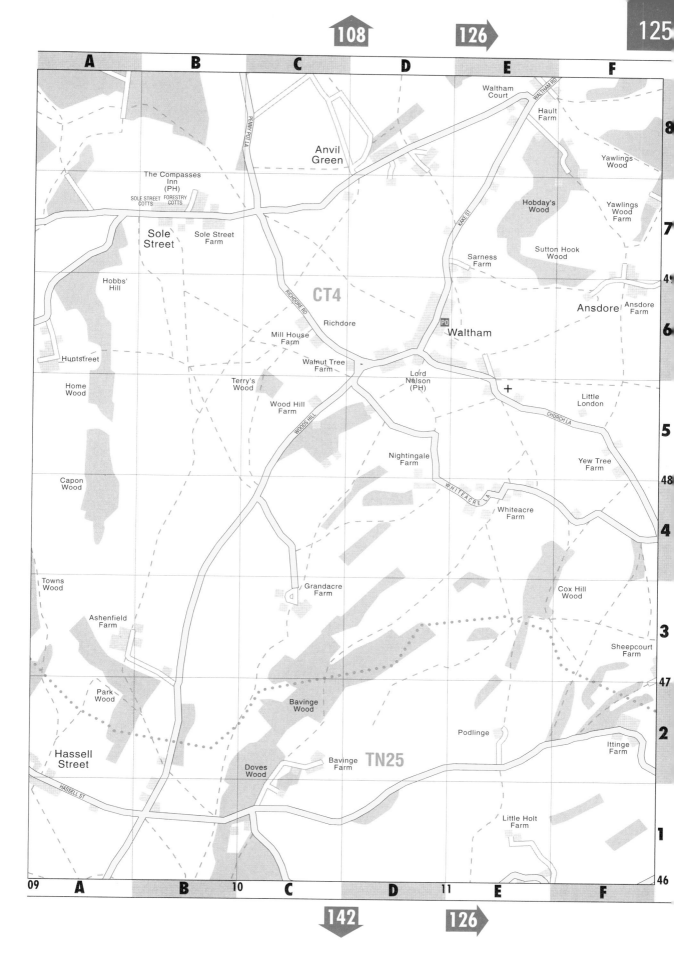

125
109

A **B** **C** **D** **E** **F**

New Barn Farm

Dane Chantry

B2068

Homestead Farm

Upper Hardres Wood

Round Wood

Waddenhall Wood

Nursery

Little Bossingham Farm

Stubb's Wood

DUCKPIT RD

Dunlies Wood

The Hollies

Stelling Lodge Farm

HOMESIDE FARM

Little Wadden Hall

Parkmead

Stelling Minnis CE Prim Sch

HARDRES COURT RD

Yockletts Banks

WADDENHALL FARM

Doghouse Farm

Church Wood

SPLIT LA

Wadden Hall Cottages

Syngate Wood

Syngate House

HARVEST LA

CT4

STONE ST

Cherry Garden Farm

Yockletts Farm

WHITEACRE LA

GODWAY

Nature Reserve

Common

BOSSINGHAM RD

Butts Farm

Yewtree Farmhouse

Holly Tree Farm

Mead Farm

PONYCART LA

Prim Farm

The Laurels

Westcroft Farm

North Leigh

Gaylees Farmhouse

⛺ 🚙

Malt Farm

CROWN LA

DEAN HILL

Little Buckett Farm

Rose & Crown (PH)

PO

Stelling Minnis

Chapel Farm

THORN LA

CURTIS LA

1
2

MILL LA

Thorn Farm

Knowler Farm

1 MINNIS GN
2 MINNIS FIELD

Little North Leigh Farm

Scarp's Farm

Windmill (dis)

Dean Farm

TN25

Courthope Farm

Great Dowles Farm

B2068

12 **A** **B** **13** **C** **D** **14** **E** **F**

A B C D E F

8
7
49
6
5
48
4
3
47
2
1
46

Reed's Mill (dis)
Little Westwood Farm
Westwood
Lynsore Bottom
Covet Wood Cottages
MARLEY LA
COVET LA
Quilters Wood
Manns Wood
Hop Packet (PH)
Great Bossingham Farm
HARDRES COURT RD
Kingswood Farm
THE STREET
Bossingham
Lynsore Court
PETT BOTTOM RD
Covet Wood
TERRACE COTTS
MANNS HILL
Clambercrown
Atchester Wood
CT4
Great Palmstead Farm
Palmstead
SPLIT LA
Split Lane Farm
Little Palmstead Farm
Dane Farm
PEAFIELD WOOD RD
Peafield Wood
High Chimney Farm
Abbotswood
Charcoal Farm
Beech Villa
Fryarne Park Wood
South Lodge Farm
Fryarne Park
Little Wildage Farm
Bladbean
Lodge Wood
Bladbean Stud Farm
Boormanhatch Farm
Farthingsole Farm
Madams Wood
Jacques Court
PARK GATE

127
111

8

MARLEY LA

Little Duskin Farm

COVET LA

Duskin Farm

Long Ruffit Wood

Heart's Delight

GREEN HILLS

Barham CE Prim Sch PO

THE STREET

Little Derringstone Farm

RAILWAY HILL

KITCHENER

HEATHFIELD WAY

BIRCH CT

FOX WAY

VALLEY RD

CROCKENDEN PL

THE GROVE

OXENDEN WAY

Red House

7

Horsehead Farm

Ham Farm

Redgate Shaw

Sussex Farm

Derringstone

OLD VALLEY RD 1
FARMHOUSE CL 2
DERRINGSTONE ST 3

BRICKFIELD RD

Derringstone Hill Farm

GRAVEL CASTLE RD

RABBIT HOLE

49

Colehill Wood

Elham Valley Way

Hoath Wood

Jumping Downs

SOUTH BARHAM RD

DERRINGSTONE HILL

Derringstone Downs

6

Covert Wood

South Barham Farm

Breach Downs

Walderchain Wood

5

Collardshill Wood

CT4

48

Little Breach Farm

The Dolls House (PH)

Clip Gate Wood

Walderchain

4

Palmtree Downs

Elham Valley Vineyards

Breach Farm

Breach

Lodge Lees

3

Red Oak

Nail Bourne

Whitehorse Wood

Lodge Lees Farm

Lodge Lees Down

Bladbean Farm

BALDOCK DOWNS

Palm Tree (PH)

47

Hillhouse Farm

Whitehall Farmhouse

The Cottage

2

Thomas Acre Wood

Middle Row

Snodehill Farm

Wingmore

Grove House Farm

1

Wingmore Court Farm

Bedlam Wood

Osierground Wood

Tappington Hall

Ivy Cottage

Hall Downs

Bunkershill Farm

46

18   19   20

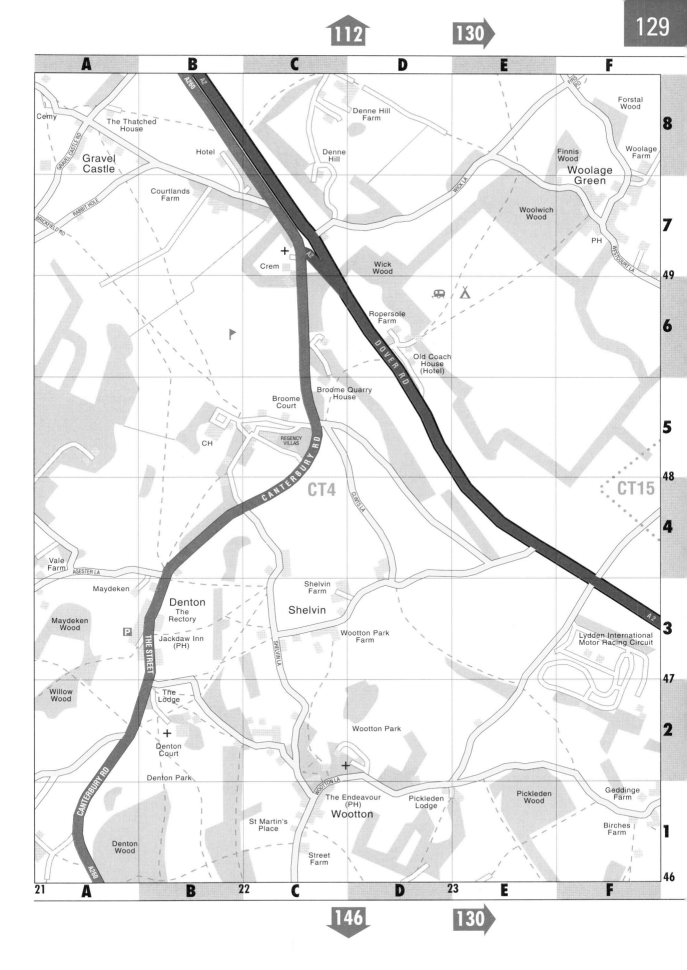

129
113

A   B   C   D   E   F

8

Leighgate Bottom

Three Barrows Down

Lower Soles Wood

CT4

Long La

Stafflands Wood

7

North Downs Way

LONG LA

49

Long Lane Farm

Golgotha

SHEPHERDSWELL RD

6

West Court Downs

LC

MEADOW VIEW RD

Crossways

CT15

Shepherdswell or Sibertswold

5

WESTCOURT LA

Shepherds Well

GLEN
PENFOLD GDNS
EYTHORNE RD
JHI
BERNARD GDNS
STATION RD
MOORWELL DR

HILL AVE

ST ANDREWS GDNS

MILL LA
HAZLING DANE

Sibert's Cl

48

THE GRANGE

THE TERRACE

Bricklayers Arms (PH)

APPROACH RD

THE OAKLeys

PO

CHURCH HILL

MOON HILL

MILL FIELDS

West Court Farm

Puckland Wood

WHITTINGTON TERR

Botolph Street Farm

MOORLAND RD

PH

Sibertswold CE Prim Sch

Upton Court Farm

4

Halfway Street

COLDRED RD

Coxhill Farm

Diamond Farm

COXHILL

Claysole Wood

3

A2

Hope Wood

Upton Wood

CHURCH RD

47

DOVER RD

2

CT4

Five Oaks

A2

Lyddenhill Wood

LYDDEN HILL

COLDRED HILL

1

46

24   A   B   25   C   D   26   E   F

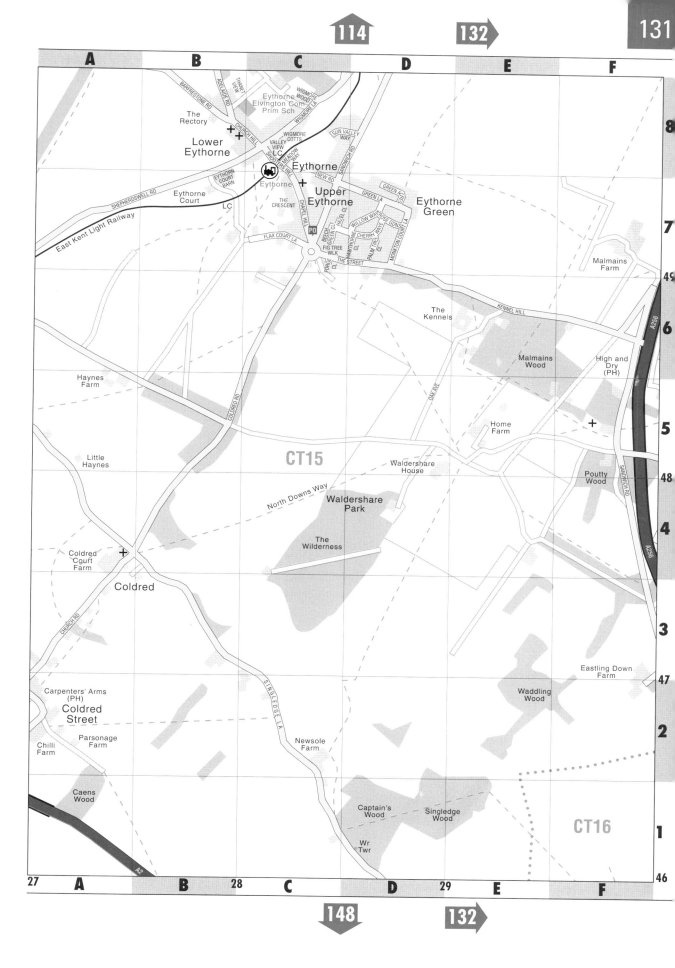

A **B** **C** **D** **E** **F**

8

THANET VIEW

BARFRESTONE RD

ADELAIDE RD

WIGMORE WOOD

Eythorne
Elvington Com
Prim Sch

WIGMORE LA

The
Rectory

CHURCH HILL

Lower
Eythorne

WIGMORE COTTS

SUN VALLEY WAY

VALLEY VIEW

MEADOW WAY

SANDWICH RD

Eythorne

SHOOTERS HILL

Eythorne
Court
Barn

NEW RD

Upper
Eythorne

GREEN LA

GREEN ACRES

Eythorne
Green

7

SHEPHERDSWELL RD

Eythorne
Court

EYTHORNE COURT BARN

LC

THE CRESCENT

CHAPEL HILL

PO

FLAX COURT LA

BEECH CL

GREEN CL

HAZEL CL

HAWTHORNE CL

CHERRY CL

PALM TREE CL

WILLOW WAY

ROSE GDNS

MONKTON COURT LA

THE STREET

FIG TREE WLK

FORGE CL

East Kent Light Railway

49

A256

The
Kennels

KENNEL HILL

Malmains
Farm

6

Malmains
Wood

High and
Dry
(PH)

Haynes
Farm

COLDRED RD

OAK AVE

Home
Farm

+

5

CT15

Little
Haynes

Waldershare
House

Pootty
Wood

48

SANDWICH RD

North Downs Way

Waldershare
Park

4

A256

Coldred
Court
Farm

+

The
Wilderness

Coldred

3

CHURCH RD

SINGLEDGE LA

Eastling Down
Farm

47

Carpenters' Arms
(PH)

Coldred
Street

Waddling
Wood

2

Chilli
Farm

Parsonage
Farm

Newsole
Farm

Caens
Wood

Captain's
Wood

Singledge
Wood

CT16

1

Wr
Twr

27 **A** 28 **B** **C** 28 **D** 29 **E** **F** 46

131
115

A   B   C   D   E   F

A256

West Studdal
Farm

Long
Plantation

STRAKERS HILL

STONEHEAP RD

NORTHBOURNE RD

OAK
COTTS

DOWNS RD

DOUGLAS
BGLWS

DOWNS CL

MEADOW
COTTS

HOMESTEAD LA

East
Studdal

The Old Downs

Nunnery Hay
Plantation

Studdal

Studdale House
Farm

Butchers Arms
(PH)

Roman Road
Cottage

Broom
Bungalow

Minacre
Farm

Chapel
Farm

NORTH DOWNS CL

WALLERSHARE RD

Ashley

North Downs Way

ROMAN RD

White Cliffs Country Trail

CT15

Chill
Wood

Eastling
Wood

North Down

FORGE LA

A256

Maydensole
Farm

Vicarage
Farm

Great Napchester
Farm

The
Fostall

Vicarage
Farm

Walk
Wood

Napchester

West
Langdon

Little Napchester
Farm

St Margaret's
Farm

White Cliffs Country Trail

Muxton's
Hole

Langdon
Abbey

SANDWICH RD

Cane
Wood

Holly
Lodge

The
Mount

CT16

Caneclose
Shaw

ROMAN RD

NAPCHESTER RD

SHEPHERD'S
CROSS

BEECHWOOD CL

A256

30   A   B   31   C   D   32   E   F

131
149

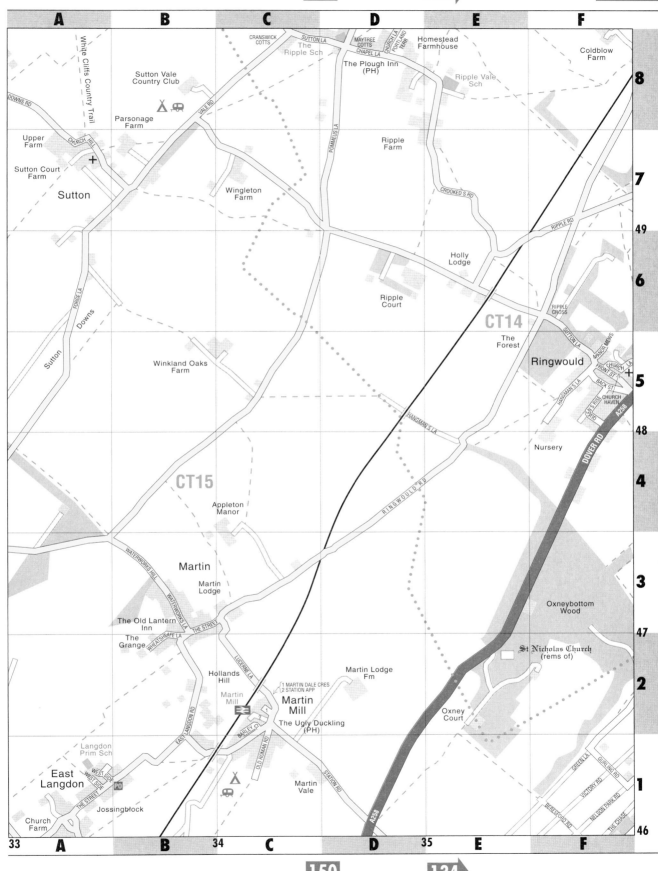

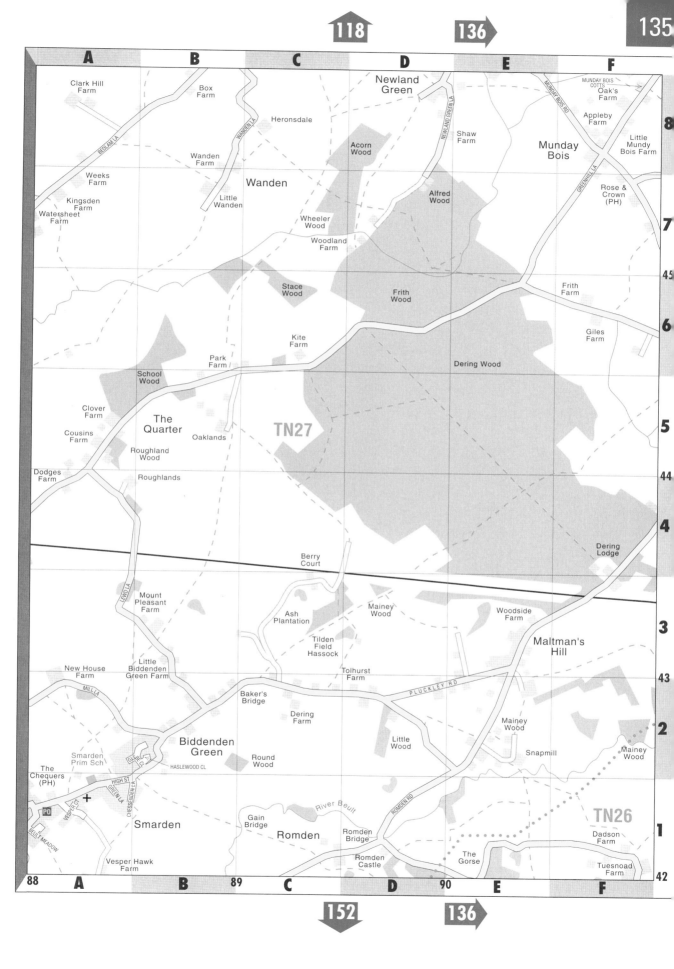

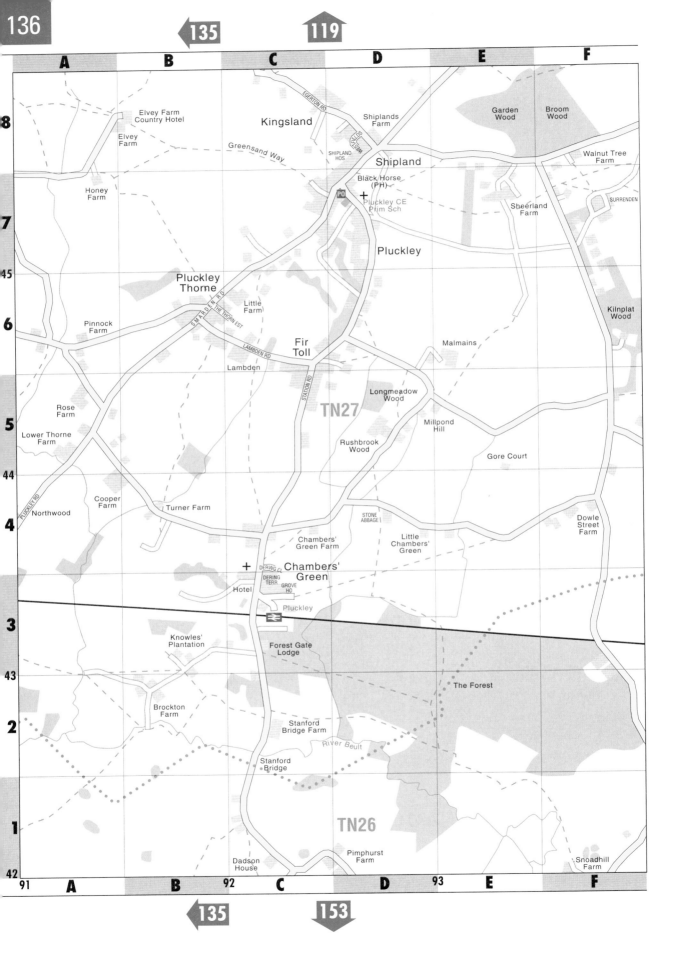

135
119

A   B   C   D   E   F

8

Elvey Farm
Country Hotel

Kingsland

Shiplands
Farm

Garden
Wood

Broom
Wood

Elvey
Farm

Greensand Way

SHIPLAND
HOS

Shipland

Walnut Tree
Farm

Honey
Farm

Black Horse
(PH)

PO

Pluckley CE
Prim Sch

Sheerland
Farm

SURRENDEN

7

45

Pluckley

Pluckley
Thorne

Little
Farm

Kilnplat
Wood

6

Pinnock
Farm

THE THORN EST

SMARDEN RD

LAMBDEN RD

Fir
Toll

Malmains

Lambden

Longmeadow
Wood

STATION RD

TN27

Rose
Farm

Millpond
Hill

5

Lower Thorne
Farm

Rushbrook
Wood

Gore Court

44

Cooper
Farm

Turner Farm

PLUCKLEY RD

Northwood

STONE
ABBAGE

Dowle
Street
Farm

4

Chambers'
Green Farm

Little
Chambers'
Green

DERING CL

Chambers'
Green

DERING
TERR

GROVE
HO

Hotel

Pluckley

3

Knowles'
Plantation

Forest Gate
Lodge

43

The Forest

Brockton
Farm

2

Stanford
Bridge Farm

River Beult

Stanford
Bridge

TN26

1

Dadson
House

Pimphurst
Farm

Snoadhill
Farm

42

91   A   B   92   C   D   93   E   F

135
153

A B C D E F

8

7

45

6

5

44

4

3

43

2

1

42

A 97 B 98 C D 99 E F

A20

P

Foxenhill Toll

Ripple Court

Waterly La

Beechbrook

Beechbrook Wood

Castle Farm

TN25

Kingsland La

Westwell La

Crouchers Manor

Kingsland

Tollhill Wood

Sch

COMMON WAY

SCHOOL RD

STATION RD

PLANTATION CL COACH RD

SACKVILLE

BEECH DR

PARK DR

TUFTON RD

PO

THANET TERR

THE STREET

MEADOW VIEW

Hothfield

TN26

MAIDSTONE RD

Railway under construction

Depot

Mill House

Woodside

Westwell La

Hords Wood Gdns

CH

Home Farm

WATERFALL RD

The Larches

Mansion Copse

Pigsbrook Wood

Marble Wood

Broomfield Wood

Potters Corner Wood

PH

POTTERS CNR

Potters Corner

Hoad's Wood

Nursery

The Warren

Godinton Plantation

GODINTON LA

Balls Wood

Eyesend Plantation

Eyesend

Lodge Wood

ASHGROVE

LODGE WOOD DR

WYNDHAM WAY

ALMOND

ORCHARD

WARREN VIEW

CHERRYWOOD

LANGTON WLK

PEMBURY

RISE

ELCREST

ROSEMOOR DR

PONDMORE

M20

A20

Balls Wood

West Lodge

Petts Hole

Godinton

Godinton Park

Chestnut Tell Plantation

SPINDLEWOOD END

LONG WLK

ORIEL RD

ORCHARD

MANOR WAY

TEMPLER WAY A28

Swinford Manor Sch

Jubilee Plantation

GREENSAND WAY

WHITEBEAM CL

SWEET BAY CRES

Loudon Wood

PH

B2074

Worten Mill

River Spinney

TN23

Great Stour

Stour Valley Wlk

BUTTERNUT COPSE

MULBERRY RD

LOUDON PATH

Godinton Prim Sch

LOUDON WAY

LOUDON

CEDAR CL

EAST LODGE RD

LIME CL

POPLAR

HORNBEAM

CHART RD

HILTON RD

BRIDGE RD

BRIDGE ROAD IND CTR

Worten Home Farm

Willow Bed

Chart Ave

THE COPSE

SPRINGWOOD DR

LOCKHOLT CL

THE SPINNEY

YEW

MAPLE CL

ROWAN CL

CYPRESS

JUNIPER CL

VIBURNUM CL

CHESTNUT CL

ST GEORGE'S BSNS CTR

BRUNSWICK RD

COBBS WOOD IND EST

BRUNSWICK IND CTR

NINN LA

Godinton Park

Bucksford Manor

WATERCRESS HO 1
KINGFISHER HO 2
HERON HO 3
ALDER HO 4
WILLOW HO 5
MEADOWSWEET HO 6

STAFFORD CL

BROOKFIELD IND PK

JEFFERSON CL

Depot

Ninn Lodge Farm

Bucksford Bridge

CHART RD

B2229

BEAVER LA

BROOKFIELD RD

Riverside Sch

RIVERVIEW

MONTPELIER BSNS PK

DENCORRA WAY

Great Chart

PH

THE STONE CL

THE PADDOCKS

SINGLETON LE

CORONATION

MIDDLE CL

HAYMAKERS

HOPPERS WAY

A28

Playing Field

Buxford Mill

Bucksford La

Singleton Lake

COVERT 1
EGGRINGE 2
HONEYFIELD 3
SILECROFT CT 4
BROUGHTON CT 5
OAKENPOLE 6
HUNTSWOOD 7

MILLBROOK MEADOW

B2229

OAKLANDS

ARLINGTON

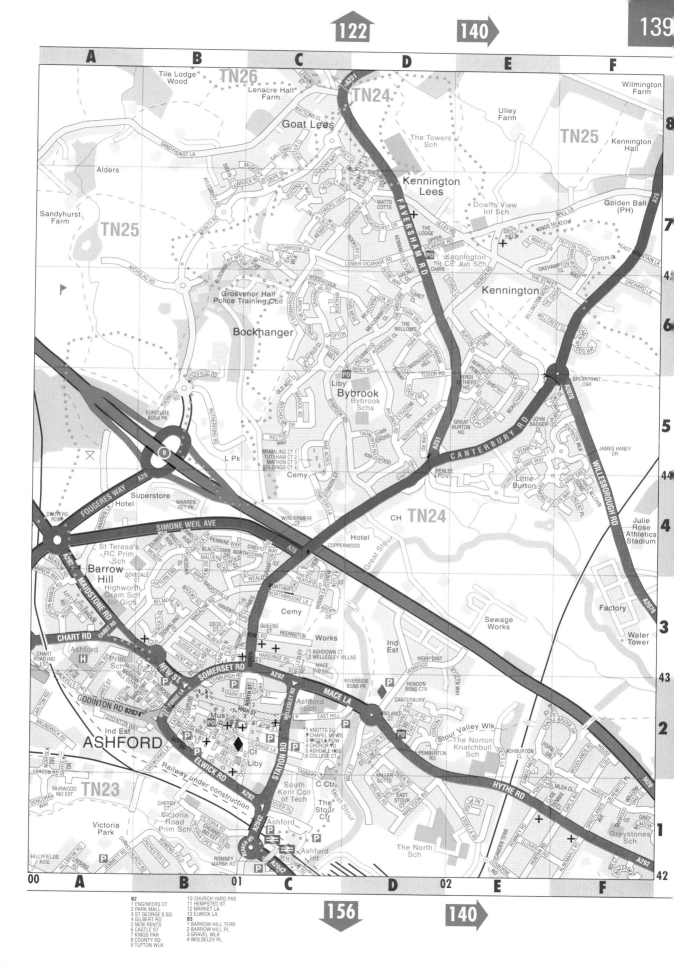

B2
1 ENGINEERS CT
2 PARK MALL
3 ST GEORGE'S SQ
4 GILBERT RD
5 NEW RENTS
6 CASTLE ST
7 KINGS PAR
8 COUNTY SQ
9 TUFTON WLK
10 CHURCH YARD PAS
11 HEMPSTED ST
12 MARKET LA
13 ELWICK LA
B3
1 BARROW HILL TERR
2 BARROW HILL PL
3 GRAVEL WLK
4 WOLSELEY PL

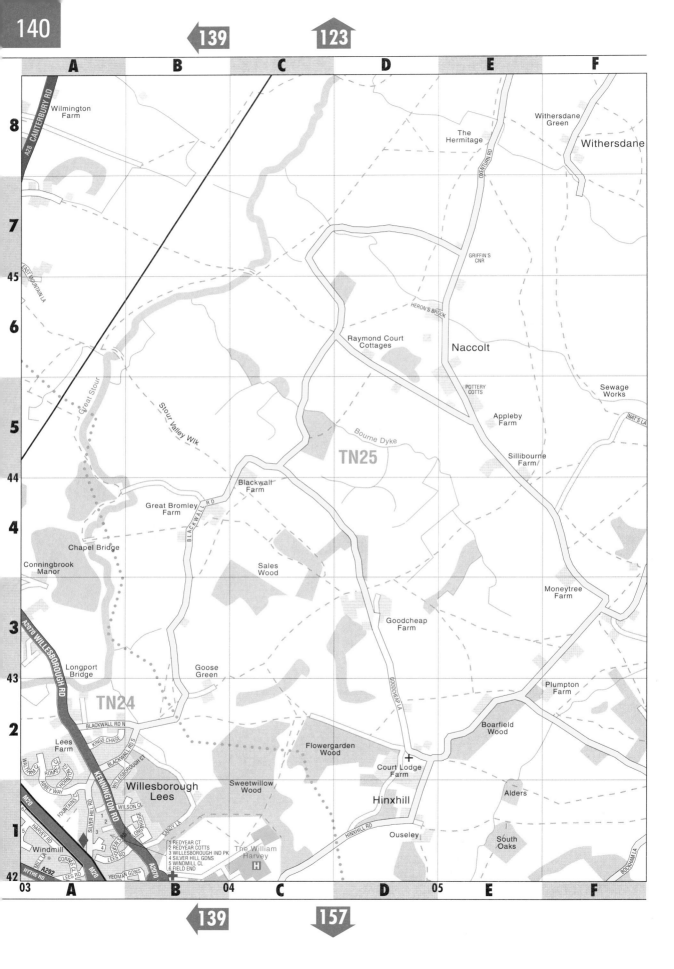

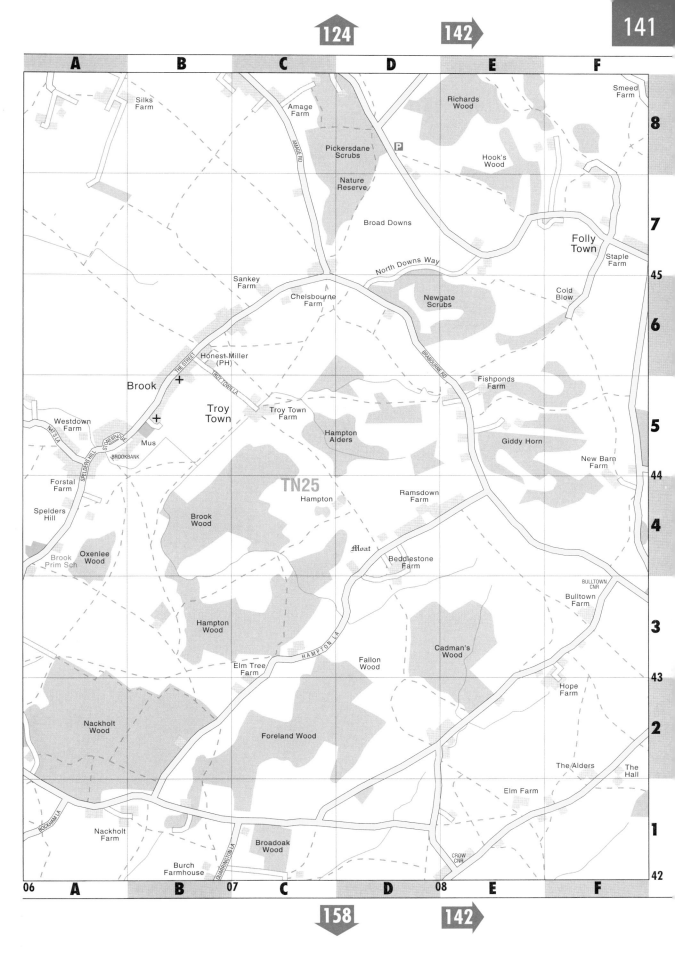

124
142
158
142

A   B   C   D   E   F

8
7
45
6
5
44
4
3
43
2
1
42

Smeed Farm
Silks Farm
Amage Farm
Richards Wood
Pickersdane Scrubs
Hook's Wood
Nature Reserve
Folly Town
Broad Downs
Staple Farm
North Downs Way
Sankey Farm
Chelsbourne Farm
Newgate Scrubs
Cold Blow
Honest Miller (PH)
Fishponds Farm
THE STREET
TROY TOWN LA
Brook
Troy Town
Troy Town Farm
Giddy Horn
BRABOURNE RD
Westdown Farm
Mus
Hampton Alders
New Barn Farm
NATS LA
STOWERBRIDGE
SPELDERS HILL
BROOKBANK
Forstal Farm
Hampton
Ramsdown Farm
TN25
Spelders Hill
Brook Prim Sch
Oxenlee Wood
Brook Wood
Moat
Beddlestone Farm
BULLTOWN CNR
Bulltown Farm
Hampton Wood
Cadman's Wood
Hope Farm
HAMPTON LA
Elm Tree Farm
Fallon Wood
Nackholt Wood
Foreland Wood
The Alders
The Hall
Elm Farm
BOCKHAM LA
Nackholt Farm
Broadoak Wood
QUARRINGTON LA
Burch Farmhouse
CROW CNR

06   A   B   07   C   D   08   E   F

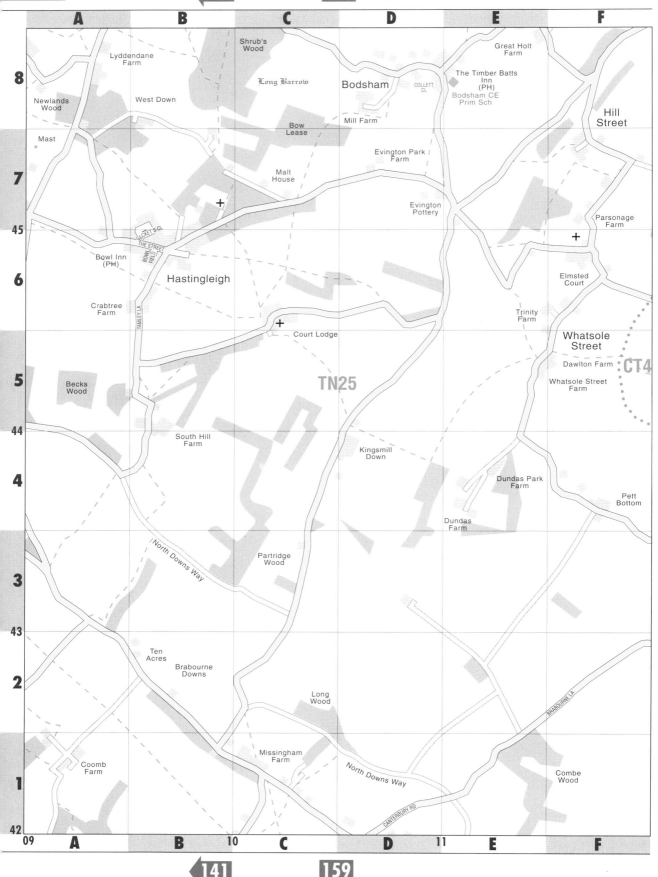

A B C D E F

8

Lyddendane
Farm

Shrub's
Wood

Long Barrow

Bodsham

Great Holt
Farm

COLLETT
CL

The Timber Batts
Inn
(PH)
Bodsham CE
Prim Sch

Hill
Street

Newlands
Wood

West Down

Mill Farm

Bow
Lease

Evington Park
Farm

Mast

7

Malt
House

Evington
Pottery

Parsonage
Farm

45

BECKET'S CL

THE STREET

BOWL
FIELD

Bowl Inn
(PH)

Hastingleigh

Elmsted
Court

6

Crabtree
Farm

TAMLEY LA

Court Lodge

Trinity
Farm

Whatsole
Street

CT4

Dawlton Farm

Becks
Wood

TN25

Whatsole Street
Farm

5

44

South Hill
Farm

Kingsmill
Down

Dundas Park
Farm

Pett
Bottom

4

Dundas
Farm

North Downs Way

Partridge
Wood

3

43

Ten
Acres

Brabourne
Downs

2

Long
Wood

BRABOURNE LA

Coomb
Farm

Missingham
Farm

North Downs Way

Combe
Wood

1

42

CANTERBURY RD

09 A B 10 C D 11 E F

A B C D E F

8

Elhampark Wood

7

45

Clavertye
Wood

Maycroft

Hawes
Farm

6

Clavertye
Wood

Grimsacre

Upper Park
Gate Farm

Little Gate
Farm

Park
Gate

Ash
Ridge
House

Works

Exted
Farm

Exted

5

Beveridge
Bottom
Wood

Elham

44

Mountbottom

CT4

East Kent Hunt
Kennels

PROSPECT TERR 1
MANORFIELD 2
CHURCH WLK 3
ST MARY S RD 4
THE SQUARE 5

PH
PO

Elham
CE Prim
Sch

STATION
MEWS

FAIRFIELD

HIGH ST
THE ROW
CHERRY GDNS
LIME
VILLAS

CULLENS RD
CULLING S HILL
HUNTERS BANK
OLD RD
NEW RD
COCK LA
WATER FARM
THE ORCHARDS
DUCK ST
THE HALL
VICARAGE
LA
PARK LA

4

Lower
Mount
Farm

Collards
Wood

Cemy

HOG GN

The
Laynes

CHAPEL LA

Fir Tree
Farm

Tye

COLLARDS LA

MAGPIE LA

CANTERBURY RD

3

Rhodes
Minnis

Tye
Wood

43

WHITE HORSE LA

The Battle
of Britain
(PH)

Wenny
Farm

Millhill
Farm

Nail Bourne

Elham Valley Way

2

Home
Farm

BOYKE LA

Bereforstal
Farm

LONGAGE HILL

Ottinge

Mill Down

CT18

1

Ottinge Court
Farm

CT18

Stonebridge
Farm

42

15 A B 16 C D 17 E F

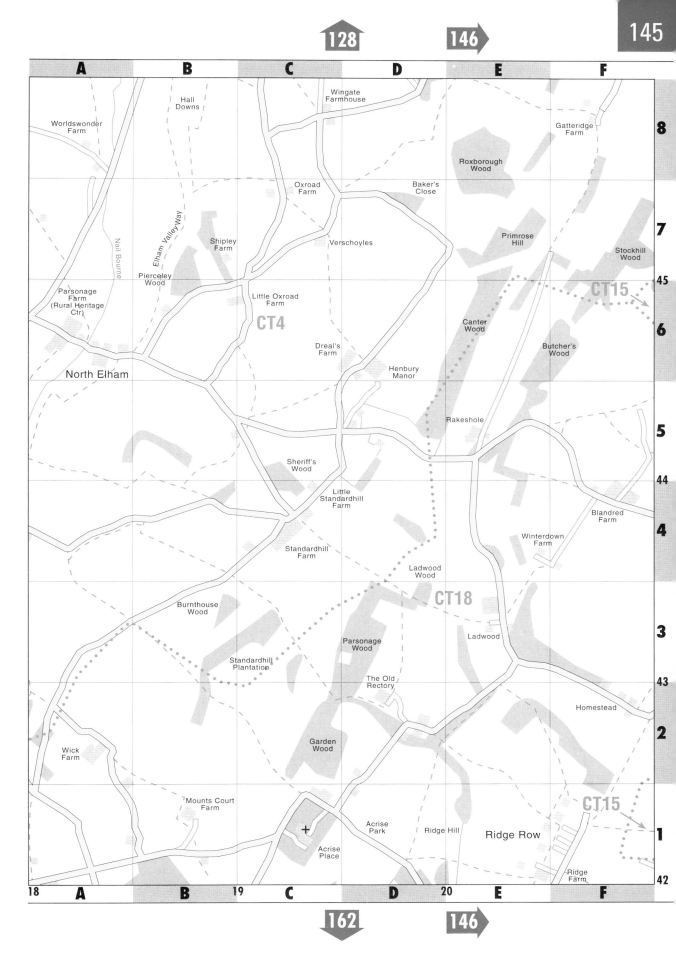

128
146

A B C D E F

8

Worldswonder
Farm

Hall
Downs

Wingate
Farmhouse

Gatteridge
Farm

Roxborough
Wood

Baker's
Close

Oxroad
Farm

7

Elham Valley Way

Shipley
Farm

Verschoyles

Primrose
Hill

Stockhill
Wood

Nail Bourne

Pierceley
Wood

45

CT15

Parsonage
Farm
(Rural Heritage
Ctr)

Little Oxroad
Farm

CT4

Canter
Wood

6

Dreal's
Farm

Butcher's
Wood

North Elham

Henbury
Manor

Rakeshole

5

Sheriff's
Wood

44

Little
Standardhill
Farm

Blandred
Farm

Standardhill
Farm

Winterdown
Farm

4

Ladwood
Wood

CT18

3

Burnthouse
Wood

Parsonage
Wood

Ladwood

Standardhill
Plantation

43

The Old
Rectory

Homestead

Wick
Farm

Garden
Wood

2

Mounts Court
Farm

CT15

Acrise
Park

Ridge Hill

Ridge Row

1

Acrise
Place

Ridge
Farm

42

18 A B 19 C D 20 E F

145
129

A   B   C   D   E   F

8

Summer House Wood

Keeper's Lodge

Hill House Farm

Park Wood

CT4

Park Side

7

Biggin Wood

Park Side Farm

West Lees Wood

45

WOOTTON LA

Park Wood

Park Wood

6

Brenstan

Chequers (PH)

Selsted Farm

Selsted CE Prim Sch

Selsted

5

Stony Lane Wood

Newland's Farm

Stockham

44

Little Smezzel Farm

MANSELL LA

St John's Commandery (rems of)

North Court

4

CT18

CT15

Smersole

Swingfield Street

North Court Wood

3

Hoad Farm

Swingfield Minnis

The Three Bells (PH)

43

Mast

Beard's Hall Farm

Ellinge House

2

Boyington Court

Foxholt Cottage

FOXHOLT RD

Boyington Wood

Everden Cottage

Little Foxholt

1

Red House Farm

Pound Farm

CANTERBURY RD

A260

Great Everden Farm

42

A260

CT18

21   A   B   22   C   D   23   E   F

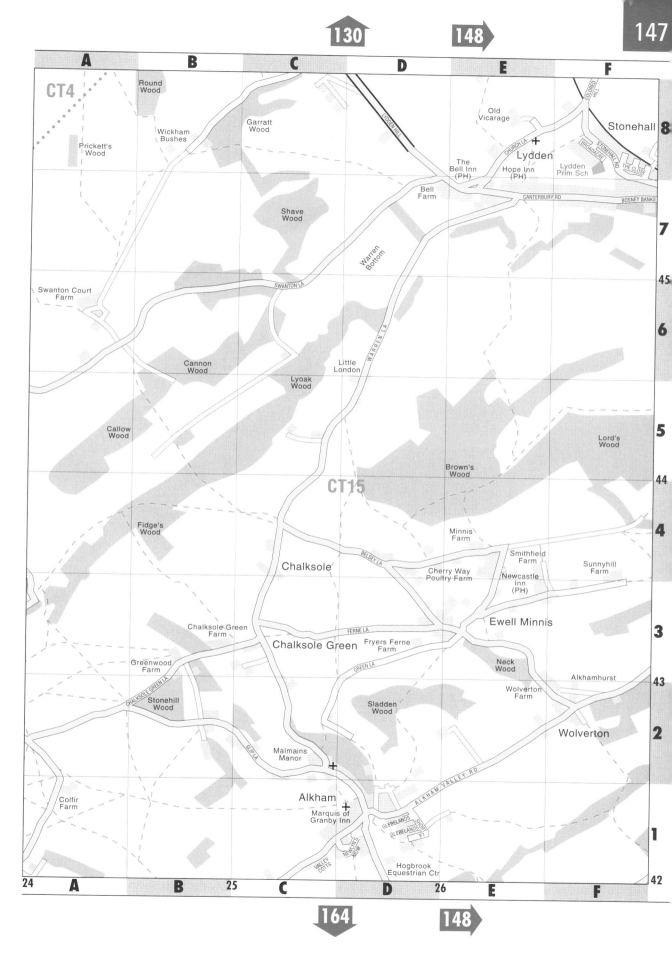

130
148
164
148

CT4

Round Wood

Prickett's Wood

Wickham Bushes

Garratt Wood

Old Vicarage

Stonehall

CHURCH LA

Lydden

The Bell Inn (PH)

Hope Inn (PH)

Lydden Prim Sch

Shave Wood

Bell Farm

CANTERBURY RD

BOSNEY BANKS

BROADACRE

STONEHALL RD

THE CLOSE

OXDRED HILL

LYDDEN HILL

Waren Bottom

SWANTON LA

Swanton Court Farm

WAREN LA

Cannon Wood

Little London

Lyoak Wood

Callow Wood

Lord's Wood

Brown's Wood

CT15

Fidge's Wood

Minnis Farm

BELSEY LA

Chalksole

Cherry Way Poultry Farm

Smithfield Farm

Newcastle Inn (PH)

Sunnyhill Farm

Ewell Minnis

Chalksole Green Farm

FERNE LA

Chalksole Green

Fryers Ferne Farm

Neck Wood

Alkhamhurst

Greenwood Farm

GREEN LA

CHALKSOLE GREEN LA

Stonehill Wood

Wolverton Farm

Wolverton

SLIP LA

Sladden Wood

Malmains Manor

Colfir Farm

Alkham

Marquis of Granby Inn

ALKHAM VALLEY RD

GLEBELANDS

GLEBELANDS

SHORT LA

NEWLYN'S MDW

VALLEY COTTS

Hogbrook Equestrian Ctr

24   25   26

42   43   44   45

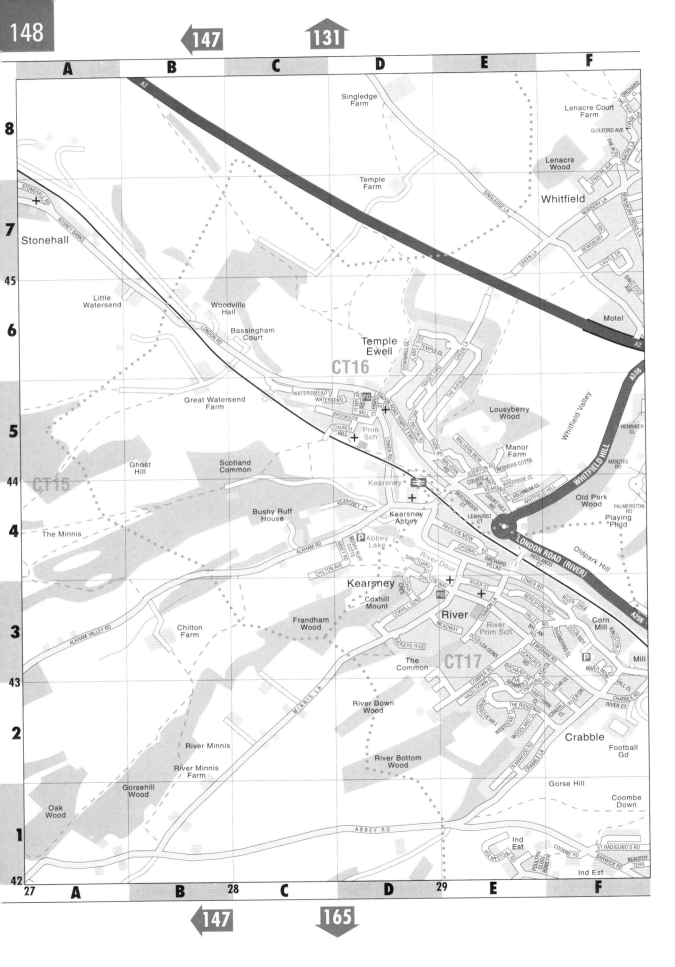

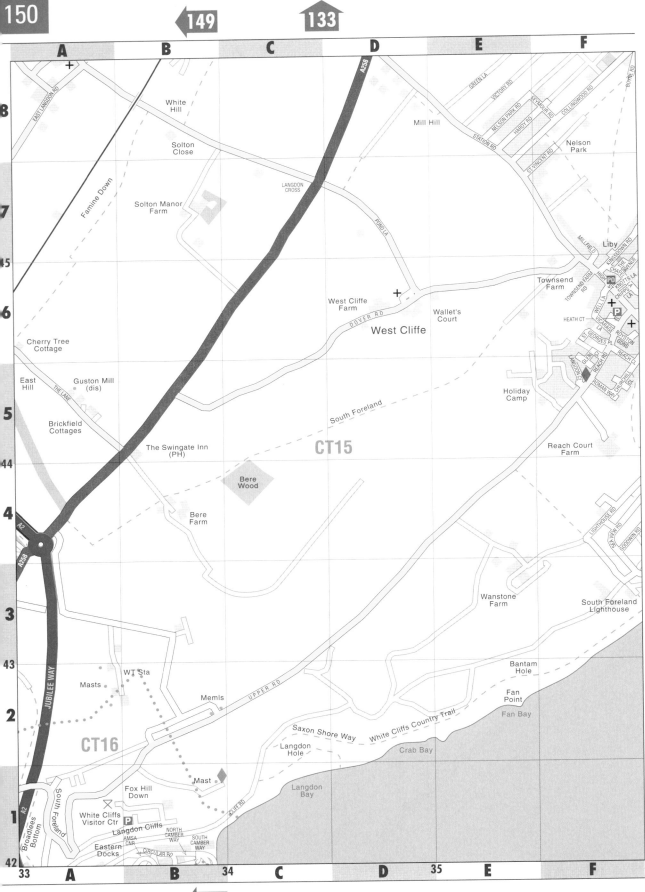

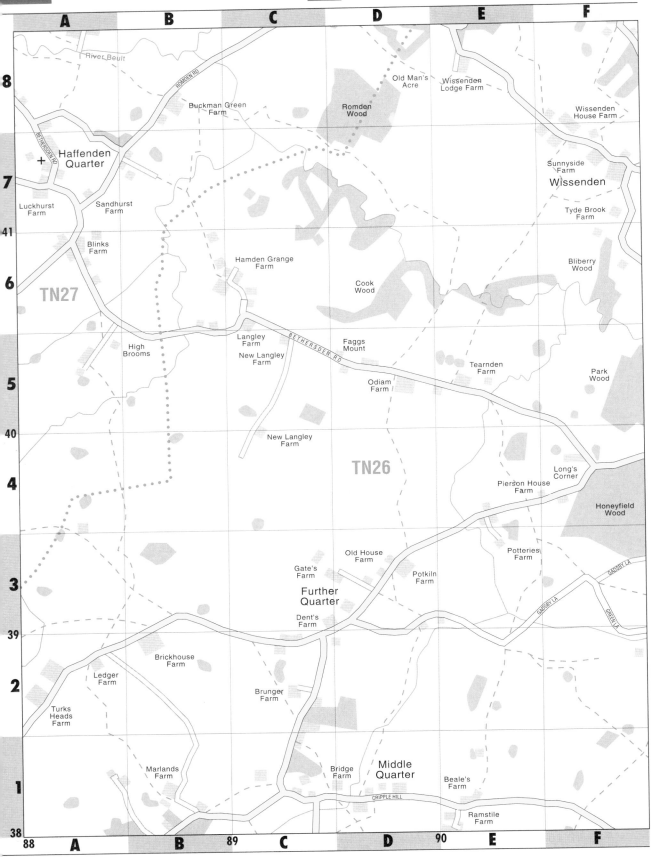

8

Snoadhill
Farm
River Beult

Buss Farm

Barnhurst
Farm

Monkery
Farm

Oakdene
Farm

Frid
Farm

FRID
CNR

Hall's Court
Nursery

Runsell
Grange

Baylisden

Tippet
Farm

Oakmead

7

Star
Farm

Little
Odiam

Runsell
Farm

PLUCKLEY RD

ETCHDEN RD

41

Odiam
Wood

Lamberden
Wood

WISSENDEN LA

Hartlands
Farm

Works

Frid
Wood

PARIS
CNR

6

New Barn
Farm

THE OLD
SAW MILL

BATEMAN
CNR

Mill
Farm

Birch
Wood

Sewage
Works

NORTON LA

TN26

Bethersden
Prim Sch

THE MILL RD

OLD SURRENDEN MANOR RD

Water
Farm

Robscott
Farm

5

Park
Wood

PO

THE STREET

THE POPLARS

CHURCH HILL

FORGEFIELD

CHESTER AVE

Thorne
Farm

KILN LA

Lovelace

LOVELACE
CT

SCHOOL RD

CC
YARD

THE TERR

FORGE HILL

Bethersden

40

WHISTON AVE

BULL LA

The Bull
(PH)

Bull
Green

BAILEY FIELDS

Works

Hoad's
Wood

4

Buckhall

Low Wood
Farm

Island
Farmhouse

A28

Honeyfield
Wood

CASSOCK LA

ASHFORD RD

Bull Bridge
Farm

Oldbury
Nurseries

3

Langham
Lodge
Farm

Twenty
Acre Wood

Whitehall
Farm

Brissenden
Green

Potten
Farm

Nursery

39

GREEN LA

Royal
Standard
(PH)

Potter's
Farm

2

Green Lane
Farm

Little Barton
Farm

Ramsden Farm

Plurenden
Wood

Northland
Wood

Wents
Wood

1

Tanden

Chequertree
Farm

Paul's
Wood

Linden
Farm

A28

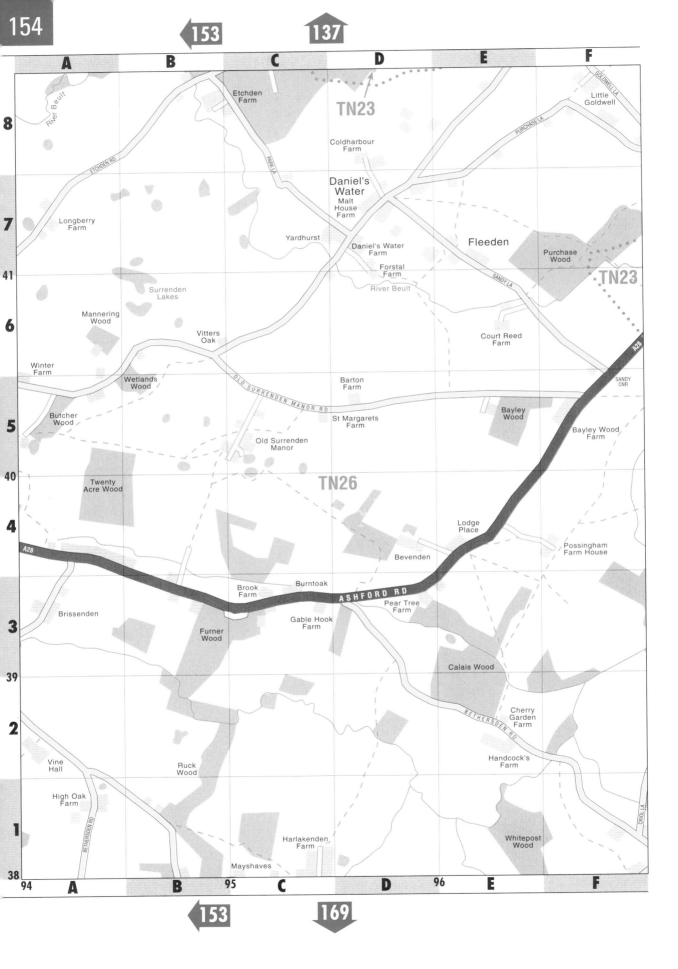

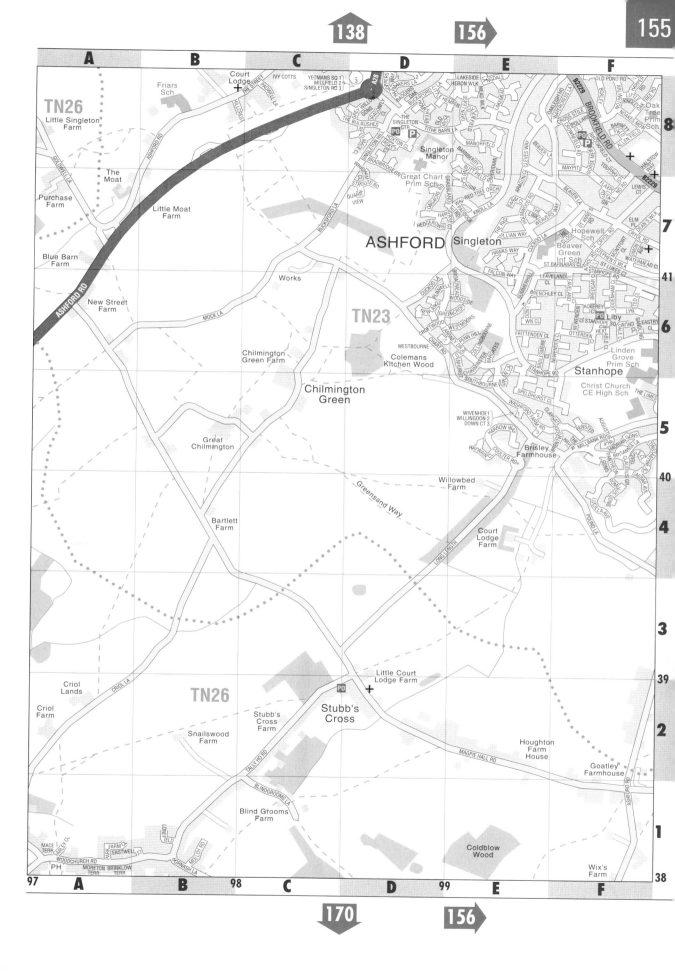

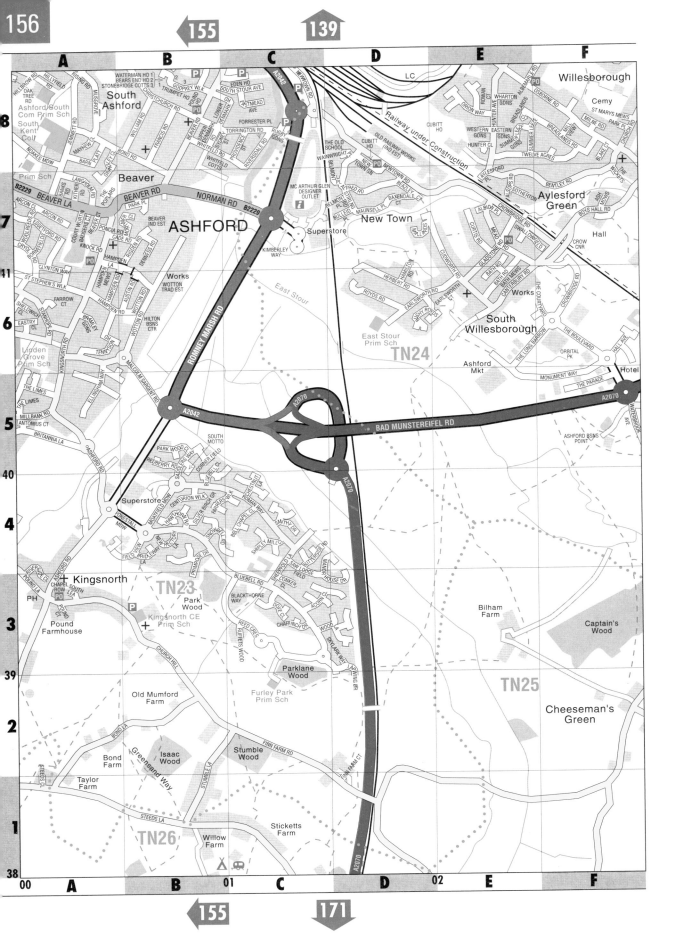

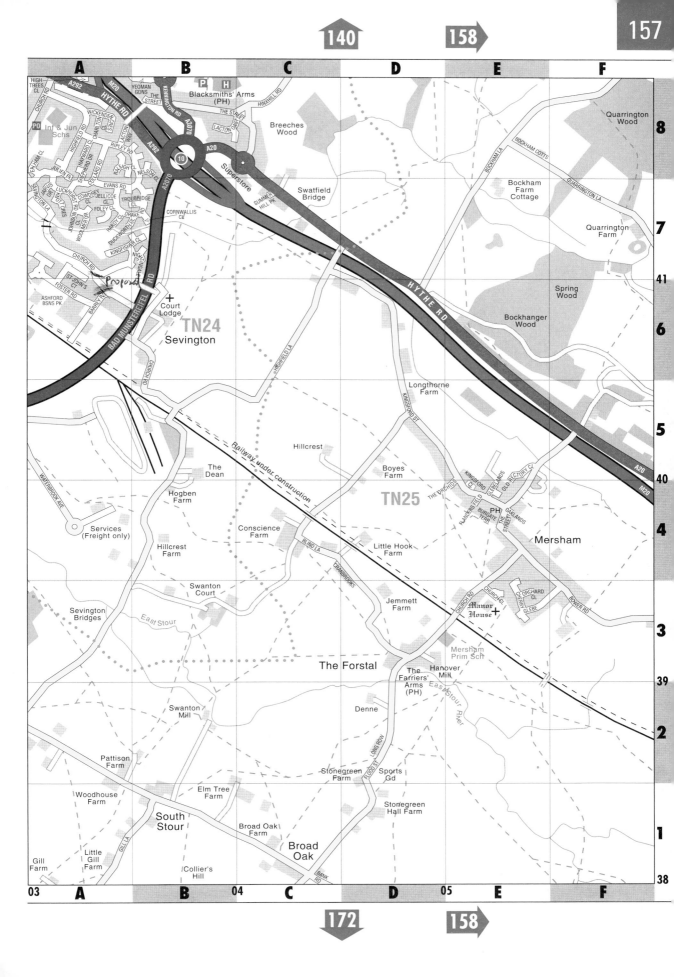

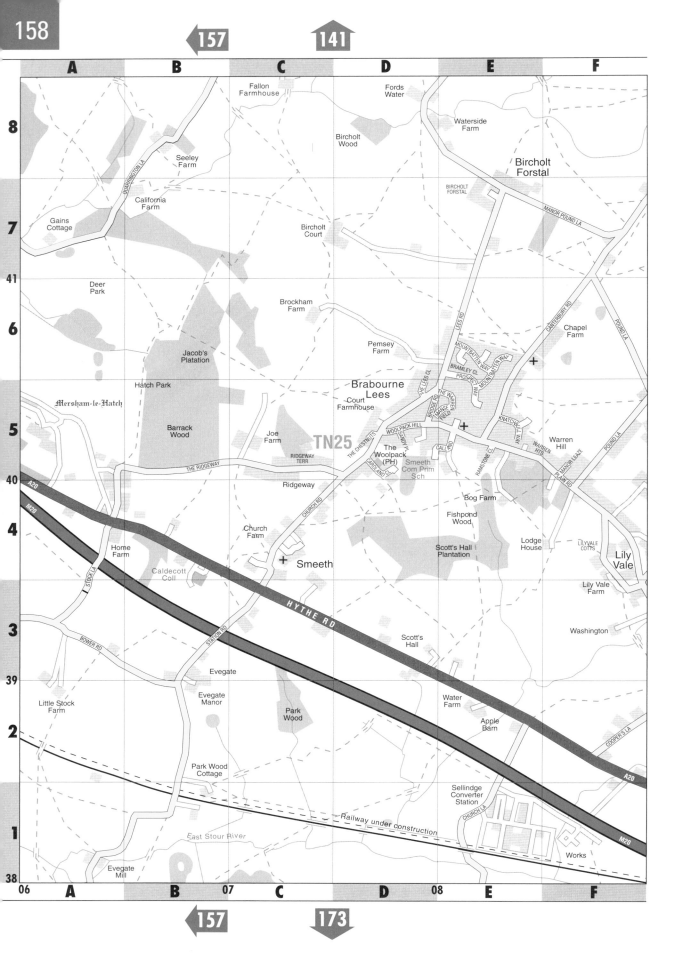

157
141

A B C D E F

8

7

41

6

Gains
Cottage

Deer
Park

Seeley
Farm

California
Farm

QUARRINGTON LA

Fallon
Farmhouse

Bircholt
Wood

Birdholt
Court

Brockham
Farm

Fords
Water

Waterside
Farm

Bircholt
Forstal

BIRCHOLT
FORSTAL

MANOR POUND LA

CANTERBURY RD

Chapel
Farm

POUND LA

Pemsey
Farm

Brabourne
Lees

MOUNTBATTEN WAY

BRAMLEY CL

PROSPECT WAY

MOUNTBATTEN WAY

THE LEES CL

THE WARREN

5

Mersham-le-Hatch

Jacob's
Platation

Hatch Park

Barrack
Wood

Joe
Farm

RIDGEWAY
TERR

TN25

THE RIDGEWAY

Ridgeway

Court
Farmhouse

WOOLPACK HILL

THE CHESTNUTS

The
Woolpack
(PH)

CANDY P

CAROLAND CL

Smeeth
Com Prim
Sch

BRIDGE RD

TANHOUSE
FIELD

CALL PID

KNATCHBULL WAY

RAMSTONE CL

WARREN
HTS

Warren
Hill

PLAIN RD

MANOR LEATE

40

A20

M20

4

Home
Farm

Church
Farm

STOCK LA

Caldecott
Coll

Smeeth

CHURCH RD

Bog Farm

Fishpond
Wood

Scott's Hall
Plantation

Lodge
House

LILYVALE
COTTS

Lily
Vale

Lily Vale
Farm

3

Bower RD

STATION RD

HYTHE RD

Scott's
Hall

Washington

39

Little Stock
Farm

Evegate

Evegate
Manor

Park
Wood

Water
Farm

COOPER'S LA

2

Park Wood
Cottage

Apple
Barn

A20

1

East Stour River

Railway under construction

Sellindge
Converter
Station

CHURCH LA

M20

Works

38

06 A B 07 C D 08 E F

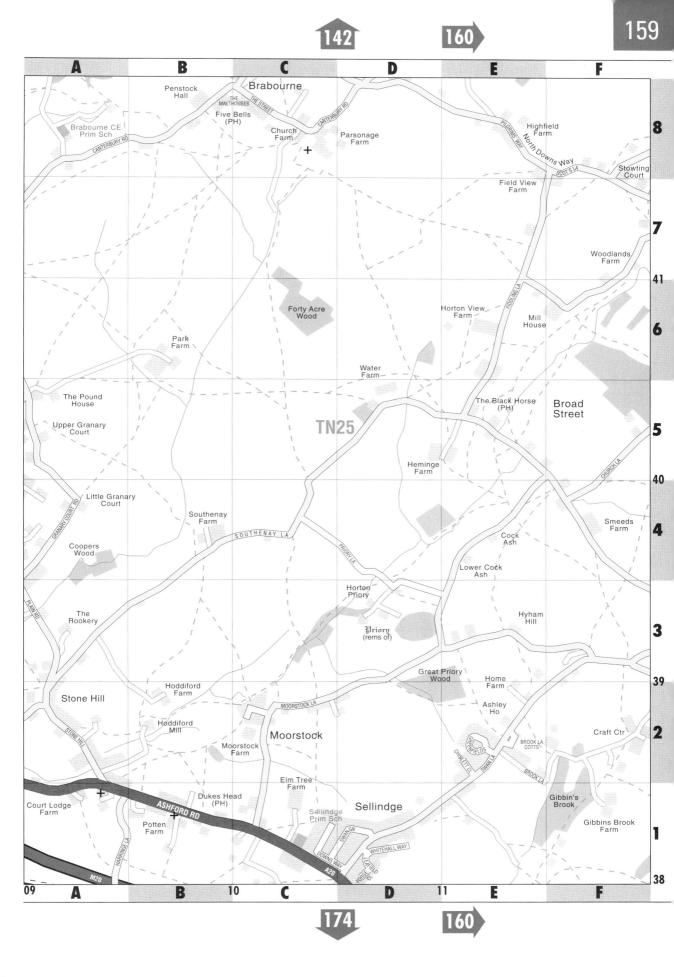

142
160

8
7
41
6
5
40
4
3
39
2
1
38

A B C D E F

174
160

Brabourne
Penstock Hall
THE MALTHOUSES
THE STREET
Five Bells (PH)
CANTERBURY RD
Church Farm
Parsonage Farm
Brabourne CE Prim Sch
CANTERBURY RD
Highfield Farm
PILGRIMS WAY
North Downs Way
SCOT'S LA
Stowting Court
Field View Farm
Woodlands Farm
FIDDLING LA
Horton View Farm
Mill House
Forty Acre Wood
Park Farm
Water Farm
The Black Horse (PH)
Broad Street
The Pound House
Upper Granary Court
TN25
Heminge Farm
CHURCH LA
Little Granary Court
GRANARY COURT RD
Southenay Farm
SOUTHENAY LA
PRIORY LA
Cock Ash
Smeeds Farm
Coopers Wood
Lower Cock Ash
PLAIN RD
The Rookery
Horton Priory
Hyham Hill
Priory (rems of)
Great Priory Wood
Home Farm
39
Stone Hill
Hoddiford Farm
MOORSTOCK LA
Ashley Ho
Craft Ctr
STONE HILL
Hoddiford Mill
Moorstock
GREENFIELDS
CHISLETT CL
SWAN LA
BROOK LA COTTS
BROOK LA
Moorstock Farm
Elm Tree Farm
Gibbin's Brook
Court Lodge Farm
Dukes Head (PH)
ASHFORD RD
Sellindge
Gibbins Brook Farm
HARRINGE LA
Potten Farm
Sellindge Prim Sch
SWAN GN
WHITEHALL WAY
DOWNS WAY
A20
FORGE CL
LEACROFT CL
M20
09 10 11

| | A | B | C | D | E | F |

8 Mill Farm
Stowting
Stowting CE Prim Sch
Curteis Farm
Round Down Wood
CH
Ridge Farm
Hemsted
Hill Top Farm
Woodland RD
Woodland

7 Tiger Inn (PH)
PILGRIMS WAY
Cobb's Hill
Palmer's Wood
STONE ST
Wick Wood
Skeete
Skeete
SKEETE RD
Dingleden Wood

41 Whiteways

6 North Downs Way
Skeete Wood
Nursery
CT18
Little Hollow Farm

5 Horton Wood
CHURCH LA
Horton Court
Hempton Lodge Farm
Hempton Farm
Nursery
Farthing Common
BRADY RD

40 TN25
Hempton Hill

4 Brickclamp Wood
Monks Horton Manor
PILGRIMS WAY

3 BLINDHOUSE LA
Blindhouse
Hayton Wood
Pent Farm

39 Craft Ctr
Postling Court Farm
Page Farm

2 Hope Farm
HAYTON RD
Hayton Manor Farm
East Stour River
CT21
ORCHARD FIELDS
THE STREET
Postling
Vicarage Farm
CUCKOO LA
Lees Farm

1 The Drum Inn (PH)
Stanford
STONE ST
B2068
Douglas Farm

38 KENNETT LA
CHURCH FIELD
YEW TREE CL

| 12 | A | B | 13 | C | D | 14 | E | F |

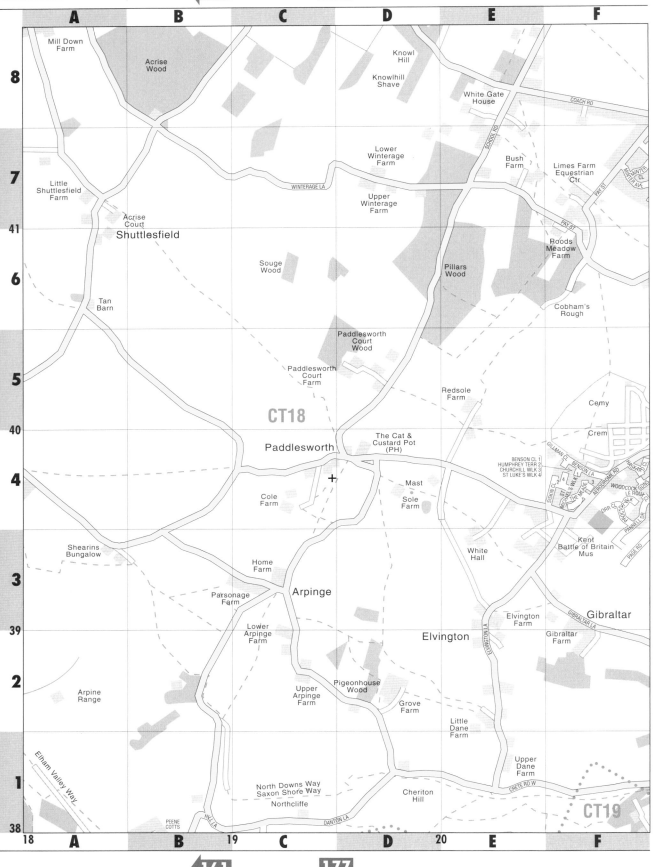

A B C D E F

8

7

41

6

5

40

4

3

39

2

1

38

Mill Down Farm

Acrise Wood

Knowl Hill

Knowlhill Shave

White Gate House

COACH RD

Lower Winterage Farm

WINTERAGE LA

Bush Farm

Limes Farm Equestrian Ctr

SCHOOL RD

PAY ST

WINTER CL
MINTER AVE

Little Shuttlesfield Farm

Acrise Court

Shuttlesfield

Upper Winterage Farm

PAY ST

Roods Meadow Farm

Souge Wood

Pillars Wood

Cobham's Rough

Tan Barn

Paddlesworth Court Wood

Paddlesworth Court Farm

Redsole Farm

Cemy

Crem

CT18

Paddlesworth

The Cat & Custard Pot (PH)

BENSON CL 1
HUMPHREY TERR 2
CHURCHILL WLK 3
ST LUKE'S WLK 4

GILLMAN CL
BENSON LA

HASKARD

+

Mast

Sole Farm

SUSKIN CL
MICHAEL'S WLK
THE MEADE
AERODROME RD

WOODCOCK GDNS
LE ROUX

Cole Farm

ORR CL
PANHELL CT

PAGE RD

Shearins Bungalow

Home Farm

White Hall

Kent Battle of Britain Mus

Arpinge

Parsonage Farm

Elvington Farm

ELVINGTON LA

GIBRALTAR LA

Gibraltar

Lower Arpinge Farm

Elvington

Gibraltar Farm

Arpine Range

Upper Arpinge Farm

Pigeonhouse Wood

Grove Farm

Little Dane Farm

Elham Valley Way

Upper Dane Farm

CRETE RD W

North Downs Way
Saxon Shore Way

Northcliffe

Cheriton Hill

CT19

PEENE COTTS

HVL LA

DANTON LA

18 A 19 B C 20 D E F

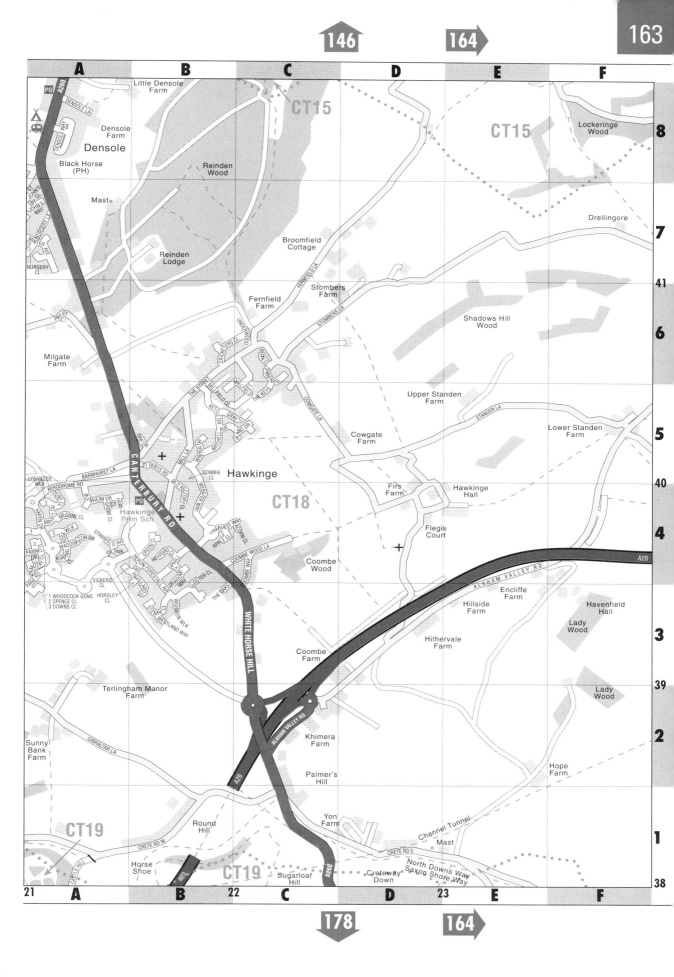

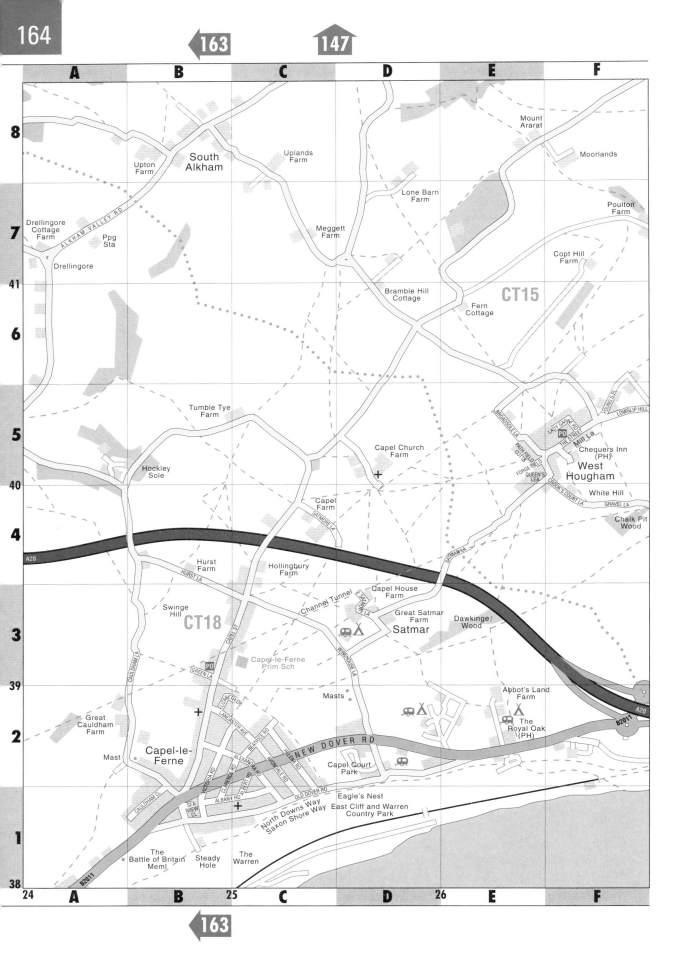

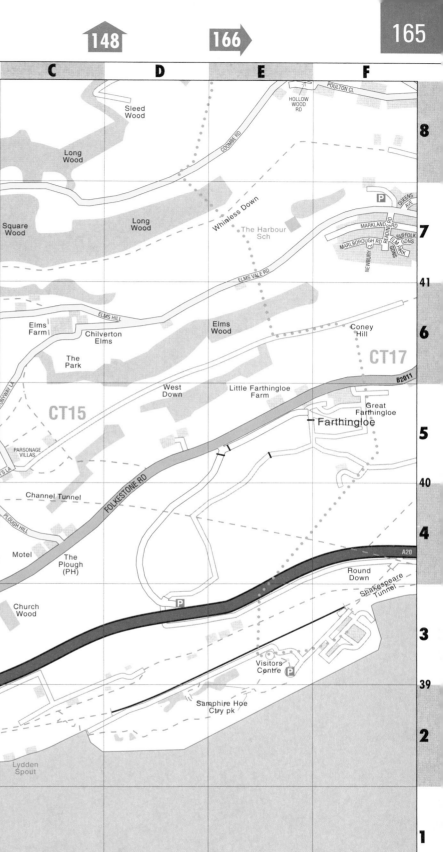

A B C D E F

8
7
41
6
CT17
5
40
4
3
39
2
1
38

St Radigund's Abbey Farm
St Radigund's Abbey (remains of)
Sleed Wood
Gorse Hill
Long Wood
Square Wood
Long Wood
Park Hill
Whinless Down
The Harbour Sch
HOLLOW WOOD RD
POULTON CL
COOMBE RD
QUEENS AVE
MARKLAND RD
MARLBOROUGH RD
NEWBURY CL
ELM PARK
SUFFOLK GDNS
HADLOW RD
ELM GDNS
ELMS VALE RD
ELMS HILL
Elms Farm
Chilverton Elms
Elms Wood
Coney Hill
The Park
B2011
LOWSLIP HILL
West Down
Little Farthingloe Farm
Great Farthingloe
Farthingloe
Cherry Tree Farm
STONYWAY LA
CT15
Church Hougham
PARSONAGE VILLAS
CHURCH LA
DOCTOR'S LA
Channel Tunnel
FOLKESTONE RD
Mast
TV Transmitting Station
PLOUGH HILL
Motel
The Plough (PH)
A20
Round Down
Shakespeare Tunnel
GRAVEL LA
Great Hougham Court Farm
HOUGHAM COURT LA
Little Hougham Court
Church Wood
Visitors Centre
Court Wood
North Downs Way
Saxon Shore Way
Samphire Hoe Ctry pk
Abbotscliff Tunnel
Abbot's Cliff
Lydden Spout

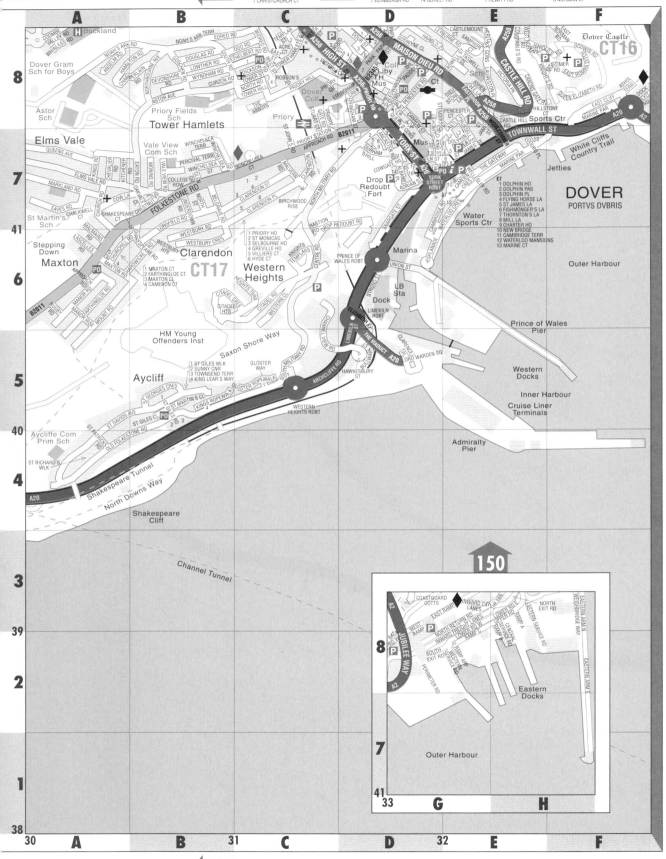

← 165   ↑ 149

C8
1 TOWER HAMLETS ST
2 DE BURGH ST
3 CHARLTON CTR
4 ST BARTHOLEMEWS CL
D7
1 CHRISTCHURCH CT

D7
2 MILITARY RD
3 LANCASTER HO
4 STEMBROOK CT
5 CORNWALL HO
6 WINDSOR HO
7 EDINBURGH HO

8 BOWLING GREEN TERR
9 DURHAM CL
10 YORK HO
11 PRINCES ST
12 MARKET SQ
13 GAOL LA
14 GORELY HO

15 ALBANY HO
16 CHAPEL PL
17 BATTLE OF BRITAIN HOMES
18 CHAPEL LA
19 BENCH ST
D8
1 HEWITT RD

2 LADYWELL HO
3 GOODFELLOW WAY
4 MAISON DIEU PL
5 ROYAL VICTORIA PL
6 PARK MEWS
7 LADYWELL
8 NORMAN ST

9 SAXON ST
10 PRIORY ST
11 WORTHINGTON ST
12 NEW ST

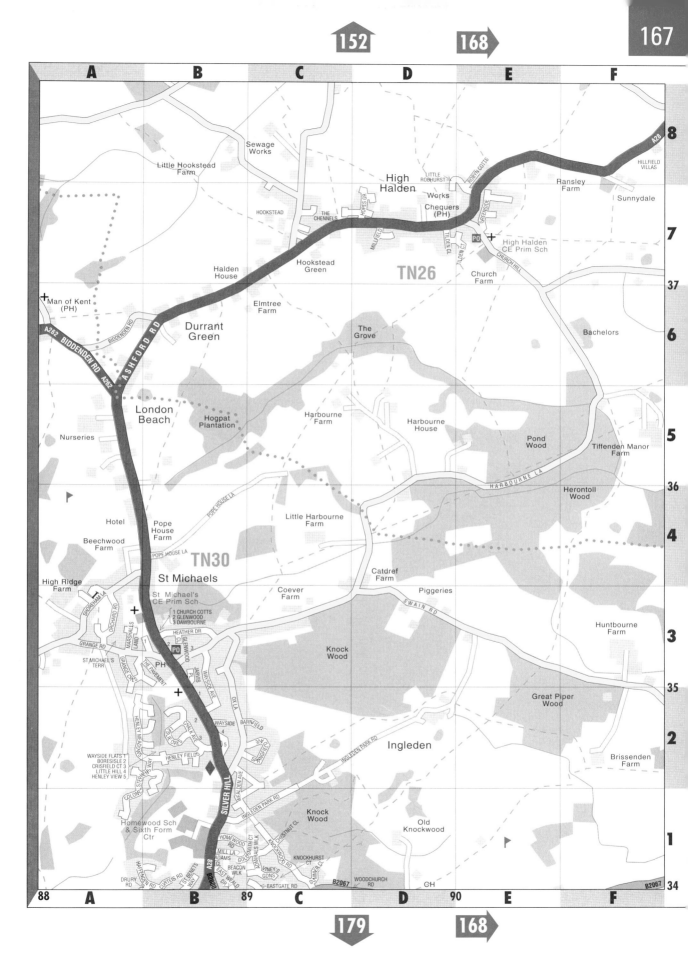

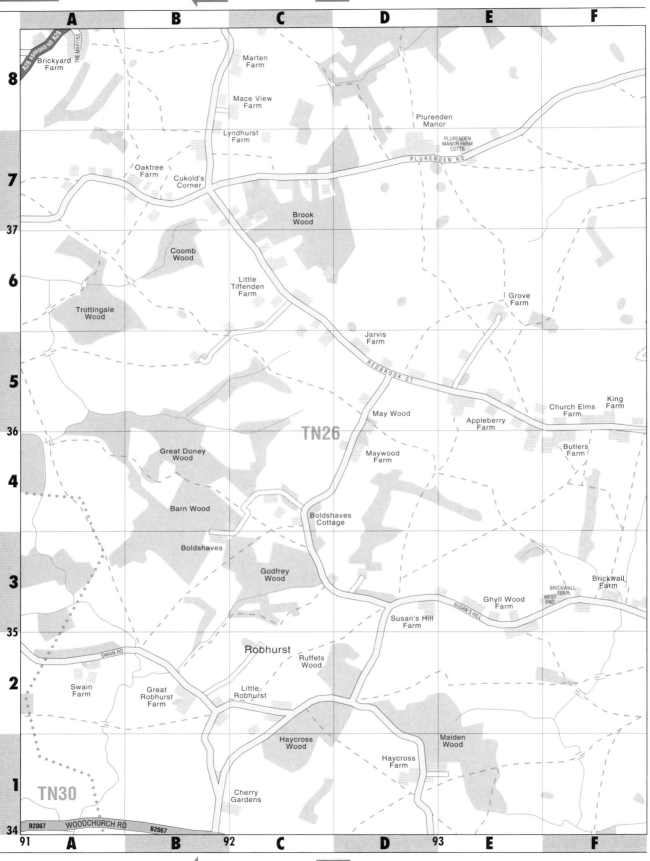

167   153

A   B   C   D   E   F

A28 ASHFORD RD A28
THE MARTINS
Brickyard Farm

Marten Farm

Mace View Farm

Plurenden Manor

PLURENDEN MANOR FARM COTTS

Lyndhurst Farm

PLURENDEN RD

8

Oaktree Farm

Cukold's Corner

7

37

Brook Wood

Coomb Wood

6

Little Tiffenden Farm

Grove Farm

Trottingale Wood

Jarvis Farm

REDBROOK ST

5

36

May Wood

Church Elms Farm

King Farm

TN26

Appleberry Farm

Great Doney Wood

Maywood Farm

Butlers Farm

4

Barn Wood

Boldshaves Cottage

Boldshaves

Godfrey Wood

BRICKWALL TERR
WEST END

Brickwall Farm

3

Ghyll Wood Farm

SUSAN'S HILL

35

Susan's Hill Farm

Robhurst

Ruffets Wood

SWAIN RD

2

Swain Farm

Great Robhurst Farm

Little Robhurst

Haycross Wood

Maiden Wood

Haycross Farm

1

TN30

Cherry Gardens

34

B2067   WOODCHURCH RD   B2067

91   **A**   **B**   92   **C**   **D**   93   **E**   **F**

167   180

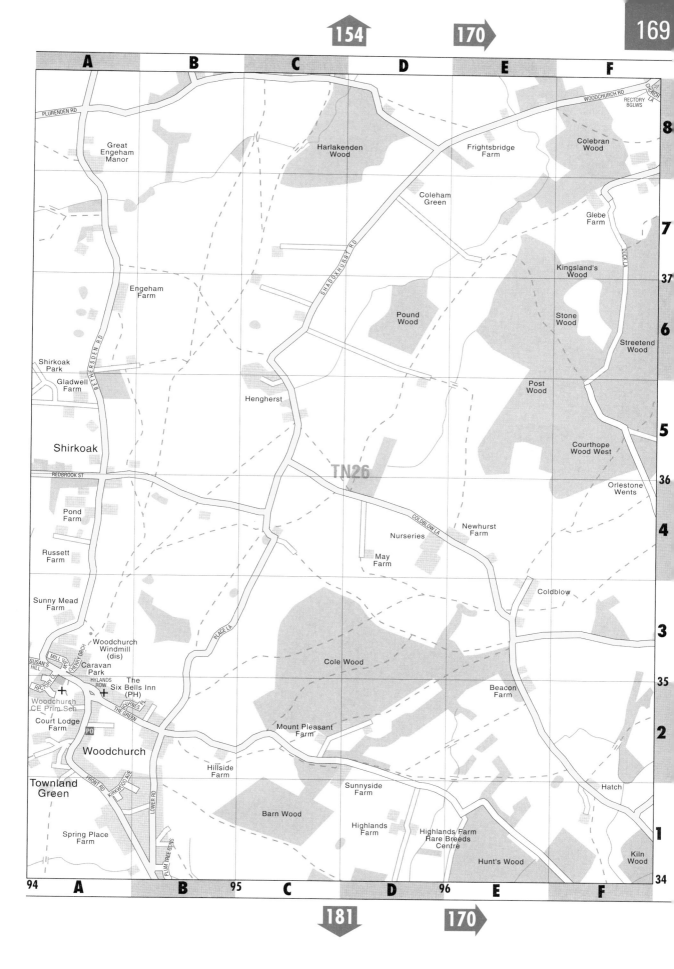

169
155

A   B   C   D   E   F

ST PETER'S WAY

MAYDE CL

Shadoxhurst

THE STREET

DUCK LA

Nursery

Kenilworth Farm

Coxland Wood

Woodside Farm

HORNASH LA

ASHFORD RD

Works

8

Alex Farm

Hillcrest Farm

Great Turrels Wood

Forty Acre Wood

7

CHURCH LA

Upper Toke's Wood

Nursery

Nickley Wood

Bambridge Wood

Manor Farm

Bromley Green

37

NICKLEY WOOD RD

Kennels

Poplar Farm

BROMLEY GREEN RD

6

Moat Farm

Dering Wood

Little Hurst

Bromley Green Farm

Courthope Wood East

Jenkey Farm

HAMSTREET RD

Long Hurst

5

Bayland Wood

TN26

Birchett Wood

Capel Wood

36

Longrope Wood

Capel House

4

Sir Edward Street's Wood

Sugarloaf

CAPEL RD

St Thomas' Cross

3

Spot House Farm

BIRCHETT LA

35

Faggs Wood Forest Wlks

P

Orlestone

2

Parsonage Farm

MALTHOUSE LA

Faggs Wood

Burnt Oak

ASHFORD RD

Court Lodge

Tucker Farm

Fifty Acre Wood

Apsley Wood

1

Lord's Wood

A2070

B2067

Adams Wood

34

97   A   B   98   C   D   99   E   F

169
182

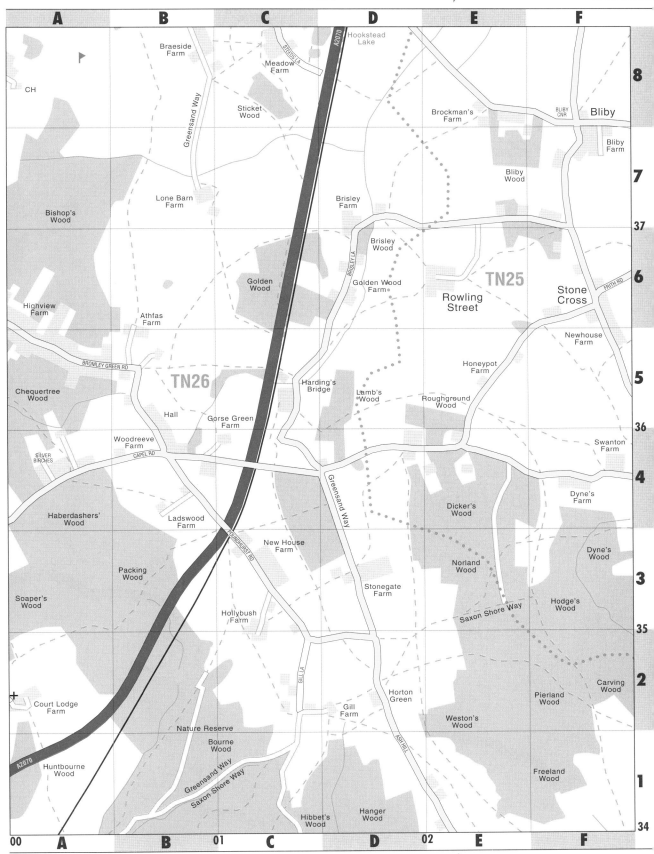

171
157

A **B** **C** **D** **E** **F**

8

GILL LA

Collier's Hill

Shelwyn

Walnut Farm

BANK RD

Handen Farm

7

CHEQUERTREE

Chequer Tree Farm

Frithfield Farm

LAWS LA

Bank Farm

Clap Hill

John Cock Farm

Little Gains Farm

37

Black Rabbit (PH)

Frithgate

FRITH RD

Aldington Frith

6

Beehive Cottage

Bourne Farm

Handen Wood

DICKSONS BOURNE

Poulton Wood

BOURNE RD

Bourne Tap Plantation

Tilelodge Wood

5

Park Wood

ROCKY BOURNE RD

Vale Farm

MILL LA

Barton Farm

36

The Priory Home Farm

TN25

NEW ROAD HILL

OAK CAER KIL RD

EASTON'S CNR

PRIORY RD

Saxon Shore Way

CHERRY ORCHARD LA

4

Fagg's Farm

May Cottage

Goddard Farm

BOAT LA

Priory Wood

Finch Wood

Bonnington Court

The Priory

Bonnington

The Park

3

Yew Tree Farm

B2067

Pinn Farm

Countryfields Wood

35

BONNINGTON CROSS

2

Crowhill Wood

Hill Farm

Gorsedown Farm

Parsonage Farm

BILSINGTON CROSS

COSWAN COT'S

1

Horn's Wood

TN26

White Horse (PH)

Mon

Court Lodge Farm

Bilsington

Marshland Sewer

St Rumwold's Church

Herne Hill

B2067

Royal Military Canal Path

Royal Military Canal (dis)

34

03 **A** **B** 04 **C** **D** 05 **E** **F**

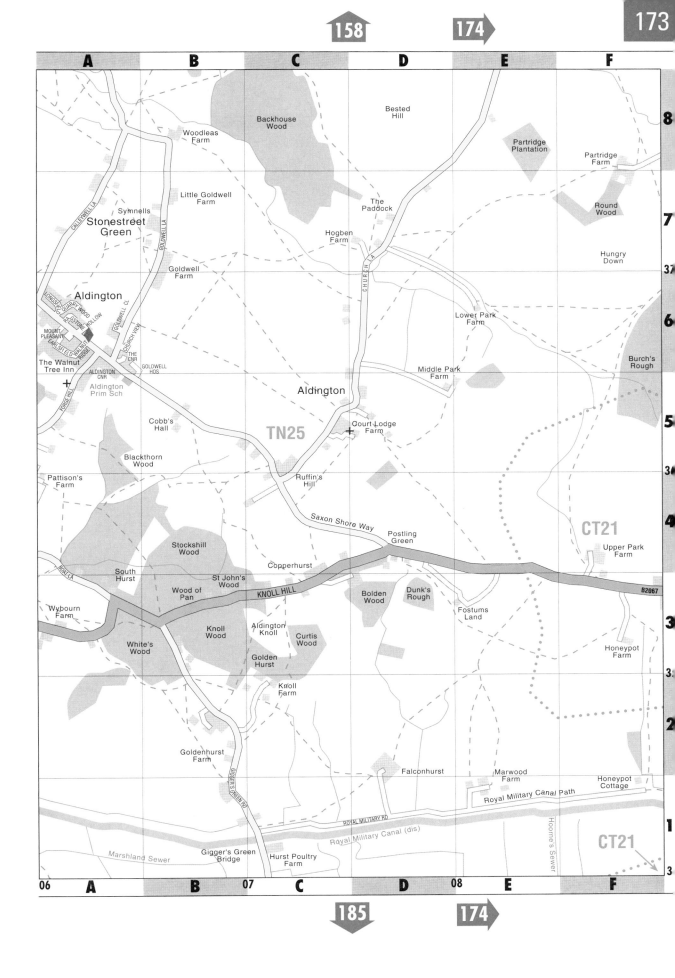

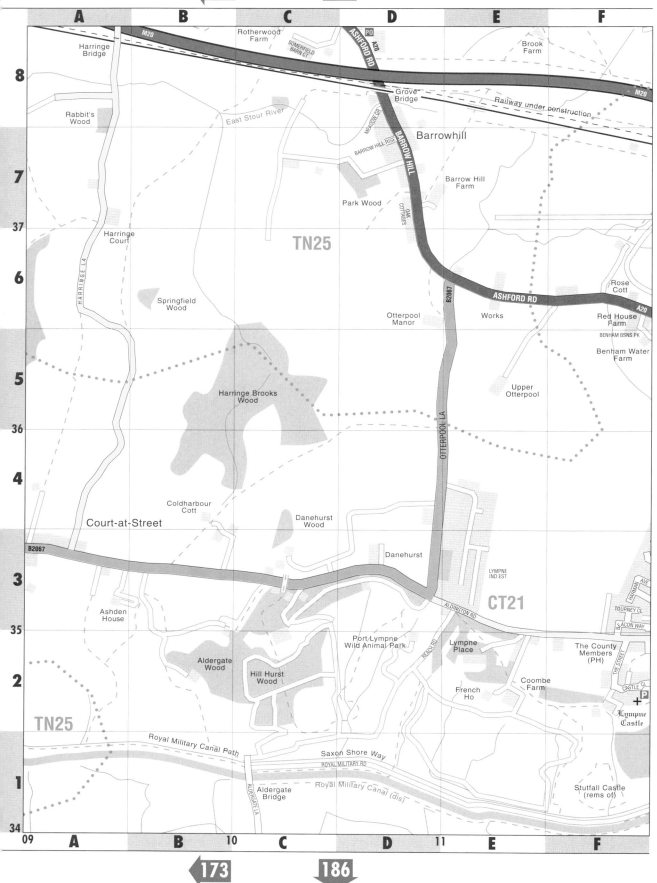

A B C D E F

8

Harringe Bridge

M20

Rotherwood Farm

SOMERFIELD BARN CT

ASHFORD RD
A20

PO

Brook Farm

M20

Grove Bridge

Railway under construction

Rabbit's Wood

East Stour River

MEADOW GRN

Barrowhill

BARROW HILL RISE

7

Harringe Court

HARRINGE LA

Park Wood

OAK COTTAGES

BARROW HILL

Barrow Hill Farm

37

TN25

Rose Cott

6

Springfield Wood

B2067

ASHFORD RD

Otterpool Manor

Works

A20

Red House Farm

BENHAM BSNS PK

Benham Water Farm

Harringe Brooks Wood

Upper Otterpool

5

36

OTTERPOOL LA

4

Coldharbour Cott

Danehurst Wood

Court-at-Street

Danehurst

B2067

LYMPNE IND EST

3

CT21

ALDINGTON RD

HARMAN AVE

TOURNEY CL

SACON WAY

35

Ashden House

Aldergate Wood

Port Lympne Wild Animal Park

REACH RD

Lympne Place

The County Members (PH)

THE STREET

2

Hill Hurst Wood

French Ho

Coombe Farm

CASTLE CL

P

Lympne Castle

TN25

Royal Military Canal Path

Saxon Shore Way

ROYAL MILITARY RD

Stutfall Castle (rems of)

1

ALDERGATE LA

Aldergate Bridge

Royal Military Canal (dis)

34

09 A B 10 C D 11 E F

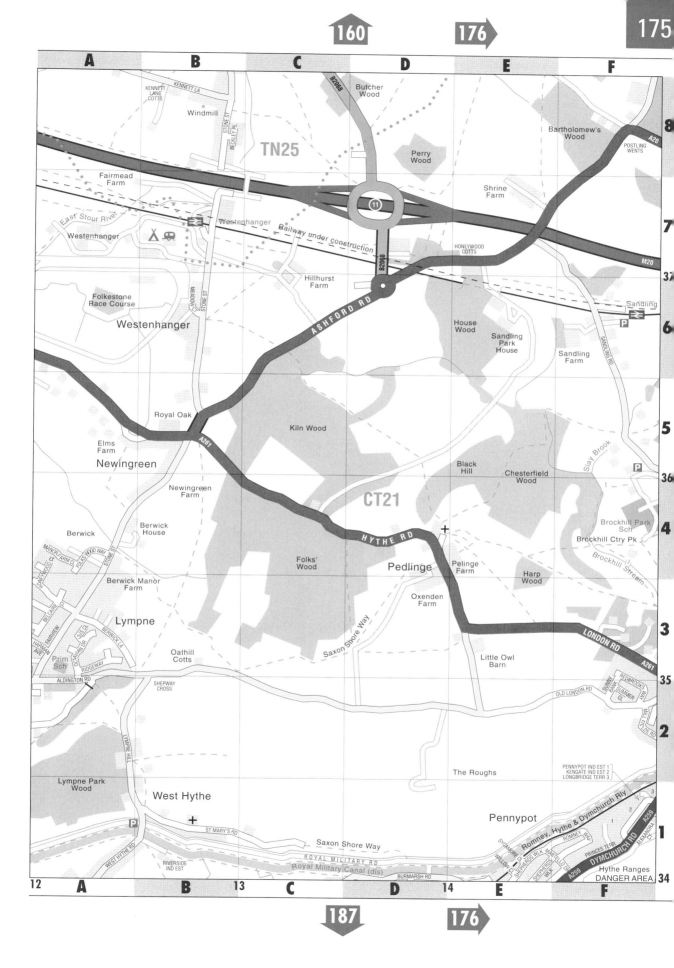

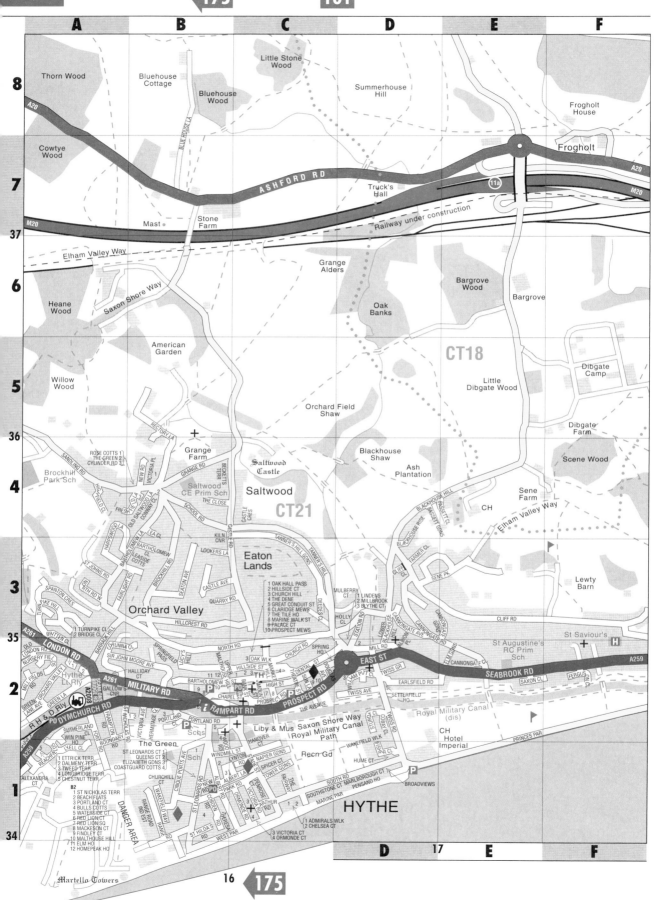

178
E3
1 HILLSIDE
2 SOUTHOVER CT
3 HOMEVALE HO
4 TOWER CT
5 SIR JOHN MOORE CT
6 RIVIERA CT
7 NORTH LA
8 WHITE CT

F3
1 MARTELLO TERR
2 LACHLAN WAY
3 JAMES MORRIS CT
4 CASTLE CL
5 VARNE LODGE
6 VARNE CT
7 BEACH MARINE
8 ZARENA CT
9 CASTLE GLEN

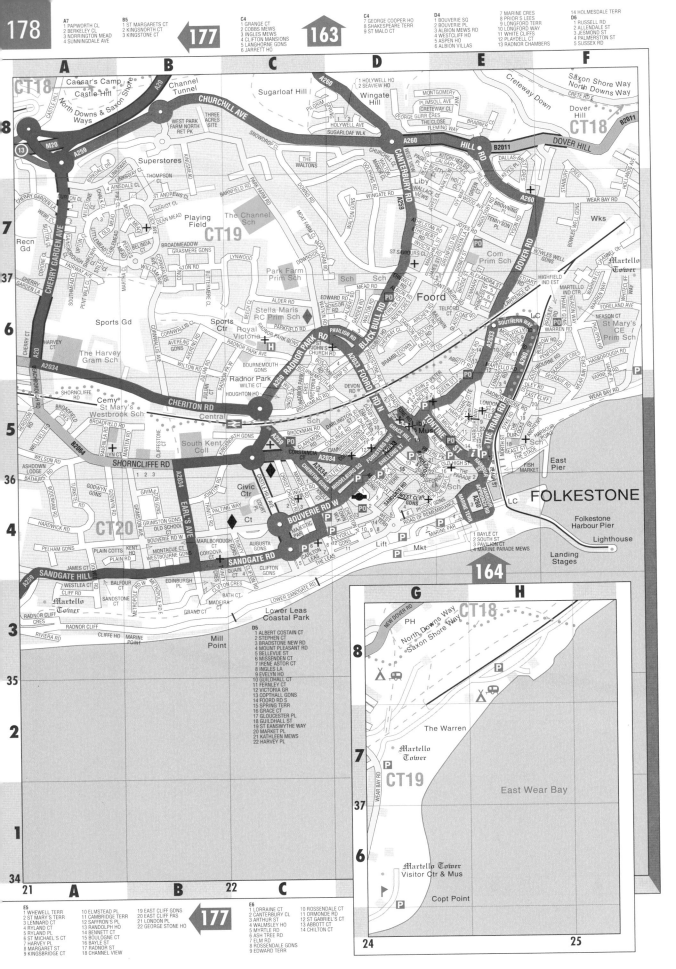

A7
1 PAPWORTH CL
2 BERKELEY CL
3 NORRINGTON MEAD
4 SUNNINGDALE AVE

B5
1 ST MARGARETS CT
2 KINGSNORTH CT
3 KINGSTONE CT

← 177

C4
1 GRANGE CT
2 COBBS MEWS
3 INGLES MEWS
4 CLIFTON MANSIONS
5 LANGHORNE GDNS
6 JARRETT HO

↑ 163

C4
7 GEORGE COOPER HO
8 SHAKESPEARE TERR
9 ST MALO CT

D4
1 BOUVERIE SQ
2 BOUVERIE PL
3 ALBION MEWS RD
4 WESTCLIFF HO
5 ASPEN HO
6 ALBION VILLAS

7 MARINE CRES
8 PRIOR S LEES
9 LONGFORD TERR
10 LONGFORD WAY
11 WHITE CLIFFS
12 PLAYDELL CT
13 RADNOR CHAMBERS

14 HOLMESDALE TERR
D6
1 RUSSELL RD
2 ALLENDALE ST
3 JESMOND ST
4 PALMERSTON ST
5 SUSSEX RD

D5
1 ALBERT COSTAIN CT
2 STEPHEN CT
3 BRADSTONE NEW RD
4 MOUNT PLEASANT RD
5 BELLEVUE ST
6 MISSENDEN CT
7 IRENE ASTOR CT
8 INGLES LA
9 EVELYN HO
10 GUILDHALL CT
11 FERNLEY CT
12 VICTORIA GR
13 COPTHALL GDNS
14 FOORD RD S
15 SPRING TERR
16 GRACE CT
17 GLOUCESTER PL
18 GUILDHALL ST
19 ST EANSWYTHE WAY
20 MARKET PL
21 KATHLEEN MEWS
22 HARVEY PL

E5
1 WHEWELL TERR
2 ST MARY'S TERR
3 LENNARD CT
4 RYLAND CT
5 RYLAND PL
6 ST MICHAEL'S CT
7 HARVEY PL
8 MARGARET ST
9 KINGSBRIDGE CT
10 ELMSTEAD PL
11 CAMBRIDGE TERR
12 SAFFRON'S PL
13 RANDOLPH HO
14 BENNETT CT
15 BOULOGNE CT
16 BAYLE ST
17 RADNOR ST
18 CHANNEL VIEW
19 EAST CLIFF GDNS
20 EAST CLIFF PAS
21 LONDON PL
22 GEORGE STONE HO

← 177

E6
1 LORRAINE CT
2 CANTERBURY CL
3 ARTHUR ST
4 WALMSLEY HO
5 MYRTLE RD
6 ASH TREE RD
7 ELM RD
8 ROSSENDALE GDNS
9 EDWARD TERR
10 ROSSENDALE CT
11 ORMONDE RD
12 ST GABRIEL'S CT
13 ABBOTT CT
14 CHILTON CT

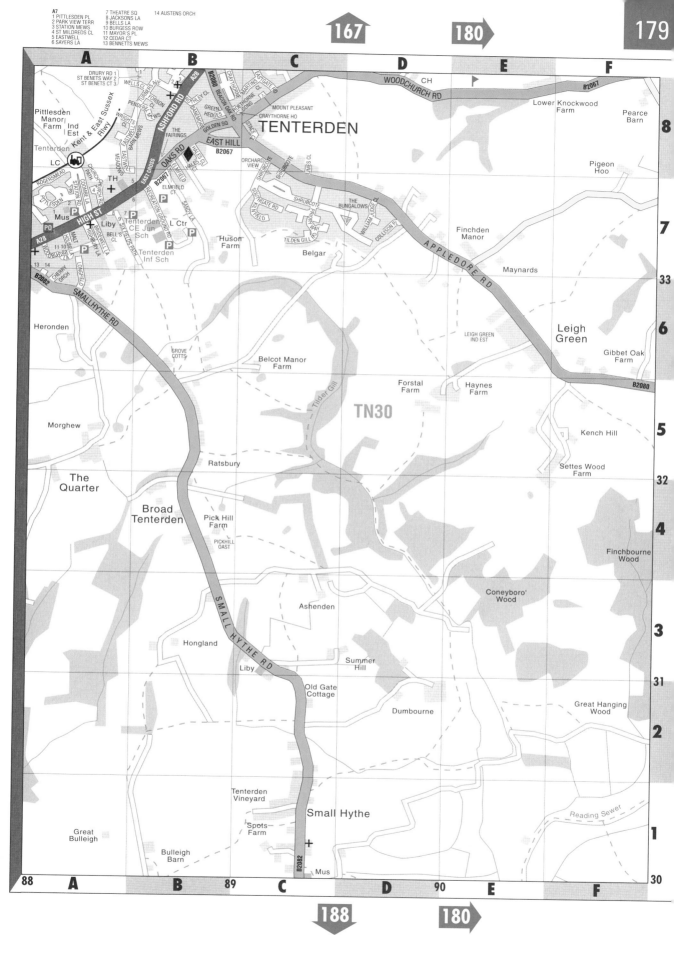

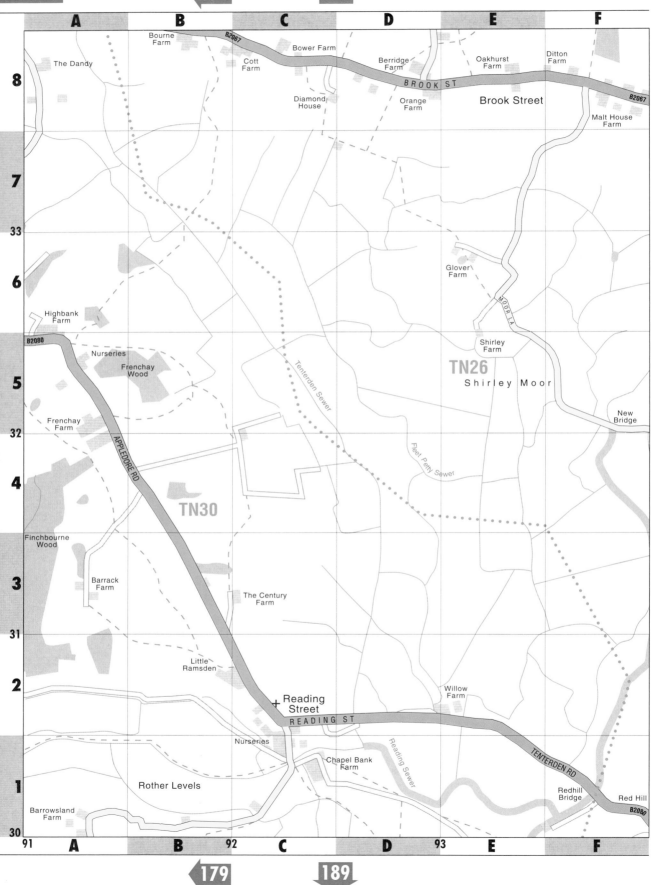

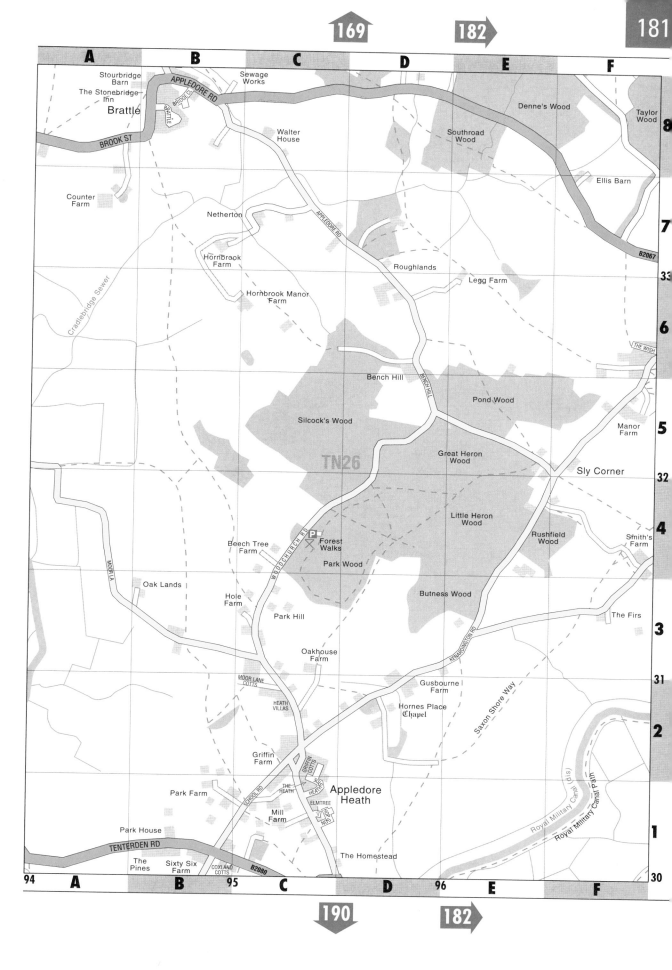

181
170

A **B** **C** **D** **E** **F**

8

High Hockley
Farm

Penfold
Wood

Birch
Wood

Hockley

Woodlands
Farm

Hamstreet
Prim Sch

Sewage
Works

Leacon
Farm

Smallman's
Wood

Burr
Farm

Elm
Farm

7

The Leacon

B2067

33

POPLARS

The World's Wonder
(PH)

Lofty
Lands

VIADUCT
TERR

Parker
Farm

Place
Farm

B2067

High House
Farm

Stone Farm

Warehorne

6

Kenardington

CORNER
COTTS

Horsemarsh
Farm

Sewage
Works

Saxon Shore Way

The
Woolpack
(PH)

Battle Hill
Farm

Tinton Manor
Farm

LC

5

Horsemarsh Sewer

32

Royal Military Canal (dis)

TN26

Bridge
Farm

4

Barncote

Royal Military Canal Path

Rentlands

Higham
Farm

Speringbrook Sewer

3

Thrift
Cottage

31

LC

The Dowels

Blackman's Arm

Terry
House

Sedbrook Sewer

1

TN29

30

181
191

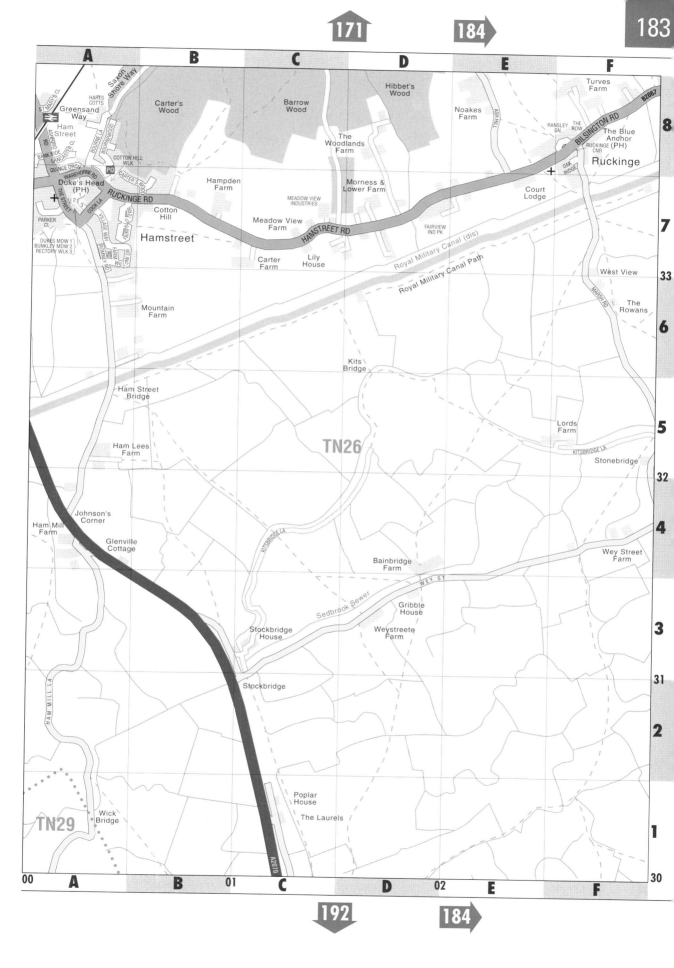

A B C D E F

8

Saxon Shore Way
ST MARY'S CL
HARTS COTTS
Greensand Way
Ham Street
Carter's Wood
Barrow Wood
Hibbet's Wood
Turves Farm
B2067
Noakes Farm
ASH HILL
BILSINGTON RD
RANSLEY GN
THE ROW
The Blue Anchor
RUCKINGE (PH)
RUCKINGE CNR
ASHFORD RD
BANK SIDE
LANCASTER CL
QUINCE ORCH
WAREHORNE RD
BOURNE LA
BOURNEWOOD
COTTON HILL WLK
PO
CARTER'S WOOD
The Woodlands Farm
Morness & Lower Farm
OAK RIDGE
Ruckinge
Duke's Head (PH)
RUCKINGE RD
Hampden Farm
MEADOW VIEW INDUSTRIES
Court Lodge
THE STREET
COCK LA
Cotton Hill
Meadow View Farm
HAMSTREET RD
FAIRVIEW IND PK
FAIRVIEW IND PK
7
PARKER CL
VILLAGE WAY
CARTER'S TERR
Hamstreet
Carter Farm
Lily House
Royal Military Canal (dis)
DUKES MDW 1
BUNKLEY MDW 2
RECTORY WLK 3
ROMNEY RD
FARM WAY
COW DR
Royal Military Canal Path
West View
33
Mountain Farm
The Rowans
6
Kits Bridge
Ham Street Bridge
Lords Farm
5
Ham Lees Farm
TN26
KITSBRIDGE LA
Stonebridge
32
Johnson's Corner
KITSBRIDGE LA
4
Ham Mill Farm
Glenville Cottage
Wey Street Farm
Bainbridge Farm
WEY ST
HAM MILL LA
Sedbrook Sewer
Gribble House
Stockbridge House
Weystreete Farm
3
Stockbridge
31
2
Poplar House
TN29
Wick Bridge
The Laurels
A2070
1
30

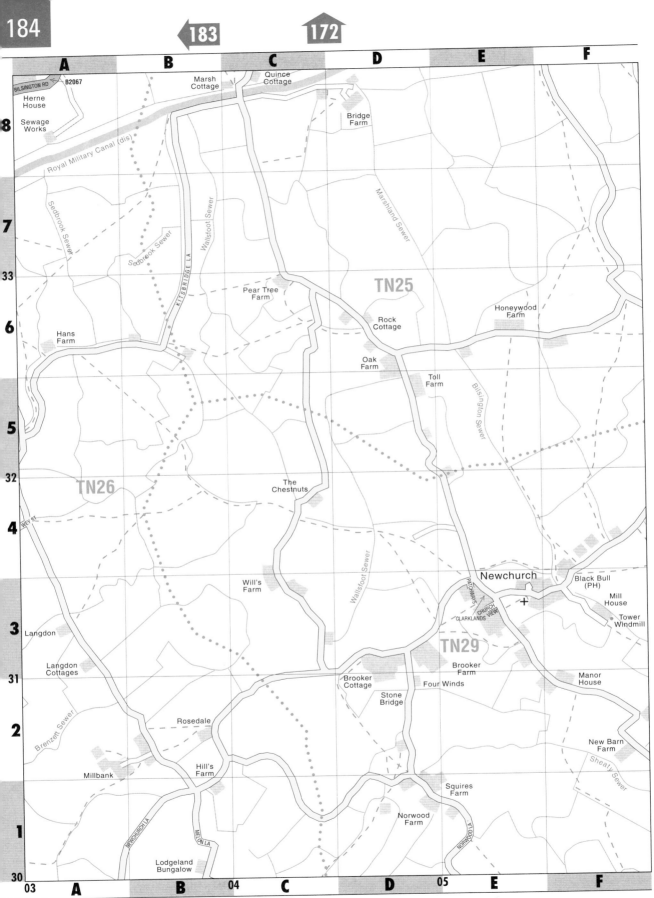

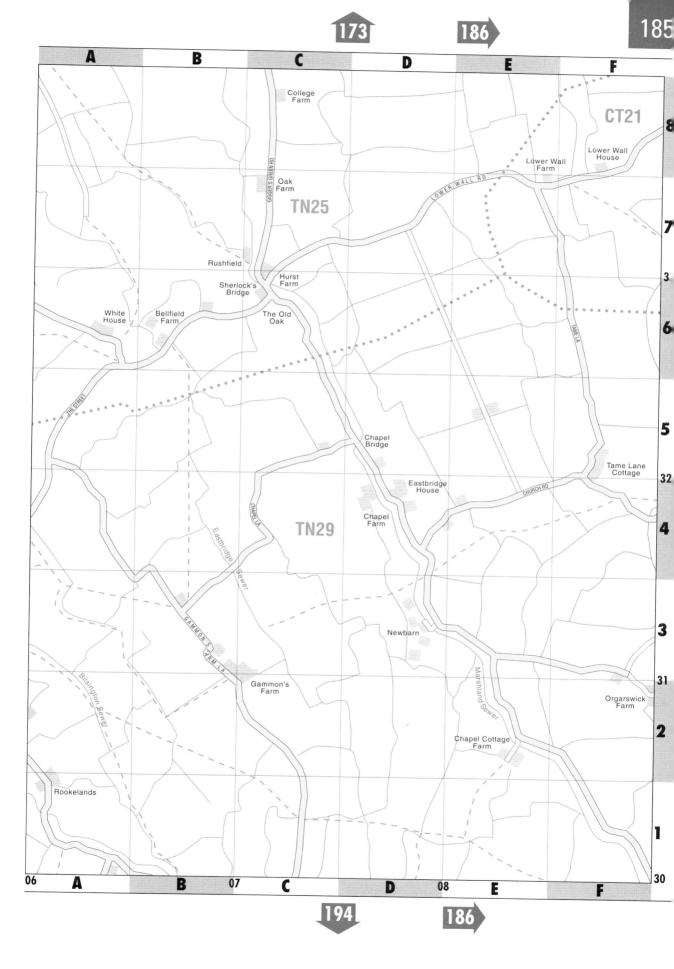

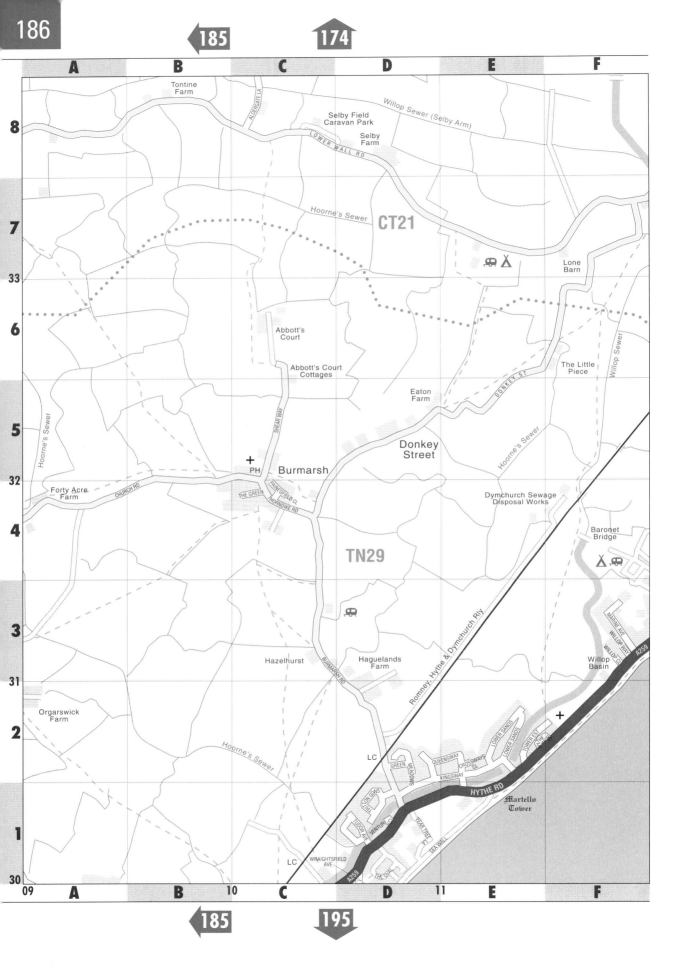

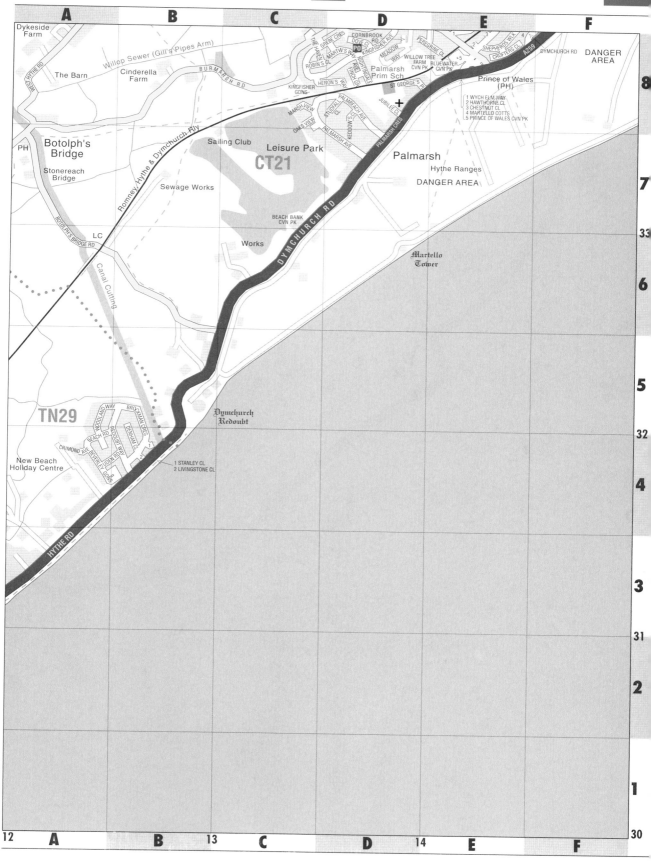

A B C D E F

Dykeside Farm

MERSE HYTHE RD

The Barn

Willop Sewer (Gill's Pipes Arm)

Cinderella Farm

BURMARSH RD

THE HAVEN
ROBIN'S CL
GREBE CRES
MARTIN'S WAY
NIGHTINGALE
FINCH DR
CORNBROOK RD
DOVE CL
PO
MEADOW WAY
KINGFISHER AVE
WILLOW TREE FARM CVN PK
PEREGRINE CL
SHEPHERDS WLK
CROFTERS CL
BLUEWATER
DYMCHURCH RD
DANGER AREA

KINGFISHER GDNS
HERON'S WAY

Palmarsh Prim Sch

ST GEORGE'S RD

A259

Prince of Wales (PH)

8

PH

Botolph's Bridge

Stonereach Bridge

Romney Hythe & Dymchurch Rly

Sailing Club

Leisure Park
CT21

MARSH VIEW
OAKS VIEW
STUDFALL CL
PALMBEACH AVE
PALMARSH AVE
KIDDOS CL
JUBILEE CL
PALMARSH CRES

+

Palmarsh

Hythe Ranges
DANGER AREA

1 WYCH ELM WAY
2 HAWTHORNE CL
3 CHESTNUT CL
4 MARTELLO COTTS
5 PRINCE OF WALES CVN PK

7

33

Sewage Works

BOTOLPH'S BRIDGE RD

Canal Cutting

LC

DYMCHURCH RD

BEACH BANK CVN PK

Works

Martello Tower

6

TN29

WOODLAND WAY
BROOKMAN CRES
CANAL WAY
REDOUBT WAY
BEACH RD
DENHAM CL
CRIMOND AVE
BEVERLEY GDNS
IDEN RD

Dymchurch Redoubt

5

32

New Beach Holiday Centre

1 STANLEY CL
2 LIVINGSTONE CL

4

HYTHE RD

3

31

2

1

12 A B 13 C D 14 E F 30

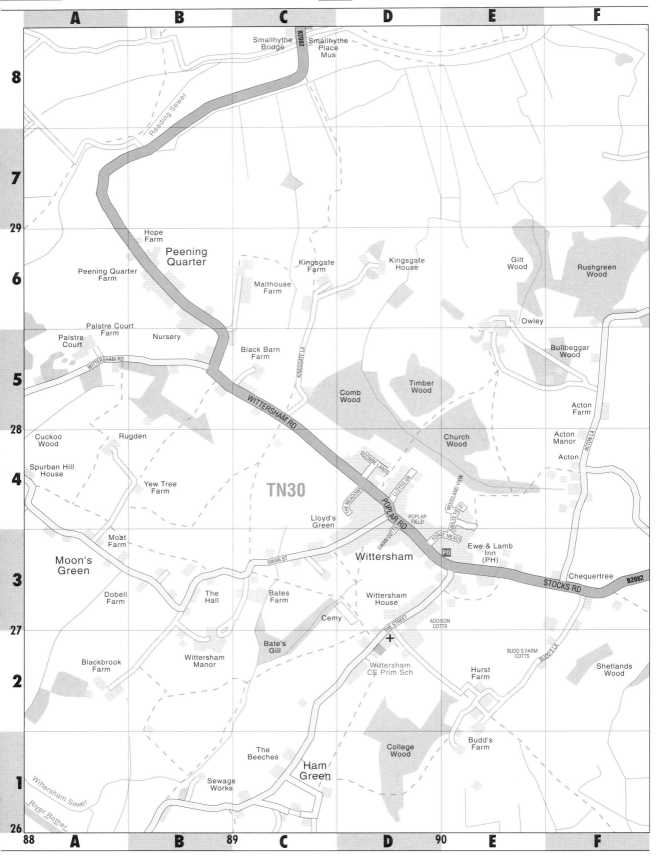

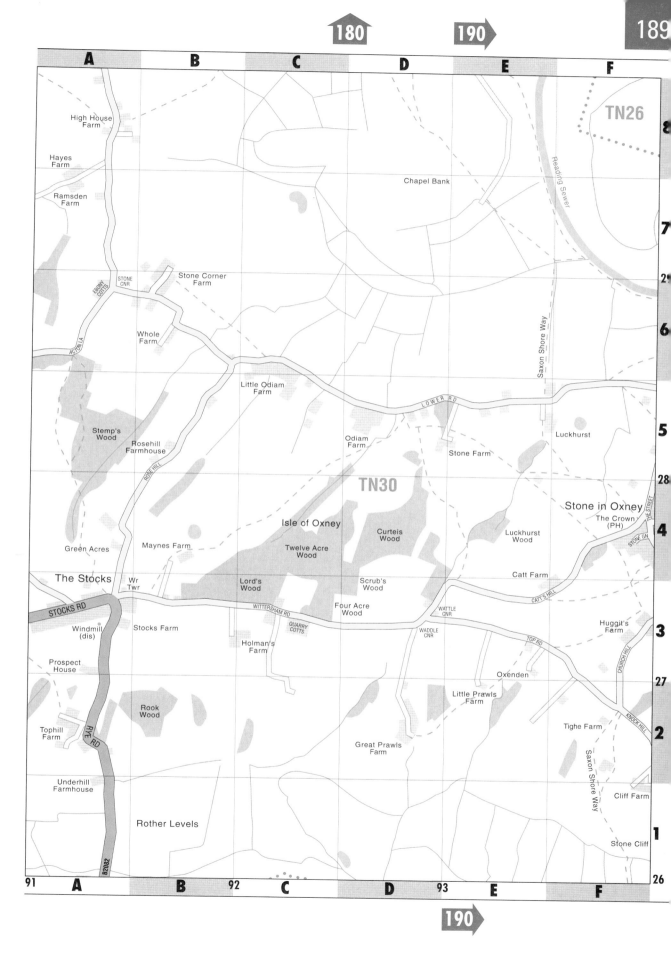

A B C D E F

8

189

B2080 TENTERDEN RD

HAWTHORN

THE STREET

Rawnie
Farm

Appledore

COURT LODGE RD

OLD WAY

7

RHEE WALL

APPLEDORE RD

Appledore
Bridge

Court Lodge

Bridge Farm

29

Saxon Shore Way

Reading Sewer

Priory
Lands

6

The Ferry Inn
(PH)

Ferry Farm

TN26

Appledore Sewer

LOWER RD

Waypost Farm

Royal Military Canal (dis)

THE STREET

Priory
Farm

5

28

ONNEY
COTTS

FORGE MDW

4

TN30

MILITARY RD

Newknock Channel

Royal Military Canal Path

Highknock Channel

Priory
Farm

Buss
Barn

Swallowstail

Ppg
Sta

CHURCH

Churchlands
Farm

3

Becket's
Bridge

27

LC

Mackley
Farm

2

TN29

Knock Hill

Knock
House

Becket Barn
Farm

Stone Bridge

1

Puddledock
Bridge

BRACK LA

26

94 A B 95 C D 96 E F

Becket's
Court

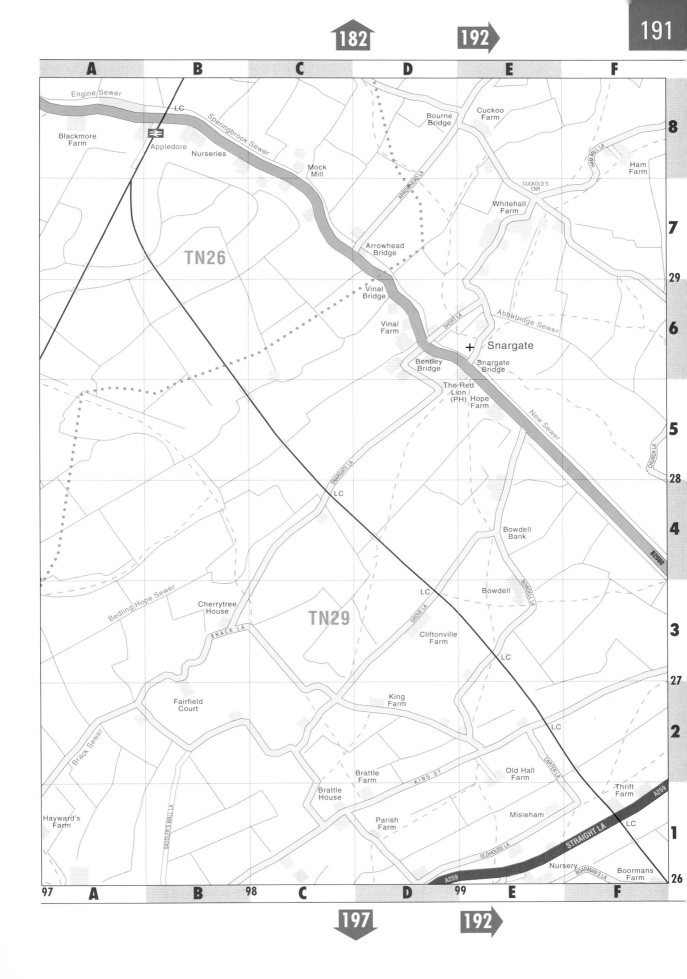

182
192

191
183

A **B** **C** **D** **E** **F**

8

TN26

Snave
Manor Farm

Court-at-Wick

Abbatridge Sewer

Walnut Tree Farm

7

Brenzett Sewer

29

Hangman's Toll Bridge

Chapel Farm

6

Codhall

Poplar Farm

Brenzett Green

Moat House

Newchurch La

CHURCH LA

Spring Farm Rd

Poplar Farm

5

Hook House

New House Farm

28

Abbatridge Sewer

Spring Farm

Moor La

Melon La

4

TN29

The Bell Inn (PH)

The Gardens

Marsh's Farm

CHURCH LA

Cemy

Brenzett Corner Bridge

B2080

Brenzett Aeronautical Mus

Oasthouse Field

Ivychurch

Knowlden Farm

PH

BRENZETT CNR

Brenzett

Brenzett Place

3

MOORE CL

PO

KING ST

THE HAVEN

B2080

Sumnerhouse Bridge

A2070

IVYCHURCH RD

27

Brenzett CE Prim Sch

A259

2

STRAIGHT LA

Blue House Farm

Owen's Bridge

WENHAM S LA

Mast

New Sewer

A259

Finn Farm

Rhee Wall

Callington Court Farm

1

TICKNER S LA

Beacon

New Sewer

YOAKES LA

TILLERY LA

Rheewall Farm

Yoakes Bridge

A259

26

00 **A** **B** 01 **C** **D** 02 **E** **F**

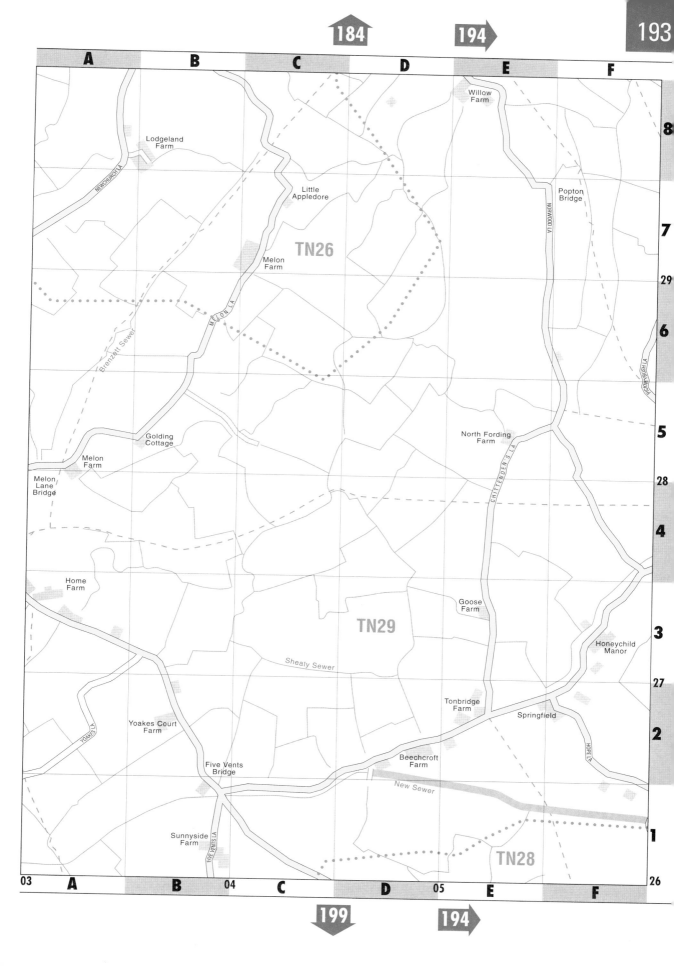

184

194

8

7

29

6

5

28

4

3

27

2

1

Willow
Farm

Lodgeland
Farm

NEWCHURCH LA

Little
Appledore

TN26

Popton
Bridge

NORWOOD LA

Melon
Farm

MELON LA

Branzett Sewer

Golding
Cottage

North Fording
Farm

CHITTENDEN S LA

Melon
Farm

Melon
Lane
Bridge

PASHURST LA

Home
Farm

Goose
Farm

TN29

Honeychild
Manor

Sheaty Sewer

YOAKES LA

Yoakes Court
Farm

Tonbridge
Farm

Springfield

HOPE LA

Five Vents
Bridge

Beechcroft
Farm

New Sewer

Sunnyside
Farm

FIVE VENTS LA

TN28

03 A   B   04   C   D   05   E   F   26

199   194

193
185

8 | **7** | **29** | **6** | **5** | **28** | **4** | **3** | **27** | **2** | **1** | **26**

A | B | C | D | E | F

Oldhouse Bridge

Blue House Farm

GAMMON'S FARM LA

Blackmanstone Bridge

Pickneybush Bridge

PICKNEYBUSH LA

Pickney Bush Farm

Shealy Sewer

Eastbridge Sewer

JEFFERSTONE Sewer

Tatnam Farm

Tatnam Bridge

Sellinge Farm

Clobsden Sewer

Marten Farm

Pickney Bush Farm Cotts

Swallowtail Bridge

TN29

Turngates Bridge

Wild Refuge

ST MARY'S RD

PICKNEY BUSH LA

Haffenden Farm

Shingle Hall Farm

Sports Gd

Golden Sands Holiday Centre

JEFFERSTONE LA

JEFFERSTONE GDNS

JEFFERSTONE LA

Jefferstone Lane

Jesson Court Caravan Park

LC

RECTORY RD

WADES CL

Star Inn

St Mary in the Marsh

OLD BAKERY

PO

JEFFERSTONE SEWER

Romney, Hythe & Dymchurch Rly

HOLLY RD

LAUREL AVE

FIR TREE RD

ASPEN CT

WILLOW DR

HAWTHORN CL

MAPLE DR

ELM RD

OAK RD

BEECH RD

CEDAR CRES

ASH TREE CL

FULMAR

School Farm

Brodnyx

MEADS WAY

GRASSMERE

NEW BRIDGE WAY

TAYLORS CL

NEWLANDS

JENNER'S WAY

FAIRWAY RD

BRIARS RD

GAZEDOWN

A259

COAST DR

TN28

Slinches

New Sewer

New Sewer

Winford Bridge

DYMCHURCH RD

The Warren

P

Paternosterford Bridge

HOPE LA

Brodynex Farm

Romney Warren Country Park

Marlie Farm

A259

06 | 07 | 08

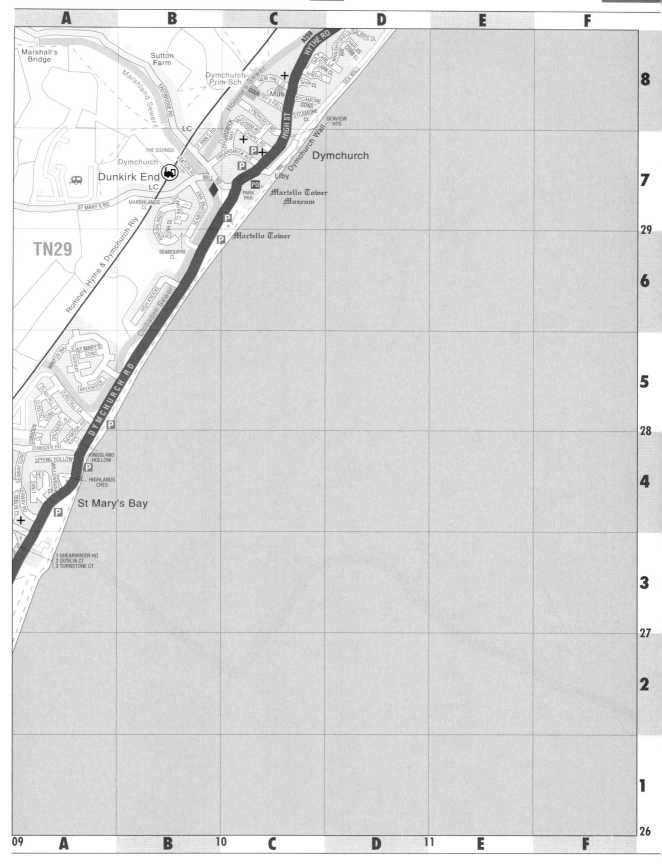

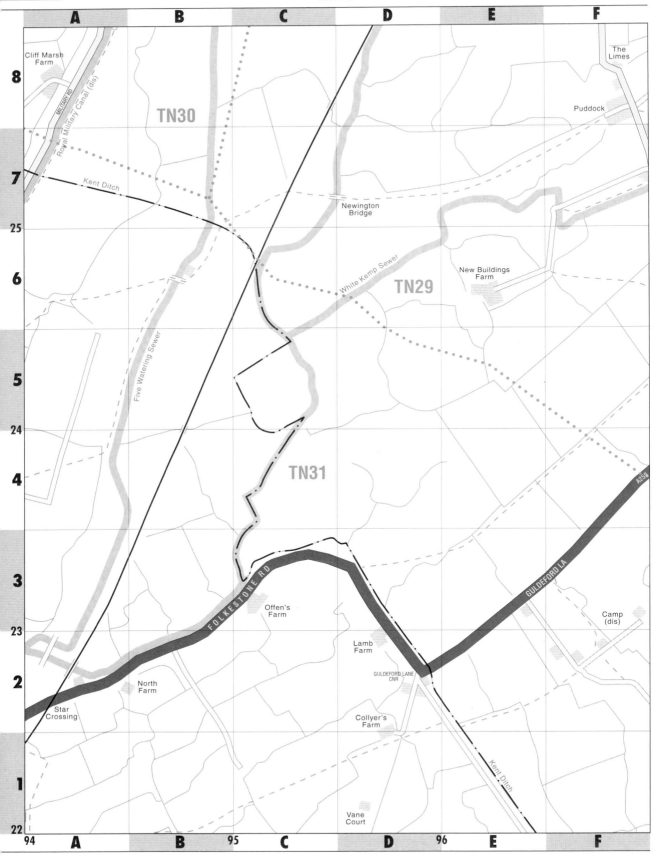

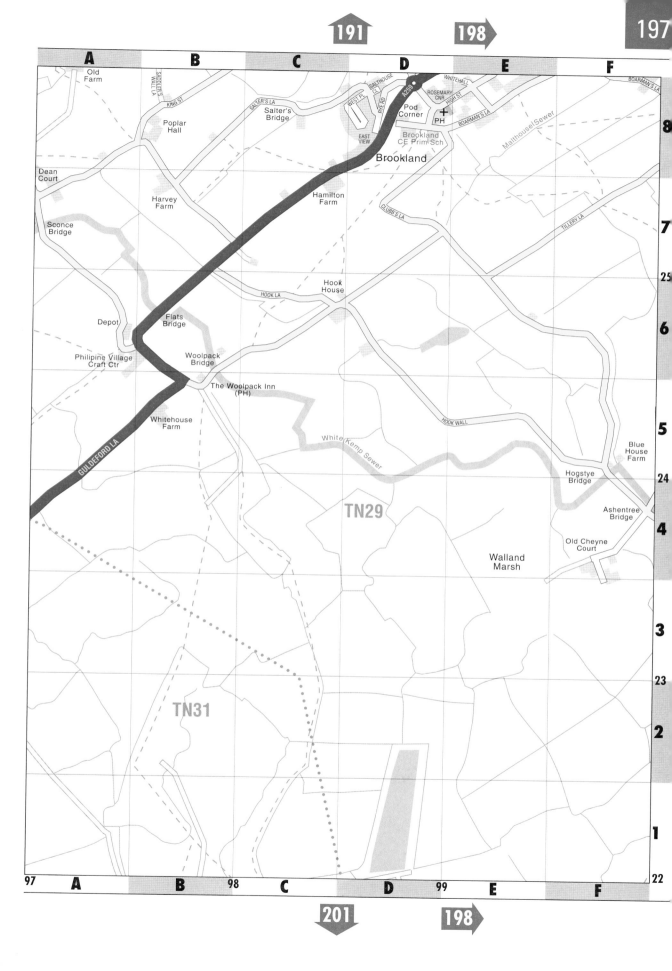

A   B   C   D   E   F

8

TICKNER'S LA
LC
Barnland Farm
TILLERY LA
LC
BARNHOUSE LA
LC
NARROWBUSH LA

Prospect Farm
A259
EIGHTEEN ACRE LA
Bush Farm
New Sewer
Vine Cottage
Sycamore House
OAKES LA
A259

7

LC
St Thomas's Innings
BEGGARSBUSH LA
Sycamore Farm

25

Mountain La
LC
WASHINGTON LA
MILLBANK LA

6

ASHENTREE LA
Coldharbour Farm
Court Lodge

White Kemp Sewer
White's House

Coldharbour Bridge
Old Romney Bridge

5

LC
COLDHARBOUR LA
Wheelsgate

24

Cutter's Bridge
Bow Bridge
Midley Cottages
LC

TN29

4

Baynham Farm
Baynham Petty Sewer

HAWTHORN CNR

3

23

Scott's Marsh House

2

Newland Bungalow

1

Newland Farm Cottage

22

00   A   B   01   C   D   02   E   F

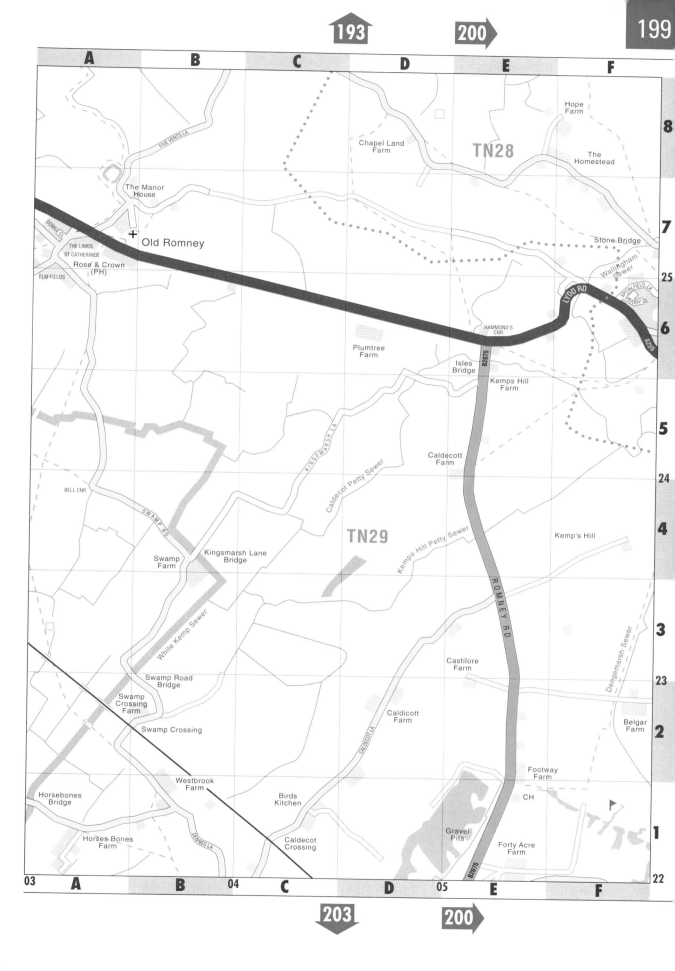

193
200

A   B   C   D   E   F

8

Hope Farm

Chapel Land Farm

TN28

The Homestead

7

Stone Bridge

The Manor House

Wallingham Sewer

DOWLE CL

FIVE VENTS LA

Old Romney

THE LIMES
ST CATHERINES

Rose & Crown (PH)

ELM FIELDS

25

LYDD RD

SPITALFIELD LA

PRIORY CL

A259

6

HAMMOND'S CNR

Plumtree Farm

Isles Bridge

B2075

Kemps Hill Farm

5

Caldecott Farm

Caldecot Petty Sewer

KINGSMARSH LA

24

BELL CNR

SWAMP RD

TN29

Kemps Hill Petty Sewer

Kemp's Hill

4

Swamp Farm

Kingsmarsh Lane Bridge

ROMNEY RD

Dengemarsh Sewer

White Kemp Sewer

3

Swamp Road Bridge

Castilore Farm

23

Swamp Crossing Farm

Swamp Crossing

Belgar Farm

2

Caldicott Farm

CALDECOT LA

Footway Farm

Horsebones Bridge

Westbrook Farm

Birds Kitchen

CH

Horses Bones Farm

DAINES LA

Caldecot Crossing

Gravel Pits

Forty Acre Farm

B2075

1

03   A   B   04   C   D   05   E   F   22

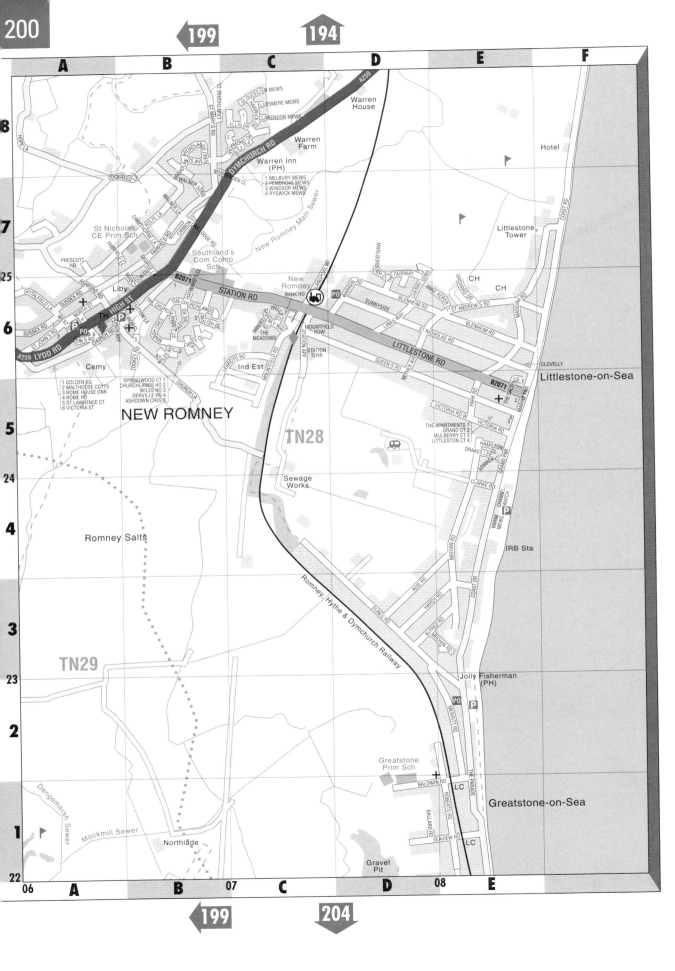

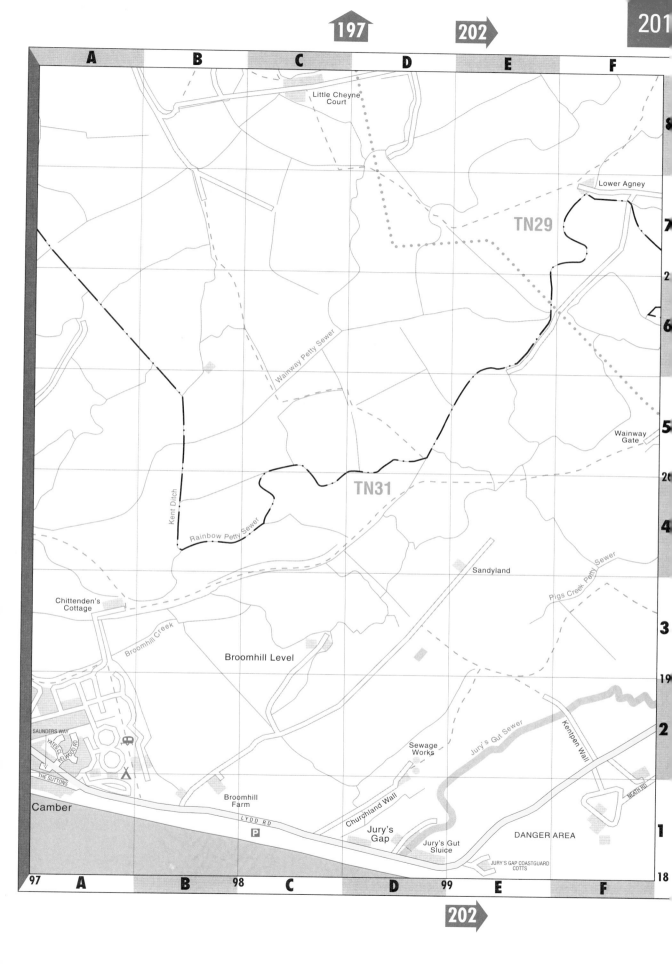

A B C D E F

8

Little Cheyne
Court

Lower Agney

TN29

7

2

6

Wainway Petty Sewer

Wainway
Gate

5

26

Kent Ditch

TN31

Rainbow Petty Sewer

Pigs Creek Petty Sewer

4

Sandyland

Chittenden's
Cottage

Broomhill Creek

19

Broomhill Level

3

Jury's Gut Sewer

Kenipen Wall

SAUNDERS WAY

YATES CL

PELWOOD RD

THE SUTTONS

2

Sewage
Works

Churchland Wall

NEATH RD

Camber

Broomhill
Farm

LYDD RD

P

Jury's
Gap

DANGER AREA

1

Jury's Gut
Sluice

JURY'S GAP COASTGUARD
COTTS

97 A 98 B C 99 D E F 18

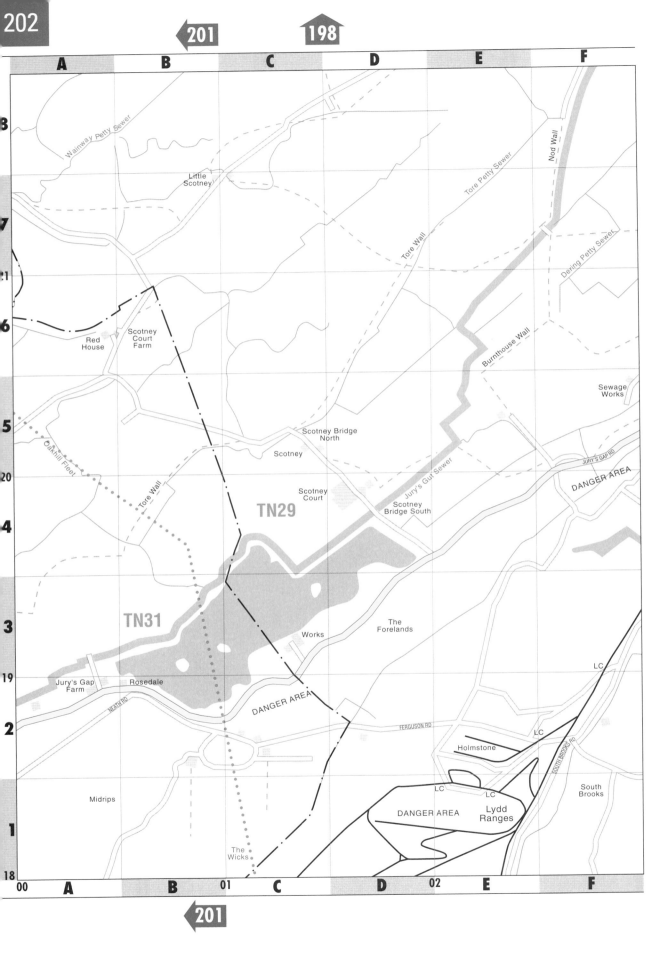

201
198

A   B   C   D   E   F

8

7

21

6

Wainway Petty Sewer

Little
Scotney

Tore Petty Sewer

Nod Wall

Tore Wall

Dering Petty Sewer

Red
House

Scotney
Court Farm

Burnthouse Wall

Sewage
Works

5

Oakhill Fleet

Scotney Bridge
North

Scotney

Jury's Gut Sewer

JURY'S GAP RD

DANGER AREA

20

Tore Wall

Scotney
Court

Scotney
Bridge South

4

TN29

TN31

The
Forelands

LC

3

Works

19

Jury's Gap
Farm

Rosedale

DANGER AREA

FERGUSON RD

LC

SOUTHBROOKS RD

2

NEATH RD

Holmstone

LC

Midrips

LC

LC

South
Brooks

1

DANGER AREA

Lydd
Ranges

18

The
Wicks

00   A   B   01   C   D   02   E   F

A B C D E F

8

Westbroke
Cottages
Whitehall
Farm
Jack's
Court
Westbroke
House
ROMNEY RD B2075
DENNES LA
The
Glebe
KITEWELL LA
LYDD TOWN
LEVEL CROSSING
LC
SAMUEL MEWSON CL
SYCAMORE
STATION RD
POPLAR LA
7
Cemy
Ind
Est
HARDEN RD
COLUMBUS CL
EASTERN RD
MILL LA
MILL RD
NESS RD
CHURCH RD
Gravel
Pits
COPPERFIELDS
CANNON ST
NEW ST
TH
WOOD CL
SOUTH
NEW ST
ST GEORGE'S
DOLPHIN RD
Grisbrook
Farm
GRISBROOK
FARM CL
6
MITTELL
CT
PADDOCK
VINE LANDS
PO
HIGH ST
PARK ST
BEAL
QUEEN'S RD
PAINE AVE
GRISBROOK RD
Mus
CORONATION
SQ
Green Hop
Farm
Denge Marsh
THE DERVIDGE
OAK
MILL
BANK
CASTLE ST
QUEENSIDE
THE
PRIORY
Lydd Prim
Sch
MANOR RD
Liby
Tourney
Hall
B2075
SKINNER RD
HAMILTON
RD
ROBIN LA
ROBIN RD
LYDD
Pigwell
THE GREEN
GREEN WAY
RYPE
OAKS WAY
DUNGENESS RD
Cockles
Bridge
TOURNEY RD
WHITING
HO
WALSELEY
TERR
TN29
JURY'S GAP RD
GALLOWAYS RD
5
Lydd Camp
CULVER'S LA
Works
20
Works
4
DANGER AREA
West
Ripe
Dengemarsh Sewer
LC
LC
LC
SOUTH BROOKS RD
DENGEMARSH RD
LC
Twr
3
LC
The
Quob
Lydd
Watersports
Centre
19
INVICTA RD
2
Hart's
Farm
Manor
Farm
LC
Brickwall
Farmhouse
DANGER AREA
1
Piper's
Pen

203
200

TN28

Lydd
Airport

Mockmill Sewer

Romney Sands
Holiday Village

Romney Sands

Caravan
Park

LA ROCCO 1
LA TAUSCO 2
LA GALAMINA 3

BEACHMONT CL

PRIOR RD

THE PARADE

CHANNON RD

DERVILLE RD

LEONARD RD

WALLER RD

COLEVILLE CRES

BEATRICE
MEWS

The Ship
(PH)

HOLT RD

STORY RD

LCs

P

TAYLOR RD

FORT CL

LADE FORT
COTTS

FORT CYS

LYDD CLOSE

FORT CRES

Lade

WILLIAMSON RD

SAXTON RD

PLEASANCE RD N

LC

Romney, Hythe & Dymchurch Railway

COAST DR

Works

Gravel
Pits

Boulderwall
Farm

TN29

Gravel
Pits

PLEASANCE ROAD CENTRAL

Works

KENTON RD

Lydd-on-Sea

DUNGENESS RD

Halfway
Bush

PLEASANCE RD SO

Mast

BATTERY RD

Denge
Marsh

Coastguard
Cottages

Walkers Outland
(RSPB Reserve)

203
205

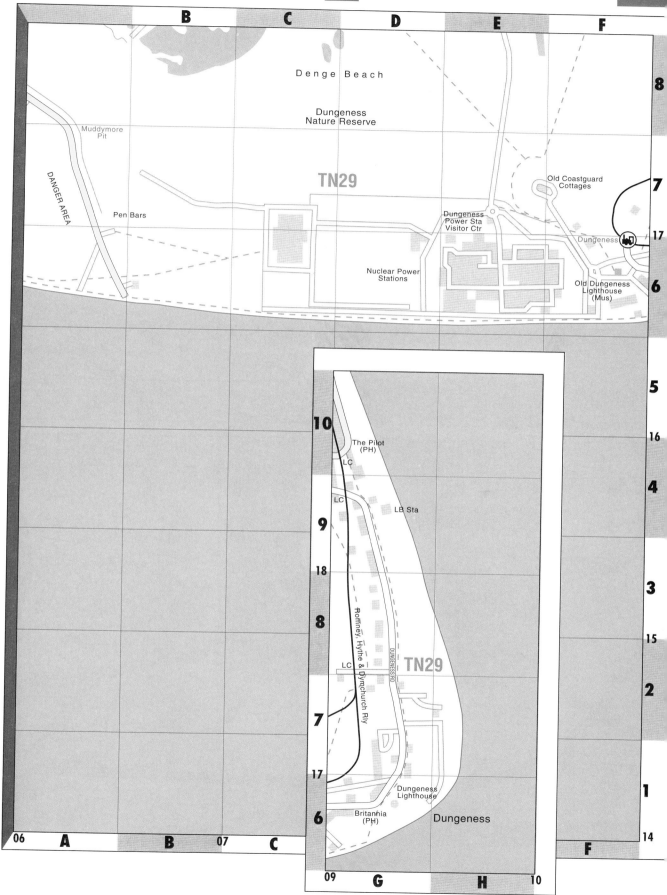

Denge Beach

Dungeness
Nature Reserve

Muddymore
Pit

DANGER AREA

TN29

Pen Bars

Old Coastguard
Cottages

Dungeness
Power Sta
Visitor Ctr

Dungeness

17

Nuclear Power
Stations

Old Dungeness
Lighthouse
(Mus)

8

7

6

5

16

4

The Pilot
(PH)

LC

LC

LB Sta

Romney, Hythe & Dymchurch Rly

DUNGENESS RD

TN29

LC

Dungeness
Lighthouse

Britannia
(PH)

Dungeness

10

9

18

8

7

17

6

3

15

2

1

14

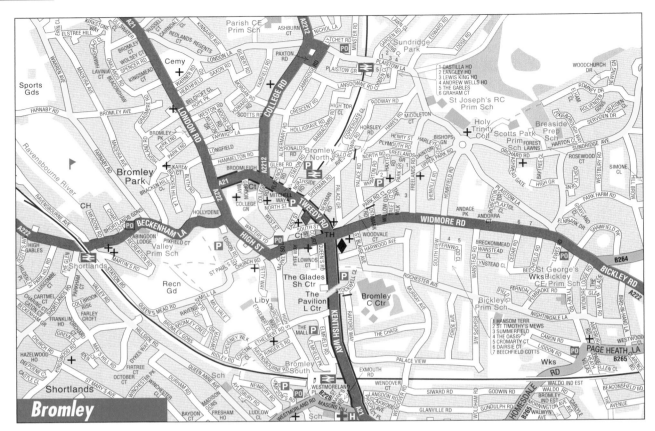

Bromley

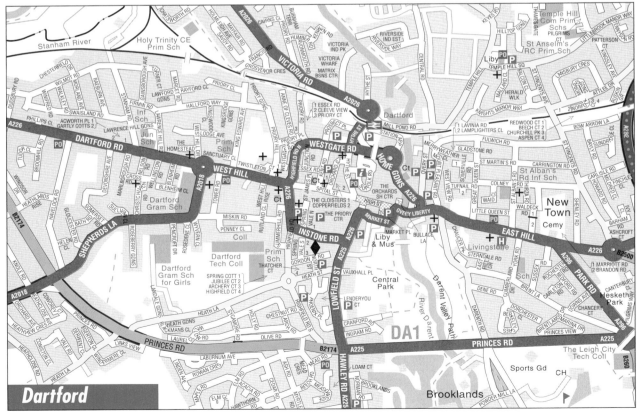

Dartford

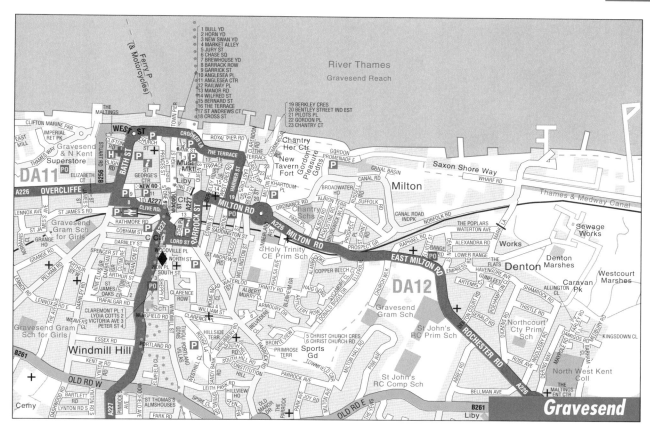

Gravesend

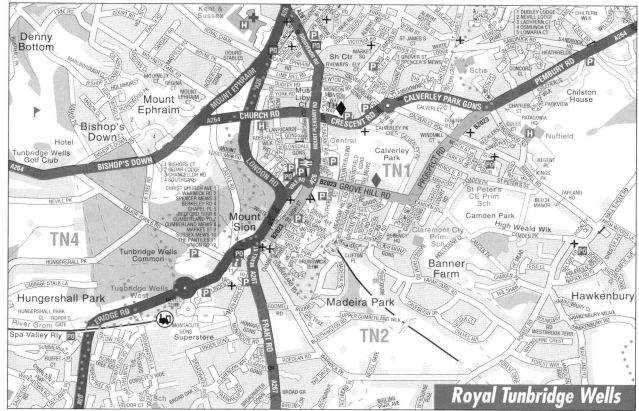

Royal Tunbridge Wells

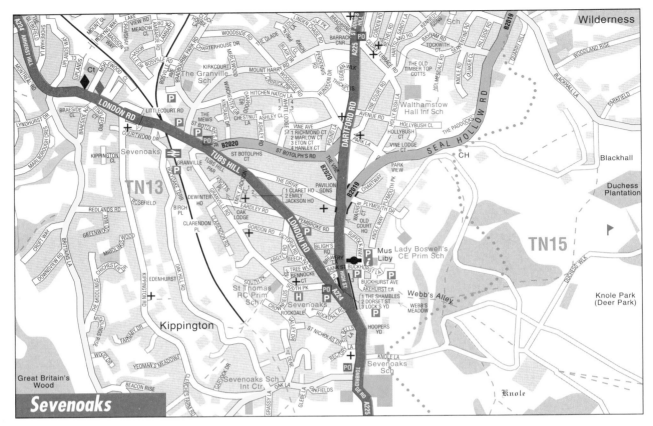

Sevenoaks

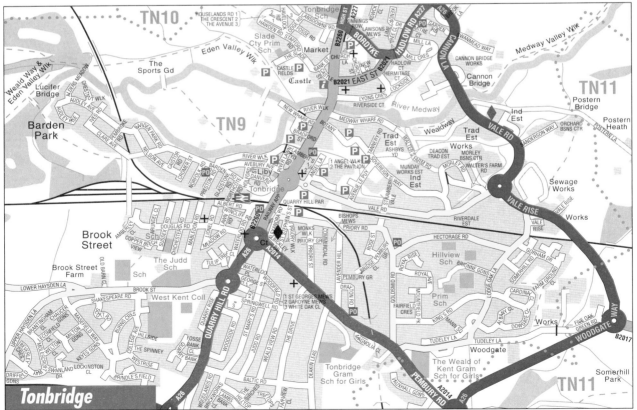

Tonbridge

Index

Archway Ct **4** Medway ME2.........**9** B8

Place name
May be abbreviated on the map

Location number
Present when a number indicates the place's position in a crowded area of mapping

Locality, town or village
Shown when more than one place has the same name

Postcode district
District for the indexed place

Page and grid square
Page number and grid reference for the standard mapping

Public and commercial buildings are highlighted in magenta   **Places of interest** are highlighted in blue with a star★

Abbreviations used in the index

App	Approach	Cl	Close	Espl	Esplanade	Orch	Orchard	Sq	Square
Arc	Arcade	Comm	Common	Est	Estate	Par	Parade	Strs	Stairs
Ave	Avenue	Cnr	Corner	Gdns	Gardens	Pk	Park	Stps	Steps
Bvd	Boulevard	Cotts	Cottages	Gn	Green	Pas	Passage	St	Street, Saint
Bldgs	Buildings	Ct	Court	Gr	Grove	Pl	Place	Terr	Terrace
Bglws	Bungalows	Ctyd	Courtyard	Hts	Heights	Prec	Precinct	Trad	Trading Est
Bsns Ctr	Business Centre	Cres	Crescent	Ind Est	Industrial Estate	Prom	Promenade	Wlk	Walk
Bsns Pk	Business Park	Dr	Drive	Intc	Interchange	Ret Pk	Retail Park	W	West
Cswy	Causeway	Dro	Drove	Junc	Junction	Rd	Road	Yd	Yard
Ctr	Centre	E	East	La	Lane	Rdbt	Roundabout		
Cir	Circus	Emb	Embankment	N	North	S	South		

Index of localities, towns and villages

Acol 27 B3
Adisham 112 C8
Aldington 173 A5
Alkham 147 C1
Appledore 190 A7
Ash 71 C2
Ashford 139 A1
Aylesford 53 A1
Aylesham 112 E4
Barham 111 E2
Bayfield 61 B3
Bekesbourne 89 C4
Bethersden 153 A2
Biddenden Green 135 B2
Birchington 26 D8
Bishopsbourne 111 C5
Blean 66 A6
Borden 36 A2
Bossingham 127 A7
Boughton Aluph 123 A4
Boughton Lees 122 E3
Boughton Monchelsea .97 B2
Boughton Street 64 A3
Boxley 54 C2
Boyden Gate 47 C7
Brabourne 159 C8
Brabourne Lees 158 D5
Bramling 90 E6
Brattle 181 C7
Bredgar 58 A5
Bredhurst 33 A1
Brenzett 192 A3
Bridge 89 A1
Broad Oak 67 D7
Broad Street 77 A6
Broadstairs 30 A1
Bromley Green 170 E5
Brook 141 A5
Brookland 197 C6
Burham 53 A8
Burmarsh 186 C3
Camber 201 A1
Canterbury 87 B6
Capel-le-F 164 B2
Challock 105 A1
Charing 120 A6
Charing Heath 119 C7
Chart Sutton 98 B1
Chartham 86 B2
Chatham 10 A1
Chestnut Street 35 D4
Chilham 107 B7

Chillenden 113 F8
Chislet 47 A5
Church Hougham 165 B5
Cliffs End 51 C2
Coldred 131 A3
Conyer 38 E6
Coxheath 96 A2
Daniel's Water 154 E6
Dargate 64 D8
Deal 117 A1
Densole 163 A7
Denton 129 A1
Detling 55 A1
Doddington 80 D7
Dover 166 A6
Dunkirk 64 E2
Dymchurch 195 B6
East Farleigh 96 A7
East Langdon 133 A1
East Studdal 132 B6
Eastchurch 5 D1
Eastling 81 E6
Eastry 93 A2
Eccles 53 A6
Egerton 118 E1
Egerton Forstal 118 C1
Elham 144 E3
Elvington 114 B1
Etchinghill 161 D3
Eyhorne Street 77 B2
Eythorne 131 B8
Faversham 62 A4
Finglesham 116 A7
Five Wents 98 D1
Folkestone 178 A3
Fordwich 68 A3
Gillingham 10 A4
Godmersham 107 B2
Goodnestone 91 D2
Great Chart 138 C1
Great Mongeham 116 C3
Greatstone-on-S 200 D1
Guston 149 E4
Halfway Houses 3 C5
Hamstreet 183 A7
Harbledown 87 A7
Harrietsham 100 B5
Hartlip 34 C3
Hastingleigh 142 B6
Hawkinge 163 A2
Herne 46 A8
Herne Bay 22 A1

Hernhill 64 B6
Hersden 46 E1
High Halden 167 A6
Hoath 46 E5
Hollingbourne 77 C2
Hothfield 138 A6
Hythe 176 A1
Ickham 69 C1
Ivychurch 192 D4
Iwade 14 C4
Kearsney 148 D4
Kenardington 182 A5
Kingsdown 134 B5
Kingsnorth 156 A3
Kingston 111 B1
Kingswood 99 A1
Kit's Coty 53 C7
Langley Heath 98 C5
Leeds 99 A6
Lenham 101 B7
Lenham Heath 119 B8
Leysdown-on-S 6 C1
Littlebourne 89 C8
Littlestone-on-S 200 D3
Loose 96 E2
Lower Halstow 13 B2
Lower Hardres 110 A3
Lydd 203 A2
Lydd-on-S 204 E6
Lydden 28 C4
Lyminge 161 C6
Lympne 175 A3
Lynsted 60 A6
Maidstone 75 B4
Manston 28 D1
Margate 7 E1
Martin Mill 133 B2
Mersham 157 C4
Milstead 58 C2
Minster (Sheppey) 4 A4
Minster (Thanet) 50 B5
Molash 105 F4
Monkton 49 A8
New Romney 200 A6
Newchurch 184 E3
Newington 35 B6
Newnham 81 C8
Nonington 113 C5
Northbourne 116 A5
Oare 40 B2
Old Romney 199 A7
Old Wives Lees 85 B3

Otham 98 A6
Park Wood 97 E5
Patrixbourne 89 B3
Pedlinge 175 D4
Pested 105 B4
Petham 109 A2
Platt's Heath 100 C1
Pluckley 136 C4
Postling 160 F2
Potter's Forstal 118 B2
Potters Corner 138 E7
Pratling Street 53 B4
Preston 70 B5
Queenborough 3 A4
Ram Lane 120 F1
Ramsgate 52 A7
Reculver 24 B5
Rhodes Minnis 144 A3
Ringwould 133 D4
Ripple 116 D1
River 148 D1
Rochester 9 A2
Rodmersham 59 B7
Rough Common 66 A2
Ruckinge 183 F6
Rushenden 2 F3
St Margaret's at Cliffe .151 A4
St Mary in the Marsh .194 B4
St Mary's Bay 195 A5
St Michaels 167 C2
St Nicholas at Wade 25 E2
Sandway 101 F4
Sandwich 73 A1
Sarre 48 E7
Sellindge 159 B1
Selling 84 A6
Sevington 157 A4
Shadoxhurst 170 A7
Sheerness 1 B1
Sheldwich 83 C4
Shepherdswell 130 D4
Shottenden 84 D8
Silver Hill 76 F1
Silver Street 57 F5
Sittingbourne 36 B5
Smarden 135 A1
Smeeth 158 B3
Snargate 191 B8
Stalisfield Green 103 A3
Stanford 160 B1
Staple 92 A4
Stelling Minnis 126 D4

Stockbury 56 D8
Stone in Oxney 189 C3
Stourmouth 48 D1
Stowting 160 A6
Stubb's Cross 155 E2
Sturry 67 F4
Sutton 133 A6
Temple Ewell 148 C4
Tenterden 179 E7
Teynham 38 A2
The Quarries 97 B4
Throwley 82 A4
Throwley Forstal 82 C7
Thurnham 76 D1
Tilmanstone 115 A2
Tyler Hill 66 E6
Upchurch 12 C2
Upstreet 47 D2
Waltham 125 F5
Warden 6 A6
Warmlake 98 E1
Warren Street 102 D7
Waterham 42 D2
West Hougham 164 F5
West Hythe 175 B1
West Minster 3 A8
Westbere 68 C7
Westenhanger 175 B6
Westfield Sole 54 B7
Westgate-on-S 27 D6
Westmarsh 71 C6
Westwell 121 B4
Whitfield 149 A5
Whitstable 20 C1
Wichling 80 B4
Wickhambreaux 69 C1
Wingham 91 A4
Wittersham 188 D4
Womenswold 112 C2
Woodchurch 169 A2
Woodnesborough 93 B5
Woodside Green 101 E8
Woolage Green 129 D6
Woolage Village 112 C1
Wormshill 79 A7
Worth 94 A4
Wye 123 D3
Yelsted 34 A1
Yorklets 42 E2

2

20/20 Ind Est ME16 .....**74** C8

A

Abbeville Ho ME1 ....**9** C4
Abbey Cl Deal CT14 .....**117** A5
  Minster (Sheppey) ME12 ...**4** D6
Abbey Ct CT8 ....**27** D7
Abbey Fields ME13 ....**62** E7
Abbey Fields Ct ME13 ...**62** E7
Abbey Gate CT11 ....**52** B5
Abbey Gate Cotts ME14 ..**53** F2
Abbey Gdns CT2 ....**67** A2
Abbey Gr
  Minster (Thanet) CT12 ...**50** C5
  Ramsgate CT11 ....**52** B5
Abbey Pl ME13 ....**62** D8
Abbey Rd Faversham ME13 .**11** A2
  Gillingham ME8 ....**11** A2
  Kearsney CT16 ....**148** D4
  River CT15,CT17 ....**148** D1
Abbey Sch The CT8 ....**27** E8
Abbey St ME13 ....**62** D8
Abbey Way TN24 ....**140** A1
Abbeyview Dr ME12 ....**4** B6
Abbot's Hill CT11 ....**52** E6
Abbots Barton Wlk CT1 ..**88** B2
Abbots Field ME16 ....**74** B2
Abbots Hill ME13 ....**61** E5
Abbots Pl CT1 ....**66** F1
Abbots Rd ME13 ....**62** F7
Abbots The CT17 ....**166** C8
Abbots Wlk TN25 ....**123** E2
Abbotsbury Hts CT2 ......**67** B4
Abbott Ct **18** CT20 ....**178** E6
Abbott Rd CT20 ....**178** E6
Abbotts Cl ME1 ....**9** B3
Aberdeen Cl CT3 ....**47** D3
Aberdeen House **9**
  ME15 ....**97** E7
Abigail Cres ME5 ....**32** A1
Abingdon Gr ME5 ....**47** D3
Abingdon Rd ME16 ....**74** A2
Abinger Dr ME5 ....**32** D2
Absalom Ct ME8 ....**11** C2
Acacia Terr ME10 ....**36** C4
Academy Dr ME7 ....**10** F1
Achilles Rd ME5 ....**32** C2
Ackerey Ct TN23 ....**155** F6
Ackholt Rd CT3 ....**113** A5
Acol Hill CT7 ....**27** B4
Acorn Cl Ashford TN23 ..**156** C2
  Hawkinge CT18 ....**163** C4
Acorn Pl ME15 ....**97** E6
Acorn Rd ME7 ....**10** F4
Acorn St ME12 ....**1** D1
Acorn Wharf Rd ME1 .....**9** C6
Acre Cl ME1 ....**9** E3
Acre Ct CT17 ....**166** C8
Acre The CT16 ....**148** F8
Acton La TN30 ....**188** F4
Acton Rd CT5 ....**20** D2
Ada Rd CT1 ....**87** D6
Adam Cl ME17 ....**96** D3
Adam Ct **1** CT9 ....**8** B2
Adams Rd TN30 ....**167** B1
Adbert Dr ME15 ....**96** B4
Addelam Cl CT14 ....**117** A4
Addelam Rd CT14 ......**117** A4
Addington Pl CT11 ......**52** E6
Addington Rd Margate CT9 .**7** J2
  Sittingbourne ME10 .....**36** E3
Addington Sq CT9 ....**7** J2
Addington St Margate CT9 .**7** J2
  Ramsgate CT11 ....**52** E6
Addiscombe Gdns CT9 ....**7** J1
Addiscombe Rd CT9 ....**8** A1
Addison Cotts TN30 ....**188** D3
Adelaide Dr ME10 ....**36** C4
Adelaide Gdns
  Halfway Houses ME12 ....**3** E6
  16 Ramsgate CT11 .....**52** E6
Adelaide Pl CT1 ....**87** F8
Adelaide Rd
  Elvington CT15 ....**114** B1
  Gillingham ME7 ....**10** C4
Aden Terr **1** ME14 ....**75** A7
Adie Rd TN28 ....**200** D3
Adisham CE Prim Sch
  CT3 ....**112** D8
Adisham Downs Rd CT3,
  CT4 ....**90** D2
Adisham Dr ME16 ....**74** B7
Adisham Gn ME10 ....**36** F8
Adisham Rd
  Bekesbourne CT4 ....**89** C3
  Wingham CT3 ....**91** A4
  Womenswold CT4,CT3 ...**112** C2
Adisham Sta CT3 ....**112** E8
Adisham Way CT9 ....**8** C1
Admiral's Wlk ME4 ....**9** F7
Admirals Wlk
  Chatham ME5 ....**32** B3
  Halfway Houses ME12 ....**3** E6
  Hythe CT21 ....**176** C1
  Tenterden TN30 ....**167** C1
Admiralty Cl ME13 ......**62** B8
Admiralty Terr **1** ME7 .**10** A7
Admiralty Wlk CT5 ......**43** A7
Adrian Mews CT8 ....**7** D1

Adrian Sq CT8 ....**7** D1
Adrian St CT17 ....**166** D7
Aerodrome Rd
  Bekesbourne CT4 ....**89** E3
  Hawkinge CT18 ....**163** A4
Afghan Rd
  Broadstairs CT10 ....**29** F8
  Chatham ME4 ....**9** E4
Agester La CT4 ....**129** A4
Agriculture & Rural Life
  Mus★ CT12 ....**50** C5
Ainsdale Cl CT19 ......**178** B7
Aintree House **1** ME15 .**97** F6
Aintree Rd ME5 ....**32** C3
Airedale Cl CT9 ....**8** A1
Airfield View ME12 .....**17** C8
Aisne Dr CT1 ....**67** D1
Ajax Rd ME1 ....**31** C8
Alamein Ave ME5 ....**31** F7
Alamein Ct CT15 ....**149** F3
Albany Dr CT6 ....**22** D4
Albany Ho **15** CT17 ...**166** D7
Albany Pl CT17 ....**166** D7
Albany Rd
  Capel-le-F CT18 ....**164** C1
  Chatham ME4 ....**10** B2
  Gillingham ME7 ....**10** D4
  Rochester ME1 ....**9** C4
  Sittingbourne ME10 .....**36** E3
Albany St ME14 ....**75** B5
Albany Terr Chatham ME4 .**9** E4
  Gillingham ME7 ....**10** D4
Albemarle Rd
  Ashford TN24 ....**139** F1
  Chatham ME5 ....**32** C2
Albert Costain Ct **1**
  CT20 ....**178** D5
Albert Ct **16** CT5 .....**20** D7
Albert La CT21 ....**176** C1
Albert Manor ME7 ....**10** B5
Albert Pl ME2 ....**9** B7
Albert Rd Ashford TN24 .**139** B3
  Broadstairs CT10 ....**29** E8
  Canterbury CT1 ....**88** B8
  Capel-le-F CT18 ....**164** C2
  Chatham ME4 ....**10** A3
  Deal CT14 ....**117** C6
  Dover CT16 ....**149** D1
  Folkestone CT19 ......**178** D6
  Gillingham ME7 ....**10** C4
  Hythe CT21 ....**176** B1
  Margate CT9 ....**7** H2
  Ramsgate CT11 ....**52** F7
  Rochester ME1 ....**9** C3
Albert Reed Gdns ME15 ..**74** C7
Albert St Maidstone ME14 .**74** F6
  Ramsgate CT11 ....**52** E6
  Whitstable CT5 ....**20** D2
Alberta Cl CT16 ....**149** B3
Albion Cl CT6 ....**46** A8
Albion Ct CT11 ....**52** E6
Albion Hill **6** CT11 ...**52** E6
Albion La CT6 ....**46** A8
Albion Mews CT11 ....**52** F6
Albion Mews Rd **3**
  CT20 ....**178** D4
Albion Pl Ashford TN24 .**156** E7
  Canterbury CT1 ....**67** A1
  Faversham ME13 ....**62** C7
  Hythe CT21 ....**176** D2
  Maidstone ME14 ....**75** B4
  Newington ME9 ....**35** B6
  Ramsgate CT11 ....**52** E6
Albion Rd Birchington CT7 .**27** A7
  Broadstairs CT10 ....**29** F6
  Chatham ME5 ....**32** B2
  Deal CT14 ....**117** D8
  Eastry CT13 ....**93** A2
  Folkestone CT19 ......**178** D6
  Margate CT9 ....**7** F7
  Ramsgate CT11 ....**52** F7
Albion St CT10 ....**30** B4
Albion Terr ME10 ....**36** E6
Albion Villas **6** CT20 .**178** D4
Albuhera Sq CT1 ....**67** D1
Albury Rd ME5 ....**32** D2
Alchins Cotts ME17 .....**96** E2
Alder Cl ME12 ....**3** A8
Alder Rd CT19 ....**178** C6
Aldergate La CT21 .....**174** C1
Alderney Gdns CT10 .....**29** E5
Aldershot Rd ME5 ....**32** A7
Aldington Cl ME5 ....**32** B5
Aldington Cnr TN25 ....**173** A6
Aldington La ME14 ......**76** D8
Aldington Prim Sch
  TN25 ....**173** A5
Aldington Rd
  Lympne CT21 ....**174** E3
  Maidstone ME14 ....**75** F4
Aldon Cl ME14 ....**75** C4
Aldon La ME14 ....**75** C6
Aldred Rd ME13 ....**62** C6
Aldridge Cl CT6 ....**22** B3
Alec Pemble Cl TN24 ...**139** C5
Alexander Cl ME13 .....**62** B8
Alexander Ct
  1 Rochester ME2 ....**9** B8
  1 Sittingbourne ME10 ...**36** E5
Alexander Dr ME13 ......**62** B7
Alexandra Ave ME7 .....**10** E4
Alexandra Cl ME10 .....**36** E7
Alexandra Ct CT21 ....**176** A1
Alexandra Gdns CT20 ...**178** D4
Alexandra Glen ME5 ....**32** A1
Alexandra Homes CT9 ....**7** I1

Alexandra Hospl The
  ME5 ....**54** A8
Alexandra Mews ME12 ....**1** C2
Alexandra Pl **1** CT17 .**149** C1
Alexandra Rd
  Birchington CT7 ....**27** A5
  Broadstairs CT10 ....**30** B4
  Capel-le-F CT18 ......**164** C2
  Chatham ME4 ....**10** B2
  Deal CT14 ....**117** D2
  Kingsdown CT14 ....**134** C5
  Margate CT9 ....**28** E8
  Ramsgate CT11 ....**52** D8
  Sheerness ME12 ....**1** E2
  Whitstable CT5 ....**43** C8
Alexandra St
  Folkestone CT19 ......**178** E6
  Maidstone ME14 ....**74** F6
Alexandra Terr CT9 ......**7** I1
Alexandria Dr CT6 ......**22** C5
Alfred Cl Canterbury CT1 .**87** C6
  Chatham ME4 ....**10** B2
Alfred Cotts CT11 ......**52** E7
Alfred Rd Ashford TN24 .**156** D7
  Birchington CT7 ....**26** D8
  Canterbury CT1 ....**87** C6
  Dover CT16 ....**149** D1
  Littlebourne-on-S TN28 ..**200** D3
  Margate CT9 ....**8** B1
Alfred Row CT14 ....**117** D7
Alfred Sq CT14 ....**117** D7
Alicia Ave CT9 ....**28** A8
Alison Cl Birchington CT7 .**27** B8
  Whitfield CT16 ....**149** A6
Alison Cres CT16 ......**149** A7
Alkham Cl CT9 ....**8** F2
Alkham Rd
  Maidstone ME14 ....**75** C5
  Temple Ewell CT15,CT16 .**148** C4
Alkham Valley Rd
  Alkham CT15 ....**147** E1
  Hawkinge CT18,CT15 ....**163** E4
All Saints CE Prim Sch
  ME15 ....**75** A3
All Saints Hospl ME4 ...**10** A2
All Saints Ind Est CT9 ...**7** I1
All Saints La **2** CT1 ...**87** F8
All Saints Rd ME10 .....**37** C4
All Saints View ME13 ...**41** E2
All Saints' Ave CT9 .....**7** H1
All Saints' CE Prim Sch
  ME4 ....**10** A3
All Saints' Cl CT5 ......**20** F1
All Souls' CE Prim Sch
  CT19 ....**177** E6
Allan Rd CT5 ....**42** E6
Alland Grange La CT12 ..**27** B2
Allen Ave CT8 ....**27** D7
Allen Cl ME5 ....**32** C6
Allen Ct ME5 ....**4** A5
Allen Field TN23 ......**155** F8
Allen St ME5 ....**75** B5
Allenby Ave CT14 ......**117** B5
Allenby Rd CT12 ....**29** C2
Allenby Wlk ME10 ....**36** B5
Allendale St **2** CT19 .**178** D6
Alliance Rd CT11 ....**52** F6
Allington Prim Sch ME16 **74** C7
Allington Rd ME8 ....**11** A3
Allington Way ME16 .....**74** B6
Allison Ave ME7 ....**10** E1
Allnutt Mill Cl ME15 ...**74** E2
Allsworth Rd ME7 ....**35** B6
Alma Pl **2** Canterbury CT1 .**67** A1
  Ramsgate CT11 ....**52** E7
  Rochester ME2 ....**9** A7
Alma Rd Folkestone CT20 .**177** D5
  Herne Bay CT6 ....**23** C5
  Margate CT9 ....**7** J1
  Ramsgate CT11 ....**52** E8
  Sheerness ME12 ....**1** D2
Alma St Canterbury CT1 ..**67** A1
  Sheerness ME12 ....**1** E2
Alma Street Pas ME12 ....**1** E2
Almarina CT9 ....**7** C1
Almon Pl ME1 ....**9** D5
Almond Cl Ashford TN23 .**138** C5
  Broadstairs CT10 ....**29** C4
  Whitstable CT5 ....**21** D1
Almond Ct CT4 ....**86** E1
Almond Gr ME7 ....**33** C8
Almond Tree Cl ME12 ....**3** A8
Almonds The ME14 ......**76** A4
Almshouse Rd ME13 ....**104** C3
Almshouses **7** CT1 ....**88** A8
Alpha Rd Birchington CT7 .**27** A7
  Ramsgate CT11 ....**52** D6
Alsager Ave ME11 ....**2** F3
Alsops Rd TN23 ....**156** E2
Alston Cl ME12 ....**4** C7
Altbarn Ind Est ME5 ....**54** C8
Alvis Ave CT6 ....**22** A4
Amage Rd TN25 ....**141** C8
Amage Road Cotts
  TN25 ....**124** B1
Amanda Cl ME5 ....**31** F3
Amber Cl ME9 ....**38** D2
Amber La ME17 ....**98** A1
Amber Way ME17 ....**98** B1
Ambleside
  Faversham ME13 ....**62** E6
  Sittingbourne ME10 .....**37** C3
Ambley Gn ME8 ....**33** A8
Ambley Rd ME8 ....**33** B8
Ambrose Hill ME5 ......**10** C2
Amels Hill ME9 ....**56** F8
Ames Ave ME14 ....**76** A4
Amethyst Ave ME5 ......**31** E6

Amherst Cl
  Maidstone ME16 ....**74** D4
  Margate CT9 ....**8** C1
Amherst Hill ME7 ....**10** A6
Amherst Rd ME1 ....**9** D3
Amherst Redoubt ME4 ...**10** A5
Amies House ME15 ......**96** F3
Amos Cl Herne Bay CT6 ..**23** C3
  Sheldwich ME13 ....**83** C5
Amsa Cnr CT17 ....**150** B1
Amsbury Rd ME15,ME17 ..**96** F3
Amshurst Villas ME15 ...**96** A4
Anatase Cl ME10 ....**36** C7
Anchor Bsns Pk ME10 ...**37** B6
Anchor Hill **4** CT9 ....**7** J2
Anchor Ho ME1 ....**9** B4
Anchor La Deal CT14 ...**117** C6
  Sheerness ME12 ....**1** B3
Anchor Rd ME1 ....**9** C1
Ancress Cl CT2 ....**67** A4
Andover Wlk **13** ME15 .**97** F6
Andrew Broughton Way
  ME14 ....**75** B4
Andrew Manor ME7 ......**10** C6
Andrews Wlk ME10 ......**36** B5
Anemone Way CT6 ......**45** E7
Anerley Cl ME16 ....**74** D7
Angel Cotts ME8 ....**12** A2
Anglesey Ave ME15 .....**97** A7
Anglesey Cl ME5 ....**32** B7
Ann's Rd CT11 ....**52** E8
Anna Pk CT7 ....**26** F8
Anne Boleyn Cl ME12 ....**5** E3
Anne Ct CT7 ....**27** B7
Anne Green Wlk **8** CT1 .**67** B2
Anne Roper Cl TN28 ...**200** E6
Anne's Rd CT10 ....**30** C7
Annvera Ho **2** ME7 ...**10** C7
Ansell Ave ME4 ....**10** A1
Anselm Cl ME10 ....**36** E4
Anselm Rd CT17 ....**166** A8
Anson Cl Broadstairs CT10 **29** D3
  Chatham ME5 ....**32** C6
Anstee Rd CT17 ....**149** C1
Anthony Cres CT5 ......**43** B6
Anthonys Way ME7 ......**9** E8
Antolin Way CT10,CT12 ..**29** A3
Antonius Ct TN23 .....**156** A5
Anvil Cl CT7 ....**27** A6
Anzio Cres CT15 ......**149** E2
Anzio Ho **15** CT1 .....**67** B2
Apartments The TN28 ..**200** E5
Apollo House ME5 ......**32** A4
Apple Cl CT18 ....**163** B4
Apple Craft Ctr★ ME13 .**62** E5
Appleby Cl ME1 ....**31** D7
Applecross Cl ME1 ......**9** B4
Appledore Ave ME12 .....**3** A8
Appledore Cl CT9 ....**8** C1
Appledore Cres CT19 ..**177** D7
Appledore Ct ME16 .....**74** C7
Appledore Rd
  Appledore TN26,TN30 ..**190** A7
  Brattle TN26 ....**181** C7
  Gillingham ME8 ....**11** A3
  Tenterden TN30 ....**179** E7
Appledown Way CT11 ....**88** D5
Appleford Dr ME12 ......**3** F7
Applegarth Pk CT5 .....**43** A6
Approach Rd
  Broadstairs CT10 ....**30** A4
  Dover CT17 ....**166** A6
  Margate CT9 ....**8** A2
  Shepherdswell CT15 ....**130** D5
  Whitstable CT5 ....**43** B7
April Rise Birchington CT7 .**26** D8
Apsley Cotts CT4 ....**86** D3
Apsley St TN23 ....**139** B2
Aragon Cl TN23 ....**155** E7
Archbishop's Sch The
  CT2 ....**66** E3
Archcliffe Rd CT17 ...**166** C5
Archer Rd Chatham ME5 ..**32** B6
  Folkestone CT19 ......**178** D6
Archer's Court Rd CT15,
  CT16 ....**149** B7
Archers Court Sch CT16 **149** B5
Archery Sq CT14 ......**117** D7
Archway Ct **4** ME2 .....**9** B8
Archway Rd
  Ramsgate CT11 ....**52** E6
  Sheerness ME12 ....**1** B3
Arcon Cl TN23 ....**156** A7
Arcon Rd TN23 ....**156** A7
Arden Bsns Pk ME2 ......**9** E8
Arden Dr TN24 ....**139** C3
Arden Grange CT4 .....**107** C8
Arden Jun Sch ME7 .....**10** B8
Arden Rd Faversham ME13 .**62** E7
  Herne Bay CT6 ....**23** C2
Arden St ME7 ....**10** C6
Ardenlee Dr ME14 ......**75** B5
Arethusa Rd ME1 ....**31** C8
Argent Bsns Pk ME11 ....**3** A3
Argent Rd ME11 ....**3** A3
Argent Way ME10 ....**36** C6
Argyle Ave CT9 ....**7** G1
Argyle Cl ME1 ....**31** E8
Argyle Gdns CT9 ....**7** G1
Argyle Rd CT5 ....**20** D1
Argyll Dr CT11 ....**29** F1
Ark Cotts CT18 ....**161** D4
Ark La CT14 ....**117** D7
Arkley Rd CT6 ....**22** F4
Arklow Sq **4** CT11 ....**52** F7
Arlington TN23 ....**155** F8
Arlington Gdns CT9 .....**29** C8

Arlington Ho CT9 ....**7** H2
Arlington Sq CT9 ....**7** H2
Arlott Cl ME14 ....**74** F6
Armada Cl TN28 ....**200** E5
Armada Ct ME4 ....**9** E1
Armada Way ME4 ....**9** F3
Armourers Wlk CT16 ...**149** A3
Armstrong Rd ME15 .....**75** A1
Armstrong Sq CT6 ......**22** A3
Arnhem Dr ME5 ....**31** F7
Arnold Rd Chartham CT4 .**86** C2
  5 Margate CT9 ....**7** J1
Arnolde Cl ME2 ....**9** E7
Arolla Rd CT6 ....**23** C4
Arran Mews **4** CT1 ....**67** B2
Arran Rd ME15 ....**97** A6
Arrowhead La TN26,
  TN29 ....**191** D7
Arthur Kennedy Cl ME13 .**63** F3
Arthur Rd Birchington CT7 .**26** D8
  Deal CT14 ....**117** A3
  Gillingham ME8 ....**33** E7
  Hythe CT21 ....**176** C1
  Margate CT9 ....**8** A3
  Rochester ME1 ....**9** D3
Arthur Salmon Cl ME13 .**62** B7
Arthur St
  3 Folkestone CT19 ...**178** E6
  Sittingbourne ME10 .....**36** E4
Artillery Gdns **12** CT1 .**67** A1
Artillery Ho **13** CT1 ...**67** A1
Artillery Rd CT11 ......**52** F7
Artillery St **11** CT1 ...**67** A1
Arundel Ave ME10 ......**36** E1
Arundel Cl ME5 ....**32** D1
Arundel Rd Cliffs End CT12 **51** D7
  Margate CT9 ....**8** B2
Arundel St ME14 ....**74** F6
Ascot Cl ME5 ....**32** C2
Ascot Gdns CT8 ....**27** E7
Ascot House **2** ME15 ..**97** F6
Ash Cl Ashford TN23 ...**138** E3
  Broadstairs CT10 ....**29** C4
  Chatham ME5 ....**10** C1
  Gillingham ME8 ....**11** B3
  Herne Bay CT6 ....**22** F1
  River CT17 ....**148** E1
Ash Cres CT3 ....**46** E1
Ash Ct CT12 ....**51** D4
Ash Gr Elvington CT15 .**114** B2
  Lydd TN29 ....**203** D7
  Maidstone ME16 ....**74** C6
Ash Hill TN26 ....**171** D1
Ash Mdws TN24 ....**156** F7
Ash Rd Aylesham CT3 ...**112** E5
  Sandwich CT13 ....**72** C3
Ash Tree Cl
  Birchington CT8 ....**27** B7
  St Mary's Bay TN29 ...**194** F3
Ash Tree La ME5 ....**10** D1
Ash Tree Rd **6** CT19 .**178** E6
Ashbank Cotts ME17 ....**99** B7
Ashbee Gdns CT6 ....**23** C5
Ashborne Cl TN24 .....**139** D6
Ashburn Gdns CT6 ......**23** C5
Ashburn Mews ME7 .....**10** E3
Ashburnham Rd
  Maidstone ME14 ....**75** B4
  Ramsgate CT11 ....**52** C7
Ashburton Cl TN24 ....**139** E2
Ashdale Hos TN23 .....**139** C2
Ashdown Cl
  Herne Bay CT6 ....**23** B2
  Maidstone ME16 ....**74** D3
Ashdown Cres TN28 ....**200** B6
Ashdown Ct TN24 .....**139** C3
Ashdown Field CT4 .....**86** B2
Ashdown Lodge CT20 ..**178** A5
Ashdown Rd ME17,ME9 ..**79** F1
Ashen Tree Cotts CT3 ...**70** B1
Ashen Tree La CT16 ...**166** E8
Ashenden Cl CT1 ....**87** C5
Ashendene Gr CT2 ......**68** A6
Ashentree La TN29 ....**198** A5
Ashford Bsns Pk TN24 .**157** A6
Ashford Bsns Point
  TN24 ....**156** F5
Ashford Dr ME17 ....**99** D3
Ashford Hospl TN23 ...**139** A3
Ashford Int Sta TN24 .**139** C1
Ashford Mus★ TN23 ...**139** B2
Ashford Rd
  Bethersden TN26,TN23 ..**153** C4
  Chartham CT4,CT1 ......**86** C3
  Folkestone CT18,CT19 ..**177** B7
  Godmersham CT4 ......**107** C4
  Great Chart TN23 .....**155** B8
  Hamstreet TN26 ....**170** F1
  Harrietsham ME17 .....**100** C6
  High Halden TN26,TN30 .**167** A6
  Kingsnorth TN23,TN26 ..**156** A4
  Maidstone,Grove Green
    ME14 ....**75** D4
  Maidstone,Silver Hill ME14 .**76** D3
  New Romney TN28 .....**200** A6
  Sellindge TN25 ....**159** B1
  Sheldwich ME13 ....**83** C4
  Tenterden TN30 ....**179** B8
  Westenhanger CT21,TN25,
    CT18 ....**175** C6
Ashford Sch TN23 .....**139** C2
Ashford South
  Com Prim Sch
  TN23 ....**156** A8
Ashford Sta TN24 .....**139** C1
Ashgrove TN23 ....**138** F5
Ashington Cl ME10 .....**36** C5
Ashley Ave CT19 ......**177** E6

Ashley Cl
Halfway Houses ME12 . . . . . .3 C5
Ramsgate CT12 . . . . .29 B2
Ashley Dr CT5 . . . . .43 A7
Ashley Ho CT19 . . . . .177 E6
Ashley Mill Cotts CT19 . .177 E7
Ashley Rd ME8 . . . . .11 C2
Ashmead Cl ME5 . . . . .32 C3
Ashtead Dr ME9 . . . . .37 D2
Ashton Cl CT14 . . . . .116 D4
Ashton Ct 4 CT14 . . . . . . .29 C5
Ashton Mews 20 CT10 . . . .30 B4
Ashtree Ho ME10 . . . . .37 B3
Ashtrees CT6 . . . . .23 B3
Ashurst Ave CT5 . . . . .43 C6
Ashurst Gdns CT9 . . . . .8 E3
Ashurst Rd ME14 . . . . .75 C5
Askes CT5 . . . . .155 D8
Aspen Cl TN29 . . . . .194 F3
Aspen Ho 6 CT2 . . . . . . .178 D4
Aspen Rd Chartham CT4 . . . .86 E1
Herne CT6 . . . . .45 E7
Aspen Way 2 ME5 . . . . . . .31 E4
Aspian Dr ME17 . . . . .96 D3
Asquith Rd ME8 . . . . .33 C6
Association Wlk ME1 . . . . . .31 C7
Astley Ave CT16 . . . . .149 C2
Astley Ct CT16 . . . . .149 C2
Astley St ME14 . . . . .75 A4
Aston Cl ME5 . . . . .32 A2
Astor Ave CT17 . . . . .166 B8
Astor Dr CT14 . . . . .117 C5
Astor of Hever Com Sch
The ME16 . . . . .74 C3
Astor Rd CT10 . . . . .29 E8
Astor Sch CT17 . . . . .166 A8
Astrid Rd CT14 . . . . .117 C8
Athelstan Gn ME17 . . . . . . .77 C2
Athelstan Pl CT14 . . . . . . .117 C8
Athelstan Rd
Canterbury CT1 . . . . .87 C5
Chatham ME4 . . . . .9 F2
Faversham ME13 . . . . .62 C6
Folkestone CT19 . . . . .178 D7
Margate CT9 . . . . .8 A1
Athol Pl ME13 . . . . .62 A8
Athol Rd Ashford TN23 . . . .155 F7
Whitstable CT5 . . . . .20 F2
Athol Terr CT16 . . . . .166 F8
Atkinson Wlk TN24 . . . . . .139 F5
Atlanta Ct ME4 . . . . .9 D3
Attlee Ave CT3 . . . . .112 C5
Attlee Way ME10 . . . . .36 E8
Atwater Ct ME17 . . . . .101 D5
Aubretia Wlk ME10 . . . . . . .37 A3
Auckland Ave CT12 . . . . . . .52 A8
Auckland Cres CT16 . . . . . .149 C3
Auckland Dr ME10 . . . . .36 C3
Auckland House 10 ME15 . . .97 E5
Audley Ave
Gillingham ME7 . . . . .10 E1
Margate CT9 . . . . .7 E1
Audley Cl ME16 . . . . .74 B5
Audley Rd CT20 . . . . .177 D5
Auger Cl ME9 . . . . .34 E5
Augusta Cl 1 ME7 . . . . . . .10 C7
Augusta Gdns CT20 . . . . . .178 C4
Augusta Pl 12 CT11 . . . . . .52 F7
Augusta Rd CT11 . . . . .52 F7
Augustine Rd
Minster (Sheppey) ME12 . . . . .4 B8
Minster (Thanet) CT12 . . . . . .50 B6
Augustus Wlk TN23 . . . . . .155 F5
Austell Manor 5 ME7 . . . . .10 C6
Austen Orch 14 TN30 . . . . .179 A7
Austin Ave CT6 . . . . .21 F4
Austin Cl Gillingham ME5 . . .10 E2
Sittingbourne ME10 . . . . .37 A8
Austin Rd TN23 . . . . .156 B6
Austins La 4 CT13 . . . . . . .73 A1
Autumn Glade ME5 . . . . . . .54 D8
Avebury Ave CT11 . . . . . . .52 G8
Aveling Ct 2 ME2 . . . . .9 B7
Avent Wlk ME9 . . . . .37 D2
Avenue Gdns CT9 . . . . .8 C3
Avenue of Remembrance
ME10 . . . . .36 F3
Avenue Rd Dover CT16 . . . .149 C1
Herne Bay CT6 . . . . .22 E5
Ramsgate CT11 . . . . .52 F7
Avenue The Deal CT14 . . . .117 C7
Hersden CT3 . . . . .46 E1
Hythe CT21 . . . . .176 C2
Kingsdown CT14 . . . . .134 D4
Margate CT9 . . . . .8 A1
St Margaret's at Cliffe
CT15 . . . . .150 F6
Temple Ewell CT16 . . . . . . .148 E5
Averenches Rd ME14 . . . . . .75 F5
Avereng Gdns CT19 . . . . . .178 B6
Avereng Rd CT19 . . . . .178 B6
Avery Cl ME15 . . . . .74 F1
Avery La ME15, ME17 . . . . . .98 D6
Aviation ME12 . . . . .5 E3
Aviemore Gdns ME14 . . . . . .75 F4
Avington Cl ME15 . . . . .74 F1
Avocet Wlk ME5 . . . . .32 D2
Avon Cl CT1 . . . . .88 C8
Avondale Cl CT5 . . . . .44 A8
Avondale Rd
Capel-le-F CT18 . . . . .164 C2
Gillingham ME7 . . . . .10 D5
Axford Ct ME8 . . . . .34 A8
Aycliffe Com Prim Sch
CT17 . . . . .166 A4
Aylesford Cres ME8 . . . . . . .11 B4
Aylesford Pl TN24 . . . . . . .156 E7

Aylesham Cnr CT3 . . . . . . .112 D3
Aylesham Prim Sch CT3 . . .112 E5
Aylesham Rd CT15,CT3 . . . .113 A4
Aylesham Sta CT3 . . . . . . .113 A5
Aylewyn Gn ME10 . . . . .36 F8
Aynsley Cl 1 CT13 . . . . . . .73 A1
Ayton Rd CT11 . . . . .52 C6

B

Babs Oak Hill CT2 . . . . .68 B7
Back La
6 Faversham ME13 . . . . . .62 D7
Maidstone ME17 . . . . .97 D3
Minster (Sheppey) ME12 . . . . .4 D6
Back Rd W CT16 . . . . .166 G8
Back St
Langley Heath ME17 . . . . . . .98 E6
Ringwould CT14 . . . . .133 F5
Backfields ME1 . . . . .9 B4
Bad Munstereifel Rd
TN23,TN24 . . . . .156 D5
Baddlesmere Rd CT5 . . . . . .21 C3
Baden Rd ME7 . . . . .10 D7
Bader Cres ME5 . . . . .32 A7
Badger Rd ME5 . . . . .32 C1
Badgers Bridge CT18 . . . . .161 D4
Badgers Cl CT2 . . . . .66 A7
Badgers Ct TN23 . . . . .156 A7
Badgers Oak TN23 . . . . . . .155 D8
Badgers Rise Deal CT14 . . .134 C8
River CT17 . . . . .148 D3
Badlesmere Cl TN23 . . . . . .155 E6
Baffin Cl ME4 . . . . .9 F2
Bagham La CT4 . . . . .107 D8
Bagham Rd CT4 . . . . .107 C8
Bagshill Rd ME13 . . . . .83 A3
Bailey Dr ME7 . . . . .11 A1
Bailey Fields TN26 . . . . . . .153 E4
Baileys Field TN23 . . . . . . .138 F1
Baird's Hill CT10 . . . . .29 F6
Bairdsley Cl CT10 . . . . .29 F6
Bakenham Ho 1 ME1 . . . . . .9 C1
Baker Cl ME9 . . . . .38 C2
Baker Ct CT19 . . . . .177 E6
Baker St ME1 . . . . .9 C3
Baker's La CT4 . . . . .86 D2
Baker's Wlk ME1 . . . . .9 C6
Bakers CT2 . . . . .87 C7
Balas Dr ME10 . . . . .36 C7
Balcomb Cres CT9 . . . . .29 C8
Baldric Rd CT20 . . . . .177 F5
Baldwin Rd
Greatstone-on-S TN28 . . . . .200 D1
Minster (Sheppey) ME12 . . . . .4 D7
Baldwin Terr CT19 . . . . . . .178 D6
Balfour Cl CT20 . . . . .178 B3
Balfour Inf Sch ME1 . . . . . . .9 E1
Balfour Jun Sch ME4 . . . . . .9 E2
Balfour Rd Chatham ME4 . . . .9 F2
Deal CT14 . . . . .117 C2
Dover CT16 . . . . .149 C1
Baliol Rd CT5 . . . . .20 E2
Ball La ME7 . . . . .139 F7
Ballard Ind Est ME5 . . . . . . .54 C8
Ballard Rd TN28 . . . . .200 D1
Ballens Rd ME5 . . . . .32 C3
Balliemoor Ct CT11 . . . . . . .29 F1
Balliol Rd CT20 . . . . .29 F8
Balmer Cl ME8 . . . . .33 D7
Balmoral House 11 ME15 . . .97 F5
Balmoral Pl 10 CT11 . . . . . .52 F7
Balmoral Rd
Gillingham ME7 . . . . .10 D5
Kingsdown CT14 . . . . .134 C6
4 Margate CT9 . . . . .28 B8
Bamford Way CT14 . . . . . . .117 C4
Bank Cotts ME17 . . . . .77 E3
Bank Ho TN28 . . . . .200 C6
Bank Rd TN25 . . . . .172 E4
Bank Side TN26 . . . . .183 A8
Bank St Ashford TN23 . . . . .139 B2
Chatham ME4 . . . . .10 B3
Faversham ME13 . . . . .62 C7
Herne Bay CT6 . . . . .22 F5
Maidstone ME14 . . . . .75 A4
Rochester ME2 . . . . .9 C8
Banks The CT10 . . . . .29 F6
Banks Yd 6 ME10 . . . . .36 F4
Bankside Canterbury CT1 . . .88 D7
Chatham ME5 . . . . .32 B8
Banky Fields CT18 . . . . .12 B1
Banner Way ME12 . . . . .3 E6
Banning St ME2 . . . . .9 B8
Banningbrook Ct CT14 . . . .117 D4
Bannister Hill ME9 . . . . .36 B2
Bannister Hos TN26 . . . . . .120 A1
Bannister Rd ME14 . . . . . . .75 A7
Bapchild & Tonge
CE Prim Sch ME9 . . . . . . .37 D3
Barbados Terr 2 ME14 . . . . .75 A7
Barberry Ave ME5 . . . . .31 E5
Barcham Ct ME15 . . . . .96 F5
Barclay St CT7 . . . . .7 C1
Bardell Terr ME1 . . . . .9 C5
Barden Ct ME14 . . . . .75 A4
Barfleur Manor 3 ME7 . . . . .10 A6
Barfreston Cl ME15 . . . . . . .74 F2
Barfrestone Rd CT15 . . . . . .114 A1
Bargates TN23 . . . . .155 E6
Bargrove Rd ME14 . . . . .75 C5
Barham CE Prim Sch
CT4 . . . . .128 F8
Barham Cl ME15 . . . . .97 E5

Barham's Mill Rd TN27 . . .118 B3
Barker Rd ME16 . . . . .74 F3
Barkers Ct ME10 . . . . .36 D4
Barkis Cl ME1 . . . . .31 D7
Barler Pl ME11 . . . . .3 A5
Barley Cl Herne Bay CT6 . . . .23 D2
Martin Mill CT15 . . . . .133 C2
Barley Fields ME14 . . . . . . .75 D4
Barleycorn Dr ME8 . . . . . . .33 E6
Barleymow Cl ME5 . . . . .32 C7
Barling Cl ME5 . . . . .31 D1
Barlow St ME4 . . . . .33 E5
Barn Cl Borden ME9 . . . . . . .36 A2
Hoath CT3 . . . . .46 E5
Yorklets CT5 . . . . .43 A3
Barn Cres CT7 . . . . .7 F1
Barn Platt TN23 . . . . .156 A8
Barn The ME9 . . . . .36 A2
Barnaby Terr ME1 . . . . .9 D2
Barnard Ct ME4 . . . . .10 A2
Barnberry Cl TN23 . . . . . . .155 E8
Barncroft ME14 . . . . .75 F4
Barncroft Dr ME7 . . . . .32 F4
Barnes Ave CT7 . . . . .7 F1
Barnes Cl ME13 . . . . .62 B8
Barnes Ct CT1 . . . . .87 D6
Barnesende Ct CT13 . . . . . . .94 A8
Barnet's La CT7 . . . . .67 C8
Barnett Ct CT12 . . . . .29 B1
Barnett Field TN23 . . . . . . .155 F8
Barnfield Chatham ME5 . . . . .32 A8
Herne Bay CT6 . . . . .22 C2
St Michaels TN30 . . . . .167 C2
Barnfield Rd
Faversham ME13 . . . . .62 C8
Folkestone CT19 . . . . .178 C7
Barnhouse La TN29 . . . . . . .198 A8
Barnhurst La CT18 . . . . . . .163 A5
Barnhurst Rd ME14 . . . . . . .75 A8
Barnsley Cl ME12 . . . . .1 F2
Barnsole Inf Sch ME7 . . . . . .10 E4
Barnsole Jun Sch ME7 . . . . .10 E4
Barnsole Rd
Gillingham ME7 . . . . .10 E3
Staple CT3 . . . . .92 B5
Barntye Cl CT15 . . . . .149 E6
Barnwell Pl ME7 . . . . .10 C5
Barnwood Cl ME1 . . . . .31 B8
Baron Cl Gillingham ME7 . . . .10 E7
Maidstone ME14 . . . . .75 F5
Barrack Hill CT21 . . . . .176 A2
Barrack Rd ME4 . . . . .10 B8
Barrey Rd TN24 . . . . .157 A6
Barrier Rd ME4 . . . . .9 F5
Barrington Cl ME5 . . . . .31 F5
Barrington Cres CT7 . . . . . . .27 B7
Barrow Gr ME10 . . . . .36 D3
Barrow Grove Jun Sch
ME10 . . . . .36 D3
Barrow Hill
Ashford TN23 . . . . .139 B2
Sellindge TN25 . . . . .174 D7
Barrow Hill Cotts TN23 . . .139 B3
Barrow Hill Pl 2 TN23 . . . .139 B3
Barrow Hill Rise TN25 . . . .174 D7
Barrow Hill Terr 1
TN23 . . . . .139 B3
Barrowfields ME5 . . . . .32 D1
Barrows Cl CT7 . . . . .27 A6
Bartholomew Ct CT21 . . . . .176 B3
Bartholomew La CT21 . . . . .176 B3
Bartholomew St
6 Dover CT16 . . . . .149 C1
Hythe CT21 . . . . .176 B2
Bartlett Cl ME5 . . . . .32 C1
Bartlett Dr CT5 . . . . .21 A1
Bartletts Cl ME12 . . . . .3 C5
Barton Bsns Pk CT1 . . . . . . .88 D6
Barton Court Gram Sch
CT1 . . . . .88 B8
Barton Field CT3 . . . . .161 B7
Barton Hill Dr ME12 . . . . . . .4 B7
Barton Jun Sch CT1 . . . . . .149 C2
Barton Mill Ct 2 CT2 . . . . . .66 F1
Barton Mill Rd CT1 . . . . . . .67 B2
Barton Rd Canterbury CT1 . . .88 C6
Dover CT16 . . . . .149 C2
Maidstone ME15 . . . . .75 A2
Rochester ME2 . . . . .9 A7
Barton View Terr 2
CT17 . . . . .149 C1
Barton's Point
Coastal Pk★ ME12 . . . . . .1 G2
Barville Rd CT15 . . . . .114 C2
Barwick Rd CT17 . . . . .148 F1
Bashford Barn La ME9 . . . . .58 A4
Basil Terr ME15 . . . . .75 A1
Basing Cl ME15 . . . . .75 B3
Baskerville TN24 . . . . .139 B3
Basmere ME14 . . . . .75 C6
Bassett Cl CT21 . . . . .176 E4
Bassett Gdns CT21 . . . . . . .176 D4
Bassett Rd ME10 . . . . .36 D4
Bastion Rd CT17 . . . . .166 C6
Batchelor St ME4 . . . . .10 A4
Bateman Ct TN26 . . . . .153 E6
Bates Cl CT3 . . . . .91 F6
Bath Ct CT20 . . . . .178 B3
Bath Hard ME1 . . . . .9 D5
Bath Mews TN24 . . . . .156 A6
Bath Pl CT9 . . . . .7 J2
Bath Rd Ashford TN24 . . . . .156 A6
Margate CT9 . . . . .7 J2
Bathurst Cl CT12 . . . . .29 B1
Bathurst Rd CT20 . . . . .178 A5
Batteries Cl ME9 . . . . .60 B8
Batteries Terr ME9 . . . . .60 B8
Battery Point CT21 . . . . . . .177 B2

Battery Rd TN29 . . . . .204 F2
Battle of Britain Homes 17
CT17 . . . . .166 D7
Bawden Cl CT2 . . . . .67 A4
Baxendale Ct TN24 . . . . . . .156 D7
Bay Banks ME13 . . . . .61 E2
Bay Cotts CT15 . . . . .151 C6
Bay Hill CT15 . . . . .151 B6
Bay Hill Cl CT15 . . . . .151 A5
Bay Mus The★ CT15 . . . . . .151 B5
Bay View Gdns ME12 . . . . . . .6 D2
Bay View Hts CT7 . . . . .26 D8
Bay View Rd CT10 . . . . .30 A2
Baye La CT3 . . . . .69 D1
Bayfield ME13 . . . . .61 E2
Bayford Rd ME10 . . . . .37 A4
Bayhill ME13 . . . . .61 E2
Bayle Ct CT20 . . . . .178 E4
Bayle St 16 CT20 . . . . .178 E5
Bayle The CT20 . . . . .178 E5
Bayswater Dr ME8 . . . . .33 E4
Bayview Rd
Kingsdown CT14 . . . . .134 C4
Whitstable CT5 . . . . .43 D7
Beach Alley 9 CT5 . . . . . . .20 D2
Beach App CT14 . . . . .6 E3
Beach Ave CT7 . . . . .26 F8
Beach Bank Cvn Pk
CT21 . . . . .187 C7
Beach Flats 2 CT21 . . . . . .176 B2
Beach Ho's CT7 . . . . .7 G2
Beach House Mews CT8 . . . .7 D1
Beach Marine 7 CT20 . . . .177 F3
Beach Rd
Dymchurch TN29 . . . . .187 A4
St Margaret's at Cliffe
CT15 . . . . .151 B5
Westgate-on-S CT8,CT9 . . . . .7 D1
Beach Rise CT9 . . . . .7 D1
Beach St Deal CT14 . . . . . . .117 D6
Folkestone CT20 . . . . .178 E4
Herne Bay CT6 . . . . .22 F5
Sheerness ME12 . . . . .1 C2
Beach Terr ME12 . . . . .1 C2
Beach The CT14 . . . . .117 D3
Beach Wlk CT5 . . . . .20 E3
Beachborough Rd CT19,
CT20 . . . . .178 A5
Beachfield Lodge ME12 . . . . .1 D2
Beachmont CT TN28 . . . . . .204 E8
Beacon Ave CT6 . . . . .23 B5
Beacon Cl ME8 . . . . .11 D8
Beacon Hill Chatham ME5 . . .10 D2
Herne Bay CT6 . . . . .23 B5
Beacon La CT13 . . . . .93 A6
Beacon Oak Rd TN30 . . . . .179 B8
Beacon Rd
Broadstairs CT10 . . . . .29 F7
Chatham ME5 . . . . .10 C2
Herne Bay CT6 . . . . .23 A5
Lenham ME17 . . . . .101 C5
Beacon Terr CT21 . . . . .177 B2
Beacon Way CT21 . . . . .174 F4
Beacon Wlk
Herne Bay CT6 . . . . .23 A5
Tenterden TN30 . . . . .167 B1
Beacons The ME17 . . . . .96 C2
Beaconsfield CT5 . . . . .42 F6
Beaconsfield Ave
Dover CT16 . . . . .149 C1
Gillingham ME7 . . . . .10 E5
Beaconsfield Gdns CT10 . . . .29 F5
Beaconsfield Rd
Canterbury CT2 . . . . .66 F2
Chatham ME4 . . . . .9 F3
Deal CT14 . . . . .117 D5
Dover CT16 . . . . .149 C1
Maidstone ME15 . . . . .74 E2
Sittingbourne ME10 . . . . .37 C4
Beamont Cl CT12 . . . . .27 F2
Beams The ME15 . . . . .75 F1
Bean Cl TN23 . . . . .138 C1
Beaney's La CT4 . . . . .84 C1
Bear's La TN23,TN26 . . . . .137 E3
Bears End Ho TN23 . . . . . . .156 B8
Bearsted ME14 . . . . .76 B5
Bearsted Cl ME8 . . . . .11 B3
Bearsted Green Bsns Ctr
ME14 . . . . .76 C4
Bearsted Rd ME14 . . . . .75 E6
Beatrice Mews TN28 . . . . . .204 E7
Beatrice Rd
Capel-le-F CT18 . . . . .164 C2
Margate CT9 . . . . .28 E8
Beatty Ave ME7 . . . . .10 F4
Beatty Cl CT19 . . . . .178 E8
Beatty Rd Chatham ME1 . . . .31 D8
Folkestone CT19 . . . . .178 D8
Beauchamp Ave CT14 . . . . . .117 A3
Beauchamp Cl TN24 . . . . . .139 C6
Beauchamps La CT15 . . . . . .113 D5
Beaufort Ave ME2 . . . . .9 E6
Beaufort Ct ME2 . . . . .9 E6
Beaufort Wlk ME15 . . . . . . .97 E4
Beaufoy Rd CT17 . . . . .149 A1
Beaufoy Terr CT17 . . . . . . .148 F1
Beauherne Com Sch CT2 . . .87 D8
Beaulieu Rise ME1 . . . . .9 D1
Beaulieu Wlk ME16 . . . . .74 D7
Beaumanor CT6 . . . . .22 D4
Beaumont Davy Cl ME13 . . . .62 C5
Beaumont Rd ME16 . . . . .74 B2
Beaumont St CT6 . . . . .22 C4
Beaumont Terr ME13 . . . . . .62 D6
Beauvoir Dr ME10 . . . . .37 A8
Beauworth Pk ME15 . . . . . . .97 E8
Beauxfield CT16 . . . . .149 C4
Beaver Ct TN23 . . . . .156 A7

Beaver Green Inf Sch
TN23 . . . . .155 E7
Beaver Ind Est TN23 . . . . . .156 B7
Beaver La Ashford TN23 . . . .138 E1
Ashford, Beaver TN23 . . . . . .155 E7
Ashford,Singleton TN23 . . . . .155 F7
Beaver Rd Ashford TN23 . . . .138 E1
Maidstone ME16 . . . . .74 B7
Beazley Ct TN24 . . . . .156 D7
Beckenham Dr ME16 . . . . . . .74 D7
Becket Ave CT2 . . . . .66 D1
Becket Cl Ash CT3 . . . . .71 D2
Deal CT14 . . . . .117 C8
Whitstable CT5 . . . . .21 B1
Becket Mews CT2 . . . . .66 F1
Becket's Cl TN25 . . . . .142 B6
Beckett St 4 ME13 . . . . . . .62 C7
Becketts Terr CT21 . . . . . . .176 B4
Beckley Mews ME5 . . . . .31 F5
Beckley Pl TN25 . . . . .175 B8
Beckley Rd ME12 . . . . .1 F2
Becksbourne Cl ME14 . . . . . .75 A8
Beckwith Gn CT20 . . . . .177 E5
Beckworth Pl ME16 . . . . .74 B2
Beddow Way ME20 . . . . .53 B3
Bede Ho CT14 . . . . .117 D8
Bedford Ave ME8 . . . . .11 D1
Bedford Pl ME16 . . . . .74 E4
Bedford Sq CT12 . . . . .29 B2
Bedford Way CT7 . . . . .25 F1
Bedgebury Cl
Chatham ME1 . . . . .31 D8
Maidstone ME14 . . . . .75 C6
Bedingfield Way CT18 . . . . .161 B7
Bedlam Court La CT12 . . . . . .50 C6
Bedlam La TN27 . . . . .135 A8
Bedson Wlk ME8 . . . . .12 B1
Bedwin Cl ME1 . . . . .31 D7
Beech Cl Faversham ME13 . . .62 B7
Folkestone CT19 . . . . .178 C6
Beech Ct Canterbury CT1 . . . .88 A7
Challock TN25 . . . . .105 A1
Beech Dr Broadstairs CT10 . . .29 D4
Elvington CT15 . . . . .114 B2
Hothfield TN26 . . . . .138 A7
Maidstone ME16 . . . . .74 C5
Beech Gr CT12 . . . . .51 C5
Beech Green Cl CT15 . . . . . .131 C7
Beech Hill CT4 . . . . .111 B8
Beech Hurst ME15 . . . . .75 B2
Beechcroft CT5 . . . . .21 D1
Beechcroft Gdns CT11 . . . . . .52 B8
Beechen Bank Rd ME5 . . . . .32 A1
Beeches The ME4 . . . . .32 A4
Beechings Gn ME8 . . . . .11 C3
Beechings Way ME8 . . . . . . .11 C3
Beechings Way Ind Ctr
ME8 . . . . .11 B4
Beechmore Dr ME5 . . . . .32 A2
Beecholme Dr TN24 . . . . . . .139 C5
Beechwood Ave
Chatham ME5 . . . . .10 D2
Deal CT14 . . . . .117 C5
Sittingbourne ME10 . . . . .36 E6
Beechwood Cl
St Mary's Bay TN29 . . . . . . .194 F3
Whitfield CT16 . . . . .132 A1
Beechwood Ct
Deal CT14 . . . . .117 C5
River CT16 . . . . .148 E4
Beecroft Cl CT2 . . . . .67 A4
Beer Cart La CT1 . . . . .87 F8
Beggars Cnr CT3 . . . . .48 C1
Begonia Ave ME8 . . . . .11 C2
Beke Rd ME8 . . . . .33 D4
Bekesbourne Hill CT4 . . . . . .89 B5
Bekesbourne La
Bekesbourne CT3,CT4 . . . . . .89 E6
Canterbury CT3 . . . . .88 F7
Littlebourne CT3 . . . . .89 F6
Bekesbourne Rd CT4 . . . . . . .88 F2
Bekesbourne Sta CT4 . . . . . .89 B5
Belcaire Cl CT21 . . . . .175 A3
Belfast Ho 14 ME15 . . . . . . .97 E7
Belgrave Cl CT11 . . . . .52 D7
Belgrave Rd Dover CT17 . . . .166 B7
Halfway Houses ME12 . . . . . . .3 C5
Margate CT9 . . . . .7 I2
Belinda Ct CT19 . . . . .178 B7
Bell Chapel Cl TN23 . . . . . .156 C4
Bell Cotts ME9 . . . . .13 B3
Bell Cres ME1 . . . . .53 A8
Bell Farm La ME12 . . . . .5 A6
Bell Gr CT3 . . . . .113 A5
Bell La Burham ME1 . . . . . . .53 A8
Maidstone ME14 . . . . .76 A5
Sandwich CT13 . . . . .73 A1
Westfield Sole ME14 . . . . . . .54 B7
Bell Meadow ME15 . . . . .97 E6
Bell Rd Park Wood ME15 . . . .97 E5
Sittingbourne ME10 . . . . .36 F3
Bell Sh Ctr ME10 . . . . .36 F4
Bell Way ME17 . . . . .99 E2
Bell Wood Com Sch
ME15 . . . . .97 E5
Bell Wood Inf Sch ME15 . . . .97 E5
Bell's Cl TN30 . . . . .179 A7
Bell-Davies Dr CT12 . . . . . . .28 A1
Belle Friday Cl ME9 . . . . . . .38 C2
Belle Vue Rd CT6 . . . . .23 B5

Bellevue Ave CT11 . . . . . .52 F7
Bellevue Rd
 Minster (Sheppey) ME12 . . .4 C6
 Ramsgate CT11 . . . . .52 F7
 Whitstable CT5 . . . . .43 F8
Bellevue St 5 CT20 . . . . .178 D5
Bellflower Ave ME12 . . . . . .4 A4
Bellgrove Ct ME5 . . . . . . .54 A8
Bells La 9 TN30 . . . . . .179 A7
Belmont CT14 . . . . .117 B1
Belmont Ct
 9 Maidstone ME15 . . . . . .75 B4
 Ramsgate CT11 . . . . .52 D7
Belmont Farm Bsns Ctr
 TN26 . . . . .137 A1
Belmont Pl TN24 . . . . . . .156 D7
Belmont Rd
 Ashford TN24 . . . . .139 D6
 Broadstairs CT10 . . . . . . .30 A4
 Faversham ME13 . . . . . . .62 C6
 Gillingham ME7 . . . . .10 C4
 Halfway Houses ME12 . . . . .3 E8
 Ramsgate CT11 . . . . .52 D7
 Sittingbourne ME10 . . . . . .36 E3
 Westgate-on-S CT8 . . . . . .27 F8
 Whitstable CT5 . . . . .20 D1
Belmont St CT11 . . . . .52 E7
Belmont Terr CT13 . . . . . . .93 B3
Belmore Pk TN24 . . . . . . .139 B3
Belnor Ave ME9 . . . . .13 F1
Belsey La CT15 . . . . .147 A5
Belting Dr CT6 . . . . .23 E5
Beltinge Rd CT6 . . . . .23 B5
Belton Cl CT5 . . . . .43 E8
Belvedere House 9
 ME15 . . . . .97 F5
Belvedere Rd
 Broadstairs CT10 . . . . . . .30 B4
 Faversham ME13 . . . . . . .62 D8
Benacre Rd CT5 . . . . .43 D6
Bench Hill TN26 . . . . . . .181 D5
Bench St 19 CT16 . . . . . .166 D7
Bendon Way ME5 . . . . . . .33 D8
Benenden Manor ME8 . . . .11 B3
Bengal Rd CT12 . . . . .29 A1
Benham Bsns Pk CT21 . . .174 F5
Bennells Ave CT5 . . . . . . .21 B3
Bennett Ct 14 CT20 . . . . .178 E5
Bennetts Cotts ME7 . . . . .55 A8
Bennetts Gdns ME13 . . . . .61 D8
Bennetts Mews 13 TN30 179 A7
Benson Cl CT18 . . . . .162 F4
Benson Ct CT18 . . . . .162 F4
Bensted TN23 . . . . .155 F5
Bensted Gr ME13 . . . . . . .62 A7
Benstede Cl CT6 . . . . .23 A1
Bentham Sq ME12 . . . . . . .1 B3
Bentley Ave CT6 . . . . .22 B4
Bentley Cl ME5 . . . . .32 D2
Bentley Rd TN24 . . . . . . .156 F7
Bentlif Cl ME16 . . . . .74 D5
Berber Rd ME2 . . . . .9 B8
Berengrave La ME8 . . . . . .11 F2
Berengrave Lane
 Chalk Pit
 (Nature Reserve)★ ME8 12 A3
Beresford Ave ME1 . . . . . . .9 E2
Beresford Ct 7 CT7 . . . . . .26 F8
Beresford Gap CT7 . . . . . . .26 F8
Beresford Gdns CT9 . . . . . .8 C3
Beresford Rd
 Gillingham ME7 . . . . .10 D4
 Kit's Coty ME20 . . . . .53 D7
 Ramsgate CT11 . . . . .52 D6
 River CT17 . . . . .148 E3
 St Margaret's at Cliffe
 CT15 . . . . .133 F1
 Whitstable CT5 . . . . .20 D1
Beresfords Hill ME17 . . . . .97 B4
Bergland Pk ME2 . . . . .9 D8
Berkeley Cl
 Boughton Street ME13 . . . .64 B3
 Chatham ME1 . . . . .31 D8
 2 Folkestone CT19 . . . . .178 A7
Berkeley Ct ME10 . . . . . . .36 D3
Berkeley Mount 8 ME4 . . . .9 F4
Berkeley Rd CT7 . . . . .26 F8
Berkshire Cl ME5 . . . . . . .32 C8
Bernard Sunley Hall
 TN25 . . . . .124 A2
Bernards Gdns CT15 . . . .130 E5
Berridge Rd ME12 . . . . . . .1 D2
Berry St ME10 . . . . .36 F4
Berwick La CT21 . . . . . . .175 A3
Berwyn Gr ME15 . . . . . . .97 A6
Best La CT1 . . . . .87 F8
Best St ME4 . . . . .9 F4
Bethany Cl CT14 . . . . . . .117 C4
Bethel Row ME1 . . . . .82 F1
Bethersden Ct ME15 . . . . .97 F7
Bethersden Cty Prim Sch
 TN26 . . . . .153 D5
Bethersden Rd
 Biddenden Green TN27,
 TN26 . . . . .152 C5
 Hothfield TN26 . . . . .137 D4
 Shadoxhurst TN26 . . . . . .154 E2
 Woodchurch TN26 . . . . . .169 A6
Betony Gdns ME14 . . . . . .75 F5
Betsham Rd ME5 . . . . . . .97 F6
Bettescombe Rd ME8 . . . . .33 E7
Betty Shelvey Ct CT14 . . .117 D4
Beult Meadow TN27 . . . . .135 A1
Bevan Way CT3 . . . . .112 E5
Beverley Cl ME8 . . . . .33 F8

Beverley Gdns TN29 . . . . .187 A4
Beverley Rd
 Canterbury CT2 . . . . .66 E2
 Maidstone ME16 . . . . . . .74 A2
Beverley Way CT12 . . . . . .29 C1
Beverly Cl CT7 . . . . .27 B8
Bewsbury Cres CT16 . . . . .148 F7
Bewsbury Cross La
 CT16 . . . . .148 F7
Bexley St CT5 . . . . .20 C2
Bexon La ME9 . . . . .58 C4
Bhutan Rd CT6 . . . . .23 C4
Bicknor Cl CT2 . . . . .67 B4
Bicknor Court Cotts ME9 57 C2
Bicknor Rd ME15 . . . . . . .97 F4
Biddenden Cl
 Maidstone ME15 . . . . . . .75 F3
 Margate CT9 . . . . .8 C1
Biddenden Rd TN26,
 TN26 . . . . .167 A6
Bierce Ct CT7 . . . . .26 F7
Bierce Ct Cotts CT7 . . . . . .26 F7
Bifrons Gdns CT4 . . . . . . .89 B3
Bifrons Hill CT4 . . . . .89 B4
Bifrons Rd CT4 . . . . .89 B4
Bigbury Rd CT2,CT4 . . . . .86 E7
Biggin St CT16 . . . . .166 D8
Biggins Wood Rd CT19 . . .177 E7
Bilberry Cl ME14 . . . . . . .75 E5
Bill Street Rd ME2 . . . . . . .9 C8
Billington Gdns TN24 . . . .139 E6
Bilsington Cl ME5 . . . . . . .32 B5
Bilsington Cross TN25 . . .172 C1
Binbury La ME14,ME9 . . . .56 A5
Bindon Blood Rd CT16 . . .149 A5
Bingley Rd 1 ME1 . . . . . . .9 E4
Binland Gr ME5 . . . . .31 D5
Binnacle Rd ME1 . . . . . . .31 C8
Binnie Cl CT10 . . . . .29 F2
Birch Cl Ashford TN24 . . . .139 F2
 Broadstairs CT10 . . . . . . .29 C3
Birch Ct Barham CT4 . . . . .128 F8
 Ramsgate CT11 . . . . .52 D8
Birch Dr ME5 . . . . .32 D1
Birch Gr ME7 . . . . .33 A4
Birch Hill Ct CT7 . . . . .27 B7
Birch Ho Sheerness ME12 . . .1 C2
 Sittingbourne ME10 . . . . . .37 B3
Birch Rd CT5 . . . . .44 A8
Birch Tree Way ME15 . . . . .75 B3
Birches The CT7 . . . . .27 B7
Birchett TN23 . . . . .138 E1
Birchett La TN26 . . . . . . .170 D3
Birchfield Cl ME15 . . . . . .97 B6
Birchfields ME5 . . . . .32 A3
Birchington CE Prim Sch
 CT7 . . . . .27 A6
Birchington-Cl CT7 . . . . . .75 C5
Birchington-On-Sea Sta
 CT7 . . . . .26 F7
Bircholt Forstal TN25 . . . .158 E7
Bircholt Rd ME15 . . . . . . .97 F4
Birchwood Rd ME10 . . . . . .74 C5
Birchwood Rise CT17 . . . .166 C7
Birchwood Wlk CT2 . . . . . .66 E2
Birds Ave CT9 . . . . .28 B7
Birdwood Ave CT14 . . . . .117 A5
Birkdale Cl CT5 . . . . .44 D8
Birkdale Ct 3 ME16 . . . . . .74 E4
Birkdale Dr CT19 . . . . . . .178 A8
Birkdale Gdns CT6 . . . . . .22 D2
Birkhall Ct ME5 . . . . .32 A5
Birling Ave Gillingham ME8 11 E1
 Maidstone ME14 . . . . . . .76 A4
Birling Ct ME14 . . . . .76 A4
Birling Rd TN24 . . . . .139 D1
Birnam Sq 1 ME16 . . . . . .74 E4
Bishop Ct 5 ME10 . . . . . . .36 E5
Bishop Jenner Ct CT3 . . . .70 C6
Bishop La ME9 . . . . .12 E3
Bishop's Ave CT10 . . . . . . .30 B6
Bishopbourne Gn ME8 . . . .11 B4
Bishopden Ct CT2 . . . . . . .66 C4
Bishops Gn TN23 . . . . . . .155 E7
Bishops Way
 Canterbury CT2 . . . . .66 D1
 Maidstone ME15 . . . . . . .74 F4
Bishops Wlk ME1 . . . . .9 C5
Bishopstone Dr CT6 . . . . . .23 F6
Bishopstone La CT6 . . . . . .23 F5
Black Bull Rd CT19 . . . . .178 D6
Black Griffin La CT1 . . . . . .87 F8
Black Post ME17 . . . . .78 E4
Black Robin La CT4 . . . . . .111 E3
Black Rock Gdns ME7 . . . .33 B4
Blackberry Way CT5 . . . . . .44 B8
Blackburn Rd CT6 . . . . . . .22 B2
Blackdown Dr TN24 . . . . .139 B4
Blacketts Cotts ME9 . . . . .38 B7
Blacketts Rd ME9 . . . . . . .38 A6
Blackfriars St 7 CT1 . . . . .66 F1
Blackhouse Hill CT18,
 CT21 . . . . .176 D4
Blackhouse Rise CT21 . . . .176 D3
Blackleys CT5 . . . . .84 F7
Blackmanstone Way
 ME16 . . . . .74 B7
Blacksmith Dr ME14 . . . . .75 D5
Blackstable Ct CT5 . . . . . .43 D8
Blackthorn Ave ME5 . . . . .32 A3
Blackthorne Rd ME8 . . . . .34 B8
Blackthorne Way TN23 . . .156 C3
Blackwall Rd TN24,TN25 140 E4
Blackwall Rd N TN24 . . . .140 A2
Blackwall Rd S TN24 . . . .140 A2
Blake Cl CT14 . . . . .134 C8
Blake Ct Ashford TN24 . . .156 F8

Ramsgate CT11 . . . . .52 D7
Blakeney Cl ME14 . . . . . . .76 B4
Blaker Ave ME1 . . . . .9 E1
Bland Dr CT18 . . . . .163 C5
Blandford Gdns ME10 . . . .36 E1
Blatcher Cl ME12 . . . . .4 B6
Blaxland Cl ME13 . . . . . . .62 B8
Bleak Ho★ CT10 . . . . .30 B4
Bleak Rd TN29 . . . . .203 C6
Bleakwood Rd ME5 . . . . . .31 F4
Blean Comm CT2 . . . . . . .66 A6
Blean Hill CT2 . . . . .66 A5
Blean Prim Sch CT2 . . . . .66 B4
Blean Rd ME8 . . . . .11 C2
Blean Sq ME14 . . . . .75 C6
Blean View Rd CT6 . . . . . .22 B2
Blendon Rd ME14 . . . . . . .75 C5
Blenheim Ave
 Canterbury CT1 . . . . .67 D1
 Chatham ME4 . . . . .9 E2
 Faversham ME13 . . . . . . .62 E5
Blenheim Cl
 Broadstairs CT10 . . . . . . .29 D3
 Herne Bay CT6 . . . . .23 A1
 Maidstone ME15 . . . . . . .75 F3
 Hawkinge CT18 . . . . . . .163 A4
Blenheim Ho CT9 . . . . .8 C3
Blenheim Rd Deal CT14 . . .117 D5
 Littlestone-on-S TN28 . . .200 D5
 Sittingbourne ME10 . . . . .37 B2
Bleriot Meml★ CT16 . . . . .149 F1
Bliby Cnr TN25 . . . . .171 E8
Blind La Bredhurst ME7 . . . .33 A1
 Challock TN25 . . . . .105 C2
 Chatham ME7 . . . . .32 F1
 Mersham TN25 . . . . .157 C4
Blind Mary's La ME9 . . . . .57 E4
Blindgrooms La TN26 . . . .155 C1
Blindhouse La TN25 . . . . .160 B3
Blockmakers Ct ME4 . . . . .9 C7
Bloomsbury Rd CT11 . . . . .52 C6
Bloomsbury Way TN24 . . .139 B7
Bloomsbury Wlk 2
 ME15 . . . . .75 A4
Bloors La ME8 . . . . .11 D3
Bloors Wharf Rd ME7 . . . .11 F4
Blowers Grove Wood
 ME7 . . . . .33 B3
Blue Boar La ME1 . . . . . . .9 D5
Blue House La CT21 . . . . .176 B8
Blue Line La TN24 . . . . . .139 B7
Bluebell Cl Gillingham ME7 10 F6
 Kingsnorth ME9 . . . . . . .156 B4
Bluebell Rd TN23 . . . . . . .156 C3
Bluebell Mews CT5 . . . . . .43 C6
Bluefield Rd CT5 . . . . .43 C6
Bluett St ME14 . . . . .75 A5
Bluewater Cvn Pk CT21 187 E8
Blythe Cl ME10 . . . . .37 C5
Blythe Ct CT21 . . . . .176 D2
Blythe Rd ME15 . . . . .75 B4
Boarley Ct ME14 . . . . .53 F1
Boarley La ME14 . . . . .53 F2
Boarman's La TN29 . . . . .197 E8
Boat La TN25 . . . . .173 A4
Boathouse Rd ME12 . . . . . .1 A3
Bob Amor Cl ME13 . . . . . .62 E7
Bobbin Lodge Hill CT4 . . . .86 B2
Bobbing Hill ME9 . . . . .36 A7
Bobbing Village Sch ME9 36 B7
Bockham Cotts TN25 . . . .157 E8
Bockham La
 Ashford TN25 . . . . .141 A1
 Mersham TN25 . . . . .141 A1
Bockhanger La TN24 . . . .139 C6
Bockingford La ME15 . . . . .96 F8
Bodenham Rd CT20 . . . . .178 A4
Bodiam Cl ME8 . . . . .11 C3
Bodiam Ct ME16 . . . . .74 F3
Bodsham CE Prim Sch
 TN25 . . . . .142 E8
Bodsham Cres ME15 . . . . .76 B3
Bogle Rd ME9 . . . . .60 C7
Bognor Dr CT6 . . . . .22 D4
Bogshole La
 Herne Bay CT6 . . . . .23 D3
 Whitstable CT5 . . . . .43 E4
Boiler Rd ME4 . . . . .10 A8
Boley Hill ME1 . . . . .9 C6
Boleyn Ave CT9 . . . . .7 E1
Boleyn Ct 8 CT1 . . . . .88 A8
Bolingbroke Ho ME16 . . . .74 F2
Bolner Cl ME5 . . . . .31 F2
Bolton Rd CT19 . . . . .178 D6
Bolton St CT11 . . . . .52 D8
Bolts Hill CT4 . . . . .86 D2
Bombay House 1 ME15 . .97 E5
Bond La TN23 . . . . .156 A2
Bond Rd Ashford TN23 . . .156 B8
 Gillingham ME8 . . . . .33 E5
Bonetta St ME12 . . . . .3 B8
Bonham Dr ME10 . . . . . . .37 B5
Bonners Alley 13 CT5 . . . .20 D2
Bonnington Cross TN25 172 E3
Bonnington Gn ME8 . . . . . .11 C3
Bonnington Rd ME14 . . . . .75 C6
Bonny Bush Hill CT4 . . . .111 D5
Bonsor Rd CT19 . . . . .178 D6
Bookins Cl ME17 . . . . .97 D5
Booth Pl CT9 . . . . .7 J3
Booth Rd ME4 . . . . .9 F2
Borden CE Prim Sch ME9 35 F3
Borden Gram Sch ME10 . .36 F3
Borden La ME10,ME9 . . . .36 F1
Boresisle TN30 . . . . .167 B2
Bornefields TN23 . . . . . . .156 A7
Borough CT1 . . . . .67 A1

Borough Rd
 Gillingham ME7 . . . . .10 D4
 Queenborough ME11 . . . . . .3 B4
Borrowdale Ave CT11 . . . . .52 A7
Borstal Ave CT5 . . . . .43 D6
Borstal Hill CT5 . . . . .43 D7
Borstal HM Prison
 & Youth Custody Ctr ME1 9 B1
Borstal Mews ME1 . . . . . . .9 B3
Borstal Rd ME1 . . . . .9 B3
Borstal St ME1 . . . . .9 B2
Boscombe Rd CT19 . . . . .178 C6
Bosney Banks CT15 . . . . .148 A7
Bossingham Rd CT4 . . . . .126 F3
Bossington Rd CT3 . . . . . .90 E1
Boston Cl 5 CT16 . . . . . .149 B3
Boston Gdns ME8 . . . . . . .11 C1
Boston Rd ME5 . . . . .32 C2
Botany Cl ME12 . . . . .1 C1
Botany Rd CT10,CT9 . . . . .8 F2
Boteler Cotts CT13 . . . . . .93 A2
Botolph's Bridge Rd
 CT21 . . . . .187 A6
Bottles La ME13 . . . . .59 A6
Bottlescrew Hill ME17 . . . .97 B4
Bottom Pond Rd ME9 . . . . .58 D3
Boughton Ave CT10 . . . . . .30 D4
Boughton Church Cotts
 ME13 . . . . .63 D1
Boughton Cl ME8 . . . . .11 B3
Boughton Cnr TN25 . . . . .123 C5
Boughton Field Cotts
 ME13 . . . . .63 A5
Boughton Hill ME13 . . . . . .64 C3
Boughton La ME15 . . . . . .97 B6
Boughton Monchelsea
 Cty Prim Sch ME17 . . . . .97 B2
Boughton Par ME15 . . . . .97 A7
Boughton Place Cotts
 ME17 . . . . .118 A8
Boughton Rd ME17 . . . . .101 B2
Boulevard Courrieres
 CT3 . . . . .112 E5
Boulevard The CT1 . . . . . .87 D7
Boulogne Ct 15 CT20 . . . .178 E5
Boundary Cl ME12 . . . . . . .4 C6
Boundary Ct CT1 . . . . .88 B6
Boundary Rd Chatham ME4 .9 E3
 Hythe CT21 . . . . .176 A2
 Kingsdown CT14 . . . . . . .134 C6
 Ramsgate CT11 . . . . .52 E7
Boundary The CT1 . . . . . . .87 D7
Bounds La ME13 . . . . .64 A7
Boundsgate Cnr ME13 . . .105 B7
Bourne Cotts CT4 . . . . . . .111 C5
Bourne Gr ME10 . . . . .36 C5
Bourne La TN26 . . . . .183 A8
Bourne Park Rd CT4 . . . .111 A7
Bourne Rd TN25 . . . . . . .172 D5
Bourne View CT4 . . . . .88 F1
Bournelodge Cl CT2 . . . . . .66 A7
Bournemouth Dr CT6 . . . .22 D4
Bournemouth Gdns
 CT19 . . . . .178 C6
Bournemouth Rd CT19 178 C5
Bournes Cl CT2 . . . . .67 F7
Bournes Pl TN26 . . . . . . .169 A2
Bourneside Terr ME17 . . . .77 D2
Bournewood CT6 . . . . . . .23 B2
Bournewood Cl ME15 . . . . .75 F1
Bournville Ave ME4 . . . . . . .9 F1
Bouverie Pl 2 CT20 . . . . .178 D4
Bouverie Rd CT20 . . . . . .178 D4
Bouverie Rd W CT20 . . . .178 C4
Bouverie Sq 1 CT20 . . . .178 D4
Bow Hill CT4 . . . . .109 F2
Bowan Ct CT11 . . . . .52 D7
Bowdell La TN29 . . . . . . .191 E3
Bowden Cres CT20 . . . . . .177 C6
Bowen Rd CT19 . . . . .177 E6
Bowens Field TN23 . . . . . .139 B1
Bower Cl ME16 . . . . .74 E4
Bower Gr ME5 . . . . .32 C1
Bower Grove Sch ME16 . . .74 E4
Bower La Maidstone ME16 .74 E2
 Maidstone ME16 . . . . . . .74 E3
Bower Mount Rd ME16 . . .74 D4
Bower Pl ME16 . . . . .74 E4
Bower Rd TN25 . . . . .158 A3
Bower St ME16 . . . . .74 E4
Bower Terr ME16 . . . . .74 E3
Bowerland La
 Chilham CT4 . . . . .85 E1
 Old Wives Lees CT4 . . . . .85 C2
Bowers Ave CT9 . . . . .7 E1
Bowes La CT6 . . . . .23 A3
Bowes Rd ME2 . . . . .9 B8
Bowes Villas CT14 . . . . . .93 E4
Bowl Field TN25 . . . . . . .142 B6
Bowl Rd TN27 . . . . .103 D2
Bowland Cl CT6 . . . . .23 C2
Bowles Well Gdns CT19 178 F7
Bowley La ME17 . . . . .118 D8
Bowling Green La CT14 . .117 B5
Bowling Green Terr 8
 CT17 . . . . .166 D7
Bowling St CT13 . . . . .72 F1
Bowman Cl ME5 . . . . .32 C5
Bowman Ct CT17 . . . . . . .149 A1
Bowser Cl CT14 . . . . .116 F4
Bowyer Rd CT5 . . . . .42 F7
Box La ME13 . . . . .61 D1
Boxley Rd TN23 . . . . .156 F8
Boxley Cl Maidstone ME14 .75 B8
 West Minst ME12 . . . . . . .3 B7
Boxley Rd Chatham ME5 . . .32 B2

Boxley Rd continued
 Maidstone ME14 . . . . . . .75 B7
Boxmend Ind Est ME15 . . .97 F3
Boxted La ME14 . . . . .13 A1
Boyces Hill ME9 . . . . .35 D6
Boyden Gate Hill CT3 . . . .47 B8
Boyes La CT3 . . . . .91 D3
Boyke La CT4 . . . . .144 C2
Boyne Rd CT15 . . . . .134 A1
Boys Hall Rd TN24 . . . . . .156 F7
Boystown Pl CT13 . . . . . . .93 C3
Brabazon Rd ME12 . . . . . . .5 C1
Brabner Cl CT19 . . . . . . .178 E8
Brabourne Ave ME8 . . . . . .11 C3
Brabourne CE Prim Sch
 TN25 . . . . .159 A8
Brabourne Cl CT2 . . . . . . .67 A4
Brabourne Gdns CT20 . . .177 E5
Brabourne La TN25 . . . . .142 F2
Brabourne Rd TN25 . . . . .141 D6
Brack La TN29 . . . . .191 B3
Bracken Cl TN24 . . . . . . .139 C6
Bracken Ct
 3 Broadstairs CT10 . . . . .29 E5
 Sittingbourne ME10 . . . . .37 C5
Bracken Hill ME5 . . . . .32 A1
Bracken Lea ME5 . . . . .10 C1
Brackley Cl ME14 . . . . . . .75 C5
Brackwood Cl ME8 . . . . . .33 D5
Bradbridge Gn TN23 . . . . .155 D8
Braddick Cl ME15 . . . . . . .97 B6
Bradfield Ave ME9 . . . . . . .38 D2
Bradfield Rd TN24 . . . . . .139 B5
Bradfields Ave ME5 . . . . . .31 F5
Bradfields Ave W ME5 . . . .31 F5
Bradfields Sch ME5 . . . . . .32 A6
Bradley Dr ME10 . . . . .36 E2
Bradley Rd
 Folkestone CT19 . . . . . . .178 E6
 Ramsgate CT12 . . . . .29 C1
Bradshaw Cl ME9 . . . . . . .12 E3
Bradstone Ave CT19 . . . . .178 C6
Bradstone New Rd 3
 CT20 . . . . .178 D5
Bradstone Rd CT20 . . . . .178 D5
Bradstow Sch CT10 . . . . . .30 A3
Bradstow Way CT10 . . . . . .30 A5
Brady Rd CT18 . . . . .161 A4
Braeside CT10 . . . . .30 B3
Braggs La CT6 . . . . .45 E6
Brake Ave ME5 . . . . .31 E5
Bramble Cl
 Maidstone ME16 . . . . . . .74 B3
 Wye TN25 . . . . .123 D3
Bramble La TN25 . . . . . . .123 C3
Brambledown
 Chatham ME5 . . . . .32 B8
 Folkestone CT19 . . . . . . .178 D6
Bramblefield La ME9,
 ME9 . . . . .14 E1
Bramblefields Cl CT6 . . . . .23 B2
Bramblehill Rd ME13 . . . . .62 C8
Brambley Cres CT20 . . . . .177 E5
Brambling Rise ME10 . . . . .36 E6
Bramley Ave
 Canterbury CT1 . . . . .87 C6
 Faversham ME13 . . . . . . .62 E6
Bramley Cl
 Brabourne Lees TN25 . . . .158 E6
 Eastchurch ME12 . . . . .5 D3
 Gillingham ME8 . . . . .34 B8
Bramley Cres ME15 . . . . . .75 F3
Bramley Gdns
 Ashford TN23 . . . . .156 A6
 Coxheath ME17 . . . . .96 C3
Bramley Way ME12 . . . . . . .5 D3
Bramling Gap CT3 . . . . . . .90 C3
Bramling Rd CT3,CT4 . . . .90 B4
Bramshaw Rd CT2 . . . . . . .66 E2
Bramshott Cl ME16 . . . . . .74 C6
Bramston Rd ME12 . . . . . . .4 C6
Bramwell Ct CT12 . . . . . . .50 D7
Branch Cl CT4 . . . . .107 C7
Branch St CT16 . . . . .149 C1
Brandon Rd CT12 . . . . . . .29 A1
Brandon Way CT7 . . . . . . .27 B6
Bransgore Cl ME8 . . . . . . .33 D7
Brasenose Rd ME7 . . . . . .10 E4
Brasier Ct ME12 . . . . .4 A5
Brassey Ave CT10 . . . . . . .29 F3
Brattle TN26 . . . . .181 B8
Braunstone Dr ME16 . . . . .74 D7
Bray Gdns ME15 . . . . .96 F5
Breach La ME9 . . . . .13 A2
Breadlands Cl TN24 . . . . .156 E8
Breadlands Rd TN24 . . . . .156 F8
Brecon Chase ME12 . . . . . .4 C7
Brecon Rise TN24 . . . . . . .139 B4
Brecon Sq CT12 . . . . .29 A1
Bredgar CE Prim Sch
 ME9 . . . . .58 A5
Bredgar Cl Ashford TN23 .155 F6
 Maidstone ME14 . . . . . . .75 C5
Bredgar Rd ME8 . . . . .11 B4
Bredhurst CE Prim Sch
 ME7 . . . . .33 B1
Bredhurst Cl ME12 . . . . . . .3 B7
Bredhurst Rd ME8 . . . . . . .33 C4
Bredlands La CT3,CT2 . . . .46 C1
Brenchley Ave CT14 . . . . .116 F4
Brenchley Cl
 Ashford TN23 . . . . .155 E6
 Chatham ME1 . . . . .9 D2
Brenchley Rd
 Gillingham ME8 . . . . .11 B2
 Maidstone ME15 . . . . . . .74 F2
 Sittingbourne ME10 . . . . .36 F2
Brendon Ave ME5 . . . . . . .32 A3

Brendon Dr TN24 ....139 B3
Brenley Cnr ME13 ....63 B4
Brenley La ME13 ....63 C2
Brent Cl ME5 ....31 E5
Brent Hill ME13 ....62 C8
Brent Rd ME13 ....62 C8
Brents Ind Est ME13 ....40 D1
Brentwood TN23 ....155 F5
Brenzett Aeronautical Mus TN29 ....192 B3
Brenzett CE Prim Sch TN29 ....192 A2
Brenzett Cl ME5 ....32 B5
Brenzett Cnr TN29 ....192 A3
Breton Rd ME1 ....9 C2
Brett Wlk ME8 ....33 D4
Brewer St Deal CT14 ....117 D6
 Maidstone ME14 ....75 A5
Brewer's Hill 177 D3
Brewery Cotts CT14 ....116 E4
Brewery La CT4 ....89 A1
Brewery Rd ME10 ....36 E6
Brewery Sq CT3 ....48 D2
Brewster Cotts ME9 ....59 E2
Brian Roberts Ho CT6 ....22 F5
Briar Cl Ashford TN24 ....139 C6
 Aylesham CT3 ....112 F5
 River CT17 ....148 F2
Briar Fields ME14 ....75 E5
Briars Rd TN29 ....194 F3
Briars The CT5 ....43 C6
Briars Wlk CT10 ....29 F3
Briary Cl CT9 ....28 A8
Briary Prim Sch CT6 ....22 C2
Brice Ave CT4 ....86 C1
Brices Alley CT5 ....20 D2
Brickfield Cotts TN25 ....123 B2
Brickfield La ME13 ....63 E2
Brickfield Rd CT4 ....128 F7
Brickmakers Ind Est ME10 ....37 B6
Brickwall Terr TN26 ....168 F3
Bridewell La TN30 ....179 A7
Bridewell Pk CT5 ....21 A1
Bridge & Patrixbourne CE Prim Sch CT4 ....89 A2
Bridge App The CT5 ....20 F1
Bridge Cl Hythe CT21 ....176 A2
 Woodchurch TN26 ....181 B8
Bridge Cotts Selling ME13 ....84 E7
 Teynham ME9 ....38 D2
Bridge Down CT4 ....111 B8
Bridge Hill Bridge CT4 ....111 B8
 Finglesham CT14 ....116 C8
Bridge Ho Chatham ME1 ....9 B4
 Ramsgate CT11 ....52 C7
Bridge Mill Way ME13 ....74 D2
Bridge Rd Ashford TN23 ....138 F2
 Brabourne Lees TN25 ....158 D5
 Bridge CT4 ....88 D1
 Deal CT14 ....117 D7
 Faversham ME13 ....62 D8
 Gillingham ME7 ....10 C7
 Margate CT9 ....7 E1
 Rochester ME1 ....9 C2
 Sheerness ME12 ....1 C3
Bridge St Dover CT16 ....149 C1
 Folkestone CT19 ....178 E6
 Loose ME15 ....96 F5
 Wye TN25 ....123 E2
Bridge View Ind Est ME11 ....3 A2
Bridgefield Rd CT1 ....21 B3
Bridgeford Way CT4 ....89 A1
Bridges Cl CT7 ....25 E2
Bridgeside CT14 ....117 C6
Bridgeway CT5 ....20 F2
Bridgewater Rd ME12 ....3 B8
Bridle Way Herne Bay CT6 ....22 D3
 Hythe CT21 ....177 A3
Bridleway Gdns CT10 ....29 E3
Bridleway La TN23 ....156 B4
Brielle Way Queenborough ME11,ME12 ....3 A6
 Sheerness ME12 ....1 B2
Brier Cl ME5 ....32 C8
Brier Rd ME10 ....36 B4
Bright Rd 3 ME4 ....10 B2
Bright's Pl CT11 ....52 F7
Brightlingsea Rd CT13 ....93 F8
Brindle Gr CT11 ....29 F1
Brindle Way ME5 ....32 C1
Brinklow Terr TN26 ....155 A1
Brisbane Ave ME10 ....36 C4
Brisbane Dr CT12 ....29 A1
Brisbane Rd ME4 ....10 A3
Brishing Cl ME15 ....97 E5
Brishing La ME17 ....97 D4
Brishing Rd ME15,ME17 ....97 F3
Brisley La TN26 ....171 D6
Brissenden Cl TN28 ....200 B8
Bristles Cnr CT3 ....46 E6
Bristol Pl CT11 ....52 D7
Bristol Rd CT1 ....87 F6
Britannia Ave CT5 ....43 B7
Britannia La TN23 ....155 F5
Britannia Rd CT14 ....117 D8
Briton Cl ME12 ....3 B8
Briton Rd ME13 ....62 C7
Britten Cl CT21 ....176 A3
Britton St ME7 ....10 B5
Broad La CT14 ....116 B7
Broad Oak Rd CT2 ....67 B3
Broad St Canterbury CT1 ....67 A1
 Deal CT14 ....117 D6
 Margate CT9 ....7 I3
 Ramsgate CT11 ....52 E7
 Sheerness ME12 ....1 C2

Broad Street Hill ME17 ....77 D7
Broadacre River,Lydden CT15 ....147 F8
 Teynham ME9 ....38 D2
Broader La ME14 ....55 B2
Broadfield Cres CT20 ....178 A5
Broadfield Rd Folkestone CT20 ....178 A5
 Maidstone ME15 ....97 A8
Broadhurst Dr TN24 ....139 D7
Broadlands CT2 ....67 F6
Broadlands Ave TN28 ....200 B8
Broadlands Cres TN28 ....200 B8
Broadlands Dr ME5 ....32 A8
Broadlands Ind Est CT2 ....66 A7
Broadley Ave CT7 ....26 F5
Broadley Rd CT10,CT9 ....29 C7
Broadmead TN23 ....155 E6
Broadmead Rd CT19 ....178 C5
Broadmeadow CT19 ....178 B3
Broadmere Terr ME16 ....74 D3
Broadoak Ave ME15 ....97 A8
Broadoak Ent Village ME9 ....58 F6
Broadoak Rd ME9 ....58 F6
Broadsole La CT15 ....164 E5
Broadstairs Rd CT10 ....29 E5
Broadstairs Sta CT10 ....30 A4
Broadview CT21 ....177 C6
Broadview Ave ME8 ....33 E8
Broadviews CT21 ....176 D1
Broadway Gillingham ME8 ....11 A3
 Maidstone ME14 ....74 F4
 Petham CT4 ....109 A2
 Sheerness ME12 ....1 D2
Broadway The Broadstairs CT10 ....30 A4
 Herne Bay CT6 ....22 C5
 Minster (Sheppey) ME12 ....4 B7
Brockbank Cl ME5 ....32 A1
Brockenhurst Ave ME15 ....75 C1
Brockenhurst Cl Canterbury CT2 ....66 E2
 Gillingham ME8 ....33 C7
Brockenhurst Rd CT11 ....52 G8
Brockhill Ctry Pk CT21 ....175 F4
Brockhill Park Sch CT21 ....175 F4
Brockhill Rd CT21 ....176 B3
Brockley Rd CT19 ....8 A2
Brockman Cres TN29 ....187 B4
Brockman Rd CT20 ....178 C5
Brockman's Cl CT12 ....50 B7
Brogdale Farm Cotts ME13 ....62 A3
Brogdale Rd ME13 ....62 B5
Brogdale World of Fruit* ME13 ....62 B4
Brogden Cres ME17 ....98 F7
Bromley Cl Chatham ME5 ....32 B4
 Newington ME9 ....35 A5
Bromley Green Rd TN26 ....171 A5
Brompton Hill ME4 ....9 F6
Brompton La ME2 ....9 A8
Brompton Rd ME7 ....10 B6
Brompton Villas CT15 ....149 E6
Brompton-Westbrook Prim Sch ME7 ....10 A5
Bromstone Mews CT10 ....29 E3
Bromstone Prim Sch CT10 ....29 D3
Bromstone Rd CT10 ....29 E3
Bronington Cl ME5 ....32 A5
Brook Cl Herne Bay CT6 ....22 C3
 Hythe CT21 ....177 B3
Brook Cotts Dean Street ME15 ....96 C7
 Teynham ME9 ....39 A4
Brook Cty Prim Sch TN25 ....141 A4
Brook La Cliffs End CT12 ....50 F4
 Reculver CT6 ....24 B5
 Sellindge TN25 ....159 E2
Brook La Cotts TN25 ....159 E2
Brook Rd Faversham ME13 ....40 D1
 Whitstable CT5 ....21 C3
Brook St Eastry CT13 ....93 C2
 Woodchurch TN26 ....180 D8
Brook The ME4 ....10 A4
Brookbank Brook TN25 ....141 A5
 Maidstone ME14 ....75 A8
Brooke Ave CT9 ....28 B7
Brooke Rd TN24 ....139 B3
Brookes Pl ME9 ....35 B6
Brookfield Ave CT16 ....149 B2
Brookfield Cl TN23 ....155 F8
Brookfield Ind Pk TN23 ....138 F1
Brookfield Pl CT16 ....149 B2
Brookfield Rd Ashford TN23 ....155 F8
 Dover CT16 ....149 A3
Brookland CE Prim Sch TN29 ....197 D8
Brooklands Cl CT2 ....67 F4
Brooklyn Paddock ME7 ....10 D6
Brooks Pl ME14 ....75 A4
Brooks Way TN29 ....203 C5
Brookside St Mary's Bay TN29 ....195 A5
 Temple Ewell CT16 ....148 D5
Broom Rd ME10 ....37 D5
Broomcroft Rd ME8 ....11 F2
Broomfield Cres CT9 ....8 F2
Broomfield Gate CT5 ....44 D5
Broomfield Rd Faversham ME13 ....62 C8
 Folkestone CT19 ....177 E6

Broomfield Rd continued
 Herne Bay CT6 ....23 C2
 Kingswood ME17 ....99 D4
Brotherhood Cl CT2 ....66 D4
Broughton Ct TN23 ....138 E1
Brown St ME8 ....11 F1
Brownelow Copse ME5 ....32 B1
Brownhill Cl ME7 ....32 A4
Browning Pl CT19 ....178 E7
Brownings Orch ME9 ....59 A7
Broxhall Rd CT4 ....110 B3
Bruce Cl CT14 ....117 B4
Bruges Cl CT14 ....14 F1
Brundell Terr CT4 ....86 B2
Brunel Way ME4 ....10 A7
Brunswick Cotts ME9 ....38 E6
Brunswick Ct 3 CT11 ....52 E7
Brunswick Field ME9 ....38 E6
Brunswick Gdns 3 CT16 ....149 B3
Brunswick House Prim Sch ME16 ....74 E5
Brunswick Ind Ctr TN23 ....138 F2
Brunswick Rd Ashford TN23 ....138 F2
 Birchington CT7 ....27 A5
Brunswick Sq CT6 ....22 C7
Brunswick St Maidstone ME15 ....75 A3
 Ramsgate CT11 ....52 E7
Brunswick St E ME15 ....75 A3
Bryant Rd ME2 ....9 A7
Bryant St ME4 ....10 A3
Brymore Cl CT1 ....67 B2
Brymore Rd CT1 ....67 B2
Bryony Sch ME8 ....33 F5
Buck St TN25 ....105 C2
Buckhurst Dr CT9 ....8 F7
Buckingham Rd 14 Broadstairs CT10 ....30 B4
 Gillingham ME7 ....10 D5
 Margate CT9 ....7 I1
 Whitstable CT5 ....21 B2
Buckingham Row ME15 ....97 E7
Buckland Ave CT16 ....149 B2
Buckland Cl ME5 ....32 A2
Buckland Cotts ME13 ....61 B8
Buckland Hill ME16 ....74 E5
Buckland Hospl CT17 ....149 A1
Buckland La Maidstone ME16 ....74 D6
 Staple CT3 ....92 A4
Buckland Pl ME16 ....74 E4
Buckland Rd ME16 ....74 E4
Bucklers Cl CT14 ....6 E4
Bucksford La TN23 ....155 C7
Buckthorn Cl CT14 ....117 C2
Buckthorne Rd ME12 ....4 A4
Budd's Farm Cotts TN30 ....188 E2
Budd's La TN30 ....188 F2
Buddle Dr ME12 ....3 E7
Buenos Ayres CT9 ....7 H2
Buffs Ave CT20 ....177 B6
Builders Sq CT3 ....90 A8
Bull Hill ME17 ....102 A1
Bull La Bethersden TN26 ....153 B4
 Boughton Street ME13 ....63 F4
 Eccles ME20 ....53 A6
 Stockbury ME9 ....34 E2
Bulldog Rd ME5 ....32 B2
Bulleid Pl TN24 ....156 D7
Buller Rd ME4 ....9 F2
Buller's Ave CT6 ....22 E4
Bullockstone Rd CT6 ....45 E7
Bulls Cotts 4 CT21 ....176 B2
Bulltown Cnr TN25 ....141 F3
Bullwark St CT17 ....166 D5
Bulrush Cl ME5 ....31 F3
Bulrushes The TN23 ....155 D8
Bulwark Rd CT14 ....117 D7
Bumbles Cl ME1 ....31 D7
Bunce Court Rd ME13,ME17 ....102 E7
Bungalow The TN26 ....137 F5
Bungalows The Faversham ME13 ....62 A4
 Tenterden TN30 ....179 D6
 Woodnesborough CT13 ....93 B5
Bunker's Hill CT17 ....149 B2
Bunkers Hill Ave CT17 ....149 A1
Bunkers Hill Rd CT17 ....149 A1
Bunkley Mdw ME20 ....183 A4
Burberry La ME17 ....99 B5
Burch Ave CT13 ....93 F8
Burdock Ho 6 ME15 ....97 D8
Burford's Alley CT3 ....71 D1
Burgate CT1 ....88 A8
Burgate La 4 CT1 ....88 A8
Burgate Terr TN25 ....157 E4
Burgess Cl Minster (Thanet) CT12 ....50 C7
 Whitfield CT16 ....149 B7
Burgess Gn CT14 ....116 C8
Burgess Hall Dr ME17 ....98 F6
Burgess Rd Aylesham CT3 ....112 F6
 Rochester ME2 ....9 B7
Burgess Row 10 TN30 ....179 A7
Burghclere Dr ME16 ....74 B2
Burgoyne Ct ME14 ....74 F7
Burgoyne Gr CT16 ....149 A5
Burgoyne Hts CT15 ....149 E3
Burial Ground La ME15 ....74 E1
Burkeston Cl ME10 ....37 A8
Burleigh Dr ME14 ....53 F1
Burleigh Rd TN27 ....120 C7
Burley Rd ME10 ....36 E4
Burlington Dr CT6 ....23 D5

Burlington Gdns Gillingham ME8 ....33 E4
 Margate CT9 ....28 C8
Burma Cres CT1 ....67 D1
Burma Way ME5 ....31 F6
Burmarsh Cl ME5 ....32 B5
Burmarsh Rd Burmarsh TN29 ....186 C3
 Hythe CT21 ....187 C8
Burn's Rd ME7 ....10 C7
Burnan Rd CT5 ....21 C2
Burnham Cl ME10 ....36 E8
Burnham Wlk ME8 ....33 E3
Burns Rd ME16 ....74 C2
Burnt House Hill CT3 ....69 B5
Burnt Oak Terr ME7 ....10 D6
Burnt Oast Rd ME13 ....64 A3
Burntwick Dr ME9 ....13 B3
Burnup Bank ME10 ....37 C5
Burritt Mews ME1 ....9 C3
Burrow Rd CT19 ....178 F6
Burrs The ME10 ....36 F3
Burrstock Way ME8 ....12 B2
Bursill Cres CT12 ....29 B1
Bursted Hill CT4 ....110 B2
Burston Rd ME17 ....96 B2
Burton Cl CT19 ....178 A7
Burton Fields CT6 ....23 B4
Burton Rd TN24 ....139 E6
Busbridge Rd ME15 ....96 E6
Bush Ave CT12 ....29 B1
Bush Cl ME9 ....57 F5
Bush Row ME20 ....53 A3
Bushey Cl ME13 ....63 F3
Busheyfields Rd CT6 ....45 F6
Bushmeadow Rd ME8 ....11 F2
Bushy Gr ME17 ....99 D2
Bushy Hill Rd CT2 ....68 D7
Bushy Royds TN24 ....156 D6
Bushy Ruff Cotts CT16 ....148 D4
Butchers La CT15 ....113 E5
Butchery La 1 CT1 ....88 A8
Butchery The 2 CT13 ....73 A1
Butler's Hill ME13 ....64 D7
Butt Field Rd TN23 ....155 E2
Butter St CT15 ....113 C4
Buttermere ME15 ....62 E6
Buttermere Cl Folkestone CT19 ....178 B6
 Gillingham ME7 ....11 B3
Buttermere Gdns CT3 ....112 F6
Butterside Rd TN23 ....156 C4
Button La ME15 ....76 B2
Butts Ct CT4 ....110 A6
Butts Hill ME13 ....63 F5
Butts Meadow CT4 ....110 A6
Butts The Sandwich CT13 ....72 F1
 Sittingbourne ME10 ....36 F4
Buxton Cl Chatham ME5 ....32 D1
 Maidstone ME15 ....97 A8
Buxton Rd CT12 ....29 B2
Bybrook Ct TN24 ....139 C4
Bybrook Cty Inf Sch TN24 ....139 D5
Bybrook Cty Jun Sch TN24 ....139 D5
Bybrook Field CT20 ....177 E3
Bybrook Rd TN24 ....139 C5
Bybrook Way CT20 ....177 E4
Bychurch Pl 6 ME15 ....75 A3
Byllan Rd CT17 ....148 E3
Byng Rd TN24 ....139 E6
Byron Ave CT9 ....7 J1
Byron Cl CT1 ....88 C7
Byron Cres CT16 ....149 B4
Byron Prim Sch ME7 ....10 C3
Byron Rd Gillingham ME7 ....10 C3
 Maidstone ME14 ....75 B2
Bysing Wood Cotts ME13 ....39 F1
Bysing Wood Prim Sch ME13 ....62 A8
Bysing Wood Rd ME13 ....39 F1
Bythorne Ct ME8 ....12 B1

C

C Ramp App CT16 ....166 G8
Cabin The TN24 ....139 D7
Cade Rd TN23 ....156 B7
Cades Orch ME13 ....61 E3
Cadnam Cl CT7 ....26 E3
Caernarvon Dr ME15 ....74 F1
Caernarvon Gdns CT10 ....30 B5
Caesar Ave ME2 ....9 A7
Caesar's Way CT19 ....177 D3
Calais Hill CT2 ....66 E6
Calcraft Mews 6 CT1 ....67 B2
Calcutta House 3 ME15 ....97 E5
Caldecot La ME14 ....74 E7
Caldecote Cl 12 B1
Caldecott Coll TN25 ....158 B4
Calder Rd ME14 ....74 E7
Caldew Ave ME8 ....11 C1
Caldew Gr ME10 ....37 A3
Caledon Terr CT1 ....88 A7
Caledonian Ct ME8 ....33 E8
Calehill Cl ME14 ....75 C6
Calgary Cres CT19 ....178 E8
California Row CT3 ....90 E6
Callams Cl ME8 ....33 D6
Calland TN25 ....158 E5
Callaways La ME9 ....35 B6
Calleywell La TN25 ....173 A7
Callis Court Rd CT10 ....29 F6
Callis Grange Inf Sch CT10 ....29 F7
Callis Way ME8 ....33 D5
Calverden Rd CT12 ....29 A1

Camborne Manor 2 ME7 ....10 C6
Cambourne Ave CT8 ....27 D8
Cambrai Ct CT1 ....67 D1
Cambridge Ave CT13 ....95 B7
Cambridge Cl CT7 ....27 B7
Cambridge Cres ME15 ....97 D7
Cambridge Gdns CT20 ....178 D5
Cambridge Ho 3 ME15 ....97 D7
Cambridge La ME9 ....60 C8
Cambridge Rd Canterbury CT1 ....87 F6
 Deal CT14 ....117 D7
 Dover CT17 ....166 D7
 Faversham ME13 ....62 B6
 Gillingham ME8 ....33 C6
 Rochester ME1 ....9 A8
 Sittingbourne ME10 ....37 B3
Cambridge Terr 1 Chatham ME4 ....9 F4
 11 Dover CT16,CT17 ....166 E7
 11 Folkestone CT20 ....178 E5
 Margate CT9 ....8 B1
Cambridge Way CT1 ....87 F6
Camden Cl ME5 ....32 B5
Camden Cres CT16 ....166 E7
Camden Rd Broadstairs CT10 ....29 E7
 Gillingham ME7 ....10 D7
 Ramsgate CT11 ....52 E6
Camden Sq 7 CT11 ....52 E7
Camden St ME14 ....75 A5
Camden Terr TN24 ....139 E1
Camellia Cl Gillingham ME8 ....33 D7
 2 Margate CT9 ....28 B8
Cameron Cl ME5 ....32 B8
Cameron Ct CT17 ....166 A6
Camomile Dr ME14 ....75 F5
Camp Way ME15 ....97 C6
Campbell Cl CT6 ....23 C3
Campbell Rd Deal CT14 ....117 D4
 Maidstone ME15 ....75 A3
Camperdown Manor 5 ME7 ....10 A6
Campion Cl ME5 ....31 E3
Campleshon Rd ME8 ....33 D5
Campus Way ME8 ....33 A8
Canada Cl CT17 ....177 C6
Canada Mews CT14 ....117 C3
Canada Rd CT14 ....117 D3
Canada Terr 3 ME14 ....75 A7
Canadian Ave ME7 ....10 F4
Canal Rd ME2 ....9 C7
Canberra Gdns ME10 ....36 C4
Canning St ME14 ....75 A6
Cannon Appleton Ct CT1 ....87 E7
Cannon Rd CT11 ....52 D7
Cannon St Deal CT14 ....117 C7
 Dover CT16 ....166 D8
 Lydd TN29 ....203 C6
 New Romney TN28 ....200 B7
Cannonbury Rd CT11 ....52 D6
Cannongate Ave CT21 ....176 D3
Cannongate Cl CT21 ....176 E2
Cannongate Gdns CT21 ....176 E3
Cannongate Rd CT21 ....176 D3
Canon Cl ME1 ....9 B2
Canon Gn CT3 ....91 A7
Canon Woods Way TN24 ....139 C6
Canons Gate Rd CT16 ....166 E8
Canterbury Cathedral* CT1 ....88 A8
Canterbury Centre The (Mus)* CT1 ....66 F1
Canterbury Christ Church Coll Post Graduate Ctr CT3 ....67 F1
Canterbury Christ Church Univ Coll CT10 ....29 C4
Canterbury Cl Broadstairs CT10 ....29 D5
 2 Folkestone CT10 ....178 E6
Canterbury Coll CT1 ....88 A7
Canterbury Ct TN24 ....139 D2
Canterbury East Sta CT1 ....87 F7
Canterbury Heritage Ctr & Mus* CT1 ....87 F8
Canterbury High Sch The CT2 ....87 D8
Canterbury Hill CT2 ....66 E5
Canterbury Ho 2 CT17 ....97 D7
Canterbury Ind Pk CT3 ....69 C8
Canterbury La Canterbury CT1 ....88 A8
 Gillingham ME8,ME9 ....12 C1
Canterbury Rd Ashford, Bybrook TN24 ....139 E5
 Ashford, South Willesborough TN24 ....156 E6
 Barham CT4 ....129 C5
 Boughton Aluph TN25 ....123 C5
 Boughton Street ME13 ....63 D4
 Brabourne TN25 ....159 C8
 Brabourne Lees TN25 ....158 F6
 Challock TN25,TN27 ....104 C1
 Chilham CT4 ....85 E1
 Denton CT4 ....129 A1
 Dunkirk ME13 ....64 D2
 Elham CT4 ....144 E3
 Etchinghill CT18 ....161 D4
 Faversham ME13 ....62 E5
 Folkestone CT19 ....178 D7
 Folkestone, Foord CT19 ....178 E6

Canterbury Rd continued
Hawkinge CT18,CT19,CT15, CT4 ....163 B4
Herne CT3,CT6 ....45 E5
Herne Bay CT6 ....23 A3
Littlebourne CT3 ....89 C8
Lyminge CT18 ....161 C7
River,Lydden CT15 ......147 E7
Sarre CT7 ....48 E7
Sittingbourne ME10 ......37 B3
Whitstable CT5 ....43 D8
Wingham CT3 ....91 A7
Canterbury Rd E CT11, CT12 ....52 A6
Canterbury Rd W CT12 .51 D7
Canterbury Road Birchington CT7 ......27 B7
Canterbury Road Cty Prim Sch ME10 .....37 B3
Canterbury Road Margate CT9 ....7 G1
Canterbury Road Westgate CT8,CT9 ......27 E8
Canterbury St ME7 ....10 C4
Canterbury Tale Mus The★ CT1 ....87 F8
Canterbury West Sta CT1 66 F1
Canute Rd Birchington CT7 26 D7
Deal CT14 ....95 C1
Faversham ME13 ....62 C6
Capel Cl Broadstairs CT10 .8 F1
Gillingham ME8 ....33 D4
Capel Rd Faversham ME13 .62 B7
Petham CT4 ....108 F3
Ruckinge TN26 ....171 B4
Sittingbourne ME10 ......36 E2
Capel St CT18 ....164 B3
Capel-le-Ferne Prim Sch CT18 ....164 C3
Capell Cl ME17 ....96 C3
Capetown House 1 ME15 ....97 F5
Capstan Row CT14 .....117 D7
Capstone Farm Ctry Pk★ ME7 ....32 D5
Capstone Rd Chatham ME5 ....10 D1
Gillingham ME7 ....32 F6
Cardinal Cl ME12 ....4 D7
Cardine Cl ME10 ....36 E7
Carey Cl TN28 ....200 B6
Carey Ho 5 CT1 ....87 F7
Caring La ME14,ME17 ....76 E1
Caring Rd ME15,ME17 ...76 C1
Carisbrooke Dr ME16 ....74 D4
Carlsden Cl CT17 ......149 A3
Carlton Ave
Broadstairs CT10 ....30 A5
Gillingham ME7 ....10 E4
Ramsgate CT11 ....52 D6
Sheerness ME12 ....1 C1
Carlton Cres 32 D8
Carlton Gdns ME15 .....97 B8
Carlton Hill CT6 ....22 C4
Carlton Leas CT20 .....178 C4
Carlton Mansions CT10 ..8 A3
Carlton Rd Ashford TN23 139 A2
Kingsdown CT14 ....134 C6
Whitstable CT5 ....43 D2
Carlton Rd E CT8 ....27 D8
Carlton Rd W CT8 ....27 D8
Carlton Rise CT8 ....27 C8
Carman's Cl ME15,ME17 ..96 F3
Carmel Ct 2 CT7 ....26 F8
Carnoustie Cl CT5 ......44 E8
Caroland Cl TN25 ....158 D5
Caroline Cl CT5 ....43 B6
Caroline Cres
Broadstairs CT10 ....29 E6
Maidstone ME16 ....74 D7
Caroline Sq CT9 ....7 J3
Carpeaux Cl ME4 ....10 A4
Carpenters Cl ME1 ......9 E2
Carpinus Cl ME5 ....32 B1
Carriage Ho The ME13 ..83 D5
Carriage Mews CT2 .....66 F1
Carrie House ME14 .....74 E5
Carrington Cl ME7 ......10 F6
Carroway's Pl CT9 ....7 J2
Carter La TN29 ....191 E2
Carter's Rd CT20 ......177 F5
Carter's Wood TN26 ...183 B7
Carton Cl ME1 ....9 D2
Cartwright & Kelsey CE Prim Sch The CT3 .71 C2
Cartwright Cl CT3 ....71 C2
Carvoran Way ME8 ......33 C5
Caslocke St 2 ME13 ....62 C7
Cassino Ho 16 CT1 ......67 B2
Cassino Sq CT15 ....149 E2
Castalla Cotts CT14 ...117 D3
Castle Ave
Broadstairs CT10 ....30 B6
Dover CT16 ....149 D1
Hythe CT21 ....176 B3
Rochester ME1 ....9 C4
Castle Bay CT20 ....177 D3
Castle Cl
4 Folkestone CT20 ....177 F3
Lympne CT21 ....174 F2
Castle Com Sch CT14 ...117 C4
Castle Cotts CT13 ......72 E5
Castle Cres CT21 ......176 C4
Castle Dene ME14 ......74 F8
Castle Dr CT16 ....148 F7

Castle Glen 9 CT20 ....177 F3
Castle Hill
Folkestone CT19,CT18 ...178 A8
Rochester ME1 ....9 C6
Thurnham ME14 ....55 D1
Castle Hill Ave CT20 ...178 C4
Castle Hill Cl ME1 ......9 C6
Castle Hill Rd CT18 ....166 E8
Castle Mayne Ave CT7 ..27 F3
Castle Mews CT14 .....117 A4
Castle Rd Chatham ME4 .10 B2
Folkestone CT20 ....177 F3
Hythe CT21 ....176 B4
Maidstone ME16 ....74 D7
Sittingbourne ME10 ......37 B5
Whitstable CT5 ....20 F2
Castle Road Bsns Prec ME10 ....37 B6
Castle Road Tech Ctr ME10 ....37 B6
Castle Rough La ME10 ..14 F1
Castle Row CT1 ....87 F7
Castle St
6 Ashford TN23 ......139 B2
Canterbury CT1 ....87 F8
Dover CT16 ....166 E8
Queenborough ME11 .....3 A5
Castle View Bsns Ctr ME1 .9 C6
Castle View Mews ME1 ..9 C6
Castle View Rd ME2 .....9 A7
Castle Wlk CT14 ....95 D1
Castleacres Ind Pk ME10 37 B6
Castlemaine Ave ME7 ...10 F6
Castlemere Ave ME11 ...3 B5
Castlemount Ct CT16 ...166 E8
Castlemount Rd CT16 ..149 D1
Castleview Ct CT17 ....149 B1
Cathedral View CT2 .....67 A2
Catherine Cl ME16 ......74 A3
Catherine St ME1 ....9 D3
Catherine Way CT10 ....30 A6
Catkin Cl ME5 ....31 F1
Catsole Hill CT3 ....91 D2
Catt's Hill TN30 ....189 E3
Catt's Wood Rd CT4 ....109 F4
Catterick Rd ME5 ....32 D2
Cattle Market CT13 .....72 F1
Cauldham Cl CT18 ......164 B1
Cauldham La CT18 ......164 B3
Causeway The
Canterbury CT1 ....66 F1
Sandwich CT13 ....72 D2
Cavalry Ct CT20 ....177 D5
Cave Hill ME15 ....74 F1
Cave La CT3 ....91 D3
Cavell Sq CT14 ....117 A3
Cavell Way CT10 ....36 D5
Cavenagh Rd CT15 .....151 B6
Cavendish Ave ME7 .....10 E6
Cavendish Ct CT6 ....23 A5
Cavendish Pl 2 CT11 ...52 E6
Cavendish Rd
Herne Bay CT6 ....23 A5
Rochester ME1 ....9 D3
Cavendish St CT11 ......52 E6
Cavendish Way ME15 ...76 B3
Caversham Cl ME8 ......11 F1
Cavour Rd
Faversham ME13 ....62 C7
Sheerness ME12 ....1 D2
Caxton Rd CT9 ....28 C8
Cayser Dr ME17 ....99 E2
Cazeneuve St ME1 ......9 C5
Cecil Ave Gillingham ME8 .11 A2
Rochester ME2 ....9 B8
Sheerness ME12 ....1 C1
Cecil Ct Ashford TN24 ..139 B3
Herne Bay CT6 ....23 A4
Cecil Pk CT6 ....23 A4
Cecil Rd Kingsdown CT14 134 D7
Rochester ME1 ....9 C3
Cecil Sq CT9 ....7 I2
Cecil St CT9 ....7 I2
Cecilia Gr CT10 ....29 F6
Cecilia Rd CT11 ....52 E8
Cedar Cl Ashford TN23 ..138 E3
Birchington CT8 ....27 B7
Broadstairs CT10 ....29 F7
Margate CT9 ....8 B1
Sittingbourne ME10 ......37 B2
Cedar Cres TN29 ......194 F3
Cedar Ct Folkestone CT20 177 E5
Maidstone ME14 ....75 B5
12 Tenterden TN30 .....179 A7
Cedar Gdns ME9 ....56 E8
Cedar Gr ME7 ....33 A5
Cedar Ho ME12 ....1 C2
Cedar Rd CT2 ....68 A6
Cedar Terr ME13 ....62 A4
Cedars Sch The
Maidstone ME16 ....74 D4
Rochester ME1 ....9 C4
Cedars The ME10 ....37 C5
Cedarview CT2 ....66 C1
Cedarwood House ME15 .96 B6
Cedric Rd CT8 ....7 C1
Ceil Villas CT14 ....94 B4
Celestine Cl ME5 ....32 A1
Cellar Hill ME9 ....60 C8
Celt Cl ME10 ....36 F8
Celtic Rd CT14 ....117 A2
Cemetery La TN24 .....139 C4
Centenary Cl TN27 ....120 C8
Centenary Gdns CT13 ..93 A2
Central Ave
Gillingham ME4 ....10 B8
Herne Bay CT6 ....22 D4
Sittingbourne ME10 ......36 E4

Central Bsns Pk ME2 ....9 E7
Central Par Herne Bay CT6 22 E5
Rochester ME1 ....9 D2
Central Park Gdns ME4 ..9 E2
Central Rd Ramsgate CT11 52 D8
Rochester ME2 ....9 A7
Central Service Rd CT16 ....166 H8
Central Sta CT19 ......178 C5
Centre 2000
Maidstone ME16 ....74 C8
Sittingbourne ME10 ......37 A4
Centre Ct ME2 ....9 E7
Centre Rd CT17 ....166 C6
Centre The Margate CT9 ..7 I2
Ramsgate CT11 ....29 A1
Centurion Cl ME8 ....10 F1
Centurion Wlk TN23 ...156 B4
Century Rd
Faversham ME13 ....62 E7
Gillingham ME8 ....33 D8
Century Wlk CT14 ......117 C6
Ceres Cl ME10 ....37 C5
Chada Ave ME7 ....10 E3
Chaffe's La ME9 ....12 E3
Chaffes Terr ME9 ....12 E3
Chaffinch Cl ME5 ....32 A7
Chaffinch Dr TN23 .....156 C3
Chaffinch Lodge 5 CT16 ....149 B2
Chafy Cres CT2 ....67 F5
Chain Gate ME17 ......118 A8
Chain The 6 CT13 ......73 A1
Chalcroft Rd CT20 .....177 E4
Chalfont Dr ME8 ....33 D6
Chalford Dr CT6 ....23 D2
Chalk Ave TN30 ....167 B2
Chalk Cl CT19 ....178 A7
Chalk Hill CT11,CT12 ....51 F6
Chalk Hill Rd CT14 .....134 C5
Chalk Pit Hill ME4 ......10 A3
Chalk Pit La CT13,CT3 ...92 C5
Chalk Rd ME11 ....3 A5
Chalkenden Ave ME8 ....11 A2
Chalkpit Hill CT4 ....89 D3
Chalksole Green La CT15 ....147 B2
Chalkwell Ct CT17 .....166 A7
Chalkwell Rd ME10 .....36 D5
Chalky Rd ME9 ....56 C6
Challenger Cl ME10 .....36 E7
Challock Ct CT9 ....8 F2
Challock Prim Sch TN25 ....105 B1
Challock Wlk ME14 .....75 C6
Chamberlain Ave ME16 ..74 C2
Chamberlain Ct ME8 ....33 B5
Chamberlain Dr CT6 ....22 B4
Chamberlain Rd
Chatham ME4 ....10 B2
Dover CT17 ....166 B8
Chance Mdw CT15 .....149 E6
Chancel Ct CT2 ....66 D1
Chancery La ME15 ......75 B3
Chanctonbury Chase CT5 ....43 A6
Chandlers Wharf ME1 ...9 B5
Chandos Rd 16 CT10 ...30 B4
Chandos Sq 15 CT10 ...30 B4
Channel Cl CT19 ....178 F7
Channel Lea CT14 ......117 C1
Channel Rd CT9 ....29 A6
Channel Sch The CT19 .178 C1
Channel Tunnel Terminal CT18 ....177 B8
Channel View 18 CT19 .178 E5
Channel View St 16 CT11 .52 F7
Channel View Rd CT17 .166 C5
Channel Watch TN28 ...200 E4
Channon Rd TN28 .....204 E7
Chantry Ct 8 CT1 ....66 F1
Chantry Pk CT7 ....48 D7
Chapel Cl CT18 ....161 D3
Chapel Cotts ME17 .....98 F5
Chapel Hill
Eythorne CT15 ....131 C7
Margate CT9 ....29 A6
Chapel Hill Cl CT9 ......28 C7
Chapel La Blean CT2 ....66 A7
Broad Oak CT2 ....67 D7
18 Dover CT16 ....166 D7
East Studdal CT15 ......132 C6
Gillingham,Hempstead ME7 .33 A4
Gillingham,Lidsing ME7 ...33 A2
Maidstone ME14 ....76 A5
Newchurch TN29 ....185 C4
Potter's Forstal TN27 ...118 B2
Rhodes Minnis CT4 ....144 B4
Ripple CT14 ....133 D8
St Margaret's at Cliffe CT15 ....150 F6
Staple CT3 ....92 B6
Sturry CT2 ....67 F5
Chapel Mews TN23 ....139 C2
Chapel Pl 16 Dover CT17 166 D7
Ramsgate CT11 ....52 D7
Chapel Place La CT11 ...52 D7
Chapel Rd
Dymchurch TN29 ....195 C7
Ram Lane TN26 ....120 F1
Ramsgate CT11 ....52 C7
Tilmanstone CT14 ......115 A3
Whitfield CT16 ....149 A8
Chapel Row Herne CT6 ..46 A8
Kingsnorth TN23 ....156 A3
Ram Lane TN26 ....120 F2
Chapel St Deal CT14 ...117 D6
Faversham ME13 ....62 D6

Chapel St continued
Herne Bay CT6 ....23 A5
Hythe CT21 ....176 B2
Minster (Sheppey) ME12 ..4 D6
Sheerness ME12 ....1 B2
Chapman Ave ME15 .....97 E8
Chapman Ho CT14 .....117 B3
Chapmans Cl TN25 ....105 C2
Chapmans Hill CT15,CT3 113 B5
Chappell Way ME10 .....36 E6
Charing CE Prim Sch TN27 ....120 C8
Charing Cl CT12 ....52 C8
Charing Cres CT8 ....27 D7
Charing Heath Rd
Charing TN27 ....120 A6
Charing Heath TN27 ...119 E3
Charing Hill TN27 ......103 E1
Charing Rd ME8 ....11 B3
Charing Sta TN27 ......120 B7
Charlbury Cl ME16 ......74 C3
Charlecote Ct ME8 ......33 D8
Charles Cobb Cl TN29 .195 D8
Charles Cres CT19 .....177 C2
Charles Ct CT8 ....27 E8
Charles Dickens Ctr (Mus)★ ME1 ....9 C5
Charles Dickens Sch The CT10 ....29 E4
Charles Drayson Ct ME13 62 E7
Charles Ho CT14 ....117 B3
Charles Lister Ct CT17 .149 B1
Charles Rd Deal CT14 ..117 B4
Ramsgate CT11 ....52 E8
Charles St Chatham ME4 ..9 E3
Herne Bay CT6 ....23 A5
Maidstone ME16 ....74 C3
Rochester ME2 ....9 A7
Sheerness ME12 ....1 B1
Charlesford Ave ME17 ..99 D3
Charleston Ct CT10 .....30 B3
Charlesworth Dr CT7 ...27 B7
Charlock Cl ME10 ....74 D8
Charlotte Cl ME5 ....32 B6
Charlotte Ct CT11 ......52 E6
Charlotte Dr ME8 ....11 C1
Charlotte Pl 2 CT9 .....7 J1
Charlotte Sq 8 CT9 ....7 J2
Charlotte St
13 Broadstairs CT10 ...30 B4
Folkestone CT20 ....178 E5
Sittingbourne ME10 ......36 E5
Charlton Ave CT16 .....149 C1
Charlton CE Prim Sch CT16 ....149 C1
Charlton Cl
Ashford TN24 ....157 A8
Ramsgate CT11 ....29 B2
Charlton Ctr 3 CT17 ...166 C8
Charlton Gn CT16 ......149 C1
Charlton La ME17 ....99 C1
Charlton Manor ME7 ...10 B5
Charlton St ME16 ....74 C2
Charltons The ME13 ....63 F4
Charminster TN23 .....155 E6
Charnock CT5 ....21 D1
Charnwood Rd CT6 .....23 B1
Charollais Cl CT2 ....67 A2
Chart Cl ME13 ....62 B7
Chart Cnr ME7 ....98 B1
Chart Gunpowder Mills★ ME13 ....62 B7
Chart Hill Rd ME17 .....98 B1
Chart Pl ME8 ....33 C3
Chart Rd
Ashford, Godinton Park TN23 ....138 F2
Ashford,Great Chart TN23 138 D1
Ashford,Singleton TN23 ..155 D6
Folkestone CT19 ....177 F2
Chart Road Ind Est TN23 ....139 A3
Charter Ho 9 CT16 ....166 F7
Charter St Chatham ME4 .9 F2
Gillingham ME7 ....10 C7
Chartham Downs Rd CT4 ....109 C2
Chartham Prim Sch CT4 .86 C1
Chartham Sta CT4 ......86 D3
Chartway St ME17 ......99 C1
Chartwell Ave CT6 .....23 D4
Chartwell Ct
Maidstone ME15 ....75 B3
Rochester ME4 ....9 E4
Chartwell Gr ME10 .....36 C3
Chase The Chatham ME4 ..9 D2
Gillingham ME8 ....11 A2
Ramsgate CT11 ....29 F1
St Margaret's at Cliffe CT15 ....133 F1
Chater Cl CT14 ....117 C4
Chatham Ct CT11 ......52 D8
Chatham Gr ME4 ....9 F1
Chatham Gram Sch for Boys ME4 ....31 F8
Chatham Gram Sch for Girls ME5 ....10 C2
Chatham Hill ME4 ....10 B3
Chatham House Boys Gram Sch CT11 ..52 E7
Chatham Pl CT11 ....52 E7
Chatham Rd
Kit's Coty ME20 ....53 D6
Maidstone ME14 ....53 E1
Maidstone,Sandling ME14 .53 E4
Chatham Ski Ctr ME7 ...32 E6
Chatham South Sch ME4 31 F8
Chatham St CT11 ....52 E7

Chatham Sta ME4 ....9 E4
Chatsworth Dr ME10 ....36 B5
Chatsworth Mews CT11 .52 C6
Chatsworth Rd 10 ME7 .10 C6
Chattenden Ct ME14 ....75 B6
Chatwell Ct ME7 ....10 C5
Chaucer Ave CT5 ....21 B1
Chaucer Cl
Canterbury CT1 ....88 C7
13 Maidstone ME15 ...97 E7
Rochester ME2 ....9 E7
Chaucer Coll CT2 ....66 D3
Chaucer Cres CT16 ....149 B3
Chaucer Ct CT1 ....88 B7
Chaucer Hospl CT4 .....88 A4
Chaucer Mews CT2 .....65 E1
Chaucer Rd
Broadstairs CT10 ....30 A3
Canterbury CT1 ....67 C5
Elvington CT15 ....114 B2
Gillingham ME7 ....10 D3
Sittingbourne ME10 ......36 D3
Chaucer Tech Coll CT1 ..88 C7
Cheddar Cl TN24 ......139 B4
Cheesmans Cl CT12 ....50 C5
Cheffins Ho ME7 ....10 C7
Chegwell Dr ME5 ....32 B4
Chegworth Gdns ME10 ..36 E1
Chegworth La ME17 ...100 A6
Chegworth Rd ME17 ....99 D5
Chelmar Rd ME7 ....10 B4
Chelmsford Ho ME15 ...97 E6
Chelsea Ct CT21 ......176 C1
Chelsea Rd CT11 ....67 C4
Chelsfield Ho ME16 .....74 D5
Cheltenham Cl ME15 ....97 F6
Cheney Cl ME8 ....33 C5
Cheney Hill ME9 ....59 A5
Cheney Rd ME13 ....62 F7
Chennels The TN26 ....167 C7
Chepstow House 3 ME15 ....97 F6
Chequer La CT3 ....71 C2
Chequer's Terr ME12 ...5 A5
Chequers Cl ME5 ....54 A8
Chequers Ctr ME15 .....75 A4
Chequers Hill CT4 ......109 C2
Chequers Pk TN25 .....123 E1
Chequers Rd ME12 ......4 E6
Chequertree TN25 .....172 B2
Cherbourg Cres ME5 ...31 F7
Cheriton Ave CT12 .....52 B8
Cheriton Court Rd CT20 177 C6
Cheriton Gdns CT20 ...178 C4
Cheriton High St CT19 .177 D6
Cheriton Intc CT19 .....177 C7
Cheriton Pl Deal CT14 ..117 C4
Folkestone CT20 ....178 D4
Cheriton Prim Sch CT18 ....177 C6
Cheriton Rd Deal CT14 .117 C4
Folkestone CT19,CT20 ...178 B5
Folkestone, Morehall CT19 177 F6
Gillingham ME8 ....33 D8
Cheriton Way ME14 .....74 C7
Cheriton Wood Ho CT19 ....177 D7
Cherries The ME16 .....74 A2
Cherry Amber Cl ME8 ...33 F8
Cherry Ave CT2 ....66 D2
Cherry Cl Lenham ME17 101 C5
Sittingbourne ME10 ......36 D6
Cherry Ct Ashford TN23 139 A1
Folkestone CT19 ....178 A6
Cherry Dr CT2 ....66 D2
Cherry Fields ME10 .....36 A5
Cherry Garden Ave CT19 ....178 A7
Cherry Garden Cres TN25 ....123 F2
Cherry Garden La
Ash CT3 ....71 E1
Folkestone CT19 ....177 F7
Wye TN25 ....123 F2
Cherry Garden Rd CT2 ..66 D2
Cherry Gdns
Broadstairs CT10 ....29 C3
Elham CT4 ....144 F5
Herne Bay CT6 ....22 F4
Littlebourne-on-S TN28 .200 D6
Teynham ME9 ....38 C2
Cherry Glebe TN25 ....157 E3
Cherry Gr CT15 ....114 B2
Cherry Hill Ct ME9 .....35 B6
Cherry La CT14 ....116 C7
Cherry Orch
Littlebourne CT3 ....68 F1
Tenterden TN30 ....179 A6
Whitstable CT5 ....44 C8
Woodchurch TN26 .....169 A3
Cherry Orchard La TN25 ....172 E4
Cherry Orchard Mews CT3 ....68 F1
Cherry Orchard Way ME16 ....74 B3
Cherry Tree Ave CT16 .149 C1
Cherry Tree Cl
Teynham ME9 ....38 D2
West Minster ME12 ......3 A8
Cherry Tree Dr ME13 ...39 F3
Cherry Tree Gdns CT12 .29 B3
Cherry Tree Rd
Charing Heath TN27 ...119 E2
Gillingham ME8 ....33 F8
Cherry View ME17 ......97 B3
Cherry Waye CT15 .....131 C7
Cherrybrook Rd CT20 ..177 D6

Cherrygarden La CT15,
CT3 . . . . .113 E7
Cherville La CT3 . . . . . .90 C7
Chervilles ME16 . . . . . .74 A2
Chesham Dr ME8 . . . . . .33 E6
Cheshire Rd
  Maidstone,Shepway ME15 .97 E7
  Maidstone,Willington ME15 .75 E2
Chessenden La TN27 . . .135 A1
Chester Ave TN26 . . . . .153 D5
Chester Rd
  Gillingham ME7 . . . . . . .10 D2
  Westgate-on-S CT8 . . . . .27 F8
Chestfield & Swalecliffe
  Sta CT5 . . . . .21 D2
Chestfield Cl ME8 . . . . . .11 E2
Chestfield Rd CT5 . . . . . .44 C7
Chestnut Ave Blean CT2 . .66 A7
  Chatham ME5 . . . . .31 F3
Chestnut Cl
  Ashford TN23 . . . . . . .138 E3
  Hythe CT21 . . . . .187 E8
  Tenterden TN30 . . . . . .167 C1
  Whitfield TN16 . . . . . .149 A8
  Chartham CT4 . . . . .86 F1
Chestnut Ct ME13 . . . . . .64 A3
Chestnut Dr
  Broadstairs CT10 . . . . . .29 D4
  Coxheath ME17 . . . . . . .96 B3
  Herne Bay CT6 . . . . . . .22 D3
  Kingswood ME17 . . . . . .99 D2
  Sturry CT2 . . . . .68 A7
  Worth CT14 . . . . .94 A4
Chestnut La TN23 . . . . .156 C4
Chestnut Rd CT17 . . . . .166 B7
Chestnut St ME9 . . . . . .35 E4
Chestnut Terr 176 A1
Chestnut Wood La ME9 . .35 E3
Chestnuts The TN25 . . . .158 D5
Chevalier Rd CT17 . . . . .166 A7
Chevening Cl ME5 . . . . . .32 A5
Cheviot Ct CT10 . . . . . . .30 B5
Cheviot Gdns ME15 . . . . .76 A1
Cheviot Way TN24 . . . . .139 C4
Cheyne Cl ME10 . . . . . . .36 F8
Cheyne Mid Sch The ME12 1 E2
Cheyne Rd ME12 . . . . . . .5 D3
Chicago Ave ME7 . . . . . .10 F5
Chichester Cl
  Ashford TN23 . . . . . . .139 B1
  Gillingham ME8 . . . . . . .34 A8
Chichester Rd
  Folkestone CT20 . . . . . .177 E4
  Ramsgate CT11 . . . . . . .29 B1
Chickfield Gdns 4 ME8 . .10 C2
Chiddingfold Cl ME12 . . . .4 D6
Chiddingstone Cl ME15 . . .97 F6
Chieftain Cl ME7 . . . . . . .11 B1
Childgate Rd CT5 . . . . . .42 F2
Childscroft Rd ME8 . . . . .11 F2
Chilham Ave CT8 . . . . . .27 D7
Chilham Castle & Gdns★
  CT4 . . . . .107 B7
Chilham Cl Chatham ME4 . .9 E3
  West Minst ME12 . . . . . . .3 B8
Chilham Ho 1 ME15 . . . . .97 E8
Chilham Rd
  Folkestone CT19 . . . . . .177 E6
  Gillingham ME8 . . . . . . .11 A3
  Maidstone ME16 . . . . . .74 C7
Chilham Sta CT4 . . . . . .107 D8
Chillenden Windmill
  (dis)★ CT3 . . . . .91 F1
Chillington St ME14 . . . . .74 F6
Chilston Rd ME17 . . . . .101 D5
Chiltern Cl ME15 . . . . . . .75 F1
Chiltern End TN24 . . . . .139 B3
Chilton Ave
  Kearsney CT16 . . . . . . .148 C4
  Sittingbourne ME10 . . . . .37 A3
Chilton Ct
  14 Folkestone CT20 . . . .178 E6
  Gillingham ME8 . . . . . . .11 E1
Chilton Field CT3 . . . . . .71 D2
Chilton Gdns CT3 . . . . . .71 D2
Chilton La CT11 . . . . . . .52 A6
Chilton Pl CT3 . . . . .71 D2
Chilton Prim Sch CT11 . . .52 A6
Chilton Sq CT3 . . . . .71 D2
Chilton Way CT17 . . . . .148 D3
Chimes The
  Ashford TN24 . . . . . . .139 C3
  Rochester ME1 . . . . .9 C5
Chineham Way CT1 . . . . .87 E6
Chippendale Cl ME5 . . . . .31 F1
Chippendale Dr ME17 . . .100 D6
Chipstead Cl ME16 . . . . .74 D6
Chipstead Rd ME8 . . . . . .33 D4
Chislehurst Cl ME15 . . . . .97 F6
Chislet CE Prim Sch CT5 47 C5
Chislet Ct CT6 . . . . .22 E5
Chislet Park Cotts CT3 . .46 F1
Chislet Wlk ME8 . . . . . . .33 D5
Chislett Cl TN29 . . . . . .159 E2
Chisnall Rd CT17 . . . . . .148 E4
Chittenden's La TN29 . . .193 E5
Chitty La CT3 . . . . .47 D6
Christ Church Cath CT1 . .88 A8
Christ Church
  CE High Sch TN23 . . . .155 F5
Christ Church
  CE Jun Sch CT11 . . . . .52 C6
Christ Church
  CE Prim Sch CT20 . . . .178 C5
Christ Church Coll CT1 . .88 B8
Christ Church Coll
  Post Graduate Ctr CT3 .67 F1
Christ Church Rd CT20 . .178 C4

Christchurch Ct
  3 Chatham ME5 . . . . . .10 C2
  1 Dover CT17 . . . . . . .166 D7
Christchurch House 11
  ME15 . . . . .97 E5
Christchurch Rd TN23 . .156 B8
Christchurch Way CT16 .149 B3
Christen Way ME15,ME17 .97 F3
Christian Ct 3 ME2 . . . . .9 C8
Christie Cl ME5 . . . . . . .32 B6
Christmas St ME7 . . . . . .10 E7
Christopher's Row ME9 . .60 A3
Chrysler Ave CT6 . . . . . .22 B4
Chunnel Ind Est TN23 . .139 B1
Church App TN28 . . . . .200 A6
Church Cl Mersham TN25 157 E3
  New Romney TN28 . . . .200 B6
Church Cliff CT14 . . . . . .134 D6
Church Cotts
  Rodmersham ME9 . . . . . .59 D8
  St Michaels TN30 . . . . . .117 C1
Church Court Gr CT10 . . .29 E6
Church Cres ME17 . . . . .100 F6
Church Ct CT18 . . . . . . .161 C6
Church Farm Rd ME9 . . . .12 E3
Church Farm Way CT13 . .93 B6
Church Field TN25 . . . . .160 B1
Church Gn
  Hollingbourne ME17 . . . .77 E3
  Rochester ME2 . . . . .9 C8
Church Haven CT14 . . . .133 F5
Church Hill
  Bethersden TN26 . . . . .153 D5
  Boughton Monchelsea
    ME17 . . . . .97 C1
  Boughton Street ME13 . . .64 A5
  Canterbury CT2 . . . . . . .66 C1
  Charing Heath ME17,TN27 119 C7
  Chatham ME5 . . . . .10 C2
  Chilham CT4 . . . . .107 B8
  Doddington ME9 . . . . . .80 F8
  Eythorne CT15 . . . . . . .131 C8
  High Halden TN26 . . . . .167 E7
  Hythe CT21 . . . . .176 C2
  Kingsnorth TN23 . . . . .156 B3
  Ramsgate CT11 . . . . . . .52 E7
  Shepherdswell CT15 . . . .130 D4
  Stockbury ME9 . . . . . . .56 F7
  Stone in Oxney TN30 . . .189 F3
  Sutton CT15 . . . . .133 A7
  Temple Ewell CT16 . . . .148 D5
Church Ho CT14 . . . . . .117 C7
Church La Adisham CT3 . .90 D1
  Aldington TN25 . . . . . .173 D7
  Boughton Aluph TN25 . .123 B4
  Boyden Gate CT3 . . . . . .47 C7
  Brenzett TN29 . . . . . . .191 F5
  Canterbury CT1 . . . . . . .87 F8
  21 Canterbury,Northgate
    CT1 . . . . .67 A1
  Challock TN25 . . . . . . .122 B8
  Chartham CT4 . . . . .86 D3
  Chatham ME4 . . . . .9 F6
  Church Hougham CT15 . .165 B5
  Deal CT14 . . . . .117 B6
  Harrietsham ME17 . . . . .100 E6
  Kingston CT4 . . . . .111 D3
  Lower Hardres CT4 . . . . .88 B2
  Maidstone ME14 . . . . . .76 C4
  New Romney TN28 . . . .200 B5
  Newington ME9 . . . . . . .35 B6
  Petham CT4 . . . . .109 C3
  Ringwould CT14 . . . . . .133 F5
  Ripple CT14 . . . . .116 D1
  River,Lydden CT15 . . . .147 E8
  Selling ME13 . . . . .84 B6
  Shadoxhurst TN26 . . . . .170 A7
  Stockbury ME9 . . . . . . .56 E8
  Stowting TN25 . . . . . . .160 A6
  Sturry CT2 . . . . .67 F5
  Waltham CT4 . . . . .125 F5
  Westbere CT2 . . . . .68 C7
  Whitstable CT5 . . . . . . .43 A6
  Womenswold CT4 . . . . .112 D2
Church Mdws CT14 . . . .117 A6
Church Mews ME8 . . . . . .33 B8
Church Path Deal CT14 . .117 B5
  Gillingham ME7 . . . . . . .10 E6
  Lower Halstow ME9 . . . .13 C3
Church Rd Ashford TN23 .139 C6
  Ashford,Kennington TN24 .139 E6
  Ashford,Aylesford Green
    TN24 . . . . .157 A7
  Ashford,Willesborough
    TN24 . . . . .157 A8
  1 Broadstairs CT10 . . . .30 B4
  Burmarsh TN29 . . . . . .185 E4
  Charing TN27 . . . . .103 D2
  Chart Sutton ME17 . . . . .98 C1
  Coldred CT15 . . . . .131 A3
  Dover CT17 . . . . .166 A7
  Eastchurch ME12 . . . . . . .5 D2
  Eastling ME13 . . . . .82 B2
  Faversham ME13 . . . . . .62 D7
  Faversham,The Brents
    ME13 . . . . .62 D8
  Folkestone CT20 . . . . . .177 C6
  Harrietsham ME17 . . . . .100 E6
  Hoath CT3 . . . . .46 E5
  Hollingbourne ME17 . . . .56 E1
  Hythe CT21 . . . . .176 C2
  Kenardington TN26 . . . .182 A5
  Lenham ME17 . . . . . . .118 A8
  Littlebourne CT3 . . . . . . .90 A8
  Lydd TN29 . . . . .203 C6
  Lyminge CT18 . . . . . . .161 C7
  Maidstone,Shepway ME15 .97 F7
  Maidstone,Tovil ME15 . . .74 E2

Church Rd *continued*
  Margate CT9 . . . . .7 J1
  Mersham TN25 . . . . . . .157 E3
  Molash CT4 . . . . .105 F5
  New Romney TN28 . . . .200 A6
  Oare ME13 . . . . .40 B3
  Ramsgate CT11 . . . . . . .52 E7
  Sevington TN24 . . . . . . .157 B6
  Sittingbourne ME9 . . . . . .37 E5
  Sittingbourne, Murston
    ME10 . . . . .37 B5
  Smeeth TN25 . . . . .158 C4
  Stalisfield Green ME13 . .103 F5
  Tenterden TN30 . . . . . .179 A7
Church Sq
  2 Broadstairs CT10 . . . .30 B4
  Lenham ME17 . . . . . . .101 D5
Church St
  Boughton Monchelsea ME17 97 B2
  Broadstairs CT10 . . . . . .29 E6
  Canterbury CT2 . . . . . . .66 E1
  Chatham ME4 . . . . .10 A4
  Deal CT14 . . . . .117 B1
  Dover CT16 . . . . .166 D7
  Eastry CT13 . . . . .93 C2
  Faversham ME13 . . . . . .62 D8
  Folkestone CT20 . . . . . .178 D4
  Gillingham ME7 . . . . . . .10 E6
  Loose ME15 . . . . .96 F5
  Maidstone ME14 . . . . . .75 A4
  Maidstone,Tovil ME15 . . .74 E2
  Margate CT9 . . . . .7 J2
  Minster (Thanet) CT12 . .50 C5
  Nonington CT15 . . . . . .113 C5
  Rochester ME1 . . . . .9 D4
  Rodmersham ME9 . . . . . .59 C8
  7 Sandwich CT13 . . . . . .73 A1
  5 Sittingbourne ME10 . . .36 E4
  Sittingbourne,Milton Regis
    ME10 . . . . .36 E5
  Whitstable CT5 . . . . . . .20 F1
  Woodnesborough CT13 . .93 B6
  Wye TN25 . . . . .123 E2
Church Street
  (St Pauls) 6 CT1 . . . . .88 A8
Church Street
  St Mary's 3 CT13 . . . . .72 F1
Church Terr Chatham ME5 .10 C2
  Minster (Sheppey) ME12 . .4 C7
Church View
  Aldington TN25 . . . . . .173 A6
  Herne Bay CT6 . . . . . . .23 C4
  Newchurch TN29 . . . . . .184 E3
  Worth CT14 . . . . .94 B5
Church Way CT5 . . . . . . .21 D3
Church Whitfield Rd
  CT16 . . . . .149 B8
Church Wlk CT4 . . . . . .144 F4
Church Wood Cl CT2 . . . .66 B2
Church Wood
  Nature Reserve★ CT2 . .65 F4
  TN23 . . . . .139 B2
Church Yd TN23 . . . . . .139 C2
Church Yard Pas 10
  TN23 . . . . .139 B2
Churchfield Pl CT9 . . . . . .7 I2
Churchfield Way TN25 . .123 E2
Churchfields
  Broadstairs CT10 . . . . . .29 F7
  Margate CT9 . . . . .7 J1
Churchfields Terr ME1 . . . .9 B4
Churchill Ave
  Chatham ME5 . . . . .32 A7
  Deal CT14 . . . . .117 C4
  Folkestone CT19 . . . . . .178 C8
  Herne Bay CT6 . . . . . . .23 D4
Churchill Cl Bridge CT4 . .88 F1
  Folkestone CT19 . . . . . .178 D8
  St Margaret's at Cliffe
    CT15 . . . . .150 F5
Churchill Cotts ME17 . . . .98 F6
Churchill Ct Hythe CT21 .176 B1
  Ramsgate CT11 . . . . . . .52 D7
Churchill Ho
  2 Folkestone CT20 . . . .177 F5
  Maidstone ME16 . . . . . .74 B2
  Sittingbourne ME10 . . . . .37 C4
  Teynham ME9 . . . . .38 C3
Churchill Rd
  Canterbury CT1 . . . . . . .88 C6
  Dover CT17 . . . . .166 A6
  Minster (Sheppey) ME12 . .4 D6
Churchill St CT16 . . . . . .149 C1
Churchill Way ME13 . . . . .40 B1
Churchill Wlk CT18 . . . . .162 F4
Churchlands ME8 . . . . . .200 B6
Churchlands The TN28 . .200 B6
Churchwood Dr CT5 . . . . .21 D1
Chute Cl ME8 . . . . .33 D4
Cinder Path CT10 . . . . . .30 A4
Cinnabar Cl ME5 . . . . . . .32 A1
Cinnabar Br ME5 . . . . . . .32 A1
Cinque Ports Ave CT21 .176 B1
Circular Rd Dover CT16 . .150 B1
  Finglesham CT14 . . . . . .116 B7
Circus The CT6 . . . . .22 E4
Citadel Cres CT17 . . . . .166 B6
Citadel Hts CT17 . . . . . .166 B6
Citadel Rd CT17 . . . . . .166 C6
Citroen Cl CT6 . . . . .22 B4
City Bsns Pk CT1 . . . . . .67 C3
City View CT2 . . . . .87 C8
City Way ME1 . . . . .9 D2
Claire Cl Birchington CT7 . .26 F7
  Broadstairs CT10 . . . . . .30 B5
Claire House ME16 . . . . .74 E5
Clandon Br ME5 . . . . . . .32 D2
Clanwilliam Rd CT14 . . . .117 D5
Clapham Hill CT5 . . . . . . .43 D5

Clapton Ct ME8 . . . . .33 D8
Clare Dr CT6 . . . . .22 C2
Clare Rd CT5 . . . . .20 E2
Claremont Cl CT14 . . . . .134 C6
Claremont Gdns CT11 . . . .52 D6
Claremont Pl CT1 . . . . . .87 F7
Claremont Rd Deal CT14 117 B5
  Folkestone CT20 . . . . . .178 C5
  Kingsdown CT14 . . . . . .134 C6
  Maidstone ME15 . . . . . .75 B5
Claremont St CT6 . . . . . .22 C4
Claremont Terr CT13 . . . .93 D7
Claremont Way 2 ME4 . . . .9 F3
Clarence Ave Margate CT9 .8 D2
  Rochester ME1 . . . . .9 C4
Clarence Ct ME14 . . . . . .75 E4
Clarence Gdns ME12 . . . . .6 E3
Clarence Pl Deal CT14 . .117 D7
  Dover CT17 . . . . .166 D5
Clarence Rd
  Capel-le-F CT18 . . . . . .164 B2
  Chatham ME4 . . . . .10 B2
  Deal CT14 . . . . .117 D3
  Herne Bay CT6 . . . . . . .22 D5
  Ramsgate CT11 . . . . . . .52 C6
Clarence Row ME12 . . . . .1 C2
Clarence St
  Folkestone CT20 . . . . . .178 D5
  Herne Bay CT6 . . . . . . .22 E5
Clarendon Cl
  Maidstone ME14 . . . . . .76 A4
  Sittingbourne ME10 . . . . .37 A5
Clarendon Gdns 7 CT11 .52 D6
Clarendon House
  Gram Sch CT11 . . . . . .52 E6
Clarendon Mews
  1 Broadstairs CT10 . . . .30 A4
  New Romney TN28 . . . .200 C8
Clarendon Pl
  Dover CT17 . . . . .166 C7
  Maidstone ME14 . . . . . .75 A4
Clarendon Rd
  Aylesham CT3 . . . . .112 F5
  Broadstairs CT10 . . . . . .30 A4
  Dover CT17 . . . . .166 C7
  Margate CT9 . . . . .8 A2
Clarendon St
  Dover CT17 . . . . .166 C7
  Herne Bay CT6 . . . . . . .22 C4
Claridge Ct ME7 . . . . . . .32 F4
Claridge Mews CT21 . . . .176 C2
Clarke Cres TN24 . . . . . .139 F4
Clarke Rd TN28 . . . . . . .200 E4
Clarke's Cl CT14 . . . . . . .116 F4
Clarklands TN29 . . . . . .184 E3
Claudius Gr TN23 . . . . . .155 F5
Clavell Cl ME8 . . . . .33 E4
Claxfield Cotts ME9 . . . . .38 A2
Claxfield Rd ME9 . . . . . . .60 A8
Claygate Ashford TN23 . .155 F5
  Maidstone ME15 . . . . . .75 D1
Clearmount Dr TN27 . . . .120 C8
Cleave Rd ME7 . . . . .10 E3
Cleaver La CT11 . . . . . . .52 E7
Clematis Ave ME8 . . . . . .33 B5
Clement Cl
  Canterbury CT1 . . . . . . .67 B1
  Sittingbourne ME10 . . . . .36 E8
Clement Ct ME16 . . . . . .74 D5
Clement's Rd CT12 . . . . .29 C2
Clementine Cl CT6 . . . . . .23 D4
Clerke Dr ME10 . . . . . . .37 A8
Clermont Cl ME7 . . . . . . .33 A4
Clevedon Ct TN25 . . . . .105 B2
Cleveland Cl CT16 . . . . .149 B3
Cleveland Ho ME16 . . . . .74 B2
Cleveland Rd ME7 . . . . . .10 D6
Cleveley Lo CT11 . . . . . .29 C2
Cleven Lo CT17 . . . . .48 D6
Cleves Way TN23 . . . . . .155 E8
Clewson Rise ME14 . . . . .75 B8
Cliff Ave CT6 . . . . .23 C5
Cliff Cl CT11 . . . . .176 D3
Cliff Dr Herne Bay CT6 . . .22 C4
  Warden ME12 . . . . .6 E4
Cliff Field CT8 . . . . .27 C8
Cliff Gdns ME12 . . . . .4 E7
Cliff Hill ME17 . . . . .97 D4
Cliff Hill Rd ME17 . . . . . .97 C4
Cliff Prom CT10 . . . . . . .30 C7
Cliff Rd Birchington CT7 . .26 F8
  Broadstairs CT10 . . . . . .30 B7
  Dover CT15,CT16 . . . . .150 C1
  Folkestone CT20 . . . . . .178 A3
  Hythe CT21 . . . . .176 E3
  Whitstable CT5 . . . . . . .20 F3
Cliff Sea Gr CT6 . . . . . . .22 C4
Cliff St CT11 . . . . .52 E6
Cliff Terr CT9 . . . . .7 J3
Cliff View Gdns
  Leysdown-on-S ME12 . . . . .6 D1
  Warden ME12 . . . . .6 E4
Cliff View Rd CT12 . . . . . .51 D6
Cliffe Ave CT9 . . . . .7 F1
Cliffe Ho CT20 . . . . .178 A3
Cliffe Rd
  Kingsdown CT14 . . . . . .134 D6
  Rochester ME2 . . . . .9 B8
Cliffestone Ct CT20 . . . . .178 B5
Clifford Gdns CT14 . . . . .117 B2
Clifford Ho 6 ME14 . . . . .75 B4
Clifford Rd CT5 . . . . .43 F8
Cliffs End Gr CT12 . . . . . .51 D5
Cliffs End Rd CT12 . . . . . .51 E5
Cliffside Dr CT10 . . . . . . .30 A1
Clifftown Gdns CT6 . . . . .22 C4
Clifton Cl ME14 . . . . .75 B5
Clifton Cres CT20 . . . . . .178 B3

Clifton Gdns
  Canterbury CT2 . . . . . . .66 D2
  Folkestone CT20 . . . . . .178 C4
  Margate CT9 . . . . .7 J3
Clifton Lawn CT11 . . . . . .52 D5
Clifton Mansions 4
  CT20 . . . . .178 C4
Clifton Pl CT9 . . . . .8 A3
Clifton Rd
  Folkestone CT20 . . . . . .178 C4
  Gillingham ME7 . . . . . . .10 C7
  Margate CT9 . . . . .8 A2
  Ramsgate CT11 . . . . . . .52 B8
  Whitstable CT5 . . . . . . .20 D1
Clifton St CT9 . . . . .7 J3
Cliftonville Ave
  Margate CT9 . . . . .8 A2
  Ramsgate CT12 . . . . . . .29 B1
Cliftonville Ct CT9 . . . . . .8 A3
Cliftonville Mews CT9 . . . .8 A3
Cliftonville Prim Sch CT9 .8 C2
Clim Down CT14 . . . . . .134 D6
Clinton Cl ME6 . . . . .96 B3
Clints La CT4 . . . . .129 D4
Clipper Cl ME2 . . . . .9 E7
Clipper Cl ME2 . . . . .9 E7
Clive Ct CT9 . . . . .8 B2
Clive Dennis Ct TN24 . . .139 E1
Clive Rd Cliffs End CT12 . .51 D6
  Margate CT9 . . . . .29 A5
  Rochester ME1 . . . . .9 C3
  Sittingbourne ME10 . . . . .36 B5
Cliveden Cl ME16 . . . . . .74 D7
Clockhouse TN25 . . . . . .138 F1
Clockhouse Pk TN25 . . . .105 C2
Cloisterham Rd ME1 . . . . .31 D7
Cloisters The
  9 Canterbury CT1 . . . . .66 F1
  Lenham ME17 . . . . . . .101 C5
  Ramsgate CT11 . . . . . . .52 D5
  8 Sittingbourne ME10 . . .36 E4
Close The Ashford TN23 . .155 F7
  Bridge CT4 . . . . .89 A1
  Canterbury,Hales Place CT2 .66 F4
  Canterbury,Thanington CT1 .87 B6
  Faversham ME13 . . . . . .62 C6
  Folkestone CT19 . . . . . .178 E8
  Hythe CT21 . . . . .176 B4
  River,Lydden CT15 . . . .147 F8
  Rochester ME1 . . . . .9 C4
  Wye TN25 . . . . .123 E2
Close The
  (St Edmunds Sch) CT2 . .66 C3
Cloudberry Cl ME16 . . . . .74 D6
Cloudesley Cl ME9 . . . . . .9 B1
Clovelly TN28 . . . . .200 C6
Clovelly Dr ME12 . . . . . . .4 B8
Clovelly Rd CT5 . . . . .43 D7
Clover Bank View ME5 . . .32 B6
Clover Ct ME10 . . . . .37 B5
Clover La ME8 . . . . .12 B2
Clover Rise CT5 . . . . .21 B1
Clover St 3 ME4 . . . . .9 F4
Clover Terr 4 ME15 . . . . .97 D8
Clowes Ct CT2 . . . . .66 C4
Clubb's La TN29 . . . . . . .197 D7
Cluny Rd ME13 . . . . .62 F7
Clyde Cotts ME12 . . . . . . .1 E2
Clyde St
  1 Canterbury CT1 . . . . .67 A1
  Sheerness ME12 . . . . . . .1 E2
Clynton Way TN23 . . . . .156 A7
Coach Dr TN26 . . . . . . .138 A7
Coach Rd Densole CT18 . .162 F8
  Egerton ME17,TN27 . . . .118 E6
Coalpit La ME9 . . . . .80 A6
Coast Dr
  Littlestone-on-S TN28 . . .200 E3
  Lydd-on-S TN29 . . . . . .204 F4
  St Mary's Bay TN29 . . . .194 F2
Coast Rd TN28,TN29 . . .200 F7
Coastguard Alley CT5 . . . .20 C1
Coastguard Cotts
  Conyer ME9 . . . . .38 E6
  Dover CT16 . . . . .166 D4
  Herne Bay CT6 . . . . . . .21 F4
  Hythe CT21 . . . . .176 B1
  Kingsdown CT14 . . . . . .134 D4
  Leysdown-on-S ME12 . . . .19 E4
  Minster (Sheppey) ME12 . .5 C5
  18 Ramsgate,East Cliff
    CT11 . . . . .52 F7
  Ramsgate,Pegwell CT11 . .52 A5
  Sandwich CT13 . . . . . . .95 B7
  Birchington CT7 . . . . . . .26 D8
Coastguard Cotts The
  ME12 . . . . .1 I1
Coastguard Hos ME12 . . . .6 C5
Coats Ave ME12 . . . . .3 A8
Cobay Cl CT21 . . . . .176 D2
Cobb Ct CT9 . . . . .7 I3
Cobb Wlk ME13 . . . . . . .62 B8
Cobblers Bridge Rd CT6 . .22 D3
Cobblestones ME7 . . . . . .32 F5
Cobbs Hill CT4 . . . . .85 C2
Cobbs Mews 2 CT20 . . . .178 C4
Cobbs Pl CT9 . . . . .7 I3
Cobbs Wood Ind Est
  TN23 . . . . .138 F2
Cobden Pl 16 CT1 . . . . . .67 A1
Cobden Rd
  4 Gillingham ME4 . . . . .10 B2
  Hythe CT21 . . . . .176 B1
Cobdown Gr ME8 . . . . . .12 A2
Cobfield ME17 . . . . .98 A1

Cobham Ave ME10 ....36 E1
Cobham Chase ME13 ..62 B8
Cobham Cl
  Canterbury CT1 ....88 C6
  Maidstone ME16 ...74 E4
Cobham Rise ME7 ....10 F5
Cobsden Cl TN29 ....195 A4
Cobsden Rd TN29 ...195 A4
Cobtree Cl ME5 ......32 C8
Cobtree Rd ME17 ....96 C3
Cobtree Wharf ME20 ..53 C2
Cobweb Cnr CT2 ......66 B4
Cock La Elham CT4 ...144 F4
  Hamstreet TN26 ....183 A4
Cockering Rd CT1,CT4 ..87 B4
Cockreed La TN28 ...200 B7
Codrington Rd CT11 ...52 D7
Cogans Terr CT1 .....87 B6
Coggan Ho **7** CT1 ...87 F7
Coinston Ave CT11 ...52 A7
Colburn Rd CT10 .....30 A2
Colchester Cl ME5 ...32 A7
Cold Harbour CT1 ....67 A2
Cold Harbour La ME9 ..35 F6
Cold Harbour Rd ME13 .103 A7
Coldblow CT14 ......117 A1
Coldblow La
  Maidstone ME14 ....56 A2
  Woodchurch TN26 ..169 D4
Coldbridge La TN27 ..118 B5
Coldharbour La
  Aylesford ME20 ....53 A1
  Bekesbourne CT4,CT3 .111 D7
  Hollingbourne ME14,ME9 .56 B1
  Old Romney TN29 ...198 C5
  Sittingbourne ME10 ..14 F1
  Wye TN25 ....124 A2
Coldred Hill CT15 ...130 F1
Coldred Rd Coldred CT15 131 B5
  Park Wood ME15 ....97 F4
  Shepherdswell CT15 .130 E3
Coldswood Rd CT12 ...28 F2
Cole Rd ME13 ....62 E7
Cole Terr ME17 .....101 C4
Colegate Dr ME14 ....76 C4
Colegates Cl ME13 ...40 B2
Colegates Ct ME13 ...40 B2
Colegates Rd ME13 ...40 A2
Coleman Cres CT12 ...29 C1
Coleman Dr ME10 .....14 F1
Coleman's Stairs Rd CT7 27 A8
Coleman's Yd **3** CT11 ..52 E6
Colemans La TN29 ...203 D7
Coleridge Gdns CT3 ..112 F6
Coleshall Cl ME15 ...97 F6
Coleshall Cotts ME9 ..14 D3
Colette Cl CT10 ......8 G2
Coleville Cres TN28 .204 E7
Colewood Rd CT5 .....21 E3
Colfe Way ME10 ......37 A8
Colin's Way CT21 ...177 A3
Collard Cl CT6 ......23 A4
Collard Rd TN24 ....157 A8
Collards Cl CT12 ....49 D2
Collards La CT4 ....144 E3
College Ave
  Gillingham ME7 .....10 B4
  Maidstone ME15 ....74 F3
College Cotts ME16 ..74 F3
College Ct Ashford TN23 .139 C2
  5 Maidstone ME15 ..75 A3
College Rd Canterbury CT1 67 B1
  Chatham ME4 ......10 A4
  Deal CT14 ....117 D8
  Maidstone ME15 ....74 F2
  Margate CT9 ....8 A1
  Ramsgate CT11 .....29 E1
  Sittingbourne ME10 ..36 D3
College Row CT17 ...166 B7
College Sq **2** CT9 ...7 J2
College Way CT3 .....91 A7
College Wlk **3** CT9 ..7 J2
College Yd ME1 ......9 C6
Collet Wlk ME8 ......33 D4
Collett Cl TN25 ....142 D8
Collingbourne TN23 .155 E6
Collings Wlk ME8 ....33 D4
Collington Terr ME15 .97 E4
Collingwood Cl
  Broadstairs CT10 ...29 E4
  Westgate-on-S CT8 ..27 D7
Collingwood Ct
  Folkestone CT20 ...177 E5
  Ramsgate CT11 .....52 D7
Collingwood Ind Ctr
  ME17 ....98 E2
Collingwood Rd
  Kit's Coty ME20 ....53 C7
  St Margaret's at Cliffe
    CT15 ....150 F8
  Whitstable CT5 .....20 C1
Collingwood Rd E CT15 134 A1
Collingwood Rise CT20 .177 E5
Collingwood Wlk ME10 .36 B5
Collins Rd CT6 ......22 C2
Collis St ME2 ....9 A8
Collison Pl TN30 ...179 D7
Colman House **4** ME14 .75 A4
Colombo Sq CT1 .....29 A1
Colonel Stephens Way
  TN30 ....167 B2
Colonel's La ME13 ...64 A3
Colorado Cl CT16 ...149 B3
Colton Cres CT16 ...149 B4
Coltsfoot Dr ME14 ...75 F4

Columbia Ave CT5 ....43 B7
Columbine Cl CT5 ....43 C6
Columbus Ave CT12 ..27 D1
Com Coll Whitstable The
  CT5 ....43 F8
Combe Cl CT18 ......163 B5
Command Rd ME14 ...74 F8
Commercial Rd ME2 ...9 A7
Commissioner's Rd ME2 .9 C8
Commodore Rd ME14 ..75 C5
Common La CT17 ....148 E3
Common Rd ME5 .....31 B1
Common The ME1 ....9 C6
Common Way TN26 ..138 A4
Commonwealth Cl ME10 37 B3
Compass Cl ME1 .....9 C1
Compass Ctr ME4 ....10 B8
Concord Ave ME5 .....31 E5
Concorde Ct CT21 ...52 D2
Condor CT12 ....6 E3
Conduit St ME13 .....62 D8
Coney Mews ME4 ....10 A1
Conference Wlk CT1 ..88 C8
Conifer Ct CT8 ....7 D1
Conifer Dr ME5 ......32 D1
Conifers The CT14 ...117 A2
Coniston Cl ME7 .....11 A6
Coniston Dr CT3 ....112 F6
Coniston Rd CT19 ...178 B2
Conker Cl TN23 .....156 C3
Connaught Barracks
  CT16 ....149 E1
Connaught Cl ME15 ..97 F4
Connaught Gdns **9** CT9 ..7 J1
Connaught Mews **2** ME4 10 C2
Connaught Rd
  Chatham ME4 ......10 C2
  Dover CT16 ....149 D1
  Folkestone CT20 ...178 B5
  Gillingham ME7 ....10 C5
  Margate CT9 ....7 J1
  Sittingbourne ME10 ..36 E3
Conquest Ind Est ME2 ..9 A6
Conrad Ave CT1 .....67 C3
Conrad Cl ME8 ......33 D4
Consort Cl ME14 ....75 B5
Constable Rd CT7 ...27 A8
Constable's Rd CT16 .166 E8
Constancia Ct CT20 .178 C7
Constantine Rd TN23 .155 C5
Constitution Hill **8** ME5 .10 B3
Constitution Rd ME5 .10 B2
Consul Cl CT6 ....22 B4
Continental App CT9 ..28 F6
Convent Cl CT15 ....151 B6
Convent Rd CT10 .....8 G1
Convent Wlk CT11 ...52 B5
Conway Cl Birchington CT7 26 E7
  Hythe CT21 ....176 B4
Conway Mews ME7 ...10 A6
Conway Rd ME16 ....74 C6
Conyer Rd ME9 ......38 F4
Conyers Wlk ME8 ....33 D4
Conyngham Cl CT12 ..29 B2
Conyngham La CT4 ...89 A2
Conyngham Rd
  Herne Bay CT6 .....23 D5
  Minster (Thanet) CT12 .50 C5
Cooden Cl ME8 ......12 A2
Cook Cl ME5 ....32 C6
Cook's Lea CT13 .....93 B2
Cookham Hill ME1 ....9 A2
Cookham Wood Rd ME1 31 B8
Cooks La ME10 ......36 F6
Cooks Wharf ME1 .....9 E4
Cooling Cl ME14 .....75 C6
Coolinge La CT20 ...177 F4
Coolinge Rd CT20 ...178 D5
Coombe Cl Chatham ME5 32 B3
  Dover CT17 ....149 A1
Coombe Ct CT17 ....149 A1
Coombe Dr ME10 .....37 C4
Coombe La Ash CT13,CT3 92 E8
  Tenterden TN30 ....179 A7
Coombe Lands TN30 .188 D4
Coombe Rd
  Dover CT15,CT17 ...165 E8
  Dover,St Radigund's CT17 148 F1
  Folkestone CT19 ...177 F6
  Maidstone ME15 ....74 F2
Coombe Valley Rd CT17 149 A1
Coombe Way CT18 ...163 C4
Coombe Wlk CT5 .....43 A2
Coombe Wood La CT18 163 C4
Cooper Rd ME5 ......32 B3
Cooper Street Dro CT3 .72 B4
Cooper's Hill CT6 ...22 F5
Cooper's La TN25 ...158 F2
Coopers La CT1 ......87 E7
Cooting La CT3 .....112 D8
Cooting Rd CT3 .....112 E4
Cop Street Rd CT3 ...71 D3
Copenhagen Rd ME7 ..10 C4
Copinger Cl CT2 .....67 A4
Copland Ave ME12 ....4 C6
Copper Tree Ct ME15 .97 A5
Copper Tree Wlk ME5 .32 C1
Copperfield ME12 .....5 F6
Copperfield Cl TN24 .139 C3
Copperfield Ct CT10 ..30 B5
Copperfield Dr ME17 .97 B8
Copperfield Ho **6** ME4 ..9 F4
Copperfield Rd ME1 ...9 C2
Copperfields TN29 ...203 B6
Copperfields The ME1 ..9 B4
Coppergate
  Canterbury CT2 .....66 F2
  Gillingham ME7 .....32 F5

Copperhouse La ME7 ..11 B6
Copperhurst Wlk CT9 ..8 F2
Copperpenny Dr ME7 ..33 B3
Copperwood TN24 ...139 C4
Coppice Ct ME7 ......33 B4
Coppice The CT2 .....67 F6
Coppice View ME14 ..75 E6
Coppin St ME9 ......117 D6
Copse Cl ME1 ....9 E1
Copse The TN23 ....138 D3
Copsewood Way ME15 .76 A3
Copt Cl CT14 ....67 F7
Copthall Gdns **13** CT20 .178 D5
Cordelia Cres ME1 ....9 A2
Cordingham Rd CT5 ..43 A6
Cordova Ct CT20 ....178 B4
Corkwell St ME4 .....9 E3
Cornbrook Rd CT21 ..187 D8
Cornelis Dr CT12 ....50 B5
Corner Cotts TN26 ..182 A6
Corner Field TN23 ...156 B5
Corner The TN25 ....173 A6
Cornes Cl TN24 ....140 A1
Cornflower Cl ME14 ..75 E4
Cornford Rd CT7 .....27 A7
Cornhill **12** CT11 .....52 E6
Corniche The CT20 ..177 C3
Cornwall Ave CT11 ...52 F8
Cornwall Cl ME15 ....97 E7
Cornwall Gdns
  Canterbury CT1 .....88 D7
  Margate CT9 ....8 B3
Cornwall Ho Deal CT14 117 A5
  5 Dover CT17 .....166 D7
Cornwall Rd Deal CT14 117 C3
  Gillingham ME7 ....10 C6
  Herne Bay CT6 .....22 B2
  Rochester ME1 ......9 C3
Cornwallis Ave
  Aylesham CT3 .....112 F6
  Chatham ME4 ....9 E1
  Folkestone CT19 ...178 B6
  Gillingham ME8 .....11 A4
  Herne Bay CT6 .....23 C3
Cornwallis Circ CT5 ..20 D1
Cornwallis Cl
  Ashford TN24 ......157 B7
  Folkestone CT19 ...178 B6
Cornwallis Cotts ME17 .96 E2
Cornwallis Gdns CT10 .30 A6
Cornwallis Rd ME16 ..74 D4
Cornwallis Rdbt ME8 .11 A4
Cornwallis Sch The ME15 96 F2
Coronation Cl CT10 ..29 E7
Coronation Cotts CT19 177 D6
Coronation Cres
  Margate CT9 ....28 B8
  Queenborough ME11 ..2 F5
Coronation Dr
  Great Chart TN24 ..138 C1
  Leysdown-on-S ME12 ..6 D2
Coronation Flats **5** ME4 ..9 F3
Coronation Rd
  Chatham ME5 ....10 C2
  Ramsgate CT11 .....52 D6
  Sheerness ME12 .....1 E1
Coronation Sq TN29 .203 C6
Corone CT19 ....178 A7
Corporation Rd ME7 ..10 D7
Corporation St ME1 ...9 C6
Corral Cl ME5 ....10 D2
Corrall Almshouses **4**
  ME15 ....75 A3
Corrance Gn ME15 ...97 A8
Corsican Wlk CT6 ....23 C3
Cortland Cl ME10 ....36 E6
Cortland Mews ME10 .36 E6
Corunna Cl CT21 ....176 A2
Corunna Pl CT15 ....149 E3
Cory's Rd ME1 ....9 D6
Corylus Dr CT5 .....43 A7
Cossack St ME1 ......9 D3
Cossington Rd
  Canterbury CT1 .....88 A7
  Chatham ME5 ......32 B1
Cosway Cotts TN25 ..172 C1
Cotswold Cl TN24 ...139 B4
Cotswold Gdns ME15 .76 A2
Cottage Rd Chatham ME4 ..9 F6
  Ramsgate CT11 .....52 E6
Cottage Row CT13 ...72 F1
Cottall Ave ME4 .....9 F2
Cottington Rd CT12 ..51 B5
Cotton Hill Wlk TN26 .183 A4
Cotton Rd CT1 ....87 E7
Coulman St ME7 .....10 D5
Coulson Gr CT14 ...116 A5
Coulter Rd Ashford TN23 155 E5
  Herne Bay CT6 .....22 B2
Coulters Cl ME14 ....75 D5
Coultrip Cl ME12 .....5 B5
Council Cotts ME15 ..96 A4
Countess Mountbatten Ct
  CT8 ....27 E8
Country Ways ME17 .102 D3
Country's Field TN29 .195 C8
County Rd ME14 .....75 A5
County Sq **8** TN23 ..139 B2
Court Cotts
  St Nicholas at Wade CT7 .25 E2
  Wingham CT3 ....91 A7
Court Dr ME16 ......74 D4
Court Flats CT3 .....91 A7
Court Hall ME11 ......2 F5
Court Hall Mus* ME10 ..36 E6
Court Hill CT3 ....68 E2

Court Hill Ho CT16 ..148 E4
Court House Farm CT15 113 E5
Court La Detling ME14 ..55 C5
  Preston CT3 ....70 B6
Court Lodge CT14 ...117 B6
Court Lodge Cotts ME15 .96 A7
Court Lodge Rd
  Appledore TN26 ....190 C7
  Gillingham ME7 ....10 F6
Court Mdw ME8 ......11 B2
Court Mdws CT3 .....89 F8
Court Pl CT20 ......178 C4
Court Rd Burham ME1 .53 A8
  Deal CT14 ....117 B1
  Sittingbourne ME10 ..36 F7
  St Nicholas at Wade CT7 25 E2
Court St ME13 ......62 D7
Court Tree Dr ME12 ...5 B5
Court Wurtin TN23 ..156 A7
Courtenay Rd
  Boughton Street CT2,ME13 .64 E5
  Deal CT14 ....117 C8
  Maidstone ME15 ....74 F2
Courtenay Rd ME8 ...33 B8
Courtfield Ave ME5 ..32 B3
Courtland Ave CT16 .149 A6
Courtland Dr CT16 ..148 A6
Courtlands Herne Bay CT6 23 B3
  Kingsdown CT14 ...134 D6
Courtlands Cl CT12 ..51 E5
Courtlands Way CT8 ...7 D1
Courts The CT9 ....7 E1
Courtyard The
  Ashford TN24 ......156 F6
  Gillingham ME8 .....33 A8
  Staple CT3 ....92 A6
Coventina Ho CT11 ...52 D7
Coventon La CT14 ....94 A5
Coventry Gdns CT6 ..23 E5
Coverdale Ave ME15 .97 D6
Coverdale Cl ME5 ....32 B7
Covert TN23 ....138 E1
Covert Rd CT3 ......112 E4
Covert The ME5 .....32 B1
Covet La CT4 ....111 C2
Cow La Canterbury CT1 .87 D7
  Dover CT17 ....166 A7
Cowbeck Cl ME8 .....33 D6
Cowden Rd ME14 ....75 C5
Cowdray Rd CT17 ...117 A3
Cowdray Sq CT14 ...117 A3
Cowdrey Cl
  Ashford TN24 ......157 A7
  Maidstone ME16 ....74 B2
  Rochester ME1 ......9 B2
Cowdrey Pl CT1 .....88 B6
Cowgate Hill CT17 ..166 D7
Cowgate La CT18 ...163 C5
Cowley Rise CT9 ....29 C8
Cowper Cl CT5 ......21 D3
Cowper Rd Deal CT14 117 C5
  Gillingham ME7 ....10 D3
  Margate CT9 ....7 J1
  River CT17 ....148 E3
  Sittingbourne ME10 ..37 B4
Cowstead Rd ME9 ....34 D2
Cox St ME14 ....55 E6
Coxes Ave CT12 .....29 B3
Coxes La CT12 ......29 B3
Coxett Hill ME13 ....61 D5
Coxheath Prim Sch ME17 96 C3
Coxhill CT15 ....130 C3
Coxhill Cres CT17 ..148 D3
Coxhill Gdns CT17 ..148 D3
Coxland Cotts TN26 .181 B1
Cozenton Cl ME8 ....11 E1
Crabble Ave CT17 ...149 A2
Crabble Cl CT17 ....148 F2
Crabble Corn Mill*
  CT17 ....148 F3
Crabble Hill CT16,CT17 .149 A2
Crabble La CT17 ....148 E2
Crabble Mdws CT17 .149 A2
Crabble Rd CT17 ....149 A3
Crabtree La ME17 ...119 B8
Crabtree Rd ME8 ....33 D8
Crabtree Rndbt ME14 .53 E2
Crackstake CT3 ......71 D2
Craddock Dr **8** CT1 ..67 B1
Craddock Rd CT1 ....67 B1
Craddock Way ME8 ..33 D5
Cradle Bridge Dr TN24 139 F2
Cradles Rd ME9 .....34 C2
Crafford St CT16 ...149 D1
Craft Ctr TN25 .....159 F2
Cragie Wlk ME8 .....33 E4
Craig Ho ME1 ....9 E1
Craighton Flats **2** CT13 72 F1
Crampton Cl CT10 ...30 A4
Cranborne Ave ME15 .75 C1
Cranborne Wlk CT2 ..66 E3
Cranbourne Cl ME15 .97 B8
Cranbourne Cl CT11 ..52 F8
Cranbrook Cl
  Gillingham ME8 .....11 C3
  Maidstone ME15 ....97 F7
  Margate CT9 ....8 E1
Cranbrook Dr ME10 ..36 D1
Cranbrooks TN25 ...157 D4
Cranford Cl ME8 .....11 D1
Cranleigh Dr CT16 ..149 B7
Cranleigh Gdns
  Chatham ME5 ....9 D3
  Maidstone ME16 ....74 C7
  Whitstable CT5 .....43 E8
Cranmer Cl ME15 ....97 B8
Cranmere Ct ME2 ....9 C5
Cranswick Cotts CT14 133 C8

Craufurd Gn CT20 ...177 D5
Craven CT21 ....28 C8
Crawford Gdns CT9 ...8 B2
Crawford Rd CT10 ...29 F5
Crayford Cl ME14 ...75 C6
Craythorne TN30 ...179 B8
Craythorne Cl
  Hythe CT21 ....177 B4
  New Romney TN28 .200 B8
Craythorne Ho TN30 179 B8
Craythorne La TN28 .200 B7
Cremer Cl CT4 ....86 C1
Cremer Pl ME13 .....62 A8
Cremers Rd ME10 ...37 B5
Crescent Ho Margate CT9 .8 A2
  Rochester ME2 ......9 C7
Crescent Rd
  Birchington CT7 ....27 A7
  Broadstairs CT10 ...30 C8
  Faversham ME13 ...62 D7
  Margate CT9 ....7 H2
  Ramsgate CT11 .....52 D7
Crescent St **1** ME10 .36 F4
Crescent The
  Aylesham CT15 ....113 A3
  Boughton Street ME13 .64 A3
  Canterbury CT2 ....66 F4
  Chartham CT4 ......86 D1
  Eythorne CT15 .....131 C7
  Folkestone CT20 ...177 E3
  Halfway Houses ME12 ..3 E6
  Lower Halstow ME9 .13 C3
  Maidstone ME14 ...74 F8
  Sandwich CT13 .....93 E6
  Sheerness ME12 .....1 D2
  Sittingbourne ME10 ..15 A1
  St Margaret's at Cliffe
    CT15 ....151 A5
  Teynham ME9 ....38 D3
Crescent Way ME5 ...31 D5
Cress Way ME13 .....62 A7
Cressey Ct **7** ME4 ...9 E4
Cressfield TN23 ....138 F1
Crest Rd ME1 ....9 C1
Cresta Cl CT6 ....21 D4
Crestway ME5 ....32 B8
Crete Rd E CT18,CT19 .163 D1
Crete Rd W CT18 ...163 B1
Creteway Cl CT19 ...178 E8
Creve Coeur Cl ME14 .76 A5
Crevequer Chambers **1**
  ME8 ....11 F1
Cricketers Cl
  Harrietsham ME17 .100 D6
  Hawkinge CT18 ....163 B6
  Sittingbourne ME10 ..36 F8
Crimond Ave TN29 ..187 A4
Criol La TN26 ......155 A2
Cripple Hill TN26 ...152 D1
Cripple St ME15 .....97 A4
Cripps Cl CT3 ......112 E5
Cripps' La CT15 ....150 F6
Crisfield Ct TN30 ..167 B2
Crismill La ME14,ME17 ..76 B3
Crispe Cl CT8 ....33 D4
Crispe Park Cl CT8 ..27 B7
Crispe Rd CT7 ......27 A3
Crispin Cl ME13 .....62 D8
Crispin Ct ME17 .....96 C3
Crittenden Bglws ME15 96 A4
Crittenden Cotts ME15 96 A4
Crocken Hill Rd TN27 118 C2
Crockham La ME13 ...64 B6
Crockham Rd ME13 ..64 C6
Crockshard Hill CT3 ..91 B4
Crockshard La CT3 ..91 B4
Croft Cl ME5 ....32 C1
Croft Gdns ME17 ...101 D4
Croft La CT20 ......177 F5
Croft Rd TN24 .....139 D2
Croft's Pl **8** CT10 ..30 B4
Crofters Cl CT21 ...187 E8
Crofters The ME8 ...33 F7
Crofton Cl TN24 ...139 C6
Crofton Rd CT8 .....27 E7
Croftwood TN23 ...155 D6
Croidene Ct ME12 ....4 A6
Cromer Rd Rochester ME2 .9 B8
  Sittingbourne ME9,ME10 ..58 F8
Crompton Gdns ME15 .75 B3
Crompton Tower
  Rly Mus* CT10 .....30 A4
Cromwell Park Pl CT20 177 D4
Cromwell Rd
  Canterbury CT1 .....88 A6
  Maidstone ME14 ....75 B5
  West Minst ME11 ....2 F7
  Whitstable CT5 .....20 E1
Cromwell Terr ME4 ..10 A3
Crook's Court La CT15 134 F4
Crooked S Rd CT14 .133 E7
Crookenden Pl CT4 .128 F8
Crosier Ct ME9 ......12 E3
Crosley Rd ME7 ......10 D3
Cross Dr ME17 ......99 B1
Cross Keys ME14 ....76 C4
Cross La Faversham ME13 62 C7
  7 Faversham ME13 .62 D7
  Sittingbourne ME10 ..36 E6
  Throwley Forstal ME13 104 C7
Cross Rd Birchington CT7 .27 B8
  Deal CT14 ....117 A2
  St Margaret's at Cliffe
    CT15 ....151 A4
Cross St
  2 Canterbury CT2 ..66 E1
  Chatham ME4 ......10 A4
  Gillingham ME7 .....10 C6

Cross St continued
Herne Bay CT6 . . . . .22 D3
Maidstone ME14 . . . . .75 A6
Rochester ME2 . . . . .9 B8
Cross Stile TN23 . . . . .155 F8
Cross The TN13 . . . . .93 B2
Cross Way ME1 . . . . .9 C3
Crossley Ave CT6 . . . . .21 F4
Crossway ME5 . . . . .31 E6
Crossways Canterbury CT2 .66 F4
Chart Sutton ME17 . . . . .98 B1
Sittingbourne ME10 . . . . . . .36 F1
Crossways Ave CT9 . . . . . . .29 A5
Crossways CI TN29 . . . . . .186 E2
Crouch Cotts ME13 . . . . . . .84 E8
Crouch Hill Ct ME9 . . . . . . .13 C3
Crouch La ME13 . . . . .84 E8
Crow Cnr Ashford TN24 . . .156 F7
Brabourne ME10 . . . . .141 E1
Rochester ME1 . . . . .9 C5
Crow Hill CT6 . . . . .30 B5
Crow Hill Rd CT9 . . . . .28 B8
Crow La ME1 . . . . .9 C5
Crowbridge Rd
Ashford,Aylesford Green
TN24 . . . . .156 E7
Ashford,South Willesborough
TN24 . . . . .156 F6
Crown Ct CT14 . . . . .117 D6
Crown Gdns CT2 . . . . .66 E1
Crown Hill Rd CT6 . . . . .22 C4
Crown Ho ME1 . . . . .9 B4
Crown La CT4 . . . . .126 D3
Crown Quay ME10 . . . . .36 F5
Crown Quay La 5 ME10 . .37 A4
Crown Rd ME10 . . . . .36 E6
Crown St ME7 . . . . .10 C6
Crownfield Rd TN23 . . . . . .155 F8
Crownfields ME14 . . . . .75 F4
Crows Camp Rd CT4 . . . . .111 A5
Croydon CT5 . . . . .32 C4
Cruise Liner Terminal
CT17 . . . . .166 F4
Crundale 2 ME14 . . . . .75 A5
Crundale Cl TN23 . . . . .155 F6
Crundale Rd ME8 . . . . .11 C3
Crundale Way CT10,CT9 . . . .8 E1
Crusader Ct ME8 . . . . .33 B8
Cryalls Bsns Est ME10 . . . . .36 C4
Cryalls La ME10,ME9 . . . . . .36 C4
Cryol Rd TN23 . . . . .156 A7
Crystal Bsns Ctr CT13 . . . . .73 B2
Ctr for European
Agricucultural Studies
TN25 . . . . .124 A1
Cubitt Ho Ashford TN24 . .156 D8
Folkestone CT19 . . . . .178 D6
Cuckold's Cnr
High Halden TN26 . . . . . . .168 B7
Snargate TN29 . . . . .191 E7
Cuckolds Cnr CT14 . . . . . . .114 A7
Cuckoo La
Ashford,Beaver TN23 . . . . .155 A4
Ashford,Singleton TN23 . . .155 D6
Postling CT21 . . . . .160 F2
Cuckoowood Ave ME14 . . . .53 F1
Cudham Cl ME14 . . . . .75 C6
Cudham Gdns CT9 . . . . .8 E2
Cudworth Rd TN24 . . . . . . .156 E7
Cullens Hill CT4 . . . . .144 F4
Culling's Hill CT4 . . . . .144 F4
Culmers Terr ME13 . . . . .41 E1
Culpeper Rd
Hollingbourne ME17 . . . . . . .77 C2
Rochester ME2 . . . . .9 E6
Culpepper Cl CT2 . . . . .67 A4
Culpepper Rd
Coxheath ME17 . . . . .96 B3
Gillingham ME8 . . . . .33 D4
Maidstone ME15 . . . . .97 C8
Culter Field TN23 . . . . .155 E8
Culver's La TN29 . . . . .203 D5
Cumberland Ave
Broadstairs CT10 . . . . .30 A5
Canterbury CT1 . . . . .88 D7
Maidstone ME15 . . . . .97 D8
Cumberland Dr ME9 . . . . . .13 C3
Cumberland Rd
Gillingham ME4,ME7 . . . . . .10 B7
Gillingham ME7 . . . . .10 C7
Margate CT9 . . . . .8 B3
1 Ramsgate CT11 . . . . .52 D6
Cundishall Cl CT5 . . . . .43 C8
Cunningham Cres
Birchington CT7 . . . . .26 E7
Chatham ME5 . . . . .32 A8
Cunningham Ho ME1 . . . . . .9 B4
Curlew Ave ME9 . . . . .13 B3
Curlew Ct CT6 . . . . .23 C2
Curlinge Ct CT11 . . . . .52 A6
Curteis Rd TN30 . . . . .167 B1
Curtis La CT4 . . . . .126 D2
Curtis Rd TN24 . . . . .156 F7
Curtis Way Chatham ME1 . .31 D7
1 Faversham ME13 . . . . . . .62 C7
Curtis Wood Park Rd
CT6 . . . . .46 A7
Curtis Wood Rd CT6 . . . . . .45 F7
Curzon Cl CT14 . . . . .117 C3
Curzon Ho 5 CT11 . . . . . . .52 D6
Curzon Rd Chatham ME4 . . .9 F3
Dover CT17 . . . . .166 B8
Maidstone ME14 . . . . .75 A6
Cushman Rd CT1 . . . . .87 E7
Cutbush & Corrall Ct 1
ME14 . . . . .75 B4
Cutbush Almshouses
2 Maidstone ME15 . . . . . . .75 A3

Cutbush Almshouses continued
3 Maidstone ME15 . . . . . . .75 A4
Cutbush Rd ME17 . . . . .100 D6
Cuthbert Rd CT8 . . . . .27 E8
Cuttings The CT12 . . . . .52 C8
Cuxton Rd ME15 . . . . .97 F5
Cygnet CI ME5 . . . . .32 C2
Cygnet Way TN23 . . . . .138 F1
Cylinder Rd CT21 . . . . .176 B4
Cypress Ave TN23 . . . . .138 E2
Cypress CI CT5 . . . . .43 C7
Cypress Ct ME7 . . . . .10 F6
Cypress Gr CT15 . . . . .114 B2
Cyprus Ct ME13 . . . . .62 E7
Cyprus Rd ME13 . . . . .62 E7

D

D'este Rd CT11 . . . . .52 F7
D2 Trad Est ME10 . . . . .37 B6
Daglish Cl TN28 . . . . .200 B6
Dagmar Rd ME4 . . . . .10 B2
Daimler Ave CT6 . . . . .22 B3
Dalby Rd CT9 . . . . .8 A3
Dalby Sq CT9 . . . . .8 A3
Dale Rd ME1 . . . . .9 C3
Dale St ME4 . . . . .9 E2
Dale Wlk TN24 . . . . .139 C7
Dalewood ME10 . . . . .37 A2
Dallas-Brett Cres CT19 . . .178 E8
Dallinger Rd 1 CT7 . . . . . . .26 F8
Dalmaney Cl CT10 . . . . .30 B5
Dalmatia Ct CT17 . . . . .149 A1
Dalmeny Ave CT9 . . . . .8 D1
Dalmeny Terr CT21 . . . . . . .176 A1
Dalton Ct 4 CT11 . . . . .52 E7
Dalton St ME7 . . . . .10 C6
Dame Janet
Comm Inf Sch CT12 . . . . . .29 B2
Dame Janet
Comm Jun Sch CT12 . . . . .29 B2
Damerham Ct CT2 . . . . .66 E3
Damiem Cl ME4 . . . . .10 A2
Dan Dr ME13 . . . . .62 A8
Danaway Cotts ME9 . . . . . .35 C3
Hartlip ME9 . . . . .34 D6
Dane Cl Chatham ME5 . . . . .32 C2
Hythe CT21 . . . . .187 D8
Dane Court Gdns CT10 . . . .29 D5
Dane Court Gram Sch
CT10 . . . . .29 E4
Dane Court Rd CT10 . . . . . .29 C6
Dane Cres CT11 . . . . .52 E8
Dane Ct ME17 . . . . .96 C2
Dane End Rd CT8 . . . . .27 D8
Dane Gdns CT9 . . . . .29 B8
Dane Hill CT9 . . . . .7 J3
Dane Hill Gr CT9 . . . . .7 J2
Dane Hill Row CT9 . . . . .7 J2
Dane John Ct 3 CT1 . . . . . .87 F7
Dane John Mews 1 CT1 . . .87 F7
Dane La ME9 . . . . .34 D6
Dane Mount CT9 . . . . .7 J2
Dane Park Rd Margate CT9 . .7 J2
Ramsgate CT11 . . . . .52 E8
Dane Park Villas CT9 . . . . . .8 A2
Dane Rd Birchington CT7 . . .26 D7
Margate CT9 . . . . .8 A2
Ramsgate CT11 . . . . .52 E8
Dane Valley Rd CT10,CT9 . .29 C8
Danecourt Sch ME8 . . . . . . .11 A2
Danedale Ave ME12 . . . . .4 F6
Danefield Ct ME14 . . . . .76 B4
Danehurst CT7 . . . . .7 C1
Danemore TN30 . . . . .179 B8
Danes Ct CT16 . . . . .149 D2
Danes Dr ME12 . . . . .6 D2
Danes Hill ME7 . . . . .11 A6
Danes Mead ME10 . . . . .14 F1
Danesmead Terr CT9 . . . . . . .7 J2
Daniel Ho ME16 . . . . .74 E5
Danley Rd ME12 . . . . .3 E7
Danley Mid Sch ME12 . . . . .3 E7
Danley Rd ME12 . . . . .3 E7
Danson Way ME8 . . . . .11 D2
Danton La CT18 . . . . .162 C1
Darby Pl CT20 . . . . .178 D5
Darby Rd CT20 . . . . .178 D5
Darenth Cl CT6 . . . . .23 B3
Darenth Rise ME5 . . . . .32 B3
Dargate Ct ME16 . . . . .74 D7
Dargate Rd
Dargate CT2,ME13 . . . . .64 F7
Yorklets CT5 . . . . .43 A3
Dargets Rd ME5 . . . . .32 A3
Dark Hill ME13 . . . . .62 C8
Darland Ave ME7 . . . . .10 E1
Darland Banks
Nature Reserve ★ ME7 . .33 A8
Darlinghurst Rd CT19 . . . .177 E7
Darlington Dr ME12 . . . . .4 A6
Darlington St CT20 . . . . . . .178 D5
Darnley Cl
Broadstairs CT10 . . . . .29 F3
Folkestone CT20 . . . . .177 F4
Darnley Rd CT2 . . . . .66 F4
Darracott Cl CT14 . . . . .117 B5
Darrell Cl CT6 . . . . .22 C3
Darren Gdns CT10 . . . . .29 F2
Darwin Coll CT2 . . . . .66 E5
Darwin Ct ME1 . . . . .9 D5
Darwin Rd Birchington CT7 .26 F8
Canterbury CT2 . . . . .66 E5
Daryngton Ave CT7 . . . . . . .26 C7
Davenport Ave ME7 . . . . . . .10 E7
David Ave CT9 . . . . .8 D2
Davids Cl CT10 . . . . .30 B3
Davidson Rd CT2 . . . . .66 D1

Davie Cl ME12 . . . . .3 B8
Davie Ct ME12 . . . . .3 B8
Davington Hill ME13 . . . . . .62 C8
Davington Prim Sch
ME13 . . . . .62 C8
Davis Ave CT14 . . . . .117 A4
Dawbourne TN30 . . . . .167 B3
Dawes Rd CT2,ME13 . . . . . .64 C4
Dawes St ME7 . . . . .10 C5
Dawn Rise ME12 . . . . .5 F6
Dawson Ct 7 ME7 . . . . . . .10 A6
Dawson Rd CT19 . . . . .178 D6
Dawson's Row CT4 . . . . . . .62 A6
Day Ho 2 ME14 . . . . .75 B4
Dayton Rd ME13 . . . . .83 C3
Daytona Way CT6 . . . . .22 A4
De Burgh Hill CT17 . . . . . .149 C1
De Burgh St 2 CT17 . . . . .166 C8
De Havilland Cl CT18 . . . . .163 B4
De Havillands CT4 . . . . .89 E3
De L'angle Ho CT4 . . . . .86 D3
De L'angle Row CT4 . . . . . . .86 D3
De Mere Cl ME8 . . . . .33 D6
Deacon Est The ME20 . . . . .53 A2
Deacon Trad Ctr ME2 . . . . . .9 A6
Deal Castle ★ CT14 . . . . . .117 D5
Deal Castle Rd CT14 . . . . .117 D5
Deal Ho ME15 . . . . .97 E8
Deal Maritime & Local
History Mus ★ CT14 . . . .117 D6
Deal Parochial
CE Prim Sch CT14 . . . . . .117 C5
Deal Rd CT13,CT14 . . . . .93 F5
Deal Sta CT14 . . . . .117 C6
Dean Croft CT6 . . . . .23 B2
Dean Ct 14 CT1 . . . . .67 A1
Dean Hill CT4,TN25 . . . . . .126 B2
Dean Mead TN19 . . . . .178 B7
Dean Rd ME10 . . . . .36 E6
Dean St ME15 . . . . .96 C6
Dean's Wlk TN23 . . . . .155 F7
Deane Cl CT5 . . . . .43 E7
Deane Ct 8 ME7 . . . . .10 C6
Deans Hill Rd ME9 . . . . .57 D5
Deans Mill Ct CT1 . . . . .66 F1
Deansway Ave CT2 . . . . .67 F7
Deanwood Cl ME8 . . . . .33 D6
Deanwood Dr ME8 . . . . .33 E6
Deanwood Prim Education
Tech Sch ME8 . . . . .33 D3
Deanwood Rd CT17 . . . . . .148 E2
Deborah Cl CT5 . . . . .43 F7
Deedes Cl CT21 . . . . .176 C3
Deerhurst Gdns ME16 . . . . .74 D4
Deerson La CT3 . . . . .70 A4
Deerton St ME9 . . . . .39 A2
Defiant Cl ME5 . . . . .32 B6
Defoe Cl ME5 . . . . .32 B6
Delacourt Cl CT12 . . . . .51 D5
Delamark Rd ME12 . . . . .1 D2
Delane Rd CT14 . . . . .117 A5
Delaware Cl CT2 . . . . .67 F6
Delce Inf Sch ME1 . . . . .9 D2
Delce Jun Sch ME1 . . . . . . .9 C2
Delce Rd ME1 . . . . .9 D4
Delf St CT13 . . . . .72 F1
Delfside CT13 . . . . .94 A8
Delmar Cl CT5 . . . . .21 D3
Demelza House Hospice
ME9 . . . . .35 F6
Demozay Cl CT18 . . . . .163 A4
Denbigh Ave ME8 . . . . .11 D1
Denbigh Cl ME10 . . . . .36 E7
Denbigh Rd CT12 . . . . .29 A1
Dence Cl CT6 . . . . .23 B5
Dence Pk CT6 . . . . .23 B4
Dencorra Way TN23 . . . . . .139 A1
Dene Farm La CT3 . . . . .91 A4
Dene The
Bethersden TN26 . . . . .153 D5
Canterbury CT1 . . . . .88 B5
Hythe CT21 . . . . .176 C2
Dene Wlk CT9 . . . . .28 F7
Dengemarsh Rd TN29 . . . .203 C3
Denham Ho TN29 . . . . .187 B4
Denham Ho ME10 . . . . .36 D5
Denham Rd ME9 . . . . .35 D7
Denmark Rd CT11 . . . . .52 E8
Denmark St CT19 . . . . .178 E6
Denne Cl CT2 . . . . .67 F7
Denne Manor La CT4 . . . . .106 C8
Dennes La TN29 . . . . .203 C4
Dennes Mill Cl TN25 . . . . .123 D2
Denness Rd TN23 . . . . .156 B7
Dennis Way CT19 . . . . .177 E7
Dennis Willocks Cl ME9 . . .35 B6
Densole La CT18 . . . . .163 A8
Densole Way CT18 . . . . . . .163 A8
Denstead Cotts CT4 . . . . . . .86 B8
Denstead Ct CT2 . . . . .66 C4
Denstead La CT4,ME13 . . . .86 C7
Denstead Oast CT4 . . . . . . .86 B8
Denstead Wlk 11 ME15 . . . .97 F6
Dent-De Lion Ct CT9 . . . . . .28 A8
Dent-De-Lion Rd
Margate CT9 . . . . .28 A8
Westgate-on-S CT8 . . . . .7 C1
Dental Cl ME10 . . . . .36 A5
Dental St CT21 . . . . .176 C2
Denton Cl ME15 . . . . .97 E8
Denton Way CT19 . . . . .8 C1
Derby Cl ME10 . . . . .36 D6
Derby Rd Gillingham ME5 . .10 E2
Maidstone ME15 . . . . .97 C8
Dering Cl Bridge CT4 . . . . . .88 F1
Pluckley TN27 . . . . .136 C4
Dering Rd Ashford TN24 . .139 D2

Dering Rd continued
Bridge CT4 . . . . .89 A1
Herne Bay CT6 . . . . .22 F7
Dering Terr TN27 . . . . .136 C3
Derings The TN29 . . . . . . .203 B6
Deringwood Dr ME15 . . . . .75 F1
Derringstone Downs
CT4 . . . . .128 F6
Derringstone Hill CT4 . . . .128 F6
Derringstone St CT4 . . . . .128 F6
Derville Ho ME18 . . . . .200 B6
Derville Rd TN29 . . . . .204 E2
Derwent Ave CT1 . . . . .52 A7
Derwent House 3 ME15 . .97 E7
Derwent Way
Aylesham CT3 . . . . .112 F6
Gillingham ME8 . . . . .33 D8
Desmond Cres ME13 . . . . . .63 A5
Detling Ave CT10 . . . . .30 A1
Detling CE Prim Sch
ME14 . . . . .55 A1
West Minst ME12 . . . . .3 B7
Detling Hill ME14 . . . . .55 B2
Devon Ave CT14 . . . . .117 C3
Devon Cl Chatham ME5 . . . .32 C7
Gillingham ME8 . . . . .11 F1
Devon Ct CT12 . . . . .29 B2
Devon Gdns CT7 . . . . .26 B7
Devon Rd Canterbury CT1 . .88 D8
Folkestone CT19 . . . . .178 D5
Maidstone ME15 . . . . .97 C8
Devonshire Gdns CT9 . . . . . .8 C3
Devonshire Rd
Dover CT17 . . . . .166 B8
Gillingham ME7 . . . . .10 D7
Devonshire Terr CT10 . . . . .30 B5
Dexter Cl TN25 . . . . .139 C8
Dhekelia Cl ME14 . . . . .75 A7
Dial Cl ME7 . . . . .10 F6
Dial Rd ME7 . . . . .10 F6
Diamond Cl ME1 . . . . .1 C1
Diamond Rd CT5 . . . . .20 E2
Diana Gdns CT14 . . . . .117 A5
Dibdin Rd CT14 . . . . .117 D7
Dickens Ave CT1 . . . . .67 D2
Dickens Cl ME17 . . . . .98 E4
Dickens Ct ME2 . . . . .9 D8
Dickens House Mus ★
CT10 . . . . .30 B4
Dickens Rd
Broadstairs CT10 . . . . .30 B5
Maidstone ME14 . . . . .74 E8
Rochester ME1 . . . . .9 C2
Dickens Wlk CT10 . . . . .30 B4
Dickley La ME17 . . . . .101 A6
Dickson Ct 7 ME10 . . . . . .37 B4
Dickson Rd CT17 . . . . .166 B8
Dickson's Cnr CT13 . . . . . . .95 A6
Dicksons Bourne TN29 . . .172 F6
Dieu Stone La CT16 . . . . . .166 E8
Digby Rd CT2 . . . . .177 E5
Dignals Cl ME8 . . . . .11 F2
Dignash TN25 . . . . .121 E2
Diligent Dr ME10 . . . . .36 F7
Dilnot La CT7 . . . . .27 B3
Diocesan & Payne Smith
CE Prim Sch CT1 . . . . .67 A1
Discovery Rd ME15 . . . . . . .76 B2
Discovery Wlk CT1 . . . . . . .88 C7
Disraeli Cl CT20 . . . . .97 E5
Dixon Cl ME15 . . . . .74 F2
Dixwell Cl ME8 . . . . .33 D5
Dixwell Rd CT20 . . . . .178 A4
Dobbie Cl ME10 . . . . .36 E6
Dock Exit Rd CT16 . . . . . . .166 F8
Dock Head Rd ME4 . . . . .10 A8
Dock Rd Chatham ME4 . . . . .9 F6
Gillingham ME4 . . . . .10 A7
Doctor's La CT15 . . . . .165 B5
Dodd's La CT16 . . . . .149 A3
Doddington Ct ME16 . . . . . .74 E5
Doddington Place
Gardens ★ ME9 . . . . .81 A7
Doddington Prim Sch
ME9 . . . . .80 F7
Doddington Rd ME8 . . . . . . .11 D3
Does Alley 4 ME10 . . . . . .36 F4
Dog Kennel La CT18 . . . . . .161 B7
Doggerel Acre CT5 . . . . .43 F7
Dogwood Cl ME5 . . . . .32 C1
Dola Ave CT14 . . . . .117 B6
Dolphin Cl CT10 . . . . .8 G3
Dolphin Dr ME8 . . . . .33 E5
Dolphin Ho 1 CT16 . . . . . .166 E7
Dolphin Pas 2 CT16 . . . . .166 E7
Dolphin Pk CT6 . . . . .23 B6
Dolphin Pl 3 CT16 . . . . . .166 E7
Dolphin St Deal CT14 . . . . .117 D7
Herne Bay CT6 . . . . .22 D5
Dolphin Yard Sailing
Barge Mus ★ ME10 . . . . . .37 A5
Dolphins Rd CT19 . . . . .178 D7
Dombey Cl ME1 . . . . .9 C3
Domneva Rd
Minster (Thanet) CT12 . . . .50 B6
Westgate-on-S CT8 . . . . . . .27 B6
Donald Moor Ave ME9 . . . . .38 C2
Doncaster Ct 7 ME15 . . . . .97 F6
Donegal Rd CT1 . . . . .88 C8
Donemowe Dr ME10 . . . . . . .36 F8
Donet Ct ME8 . . . . .33 C5
Dongola Rd ME2 . . . . .9 B8
Donkey La CT3 . . . . .112 C8
Donkey St CT21,TN29 . . . .186 E5

Cro – Dow **217**

Donnahay Rd CT12 . . . . . . .29 C3
Donnithorne Ho CT6 . . . . . .22 E5
Dorcas Gdns CT10 . . . . .30 A6
Doric Ct CT11 . . . . .52 C5
Dorman Ave N CT3 . . . . . .112 E6
Dorman Ave S CT3 . . . . . .112 F5
Dornden Gdns ME5 . . . . . . .32 B2
Dorne Cotts TN12 . . . . .118 C6
Dorothy Dr CT9 . . . . .29 C2
Dorrit Way ME1 . . . . .9 D2
Dorset Cl CT5 . . . . .43 B7
Dorset Ct Deal CT14 . . . . . .117 D2
Ramsgate CT11 . . . . .29 B2
Dorset Gdns
Birchington CT7 . . . . .26 F7
Deal CT14 . . . . .117 C2
Dorset Pl ME13 . . . . .62 C7
Dorset Rd
Canterbury CT1 . . . . .88 D7
West Minst ME12 . . . . .3 A7
Dorset Sq ME13 . . . . .11 D1
Dorset Way ME15 . . . . .97 C8
Dossett Ct CT14 . . . . .117 A2
Dotterel Cl ME5 . . . . .32 D2
Doubleday Dr ME9 . . . . .37 E2
Douglas Almshouses
ME17 . . . . .101 D5
Douglas Ave Hythe CT21 . .176 C2
Whitstable CT5 . . . . .20 E1
Douglas Bglws CT15 . . . . . .132 E8
Douglas Cl CT10 . . . . .29 E5
Douglas Rd Deal CT14 . . . .117 A3
Dover CT17 . . . . .166 B8
Herne Bay CT6 . . . . .23 A4
Lenham ME17 . . . . .101 D5
Maidstone ME16 . . . . .74 E3
Douglas Terr CT14 . . . . . . .117 C5
Dour Side CT17 . . . . .148 F3
Dour St CT16 . . . . .166 D8
Douro Cl CT1 . . . . .67 D1
Douro Pl CT16 . . . . .166 E7
Doust Way ME1 . . . . .9 D5
Dove Cl Ashford TN23 . . . .156 C3
Chatham ME5 . . . . .32 B6
Hythe CT21 . . . . .187 D8
Whitstable CT5 . . . . .43 C7
Dove Lea Gdns CT17 . . . . .148 E3
Dovecote Cl CT14 . . . . .107 B8
Dovedale CT7 . . . . .27 B7
Dovedale Ct
Ashford TN24 . . . . .139 B4
Birchington CT7 . . . . .27 B7
Dover Castle & Mus ★
CT16 . . . . .166 F8
Dover Coll CT17 . . . . .166 C8
Dover Gram Sch
for Boys CT17 . . . . .166 A8
Dover Gram Sch
for Girls CT16 . . . . .149 C1
Dover Hill CT19 . . . . .178 D8
Dover Ho 2 ME15 . . . . .97 E8
Dover Mus ★ CT16 . . . . . .166 D7
Dover Pl TN23 . . . . .139 C1
Dover Rd Barham CT4 . . . . .112 A1
Bishopsbourne CT4 . . . . . . .111 D5
Folkestone CT19,CT20 . . . .178 E7
Guston CT15 . . . . .149 E4
Ringwould CT14 . . . . .134 A6
Sandwich CT13 . . . . .93 F6
St Margaret's at Cliffe
CT15 . . . . .150 D6
Tilmanstone CT13,CT14 . . .115 B5
Woolage Green CT4 . . . . . .129 D6
Dover St Canterbury CT1 . .88 A7
Maidstone ME16 . . . . .74 C2
1 Sittingbourne ME10 . . . .36 E4
Doves Cnr CT14 . . . . .115 A4
Dowle Ct TN29 . . . . .29 A7
Down Barton Rd CT7 . . . . . .25 E1
Down Court Rd ME9 . . . . . . .59 C1
Down Ct TN23 . . . . .155 E5
Downer Ct ME1 . . . . .31 E8
Downhill Cl CT16 . . . . .148 D6
Downings The CT6 . . . . .23 A2
Downland Ct TN24 . . . . . . .139 B3
Downlands Deal CT14 . . . . .134 B8
Harrietsham ME17 . . . . . . .100 F6
Downs CE Prim Sch The
CT4 . . . . .117 B2
Downs Cl Charing TN27 . . .120 C8
East Studdal CT15 . . . . . . .132 D8
Hawkinge CT18 . . . . .163 A4
Maidstone ME14 . . . . .75 B8
Sittingbourne ME10 . . . . . . .36 D2
Downs Pk CT6 . . . . .23 A5
Downs Rd Canterbury CT2 . .66 F4
Deal CT14 . . . . .117 C3
East Studdal CT15 . . . . . . .132 E8
Folkestone CT19 . . . . .178 C7
Maidstone ME14 . . . . .75 B8
Ramsgate CT11 . . . . .52 B6
Downs The Chartham CT4 . .86 C1
Chatham ME5 . . . . .31 D1
Preston CT3 . . . . .70 C6
Downs View Inf Sch
TN24 . . . . .139 E7
Downs View Rd ME14 . . . . .75 B8
Downs Way
Charing TN27 . . . . .120 C8
Sellindge TN25 . . . . .159 C1
Downside
Bekesbourne CT4 . . . . .89 E3
Folkestone CT19 . . . . .178 C7
Rochester ME2 . . . . .9 A7

Downside *continued*
St Margaret's at Cliffe CT15 151 A6
Downside Rd CT16 149 B7
Downsview ME5 32 C8
Dragonfly Cl TN23 155 D8
Dragonfly Way CT18 163 B4
Dragoon Ho 10 CT1 67 A1
Drainless Rd CT13 93 A5
Drake Ave ME12 4 D5
Drake Ct 3 CT11 52 F8
Drake Rd TN24 157 B7
Drakes Cl ME9 12 E2
Drakes Lee TN28 200 E5
Drapers Almshouses CT9 29 A8
Drapers Ave CT9 28 F8
Drapers Cl CT9 29 A8
Drapers Mill (dis)★ CT9 8 A1
Drapers Mills Prim Sch CT9 29 A8
Drawbridge Cl ME15 97 E8
Dray's Field ME9 79 A7
Dreadnought Ave ME12 4 B6
Dreamland Fun Pk★ CT9 7 I2
Dresden Ct CT8 27 D8
Drew La CT14 117 C4
Drewery Dr ME8 33 C5
Drill La CT3 69 B1
Drive The Canterbury CT1 88 B6
Deal CT14 117 C5
Whitstable CT5 44 D8
Drop Redoubt Fort★ CT17 166 D7
Drop Redoubt Rd CT17 166 D7
Drove Rd ME12 3 E7
Drove The Fordwich CT2 68 A4
Monkton CT12 49 B6
Northbourne CT14 116 A5
Whitfield CT16 149 A8
Whitstable CT5 44 D8
Drovers Rdbt TN24 139 A4
Droveway Gdns CT15 151 A6
Droveway The CT15 151 B6
Drum La TN23 139 B2
Drury Rd TN30 167 B1
Drybeck Ave CT11 51 F7
Dryden Cl CT1 88 C7
Dryden Rd CT16 149 B3
Drywall Ind Est ME10 37 B6
Dublin Ho 16 ME15 97 E7
Duchess Of Kent Dr ME5 32 B3
Duck La Canterbury CT1 67 A1
Shadoxhurst TN26 169 F7
Duck St CT4 144 F4
Duckpit Rd CT4 126 A6
Duckworth Cl TN24 157 B7
Dudley Ave CT8 27 C8
Dudley Rd Ashford TN24 139 E5
Folkestone CT19 178 E5
Duke of Clarence Trad Est The ME12 1 B3
Duke of York's Royal Military Sch CT15 149 F4
Duke St Deal CT14 117 D7
Margate CT9 7 I3
Dukes Mdw TN26 183 A7
Dukes Meadow Dr ME7 32 F6
Dukes Wlk 7 ME15 75 A4
Dukeswood CT5 44 D6
Dully Rd ME9 59 E6
Dumergue Ave ME11 3 B5
Dumpton Gap Rd CT10 30 A2
Dumpton La CT11 29 E1
Dumpton Park Dr CT10, CT11 30 A2
Dumpton Park Rd CT11 52 E8
Dumpton Park Sta CT11 29 F1
Duncan Dr CT7 26 E8
Duncan Rd
Gillingham ME7 10 D5
Ramsgate CT11 52 D7
Whitstable CT5 43 D7
Dundein Dr CT16 149 B3
Dundonald Rd
11 Broadstairs CT10 30 B4
Ramsgate CT11 52 C7
Dunedin Cl ME10 36 C3
Dunedin House 9 ME15 97 E5
Dunedin Rd CT12 29 A1
Dunera Dr ME14 75 A7
Dunes Rd TN28 200 D3
Dungeness Nature Reserve★ TN29 205 D8
Dungeness Power Sta Visitor Ctr★ TN29 205 E6
Dungeness Rd TN29 204 C3
Dungeness Sta★ TN29 205 F6
Dunkeld Ho 6 ME15 97 E7
Dunkery Rise TN24 139 B4
Dunkirk Cl TN29 195 B7
Dunkirk Dr ME5 31 F6
Dunkirk Rd N ME13 64 B2
Dunkirk Rd S ME13 64 B1
Dunkirk Sq CT15 149 F3
Dunkirk Village Sch ME13 64 D2
Dunlin Ct TN29 195 A3
Dunn Street Rd ME7 55 A8
Dunnett Rd CT19 177 E6
Dunning's La ME1 9 C4
Dunnings The ME16 74 A2
Dunnock Rd TN25 139 B7
Dunoon Ct CT11 29 F1
Dunstall Cl TN29 195 A5
Dunstall Gdns TN29 195 A5
Dunstall La TN29 195 A5
Dunstan Ave CT8 27 D7
Dunster Terr 3 ME15 97 E8
Dunston Ho CT14 117 D8
Durban Cl CT12 29 A2
Durban Cres CT16 149 C4
Durban House 7 ME15 97 E5
Durban Rd CT9 8 A1
Durham Cl Canterbury CT1 87 F6
9 Dover CT17 166 D7
Maidstone ME15 75 E1
Durham Hill CT17 166 D7
Durham Rd ME8 33 C7
Durling Ct ME8 12 A1
Durlock CT12 50 C5
Durlock Ave CT11 52 B5
Durlock Rd CT3 92 B7
Durlocks The CT19 178 E5
Durnford Cl CT2 66 E2
Durovernum Ct CT1 88 A7
Durrell Gdns ME5 10 C1
Duval Dr ME1 31 E8
Duvard's Pl ME9 35 F1
Dyke Rd CT19 178 E5
Dymchurch Ho CT1 88 B8
Dymchurch Prim Sch TN29 195 C8
Dymchurch Rd
Hythe CT21 176 A2
Hythe,Palmarsh CT21, TN29 187 C6
St Mary's Bay TN29,TN28 195 A5
Dymchurch Sta★ TN29 195 B7
Dyngley Cl ME10 36 E6

E

Eagle Hill CT11 52 D7
Eagles Cl ME10 37 C4
Ealham Cl Ashford TN24 157 A8
Canterbury CT4 88 B5
Ealing Cl ME5 32 C4
Earl Cl ME5 32 B4
Earl St ME14 74 F4
Earl's Ave CT20 178 B4
Earls Ave TN24 139 F1
Earlsfield TN25 173 A6
Earlsfield Rd CT21 176 D2
Earlsmead Cres CT12 51 C5
Earlsworth Ct TN24 156 E6
Earlsworth Rd TN24 156 D6
Easole Hts CT15 113 D5
Easole St CT15 113 D5
East Blean Wood (Nature Reserve)★ CT3,CT6 46 B6
East Borough Prim Sch ME14 75 B5
East Cliff Dover CT16 166 F8
Folkestone CT19 178 F6
East Cliff & Warren Ctry Pk★ CT18 164 D1
East Cliff Gdns 19 CT19 178 E5
East Cliff Par CT6 23 A5
East Cliff Pas 20 CT19 178 E5
East Court (Sch for Dyslexics) CT11 52 G7
East Cross TN30 179 B7
East Ct ME15 75 A1
East End Rd ME4,ME7 10 D8
East Farleigh Prim Sch ME15 96 B6
East Farleigh Sta ME16 96 B8
East Gn ME10 15 A1
East Hall La ME10 37 C5
East Hill Ashford TN24 139 C2
Tenterden TN30 179 B8
East Kent Light Rly★ CT15 131 A7
East Kent Ret Pk CT10 29 B4
East La ME12 1 B2
East Langdon Rd
Guston CT15 149 F7
Martin Mill CT15 133 B2
East Lodge Rd TN23 138 F3
East Mountain La TN24 139 F7
East Norman Rd CT16 149 E1
East Northdown Cl CT9 8 E1
East Park Rd ME20 74 A8
East Ramp CT16 166 G8
East Rd Chatham ME4 10 A7
Folkestone CT20 177 D4
Gillingham ME4 10 A8
Sandwich CT13 73 A8
East Rise CT12 29 B1
East Roman Ditch CT16 166 F8
East Row ME1 9 C5
East St Ashford TN23 139 B2
Canterbury CT1 67 C3
Chatham ME4 10 A3
Dover CT17 166 C8
Faversham ME13 62 D7
Folkestone CT19 178 E5
Gillingham ME7 10 D6
Harrietsham ME17 100 E5
Herne Bay CT6 23 A5
Hythe CT21 176 D2
Sittingbourne ME10 37 A4
East Stour Ct TN24 139 D1
East Stour Prim Sch TN24 156 D6
East View
Brookland TN29 197 D8
Hersden CT3 46 F1
East Weald Dr TN30 167 B1
East Wootton Cotts CT4 109 A4
Eastbridge Rd TN29 195 B8
Eastbrook Pl CT16 166 E8
Eastchurch CE Prim Sch ME12 5 D3
Eastchurch Rd Margate CT9 8 E3
Minster (Sheppey) ME12 5 B5
Eastcourt Gn ME8 11 B4
Eastcourt La
Gillingham ME8 11 B3
Gillingham,Lower Twydall ME7,ME8 11 B4
Eastern Arm N CT16 166 H8
Eastern Arm S CT16 166 H8
Eastern Ave
Ashford TN23 139 A2
Halfway Houses ME12 3 D6
Queenborough ME11 3 B4
Eastern Espl
Broadstairs CT10 30 B5
Margate CT9 8 B3
Eastern Gdns TN24 156 E8
Eastern Rd Gillingham ME7 10 F6
Leysdown-on-S ME12 6 G2
Lydd TN29 203 D7
Eastern Service Rd CT16 166 H8
Eastfield House ME16 74 B2
Eastfield Rd 1 CT7 27 A7
Eastfields CT19 178 D6
Eastgate ME1 9 C5
Eastgate Cl CT6 23 B3
Eastgate Ct ME1 9 C5
Eastgate Rd TN30 179 C8
Eastgate Terr ME1 9 C5
Eastling Cl ME8 11 D3
Eastling Prim Sch ME13 81 F5
Eastling Rd Bayfield ME13 61 D2
Eastling ME13 81 F7
Eastmead Ave TN23 156 C8
Easton's Cnr TN25 172 F4
Eastry CE Prim Sch CT13 93 B2
Eastry Cl Ashford TN23 156 A6
Maidstone ME16 74 C7
Eastry Ct CT3 112 F5
Eastry Park CT13 93 C1
Eastwell 5 TN30 179 A7
Eastwell Barn Mews TN30 179 A8
Eastwell Cl
Maidstone ME14 75 C5
Shadoxhurst TN26 155 B1
Eastwell Meadows TN30 179 A8
Eastwell Terr TN25 122 E3
Eastwood Cotts ME9 38 E6
Eastwood Rd ME10 36 D5
Eaton Hill CT9 7 I2
Eaton Rd Dover CT17 166 B7
Margate CT9 7 I1
Eaves Ct ME10 37 B5
Eaves Rd CT17 166 A7
Ebbsfleet La CT12 51 A3
Ebony Cotts TN30 189 A6
Ebony Wlk ME16 74 B3
Eccleston Rd ME15 74 F2
Echo Cl ME15 97 F6
Echo Ho ME10 37 B3
Echo Wlk ME12 4 D6
Eclipse Dr ME10 36 E8
Eddie Willet Rd CT6 22 B3
Eddington Cl ME15 97 B6
Eddington La CT6 22 F3
Eddington Way CT6 22 E3
Eden Ave ME5 32 A7
Eden Ho TN23 156 C8
Eden Rd CT5 43 A7
Edenbridge Dr ME12 3 B8
Edenbridge Ho CT1 88 B8
Edenfield CT7 27 B7
Edgar Cl CT5 21 D3
Edgar Ho CT14 117 B3
Edgar Rd Canterbury CT1 67 B1
Dover CT17 149 B1
Margate CT9 8 A3
Minster (Thanet) CT12 50 B6
Edge End Rd CT10 29 F4
Edgehill Cl CT20 177 D4
Edger Pl 5 ME15 75 A4
Edinburgh Ho Deal CT14 117 A5
7 Dover CT17 166 D7
Edinburgh Pl CT20 178 B3
Edinburgh Rd
Ashford TN24 139 B2
Chatham ME4 10 C2
Gillingham ME7 10 D5
Margate CT9 28 B8
Edinburgh Sq ME15 97 D7
Edinburgh Wlk 5 CT9 28 B8
Edisbury Wlk ME8 33 D5
Edith Rd Faversham ME13 62 C6
Ramsgate CT11 52 C6
Westgate-on-S CT8 7 D1
Edmanson Ave CT9 7 E1
Edmund Cl ME16 74 A3
Edmund St CT3 91 A8
Edna Rd ME14 74 F8
Edred Rd CT17 166 B8
Edward Ct ME5 10 C1
Edward Dr CT7 27 B7
Edward Rd Canterbury CT1 88 A8
Folkestone CT19 178 D6
Kingsdown CT14 134 C6
Queenborough ME11 3 B5
Edward St Chatham ME4 10 A3
Rochester ME2 9 B7
Sheerness ME12 1 B3
Edward Terr 9 CT20 178 E6
Edwards Cl ME8 33 C5
Edwards Rd CT16 166 D8
Edwin Rd ME8 33 C8
Edwina Ave ME12 4 A7
Edwina Pl ME9 35 C7
Edyngham Cl ME10 37 A8
Effingham Cres CT17 166 D8
Effingham St
Dover CT17 166 D8
Ramsgate CT11 52 E6
Egbert Rd Birchington CT7 26 D8
Faversham ME13 62 C6
Minster (Thanet) CT12 50 B6
Westgate-on-S CT8 7 C1
Egerton CE Prim Sch TN27 118 F3
Egerton Dr CT9 8 E2
Egerton House Rd TN27 118 E4
Egerton Rd
Charing Heath TN27 119 C7
Maidstone ME14 74 E7
Pluckley TN27 119 B1
Temple Ewell CT16 148 E5
Eggarton La CT4 107 C2
Eggringe TN23 138 E1
Egremont Rd ME15 75 F2
Eighteen Acre La TN29 198 D8
Elder Cl ME17 99 D2
Elder Ct ME8 33 B6
Elders The CT3 68 F1
Eldon Pl 4 CT10 30 B4
Eldon St ME4 10 A4
Eleanor Dr ME10 36 F8
Elfrida Cl CT9 29 C8
Elgar Pl CT11 52 D7
Elham CE Prim Sch CT4 144 F4
Elham Cl Gillingham ME8 11 B3
Margate CT9 8 C1
Elham Rd CT1 87 E6
Elham Valley Railway Mus★ CT18 177 A8
Elham Valley Vineyards★ CT4 128 D4
Elham Way CT10 30 A2
Eling Ct ME15 97 A8
Eliot Coll CT2 66 E4
Elisons Wlk CT1 88 C8
Elizabeth Carter Ave CT14 116 F4
Elizabeth Ct
Broadstairs CT10 30 B6
Chatham ME5 32 A7
Gillingham ME8 11 C1
Herne Bay CT6 22 F5
Elizabeth Dr CT18 164 B2
Elizabeth Gdns CT21 176 B1
Elizabeth House ME14 75 A6
Elizabeth Kemp Ct CT12 29 C1
Elizabeth Rd CT11 52 F6
Elizabeth St CT17 166 D6
Elizabeth Way CT6 23 B3
Elizabethen Ct TN27 120 C7
Ellen Ave CT11 29 E2
Ellen's Hill CT14 116 E3
Ellen's Pl ME9 35 C6
Ellenden Ct CT2 66 C4
Ellens Rd CT14 116 F2
Ellenswood Cl ME15 76 A1
Ellesmere Mews TN28 200 C8
Ellingham Leas ME15 97 C7
Ellingham Way TN23 156 A5
Ellington Ave CT9 28 B8
Ellington High Sch CT11 52 C7
Ellington Inf Sch CT11 52 C7
Ellington Pl CT11 52 C7
Ellington Rd CT11 52 D7
Elliot Cl CT1 67 C3
Elliots Pl ME13 62 D7
Elliott Park Sch ME12 4 A7
Ellis Dr TN28 200 C8
Ellis Ho 7 ME14 75 B4
Ellis Rd CT5 21 A3
Ellis Way CT6 23 C2
Ellison Cl CT5 21 C1
Ellison Ct ME13 62 E6
Ellison Way ME8 12 A2
Elm Ave ME4 9 E1
Elm Cl TN27 118 F3
Elm Cotts TN25 122 E3
Elm Court Ind Est ME7 32 E3
Elm Ct CT8 27 E8
Elm Fields TN29 199 A6
Elm Gdns CT21 176 E2
Elm Gr Maidstone ME15 75 B3
Manston CT12 28 D1
Sittingbourne ME10 37 B4
Westgate-on-S CT8 27 E8
Elm Ho 11 CT21 176 B2
Elm La ME12 4 E5
Elm Park Gdns CT17 165 F7
Elm Pl TN23 155 F7
Elm Rd Aylesham CT3 112 E5
7 Folkestone CT19 178 E6
Gillingham ME7 10 E6
St Mary's Bay TN29 194 F3
Elm Tree Dr ME1 9 A2
Elm Wood Cl CT5 21 C2
Elm Wood W CT5 21 C2
Elmfield Gillingham ME8 11 A3
Tenterden TN30 179 B8
Elmfield Ct
Coxheath ME17 96 C3
Tenterden TN30 179 B8
Elmhurst Gdns ME4 9 E3
Elmleigh Rd CT3 90 A8
Elmley Ind Est ME11 3 A2
Elmley Marshes Nature Reserve★ ME12 16 F4
Elmley Rd ME12 4 D3
Elmley Way CT9 28 F6
Elms Ave CT11 52 D6
Elms Hill CT15 165 D6
Elms The Hersden CT3 46 E1
Teynham ME9 39 A2
Elms Vale Rd CT15,CT17 165 E7
Elmstead Pl 10 CT20 178 E5
Elmstone Cl ME16 74 B2
Elmstone Gdns CT9 8 E2
Elmstone Hole Rd ME17 100 D1
Elmstone La ME16 74 B2
Elmstone Rd
Gillingham ME8 33 D7
Ramsgate CT11 52 D7
Elmton La CT15 114 C1
Elmtree TN26 181 C1
Elmway ME12 5 F6
Elmwood Ave CT10 30 A8
Elmwood Cl CT10 30 A7
Elventon Cl CT19 177 E7
Elverland La ME13,ME9 61 B2
Elvington Cl ME16 74 D5
Elvington La CT18 162 E2
Elwick La 13 TN23 139 B2
Elwick Rd TN23 139 B2
Ely Cl ME8 11 E2
Embassy Cl ME7 10 F1
Emerald Cl ME1 31 D7
Emerald View ME12 6 E4
Emily Rd ME5 32 B6
Emmerson Gdns CT5 21 D3
Empire Terr CT9 28 E8
Empress Gdns ME12 6 D4
Emsworth Gr ME14 75 D6
Enbrook Rd CT20 177 E4
Enbrook Valley CT20 177 E5
Encombe CT20 177 D3
Enfield Rd CT14 117 D7
Engineers Ct 1 TN23 139 B2
English Martyrs' RC Prim Sch ME2 9 B8
Ennerdale ME13 62 E6
Ennerdale Gdns CT3 112 F6
Enterprise Bsns Est ME2 9 E7
Enterprise Cl ME2 9 D8
Enterprise Ctr The ME5 54 C8
Enterprise Rd
Maidstone ME15 75 A1
Margate CT9 29 A6
Enticott Cl CT5 21 A1
Epaul La ME1 9 C6
Eppe Cl 2 ME2 9 B8
Epping Cl CT6 23 B2
Epple Bay Ave CT7 27 B8
Epple Bay Rd CT7 27 A8
Epple Rd CT7 27 B8
Epps Rd ME10 36 E3
Epsom Cl ME15 97 F6
Eric Rd CT17 149 B2
Erith Cl ME14 75 A8
Erith St CT17 149 B1
Ernest Dr ME16 74 B5
Ernest Rd ME4 10 A3
Ernwell Rd CT19 178 D6
Ersham Rd CT1 88 A7
Eskdale Ave CT11 52 A7
Esmonde Dr CT12 27 F2
Esplanade Dover CT17 166 D6
Rochester ME1 9 B5
Westgate-on-S CT8,CT9 7 C1
Essella Pk TN24 139 E1
Essella Rd TN24 139 E1
Essetford Rd TN23 156 A7
Essex Ave CT6 22 B4
Essex Gdns CT7 26 F6
Essex Rd Canterbury CT1 88 D7
Maidstone ME15 97 E6
Westgate-on-S CT8 27 F8
Essex St CT5 43 D8
Estelle Cl ME1 31 D7
Esther Ct ME10 36 E8
Estuary Cl CT5 21 E3
Estuary Rd ME12 1 C1
Etchden Rd TN26 154 A8
Ethel Rd CT10 29 F5
Ethel-Maud Ct ME7 10 D7
Ethelbert Cres CT9 8 A3
Ethelbert Gdns CT9 7 J3
Ethelbert Rd
Birchington CT7 26 D8
Canterbury CT1 88 B6
Deal CT14 95 C1
Dover CT17 166 C8
Faversham ME13 62 C6
Folkestone CT19 178 D7
Margate CT9 7 J3
Ramsgate CT11 52 D6
Rochester ME1 9 C4
Ethelbert Road Inf Sch ME13 62 C6
Ethelbert Sq CT8 7 C1
Ethelbert Terr Margate CT9 8 A3
Westgate-on-S CT8 7 C1
Ethelburga Dr CT18 161 B7
Ethelred Ct ME13 62 C6
Ethelred Rd CT8 7 C1
Eton Cl ME5 31 F4
Ettrick Terr CT21 176 A2
Eurogate Bsns Pk TN24 139 B5
Eurolink Way ME10 36 F4
Eva Rd ME7 10 D3
Evans Rd TN24 157 A7
Evelings Alley 12 CT5 20 D2
Evelyn Cl ME2 9 C8
Evelyn Ct CT21 177 A2
Evelyn Ho
9 Folkestone CT20 178 D5
5 Rochester ME2 9 C8
Evelyn Rd ME16 74 E3

Evenhill Rd CT3 ....89 E8
Everard Way ME13 ....62 B8
Everglades The ME7 ....32 F6
Evergreen Cl
  Gillingham ME7 ....33 A5
  Iwade ME9 ....14 D4
Everist Ct CT18 ....161 C6
Eversley Cl ME16 ......74 C6
Eversley Coll CT20 ...177 A3
Eversley Rd CT21 .....177 B3
Eversley Way CT20 ...177 F5
Evington Pottery TN25 .142 D7
Evison Cl CT16 ....149 B2
Ewart Rd ME4 ....9 E1
Exchange St CT14 ....117 D7
Exeter Cl CT19 ....177 D6
Exeter Wlk ME1 ....31 C7
Exmoor Rise TN24 ....139 B4
Exmouth Rd ME7 ......10 C7
Exton Cl ME5 ....32 C2
Exton Gdns ME14 .....75 F5
Eyhorne St ME17 ......77 D2
Eynsford Cl CT9 ....8 F2
Eynsford Rd ME16 ....74 D7
Eythorn Court Barn
  CT15 ....131 B7
Eythorne Cl TN24 ....139 D5
Eythorne Elvington
  Com Prim Sch CT15 ..131 C8
Eythorne Rd CT15 ....130 E6
Eythorne Sta CT15 ...131 C8

F

Faggs Wood
  Forest Wlks★ TN26 ...170 D2
Fagus Cl ME5 ....32 B1
Fair St CT10 ....29 E4
Fair View Com Inf Sch
  ME8 ....33 C5
Fair View Com Jun Sch
  ME8 ....33 C5
Fairacre CT10 ....29 E4
Fairacres Cl CT6 ......23 C4
Fairbourne Heath Cotts
  ME17 ....100 B1
Fairbourne La ME17 ..100 C4
Fairfax Bsns Ctr ME15 .97 F4
Fairfax Cl
  Folkestone CT20 .....177 D5
  Gillingham ME8 ....33 D4
Fairfax Dr CT6 ....23 F5
Fairfield Deal CT14 ...116 F6
  Elham CT4 ....144 F5
Fairfield Cl TN28 ....200 B7
Fairfield Pk CT10 .....29 E4
Fairfield Rd
  Broadstairs CT10 .....29 E4
  Minster (Thanet) CT12 ..50 B7
  New Romney TN28 ....200 B7
  Ramsgate CT11 ....29 E2
Fairfield Terr TN26 ..183 A4
Fairhurst Dr ME15 ....96 B4
Fairings The TN30 ...179 B8
Fairlawn CT5 ....21 D1
Fairlawn Rd CT12 .....29 B3
Fairlead Rd ME1 ....9 D1
Fairleas ME10 ....37 B2
Fairlight Ave CT12 ...52 B8
Fairlight Rd CT21 ....176 A3
Fairmeadow ME14 ....74 F4
Fairoaks CT6 ....23 B3
Fairservice Cl ME10 ..37 C5
Fairview CT21 ....175 A3
Fairview Ave ME8 .....33 B5
Fairview Cl CT9 ....8 A2
Fairview Cotts ME15 ..96 F5
Fairview Gdns
  Deal CT14 ....117 A2
  Sturry CT2 ....68 A6
Fairview Ind Pk TN26 .183 D7
Fairview Rd
  Elvington CT15 ....114 B1
  Sittingbourne ME10 ...37 A3
Fairway Ave CT19 ....178 A7
Fairway Cl Rochester ME1 ..9 C1
  St Mary's Bay TN29 ..194 F3
Fairway Cres CT5 .....43 A7
Fairway The Deal CT14 ..117 C8
  Herne Bay CT6 ....22 D2
  Hythe CT21 ....176 C1
  Littlebourne-on-S TN28 ..200 D6
  Rochester ME1 ....9 C1
  Sittingbourne ME10 ...36 E1
  St Mary's Bay TN29 ..195 A3
Fairways The ME13 ...62 A6
Fairwood Ind Est TN23 .139 A1
Falcon Cl CT6 ....45 F7
Falcon Ct
  Sittingbourne,Fernleigh
  ME10 ....37 A2
  3 Sittingbourne,Murston
  ME10 ....37 A4
Falcon Gdns ME12 .....4 D7
Falcon Way TN23 ....155 E7
Falkland Pl ME5 ....31 E1
Fallowfield Chatham ME5 ..32 B8
  Sittingbourne ME10 ...37 A2
Fallowfield Cl ME14 ..75 E4
Fan The CT16 ....166 H8
Fanconi Rd ME5 ....32 B3
Fancy Row ME14 .....76 C5
Fane Way ME8 ....33 D4
Fans La ME9 ....14 D4
Fant La ME16 ....74 B2
Faraday Rd ME14 .....75 C7
Fareham Wlk [10] ME15 ..97 F6

Farleigh Ct ME16 .....74 A2
Farleigh Hill ME15 ...74 E1
Farleigh Hill Ret Pk
  ME15 ....74 E1
Farleigh La ME16 .....74 A1
Farleigh Rd CT2 ......67 A3
Farleigh Trad Est ME15 .74 E1
Farley Cl Chatham ME5 ..32 A1
  Shadoxhurst TN26 ....155 A1
Farley Rd CT9 ....28 F7
Farm Cl TN23 ....155 E7
Farm Cres ME10 ......37 A2
Farm House Cl ME5 ...43 F8
Farm La CT14 ....116 F6
Farm Rd Chatham ME5 ..31 E3
  Hamstreet TN26 ......183 A7
  Leeds ME17 ....99 A6
Farmhouse Cl CT4 ...128 F7
Farnborough Cl ME16 .74 C2
Farncombe Way CT16 .149 B7
Farne Cl ME15 ....97 A6
Farnham ME8 ....12 B1
Farningham Cl ME14 ..75 C6
Farraday Cl ME1 ......31 D8
Farrar Cl CT7 ....27 A6
Farrers Wlk TN23 ....156 B4
Farrier Cl Ashford TN23 ..138 F5
  Maidstone ME14 ......75 E5
Farrier St CT14 ......117 D7
Farriers Ct ME8 ....34 C8
Farrow Ct TN23 ......156 A6
Farthing Cnr ME9 .....33 E3
Farthingloe Ct CT17 .166 A6
Farthingloe Rd CT17 .166 A6
Farthings Cotts ME14 ..53 F1
Farthings Ct CT2 .....66 C4
Fauchon's Cl ME14 ...75 F3
Fauchon's La ME14 ...75 F4
Faulkners La CT2 .....66 A1
Faussett Hill CT4 ....109 F8
Faversham
  Cottage Hospl ME13 ..62 C7
Faversham
  Miniature Rly★ ME13 ..61 A8
Faversham Rd
  Boughton Lees TN24,TN25 ..122 E5
  Challock ME13,TN27 ..104 C3
  Charing TN27 ....103 E1
  Faversham ME13,ME9 ..61 B5
  Lenham ME17 ....101 E2
  Pested TN25,ME13 ...105 B4
  Whitstable CT5 ......42 C6
  Wichling ME17,ME9 ...80 B4
Faversham Reach ME13 .62 D8
Faversham Sta ME13 ..62 D6
Faversham Stone Chap★
  ME13 ....61 E7
Fawley Cl ME14 ....74 E7
Fay Cl ME1 ....9 B3
Featherbed La
  Selling ME13 ....84 A7
  Sittingbourne ME9 ...14 E2
Featherby Cotts ME7 ..10 F6
Featherby Inf Sch ME8 ..11 A3
Featherby Jun Sch ME8 ..11 A3
Featherby Rd
  Gillingham,Lower Twydall
  ME7 ....11 A5
  Gillingham,Twydall ME8 ..11 A3
Felborough Cl CT4 ...107 C8
Felderland Cl
  Park Wood ME17 .....97 E5
  Sandwich CT14 ....93 F5
Felderland Dr ME17 ..97 E5
Felderland La CT14 ...93 E4
Felderland Rd ME17 ..97 E5
Feldspar Cl ME5 ......32 A1
Fellows Cl ME8 ....33 B6
Fennel Cl ME16 ....74 B3
Fennell Cl ME1 ....9 B3
Fenner Cl CT20 ......177 E4
Fenoulhet Way CT6 ...23 A5
Fenton Ct CT14 ......117 B6
Ferdi Lethert Ho TN24 .139 E5
Ferguson Cl CT21 ....176 F2
Ferguson Rd TN29 ...202 D2
Fern Bank Cres CT19 .178 D6
Fern Cl Hawkinge CT18 .163 C6
  Whitstable CT5 ......21 C1
Fern Ct CT10 ....30 B5
Fern Wlk ME10 ....37 C5
Fernbank Cl ME5 .....31 F2
Ferndale Cl ME12 ......3 D6
Ferndale Ct CT7 ......27 A6
Ferndale Rd ME7 .....10 E5
Ferndown CT7 ....26 D8
Ferndown Cl ME7 ....33 A5
Ferne La CT15 ....147 D3
Ferne Way CT20 .....177 E6
Fernfield CT18 ....163 C6
Fernfield La CT18 ...163 C7
Fernhill Rd ME16 ....74 A2
Fernlea Ave CT6 ......22 E4
Fernleigh Cl ME13 ...64 B3
Fernley Ct [11] CT20 .178 D5
Ferrier Cl ME8 ....33 E4
Ferry Rd Iwade ME9 ..14 E4
  Queenborough ME11,ME12 ..3 D1
Ferry View ME11 ....2 F3
Fiddling La TN25 ....159 E6
Field Ave CT1 ....67 D3
Field Cl ME5 ....31 E6
Field End TN24 ......140 A1
Field End Pl ME13 ....64 A3
Field Mill Rd TN27 ..119 B5
Field View
  Kingsnorth TN23 ....156 B4

Field View continued
  Whitstable CT5 ....43 B7
Field View Cl ME12 ....3 C6
Field Way CT2 ....67 F5
Fielder Cl ME10 ......37 C5
Fielding St ME13 .....62 C7
Fieldings The ME10 ..36 E2
Fieldworks Rd ME7 ...10 A7
Fiesta Wlk CT1 ....88 C7
Fife Rd CT6 ....22 B3
Fifth Ave CT9 ....8 B3
Fig Tree Rd CT10 .....29 F7
Fig Tree Wlk CT15 ..131 C7
Fiji Terr ME14 ....75 A7
Filer Rd ME12 ....3 E7
Filmer Rd CT4 ....88 F1
Finch Cl ME14 ....74 E7
Finch Gr CT21 ....187 D8
Finch Mews CT14 ...117 C4
Finches The
  Sittingbourne ME10 ...36 F3
  St Nicholas at Wade CT7 ..25 E2
Findlay Cl ME8 ....33 D6
Findley Ct [9] CT21 ..176 B2
Finglesham Ct ME15 .97 C8
Finlay Cl ME13 ....62 B7
Finn Farm Ct TN23 ..156 D1
Finn Farm Rd TN23 ..156 C2
Finsbury Ct CT11 .....52 E8
Finsbury Rd CT11 ....52 E8
Fintonagh Dr ME14 ..75 B6
Finwell Rd ME8 ....12 A2
Fir Ct TN24 ....139 F1
Fir Tree Cl CT11 .....52 C6
Fir Tree Gr Bredhurst ME7 ..33 B1
  Chatham ME5 ....32 D1
Fir Tree Hill CT13 ....93 B6
Firbank Gdns CT9 ....28 D7
Firbanks CT5 ....43 F8
Firethorn Cl ME7 .....10 E6
Firmin Ave ME17 .....97 D5
Firs Cl CT19 ....177 D7
Firs La CT19 ....177 D7
Firs Rd CT4 ....112 F1
Firs The Deal CT14 ..117 C8
  Hersden CT3 ....46 E1
First Ave Broadstairs CT10 ..8 F2
  Chatham ME4 ....10 C2
  Eastchurch ME12 ......5 E5
  Gillingham ME7 ....10 E3
  Margate CT9 ....8 B3
  Rushenden ME11 ......2 F3
  Sheerness ME12 ....1 D1
First La ME15 ....76 E2
Firtree Cl CT20 ......178 E5
Fish Market CT19 ...178 E5
Fisher Cl CT21 ....176 D1
Fisher Rd Canterbury CT2 ..66 D1
  Chatham ME5 ....32 B7
Fisher St Maidstone ME14 ..75 A6
  Sandwich CT13 ....73 A1
Fisher Street Rd ME13 ..83 E2
Fishermans Ctyd CT14 .117 D3
Fishmonger's La [6]
  CT16 ....166 E7
Fitzgerald Ave CT6 ...22 C4
Fitzmary Ave CT9 ......7 E1
Fitzroy Ave
  Broadstairs CT10 ......8 G2
  Margate CT9 ....8 B1
  Ramsgate CT12 ....29 B2
Fitzroy Rd CT5 ....20 F2
Fitzthorold Ho ME7 ..10 E7
Fitzwalter Rd [1] CT16 ..149 B3
Fitzwilliam Rd ME14 ..75 F5
Five Acre Wood Sch
  ME15 ....97 B7
Five Bells La ME1 ......9 D4
Five Vents La TN29 ..199 B8
Five Ways Ct ME4 ....10 A4
Fiveways L Ctr ME4 ..10 A4
Fiveways Rise CT14 ..116 F5
Flamingo Cl ME5 .....32 A7
Flamingo Dr CT6 .....22 E3
Flanders Cl ME10 .....14 F1
Flanders Field TN25 .157 E4
Flax Court La CT15 ..131 C2
Flaxman Ct [18] ME7 ..10 A6
Flaxman Dr ME16 .....74 C6
Flaxpond Rd TN23 ...155 F7
Fleet Ave ME12 ....1 C1
Fleet Rd Rochester ME1 ..9 D1
  St Margarets' at Cliffe
  CT15 ....134 A1
Fleet Villas TN24 ....139 D7
Fleets La CT2 ....66 D7
Fleetwood Ave CT6 ...22 D4
Fleetwood Cl ME12 ....4 B6
Fleming Rd CT13,CT3 ..92 D6
Fleming Way CT19 ...178 E8
Fletcher Rd CT5 ......21 B1
Flete Rd CT9 ....28 D5
Fleur de Lis
  Heritage Ctr★ ME13 ..62 D7
Flimwell TN23 ....155 D6
Flint Cl ME10 ....36 E8
Flint Cotts CT7 ....26 F6
Flint Gn ME5 ....32 C3
Flint La ME17 ....79 C1
Flood Hatch ME15 ...74 D2
Flood La ME13 ....62 C8
Flood St TN25 ....157 D2
Flora Rd CT11 ....52 E8
Florence Ave CT5 .....43 B7
Florence Cotts CT11 ..52 D6
Florence Ct CT9 ....8 B3
Florence Rd
  Maidstone ME16 .....74 E3

Florence Rd continued
  3 Ramsgate CT11 .....52 D6
Florence St [3] ME2 ...9 B8
Florida Cl CT16 ......149 B3
Florin Dr ME1 ....9 B4
Flower Rise ME14 ....74 F7
Flume End ME15 .....74 D2
Flying Horse La [4]
  CT16 ....166 E7
Foads Hill CT12 ......51 D6
Foads La CT12 ....51 D5
Fodbury Ct CT8 ....7 C1
Foley Cl ME14 ....75 A5
Foley St ME14 ....75 A5
Folkestone Mus★ CT20 ..178 D5
Folkestone Race Course
  CT21 ....175 A6
Folkestone Rd
  Brookland TN31 ......196 B3
  Church Hougham CT15 ..165 D4
  Dover CT17,CT15 ....166 B7
Folkestone Sch for Girls
  The CT20 ....177 F4
Folkestone West Sta
  CT18 ....177 F5
Folks Wood Way CT21 .175 A4
Folkstone House [4]
  ME15 ....97 F6
Folly Rd CT20 ....178 E6
Fonblanque Rd ME12 ..1 D2
Fontwell Cl ME15 .....97 F6
Foord Almshouses
  ME1 ....9 B3
Foord Rd ME17 ......101 D5
Foord Rd S ME13 ....40 C1
Foord Rd S [14] CT20 ..178 D5
Foord St ME1 ....9 C4
Forbes Rd ME13 .....62 C6
Ford Cl Bridge CT4 ...88 F1
  Herne Bay CT6 ....22 A4
Ford Hill CT3,CT6 ....46 E8
Ford Way TN23 ......138 F1
Ford Wlk CT5 ....43 A3
Fordcombe Cl ME15 ..97 F7
Fordingbridge Cl ME16 .74 B5
Fordoun Rd CT10 .....29 F5
Fordwich Cl ME16 ...74 B7
Fordwich Gn ME8 ....11 C3
Fordwich Gr CT10 ...29 E7
Fordwich Pl CT13 ....93 F8
Fordwich Rd CT2 .....67 F4
Fordwich TH★ CT2 ...68 A4
Foreland Ave
  Folkestone CT19 ....178 F6
  Margate CT9 ....8 D1
Foreland Ct
  Birchington CT7 ......26 D8
  Ramsgate CT11 ....52 D5
  St Margaret's at Cliffe
  CT15 ....151 A5
Foreland Hts CT10 ...30 B7
Foreland Park Ho CT10 .30 B7
Foreland Rd CT15 ...151 A4
Foreland Sch The CT10 ..30 A6
Foreland The CT1 .....88 B5
Forelands Sq CT14 ...117 B3
Foreness Cl CT10,CT9 ..8 G3
Forest Cotts TN25 ...105 C2
Forest Dr ME5 ....31 F2
Forest Hill ME15 .....74 F1
Forestall Mdw TN23 .156 B4
Forestdale Rd ME5 ...54 A8
Foresters Cl ME5 .....31 F2
Foresters Way CT20 .178 D5
Forestry Cotts CT4 ..125 E7
Forge Cl Eythorne CT15 .131 C7
  Sellindge TN25 ......159 D1
  Sturry CT2 ....67 F5
Forge Cotts CT3 ......47 C8
Forge Field CT15 ....164 E5
Forge Hill
  Aldington TN25 ......173 A5
  Bethersden TN26 ....153 E5
Forge Ho Canterbury CT1 ..87 E6
  Ickham CT3 ....69 C1
Forge La Ashford TN23 ..139 B2
  Boxley ME14 ....54 C2
  Boyden Gate CT3 .....47 C8
  Bredhurst ME7 ....33 A1
  Dean Street ME15 ....96 C7
  Egerton Forstal TN27 .118 C1
  Gillingham ME7 ....10 E7
  Leeds ME17 ....98 F7
  Ramsgate CT12 ....52 C7
  Sutton CT15 ....133 A6
  Upchurch ME9 ....12 F3
  Whitfield CT16 ......149 A8
  Whitstable CT5 ......43 D8
Forge Lane Cty Inf Sch
  ME7 ....10 E6
Forge Mdw TN30 ....190 A4
Forge Meadow ME17 .100 D6
Forge Meads TN30 ..188 E3
Forge Path CT16 ....149 A8
Forge Rd ME10 ....36 E6
Forgefield TN26 .....153 D5
Forgefields CT6 ......46 B8
Forrens The [15] CT1 ..67 A1
Forrester Cl CT1 .....67 C2
Forson Cl TN30 .....179 B8
Forstal Cotts
  Aylesford ME20 ......53 B2
  Lenham Heath ME17 ..102 A1
Forstal La ME17 ......96 D4
Forstal Rd
  Egerton Forstal TN27 .118 C1
  Pratling Street ME20 .53 C2
  Woolage Village CT4 ..112 E1

Eve – Fre 219

Forstal The Preston CT3 ..70 B6
  Wye TN25 ....123 E2
Forsters ME17 ....98 E4
Fort Amherst Heritage Pk
  & Caverns★ ME4 ......9 F5
Fort Burgoyne (Casemated
  Barracks) CT15 .....149 E2
Fort Burgoyne Rd CT16 .149 E1
Fort Cl TN29 ....204 E6
Fort Cotts CT10 ......30 B4
Fort Cres CT9 ....7 J3
Fort Hill CT9 ....7 J3
Fort Lower Prom CT9 ..7 J3
Fort Luton Model Mus★
  ME4 ....10 A1
Fort Paragon CT9 ......7 J3
Fort Pitt Gram Sch ME4 ..9 E4
Fort Pitt Hill ME1,ME4 ..9 E4
Fort Pitt St ME4 ....9 E3
Fort Prom CT9 ....7 J3
Fort Rd Broadstairs CT10 ..30 B4
  Hythe CT21 ....176 A2
  Margate CT9 ....7 I3
Fort St ME1 ....9 D4
Fortuna Ct CT11 ......52 D7
Forty Acres Hill ME12 ..4 C4
Forty Acres Rd CT2 ..66 E2
Forum The [2] ME5 ...36 F4
Forward Way ME1 ....31 C6
Fostall Gn TN23 .....155 F7
Fostall Rd ME13 ......40 C1
Foster Cl CT19 ......177 E7
Foster Clark Est ME15 .75 B2
Foster Clarke Dr ME17 .97 D5
Foster Rd TN24 .....157 A6
Foster St ME15 ....75 A3
Foster Way CT14 ....117 B5
Foster's Ave CT10 ...29 E7
Foster's Ct CT13 .....94 A7
Fostington Way ME5 ..31 F1
Foulds Cl ME8 ....33 B5
Foundry Wharf ME1 ...9 E4
Fountain Ent Pk ME15 .75 A1
Fountain Inn Ct CT9 ...7 I3
Fountain La ME16 ....74 A2
Fountain St
  [2] Sittingbourne ME10 ..36 E4
  [3] Whitstable CT5 ...20 D2
Fountains Cl TN24 ..140 A1
Four Oaks ME13 .....61 E8
Four Turnings CT3 ...70 B3
Four Wents
  Langley Heath ME17 ..98 E3
  Maidstone ME17 ......97 F2
Fouracre Cotts ME9 ..34 E6
Fourth Ave Eastchurch ME12 .5 F5
  Gillingham ME7 ......10 E4
Fowey Cl ME5 ....32 C5
Fowler Cl ME8 ....33 C3
Fox Cl CT18 ....161 B7
Fox Hill ME10,ME9 ...37 D3
Fox Holt Rd CT15 ...146 B2
Fox St ME7 ....10 C6
Fox Way CT4 ....128 F8
Fox's Cross CT5 ......43 B4
Fox's Cross Hill CT5 ..43 A3
Fox's Cross Rd CT5 ..43 C3
Foxborough Cl CT13 ..93 B6
Foxborough Hill CT13 ..93 B5
Foxborough La CT12 ..50 C6
Foxburrow Cl ME8 ...33 D5
Foxden Dr ME15 .....75 F1
Foxdown Cl CT2 ......66 E2
Foxglove Cres ME14 ..31 E4
Foxglove Gn TN24 ..139 E2
Foxglove Rd TN24 ..139 E1
Foxglove Rise ME14 ..74 E7
Foxgrove ME10 ....36 E7
Foxgrove Rd CT5 .....21 A1
Foxhunter Pk The CT12 ..49 D6
Foxley Rd ME11 ....3 A5
Frampton Rd CT21 ..176 A2
France Rd CT16 .....149 A5
Frances Gdns CT11 ..52 F8
Francis Ave CT13 .....95 B7
Francis Dr ME5 ....32 A2
Francis La ME15 ......97 F5
Francis Rd Ashford TN23 .156 B8
  Broadstairs CT10 .....30 B7
Frank Walters Bsns Pk
  The CT10 ....29 D3
Frankapps Cl ME9 ...35 B6
Franklin Dr ME14 ....75 D4
Franklin Rd ME7 .....10 D5
Franklins Cotts ME15 .96 C5
Franklyn Rd CT2 .....87 C8
Franks Ct ME8 ....11 B2
Freda Cl CT10 ....29 F1
Frederick Rd Deal CT14 .117 A3
  Gillingham ME7 ......10 C4
Frederick St ME10 ....36 E4
Freedown The CT15 .151 A7
Freeman Ct [3] ME10 .36 E4
Freeman Gdns ME4 ...9 F2
Freeman Way ME15 ..97 E7
Freeman's Cl CT5 ....43 A6
Freeman's Rd CT12 ..50 B6
Freemen's Way CT14 .117 B3
Freesia Cl ME7 ....10 F6
Fremantle Rd CT20 ..177 E5
Fremlins Rd ME14 ...76 C4
French's Row ME9 ...38 D2
Frencham Cl CT2 .....67 A4
Frensham Cl ME10 ...37 B4
Frensham Wlk ME5 ..31 F1

Freshfield La CT21 .....176 B4
Freshland Rd ME16 ....74 B4
Freshlands CT6 ....23 E5
Freshwater Cl CT6 .....22 B3
Freshwater Rd ME5 ....32 B7
Friars Ave ME5 ....31 F2
Friars Cl CT5 ....21 A1
Friars Sch TN23 ....155 B8
Friars The CT1 ....66 F1
Friars Way CT16 ......149 A3
Friary Pl 3 ME2 ....9 B7
Friary Prec ME2 ....9 B7
Friary Way CT2 ....66 D2
Frid Cnr TN26 ....153 E2
Friendly Cl CT9 ....8 D1
Friends Ave CT9 ....29 D8
Friesian Way TN24 ...139 C8
Frindsbury Rd ME2 .....9 B8
Frinstead Wlk ME16 ...74 B7
Frinsted Cl ME8 ....11 C3
Frinsted Rd ME9 ....58 E2
Friston Way ME1 ......172 C6
Frith Rd Aldington TN25 .172 C6
   Dover TN16 ....149 C1
Frithwood Cl ME15 ....75 F1
Frittenden Cl TN23 ...155 E6
Frobisher Cl ME10 .....36 E7
Frobisher Ct 2 CT11 ...52 F8
Frobisher Gdns ME1 ....9 C2
Frog Farm Cotts ME9 ..13 A4
Frog La CT4 ....111 C6
Frogmore Wlk ME17 ..101 C5
Frognal Cl ME9 ....38 B2
Frognal Gdns ME9 .....38 C2
Frognal La ME9 ....38 B2
Front Brents ME13 .....62 D8
Front Rd TN26 ....169 A1
Front St CT14 ....133 F5
Front The CT15 ....151 A4
Frost Cres ME5 ....32 A7
Froyle Cl ME16 ....74 C6
Fruiterer's Cl ME9 .....59 B7
Fulbert Dr ME14 ....75 F5
Fulbert Rd CT16 ......149 B5
Fulham Ave CT9 ....28 C7
Fullers Cl ME14 ....76 A4
Fullers Yd ME9 ....7 J2
Fulmar Ct TN29 ......194 F3
Fulsam Pl ME2 ....7 H1
Fulston Manor Sch ME10 36 F2
Fulston Pl ME10 ....37 A3
Furfield Cl ME17 ....97 E5
Furley Park Prim Sch
   TN23 ....156 C2
Furrell's Rd ME1 ....9 D5
Furze Hill Cres ME12 ...3 E6
Fusilier Ave CT20 ....177 B5
Fyndon Ho CT1 ....88 C7

G

Gabriel's Hill ME15 ....75 A4
Gadby Rd ME10 ....36 C5
Gads Hill ME7 ....10 F6
Gadsby La TN26 ......153 A3
Gagetown Terr 1 ME14 .74 F7
Gainsboro Rd 4 CT7 ...26 F8
Gainsborough Ave CT9 .29 C8
Gainsborough Cl
   Folkestone CT19 ....178 A7
   Gillingham ME8 ......33 D6
   Sittingbourne ME10 ...36 B5
Gainsborough Dr
   Herne Bay CT6 ....23 C5
   Maidstone ME16 ......74 B4
Gainsborough Ho ME1 ..9 D5
Galena Cl Chatham ME5 .32 A1
   Sittingbourne ME10 ...36 C6
Gallants La ME15 ......96 A4
Galleon Cl ME1 ....31 C8
Galliard St CT13 ....94 A8
Gallow's Cnr CT21 ....176 A2
Galloway Dr TN25 ....139 C8
Galloways Rd TN29 ...203 C5
Gallwey Ave CT7 ....26 E7
Galway Rd ME12 ....1 D1
Gammon's Farm La
   TN29 ....185 B3
Gandy's La ME17 ......97 C2
Gange Mews 3 ME13 ..62 D7
Gann Rd CT5 ....20 F2
Gaol La 13 CT6 ....166 D7
Gap House Sch CT10 ..30 B2
Gap The Blean CT2 .....66 A7
   Canterbury CT1 ......88 B5
Garden Cl Maidstone ME15 97 E4
   Rough Common CT2 ...66 A2
Garden Cotts CT3 .....91 A7
Garden Hall The TN25 124 A1
Garden of England Pk
   (Mobile Home Pk)
   ME17 ....100 B7
Garden Pl TN24 ......139 E6
Garden Rd CT19 ......178 D6
Garden St ME7 ....10 A6
Gardeners Pl CT4 ......86 F1
Gardens The
   Coxheath ME17 ....96 C3
   Ivychurch TN29 .....192 F4
Gardiner St ME7 ......10 C6
Garfield Pl 4 ME13 ....62 D7
Garfield Rd
   Gillingham ME7 ......10 D6
   Margate CT9 ....7 H2

Garlinge Green Rd CT4 .108 E6
Garlinge Inf Sch CT9 ..28 C8
Garlinge Jun Sch CT9 ..28 B8
Garrard Ave CT9 ......28 B8
Garrington Cl ME14 ...75 C6
Garrison Rd ME12 ......1 B3
Gas House Rd ME1 ......9 C6
Gas La ME13 ....63 F3
Gas Rd Sittingbourne ME10 .36 F5
   Sittingbourne,Murston
   ME10 ....37 B6
Gas St CT1 ....87 F7
Gascoyne Cl ME15 ....76 B2
Gasworks La TN23 ...139 B2
Gatcombe Cl
   Chatham ME5 ....32 A5
   Maidstone ME16 .....74 B5
Gate Quays CT9 ....7 I2
Gateacre Rd CT5 ......43 A6
Gatefield La 9 ME13 ..62 D7
Gatekeeper Chase ME8 .33 F8
Gateway Ct 13 CT11 ...52 F7
Gateway The CT16 ...166 E2
Gatland La ME16 ......74 B2
Gault Cl ME15 ....76 A2
Gaunt's Cl CT14 ......117 A4
Gayhurst Cl ME8 ......33 D6
Gayhurst Dr ME10 .....36 C5
Gaze Hill Ave ME10 ...37 A3
Gazedown ME29 ......194 F3
Gean Cl ME5 ....54 A8
Genesta Ave CT5 ......43 B7
Genesta Cl ME10 ......36 E7
Geneva Ave ME8 ......11 A2
Gentian Cl
   4 Chatham ME5 ......31 E4
   Maidstone ME14 .....75 B5
Geoffrey Cl CT7 ....27 A7
George Alley CT14 ...117 D6
George Cooper Ho 7
   CT20 ....178 C4
George Gurr Cres CT19 178 D8
George Hill Rd
   Broadstairs CT10 .....29 F8
   Margate CT10,CT9 .....8 C1
George La
   Boughton Street ME13 .63 F3
   Folkestone CT20 ....178 C4
   Leeds ME17 ....99 B7
   New Romney TN28 ...200 B7
   Rochester ME1 ....9 C6
George Marsham House
   ME15 ....96 F3
George Parris Ct ME12 ..4 C6
George Pk CT9 ....7 F1
George Roche Rd CT1 ..88 A6
George Spurgen
   Com Prim Sch CT19 ..178 E7
George St Ashford TN23 139 B1
   Deal CT14 ....117 D7
   Dover CT17 ....149 C1
   Maidstone ME15 .....75 A3
   Ramsgate CT11 ......52 E7
   Sittingbourne ME10 ...37 B4
George Stone Ho 22
   CT20 ....178 E5
George V Ave CT9 .....28 C8
George Warren Ct 1 CT9 .7 J1
George Williams Way
   TN24 ....139 C5
George Wood Cl TN29 ..203 C6
George's Ave CT5 .....43 A7
Georgian Cl ME11 ......3 A3
Georgian Dr ME17 .....96 D3
Georgian Way ME8 ....33 C4
Gerald Ave ME4 ....9 F2
Gerald Palmby Ct CT14 .117 C7
Gerrard Ave ME1 ......31 E8
Gerrards Dr ME10 .....36 F2
Gibbons Rd ME10 .....36 B5
Gibraltar Ave ME7 ....10 B7
Gibraltar Hill ME4 ......9 F4
Gibraltar La
   Hawkinge CT18 ......163 A2
   Maidstone ME14 .....74 F8
Gibraltar Sq CT15 ....149 E3
Gibson St ME10 ....36 E4
Gidd's Pond Cotts ME14 .75 E6
Giddyhorn La ME16 ...74 C5
Gifford Cl ME8 ....11 C3
Gigger's Green Rd TN25 185 C7
Gilbert Cl ME7 ....33 A5
Gilbert Rd
   4 Ashford TN24 ....139 B2
   Ramsgate CT11 ......52 D8
Gilbert Terr 2 ME14 ...74 F7
Gilchrist Ave CT6 .....22 C2
Giles Gdns CT9 ....28 F8
Giles La CT2 ....66 D4
Giles-Young Ct 8 ME10 .36 E5
Gilford Cl CT14 ......117 D5
Gilham Gr CT14 ......117 B4
Gill La Mersham TN25 .172 A8
   Ruckinge TN26 ......171 C2
Gillett Rd TN29 ......203 D2
Gillingham Coll The ME7 .10 F4
Gillingham Gate ME7 ..10 C8
Gillingham Gate Rd ME7 10 C8
Gillingham Gn ME7 ...10 E6
Gillingham Rd ME7 ...10 D5
Gillingham Sta ME7 ..10 D5
Gillman Cl CT18 ......162 F4
Gillon Mews 9 CT1 ...67 B2
Gills Terr ME8 ....12 C3
Ginsbury Cl ME2 ......9 E6
Giraud Dr ME13 ......62 B8

Glack Rd CT14 ....116 F4
Glade The Chatham ME5 .32 A2
   Deal CT14 ....116 F6
Gladstone Ct CT10 .....29 F4
Gladstone Dr ME10 ....37 C4
Gladstone Rd
   Ashford TN24 ....156 E7
   Broadstairs CT10 .....29 F4
   Chatham ME4 ....9 E2
   Deal CT14 ....117 C4
   Folkestone CT19 ....178 E6
   Maidstone ME14 .....75 A6
   Margate CT9 ....7 I1
   Whitstable CT5 ....20 D2
Gladwyn Cl ME8 ......33 D4
Glamis Cl ME5 ....32 A5
Glanville Rd
   Gillingham ME7 ......10 D5
   Rochester ME2 ....9 A8
Glasgow House 8 ME5 .32 A1
Gleaming Wood Dr ME5 54 D8
Gleaners Cl ME14 .....75 A4
Gleanings Mews ME1 ...9 C5
Glebe Cl
   Biddenden Green TN27 .135 E2
   St Margaret's at Cliffe
   CT15 ....150 F6
Glebe Cotts ME13 .....81 E7
Glebe Ct CT12 ....50 B5
Glebe Gdns
   Lenham ME17 ....101 E5
   6 Margate CT9 ......28 B8
Glebe La Maidstone ME16 .74 A1
   Sittingbourne ME10 ...37 B2
Glebe Rd Gillingham ME7 .10 E3
   Margate CT9 ....28 B8
Glebe The TN27 ......120 D7
Glebe Way Ashford TN24 .156 E7
   Whitstable CT5 ....43 D8
Glebeland TN27 ......118 F4
Glebelands Alkham CT15 147 D1
   Ash CT3 ....71 C2
   Mersham TN25 ......157 E4
Glemsford Cotts CT2 ..65 E1
Glen Ave CT6 ....23 C5
Glen Gr CT17 ....166 C2
Glen Iris Ave CT2 .....66 C2
Glen Iris Cl CT2 ......66 C2
Glen Rd CT14 ....134 C6
Glen The
   Minster (Sheppey) ME12 ..4 B7
   Minster (Sheppey) ME12 ..4 C7
   Shepherdswell CT15 ..130 D5
   Upstreet CT3 ....47 D3
Glen Wlk CT5 ....43 A3
Glenavon Ho CT10 ....30 B7
Glenbervie Dr CT6 ....23 E5
Glenbrook Cl CT6 .....23 D5
Glenbrook Gr ME10 ...36 E7
Glencoe Inf Sch ME4 ..10 A2
Glencoe Jun Sch ME4 .10 A2
Glencoe Rd Chatham ME4 .10 A2
   Margate CT9 ....8 A1
Glendale Rd ME12 ......4 B7
Gleneagles Ct ME5 ....31 F2
Gleneagles Dr ME5 ....75 A1
Glenfield Rd CT16 ....149 B3
Glenside CT5 ....44 A8
Glenside Ave CT1 .....67 B2
Glenwood TN30 ......167 B3
Glenwood Cl
   Chatham ME5 ....10 C1
   Gillingham ME7 ......33 A7
   Maidstone ME16 .....74 C5
   St Michaels TN30 ...167 B3
Glenwood Dr ME12 .....4 A8
Glistening Glade ME8 .33 E6
Globe La ME4 ....9 F5
Gloster Cl CT18 ......163 B3
Gloster Ropewalk CT17 166 C5
Gloster Way CT17 ...166 C5
Gloucester Ave
   Broadstairs CT10 .....29 F3
   Margate CT9 ....8 D2
Gloucester Cl ME8 ....34 A8
Gloucester Mews TN28 200 C8
Gloucester Pl 17 CT20 .178 D5
Gloucester Rd
   Maidstone ME15 .....97 D8
   Whitstable CT5 ....20 F2
Glover Cl ME10 ....14 F1
Glover Rd TN24 ......139 E1
Glovers Cres ME10 ....36 F3
Glovers Mill ME4 ......9 D3
Glynne Cl ME8 ....33 D6
Goad Ave ME5 ....32 B3
Goat Lees La TN25 ...139 D8
Gobery Hill CT3 ....70 B1
Godden Rd CT2 ....67 A4
Goddings Dr ME1 ......9 A3
Goddington La ME17 ..100 B6
Goddington Rd ME2 ....9 B8
Godfrey Ho CT5 ....43 E8
Godfrey Wlk TN23 ...156 B8
Godfrey's Grave ME13 ..64 B7
Godfreys Cotts ME13 ..105 C8
Godinton* ME13 .....138 C4
Godinton Cty Prim Sch
   TN23 ....138 D3
Godinton La TN23,TN26 .138 D5
Godinton Rd TN23 ...139 A2
Godinton Way TN23 ..139 A2
Godwin Bglws CT9 .....8 B3
Godwin Cl ME10 ......14 F1
Godwin Cotts CT9 .....8 A3
Godwin Rd Canterbury CT1 87 F7
   Dover CT16 ....166 F8
   Margate CT9 ....8 A3

Godwyn Gdns CT20 ...178 A4
Godwyn Rd Deal CT14 .117 C8
   Folkestone CT20 ....178 A4
Godwyne Cl CT16 ....166 D8
Godwyne Ct CT16 ....149 D1
Godwyne Rd CT16 ....149 D1
Gogway CT4 ....126 B4
Gold Hill TN25 ....121 D4
Goldcrest Wlk CT19 ...43 B6
Golden Acre La CT8 ...27 D7
Golden Cl CT8 ....27 D7
Golden Hill CT5 ....43 F6
Golden Sq
   New Romney TN28 ...200 A6
   Tenterden TN30 ....179 B8
Golden St CT14 ......117 D7
Golden Wood Cl ME5 ..54 D8
Goldfinch Cl
   Faversham ME13 .....40 C1
   Herne Bay CT6 ....23 C2
Goldings The
   Gillingham ME8 ......33 C8
   Monkton CT12 ....49 C7
Goldsmith Ct TN30 ...167 B1
Goldsmith Rd ME8 ....33 E5
Goldstone Dro CT3 ....71 E7
Goldstone Wlk ME5 ...32 A1
Goldthorne Cl ME14 ..75 C5
Goldups La CT4 ......84 C1
Goldups Lane Cotts CT4 .84 C1
Goldwell Cl CT14 ....173 A6
Goldwell Hos TN25 ..173 A6
Goldwell La
   Aldington TN25 .....173 B7
   Great Chart TN23,TN26 .154 F8
Golf Ct CT14 ....95 C1
Golf Rd CT14 ....117 C8
Golf Road Pl CT14 ...117 C8
Gooch Cl ME16 ....74 D8
Good Hope CT14 .....117 C8
Good Intent Cotts TN27 119 A5
Goodall Cl ME8 ....33 E5
Goodban Sq CT3 ......71 D1
Goodcheap La TN25 ..140 D2
Goodfellow Way 3
   CT16 ....166 D8
Goodnestone
   CE Prim Sch CT3 .....91 C2
Goodnestone Gdns *
   CT3 ....91 C1
Goodnestone Hill CT3 .91 D2
Goodnestone Rd
   Sittingbourne ME10 ...37 B4
   Wingham CT3 ....91 B5
Goodwin Ave CT5 .....21 E2
Goodwin Dr ME14 .....75 B8
Goodwin Pk CT9 ......29 A5
Goodwin Rd
   Ramsgate CT11 ......52 B5
   St Margaret's at Cliffe
   CT15 ....151 A4
Goodwood Cl ME15 ...97 F6
Goose Cl ME5 ....32 A7
Gordon Ave ME11 ......3 A4
Gordon Cl Ashford TN24 .139 D2
   Sittingbourne ME10 ...37 D2
Gordon Cotts ME9 ....58 B6
Gordon Ct ME17 ......96 E3
Gordon Cty Inf Sch ME2 .9 A8
Gordon Gr CT8 ....7 C1
Gordon Rd Canterbury CT1 87 F7
   Chatham ME4 ....10 B2
   Faversham ME13 .....62 E8
   Folkestone CT20 ....177 D6
   Gillingham ME7 ......10 E5
   Gillingham,Brompton ME4 .10 B7
   Herne Bay CT6 ....22 F4
   Margate CT9 ....7 J3
   Margate, Westwood CT9 .29 A5
   Ramsgate CT11 ......52 D8
   Rochester ME2 ....9 A8
   Whitfield CT16 ......149 A5
   Whitstable CT5 ....43 D8
Gordon Sq Birchington CT7 26 E7
   Faversham ME13 .....62 E7
Gordon Terr ME1 ....9 C4
Gore Cl CT13 ....93 B3
Gore Cotts ME9 ....12 E1
Gore Court Rd
   Maidstone ME15 .....97 F5
   Sittingbourne ME10 ...36 E2
Gore End Cl CT7 ......26 F7
Gore Farm Trails * ME9 .12 D1
Gore La CT13 ....93 B2
Gore Mews 3 CT1 .....67 B2
Gore Rd Eastry CT13 ..93 B3
   Silver Street ME9 ....57 F5
Gore St CT12 ....49 A7
Gore Terr CT13 ....93 B3
Gorely Ho 14 CT17 ...166 D7
Goretop La CT14 ......94 C6
Gorham Dr ME15 .....76 A1
Gorrell Rd CT5 ....20 E1
Gorse Ave ME5 ....31 F5
Gorse La CT6 ....23 C2
Gorse Mead TN23 ...155 F8
Gorse Rd ME10 ....37 C5
Goschen Rd CT17 ....166 B8
Gosfield Rd CT6 ......23 A4
Goshawk Ho 1 ME10 ..37 A4
Goss Hall La CT3 .....72 A2
Gosselin St CT5 ......43 E8
Goteley Mere TN24 ..139 C2
Gothic Cl CT14 ......117 B1
Gothic Cotts TN26 ...121 A1
Goudhurst Cl
   Canterbury CT2 ......67 A4
   Maidstone ME16 .....74 E4

Goudhurst Rd ME8 ....11 B3
Gough Rd CT20 ......177 E3
Gould Rd ME5 ....32 B3
Grace Ave ME16 ......74 D6
Grace Ct 16 CT20 ....178 D5
Grace Hill CT20 ......178 D5
Grace Mdw CT16 ....149 A7
Grace Rd ME12 ....1 B1
Grace Wlk CT14 .....117 A5
Grafton Ave ME1 .....31 E8
Grafton Rd
   Broadstairs CT10 .....29 F8
   Sittingbourne ME10 ...36 F4
Grafton Rise CT6 .....22 C4
Grain Rd ME8 ....33 C3
Grainey Field ME9 ....34 E4
Grampian Way ME15 ..76 A1
Grampion Cl TN24 ...139 C4
Granada House 8 ME15 75 A4
Granada St 9 ME15 ...75 A4
Granary Cl Gillingham ME8 11 F1
   Maidstone ME14 .....75 E5
Granary Court Rd TN25 159 A4
Granary Pl CT5 ....43 D8
Grand Ct Folkestone CT20 178 B3
   17 Gillingham ME7 ...10 C6
   Littlestone-on-S TN28 200 E5
Grand Dr CT6 ....22 C4
Grand Mans CT10 .....30 B3
Grand Par ME7 ......200 E5
Grange Cres TN30 ...167 A3
Grange Ct 1 CT20 ...178 C4
Grange Hill ME5 ....10 B3
Grange Ho ME16 ......74 A2
Grange La ME14 ......54 A1
Grange Rd
   Broadstairs CT10 .....29 F6
   Deal CT14 ....117 B5
   Folkestone CT19 ....177 C6
   Gillingham,Grange ME7 .11 A6
   Gillingham,Lower Twydale
   ME7 ....11 B5
   Herne Bay CT6 ....23 C4
   Hythe CT21 ....176 B4
   Ramsgate CT11 ......52 C6
   Rochester ME2 ....9 B7
   Tenterden TN30 ....167 A3
Grange Rdbt ME7 .....11 A6
Grange The
   Shepherdswell CT15 ..130 D5
   Whitstable CT5 ....43 A6
Grange Way
   Broadstairs CT10 .....29 F2
   Rochester ME1 ....9 C3
Grant Cl Broadstairs CT10 29 E6
   Gillingham ME7 ......11 B1
Grant Dr ME5 ....97 D6
Grant's Cotts ME17 ..101 B5
Grantham Ave CT14 ..117 A5
Grantley Cl TN23 ....156 A8
Granville Ave
   Broadstairs CT10 .....30 B3
   Ramsgate CT12 ......29 B1
Granville Cl ME13 .....62 C7
Granville Dr CT6 ......22 B2
Granville Farm Mews 19
   CT11 ....52 F7
Granville Marina 17 CT11 52 F7
Granville Par CT20 ...177 E3
Granville Pl ME12 ......1 D2
Granville Rd
   Broadstairs CT10 .....30 B3
   Deal CT14 ....117 C2
   Gillingham ME7 ......10 E5
   Kingsdown CT14 ....134 D3
   Maidstone ME14 .....75 A6
   Sheerness ME12 ......1 D2
   St Margaret's at Cliffe
   CT15 ....151 B6
Granville Rd E CT20 ..177 F3
Granville St Deal CT14 .117 D5
   Dover CT16 ....149 C1
Granville The CT15 ..151 B6
Grapple Rd ME14 .....75 A4
Grasmere Ave CT11 ...52 A7
Grasmere Gdns CT19 .178 B7
Grasmere Rd
   Ashford TN24 ....139 C6
   Whitstable CT5 ....44 B8
Grasmere Way CT3 ..112 F6
Grasslands Ashford TN23 155 D7
   Langley Heath ME17 ..98 E4
Grassmere TN29 .....194 E3
Grassy Glade ME7 ....33 B6
Gravel Castle Rd CT4 129 A8
Gravel Hill ME13 ....103 C8
Gravel La CT15 ......165 A4
Gravel Wlk
   3 Ashford TN23 ....139 B3
   12 Canterbury CT1 ...87 F8
   Rochester ME1 ....9 D5
Gravelly Bottom Rd
   ME17 ....99 B2
Graveney Prim Sch
   ....41 E1
Graveney Rd
   Faversham ME13 .....62 F7
   Maidstone ME15 .....97 F7
Gray Cl CT18 ....163 B5
Graylen Cl CT14 .....117 C7
Graylings Cl ME10 ....36 C2
Graylings The ME1 ....9 B3
Grays Way CT1 ....87 B6
Grayshott Cl ME10 ...36 F3
Graystone Rd CT5 ....21 A2
Great Basin Rd ME12 ..1 A2
Great Burton Ho TN24 .139 E5

Great Chart Prim Sch TN23 155 D8
Great Conduit St CT21 176 C2
Great Ivy Mill Cotts ME15 96 F7
Great Lines ME7 10 B5
Great South Ave ME4 10 A1
Greatstone Prim Sch TN28 200 D2
Grebe Apartments 15 ME15 97 E5
Grebe Cl CT18 163 A4
Grebe Cres CT21 187 C8
Grecian St ME14 75 A6
Green Acres CT15 131 D7
Green Acres Cl CT6 23 B3
Green Bank Cl ME7 33 A5
Green Cl Hawkinge CT18 163 B4
Rochester ME1 9 D2
Green Cloth Mews 2 CT1 67 B2
Green Ct Bridge CT4 89 A1
Folkestone CT19 178 E7
Green Dell CT2 66 F4
Green Gates CT16 149 A8
Green Hedges TN30 179 B8
Green Hill ME15 76 B1
Green Hill La ME17 100 D1
Green Hills CT4 128 D8
Green La Alkham CT15 147 D3
Ashford TN23 155 E5
Bethersden TN26 153 A2
Boughton Monchelsea ME17 97 C3
Broadstairs CT10 29 E5
Capel-le-F CT18 164 B3
Challock TN25 105 A2
Chilham CT4 85 C2
Deal CT14 117 B1
Dover CT16 149 B3
Eythorne CT15 131 D7
Folkestone CT19 178 E7
Goodnestone CT3 92 B3
Hythe CT21 176 A2
Langley Heath ME17 98 E3
Margate CT9 29 E8
Platt's Heath ME17 100 F2
Rhodes Minnis CT4,CT18 143 E2
Rodmersham ME9 59 B7
Smarden TN27 135 A1
St Margaret's at Cliffe CT15 133 F1
Stockbury ME9 34 F1
Temple Ewell CT16 148 E6
Whitfield CT16 148 E7
Whitstable CT5 43 D8
Green Lane Ave CT21 176 A2
Green Lane Cotts ME17 98 E3
Green Leas CT5 21 D1
Green Lees ME13 61 E2
Green Meadows TN29 186 D2
Green Porch Cl ME10 36 F7
Green Rd Birchington CT7 26 F8
Stalisfield Green ME13 103 C6
Green Sands ME5 54 C8
Green St ME7 10 C5
Green The Blean CT2 66 A6
Burmarsh TN29 186 C4
Chartham CT4 86 D3
East Farleigh ME15 96 B7
Harbledown CT2 65 E1
Hythe CT21 176 B4
Littlebourne CT3 89 F7
Lower Halstow ME9 13 B3
Lydd TN29 203 B5
Manston CT12 28 D1
Sheerness ME12 1 I1
Woodchurch TN26 169 A2
Wye TN25 123 E2
Green Way Lydd TN29 203 C5
Maidstone ME16 74 B3
Green's Cotts ME15 96 A4
Greenacre CT4 111 D3
Greenacre Cl ME5 32 A5
Greenacre Dr CT14 117 C1
Greenacre Sch ME5 31 F5
Greenbank Ashford TN24 139 D6
Chatham ME5 32 B8
Greenbanks CT18 161 C6
Greenborough Cl ME15 97 E6
Greencroft TN23 155 E6
Greenfield Cl ME20 53 A6
Greenfield Cotts
9 Canterbury CT1 87 F7
Maidstone ME14 54 A1
Greenfield Rd
Folkestone CT19 178 E7
Gillingham ME7 10 D6
Ramsgate CT12 29 C2
Greenfields
Maidstone ME15 97 E8
Sellindge TN25 159 E2
Greenfinches ME7 32 F6
Greenhill Bridge Rd CT6 22 D3
Greenhill Cl CT12 50 B7
Greenhill Gdns
Herne Bay CT6 22 D3
Minster (Thanet) CT12 50 B7
Greenhill La TN27 135 F7
Greenhill Rd CT6 22 C2
Greenhithe 3 ME15 75 A3
Greenhouse La CT2 66 E2
Greenly Way TN28 200 C6
Greensand Rd ME15 76 A2
Greenside
High Halden TN26 167 E7
Maidstone ME15 75 B3
Greenvale Gdns ME8 11 B2
Greenview Wlk ME8 11 A4
Greenway Chatham ME5 31 D6
Faversham ME13 62 B8
Greenway Court Farm Cotts ME17 78 A1
Greenway Court Rd ME17 78 A1
Greenway La ME17 100 A7
Greenways
Lower Halstow ME9 13 B3
Maidstone ME14 75 F5
Sittingbourne ME10 37 B3
Greenwich Cl
Chatham ME5 32 B4
Maidstone ME16 74 D4
Gregory Cl Gillingham ME8 33 E4
Sittingbourne ME10 37 A8
Gregory Ct TN25 123 E2
Grenadier Cl
Gillingham ME8 12 B2
Maidstone ME15 75 F2
Grenham Bay Ave CT7 26 E8
Grenham Rd CT7 26 F8
Grenville Gdns CT7 26 E8
Grenville Way CT10 29 E4
Gresham Ave CT9 7 E1
Gresham Cl 3 ME8 11 F1
Gresham Rd ME17 96 D3
Greville Homes CT13 93 B2
Grey Friars Cotts 8 CT1 87 F8
Grey Wethers ME14 53 E4
Grey Willow Gdns TN23 155 D8
Greyfriars Cl ME16 74 D5
Greyfriars Ct CT10 8 F1
Greystones Rd
Cliffs End CT12 51 D5
Maidstone ME15 76 A2
Greystones Sch TN24 139 F1
Grieveson Ho ME4 10 A4
Griffin Cotts TN26 181 C2
Griffin St CT14 117 D7
Griffin's Cnr TN25 140 E7
Grimshill Ct CT2 66 C4
Grimshill Rd CT5 43 E8
Grimston Ave CT20 178 B4
Grimston Gdns CT20 178 B4
Grimthorpe Ave CT5 43 C7
Grinsell Hill CT12 50 E6
Grisbrook Farm Cl TN29 203 D6
Grisbrook Rd TN29 203 D6
Grizedale Cl ME1 31 D8
Groombridge Sq 13 ME15 97 F6
Grosvenor Ave ME4 9 E3
Grosvenor Cotts CT7 27 B3
Grosvenor Gdns CT9 7 I1
Grosvenor Hill CT9 7 I2
Grosvenor House 5 ME15 97 F5
Grosvenor Pl CT9 7 I2
Grosvenor Rd
Ashford TN24 139 D7
Broadstairs CT10 30 A4
Gillingham ME7 11 A1
Ramsgate CT11 52 C7
Whitstable CT5 43 D7
Grotto Gdns CT9 7 J2
Grotto Hill CT9 7 J2
Grotto Rd 5 CT9 7 J2
Grove Ave ME12 6 G2
Grove Cl ME13 62 A6
Grove Cotts TN30 179 B6
Grove Court Farm ME13 64 A3
Grove Ct 4 ME2 9 B7
Grove Dairy Farm ME9 36 A6
Grove Ferry Hill CT3 47 E3
Grove Ferry Rd CT3 48 A2
Grove Gdns 6 CT9 7 G1
Grove Green La ME14 75 E5
Grove Green Rd ME14 75 F5
Grove Ho TN27 136 C3
Grove La TN29 191 D3
Grove Park Ave ME10 36 B5
Grove Park Com Prim Sch ME10 36 B6
Grove Pl ME13 62 A6
Grove Rd Chatham ME4 10 B2
Deal CT14 117 D3
Folkestone CT20 178 E6
Gillingham ME7 11 A6
Maidstone ME15 97 C7
Preston CT3 70 B8
Ramsgate CT11 52 D6
Rochester ME2 9 B8
Selling ME13 84 B4
Staple CT3 91 F6
Wickhambreaux CT3 69 D6
Grove Road Cotts
Wickhambreaux CT3 69 C2
Wickhambreaux CT3 69 C3
Grove Terr CT1 87 E7
Grove The Ashford TN24 139 E6
Barham CT4 128 F8
Deal CT14 117 C6
Dover CT16 149 C1
Herne Bay CT6 22 C2
Maidstone ME14 76 A3
Westgate-on-S CT8 27 F8
Grove Way CT3 70 C7
Grovehurst Ave ME10 14 F1
Grovehurst Rd ME10,ME9 14 E2
Grovelands ME17 101 E5
Groveway ME12 6 F2
Grovewood Ct ME14 75 E4
Grovewood Dr ME14 75 E4
Grummock Ave CT11 52 B7
Grundy's Hill 10 CT11 52 E6
Guardian Ct ME8 11 C1
Guestling Mill Ct 1 CT13 72 F1
Guildcount La 5 CT13 72 F1
Guildford Ave CT8 27 E8
Guildford Lawn 1 CT11 52 E6
Guildford Rd CT1 87 F6
Guildhall Ct 10 CT20 178 D5
Guildhall Mus* ME1 9 C6
Guildhall St
4 Canterbury CT1 87 F8
18 Folkestone CT20 178 D5
Guildhall St N CT19, CT20 178 D5
Guilford Ave CT16 149 A8
Guilford Ct CT14 117 D2
Guilford Rd CT13 94 E8
Guilton CT3 71 B1
Guldeford La TN29,TN31 196 F3
Guldeford Lane Cnr TN31 196 D2
Gulland Ho 4 ME14 75 B4
Gullands ME17 98 E4
Gun La ME2 9 B7
Gundulph Rd ME1 9 E4
Gundulph Sq ME1 9 C6
Gunnis Cl ME8 33 D4
Gurling Rd CT15 133 F1
Guston CE Prim Sch CT15 149 E3
Guston Rd ME14 75 C6
Guy Cl CT10 30 A7
Gwyn Rd CT12 29 C2
Gypsy Cnr CT5 44 D3

H

Hackfield TN23 138 F1
Hackington Cl CT2 66 E4
Hackington Pl CT2 66 F2
Hackington Rd CT2 66 E7
Hackington Terr CT2 66 F2
Hacklinge Hill CT14 94 B2
Hackney Rd ME16 74 C2
Haddon Dene Sch CT10 29 F4
Hadleigh Ct ME7 33 A3
Hadleigh Gdns CT6 23 B5
Hadley Gdns ME17 77 E2
Hadlow Coll of Agriculture & Hort (Horticultural Unit) CT1 88 B8
Hadlow Dr CT9 8 E2
Hadlow Rd ME14 75 C5
Hadrian Gdns TN23 155 F5
Haffenden Meadow TN27 120 C8
Haffenden Rd TN30 167 B1
Haig Ave Chatham ME1 9 D1
Chatham,Luton ME4 10 A2
Gillingham ME7 10 E4
Haine Ind Est CT12 28 F1
Haine Rd CT12,CT10 28 F2
Halden Cl ME15 97 F6
Hales Cl TN30 179 B8
Hales Ct TN30 179 B8
Hales Dr CT2 66 F3
Hales Rd ME10 36 D1
Haleys Pl ME1 53 A8
Halfmile Ride CT9 28 E6
Halford Cl CT6 23 B2
Halfpenny Cl ME16 74 A2
Halfway Houses Prim Sch ME12 3 D6
Halfway Rd ME12 3 D8
Halifax Cl ME5 32 B6
Hall Ave TN24 156 F6
Hall Cl ME10 36 E6
Hall Cres CT14 116 F5
Hall Rd ME5 32 C3
Hallcroft Ct CT11 52 C7
Hallett Wlk 10 CT1 67 B2
Halliday Ct CT21 176 A2
Hallsfield Rd ME5 31 D2
Hallwood Cl ME8 33 D5
Hallwood House ME5 32 C2
Halstatt Rd CT14 117 A3
Halstead Cl CT2 67 B4
Halstead Gdns CT9 8 F3
Halstead Wlk ME16 74 C7
Halstow Cl ME15 97 B6
Halstow Way TN23 155 F8
Halt The Elham CT4 144 F4
Whitstable CT5 44 A7
Ham Farm Cotts CT14 93 F2
Ham La Gillingham ME7 32 E3
Lenham ME17 101 C5
Ham Mill La TN26,TN29 183 A2
Ham Rd ME13 40 C1
Ham Shades La CT5 21 A1
Ham Street Sta TN26 183 A8
Hambledon Ct ME16 74 B3
Hambrook Cl CT4 107 B8
Hambrook La CT4 107 C8
Hambrook Wlk ME10 36 F8
Hamelin Rd ME7 32 F8
Hamels The CT2 67 F5
Hamilton Cl
Littlestone-on-S TN28 200 E5
Ramsgate CT12 29 B1
Hamilton Cres ME10 36 C3
Hamilton Ho ME17 96 C3
Hamilton Rd
Ashford TN24 156 D6
Deal CT14 117 C4
Dover CT17 166 B8
Gillingham ME7 10 D7
Lydd TN29 203 C6
Whitstable CT5 20 D1
Hammond Cl CT15 113 E5
Hammond's Cnr TN29 199 E6
Hammond's Rd CT20 177 E5
Hamond Hill 6 ME4 9 E4
Hampden La TN23 156 A7
Hampden Mews TN23 156 A7
Hampden Rd TN23 156 A6
Hampshire Cl ME5 32 C7
Hampshire Dr ME15 97 C8
Hampshire Rd CT1 88 D7
Hampson Way ME14 76 A4
Hampton Cl Chatham ME5 32 A5
Herne Bay CT6 22 A3
Hampton Gdns CT6 22 A3
Hampton La TN25 141 C3
Hampton Pier Ave CT6 22 B4
Hampton Prim Sch CT6 22 C4
Hampton Rd ME14 75 C6
Hampton Vale CT21 177 B4
Hamstreet Prim Sch TN26 182 F8
Hamstreet Rd
Bromley Green TN26 170 E5
Hamstreet TN26 183 C7
Hamwick Gn ME5 32 C1
Hancocks Field CT14 117 A5
Hangman's La
Ringwould CT14 133 F5
Ripple CT14 133 D5
Hanover Cl Ashford TN23 138 F2
Deal CT14 117 D2
Margate CT9 8 E2
Sittingbourne ME10 36 E2
Hanover Ct
Broadstairs CT10 29 F4
Faversham ME13 62 B8
Hythe CT21 176 C1
Maidstone ME14 75 B5
Hanover Dr ME8 33 C4
Hanover Pl CT2 66 F2
Hanover Rd ME17 96 C3
Hanover Sq CT6 22 F5
Hanover St CT6 22 F5
Hanscomb Ho CT2 66 E2
Hanslett's La ME13 61 D3
Hanway ME8 11 A2
Harbledown Gdns CT9 8 E3
Harbledown Manor ME8 11 B3
Harbledown Pk CT2 66 C1
Harbour Approach Rd CT20 178 E4
Harbour Par CT11 52 E6
Harbour Point CT19 178 F5
Harbour Sch The CT15 165 E7
Harbour St
Broadstairs CT10 30 B4
Folkestone CT20 178 E5
Ramsgate CT11 52 E6
Whitstable CT5 20 D2
Harbour Twrs 13 CT11 52 E6
Harbour Way CT20 178 E5
Harbourland Cl ME14 75 B8
Harbourne La TN26, TN30 167 E5
Harcourt Dr
Canterbury CT2 66 D2
Herne Bay CT6 22 B5
Harcourt Gdns ME8 33 E4
Harcourt Prim Sch CT19 177 E7
Harcourt Rd CT19 177 F7
Harden Rd TN29 203 D7
Hardinge Cl ME8 33 D4
Hardinge Rd TN24 139 C3
Hardres Court Rd
Lower Hardres CT4 110 A3
Stelling Minnis CT4 126 F6
Hardres Rd CT11 52 E8
Hardres St CT11 52 E7
Hards Town ME4 10 A4
Hardwick Rd CT20 178 A4
Hardwicke Rd CT17 166 B6
Hardy Cl Ashford TN24 157 A7
Canterbury CT2 66 C1
Chatham ME5 32 B6
Hardy Rd
Littlestone-on-S TN28 200 D3
St Margaret's at Cliffe CT15 150 E8
Hardy St ME14 75 A6
Hare St 2 ME4 10 B3
Harebell Cl
3 Chatham ME5 31 F4
Maidstone ME14 75 E5
Minster (Sheppey) ME12 4 A4
Haredale Cl ME1 31 D7
Harkness Ct 6 ME10 37 B4
Harkness Dr CT2 66 E2
Harman Ave CT21 174 F3
Harman Ct ME5 32 B3
Harmers Way TN27 118 F3
Harmsworth Gdns CT10 30 A5
Harnet St 6 CT13 72 F1
Harold Ave Gillingham ME7 10 E4
Westgate-on-S CT8 27 E8
Harold Ct ME13 62 C6
Harold Rd Birchington CT7 26 E8
Deal CT14 117 D8
Margate CT9 8 B3
Sittingbourne ME10 37 B4
Harold St Dover CT16 166 D8
Queenborough ME11 3 A4
Harold's Rd CT16 166 E8
Harp Farm Rd ME14 54 C6
Harper Rd TN23 155 F8
Harple La ME14 54 F1
Harps Ave ME12 4 C6
Harpswood ME17 77 F1
Harpswood La CT21 176 A4
Harptree Dr ME5 31 F5
Harrier Dr ME10 37 A2
Harrietsham Sta ME17 100 D6
Harriet Dr ME1 9 B3
Harriets Cnr CT5 43 B5
Harringe La CT21,TN25 174 A6
Harriot Cl CT19 178 B7
Harris Gdns ME10 37 C5
Harris Rd ME12 1 D2
Harris's Alley CT3 91 A7
Harrison Ct 4 ME8 11 F1
Harrison Dr ME17 100 E6
Harrison Rd 4 CT11 52 D6
Harrison Terr ME13 40 A2
Harrow Ct Chatham ME5 32 C4
Stockbury ME9 56 D8
Harrow Dene CT10 29 E6
Harrow Rd ME7 32 F6
Harrow Way
Ashford TN23 155 E5
Maidstone ME14 75 E5
Harry Wells Rd CT6 22 B3
Harrys Rd ME9 38 D3
Hart Cl CT18 163 A4
Hart Hill TN27 103 A2
Hart St ME16 74 F3
Hart Street Bsns Ctr ME16 74 F3
Hartington St ME4 10 A3
Hartley Cl ME15 97 F6
Hartlip Cl ME12 3 B7
Hartlip Endowed CE Prim Sch ME9 34 D5
Hartlip Hill ME9 34 F7
Hartnup St ME16 74 C2
Hartpiece Cl ME8 11 F2
Harts Cotts TN26 183 A8
Harts La 6 CT5 20 D2
Hartsdown Rd CT9 28 D8
Hartsdown Tech Coll CT9 28 D8
Harty Ave ME8 33 B3
Harty Ferry Cotts ME13 40 C5
Harty Ferry Rd ME12 18 E4
Harty Ferry View CT5 43 C6
Harty Terr ME12 5 A5
Harvest La CT4 126 E5
Harvest Way
Ashford TN23 155 D7
Hawkinge CT18 163 B4
Harvesters Cl ME8 33 E7
Harvesters Way ME14 75 D4
Harvey Ct CT19 178 A6
Harvey Dr
Sittingbourne ME10 37 A2
Whitstable CT5 21 B1
Harvey Gram Sch The CT19 178 B6
Harvey Pl
22 Folkestone CT20 178 D5
7 Folkestone CT20 178 E5
Harvey Rd Ashford TN24 139 F1
Gillingham ME8 33 E8
Harvey St CT20 178 E5
Harville Rd TN25 123 C2
Harwich St CT5 43 D8
Harwick Dr TN28 200 C8
Harwood Ho TN25 123 E1
Harwood Rd ME8 12 B1
Hasborough Rd CT19 178 F6
Haskard Cl CT18 162 F4
Haslemere Est ME15 97 F5
Haslewood Cl TN27 135 B2
Hassall Reach CT1 87 B6
Hassell St TN25 124 F2
Haste Hill Cl ME17 97 B3
Haste Hill Rd ME17 97 B3
Hasted Rd ME9 35 B7
Hasteds ME17 77 D2
Hastings Ave CT9 8 A1
Hastings Pl CT13 93 F8
Hastings Rd ME15 75 B3
Hatch La CT4 86 C5
Hatch Rd ME17 101 C5
Hatch St 3 ME13 62 C7
Hatfield Rd Margate CT9 7 G2
Ramsgate CT11 52 D7
Rochester ME2 9 A8
Hathaway Ct
Gillingham ME8 33 D8
Rochester ME1 9 B5
Hatherall Rd ME14 75 B6
Hatherley Ct CT9 8 A3
Hatton Rd ME5 32 C3
Havant Wlk 8 ME15 97 F6
Havelock Pl CT3 71 E1
Havelock Rd CT14 117 C3
Havelock St CT1 67 A1
Haven Cl ME1 9 C2
Haven Dr Hawkinge CT18 163 A4
Herne Bay CT6 23 F6
Haven The Ashford TN23 155 F5
Brenzett TN29 192 A3
Hythe CT21 187 C8
Haventhorpe TN24 139 C3
Havisham Cl ME1 9 D2
Havock La 1 ME14 74 F4
Hawbeck Rd ME8 33 C3
Hawe Cl CT2 67 A4
Hawe Farm Way CT6 23 B2
Hawe La CT2 68 A7
Hawes Ave CT11 52 B7
Hawk Cl CT5 43 C7
Hawk's La CT1 87 F8
Hawkesbury St CT17 166 D5
Hawkhurst Cl CT7 27 B8

Hawkhurst Rd ME8 . . . . . .11 B3
Hawkhurst Way CT10 . . . .30 A2
Hawkinge Prim Sch
CT18 . . . . .163 B4
Hawkins Cl Chatham ME7 .10 A6
Sittingbourne ME10 . . . . . .36 E7
Hawkins Rd CT19 . . . . . . .177 D6
Hawks Rd CT6 . . . . .22 B2
Hawks Way TN23 . . . . . . .155 E2
Hawksdown CT14 . . . . . . .134 B8
Hawksdown Rd CT14 . . . .134 C8
Hawkshill Rd CT14 . . . . .134 C8
Hawkwood ME16 . . . . .74 B5
Hawkwood Cl ME1 . . . . .9 D5
Hawley Ct ME16 . . . . .74 E4
Hawley Sq CT9 . . . . .7 J2
Hawley St CT9 . . . . .7 I2
Hawser Rd ME1 . . . . .9 C1
Hawthorn Ave
Canterbury CT2 . . . . .67 A2
West Minst ME12 . . . . .3 A8
Hawthorn Cl Hythe CT21 187 B8
Ramsgate CT11 . . . . .29 E1
River CT17 . . . . .148 E2
St Mary's Bay TN29 . . . . .194 F3
Womenswold CT3 . . . . . . .112 E4
Hawthorn Cnr
Herne Bay CT6 . . . . .24 A3
Old Romney TN29 . . . . . . .198 E3
Hawthorn House 5 ME5 .31 F5
Hawthorn Rd
Kingsnorth TN23 . . . . . . .156 B4
Sittingbourne ME10 . . . . . .36 E4
Hawthorne Ave ME8 . . . . .11 C2
Hawthorne Cl CT15 . . . . .131 D7
Hawthorns ME5 . . . . .31 F1
Hawthorns The CT10 . . . . .29 C4
Hay Hill CT13,CT14 . . . . . .93 D2
Hay La CT14 . . . . .93 F2
Hayes Alley 11 CT5 . . . . . .20 D2
Hayes La ME9 . . . . .56 F6
Hayfields ME5 . . . . .32 D2
Haygate Ho ME1 . . . . .9 C4
Hayle Mill Cotts ME15 . . .96 F4
Hayle Mill Rd ME15 . . . . . .96 F8
Hayle Rd ME15 . . . . .75 A3
Haymakers La TN23 . . . . .155 D8
Haymen St ME4 . . . . .9 E3
Haynes Ho 3 ME14 . . . . . .75 B4
Hayrick Cl ME14 . . . . .75 E5
Haysel ME10 . . . . .37 A2
Hayton Rd TN25 . . . . .160 A2
Haywain Cl Ashford TN23 155 E5
Maidstone ME14 . . . . .75 F4
Hayward Ave ME2 . . . . .9 B8
Hayward Cl
Ashford TN24 . . . . .157 A8
Deal CT14 . . . . .117 A4
Hayward's Cl TN28 . . . . .200 B6
Hayward's Hill ME13 . . . . .82 C4
Hayward's Ho ME1 . . . . . . .9 C6
Hazebrouck Rd ME13 . . . .62 A7
Hazel Ave ME16 . . . . .74 C5
Hazel Cl CT15 . . . . .131 C7
Hazel Ct CT17 . . . . .26 D8
Hazel Gr Chatham ME5 . . .32 B8
Sheerness ME12 . . . . .1 H1
Hazel Street Rd ME9 . . . . .57 A4
Hazel Wlk CT10 . . . . .29 C4
Hazeldene ME12 . . . . .5 F6
Hazeldown Cl CT17 . . . . .148 E2
Hazelmere Dr CT6 . . . . . . .23 D5
Hazels The ME8 . . . . .33 B5
Hazelwood Dr ME14 . . . . .74 B4
Hazelwood Mdw CT13 . . .93 F7
Hazlemere Dr ME7 . . . . . . .11 A5
Hazlemere Rd CT5 . . . . . . .43 A7
Hazling Dane CT15 . . . . .130 F5
Hazlitt Dr ME16 . . . . .74 D5
Head Hill ME13 . . . . .63 D7
Head Hill Rd ME13 . . . . . .63 D8
Head Race The ME15 . . . .74 D2
Headcorn Dr CT2 . . . . .67 B4
Headcorn Gdns CT9 . . . . . .8 E2
Headcorn Rd
Gillingham ME8 . . . . .11 A4
Platt's Heath ME17 . . . . . .100 F1
Headingley Rd ME16 . . . . .74 B6
Heard Way ME10 . . . . .37 B5
Heart In Hand Cnr CT3 . . .23 F2
Heart In Hand Rd CT6 . . .23 F2
Heart's Delight La CT3 . . .70 B3
Hearts Delight Rd ME9 . . .36 B1
Heath Cl CT2 . . . . .67 F7
Heath Ct CT15 . . . . .150 F6
Heath Ho CT3 . . . . .46 E5
Heath Rd Coxheath ME17 . .96 C3
Langley Heath ME17 . . . . . .98 E4
Maidstone ME16 . . . . .74 A2
Heath The
Appledore TN26 . . . . .181 C1
Whitstable CT5 . . . . .21 B1
Heath Villas TN26 . . . . . .181 C2
Heather Cl Chatham ME5 . .31 F4
Margate CT9 . . . . .28 C8
Sittingbourne ME10 . . . . . .37 A3
Heather Dr
Maidstone ME15 . . . . .75 B2
St Michaels TN30 . . . . . . .167 B3
Heatherwood Cl ME17 . . .99 E2
Heathfield ME17 . . . . .98 E4
Heathfield Ave
Dover CT16 . . . . .149 B2

Heathfield Ave continued
Maidstone ME14 . . . . .75 C7
Heathfield Bglws ME17 .102 B1
Heathfield Cl
Chatham ME5 . . . . .32 B7
Maidstone ME14 . . . . .75 B7
Heathfield Rd
Ashford TN24 . . . . .139 C3
Maidstone ME14 . . . . .75 C7
Heathorn St ME14 . . . . . . .75 B5
Heathside TN26 . . . . .181 C1
Heathside Ave ME17 . . . . .96 C4
Heathwood Dr CT11 . . . . .29 E1
Heaton Rd CT1 . . . . .87 F6
Hedgend Ind Est CT17 . . .25 F3
Hedgerow The ME14 . . . . .75 E5
Hedgerows TN23 . . . . . . .155 D7
Hedges The ME14 . . . . . . .75 A7
Hedley St ME14 . . . . .75 A5
Heel La CT2 . . . . .67 C8
Heel Rd ME13 . . . . .104 B7
Heights Terr CT17 . . . . . .166 C6
Heights The CT5 . . . . .43 C6
Helding Cl CT6 . . . . .23 B2
Helen Thompson Cl ME9 .14 E4
Helena Ave CT9 . . . . .28 E8
Helena Corniche CT20 . . .177 C3
Hellyar Ct ME1 . . . . .9 C4
Helmdon Cl CT12 . . . . . . .29 C2
Helvellyn Ave CT11 . . . . . .52 B7
Hempstead Inf Sch ME7 .33 A5
Hempstead Jun Sch ME7 33 A5
Hempstead La ME9 . . . . . .37 E3
Hempstead Rd
Gillingham ME7,ME8 . . . . . .33 B6
Gillingham,Hempstead ME7 .33 A5
Hempstead Valley Dr
ME7 . . . . .33 A4
Hempstead Valley Sh Ctr
ME7 . . . . .33 A3
Hempsted St 11 TN23 . . .139 B2
Henbane Cl ME14 . . . . . . .75 E5
Hendon Bsns Ctr TN24 . .139 D2
Hengist Ave CT9 . . . . .8 B1
Hengist Rd
Birchington CT7 . . . . .26 C7
Deal CT14 . . . . .117 D7
Westgate-on-S CT8 . . . . . . .27 E8
Henley Bsns Pk ME2 . . . . . .9 D7
Henley Cl Chatham ME5 . . .32 A6
Gillingham ME8 . . . . .33 D8
Henley Fields
Maidstone ME14 . . . . .75 E6
St Michaels TN30 . . . . . . .167 B2
Henley Meadows TN30 . .167 A4
Henley View TN30 . . . . . .167 B2
Henniker Ct CT16 . . . . . . .149 A5
Henry Ct CT1 . . . . .87 F7
Henry St Chatham ME4 . . . .10 B3
Gillingham ME8 . . . . .12 A1
Henwood TN24 . . . . .139 D3
Herbert Dane Ct 10
ME13 . . . . .62 D7
Herbert Rd Ashford TN24 156 D7
Chatham ME4 . . . . .10 A3
Gillingham ME8 . . . . .33 E8
Ramsgate CT11 . . . . .52 C6
Herbert St CT17 . . . . .149 B1
Herdson Rd CT20 . . . . . . .178 A5
Hereford Cl ME8 . . . . .11 D2
Hereford Gdns CT7 . . . . . .26 F6
Hereford Rd ME15 . . . . . . .97 D7
Hereson Rd CT11 . . . . .52 E8
Hereson Sch Boys Sch
CT10 . . . . .30 A3
Hereward Ave CT7 . . . . . . .26 E8
Heritage Cl CT5 . . . . .43 A6
Heritage Dr ME7 . . . . .10 F1
Heritage Gdns CT16 . . . .166 E8
Heritage Rd Chatham ME5 32 A6
Folkestone CT20 . . . . .177 D6
Herman Terr ME4 . . . . . . .10 A3
Hermitage Cl CT21 . . . . . .176 B2
Hermitage La
Detling ME14 . . . . .55 B4
Maidstone ME16 . . . . .74 A4
Herne Ave CT6 . . . . .23 A4
Herne Bay High Sch CT6 22 D3
Herne Bay Inf Sch CT6 . .22 F4
Herne Bay Jun Sch CT6 . .22 F4
Herne Bay Mus★ CT6 . . . .22 F5
Herne Bay Rd Sturry CT3 . .45 E2
Whitstable CT5 . . . . .21 C3
Herne Bay Sta CT6 . . . . . .22 E3
Herne CE Inf Sch CT6 . . .46 B8
Herne CE Jun Sch CT6 . . .46 A8
Herne Cl CT19 . . . . .177 C6
Herne Dr CT6 . . . . .22 C2
Herne Rd ME8 . . . . .11 C2
Herne St CT6 . . . . .46 A8
Herne Windmill★ CT6 . . . .23 B4
Herneville Gdns CT6 . . . . .23 B4
Hernhill CE Prim Sch
ME13 . . . . .64 B6
Hero Ho ME12 . . . . .1 C1
Hero Wlk ME1 . . . . .31 C7
Heron Apartments 3
ME15 . . . . .97 F5
Heron Cl ME9 . . . . .13 B3
Heron Dr ME12 . . . . .4 B5
Heron Forestall Ave
CT18 . . . . .163 B4
Heron Lodge 6 CT16 . . . .149 B2
Heron Way ME5 . . . . .32 B7
Heron Wlk TN23 . . . . .155 E8

Heron's Brook TN25 . . . .140 E6
Heron's Way CT21 . . . . . .187 D8
Heronden Rd Eastry CT13 .92 F1
Park Wood ME15 . . . . .97 F4
Herons Ct CT4 . . . . .107 C8
Herschell Rd CT7 . . . . .26 F8
Herschell Rd E CT14 . . . .117 C3
Herschell Rd W CT14 . . . .117 C3
Herschell Sq CT14 . . . . . .117 C3
Hersden Com Prim Sch
CT3 . . . . .46 C1
Hertford Ct CT1 . . . . .88 C8
Hertford Ho
Herne Bay CT6 . . . . .23 A5
14 Ramsgate CT11 . . . . . . .52 E6
Hertford Pl CT11 . . . . .52 E6
Hertford Rd CT9 . . . . .29 C8
Hertford St CT11 . . . . .52 E6
Herts Cres ME15 . . . . .96 F3
Hever Cl ME15 . . . . .97 F6
Hever Gdns ME16 . . . . . . .74 E3
Hever Pl Canterbury CT2 . .67 A3
Sittingbourne ME10 . . . . . .36 D3
Hewitt Cl Gillingham ME7 . .10 F6
Maidstone ME16 . . . . .74 D7
Hewitt Rd 1 CT16 . . . . . .166 D8
Hewitts Pl TN24 . . . . .139 F1
Hextable Cl
Ashford TN23 . . . . .155 F6
Maidstone ME16 . . . . .74 D7
Heyford Ct CT18 . . . . . . .163 B4
Hibernia St 5 CT11 . . . . . .52 E6
Hickory Dell ME7 . . . . .33 A5
Hicks Forstal Rd CT3 . . . . .46 B5
Hidden Mdw ME13 . . . . . .62 B7
Higgins' La ME14 . . . . .9 F5
High Banks Loose ME15 . .96 F5
Rochester ME1 . . . . .9 B5
High Dewar Rd ME8 . . . . .34 A8
High Elms ME8 . . . . .11 E1
High Halden
CE Prim Sch TN26 . . . . . .167 E7
High Knocke TN29 . . . . . .195 B6
High Mdw CT17 . . . . .149 C1
High Minnis CT4 . . . . .143 F8
High Oak Hill ME9 . . . . . . .13 E1
High Snoad Wood TN25 105 A1
High St Ashford TN23 . . . .139 C2
Aylesford ME20 . . . . .53 A2
Bridge CT4 . . . . .89 A1
Broadstairs CT10 . . . . .29 E5
Broadstairs, St Peter's
CT10 . . . . .30 A4
Brookland TN29 . . . . .197 E8
Canterbury CT1 . . . . .87 F8
8 Canterbury,Northgate
CT1 . . . . .67 A1
Chatham ME4 . . . . .10 A4
Deal CT14 . . . . .117 D6
Dover CT16 . . . . .166 C8
Dymchurch TN29 . . . . . . .195 C6
Eastchurch ME12 . . . . .5 D3
Eastry CT13 . . . . .93 B2
Elham CT4 . . . . .144 F5
Fordwich CT2 . . . . .68 A4
Gillingham ME7 . . . . .10 C5
Gillingham,Brompton ME7 . .10 A6
Gillingham,Rainham ME8 . .33 F8
Herne Bay CT6 . . . . .22 F5
Hythe CT21 . . . . .176 C2
Lenham ME17 . . . . .101 D5
Littlebourne CT3 . . . . .89 F7
Lydd TN29 . . . . .203 B6
Lyminge CT18 . . . . .161 C6
Maidstone ME14 . . . . .74 F4
Manston CT12 . . . . .51 D8
Margate CT9 . . . . .7 I2
Margate, Garlinge CT9 . . . .28 B7
Minster (Sheppey) ME12 . . .4 C5
Minster (Thanet) CT12 . . . .50 C6
New Romney TN28 . . . . . .200 B6
Newington ME9 . . . . .35 C6
Queenborough ME11 . . . . . .2 F5
Ramsgate CT11 . . . . .52 D7
Rochester ME4 . . . . .9 E4
Rochester,Strood ME2 . . . . .9 B7
Rochester,Troy Town ME1 . .9 C6
Sandwich CT13 . . . . .73 A1
Sheerness ME12 . . . . .1 D2
Sheerness,Blue Town ME12 . .1 B3
Sittingbourne ME10 . . . . . .36 F4
Sittingbourne,Milton Regis
ME10 . . . . .36 E6
Smarden TN27 . . . . .135 A1
St Margaret's at Cliffe
CT15 . . . . .150 F6
Sturry CT2 . . . . .67 C2
Temple Ewell CT16 . . . . . .148 D5
Tenterden TN30 . . . . .179 A7
Whitstable CT5 . . . . .20 D2
Wingham CT3 . . . . .91 A8
Wye TN25 . . . . .123 D2
High St The TN27 . . . . . . .120 C7
High Street St Lawrence
CT11 . . . . .52 B7
High Trees Cl TN24 . . . . .157 A8
High View Ave CT6 . . . . . . .22 B5
Higham Cl ME15 . . . . .74 E2
Higham La CT4 . . . . .111 B8
Higham Pk★ CT4 . . . . . . .111 C8
Higham View ME14 . . . . . .53 E4
Highbury Gdns CT12 . . . . .29 B3
Highbury La TN30 . . . . . . .179 A7
Highbury Wlk CT12 . . . . . .29 B2
Highcroft Gn ME15 . . . . . .97 F4
Highfield Cl
Gillingham ME8 . . . . .33 D7
Hythe CT21 . . . . .176 A4

Highfield Cl continued
Ramsgate CT12 . . . . .29 B3
Rough Common CT2 . . . . . .66 B3
Highfield Ct
5 Margate CT9 . . . . .8 B2
Ramsgate CT12 . . . . .29 B2
Highfield Gdns CT12 . . . . . .7 H1
Highfield Ind Est CT19 . .178 F6
Highfield La TN24,TN25 .157 C6
Highfield Rd
Ashford TN24 . . . . .157 A8
Gillingham ME8 . . . . .33 D7
Halfway Houses ME12 . . . . .3 E6
Ramsgate CT12 . . . . .29 B3
Highfields Ave CT6 . . . . . .23 D4
Highfields View CT6 . . . . . .23 C4
Highgate Rd CT5 . . . . .21 B1
Highgrove Rd ME5 . . . . . . .32 A5
Highland Cl CT20 . . . . . . .177 F4
Highland Rd
Chartham CT4 . . . . .86 D1
Maidstone ME15 . . . . .79 B8
Highlands Cres TN29 . . . .195 A4
Highlands Farm Rare
Breeds Ctr★ TN26 . . . . . .169 D1
Highpoint TN24 . . . . .139 D3
Highridge Gillingham ME7 . .10 F1
Hythe CT21 . . . . .177 A3
Highridge Cl TN24 . . . . . . .75 F5
Highsted Gram Sch ME10 36 F2
Highsted Rd ME9 &10 . . . .58 F7
Highsted Valley ME9 . . . . .58 F7
Highstreet Rd
Waterham ME13 . . . . .42 D2
Yorklets CT5,ME13 . . . . . .42 E2
Highview Cl
Boughton Street ME13 . . . .64 B3
Maidstone ME15 . . . . .97 A8
Highview Dr ME5 . . . . .31 D5
Highview Rd ME12 . . . . . . .4 C7
Highview Sch CT19 . . . . .178 D6
Highworth Gram Sch
for Girls TN24 . . . . .139 A3
Hilary Cl CT6 . . . . .23 C4
Hilda Rd Chatham ME4 . . . .10 A3
Halfway Houses ME12 . . . . .3 D6
Hildenborough Cres
ME16 . . . . .74 C7
Hildersham Cl CT10 . . . . . .29 E5
Hill Ave CT15 . . . . .130 E5
Hill Brow Maidstone ME14 .76 A5
Sittingbourne ME10 . . . . . .36 D2
Hill Chase ME5 . . . . .31 E3
Hill Cres Aylesham CT3 . . .112 C5
Lenham ME17 . . . . .101 D5
Hill Ct TN27 . . . . .103 E1
Hill Dr CT13 . . . . .93 B3
Hill Green Rd ME9 . . . . . . .56 D8
Hill House Dr CT12 . . . . . .50 C7
Hill La CT18 . . . . .162 B1
Hill Rd Burham ME5 . . . . . .31 A3
Folkestone CT19 . . . . .178 E8
Folkestone,Foord CT19 . . .178 E7
Rochester ME1 . . . . .9 A2
Hill The Charing TN27 . . . .120 D8
Littlebourne CT3 . . . . .89 F8
Hill Top Cotts ME17 . . . . .96 E2
Hill Top Rd CT6 . . . . .23 B5
Hill View Ashford TN24 . . . .139 A1
Margate CT9 . . . . .28 D7
Hill View Terr CT18 . . . . .161 D3
Hill View Way ME5 . . . . . .31 E5
Hill's Terr ME4 . . . . .9 F3
Hillary Rd ME14 . . . . .75 A7
Hillborough Dr CT6 . . . . . .23 F5
Hillborough Gr ME5 . . . . . .32 A3
Hillborough Rd CT6 . . . . . .23 B5
Hillbrow Ave
Herne Bay CT6 . . . . .23 B2
Sturry CT2 . . . . .67 F7
Hillbrow La TN23 . . . . . . .138 F1
Hillbrow Rd
Ashford TN23 . . . . .139 A1
Ramsgate CT11 . . . . .52 D8
Hillcrest TN23 . . . . .155 B8
Hillcrest Cl TN24 . . . . . . .139 E6
Hillcrest Gdns
Deal CT14 . . . . .117 A2
Ramsgate CT11 . . . . .52 B6
Hillcrest Rd
Chatham ME4 . . . . .9 F2
Hythe CT21 . . . . .176 B3
Kingsdown CT14 . . . . .134 D4
Littlebourne CT3 . . . . .89 E8
Hillcroft Rd CT6 . . . . .23 B3
Hilden Shaw ME15 . . . . . . .97 A8
Hiller Cl CT10 . . . . .30 A6
Hillfield Villas TN23 . . . . .167 F8
Hillman Ave CT6 . . . . .22 A4
Hillside
1 Folkestone CT20 . . . . . .177 E3
Rochester ME1 . . . . .9 A2
Hillside Ave
Canterbury CT2 . . . . .66 C2
Rochester ME2 . . . . .9 B8
Rushenden ME11 . . . . .2 F3
Hillside Cl Hythe CT21 . . . .176 C2
2 Rochester ME2 . . . . .9 A7
Hillside Ind Est CT20 . . .177 E4
Hillside Rd
Chatham ME4 . . . . .10 A4
Dover CT17 . . . . .149 A2
Minster (Sheppey) ME12 . . .4 B7
Stalisfield Green ME13 . . .103 E6
Whitstable CT5 . . . . .21 A1
Hillside St CT1 . . . . .176 C2
Hillstone Ct CT16 . . . . . . .166 E8
Hilltop Rd ME12 . . . . .4 A5

Hilltop Spinning
& Weaving Ctr★ TN25 .160 A2
Hillview Rd
Canterbury CT2 . . . . .66 C2
Whitstable CT5 . . . . .43 B6
Hillyfield Rd TN23 . . . . . .156 A8
Hillyfields Jun Sch ME7 . .10 E6
Hillyfields Rise TN23 . . . .139 A1
Hilton Bsns Ctr TN23 . . . .156 B6
Hilton Dr ME10 . . . . .36 B6
Hilton Rd TN23 . . . . .138 F2
Hinchliffe Way CT9 . . . . . .29 D8
Hind Cl TN29 . . . . .195 C8
Hinde Cl ME10 . . . . .36 F7
Hinde Ho ME10 . . . . .36 E6
Hines Terr ME5 . . . . .10 C1
Hinton Cres ME7 . . . . .33 A6
Hinxhill Rd TN24,TN25 . .140 D1
Hirst Cl CT16 . . . . .149 B4
Historic Dockyard The★
ME4 . . . . .10 A7
Hither Field TN27 . . . . . . .120 C7
Hoades Wood Rd CT2 . . . .68 A7
Hoath Cl ME8 . . . . .33 B7
Hoath La ME8 . . . . .33 B7
Hoath Prim Sch CT3 . . . . .46 E5
Hoath Rd CT3 . . . . .46 C3
Hoath Way ME7,ME8 . . . . .33 B5
Hobart Cres CT16 . . . . . . .149 C3
Hobart Gdns ME10 . . . . . .36 C4
Hobart Rd CT12 . . . . .29 F8
Hockeredge Gdns CT8 . . . .27 F8
Hockers Cl ME14 . . . . .76 A8
Hockers La ME14 . . . . .76 A7
Hodge's Gap CT9 . . . . .8 C3
Hodgson Rd CT5 . . . . .42 F7
Hog Gn CT4 . . . . .144 F4
Hog Hill ME14 . . . . .76 B5
Hogarth Cl CT6 . . . . .23 E5
Hogbarn La ME17 . . . . . . .79 A3
Hogben Cl CT18 . . . . .161 B7
Hogg La CT4 . . . . .109 E2
Holbeam Rd ME13 . . . . . . .82 A1
Holborn La ME4 . . . . .9 F5
Holbourn Cl CT6 . . . . .46 B8
Holbrook Dr CT12 . . . . . . .29 B1
Holcombe Rd Chatham ME4 .9 F2
Rochester ME1 . . . . .9 C3
Holdenhurst TN23 . . . . . .155 E6
Holder Cl ME5 . . . . .32 C6
Holding St ME8 . . . . .11 F1
Holland Cl Broadstairs CT10 8 G2
Sheerness ME12 . . . . .1 C1
Holland Ho ME1 . . . . .9 D5
Holland Rd Chatham ME5 . .31 E4
Maidstone ME14 . . . . .75 B5
Hollands Ave CT19 . . . . . .178 F7
Hollicondane Rd CT11 . . . .52 E8
Hollingbourne Hill ME17 . .77 F4
Hollingbourne Prim Sch
ME17 . . . . .77 E2
Hollingbourne Rd ME8 . . .11 C2
Hollingbourne Sta ME17 . .77 F3
Hollington Pl TN24 . . . . . .139 B3
Hollingworth Rd ME15 . . .97 F5
Hollow La Canterbury CT1 . .87 E5
Hartlip ME9 . . . . .34 E5
Hollow Rd CT3 . . . . .47 B6
Hollow St CT3 . . . . .47 C5
Hollow Wood Rd CT17 . . .165 E8
Hollowmede CT1 . . . . .87 E6
Holly Cl Broadstairs CT10 . .29 C4
Chatham ME5 . . . . .32 C8
Eastry CT13 . . . . .93 B2
Folkestone CT19 . . . . .178 E7
Gillingham ME7 . . . . .10 E6
Hythe CT21 . . . . .176 D3
Holly Farm Rd ME15 . . . . .98 C6
Holly Gdns CT9 . . . . .8 C2
Holly Hill Rd ME13 . . . . . .64 D5
Holly La CT9 . . . . .8 C2
Holly Rd Ramsgate CT11 . . .52 E8
St Mary's Bay TN29 . . . . .194 F4
Holly Tree Cl ME17 . . . . . .99 E2
Hollybrook Hill ME10 . . . .36 D4
Hollybush Cnr CT4 . . . . . . .90 A3
Hollybush La CT3 . . . . .69 A4
Holm Mill La ME17 . . . . . .100 B6
Holm Oak Gdns CT10 . . . .29 F4
Holman Mews CT1 . . . . . . .88 A7
Holme Oak Cl CT1 . . . . . . .87 F6
Holmesdale Cl ME15 . . . . .96 F3
Holmesdale Terr 14
CT20 . . . . .178 D4
Holmestone Rd CT17 . . . .148 E1
Holmlea Cl TN24 . . . . . . .139 E1
Holmoaks Gillingham ME8 . .11 C3
Maidstone ME7 . . . . .75 C5
Holmside ME7 . . . . .10 E3
Holmscroft Rd CT6 . . . . . .23 D5
Holmside Ave ME12 . . . . . .3 D6
Holmwood Rd TN23 . . . . .155 E7
Holness Rd CT3 . . . . .71 D2
Holt St CT15 . . . . .113 C4
Holters Mill CT2 . . . . .66 F2
Holton Cl CT7 . . . . .27 A6
Holtwood Cl ME8 . . . . .33 D6
Holtye Cres ME15 . . . . . . .75 B2
Holy Family RC Prim Sch
ME15 . . . . .97 F4
Holy Trinity & St John's
CE Prim Sch CT9 . . . . .7 J2
Holy Trinity CE Prim Sch
CT10 . . . . .30 A1
Holyrood Dr ME12 . . . . .4 A5
Holywell Ave CT19 . . . . . .178 D8
Holywell Ho CT19 . . . . . . .178 D8
Holywell La ME9 . . . . .12 F2

Holywell Prim Sch ME9 ..12 F3
Home Farm Cotts CT14 .115 E6
Homebirch Ho 6 CT7 ..26 F8
Homefern Ho CT9 ....7 I3
Homefield Ave CT14 ..117 B6
Homefield Dr ME8 ....12 B2
Homefield Row CT14 ...117 B6
Homefleet Ho 11 CT11 ...52 F7
Homeleigh Rd CT12 .....29 B3
Homepeak Ho 12 CT12 ..176 B2
Homeside Farm CT4 ....126 F6
Homespire Ho 19 CT1 ...67 A1
Homestall Ct CT2 ....66 C4
Homestall La ME13 ......63 B5
Homestead TN23 ....155 D8
Homestead Cl 7 CT9 ......7 J1
Homestead Ct CT14 ....117 A4
Homestead La CT15 ....132 C7
Homestead View 36 B2
Homestead Village CT11 .52 C5
Homevale Ho 3 CT20 ...177 E3
Homeview 3 ME10 ......37 B4
Homeview Terr 2 ME10 .37 B4
Homewood Ave ME10 ....36 D3
Homewood Inf Sch ME10 36 D4
Homewood Rd
  Sturry CT2 ....68 A6
  Tenterden TN30 ....167 B1
Homewood Sch &
  Sixth Form Ctr TN30 .167 B1
Honduras Terr 8 ME14 ..75 A7
Hone St ME2 ....9 B8
Honey Bee Glade ME8 ...33 A5
Honey Cl ME7 ....33 A5
Honey Hill CT2,CT5 ......65 F8
Honey La ME15 ....98 B6
Honeyball Wlk ME9 .....38 C2
Honeycrock Hill ME9 ....56 F8
Honeyfield TN23 ....138 E1
Honeypot Cl ME2 ....9 B8
Honeysuckle Cl
  3 Chatham ME5 ....31 E4
  Gillingham ME7 ....32 F4
  Margate CT9 ....28 C8
Honeysuckle Ct ME10 ...37 B5
Honeysuckle La ME11 ...52 F8
Honeysuckle Way CT6 ...23 D2
Honeywood Cl
  Canterbury CT1 ....67 B2
  Lympne CT21 ....175 A4
  Whitfield CT16 ....149 B6
Honeywood Parkway
  CT16 ....149 B5
Honeywood Rd CT16 ...149 A6
Honfleur Rd CT13 ....93 F8
Honiton House Sch CT9 ..8 B2
Honywood Rd ME17 ....101 C4
Hook Cl Chatham ME5 ...31 E5
  Folkestone CT20 ......177 F5
Hook La Brookland TN29 .197 C6
  Charing TN27 ....120 A7
  Harrietsham ME17 ....100 A3
Hook St ME17 ....118 F8
Hook Wall TN29 ....197 E5
Hookstead TN26 ....167 C7
Hooper's Pl ME1 ....9 C4
Hooper's Rd ME1 ....9 C4
Hoopers La CT6 ....23 D3
Hop Garden Way CT1 ...87 E6
Hop Gdn TN26 ....181 C1
Hope La
  New Romney TN28 ....200 A8
  St Mary in the Marsh TN29 193 F2
Hope Rd CT14 ....117 D5
Hope St Chatham ME4 ...10 A3
  Maidstone ME14 ....74 F6
  Sheerness ME12 ....1 C2
Hope's La CT12 ....29 C3
Hopes Gr TN26 ....167 D7
Hopeville Ave CT10 .....29 E6
Hopewell Dr ME5 ....32 C8
Hopewell Sch TN23 ....155 E7
Hoppers Way TN23 ....155 D8
Hopsons Pl ME12 ....4 C5
Horn Hill ME9 ....58 E2
Horn St CT19,CT20,CT21 .177 B4
Hornash La TN26 ......170 D8
Hornbeam Ave ME5 .....32 B2
Hornbeam Cl TN23 ....138 F3
Hornes Place Chapel*
  TN26 ....181 D2
Hornet Cl CT10 ....29 D3
Horsa Rd Birchington CT7 .26 D7
  Deal CT14 ....117 D8
Horse Wash La ME1 .....9 C6
Horsebridge Rd CT5 ....20 D2
Horselees Rd ME13 .....64 A2
Horseshoe Cl
  Gillingham ME7 ....32 F5
  Maidstone ME14 ....75 E5
Horseshoes La ME17 ....98 E4
Horsford Wlk ME13 .....62 A8
Horsham Hill ME9 ......12 E4
Horsham La ME8,ME9 ...12 D3
Horshams The CT6 ......23 D5
Horsley Cl CT18 ....163 B4
Horsley Rd ME1 ....9 B4
Horsted Ave ME4 ....10 A4
Horsted Cty Inf Sch ME4 31 D5
Horsted Cty Jun Sch
  ME5 ....31 D5
Horsted Way ME1 ....31 D7
Horton Cotts CT4 ......86 E4
Horton Downs ME15 ....75 F1
Horton Gdns CT4 ....86 E4
Horwood Cl ME11 ......31 B8
Hoser Gdns CT7 ....27 A4
Hospital Hill CT20,CT21 .177 C3

Hospital La
  Canterbury CT1 ....87 F8
Hospital La 3 ME9 ......9 E4
Hospital Meadow Cotts
  CT3 ....91 D2
Hospital Rd ME17 ....99 E8
Hotel Rd Gillingham ME8 .11 A2
  St Margaret's at Cliffe
  CT15 ....151 B6
Hothfield Common
  Nature Reserve* TN26 137 F8
Hothfield Cty Prim Sch
  TN26 ....138 A7
Hothfield Rd ME8 ......11 F1
Hougham Court La
  CT15 ....165 A3
Houghton Ave ME7 .....33 B3
Houghton Ho CT19 ....178 C5
House Field TN24 ......139 F2
Housefield Rd ME13 ...104 C6
Hovenden Cl CT2 ....67 A4
Howard Ave Rochester ME1 9 D3
  Sittingbourne ME10 ....36 D6
Howard Cl ME12 ....4 C7
Howard Dr ME16 ......74 B5
Howard Rd CT10 ....30 A3
Howard Sch The ME8 ...33 D8
Howbury Wlk ME8 .....33 D4
Howfield La CT4 ....86 E5
Howletts Oast CT4 .....89 C5
Howletts Zoo Pk* CT4 ..89 D6
Hoxton Cl TN23 ....155 D8
Hoystings Cl The CT1 ...88 A7
Hubbard's La ME15 .....97 A3
Hubbards Cotts ME8 ...12 C2
Hubbards Hill ME17 ...102 B6
Hubble Dr ME15 ....97 E7
Hubert Way CT10 ......29 E6
Huckleberry Cl ME5 ....32 B3
Hudson Cl
  7 Dover CT16 ....149 B3
  Gillingham ME8 ....11 C1
  Sturry CT2 ....67 F6
Hudson Rd CT1 ....67 B2
Hugh Pl 5 ME13 ....62 D7
Hugh Price Cl ME10 ....37 C5
Hugin Ave CT10 ....29 E7
Hulkes La ME1 ....9 F4
Hull Pl CT14 ....116 F6
Hull Rd TN29 ....204 E6
Humber Ave CT6 ....21 F4
Hume Ct CT21 ....176 D1
Humphrey Terr CT18 ..162 F4
Hundreds Cl CT8 ....27 D7
Hunger Hatch La TN27 .119 F4
Hunstanton Cl ME8 .....33 E3
Hunt Cl CT18 ....163 A4
Hunter Ave CT24 .....156 E8
Hunter Cl TN24 ....156 E8
Hunter Rd TN24 ......139 E1
Hunters Bank CT4 ....144 F4
Hunters Chase
  Herne Bay CT6 ....23 C2
  Whitstable CT5 ....43 E7
Hunters Cl 5 ME7 ......10 C7
Hunters Forstal Rd CT6 .23 C2
Hunters Way
  Gillingham ME7 ....10 E1
  Sheldwich ME13 ....83 C5
Hunters Way W ME5 ...10 E1
Hunters Wlk CT14 ....117 B6
Huntersfield Cl ME5 ....32 C1
Hunting Gate CT7 ......26 F8
Huntingdon Wlk 2 ME15 97 E7
Huntington Rd ME17 ...96 B3
Huntsman La ME14 .....75 B4
Huntsman's Cnr ME4 ...31 E8
Huntsmans Cl ME1 ......9 E1
Huntswood TN23 .....138 E1
Hurst Cl ME5 ....31 E6
Hurst Gr CT12 ....29 C1
Hurst Hill ME5 ....31 E2
Hurst La Capel-le-F CT18 .164 B4
  Charing Heath TN27 ..119 E6
  Sittingbourne ME10 ....14 F1
Hurst Pl ME8 ....33 F8
Hurst Rd TN24 ....139 C7
Hurstford La TN26,TN27 .120 C2
Hurstings The ME15 ....74 D2
Hurstwood ME5 ....31 E4
Hurstwood Rd
  Bredhurst ME7 ....33 B1
  Detling ME14 ....55 B7
  Warren Street ME13 ..102 E8
Hussar Rd ME1 ....9 C3
Hutchings Cl ME10 .....37 C5
Hutsford Cl ME8 ....33 D5
Huxley Cl ME1 ....9 D4
Hybrid Cl ME1 ....9 D1
Hyde Ct CT17 ....166 C7
Hyde Pl CT3 ....112 F5
Hyde Rd ME16 ....74 D6
Hyde The CT4 ....86 B2
Hythe Cl CT20 ....177 F5
Hythe Com Sch CT21 ..176 B1
Hythe Light Railway Sta*
  CT21 ....176 A2
Hythe Pl CT13 ....94 A8
Hythe Rd Ashford TN24 .139 E1
  Dymchurch TN29 .....186 E1
  Pedlinge CT21 ....175 D4
  Sittingbourne ME10 ....36 D5
  Smeeth TN25,TN24 ...158 C3
Hythe, St Leonard's
  CE Jun Sch CT21 .....176 B2

Ian's Wlk CT21 ....177 A3
Ice Bowl The* ME8 .....11 A1
Iden La TN27 ....119 B4
Idenwood Cl ME8 ......33 D6
Iffin La CT4 ....87 E2
Ifield Cl ME15 ....97 F7
Ilex Rd CT7 ....177 F6
Illustrious Cl ME5 ......32 A6
Imbert Cl TN28 ....200 C6
Imperial Ave ME12 ......4 D7
Imperial Dr ME12 ......4 D7
Imperial Rd ME7 ....10 C3
Impton La ME5 ....32 A1
Ince Rd CT7 ....67 F7
Ingle Cl CT7 ....27 B7
Ingle Rd ME4 ....9 F2
Ingleden Cl ME10 ......36 F8
Ingleden Park Rd TN30 .146 C1
Ingles La CT20 ....178 D5
Ingles Mews 3 CT20 ..178 C4
Ingles Rd 3 CT20 .....178 C4
Ingoldsby Rd
  Birchington CT7 ....26 E7
  Canterbury CT1 ....87 D6
  Folkestone CT19 .....178 E7
Ingram Rd ME7 ....10 E6
Inner Lines ME7 ....10 D4
Institute Rd Chatham ME4 10 A4
  Faversham ME13 ....62 D7
Inverary Ct CT11 ......29 E1
Inverness House 7 ME15 97 E7
Inverness Terr CT10 ....30 A3
Invicta Cl ME10 ....36 F7
Invicta Gram Sch ME14 .75 C4
Invicta Ho Canterbury CT1 .87 F7
  Margate CT9 ....8 C1
Invicta Rd
  Folkestone CT19 .....178 D7
  Lydd TN29 ....203 A2
  Margate CT9 ....29 B8
  Sheerness ME12 ....1 D2
  Whitstable CT5 ....43 F8
Invicta Villas ME14 ....76 C4
Inward Car Lanes CT16 .166 G8
Inward Freight Lanes
  CT16 ....166 G8
Iona Cl ME5 ....32 D1
Iona Rd ME15 ....97 A7
Irchester St 9 CT11 ....52 F7
Ireland Rd TN24 ......139 D2
Irene Astor Ct 7 CT20 .178 D5
Iris Cl ME5 ....54 A8
Iron Bar La 3 CT1 .....88 A8
Ironside Cl ME5 ....32 A8
Irvine Dr CT9 ....29 C8
Isis Cl CT21 ....175 A3
Island Rd
  Upstreet CT3,CT7 ......47 D2
  Westbere CT2,CT3 .....68 C7
Island Wall CT5 ....20 C1
Ivanhoe Rd Herne Bay CT6 23 A4
  Westgate-on-S CT8 .....7 C1
Ivens Way ME17 ......100 D6
Iversgate Cl ME8 ......11 F2
Ivory Cl ME3 ....40 A1
Ivy Cl Etchinghill CT18 .161 D3
  Kingswood ME17 ......99 D2
Ivy Cottage Hill CT12 ..50 E7
Ivy Cotts TN23 ....155 C8
Ivy Ct CT2 ....66 E6
Ivy House Rd CT5 ......20 D7
Ivy La Canterbury CT1 ...88 A8
  Ramsgate CT11 ....52 D6
Ivy Mews ME17 ....99 E2
Ivy Pl Canterbury CT1 ...87 E7
  Deal CT14 ....117 D7
  Rochester ME1 ....9 A2
Ivy St ME8 ....33 F8
Ivy Way CT19 ....178 E7
Ivychurch Gdns CT9 .....8 E2
Ivychurch Rd TN29 ...192 B3
Ivyside CT9 ....7 C1
Iwade Com Prim Sch
  ME9 ....14 D4

Jaarlen Rd TN29 ......203 B6
Jacinth Dr ME10 ....36 C6
Jacklin Cl ME5 ....31 F2
Jackson Ave ME1 ......31 E8
Jackson Cl ME8 ....11 C1
Jackson Rd CT1 ....139 D2
Jacksons La 8 TN30 ..179 A7
Jacob Cl CT9 ....28 E7
Jacob Yd 8 ME13 ......62 D7
Jacobs Ho ME12 ....1 D2
Jaffa Ct CT5 ....43 D8
Jamaica Terr ME14 ....75 A7
James Allchin Gdns
  TN24 ....139 F4
James Cl Ash CT3 ......71 D2
  Lyminge CT18 ....161 C7
James Ct
  Folkestone CT20 ......178 A4
  2 Margate CT9 ....8 B2
James Hall Gdns CT14 .117 C3
James Haney Dr TN24 .139 F5
James Morris Ct 3
  CT20 ....177 F3
James St Ashford TN23 .139 A3
  5 Chatham ME4 ....9 F4
James St continued
  Maidstone ME14 ....75 A5
  8 Ramsgate CT11 ......52 E6
  Rochester ME1 ....9 C4
  Sheerness ME12 ....1 E2
James Whatman Way
  ME14 ....74 F5
Japonica Cl ME5 ....32 C2
Jarman's Field TN25 ..123 F2
Jarrett Ho 6 CT20 ....178 C4
Jarrett's Ct 1 ME10 ....37 B4
Jarvis Dr TN24 ....157 A7
Jarvis Ho 4 ME14 ......74 F7
Jarvis Pl TN30 ....167 B3
Jarvist Pl CT14 ....134 D6
Jasmine Cl Chartham CT4 .86 E1
  2 Chatham ME5 ....31 F4
Jasper Ave ME1 ....9 D2
Jayne Wlk CT5 ....43 B6
Jefferson Cl TN23 ....138 F1
Jefferson Dr ME8 ......11 C1
Jefferson Rd ME12 ......1 E2
Jefferstone Gdns TN29 .194 F4
Jefferstone La TN29 ..194 E4
Jefferstone Lane Sta
  TN29 ....194 F4
Jeffery St ME7 ....10 C6
Jeffrey St ME14 ....75 A5
Jellicoe Cl TN24 ......157 A7
Jemmett Rd TN23 ....156 A8
Jenkins Dr ME15 ......97 E5
Jenkins' Dale ME4 ......9 F3
Jenner Rd ME1 ....9 C4
Jenner's Way TN29 ...194 F3
Jennifer Gdns CT9 .....29 C8
Jersey Cl TN24 ....139 C8
Jersey La CT4 ....109 C6
Jersey Rd ME2 ....9 A8
Jesmond St 3 CT19 ..178 D6
Jesse's Hill CT4 ......111 B1
Jessica Mews
  2 Canterbury CT1 .....67 B1
  Sittingbourne ME10 ....36 E7
Jesuit Ct CT2 ....67 A4
Jesus Hospl CT1 ....67 A1
Jetty Rd Sheerness ME12 ..1 B3
  Warden ME12 ....6 E4
Jewry La CT1 ....87 F8
Jeyes Rd ME7 ....10 C4
Jezreels Rd ME7 ....10 D3
Jillian Way TN23 .....155 E7
Jiniwin Rd ME1 ....31 D7
Jo-Ann's Ct 5 CT10 ...30 A4
Joey's La TN24 ....139 E2
Johannesburg House 2
  ME15 ....97 F5
Johannesburg Rd CT16 .149 C4
John Anderson Ct 11
  ME13 ....62 D7
John Badger Cl TN24 ..139 E5
John Bowley Ho CT19 .177 H6
John Graham Ct CT1 ...88 A6
John Hall Cl ME13 .....40 B2
John Nash Cl ME9 .....60 B8
John Newington Cl
  TN24 ....139 F5
John St Broadstairs CT10 .30 B4
  Maidstone ME14 ....75 A6
  Rochester ME1 ....9 C4
John Tapping Cl CT14 .117 B1
John Wilson Bsns Pk
  CT5 ....21 B1
John's Gn CT13 ....93 E6
Johnson Ave ME1 ......10 C7
Johnson Cl TN24 .....157 A7
Johnson Ct ME13 ......40 B1
Johnson Rd ME10 .....36 D4
Johnson Way ME12 .....4 A7
Joiners St ME4 ....10 B2
Jointon Rd CT20 .....178 B4
Jordan Cl ME15 ....97 E5
Joseph Conrad Ho CT2 .66 D1
Joseph Wilson Ind Est
  CT5 ....44 A7
Joss Gap Rd CT10 ......8 H1
Joy La CT5 ....43 B8
Joy Lane Inf Sch CT5 ..43 C7
Joy Lane Jun Sch CT5 ..43 C7
Joy Wood ME17 ....97 D5
Joyes Cl Folkestone CT19 178 E7
  Whitfield CT16 ....149 B7
Joyes Rd
  Folkestone CT19 .....178 E7
  Whitfield CT16 ....149 B7
Jubilee Cl CT21 ......187 D8
Jubilee Cotts
  Throwley ME13 ....82 D1
  Worth CT14 ....94 B4
Jubilee Cres ME11 ......2 F5
Jubilee Ct 18 CT10 .....30 B4
Jubilee Field TN30 ...188 E4
Jubilee Rd
  Littlebourne CT3 ....89 F8
  Sandwich CT13 ....93 F8
  Worth CT14 ....94 B4
Jubilee St ME10 ....36 E5
Jubilee Terr ME7 ......10 C6
Jubilee Way Dover CT16 166 E8
  Guston CT15,CT16 ....150 A2
Judd Rd ME13 ....62 A7
Judkins Cl ME5 ....32 C6
Julian Ct CT19 ....178 B5
Julian Rd CT19 ....178 B6
Julie Cl CT10 ....30 A7
Julien Pl TN24 ....157 A4
Junction Rd
  Gillingham ME7 ....10 D4
  Herne Bay CT6 ....22 C2

Junior King's Sch CT2 ..67 E5
Juniper Cl Ashford TN23 .138 E2
  Canterbury CT1 ....88 A6
  Chatham ME5 ....32 A4
  Maidstone ME16 ....74 B6
  Whitstable CT5 ....20 F1
Jury's Gap Coastguard Cotts
  TN31 ....201 E1
Jury's Gap Rd TN29 ...203 A5

Kain Ct CT12 ....29 B1
Kake St CT4 ....125 E7
Katherine Ct ME5 .....32 B2
Kathleen Mews 21 CT20 178 D5
Kearsney Abbey* CT16 148 D4
Kearsney Ave CT16 ...148 E4
Kearsney Cl CT16 ....148 D4
Kearsney Sta CT16 ...148 D4
Keat Farm Cl CT6 .....23 F5
Keating Cl ME1 ....9 A3
Keddow's Cl CT21 ...187 D8
Keefe Cl ME1 ....31 D1
Keeley Mews ME7 .....10 E3
Keeper's Hill CT4 .....89 D2
Keith Ave CT12 ....52 A8
Kellaway Rd ME5 .....32 A2
Kelly Dr ME7 ....10 C7
Kelly House ME1 ......31 C7
Kelvedon Rd CT14 ...117 C2
Kemp Alley 2 CT5 .....20 D1
Kemp Cl ME5 ....31 E4
Kemp Rd CT5 ....21 C2
Kempes Pl TN25 .....123 E2
Kempton Cl ME5 ......32 C2
Kemsdale Rd ME13 ....63 F6
Kemsing Gdns CT2 ....67 B4
Kemsley Down Sta ME10 15 C1
Kemsley Sta ME10 .....14 E1
Kemsley Street Rd ME7 .33 C1
Kenardington Rd TN26 .181 E3
Kendal Cl CT11 ....52 B6
Kendal Mdw CT5 ......21 E1
Kendal Rise CT10 .....30 A5
Kendal Way ME8 ......33 D8
Kendall Pl 1 ME15 ....97 D8
Kendon Bsns Pk ME2 ...9 D8
Kenfield Rd CT4 .....109 A6
Kengate Ind Est CT21 .175 F1
Kenilworth Cl CT15 ..151 A6
Kenilworth Ct ME10 ...36 C5
Kenilworth Dr ME8 ....33 D6
Kenilworth Gdns ME16 .74 B2
Kenilworth House ME16 74 B2
Kennedy Cl ME13 .....62 D8
Kennedy Dr CT14 ....117 B2
Kennedy Ho 6 CT11 ...52 F7
Kennel Barn Rd ME9 ..57 C5
Kennel Hill CT15 .....131 E6
Kennelling Rd ME13,
  TN27 ....103 D5
Kennett Dr CT14 .....117 A2
Kennett La TN25 .....175 B8
Kennett Lane Cotts
  TN25 ....175 B8
Kennington CE Jun Sch
  TN24 ....139 E7
Kennington Cl
  Gillingham ME8 ....11 B4
  Maidstone ME15 ....97 F7
Kennington Pl TN24 ..139 D7
Kennington Rd TN24 .140 A1
Kensington House ME16 74 A2
Kensinton Rd CT1 .....67 C4
Kent & Canterbury Hospl
  CT1 ....88 A5
Kent & East Sussex Rly*
  TN30 ....179 A8
Kent Ave Ashford TN24 .139 B3
  Canterbury CT1 ....88 D8
  Maidstone ME15 ....75 C1
  Minster (Sheppey) ME12 ..4 B6
  Sittingbourne ME10 ....36 D3
Kent Battle of Britain
  Mus* CT18 ....162 F4
Kent Cl ME1 ....31 C8
Kent Coll CT2 ....66 C3
Kent County Opthalmic
  & Aural Hospl ME14 ..75 A4
Kent County Show Gd
  ME14 ....55 C3
Kent Gdns CT7 ....26 F7
Kent Ho
  4 Broadstairs CT10 ...30 A4
  Folkestone CT20 .....178 B4
Kent Inst of Art & Design
  Chatham ME1 ....9 E4
  Maidstone ME16 ......74 C3
  Canterbury CT1 ....88 B7
Kent Music Sch CT1 ...66 F1
Kent Pl CT11 ....52 F6
Kent Rd Folkestone CT19 177 E2
  Margate CT9 ....29 B8
  Sheerness ME12 ....1 C1
Kent St CT5 ....43 D8
Kent Terr Gillingham ME8 .12 C2
  Ramsgate CT11 ....52 F6
Kent View Dr ME12 .....5 D1
Kentmere Ave ME11 ...51 F7
Kenton Gdns CT12 ....50 B6
Kentstone Ct ME4 .....10 A4
Kenward Rd ME16 .....74 C5

Kenwood Ave ME5 . . . .32 A4
Kenya Terr 7 ME14 . . . . .75 A7
Kenyon Wlk ME8 . . . . . .33 B3
Kerton Rd TN29 . . . . . .204 F3
Keston Ct ME8 . . . . .11 A2
Kestrel Cl ME10 . . . . . . .37 A2
Kestrel Ct 4 ME10 . . . . .37 A4
Kestrel Ho 8 ME7 . . . . . .10 B6
Kestrel Rd ME5 . . . . . . .32 C2
Keswick Dr ME16 . . . . . .74 B5
Keswick Rd ME10 . . . . . .37 C3
Kettle Dr CT18 . . . . . .163 B5
Kettle Hill ME13 . . . . . .81 F4
Kettle Hill Rd
 Eastling ME13 . . . . .81 F5
 Throwley ME13 . . . . . . .82 A4
Kevin Dr CT11 . . . . .52 B6
Kewlands ME14 . . . . . . .75 C6
Key St ME10 . . . . .36 A5
Keycol Hill ME9,ME10 . . .35 F5
Keycol Hospl ME9 . . . . . .35 E6
Keyes Ave ME4 . . . . .9 F2
Keyes Pl CT19 . . . . . . .178 E7
Keynes Coll CT2 . . . . . . .66 D4
Keys The CT18 . . . . . . .163 C5
Keyworth Mews 7 CT1 . .67 B2
Khartoum Rd Chatham ME4 .9 F6
 Gillingham ME7 . . . . . . .10 A6
Khartoum Sq CT16 . . . .149 A6
Khyber Rd ME4,ME7 . . . .10 B7
Kilbride Ct CT11 . . . . . . .29 F1
Kilburn Ho 6 ME14 . . . . .75 A5
Kiln Cl Challock TN25 . . .105 B1
 Sittingbourne ME10 . . . . .37 A3
Kiln Cnr CT21 . . . . . . .176 B4
Kiln Field TN30 . . . . . .179 C7
Kiln La TN26 . . . . .153 F5
Kiln Rd TN25 . . . . .172 F4
Kilnbridge Cl ME15 . . . . .96 B7
Kilndown Cl
 Ashford TN23 . . . . . . .155 E6
 Maidstone ME16 . . . . . .74 C7
Kilndown Gdns
 Canterbury CT2 . . . . . . .67 A4
 Margate CT9 . . . . .8 E2
Kimberley Cl CT19 . . . .149 C3
Kimberley Cnr CT10 . . . .29 F8
Kimberley Ct CT7 . . . . . .7 C1
Kimberley Gr CT5 . . . . . .42 F6
Kimberley Rd
 Gillingham ME7 . . . . . . .10 D3
 Ramsgate CT12 . . . . . . .29 A1
Kimberley Way TN24 . . .156 C7
Kimberly Terr CT18 . . . .161 C7
King Arthur Ct ME10 . . . .36 E3
King Arthur Rd CT12 . . . .51 D7
King Charles Ct CT14 . . .117 D2
King Edward Ave
 Broadstairs CT10 . . . . . .30 A4
 Herne Bay CT6 . . . . . . .23 B4
King Edward Ct CT6 . . . .23 B4
King Edward Rd
 Birchington CT7 . . . . . . .27 A5
 Chatham ME4 . . . . .9 F2
 Deal CT14 . . . . .117 D8
 Gillingham ME7 . . . . . . .10 F6
 Maidstone ME15 . . . . . .74 F2
 Ramsgate CT11 . . . . . . .52 C6
 Rochester ME1 . . . . .9 C5
King Edward St CT5 . . . .20 C1
King Ethelbert Sch CT8 . .27 C7
King George Rd ME5 . . . .31 E4
King George V
 Meml Houses ME8 . . . . .11 C2
King George Villas CT1 . .94 B3
King Lear's Way CT17 . .166 B5
King St Brookland TN29 . .191 D2
 Canterbury CT1 . . . . . . .66 F1
 Chatham ME4 . . . . .10 A4
 Deal CT14 . . . . .117 D6
 Deal, Walmer CT14 . . . .117 D3
 Dover CT16 . . . . .166 D7
 Fordwich CT2 . . . . .68 A4
 Gillingham ME7 . . . . . . .10 C6
 Maidstone ME14 . . . . . .75 A4
 Margate CT9 . . . . .7 J3
 Ramsgate CT11 . . . . . . .52 E7
 Rochester ME1 . . . . .9 C4
 Sandwich CT13 . . . . . . .73 A1
 Sheerness ME12 . . . . . . .1 B2
 Sittingbourne ME10 . . . . .36 E5
King William Rd 6 ME7 . .10 C7
King's Ave Ashford TN23 .139 A2
 Birchington CT7 . . . . . . .26 D7
 Broadstairs CT10 . . . . . .30 B6
 Ramsgate CT12 . . . . . . .29 B1
 Rochester ME1 . . . . .9 C3
 Sandwich CT13 . . . . . . .95 A8
 Whitstable CT5 . . . . . . .20 E1
King's Bastion ME7 . . . . .10 A5
King's Cl CT14 . . . . . . .134 D6
King's Head Alley ME12 . . .1 B3
King's Orch ME1 . . . . . . .9 C5
King's Pk CT1 . . . . .67 B1
King's Pl 4 CT11 . . . . . .52 E6
King's Rd Birchington CT7 .27 A6
 Chatham ME5 . . . . .10 D1
 Faversham ME13 . . . . . .62 C7
 Herne Bay CT6 . . . . . . .22 F5
 Ramsgate CT11 . . . . . . .52 D8
King's Sch CT1 . . . . .88 A8
King's Sch ME1 . . . . .9 C5
King's Sch The CT1 . . . . .67 A1
Kingfisher Apartments 13
 ME15 . . . . .97 E5

Kingfisher Ave CT21 . . .187 D8
Kingfisher Cl Iwade ME9 .14 E4
 Margate CT9 . . . . .28 B8
 Sevington TN24 . . . . . .157 A7
 Whitstable CT5 . . . . . . .43 C7
Kingfisher Ct
 Herne Bay CT6 . . . . . . .22 D3
 11 Maidstone ME15 . . . . .75 B4
Kingfisher Cty Prim Sch
 ME5 . . . . .32 B7
Kingfisher Dr ME15 . . . .32 C7
Kingfisher Gdns CT21 . .187 D8
Kingfisher Wlk CT10 . . . .29 F5
Kings Acre ME15 . . . . . .76 A1
Kings Chase TN24 . . . . .140 A2
Kings Cotts ME17 . . . . . .98 F6
Kings Ct CT14 . . . . . . .117 D3
Kings Meadow TN24 . . .139 E7
Kings Mews 7 CT1 . . . . .67 A1
Kings Mill Cl ME10 . . . . .36 E5
Kings Par 7 TN24 . . . . .139 B2
Kings Rd Aylesham CT3 . .112 F6
 Dover CT17 . . . . .166 A7
 Folkestone CT20 . . . . .177 D6
 Minster (Sheppey) ME12 . . .4 D7
Kings Reach ME15 . . . . .97 D8
Kings Ropewalk CT17 . .166 B5
Kings Row Chatham ME1 . . .9 B4
 Maidstone ME15 . . . . . .75 A1
Kings Wood
 Forest Walks★ TN25 . . .105 F1
Kingsbridge Ct 9 CT20 .178 E5
Kingsdale Ct ME5 . . . . . .10 C1
Kingsdown Cl
 Gillingham ME7 . . . . . . .33 B4
 Maidstone ME16 . . . . . .74 E4
Kingsdown Hill CT14 . . .134 D4
Kingsdown Hos ME9 . . . .59 E4
Kingsdown Pk CT5 . . . . .20 F2
Kingsdown Rd
 Kingsdown CT14 . . . . . .134 D7
 Lynsted ME9 . . . . .59 D4
St Margaret's at Cliffe
 CT15 . . . . .151 A7
Kingsfield Rd CT6 . . . . . .23 B2
Kingsford Cl TN25 . . . . .157 E4
Kingsford Ct CT17 . . . . .149 B1
Kingsford St TN25 . . . . .157 D5
Kingsgate Ave CT10 . . . . .8 F1
Kingsgate Bay Rd CT10 . . .8 H2
Kingsgate Cl ME16 . . . . .74 C4
Kingsgate Coll CT10 . . . .30 A8
Kingsgate La TN30 . . . .188 C5
Kingsland Gdns CT14 . . .134 B8
Kingsland Hollow TN29 .195 A4
Kingsland La
 Egerton TN27 . . . . .118 E1
 Westwell TN25 . . . . . . .121 F1
Kingsley Rd
 Maidstone ME15 . . . . . .75 A3
 Whitstable CT5 . . . . . . .43 E8
Kingsmarsh La TN29 . . .199 C5
Kingsmead CT19 . . . . . .178 B8
Kingsmead Prim Sch
 CT1 . . . . .67 A1
Kingsnorth CE Prim Sch
 TN23 . . . . .156 B3
Kingsnorth Ct 2 CT20 . .178 B5
Kingsnorth Gdns CT20 . .178 C5
Kingsnorth Rd
 Ashford TN23 . . . . . . .156 A6
 Faversham ME13 . . . . . .62 C6
 Gillingham ME8 . . . . . . .11 C4
Kingston Ave CT19 . . . . .28 C7
Kingston Cl Herne Bay CT6 23 F5
 Ramsgate CT12 . . . . . . .29 B2
 River CT17 . . . . .166 C7
Kingston Cres ME5 . . . . .32 C4
Kingston Dr ME15 . . . . . .97 A8
Kingstone Ct 3 CT20 . .178 B5
Kingsway Chatham ME5 . .10 D1
 Dymchurch TN29 . . . . .186 B2
 Gillingham ME7 . . . . . . .10 E1
Kingswear Gdns ME2 . . . .9 C7
Kingswood TN24 . . . . . .139 D5
Kingswood Ave ME4 . . . . .9 F2
Kingswood Prim Sch
 ME17 . . . . .99 E2
Kingswood Rd
 Gillingham ME7 . . . . . . .10 D6
 Kit's Coty ME20 . . . . . .53 D8
Kingswood Villas ME17 .149 A2
Kinross Cl ME5 . . . . . . .32 B7
Kipling Rd TN23 . . . . . .139 B2
Kipping Cl CT18 . . . . . .163 A4
Kirby's La CT2 . . . . .66 F1
Kirk Gdns CT14 . . . . . .117 B2
Kirkdale ME15 . . . . .96 F5
Kirkdale Cl ME5 . . . . . . .32 D1
Kirkdale Cotts ME15 . . . .96 F5
Kirkdale Rd ME15 . . . . . .96 F6
Kirkstone Ave CT11 . . . . .51 F7
Kirkwood Ave TN26 . . . .169 A1
Kit Hill ME13 . . . . .84 D8
Kit Hill Ave ME5 . . . . . . .31 E3
Kit's Coty House★ ME20 .53 C6
Kitchener Ave ME4 . . . . .10 A1
Kitchener Cl CT4 . . . . . .128 F8
Kitchener Rd
 Dover CT17 . . . . .166 A7
 Rochester ME2 . . . . .9 A4
Kitchener Sq CT19 . . . . .178 E8
Kite Farm CT5 . . . . .21 D3
Kitewell La TN29 . . . . . .203 D8
Kither Rd TN23 . . . . . . .156 A7
Kitsbridge La
 Hamstreet TN26 . . . . . .183 C4

Kitsbridge La continued
 Ruckinge TN25,TN26 . . .184 B6
Klondyke Ind Est ME11 . . . .2 F4
Knatchbull Way TN25 . . .158 E5
Knavesacre Ct ME8 . . . . .33 D5
Knight Ave
 Canterbury CT2 . . . . . . .87 D8
 Gillingham ME7 . . . . . . .10 D7
Knight Rd ME2 . . . . .9 A6
Knight's Ave CT10 . . . . . .30 B6
Knight's Rd CT16 . . . . .166 E8
Knightrider Ct ME15 . . . .75 A3
Knightrider St
 1 Maidstone ME15 . . . . .75 A3
 Sandwich CT13 . . . . . . .73 A1
Knights Alley 14 CT5 . . . .20 D2
Knights Ct Dover CT17 . .149 B1
 Sittingbourne ME10 . . . . .36 E3
Knights Pk ME2 . . . . .9 A6
Knights Templars CT17 .166 C6
Knights Way CT16 . . . . .149 A3
Knightsfield Rd ME10 . . . .36 D7
Knock Hill TN30 . . . . . .190 A4
Knock Rd TN23 . . . . . . .156 A7
Knockholt Rd CT9 . . . . . . .8 F3
Knockhurst Ct TN30 . . .167 C1
Knockwood Rd TN30 . . .167 C1
Knold Pk CT9 . . . . .28 E8
Knole Rd ME5 . . . . .32 C3
Knole The ME13 . . . . . . .62 B7
Knoll Ct CT20 . . . . .178 C4
Knoll Hill TN25 . . . . . . .173 C3
Knoll La TN23 . . . . .155 E7
Knoll Pl CT14 . . . . .117 C2
Knoll Way ME12 . . . . .6 D4
Knott Cres TN24 . . . . . .157 A7
Knott Ct ME14 . . . . .74 F6
Knott's La 20 CT1 . . . . . .67 A1
Knotts La CT15 . . . . . . .150 F6
Knotts Sq TN23 . . . . . . .139 C2
Knowle Rd ME14 . . . . . .75 B6
Knowler Way CT6 . . . . . .23 C5
Knowlton Gdns ME16 . . . .74 B2
Knowlton Wlk 1 CT1 . . . .67 B1
Kohima Pl CT15 . . . . . .149 F2
Kyetop Wlk ME8 . . . . . . .33 D6
Kymbeline Ct CT14 . . . .117 B4

L

La Belle Alliance Sq 6
 CT11 . . . . .52 E7
La Galamina TN28 . . . . .204 E8
La Rocco TN28 . . . . . . .204 E8
La Tausco TN28 . . . . . .204 D8
La-Tene CT14 . . . . .117 B2
Laburnum Ave CT13 . . . .93 F8
Laburnum Cl CT16 . . . . .148 E4
Laburnum Gr ME12 . . . . . .1 I1
Laburnum Ho ME12 . . . . .1 C2
Laburnum La CT2 . . . . . .68 B7
Laburnum Pl ME10 . . . . .36 E4
Labworth Ct ME12 . . . . . .3 E6
Lacey Cl ME17 . . . . .98 E4
Lachlan Way 2 CT20 . . .177 F3
Lacton Oast TN24 . . . . .157 B8
Lacton Way TN24 . . . . .157 A8
Lacy Cl ME16 . . . . .166 C6
Ladbrooke Ho 7 ME14 . .75 A5
Ladds Cnr ME7 . . . . .11 B5
Lade Fort Cotts TN29 . . .204 E6
Lade Fort Cres TN29 . . .204 E6
Lady Garne Rd CT15 . . .164 F5
Lady J Thornhill's Endowed
 Prim Sch TN25 . . . . . .123 E2
Lady Wootton's Gn 5
 CT1 . . . . .88 A8
Ladyfields Chatham ME5 . .32 D2
 Herne Bay CT6 . . . . . . .23 D2
Ladyfields Cl ME9 . . . . . .35 F5
Ladysmith Gr CT5 . . . . . .42 F6
Ladysmith Rd CT5 . . . . . .43 C5
Ladywell 7 CT16 . . . . . .166 D8
Ladywell Ho 2 CT16 . . .166 D8
Ladywood Rd CT2 . . . . . .67 F7
Lagos Ave CT12 . . . . . . .29 A1
Lakelands
 Harrietsham ME17 . . . . .100 E6
 Maidstone ME15 . . . . . .97 A7
Lakemead TN23 . . . . . .155 E8
Laker Rd ME1 . . . . .31 C6
Lakeside TN23 . . . . . . .155 E8
Lakeside Gdns TN26 . . . .120 F1
Lakeside Pk ME2 . . . . . . .9 E7
Lakewood Dr ME8 . . . . . .33 C6
Laking Ave CT10 . . . . . .30 B7
Laleham Gdns CT9 . . . . . .8 B2
Laleham Rd CT9 . . . . .8 B1
Laleham Sch CT9 . . . . . . .8 B1
Laleham Wlk CT9 . . . . . . .8 B1
Lamb's Wlk CT5 . . . . . . .43 C6
Lambard House 8 ME14 .75 A5
Lambden Rd TN27 . . . . .136 C6
Lamberhurst Gn ME8 . . . .11 B3
Lamberhurst Rd ME16 . . .74 B7
Lamberhurst Way CT9 . . . .8 F3
Lambert Ho CT14 . . . . . .117 B3
Lambes Ct ME8 . . . . .33 D5
Lambeth Cl ME5 . . . . . . .32 B4
Lambeth Rd CT1 . . . . . . .67 C4
Lambourn Way ME5 . . . . .32 C2
Lambourne Pl ME8 . . . . .12 A2
Lambourne Rd ME15 . . . .75 F2
Lambourne Wlk CT1 . . . .88 C8
Lambsfrith Gr ME7 . . . . . .33 B3
Lambton Rd CT17 . . . . .149 A1
Laming Rd CT7 . . . . .27 B6

Lammas Dr ME10 . . . . . .36 E6
Lamplighters Cl ME7 . . . .32 F5
Lancashire Rd ME15 . . . .97 E7
Lancaster Ave CT18 . . . .164 C2
Lancaster Cl
 Hamstreet TN26 . . . . . .183 A8
 Ramsgate CT12 . . . . . . .29 B1
Lancaster Ct ME8 . . . . . .33 C7
Lancaster Gdns
 Birchington CT7 . . . . . . .26 F6
 Herne Bay CT6 . . . . . . .23 D5
Lancaster Ho Deal CT14 .117 A5
 3 Dover CT17 . . . . . . .166 D7
Lancaster Rd
 Canterbury CT1 . . . . . . .87 F6
 Dover CT17 . . . . .166 D7
Lance Cl ME10 . . . . .36 F8
Lancer Ho ME1 . . . . .9 C3
Lancet La ME15 . . . . . . .97 A6
Lanchester Cl CT6 . . . . . .22 A3
Landbury Wlk TN23 . . . .138 F4
Landon Rd CT6 . . . . .23 C4
Landor Ct ME7 . . . . .33 A3
Landrail Rd ME9 . . . . . . .13 B3
Landway The ME14 . . . . .76 A4
Lane End CT6 . . . . .22 D5
Lane The CT15 . . . . . . .149 F6
Lane's Wlk CT5 . . . . . . .20 E2
Lanes The CT12 . . . . . . .50 D6
Lanfranc Gdns CT2 . . . . .66 C1
Lanfranc Ho 5 CT1 . . . . .67 A1
Lanfranc Rd CT14 . . . . .117 C8
Lang Ct CT5 . . . . .21 C3
Langdale TN23 . . . . . . .155 E8
Langdale Ave CT11 . . . . .52 A7
Langdale Cl ME8 . . . . . . .11 D1
Langdale Rise ME16 . . . .74 C5
Langdon Ave CT3 . . . . . .71 F1
Langdon Cl CT15 . . . . . .150 F5
Langdon Cross CT15 . . .150 C7
Langdon Prim Sch
 CT15 . . . . .133 A1
Langdon Rd
 Folkestone CT19 . . . . . .177 D7
 Rochester ME1 . . . . .9 C4
Langham Cl CT9 . . . . .7 F1
Langham Gr ME15 . . . . . .74 C4
Langholm Rd TN23 . . . .156 A7
Langhorne Gdns 5
 CT20 . . . . .178 C4
Langley Gdns CT9 . . . . . .8 E3
Langley Rd ME10 . . . . . .36 F7
Langney Dr TN23 . . . . . .155 E6
Langport Rd TN28 . . . . .200 C6
Langton Cl ME14 . . . . . .75 C5
Langton Cotts CT3 . . . . .70 B5
Langton La CT4 . . . . .88 A4
Lankester Parker Rd
 ME1 . . . . .31 C6
Lansdown Rd
 Canterbury CT1 . . . . . . .88 A7
 Sittingbourne ME10 . . . . .37 C4
Lansdowne Ave ME5 . . . .97 C6
Lansdowne Ct 9 ME4 . . . .9 F4
Lansdowne Prim Sch
 ME10 . . . . .37 C3
Lansdowne Rd ME4 . . . . .9 E2
Lanthorne Rd CT10 . . . . .30 A6
Lapwing Cl ME12 . . . . . . .4 B5
Lapwing Dr
 Ashford TN23 . . . . . . .156 D3
 Lower Halstow ME9 . . . . .13 B3
Larch Cl CT10 . . . . .29 D4
Larch Ct CT15 . . . . .114 B1
Larch Terr ME12 . . . . .3 A8
Larch Wlk TN24 . . . . . .139 C6
Larch Wood Cl ME5 . . . . .32 D1
Larchcroft ME5 . . . . .32 A2
Larches The
 Faversham ME13 . . . . . .62 A8
 Whitstable CT5 . . . . . . .43 C8
Larkescliff Ct CT7 . . . . . .26 D8
Larkey View CT4 . . . . . . .86 E1
Larkfield Ave
 Gillingham ME7 . . . . . . .10 E4
 Sittingbourne ME10 . . . . .36 E6
Larking Dr ME16 . . . . . .74 D7
Larksfield Rd ME13 . . . . .40 C1
Larkspur Rd ME5 . . . . . . .31 E4
Lascelles Rd CT17 . . . . .166 A6
Laser Quay ME2 . . . . .9 D6
Latchgate CT20 . . . . . . .177 C3
Lathe Barn Mus★ TN29 .186 D5
Latimer Ct ME6 . . . . .22 B2
Latimer Pl 4 ME7 . . . . . .10 C7
Launder Way ME15 . . . . .74 E2
Laundry Rd CT12 . . . . . .50 D7
Laura Pl ME1 . . . . .9 A2
Laura Villas CT6 . . . . . . .22 E5
Laureate Cl CT9 . . . . .8 B2
Laurel Ave TN29 . . . . . .194 F4
Laurel Cl CT20 . . . . . . .177 E6
Laurel Gr ME17 . . . . .99 D2
Laurel Ho ME12 . . . . .1 C2
Laurel Rd ME7 . . . . .10 C7
Laurel Way CT4 . . . . .86 E1
Laurel Wlk ME8 . . . . .33 E6
Laurels The ME16 . . . . . .74 C7
Laureston Pl CT16 . . . . .166 E8
Laurie Gray Ave ME5 . . . .31 D1
Lauriston Cl CT10 . . . . . .52 A5
Lauriston Mount CT10 . . .30 A5
Lausanne Rd CT9 . . . . . . .7 J2
Lausanne Terr 11 CT9 . . . .7 J2
Lavenda Cl ME7 . . . . . . .33 A4
Lavender Cl
 1 Chatham ME5 . . . . . . .31 E4
 Margate CT9 . . . . .28 C8

Lavender Cl continued
 Whitstable CT5 . . . . . . .21 C2
Lavender Ct ME10 . . . . . .37 A3
Lavender Ho 3 ME6 . . . . .97 C8
Laverstoke Rd ME16 . . . .74 C8
Lawley Cl CT12 . . . . .29 C1
Lawn Cl ME4 . . . . .10 B2
Lawn Rd Broadstairs CT10 .30 A4
 Deal CT14 . . . . .117 C1
Lawn Villas CT11 . . . . . .52 E6
Lawns The 18 CT11 . . . . .52 F7
Lawrence Cl
 Folkestone CT19 . . . . . .177 F6
 Maidstone ME15 . . . . . .97 A7
Lawrence Ct CT19 . . . . .178 E6
Lawrence Gdns CT6 . . . . .23 C4
Lawrence St ME7 . . . . . . .10 C5
Laws La TN25 . . . . .172 D7
Lawson Cl CT4 . . . . .86 D2
Laxey The ME15 . . . . . . .74 E1
Laxton Cl ME15 . . . . . . .75 F3
Laxton Dr ME17 . . . . . . .98 A1
Laxton Way
 Canterbury CT1 . . . . . . .88 C7
 Faversham ME13 . . . . . .62 E5
 Sittingbourne ME10 . . . . .36 D6
 Whitstable CT5 . . . . . . .21 C1
Lay La CT3 . . . . .71 D2
Layfield Cotts ME9 . . . . .14 C1
Layfield Rd ME7 . . . . . . .10 F7
Laylam Ct CT10 . . . . . . .29 D5
Lazarus Hart Havens
 of Rest The CT11 . . . . .52 F8
Le Roux Cl CT18 . . . . . .162 F4
Lea Cl CT21 . . . . .176 B4
Lea Ct ME4 . . . . .9 E1
Leach Ho ME13 . . . . . . .64 A3
Leacon Cotts TN27 . . . .120 E4
Leacon Cotts The TN27 .120 E4
Leacon Rd TN23 . . . . . .138 F2
Leafield TN25 . . . . .159 D1
Leafy Glade ME8 . . . . . . .33 B6
Leahurst Ct ME16 . . . . . .148 E4
Leander Rd ME1 . . . . . . .31 C7
Learoyd Rd TN28 . . . . . .200 C6
Leas Gn CT10 . . . . .29 D4
Leas Rd CT14 . . . . .117 B4
Leas The Faversham ME13 .62 B8
 Folkestone CT20 . . . . . .178 C4
 Kingsdown CT14 . . . . . .134 D3
 Minster (Sheppey) ME12 . . .4 C8
 Sheerness ME12 . . . . . . .1 I1
 Whitstable CT5 . . . . . . .21 D1
Leaside Cotts CT21 . . . .176 B3
Leatt Cl CT10 . . . . .29 F4
Leaveland Cl TN23 . . . . .155 F6
Leaveland Cotts ME13 . . .83 B2
Leda Cotts TN25 . . . . . .120 F3
Leeds & Broomfield
 CE Prim Sch ME17 . . . . .99 A7
Leeds Castle & Gdns★
 ME17 . . . . .99 D7
Leeds Rd ME17 . . . . .98 E3
Leeds Sq ME8 . . . . .11 B3
Leeke Ho 2 ME1 . . . . . . .9 C1
Leelands Ho CT14 . . . . .117 B1
Lees Cl The TN25 . . . . . .158 D5
Lees Court Rd ME13 . . . .83 C5
Lees Rd Ashford TN23 . . .140 A1
 Brabourne Lees TN25 . . .158 E6
Lees Terr CT4 . . . . .85 C2
Lees The CT6 . . . . .23 C5
Leet Cl Gillingham ME7 . . .10 E6
 Minster (Sheppey) ME12 . . .5 B5
Leeward Rd ME1 . . . . . . .9 C1
Leggett's La 4 CT5 . . . . .20 D2
Leicester Ave CT9 . . . . . .8 C2
Leicester Ct CT9 . . . . . . .8 D3
Leicester Gdns ME12 . . . .6 E3
Leicester Rd ME15 . . . . .97 D7
Leigh Ave ME15 . . . . . . .97 B6
Leigh Ct ME12 . . . . .3 F5
Leigh Green Ind Est
 TN30 . . . . .179 C6
Leigh Rd CT12 . . . . .28 F1
Leighton Ct 3 CT16 . . . .149 C1
Leighton Rd CT16 . . . . .149 C1
Leighville Dr CT6 . . . . . .22 D4
Leitch Row ME7 . . . . . . .10 A7
Leivers Rd CT14 . . . . . .117 A3
Len Valley Wlk CT15 . . . .75 F1
Lenacre Ave CT16 . . . . .148 F7
Lenacre La CT16 . . . . . .148 F8
Lenacre St TN25,TN26 . .122 B2
Lendrim Cl 11 ME7 . . . . .10 A6
Lenfield Ave ME14 . . . . . .75 B4
Length The CT7 . . . . .25 F2
Lenham Ct CT10 . . . . . . .30 A2
Lenham Ct 10 ME15 . . . .75 B4
Lenham Forstal Rd
 ME17 . . . . .119 B8
Lenham Gdns CT9 . . . . . .28 B8
Lenham Heath Rd
 ME17 . . . . .101 E5
Lenham Ho ME17 . . . . . .101 E5
Lenham Prim Sch ME17 101 C5
Lenham Rd ME17 . . . . . .100 C1
Lenham Sta ME17 . . . . .101 C4
Lenham Way ME8 . . . . . .11 A3
Lennard Ct 3 CT20 . . . .178 E5
Lennard Rd CT20 . . . . . .178 E5
Lenside Dr ME15 . . . . . . .76 A2
Leona Ct 8 CT9 . . . . .8 B2
Leonard Cl ME16 . . . . . .74 B6
Leonard Rd
 7 Chatham ME4 . . . . . .10 B3
 Greatstone-on-S TN28 . .204 E7
Leonard's Ave CT11 . . . . .29 E1

Leopold Rd
Chatham ME4 [2] 10 A3
Ramsgate CT11 ....52 E8
Leopold St CT11 ....52 E6
Lerryn Gdns CT10 ....29 F8
Les Spickett Cl ME13 ....62 E6
Lesley Ave CT1 ....88 A6
Lesley Pl ME16 ....74 E5
Leslie Ave CT9 ....28 B8
Leslie Cres TN30 ....167 B2
Leslie Rd Birchington CT7 ....27 A8
Gillingham ME7 ....10 D7
Leslie Smith Dr ME13 ....62 C7
Lested La ME17 ....98 E6
Lester Rd ME4 ....10 A3
Letchworth Ave ME4 ....9 F1
Lewd La TN27 ....135 A3
Lewis Ave ME4 ....11 B2
Lewis Cl ME13 ....62 A7
Lewis Court Dr ME17 ....97 C3
Lewis Cres CT9 ....8 B3
Lewis St TN23 ....155 F7
Lewisham Rd CT17 ....148 E3
Lewson Street Rd ME9 ....60 E8
Leybourn Rd CT10 ....30 B2
Leybourne Cl ME5 ....32 A2
Leybourne Dr CT9 ....28 B8
Leyburne Rd CT16 ....166 D8
Leycroft Cl CT2 ....66 E3
Leys The CT12 ....28 D1
Leysdown Rd
Eastchurch ME12 ....5 E3
Leysdown-on-S ME12 ....6 C1
Leysdown View CT5 ....43 C6
Leyton Ave ME7 ....10 E1
Library Rd CT2 ....66 D4
Libya Terr [6] ME14 ....75 A7
Lichfield Ave CT1 ....88 B6
Lichfield Cl ME8 ....11 D2
Lichfield Ho [12] ME15 ....97 E7
Lidsing Rd ME14 ....54 E6
Liege Cl ME10 ....14 F1
Lighthouse Rd CT15 ....151 A5
Lilk Hill ME14 ....76 C3
Lillian Rd CT11 ....52 F8
Lilyvale Cotts TN25 ....158 F4
Lime Cl TN23 ....138 F3
Lime Ct ME8 ....33 C3
Lime Gr
Halfway Houses ME12 ....3 D5
Sittingbourne ME10 ....37 A4
Lime Kiln Rd CT1 ....87 F6
Lime Kiln Wharf ME11 ....3 A5
Lime Villas CT4 ....144 F5
Limekiln Rdbt CT17 ....166 D6
Limekiln St CT17 ....166 D5
Limepits Cross ME9 ....35 F3
Limes Cl TN30 ....179 C8
Limes Pl [15] ME13 ....62 D7
Limes Rd Dover CT16 ....149 C1
Folkestone CT19 ....177 F6
Limes The Ashford TN23 ....156 A5
Lenham ME17 ....101 D5
Old Romney TN29 ....199 A4
Limetree Cl ME5 ....32 B8
Limetree Terr ME17 ....101 E6
Linces The CT16 ....149 B4
Lincoln Ave CT1 ....88 B7
Lincoln Cl CT5 ....21 D3
Lincoln Gdns CT7 ....26 F7
Lincoln Rd ME15 ....97 D8
Lincon Rd ME7 ....10 D7
Linden Ave
Broadstairs CT10 ....30 B5
Herne Bay CT6 ....22 E4
Whitstable CT5 ....20 F1
Linden Chase CT2 ....66 E1
Linden Cl
Sittingbourne ME10 ....36 D3
Westgate-on-S CT8 ....27 E7
Linden Cres CT19 ....178 D6
Linden Dr ME12 ....3 A7
Linden Gr CT2 ....66 E1
Linden Grove Prim Sch
TN23 ....155 F6
Linden House [5] ME5 ....31 F4
Linden Rd Ashford TN24 ....139 D1
Chartham CT4 ....86 E1
Coxheath ME17 ....96 C4
Gillingham ME7 ....10 E5
Westgate-on-S CT8 ....27 F8
Lindens CT21 ....176 D2
Lindenthorpe Rd CT10 ....30 A6
Lindfield Cotts ME13 ....62 A6
Lindisfarne Gdns ME16 ....74 E3
Lindridge Cl CT6 ....46 A8
Lineacre Cl ME8 ....33 D6
Lines Terr ME4 ....10 A4
Linington Rd CT7 ....27 A6
Link Hill La TN27 ....118 D3
Link La CT1 ....88 A8
Link Rd Broadstairs CT10 ....29 F7
Tyler Hill CT2 ....66 E5
Link The TN23 ....155 E7
Links Cl CT6 ....23 A3
Links Cres TN29 ....195 A4
Links Ct CT14 ....95 C1
Links Rd CT14 ....117 C8
Links The ME5 ....32 B8
Links Way TN28 ....200 D6
Linksfield Ct CT8 ....27 D7
Linksfield Rd CT8 ....27 D7
Linksway CT19 ....178 B8
Linksway Cl CT19 ....178 B8
Linkway ME9 ....14 D4
Linley Ho CT10 ....29 E7
Linley Rd CT10 ....29 E7

Linnet Ave CT5 ....43 B6
Linton Gore ME17 ....96 D3
Linton Hill ME17 ....96 E1
Linton Rd ME15 ....96 F4
Lion Ct CT14 ....117 C5
Lion Field ME13 ....62 B7
Lion Yd Faversham ME13 ....62 A6
[3] Sittingbourne ME10 ....36 F4
Lion's Rd TN28 ....200 A6
Lionard Ho [3] CT2 ....66 E1
Liphook Way ME16 ....74 C8
Lisa Ct CT5 ....21 A2
Lismore Cl ME15 ....97 A7
Lismore Rd Herne Bay CT6 ....23 D5
Whitstable CT5 ....44 B8
Liss Rd CT13 ....93 A1
List The CT3 ....69 C2
Lister Cl Deal CT14 ....117 C5
Dover CT17 ....149 B1
Lister Ho CT9 ....29 A8
Lister Rd CT9 ....29 A8
Lister Way CT20 ....177 F3
Listmas Rd Chatham ME4 ....10 B3
[2] Gillingham ME4 ....10 B2
Listways Cotts CT3 ....113 B6
Little Ave CT14 ....116 F3
Little Brook Rd TN23 ....139 A3
Little Buckland Ave
ME16 ....74 D6
Little Charles St CT6 ....22 F5
Little Chequers TN25 ....123 E2
Little Copse Cl CT4 ....86 E1
Little Ct ME16 ....74 D2
Little Glovers TN23 ....155 D8
Little Hempen TN23 ....155 D8
Little Hill TN30 ....167 B2
Little John Ave ME5 ....31 F2
Little Kit's Coty House ★
ME20 ....53 C5
Little Knoll TN23 ....155 F8
Little Meadow CT2 ....65 E1
Little Orch ME17 ....96 D3
Little Paddocks CT5 ....44 D7
Little Robhurst TN26 ....167 D8
Little Stone Stile Cotts
ME13 ....84 F4
Little Walton CT5 ....93 C3
Littlebourne Ave ME8 ....11 B4
Littlebourne CE Prim Sch
CT3 ....89 F8
Littlebourne Rd
Canterbury CT1,CT3 ....88 E8
Maidstone ME14 ....75 C6
Littlebrook Cl TN23 ....139 A3
Littlefield Cl ME8 ....12 B2
Littlemead CT9 ....178 A7
Littleston Ct TN28 ....200 E5
Littlestone Rd TN28 ....200 D6
Liverpool Lawn [15] CT11 ....52 E8
Liverpool Rd CT14 ....117 D2
Livingstone Bldgs ME7 ....10 D5
Livingstone Circ ME7 ....10 D5
Livingstone Ct TN29 ....187 B4
Livingstone Rd
Broadstairs CT10 ....29 E6
Gillingham ME7 ....10 E5
Livingstone Wlk [16] ME15 ....97 F5
Llamas Gate ME13 ....62 D8
Lloyd Rd CT10 ....30 A4
Lloyds Gn TN30 ....188 B2
Loading Bay App CT13 ....73 A8
Loaland Bsns Ctr ME2 ....9 D8
Lobelia Cl ME7 ....10 E6
Locarno Ave ME8 ....11 A2
Lock La ME14 ....53 D1
Lock St ME7 ....10 C5
Lockenden Cotts CT3 ....89 D6
Lockham Farm Ave
ME17 ....97 D5
Lockholt Cl TN23 ....138 E3
Lockington Gr ME1 ....9 C5
Locksley Cl ME5 ....31 E2
Lockswood ME16 ....74 D7
Loddington La ME17 ....97 A1
Loder Rd ME17 ....101 B5
Lodge The TN24 ....139 D7
Lomas Rd ME10,ME9 ....37 D5
Lombard St CT9 ....7 I3
Lombardy Cl ME7 ....33 A6
Lombardy Dr ME14 ....75 C5
London Manston Airport
CT12 ....28 B1
London Rd [21] CT20 ....178 E5
London Rd Canterbury CT2 ....66 D1
Deal CT14 ....117 B5
Dover CT16,CT17 ....149 B1
Faversham, Ospringe ME13 ....62 B6
Faversham,Norton Ash
ME13,ME9 ....61 C7
Faversham,Preston ME13 ....63 A5
Gillingham ME8 ....11 C1
Hartlip ME8,ME9 ....34 D7
Hythe CT21 ....175 D7
Maidstone ME16 ....74 C6
Newington ME9 ....35 A6
Ramsgate CT11 ....52 B6
Rochester ME2 ....9 A7
Sittingbourne ME10 ....36 C4
Temple Ewell CT15,CT16 ....148 B6
Teynham ME9 ....38 C1
London Road (River)
CT16,CT17 ....148 F4
London Rd Trad Est
ME10 ....36 D4
London St CT20 ....178 E5

Londonderry Ho [15] ME15 ....97 E7
Lone Barn Rd ME17 ....102 B8
Lonefield TN26 ....155 B1
Long Acre Cl CT2 ....66 E2
Long Barrow The TN24 ....156 E6
Long Beech TN23 ....138 E1
Long Catlis Rd ME8 ....33 D4
Long Dr CT13 ....93 C2
Long Hill CT4 ....85 C1
Long La CT15 ....130 D7
Long Length TN23 ....155 D4
Long Market [2] CT1 ....88 A8
Long Meadow Way CT2 ....67 A4
Long Reach CT5 ....43 C6
Long Rede La ME16 ....74 A2
Long Rock TN25 ....21 C3
Long Row TN25 ....157 D2
Long Wlk TN23 ....138 E4
Long's Acre TN25 ....123 E1
Longacre CT5 ....21 D1
Longacre Rd TN23 ....155 D7
Longage Hill CT18,CT4 ....144 A1
Longbridge TN24 ....140 B1
Longbridge Terr CT21 ....175 F1
Longfellow Rd ME7 ....10 C3
Longfield TN30 ....179 A6
Longfield Cl CT5 ....21 D2
Longfield Pl ME15 ....97 C8
Longfield Rd CT17 ....166 B7
Longfields Dr ME14 ....76 A5
Longford Cl ME8 ....34 A8
Longford Ct ME8 ....34 A8
Longford Terr [9] CT20 ....178 D4
Longford Way [10] CT20 ....178 D4
Longham Copse ME15 ....75 F1
Longhill Ave ME5 ....10 B3
Longhurst Dr ME5 ....31 F2
Longley Rd Gillingham ME8 ....11 F1
Rochester ME1 ....9 C4
Longmead CT6 ....22 C3
Longmete Rd CT3 ....70 C5
Longmore Dr ME12 ....5 C1
Longparish CT15 ....97 F6
Longridge ME10 ....37 B2
Longshaw Rd ME15 ....97 F5
Longtye Dr CT5 ....44 C7
Longwood ME5 ....32 B1
Lonsdale Ave CT9 ....8 C3
Lonsdale Dr
Gillingham ME8 ....33 E7
Herne Bay CT6 ....22 B5
Sittingbourne ME10 ....36 C5
Lookers La CT21 ....176 B3
Loop Court Mews [9]
CT13 ....72 F1
Loop St CT13 ....72 F1
Loose Down Rd ME13 ....104 F3
Loose Inf & Jun Schs
ME15 ....97 A6
Loose Rd ME15 ....97 A7
Lord Romney's Hill ME14 ....75 F3
Lord Warden Ave CT14 ....117 D2
Lord Warden Sq CT17 ....166 D5
Lords Cl ME9 ....37 E2
Lords Cotts ME15 ....83 C4
Lords Wood Cl ME5 ....32 B3
Lords Wood La ME5 ....32 B3
Lordswood Ind Est ME5 ....54 C8
Lordswood Jun Sch ME5 ....32 B3
Lorenden Park Nature
Reserve ★ ME13 ....61 F3
Lorenden Prep Sch ME13 ....61 E3
Lorina Rd CT17 ....149 B1
Lorne Cotts CT14 ....117 C7
Lorne Rd
Dover CT16,CT17 ....149 B2
Ramsgate CT11 ....52 C6
Lorraine Ct [1] CT19 ....178 E6
Loudon Ct TN23 ....138 E3
Loudon Path TN23 ....138 E3
Loudon Way TN23 ....138 E3
Loughborough Ct [2]
CT11 ....52 E7
Louisville Ave ME7 ....10 D4
Love La Adisham CT3 ....90 F2
Canterbury CT1 ....88 A8
Faversham ME13 ....62 F6
Margate CT9 ....7 I3
Minster (Sheppey) ME12 ....4 D7
Rochester ME1 ....9 C5
Love Street Cl CT6 ....22 C2
Lovelace Cl ME8 ....33 D4
Lovelace Ct TN26 ....153 C5
Lovell Rd
Minster (Sheppey) ME12 ....4 A5
Rough Common CT2 ....66 B3
Lower Blackhouse Hill
CT21 ....176 D3
Lower Bloors La ME8 ....11 E3
Lower Boxley Rd [10]
ME14 ....75 A5
Lower Bridge St CT1 ....88 A8
Lower Chantry La CT1 ....88 A8
Lower Denmark Rd
TN23 ....156 C8
Lower East Rd ME4 ....10 B8
Lower Ensden Rd CT4 ....85 D4
Lower Fant Rd ME16 ....74 D2
Lower Gore La CT13 ....93 B3
Lower Halstow Sch
ME9 ....13 B2
Lower Hartlip Rd ME9 ....34 E5
Lower Herne Rd CT6 ....45 E8
Lower Lees Rd CT4 ....85 D2
Lower Mill La CT14 ....117 C5

Lower Northdown Ave
CT9 ....8 B2
Lower Rainham Rd
Gillingham, Lower Rainham
ME8 ....12 A3
Gillingham,Lower Twydall
ME7 ....11 D5
Lower Rd
East Farleigh ME15 ....96 B7
Faversham ME13 ....61 C8
Maidstone ME15 ....75 B3
Minster (Sheppey) ME12 ....3 E4
River CT17 ....148 E3
Staple CT3 ....92 B6
Temple Ewell CT16 ....148 D5
Teynham ME9 ....38 B3
Teynham,Lower Newlands
ME9,ME13 ....38 E2
Wittersham TN30 ....189 D5
Woodchurch TN26 ....169 B1
Lower Rd E CT16 ....166 H8
Lower Rd W CT16 ....166 G8
Lower Sandgate Rd
CT20 ....178 C3
Lower Sands TN29 ....186 E2
Lower Santon La CT3 ....70 D7
Lower St Eastry CT13 ....93 B1
Leeds ME17 ....99 A1
Tilmanstone CT14 ....115 A2
Lower Stone St ME15 ....75 A3
Lower Tovil ME15 ....74 D2
Lower Twydall La ME7,
ME8 ....11 C4
Lower Vicarage Rd
TN24 ....139 D7
Lower Wall Rd CT21 ....186 D8
Lower Warren Rd ME20 ....53 C6
Lower Woodlands Rd
ME7 ....11 A6
Lowfield Rd ME12 ....3 E6
Lowslip Hill CT15 ....165 A5
Lowther Rd CT17 ....166 A5
Loxwood Cl CT16 ....149 B7
Lubbock Cl ME15 ....97 E5
Lubbock Wlk ME8 ....33 D5
Lucerne Ct CT5 ....42 F6
Lucerne Dr ME10 ....42 F6
Lucerne La CT15 ....133 C2
Lucerne St ME14 ....75 A5
Lucilla Ave TN23 ....155 F4
Luckhurst Gdns CT9 ....8 E3
Luckhurst Rd
Ashford TN24 ....157 A7
River CT17 ....148 E3
Lucknow Ct CT15 ....149 F3
Lucy Ave CT19 ....178 B7
Lucy's Hill CT21 ....176 B2
Luddenham Cl
Ashford TN23 ....155 F6
Maidstone ME14 ....75 C6
Luddenham Sch ME13 ....39 E1
Ludgate Rd ME9 ....59 F5
Lukes Cl CT17 ....149 B1
Lullingstone Cl ME7 ....33 B3
Lullingstone Ct [15] CT1 ....87 F8
Lullingstone Rd ME16 ....74 C2
Lumsden Terr [8] ME4 ....9 E4
Lushington Rd ME14 ....74 E7
Luton Ave CT10 ....29 F3
Luton Ct CT10 ....29 F3
Luton High St ME5 ....10 C2
Luton Inf Sch ME5 ....10 C2
Luton Jun Sch ME4 ....10 C2
Luton Rd
Chatham ME4,ME5 ....10 B2
Faversham ME13 ....62 E7
Lyall Way ME8 ....33 E4
Lychfield Dr ME2 ....9 A8
Lydbrook Cl ME10 ....36 D4
Lydd Airport TN29 ....204 D4
Lydd Prim Sch TN29 ....203 C6
Lydd Rd Chatham ME5 ....32 B5
New Romney TN28,TN29 ....199 F6
Lydd Town Crossing
TN29 ....203 D8
Lydden Hill CT15 ....130 C1
Lydden International Motor
Racing Circuit CT4 ....129 C3
Lydden Prim Sch CT15 ....147 F8
Lydia Rd CT14 ....117 A2
Lydos Cl TN29 ....204 E5
Lyeat Ct CT14 ....66 C4
Lyell Cl CT21 ....176 A1
Lyell Ct [5] CT7 ....26 F8
Lyell Rd CT7 ....26 F8
Lyle Cl ME2 ....9 B8
Lyle Ct ME16 ....74 C5
Lyminge CE Prim Sch
CT18 ....161 C7
Lyminge Cl ME8 ....11 C2
Lyminge Way CT9 ....8 C1
Lymington Ct ME15 ....97 F4
Lymington Rd CT8 ....27 E7
Lympne Castle ★ CT21 ....174 F2
Lympne CE Prim Sch
CT21 ....175 A3
Lympne Hill CT21 ....175 A2
Lympne Ind Est CT21 ....174 E3
Lyn Ct CT20 ....178 A5
Lyndhurst Ave
Gillingham ME8 ....33 C7
Margate CT9 ....8 D2
Lyndhurst Cl CT2 ....66 E3
Lyndhurst Gr ME10 ....36 E2
Lyndhurst Rd
Broadstairs CT10 ....30 A6
Dymchurch TN29 ....195 C6
Maidstone ME15 ....97 C8

Leo – Mai 225

Lyndhurst Rd continued
Ramsgate CT11 ....52 F7
River CT17 ....148 E2
Lyndon Way CT18 ....161 C7
Lyngate Ct CT9 ....8 D2
Lynmouth Dr ME12 ....4 C7
Lynstead House ME16 ....74 A1
Lynsted & Norton Sch
ME9 ....60 A7
Lynsted Cl TN23 ....155 F6
Lynsted La ME9 ....60 B7
Lynsted Rd Gillingham ME8 ....11 B3
Halfway Houses ME12 ....3 E7
Lynton Court Mansions
CT9 ....8 B3
Lynton Dr ME5 ....32 B3
Lynton Pl CT4 ....89 A1
Lynton Rd CT21 ....176 C1
Lynwood CT19 ....178 C7
Lysander Cl
Broadstairs CT10 ....29 C3
Littlebourne CT4 ....89 E4
Lysander Wlk CT18 ....163 A4
Lytham Ave CT6 ....22 D1

M

Mabledon Ave TN24 ....139 D1
Mabledon Cl TN28 ....200 B6
Macdonald Par CT5 ....43 A6
Macdonald Rd
Dover CT17 ....149 A1
Gillingham ME7 ....10 D6
Mace Ind Est TN24 ....139 C3
Mace La TN24 ....139 C2
Mace Terr TN26 ....155 A1
Mackenders Cl ME20 ....53 A6
Mackenders Gn ME20 ....53 A6
Mackenders La ME20 ....53 A6
Mackenzie Dr CT20 ....177 E5
Mackeson Ct [8] CT21 ....176 B2
Macklands Way ME8 ....12 A2
Madden Ave ME5 ....31 E5
Madeira Ct CT20 ....178 B3
Madeira Rd
Littlestone-on-S TN28 ....200 E6
Margate CT9 ....8 A2
Madeira Wlk CT11 ....52 E6
Madginford Cl ME15 ....76 A2
Madginford Park Inf Sch
ME15 ....76 A2
Madginford Park Jun Sch
ME15 ....76 A2
Madginford Rd ME15 ....75 F2
Madras House [2] ME15 ....97 E5
Mafeking Rd ME5 ....31 F3
Magazine Rd TN24 ....139 B3
Magdala Rd
Broadstairs CT10 ....29 E6
Dover CT17 ....149 B1
Magdalen Cl ME7 ....33 A4
Magdalen Ct
Broadstairs CT10 ....30 A6
Canterbury CT1 ....88 B7
Magness Rd CT14 ....117 A2
Magnolia Ave
Gillingham ME8 ....33 B5
Margate CT9 ....8 D2
Magnolia Dr CT4 ....86 E1
Magnolia Rise CT6 ....23 D2
Magpie Ct ME12 ....4 A6
Magpie Hall Rd
Chatham ME4 ....10 A2
Stubb's Cross TN26 ....155 E2
Magpie La
Rhodes Minnis CT4 ....144 B3
Yelsted ME9,ME14 ....33 F1
Magpie Lodge [4] CT16 ....149 B4
Magwitch Cl ME1 ....9 B4
Maida Rd ME4 ....10 B2
Maiden La CT1 ....87 D6
Maidstone Barracks Sta
ME16 ....74 F5
Maidstone East Sta ME14 ....74 F5
Maidstone Gram Sch
ME15 ....75 B2
Maidstone Gram Sch
for Girls ME16 ....74 E5
Maidstone Hospl The
ME16 ....74 A4
Maidstone Ind Ctr ME14 ....74 F4
Maidstone L Ctr ME15 ....75 C2
Maidstone Mus & Bentlif
Art Gallery ★ ME14 ....74 F5
Maidstone Rd
Ashford TN23,TN24,TN25,
TN26 ....138 D7
Charing TN25,TN26,TN27 ....120 D6
Chatham ME4 ....9 F2
Chatham,Walderslade ME5 ....31 D4
Chestnut Street ME9 ....35 D4
Five Wents ME17 ....98 E2
Gillingham ME8 ....33 C6
Gillingham,Bredhurst ME7,
ME8 ....33 B2
Lenham ME17 ....101 D5
Rochester ME1 ....9 C3
Maidstone West Sta
ME16 ....74 F3
Mailyns The ME8 ....33 D7
Main Gate Rd ME4 ....9 F7
Main Rd
Queenborough ME11,ME12 ....3 B5
Sheerness ME12 ....1 B3

Maine Cl CT16 . . . . .149 B3
Maison Des Fleurs ME16 .74 C2
Maison Dieu★ ME13 . . . .62 A6
Maison Dieu Pl 4 CT16 166 D8
Maison Dieu Rd CT16 . .166 D8
Maitland Dr ME13 . . . . . . .40 B1
Majestic Par CT20 . . . . . .178 C4
Makenade Ave ME13 . . . . .62 E6
Malcolm Sargent Rd
  TN23 . . . . .156 B5
Malden Dr ME14 . . . . .75 A8
Malham Dr CT9 . . . . .8 A1
Mall The ME15 . . . . .62 C6
Mallard Apartments 14
  ME15 . . . . .97 E5
Mallard Cl CT6 . . . . .22 C2
Mallard Ct ME12 . . . . .4 A6
Mallards TN24 . . . . .156 A1
Mallards Way ME15 . . . . . .76 A1
Malling Terr ME16 . . . . . . .74 C4
Mallings Dr ME14 . . . . . . .76 C4
Mallings La ME14 . . . . . . .76 C4
Mallory Cl CT12 . . . . .29 C2
Mallow Way 1 ME5 . . . . .31 F4
Mallows The ME14 . . . . . .74 E7
Malmains Rd CT17 . . . . . .166 A6
Malmedy Ct CT14 . . . . . . .117 A1
Malt House La TN30 . . . .179 A7
Malt Mews ME1 . . . . .9 C5
Malta Ave ME5 . . . . .32 A7
Malta Ho 17 CT1 . . . . .67 B2
Malta Terr 5 ME14 . . . . . .75 A7
Malthouse Cl ME17 . . . .100 D5
Malthouse Cotts TN28 . .200 A6
Malthouse Hill
  10 Hythe CT21 . . . . . . .176 B2
  Loose ME15 . . . . .96 F4
Malthouse La TN26 . . . . .170 D1
Malthouse Rd CT2 . . . . . .66 F2
Malthouse The CT7 . . . . . .26 F7
Malthouses The TN25 . . .159 B8
Maltings The
  9 Canterbury CT1 . . . . . .88 B8
  Deal CT14 . . . . .134 B8
  Faversham ME13 . . . . . . .62 D8
  Gillingham ME8 . . . . .34 A8
  Littlebourne CT3 . . . . . . .89 F7
  Maidstone ME14 . . . . . . .75 E5
  Ramsgate CT11 . . . . .52 D7
  The Quarries ME17 . . . . .97 B4
Malus Cl ME5 . . . . .32 B1
Malvern Mdw CT16 . . . . .148 E5
Malvern Pk CT6 . . . . .23 D4
Malvern Rd
  Ashford TN24 . . . . .139 B4
  Dover CT17 . . . . .166 C7
  Gillingham ME7 . . . . .10 E3
  Temple Ewell CT16 . . . . .148 E5
Mamignot Cl ME14 . . . . . .76 A5
Manchester Cl ME5 . . . . . .32 C6
Manciple Cl CT2 . . . . .87 C8
Mandeville 1 ME14 . . . . .75 A5
Mandeville Rd CT2 . . . . . .66 E2
Mangers La CT16 . . . . . . .149 A2
Mangers Pl CT16 . . . . . . .149 A3
Mangravet Ave ME15 . . . .97 C7
Manktelow Ct CT10 . . . . . .29 F2
Manley Cl CT16 . . . . .149 A4
Mannering Ct CT17 . . . . .148 E3
Mannock Ho 6 CT1 . . . . .67 B1
Manns Hill CT4 . . . . .127 A6
Manor Ave CT14 . . . . . . .117 B4
Manor Cl Canterbury CT1 .87 C5
  Deal CT14 . . . . .117 A4
  Herne Bay CT6 . . . . .23 F6
  Maidstone ME14 . . . . . . .76 B3
  Rushenden ME11 . . . . .3 A3
Manor Cotts
  Hernhill ME13 . . . . .64 B6
  Langley Heath ME17 . . . .98 C5
Manor Ct Canterbury CT1 .87 F7
  Gillingham ME7 . . . . .11 C4
  Maidstone ME14 . . . . . . .76 B3
Manor Dr CT7 . . . . .26 F6
Manor Farm Cl CT21 . . .175 A4
Manor Gdns Chatham ME5 31 F4
  Whitfield CT16 . . . . .149 A8
Manor Gr ME10 . . . . .36 E3
Manor Ho 14 ME7 . . . . . .10 A6
Manor House Dr
  Ashford TN23 . . . . .156 D3
  Maidstone ME16 . . . . . . .74 D3
Manor La ME1 . . . . .9 A2
Manor Lea Rd CT7 . . . . . .25 F1
Manor Leaze TN25 . . . . .158 F5
Manor Mews CT14 . . . . .133 F5
Manor Pound La TN25 . .158 F7
Manor Rd
  3 Broadstairs CT10 . . . .30 A4
  Chatham ME4 . . . . .9 F4
  Deal CT14 . . . . .117 A4
  Dover CT17 . . . . .166 A6
  Folkestone CT20 . . . . . .178 C4
  Herne Bay CT6 . . . . .23 F6
  Lydd TN29 . . . . .203 C6
  Milstead ME9 . . . . .58 F2
  Monkton CT7,CT12 . . . . . .49 A8
  Rushenden ME11 . . . . .3 A3
  St Nicholas at Wade CT7 .25 F1
  Whitstable CT5 . . . . .21 A4
Manor Rise Dover CT17 .166 A6
  Maidstone ME14 . . . . . . .76 B3
Manor St ME7 . . . . .10 A6
Manor Way Ashford TN23 138 D4
  Leysdown-on-S ME12 . . . . .6 H2

Manor Way continued
  Warden ME12 . . . . .6 D6
Manorfield Ashford TN23 155 E8
  Elham CT4 . . . . .144 F4
Manse Field TN25 . . . . . .158 E5
Mansel Dr ME1 . . . . .9 A2
Mansell La CT15 . . . . . . .146 B4
Mansfield Wlk ME16 . . . .74 E2
Mansion Gdns CT16 . . . .149 A4
Mansion Row ME7 . . . . . .10 A6
Mansion St CT9 . . . . .7 I2
Mansions The CT10 . . . . . .29 E4
Manston Court Cotts
  CT12 . . . . .28 C2
Manston Court Rd CT12,
  CT9 . . . . .28 D3
Manston Park Bglws
  CT12 . . . . .27 F2
Manston Pk CT12 . . . . . . .27 D2
Manston Rd
  Acol CT12,CT7 . . . . .27 D4
  Lydden CT12,CT9 . . . . . . .28 C4
  Ramsgate CT11,CT12 . . . .52 A8
Mansum Ct CT7 . . . . .25 F2
Mantles Hill CT14 . . . . . .116 D1
Manwood Ave CT2 . . . . . .66 F3
Manwood Cl ME10 . . . . . .36 F2
Manwood Rd CT13 . . . . . .94 A8
Maple Ave Gillingham ME7 10 E8
  Maidstone ME16 . . . . . . .74 C6
Maple Cl Ashford TN23 . .138 E3
  Rough Common CT2 . . . . .66 B3
Maple Ct CT3 . . . . .68 E8
Maple Dr CT9 . . . . .194 F4
Maple Gdns CT3 . . . . .68 E8
Maple St 12 ME12 . . . . . . .1 D1
Maples The
  Broadstairs CT10 . . . . . . .29 D4
  Minster (Sheppey) ME12 . .4 B6
Maplesden Noakes Sch
  The ME16 . . . . .74 E6
Maplins Cl 5 ME8 . . . . . .11 F1
Mara Ct ME4 . . . . .9 F1
Marathon Paddock ME7 .10 D4
Marconi Way ME1 . . . . . . .31 D7
Marcroft CT10 . . . . .30 B7
Mardale Cl ME8 . . . . .12 A1
Marden Ave CT12 . . . . . . .52 B8
Mardol Rd TN24 . . . . .139 C5
Maresfield Cl CT16 . . . . .149 B2
Margaret Ct CT6 . . . . .22 F4
Margaret St 8 CT20 . . . .178 E5
Margarets Rd CT15 . . . . .134 A1
Margate Caves★ CT9 . . . . .7 J3
Margate Hill CT7 . . . . . . .27 C4
Margate Rd
  Herne Bay CT6 . . . . .23 C3
  Herne Bay, Broomfield CT6 .23 D2
  Ramsgate CT10,CT12,CT11 .29 B3
  Margate Sta CT9 . . . . .7 H2
Marian Ave ME12 . . . . .4 A7
Marilyn Cres CT7 . . . . . . .27 B7
Marina Ct CT14 . . . . .117 D8
Marina Dr ME12 . . . . .4 A7
Marina Espl CT11 . . . . . . .52 F7
Marina Rd CT11 . . . . .52 F7
Marina The CT14 . . . . . . .117 D8
Marine Ave TN29 . . . . . . .186 F3
Marine Cres
  7 Folkestone CT20 . . . .178 D4
  Whitstable CT5 . . . . .21 B3
Marine Ct 13 CT16 . . . . .166 E7
Marine Dr Broadstairs CT10 8 G3
  Margate CT9 . . . . .7 I2
Marine Gap CT5 . . . . .20 C1
Marine Gdns CT9 . . . . .7 I2
Marine Par Dover CT16 .166 E7
  Folkestone CT20 . . . . . .178 E4
  Hythe CT21 . . . . .176 C1
  Littlestone-on-S TN28 . . .200 D5
  Sheerness ME12 . . . . .1 F2
  Whitstable CT5 . . . . .21 A3
Marine Parade Mews
  CT20 . . . . .178 E4
Marine Point CT20 . . . . .178 A3
Marine Rd CT14 . . . . .117 D4
Marine Terr
  Folkestone CT20 . . . . . .178 E4
  Margate CT9 . . . . .7 H2
  Whitstable CT5 . . . . .20 C1
Marine Walk St CT21 . . .176 C2
Mariners Lea CT10 . . . . . .29 D4
Mariners The ME1 . . . . . . .9 B4
Marion Ct ME5 . . . . .32 A2
Marion Cres ME15 . . . . . .97 B8
Maritime Ave CT6 . . . . . . .23 C4
Maritime Cl ME2 . . . . .9 D8
Maritime Est ME2 . . . . .9 D8
Maritime Way ME4 . . . . . .10 A8
Marjan Cl CT17 . . . . .149 A1
Mark Ave CT11 . . . . .52 B5
Market Bldgs 4 ME14 . .74 F4
Market Colonnade 3
  ME14 . . . . .74 F4
Market Hill CT21 . . . . . . .176 C2
Market La CT21 . . . . .139 B2
Market Pl Aylesham CT3 .112 F5
  Charing TN27 . . . . .120 C7
  1 Faversham ME13 . . . . .62 D7
  20 Folkestone CT20 . . . .178 D5
  Margate CT9 . . . . .7 I3
Market Sq 12 CT16,CT17 .166 D7
Market St Deal CT14 . . . .117 D6
  Faversham ME13 . . . . . . .62 D7
  Herne Bay CT6 . . . . .22 F5
  2 Maidstone ME14 . . . . .74 F4
  Margate CT9 . . . . .7 I3

Market St continued
  Sandwich CT13 . . . . .73 A1
Market View CT3 . . . . . . .112 F5
Market Way CT2 . . . . .67 A2
Markland Rd CT17 . . . . . .165 F7
Marlborough Cl
  Broadstairs CT10 . . . . . . .29 E3
  Littlestone-on-S TN28 . . .200 D6
Marlborough Ct
  Folkestone CT20 . . . . . .178 B4
  Hythe CT21 . . . . .176 D1
Marlborough Ho
  4 Gillingham ME8 . . . . .33 F8
  Margate CT9 . . . . .8 C3
Marlborough Rd
  Deal CT14 . . . . .117 A2
  Dover CT17 . . . . .165 F7
  Gillingham ME7 . . . . .10 B5
  Margate CT9 . . . . .7 I1
  6 Ramsgate CT11 . . . . . .52 D6
  Whitstable CT5 . . . . .43 D5
Marlborough Way TN24 139 F7
Marler Rd CT19 . . . . .177 E6
Marley Ct CT2 . . . . .66 C4
Marley La Chislet CT3 . . . .47 A5
  Finglesham CT14 . . . . . .116 A8
  Kingston CT4 . . . . .111 B1
Marley Rd ME17 . . . . . . .100 F6
Marley Way ME1 . . . . .9 C2
Marlow Cl CT5 . . . . .21 B1
Marlow Copse ME5 . . . . .31 F1
Marlow Mdws CT2 . . . . . .67 F5
Marlowe Arc 11 CT1 . . . .87 F8
Marlowe Ave CT1 . . . . . . .87 F8
Marlowe Ct 13 CT1 . . . . .87 F8
Marlowe Rd
  Ashford TN23 . . . . .139 B2
  Dover CT16 . . . . .149 B3
  Margate CT9 . . . . .29 C8
Marlpit Cotts ME17 . . . . . .97 E2
Marquis Dr ME7 . . . . .33 B3
Marr Cl ME12 . . . . .3 F7
Marrians View 1 ME5 . .10 C2
Marrose Ave CT12 . . . . . .29 B3
Marrowbone Hill ME12 . . .5 B5
Marsh Cres TN28 . . . . . . .200 B6
Marsh Farm Rd CT12 . . . .50 B4
Marsh La Deal CT14 . . . . .117 A7
  Teynham ME9 . . . . .39 A4
Marsh St ME2 . . . . .9 B7
Marsh View CT21 . . . . . . .187 C8
Marshall Cres
  Broadstairs CT10 . . . . . . .29 E4
  Rushenden ME11 . . . . .2 F3
Marshall Rd ME8 . . . . .33 C8
Marshall St CT19 . . . . . . .178 E7
Marsham St ME14 . . . . . . .75 A4
Marshborough Rd CT13 . .93 B7
Marshlands TN29 . . . . . . .195 B7
Marshlands Cl TN29 . . . .195 B7
Marshwood Cl CT1 . . . . . .67 C3
Marstan Cl ME9 . . . . .12 E2
Marston Cl ME5 . . . . .31 E3
Marston Dr ME14 . . . . . . .75 C5
Marston Wlk ME5 . . . . . . .31 E3
Martello Cotts CT15 . . . .187 E8
Martello Dr CT21 . . . . . . .175 F1
Martello Ind Ctr CT19 . .178 F6
Martello Rd
  Folkestone CT20 . . . . . .178 E6
  Folkestone, Sandgate
  CT20 . . . . .177 E3
Martello Terr 1 CT20 . . .177 F3
Martello Tower Mus
  TN29 . . . . .195 C7
Marten Rd CT20 . . . . .178 B5
Martha Ct CT19 . . . . .178 B7
Martin Ct ME7 . . . . .33 A3
Martin Dale Cres CT15 . .133 C2
Martin Ho TN25 . . . . .123 E2
Martin Mill Sta CT15 . . .133 C2
Martin Rd ME2 . . . . .9 B8
Martin's Cl CT12 . . . . .29 C2
Martin's Way CT12 . . . . .187 D8
Martindale Cl CT1 . . . . . . .88 A7
Martindown Rd CT5 . . . . .43 C7
Martins Cl TN30 . . . . .179 C8
Martins The TN26 . . . . . .168 A8
Martyrs' Field Rd CT1 . . .87 F7
Mary Green Wlk 5 CT1 .67 B2
Mary Haugham
  Almshouses CT14 . . . . .117 D7
Mary Rd CT14 . . . . .117 A3
Maryland Ct ME8 . . . . . . .33 E5
Maryland Gr CT1 . . . . .88 C6
Mason's Rise CT10 . . . . . .30 A5
Masons Rd CT15 . . . . . . .149 B1
Matfield Cres ME14 . . . . .75 C5
Matilda Cl ME8 . . . . .33 B8
Matthew's Pl 8 CT16 . .149 C1
Matthews Cl CT14 . . . . . .117 C6
Matthews Rd CT6 . . . . . . .22 C2
Mattinson Pl ME9 . . . . . . .78 F7
Matts Hill Rd ME9 . . . . . .33 E2
Maugham Ct CT5 . . . . . . .43 D8
Maundene Sch ME5 . . . . .32 B5
Maunders Cl ME5 . . . . . . .32 C8
Maurice Ct CT9 . . . . .8 B3
Maxine Gdns CT10 . . . . . .29 F5
Maxted Ct CT6 . . . . .23 C4
Maxton Cl Dover CT17 . .166 A6
  Maidstone ME14 . . . . . . .75 F5
Maxton Ct CT17 . . . . .166 A6
Maxton Rd CT17 . . . . . . .166 A6

Maxwell Dr ME16 . . . . . . .74 B6
Maxwell Pl CT14 . . . . . . .117 C4
Maxwell Rd ME7 . . . . .10 A6
May Lodge CT14 . . . . . . .117 D5
May Rd Gillingham ME7 . .10 C4
  Rochester ME1 . . . . .9 C3
May St CT5 . . . . .23 F4
May Terr 2 ME7 . . . . .10 A7
Maybrook Ind Est CT1 . . .67 C3
Maydowns Rd CT5 . . . . . .21 D2
Mayers Rd CT14 . . . . . . .117 A1
Mayfair 2 ME2 . . . . .9 C8
Mayfair Ho ME5 . . . . .97 A8
Mayfield Ave CT16 . . . . .149 C6
Mayfield Cl Chatham ME5 .32 A1
  Gillingham ME8 . . . . .11 E2
Mayfield Ct 3 CT16 . . . .149 B2
Mayfield Gdns CT16 . . . .149 C2
Mayfield Rd
  Herne Bay CT6 . . . . .23 A3
  Lyminge CT18 . . . . .161 C6
  Whitfield CT16 . . . . .149 A7
Mayflower Ho ME1 . . . . . .9 B4
Mayfly Dr CT18 . . . . .163 A4
Mayford Rd ME5 . . . . .32 D2
Mayforth Gdns CT11 . . . .52 B6
Mayhew Cl TN23 . . . . . . .156 A8
Maymills Cotts CT13 . . . .93 B2
Maynard & Cotton's
  Spital 9 CT1 . . . . .87 F8
Maynard Ave CT9 . . . . . . .28 B8
Maynard Pl ME5 . . . . .10 D2
Maynard Rd CT1 . . . . .87 E7
Mayor's Pl 11 TN30 . . . .179 A7
Maypits TN23 . . . . .155 F8
Maypole La CT3 . . . . .46 E6
Maypole Rd CT3 . . . . .46 E6
Mays Rd CT11 . . . . .52 C6
Maystreet Cross CT6 . . . .23 F3
Mayton Cl CT2 . . . . .45 C1
Maytree Cotts CT14 . . . .133 D8
Mayville Rd CT10 . . . . . . .29 E6
Mayweed Ave ME5 . . . . . .31 E4
McArthur Glen
  Designer Outlet TN24 .156 C7
Mc Kenzie Dr ME5 . . . . . .32 A3
McAlpine Cres ME15 . . . .96 F3
McCarthy Ave CT2 . . . . . .67 F7
McClean Wlk ME12 . . . . . .3 D8
McCudden Row 8 ME7 . .10 A6
McKinlay Ct CT7 . . . . .26 D8
McPhie Ho 3 ME14 . . . . .74 F7
Mead Gn ME5 . . . . .32 C3
Mead Rd Ashford TN24 . .156 C7
  Folkestone CT19 . . . . . .178 D6
Mead Way CT2 . . . . .66 E1
Meade The CT18 . . . . . . .162 F4
Meadow Bank ME13 . . . . .61 F2
Meadow Brook Ct CT20 177 E4
Meadow Cl Bridge CT4 . . .89 A1
  Chatham ME5 . . . . .31 F5
  Chilham CT4 . . . . .107 E8
  Herne Bay CT6 . . . . .23 C4
  Iwade ME9 . . . . .14 D4
Meadow Cotts
  East Studdal CT15 . . . . .132 D8
  Goodnestone CT3 . . . . . .92 A2
Meadow Ct
  Broadstairs CT9 . . . . .29 B8
  Margate CT9 . . . . .8 B1
  Westenhanger CT21 . . . .175 B6
Meadow Dr CT5 . . . . .44 D8
Meadow Gr TN23 . . . . . . .174 D8
Meadow Rd
  Ashford TN24 . . . . .139 A4
  Canterbury CT2 . . . . .66 C2
  Margate CT9 . . . . .7 F1
  Sturry CT2 . . . . .67 F6
Meadow Rise ME9 . . . . . .14 D4
Meadow View TN26 . . . .138 A6
Meadow View Industries
  TN26 . . . . .183 C7
Meadow View Rd
  Boughton Monchelsea ME17 97 B3
  Shepherdswell CT15 . . . .130 E5
Meadow Way
  Eythorne CT15 . . . . .131 C8
  Hythe CT21 . . . . .187 D8
Meadow Wlk
  Maidstone ME15 . . . . . . .75 B3
  Whitstable CT5 . . . . .43 C6
Meadowbank Rd ME4 . . . .10 A4
Meadowbrook Cl TN24 . .139 D6
Meadowbrook Rd TN24 139 D6
Meadowdown ME14 . . . . .75 C4
Meadowdown Ct ME7 . . . .33 A4
Meadows The
  Herne Bay CT6 . . . . .23 D2
  Maidstone ME15 . . . . . . .74 B2
  New Romney TN28 . . . . .200 C6
  Sittingbourne ME10 . . . . .36 F2
  Wittersham TN30 . . . . . .188 D4
Meads Ave The ME10 . . . .36 D7
Meads Way TN29 . . . . . . .194 E3
Meadside Wlk ME5 . . . . . .31 F6
Meadway CT17 . . . . .148 E3
Medina Ave CT5 . . . . .43 B7
Medlar Cl ME9 . . . . .58 A6
Medlar Gr ME7 . . . . .33 A4
Medlars The ME7 . . . . . . .33 A4
Medway Cl ME10 . . . . .36 D4
Medway Com Coll ME4 . .10 A1
Medway Ent Ctr ME2 . . . .9 D8
Medway Gdns ME4 . . . . . .9 F7
Medway Heritage Ctr★
  ME4 . . . . .9 F5

Medway Hospl ME7 . . . . .10 B4
Medway Hts 5 ME4 . . . . . .9 E4
Medway Rd
  Gillingham ME7 . . . . .10 C7
  Sheerness ME12 . . . . .1 C1
Medway St Chatham ME4 . .9 F5
  Maidstone ME14 . . . . . . .74 F4
Medway Trad Est ME16 . .74 F3
Medway Villas ME15 . . . .96 B7
Meehan Rd TN28 . . . . . . .200 E4
Meehan Rd S TN28 . . . . .200 E3
Meeres Court La ME10 . . .37 C5
Meeson's Cl ME13 . . . . . .81 E6
Meeting House La 2 ME4 .9 F4
Meeting St CT11 . . . . .52 E7
Megan Cl TN29 . . . . .203 D7
Megby Cl ME8 . . . . .33 D6
Megone Cl CT18 . . . . . . .163 A4
Meirs Court Rd ME8 . . . . .33 E6
Melbourne Ave
  Dover CT16 . . . . .149 C4
  Ramsgate CT12 . . . . .29 B1
Melbourne
  Com Prim Sch CT16 . . .149 C4
Melbourne Rd ME4 . . . . . .10 A3
Melbury Mews TN28 . . . .200 C8
Melford Dr ME16 . . . . . . .74 C4
Mellanby Cl CT7 . . . . .27 A6
Mellor Row ME10 . . . . . . .14 F1
Melody Ct Gillingham ME8 .33 C4
  Warden ME12 . . . . .6 E4
Melon La TN26,TN29 . . . .193 B6
Melrose Cl ME15 . . . . .97 A1
Melsetter Cl CT7 . . . . .27 B7
Melville Ct ME4 . . . . .9 F6
Melville Lea CT13 . . . . . . .93 C7
Melville Rd ME15 . . . . . . .75 A3
Memorial (General)
  Hospl ME10 . . . . .36 F3
Mendfield St 5 ME13 . . . .62 C7
Mendip TN24 . . . . .139 B4
Menin Rd ME10 . . . . .14 F1
Mentmore Ho CT12 . . . . .29 C3
Mentmore Rd CT12 . . . . . .29 C3
Menzies Ave CT14 . . . . . .117 B1
Menzies Ct ME12 . . . . .4 A5
Menzies Rd CT16 . . . . . . .149 A5
Mercer Dr ME17 . . . . . . .100 F6
Mercer Way ME17 . . . . . . .98 B1
Mercery La 5 CT1 . . . . . .87 F8
Merchant Store The 1
  CT2 . . . . .66 F1
Merchants Way CT2 . . . . .87 C8
Mercury Cl ME1 . . . . .9 A3
Mere Gate CT9 . . . . .7 I1
Meredale Inf Sch ME8 . . .12 A1
Meresborough Cotts
  ME8 . . . . .33 F5
Meresborough La ME8,
  ME9 . . . . .34 B5
Meresborough Rd ME8 . . .34 A7
Mereworth Cl ME8 . . . . . .11 A3
Meridian Ct TN23 . . . . . .155 E7
Meridian Pk ME2 . . . . .9 E6
Meridian Wlk CT18 . . . . .161 D3
Merivale Gr ME5 . . . . .32 B4
Merleburgh Dr ME10 . . . .36 F8
Merlin Cl ME10 . . . . .37 A3
Merlin Ho 2 ME10 . . . . . .37 A4
Mermaid Cl ME5 . . . . .32 A6
Merritt Rd TN28 . . . . .200 E2
Merrivale Hts CT10 . . . . . .30 A2
Merrywood Gr CT6 . . . . . .23 D2
Mersham Prim Sch
  TN25 . . . . .157 E3
Merton Cl ME5 . . . . .32 C5
Merton La CT4 . . . . .87 F4
Merton Rd ME15 . . . . .75 F2
Meryl Gdns CT14 . . . . . . .117 C1
Metcalfe Mews 1 CT1 . . .67 B2
Meteor Ave CT5 . . . . .43 B7
Meteor Ct ME10 . . . . .36 E8
Metropole Rd E CT20 . . .178 B3
Metropole Rd W CT20 . .178 B3
Meverall Ave CT12 . . . . . .51 E5
Mews The Maidstone ME16 74 E5
  Sittingbourne ME10 . . . . .36 F2
Meyrick Rd ME12 . . . . .1 D2
Micawber Cl ME5 . . . . . . .32 A1
Michael Ave CT11 . . . . . . .52 G8
Michelle Gdns CT9 . . . . . .28 A8
Mickleburgh Ave CT6 . . . .23 B4
Mickleburgh Hill CT6 . . . .23 B4
Mid Kent Coll of H
  & F Ed Maidstone,
  Cherry Orchard ME16 . . .74 C3
  Rochester ME1 . . . . .9 E4
Mid Kent Coll of Higher
  & F Ed ME1,ME4 . . . . . .31 E6
Mid Kent Sh Ctr The
  ME16 . . . . .74 C7
Middelburg Ho CT19 . . . .177 D6
Middelburg Sq CT20 . . . .178 D4
Middle Cl TN23 . . . . .138 C1
Middle Deal Rd CT14 . . .117 B5
Middle Mead CT19 . . . . .178 B7
Middle Row
  Ashford TN23 . . . . .139 C2
  2 Faversham ME13 . . . . .62 D7
  6 Maidstone ME14 . . . . .74 F4
Middle St Ashford TN23 . .139 B2
  Deal CT14 . . . . .117 D6
  4 Gillingham ME7 . . . . . .10 A6
Middle Wall CT5 . . . . .20 D2
Middle Way ME10 . . . . . . .37 B3
Middlefields ME8 . . . . . . .34 A8
Middlesex Rd ME15 . . . . .97 D7
Middleton Cl ME8 . . . . . . .33 E4

Middleton Cotts TN25 ...122 E3
Middleton Ct **9** ME10 ...36 E4
Middletune Ave ME10 ...36 E7
Midhurst Ct ME15 ...75 A3
Midley Cl ME16 ...74 C7
Midsummer Hill TN24 ...139 D6
Miers Court Prim Sch
ME8 ...33 F7
Mierscourt Cl ME8 ...34 A8
Mierscourt Rd ME8 ...33 D4
Mikyle Ct CT1 ...88 A6
Milbourne Gr ME10 ...36 E7
Milburn Rd ME7 ...10 C7
Mildred Cotts CT19 ...177 F7
Mile Rd CT12,CT3 ...48 F6
Miles Ct CT3 ...91 A8
Miles Pl ME1 ...9 D3
Miles Way CT7 ...26 F7
Milestone Cl CT19 ...178 A7
Milestone Rd CT14 ...117 B5
Milford Cl ME16 ...74 D5
Military Rd
Canterbury CT1 ...67 A1
Chatham ME4 ...9 F5
2 Dover CT17 ...166 D7
Folkestone CT20 ...177 E4
Hythe CT21 ...176 B2
Ramsgate CT11 ...52 E6
Stone in Oxney TN26,TN30 ...190 B4
Mill Bank TN29 ...203 B6
Mill Bank Cotts CT13 ...93 A2
Mill Bay CT3 ...178 C5
Mill Cl Lenham ME17 ...101 C4
River CT17 ...148 F2
Sandwich CT13 ...72 E2
Wickhambreaux CT3 ...69 C2
Mill Cotts
Queenborough ME11 ...3 A5
Ramsgate CT11 ...52 D6
Worth CT14 ...94 A4
Mill Ct Ashford TN24 ...139 D2
Sittingbourne ME10 ...37 A3
Mill Field Ash CT3 ...71 E1
Broadstairs CT10 ...29 F5
Mill Fields Rd CT21 ...175 F2
Mill Gn CT13 ...93 A2
Mill Hamlet CT3 ...69 C2
Mill Hill CT14 ...117 A3
Mill La Aldington TN25 ...172 E5
Ashford TN24 ...140 A1
Biddenden Green TN27 ...135 A2
Birchington CT7 ...26 F6
Bridge CT4 ...88 F1
Canterbury CT1 ...66 F1
Canterbury, Harbledown
CT2 ...87 C8
Chatham,Bluebell Hill ME5 ...31 D1
Chatham,Luton ME5 ...10 C1
Chilham CT4 ...107 D7
Coxheath ME17 ...96 D4
8 Dover CT16 ...166 E7
Eastry CT13 ...93 B2
Hartlip ME9 ...34 E6
Hawkinge CT18 ...163 B5
Herne Bay CT6 ...23 B1
Lydd TN29 ...203 D7
Lynsted ME9 ...60 C5
Margate CT9 ...7 I2
Nonington CT15 ...113 F4
Northbourne CT14 ...115 F4
Preston CT3 ...70 D6
Shepherdswell CT15 ...130 F5
Stelling Minnis CT4 ...126 F2
Tenterden TN30 ...167 B1
Whitfield CT16 ...149 A8
Worth CT14 ...94 A4
Mill Lane Cotts CT14 ...116 A4
Mill Mews CT14 ...117 B4
Mill Pl ME13 ...62 D8
Mill Rd Bethersden TN26 ...153 E5
Bramling CT3 ...90 E6
Deal CT14 ...117 C4
Dymchurch TN29 ...195 B7
Gillingham ME7 ...10 C6
Hoath CT3 ...46 F5
Hythe CT21 ...176 D2
Lydd TN29 ...203 D7
Rochester ME2 ...9 B8
Staple CT3 ...92 B5
Sturry CT2 ...67 F5
Mill Row CT7 ...26 F6
Mill St Loose ME15 ...96 F5
Maidstone ME15 ...74 F4
Sittingbourne ME10 ...36 E5
Temple Ewell CT16 ...148 D5
Mill Terr Bridge CT4 ...88 F1
Chartham CT4 ...86 D3
Mill View Ashford TN24 ...156 F8
Woodchurch TN26 ...169 A3
Mill View Rd CT6 ...23 A1
Mill Wall CT13 ...94 A8
Mill Way ME10 ...36 F6
Mill Wlk ME16 ...74 A3
Millais Rd CT16 ...149 C1
Millbank La TN29 ...198 E7
Millbank Rd TN23 ...155 F5
Millbrook CT21 ...176 D2
Millbrook CT16 ...74 F1
Millbrook Meadow
TN23 ...138 E1
Milldale Cl CT14 ...117 B4
Millen Rd ME10 ...36 E5
Millen's Row ME13 ...83 B3
Millenium Terr CT1 ...87 C6
Millennium Way
Broadstairs CT10 ...29 C4
Sheerness ME12 ...1 C2

Miller Ave CT2 ...87 D8
Miller Cl Ashford TN24 ...139 D2
Sittingbourne ME10 ...37 A8
Miller Cotts TN24 ...139 D2
Miller Ct ME12 ...4 A5
Millers Ct Ramsgate CT12 ...29 B1
Whitstable CT5 ...43 D7
Millers La CT12 ...49 C7
Millers Wharf ME15 ...74 E2
Millers Yd ME15 ...87 E7
Millfield Ashford TN23 ...155 D8
Folkestone CT20 ...178 D5
Hawkinge CT18 ...163 C6
High Halden TN26 ...167 D5
Sittingbourne ME10 ...37 A3
St Margaret's at Cliffe
CT15 ...150 F7
Millfield Cl CT13 ...163 B5
Millfield Manor CT5 ...20 E1
Millfield Rd
Faversham ME13 ...62 E7
Ramsgate CT12 ...29 B3
Millfields Chatham ME5 ...32 D2
Shepherdswell CT15 ...130 E4
Millmead Ave CT9 ...8 D1
Millmead Gdns CT9 ...8 D1
Millmead Rd CT9 ...8 C1
Millpond Cl ME2 ...9 B8
Mills Cl ME12 ...3 F6
Mills Terr ME4 ...10 A3
Millstock Terr ME15 ...74 E2
Millstream Cl
Faversham ME13 ...62 C7
Whitstable CT5 ...20 E1
Millstrood Rd CT5 ...43 E8
Millwood Ct **4** ME4 ...9 F3
Milne Rd ME4 ...156 F8
Milner Cl CT15 ...114 B1
Milner Cres CT3 ...112 E5
Milner La CT7 ...67 F5
Milner Rd Elvington CT15 ...114 F1
Gillingham ME7 ...10 D7
Whitstable CT5 ...43 A6
Milstead & Frinstead
CE Prim Sch ME9 ...58 E1
Milstead Cl
Maidstone ME14 ...75 C5
West Minst ME12 ...3 B7
Milsted Rd ME8 ...11 C3
Milton Ave CT9 ...7 J1
Milton Cl Canterbury CT1 ...88 C6
Dover CT16 ...149 B4
Milton Court Prim Sch
ME10 ...36 E6
Milton Rd Ashford TN23 ...139 B2
Canterbury CT1 ...88 A6
Dover CT16 ...149 B4
Gillingham ME7 ...10 C3
Sittingbourne ME10 ...36 E4
Milton Sq **4** CT9 ...7 J1
Milton St ME16 ...74 C2
Mincers Cl ME5 ...32 C2
Minerva Ave CT16 ...149 C2
Minerva Ho CT11 ...52 D7
Minerva Rd ME2 ...9 A8
Minnis Field CT4 ...126 A8
Minnis Gn CT4 ...126 E2
Minnis La CT15,CT17 ...148 C2
Minnis Rd CT7 ...26 E7
Minnis Terr CT17 ...149 A2
Minnis Way CT4 ...94 B5
Minster Abbey
Minster (Sheppey) ME12 ...4 D6
Minster (Thanet) CT12 ...50 C5
Minster CE Prim Sch
CT12 ...50 B5
Minster Cl CT10 ...30 A2
Minster Coll ME12 ...4 A8
Minster Dr Herne Bay CT6 ...22 D4
Minster (Sheppey) ME12 ...4 B8
Minster Gatehouse Mus★
ME12 ...4 D6
Minster Lodge CT11 ...52 C6
Minster Rd Acol CT12,CT7 ...27 C2
Faversham ME13 ...62 E7
Gillingham ME8 ...11 C3
Minster (Sheppey) ME12 ...4 B6
Ramsgate CT11 ...52 B5
Westgate-on-S CT8 ...27 F7
Minster Sta CT12 ...50 C5
Minster-in-Sheppey
Prim Sch ME12 ...4 C7
Mint The CT2 ...66 C1
Mintching Wood La ME9 ...58 F2
Minter Ave CT18 ...162 F7
Minter Cl CT18 ...162 F7
Minterne Ave ME10 ...36 D2
Minterne Com Jun Sch
ME10 ...36 D2
Miranda Ct ME12 ...1 C1
Misling La CT4 ...143 C7
Missenden Ct **6** CT20 ...178 D5
Mitcham Rd TN29 ...195 C8
Mitchell Ave Chatham ME4 ...9 F2
Hawkinge CT18 ...163 B5
Mitchell Cl ME17 ...101 C5
Mitchell St CT19 ...177 D6
Mitre Rd ME1 ...9 B4
Mittell Ct TN29 ...203 B6
Moat Farm Cl CT19 ...178 C7
Moat Farm Rd CT19 ...178 C7
Moat Ho Canterbury CT1 ...87 F7
Charing TN27 ...120 C7
Moat La Ash CT3 ...71 E1
Fordwich CT2 ...68 A3
Rough Common CT2 ...66 B4
Moat Pk TN27 ...120 C6
Moat Sole CT13 ...72 F1

Moat The TN27 ...120 C7
Moat Way ME11 ...3 A5
Moatfield Mdw TN23 ...156 B6
Mock La TN23 ...155 B6
Mockett Ct **4** ME10 ...36 E4
Mockett Dr CT10 ...29 C7
Molehill Cnr CT5 ...44 D8
Molehill Copse Prim Sch
ME15 ...97 D7
Molehill Rd Herne Bay CT6 ...22 A1
Whitstable CT5,CT6 ...44 E8
Molineux Rd CT12 ...50 B6
Molland Cl CT3 ...71 C2
Molland La Ash CT3 ...71 C2
Westmarsh CT3 ...71 B6
Molland Lea CT3 ...71 C2
Molloy Rd TN26 ...155 B1
Monarch Cl ME5 ...32 A6
Monastery Ave CT1 ...149 E1
Monastery St CT1 ...88 A8
Monckton Church Cl
CT14 ...116 D3
Mongeham Prim Sch
CT14 ...116 F4
Mongeham Rd CT14 ...116 E3
Mongeham View CT14 ...116 E3
Monica CT ME13 ...84 E6
Monins Rd CT17 ...166 B7
Monkdown ME15 ...76 A1
Monkery La TN25,TN27 ...104 D2
Monks Cl Canterbury CT2 ...67 A2
Faversham ME13 ...62 B8
Monks Way CT16 ...149 A3
Monks Wlk TN27 ...120 C7
Monkshill Rd ME13 ...42 B2
Monkton CE Prim Sch
CT12 ...49 D7
Monkton Court La CT15 ...131 D7
Monkton Gdns CT9 ...8 E3
Monkton Manor CT12 ...49 D7
Monkton Pl CT11 ...52 D7
Monkton Rd CT12 ...50 A6
Monkton Rdbt CT12 ...49 D8
Monkton St CT12 ...49 D7
Monkwood Cl ME1 ...31 B8
Monmouth Cl ME8 ...11 D2
Mons Ct ME10 ...14 F1
Montacue Ct CT20 ...178 B4
Montague Ct ME12 ...1 C1
Montague Rd CT11 ...52 E8
Montague St CT6 ...22 D5
Montefiore Ave
Broadstairs CT10 ...30 A1
Ramsgate CT11 ...29 F1
Montefiore Cotts CT11 ...52 F8
Montfort Cl
Ashford TN23 ...155 F7
Canterbury CT2 ...67 A4
Montfort Rd Chatham ME5 ...31 F2
Rochester ME2 ...9 A8
Montgomery Ave ME5 ...32 A7
Montgomery Rd ME7 ...10 C3
Montgomery Sch CT2 ...68 C8
Montgomery Way CT19 ...178 E8
Montpelier Ave CT5 ...43 D6
Montpelier Bsns Pk
TN23 ...138 F1
Montpelier Gate ME16 ...74 B5
Montreal Cl **8** CT16 ...149 B3
Montrose Ave ME5 ...10 E2
Monument Way TN24 ...156 F5
Moon Hill CT15 ...130 E4
Moonstone Dr ME5 ...32 B2
Moor La Ivychurch TN29 ...192 D4
Woodchurch TN26 ...180 E6
Moor Lane Cotts TN26 ...181 C2
Moor Park Cl ME8 ...34 A8
Moor St ME8 ...34 B8
Moore Cl TN29 ...192 A3
Moore St ME2 ...9 A8
Moorfield Ct CT2 ...66 F4
Mooring Rd ME1 ...9 D1
Moorings The ME9 ...38 E6
Moorland Rd CT15 ...130 E4
Moorstock La TN25 ...159 C2
Moorwell Dr CT15 ...130 D5
Moray Ave CT7 ...26 F6
Mordaunt Ave CT8 ...27 E8
Morden St ME1 ...9 C4
Morehall Ave CT19 ...177 F6
Morehall Prim Sch
CT19 ...177 F6
Morella Wlk ME17 ...101 C5
Morello Cl ME9 ...38 C2
Moreton Ct CT14 ...117 C2
Moreton Terr TN26 ...155 A1
Morgan Kirby's Gdn
ME13 ...83 D5
Morgan Rd ME2 ...9 A8
Morris Ave CT6 ...21 C4
Morris Court Cl ME9 ...37 D2
Morrison Rd CT20 ...178 E6
Morry La ME17 ...99 D1
Mortimer Rd TN23 ...156 B7
Mortimer Rd CT16 ...166 F8
Mortimer St CT6 ...22 F5
Morton Cl ME15 ...97 D5
Mossbank ME5 ...32 A3
Mossend Mews CT11 ...29 E2
Mossy Glade ME8 ...33 E6
Mostyn Rd ME14 ...75 C4
Mote Ave ME15 ...75 B3
Mote Hall Villas ME14 ...76 C4
Mote Pk ME15 ...75 D2

Mote Rd ME15 ...75 A3
Motney Hill Rd ME8 ...12 A4
Mouat Ct ME5 ...32 A3
Mount Charles Wlk CT4 ...88 F1
Mount Dr ME4 ...76 B4
Mount Ephraim★ ME13 ...64 A4
Mount Field
Faversham ME13 ...62 B6
Queenborough ME11 ...3 A5
Mount Green Ave CT12 ...51 D5
Mount La Hartlip ME9 ...34 D4
Maidstone ME14 ...76 B4
Mount Lodge ME1 ...9 B2
Mount Pleasant
Aldington TN25 ...173 A6
Aylesford ME20 ...53 A3
Blean CT2 ...66 A6
Gillingham ME5 ...10 B3
Kingsdown CT14 ...134 D5
Oare ME13 ...40 B2
Tenterden TN30 ...167 C7
Mount Pleasant Dr ME14 ...76 A5
Mount Pleasant Rd **4**
CT20 ...178 D3
Mount Pleasant Terr
ME17 ...100 E2
Mount Rd Canterbury CT1 ...88 C6
Chatham ME4 ...9 F3
Dover CT17 ...166 A6
Rochester ME1 ...9 B2
Mount St CT21 ...176 C2
Mount View ME13 ...62 A5
Mount View Ct **3** ME4 ...9 F3
Mount View Rd CT6 ...23 A2
Mountain St CT4 ...107 B6
Mountbatten Ave ME5 ...32 A7
Mountbatten Way TN25 ...158 F6
Mountfield Rd TN28 ...200 C6
Mountfield Row TN28 ...200 C6
Mountfield Way CT8 ...27 D6
Mountpleasant Ct CT18 ...161 C7
Mounts CT14 ...117 A5
Mountsfield Ct ME16 ...74 D5
Mountview ME9 ...36 B2
Moyes Cl CT12 ...51 D5
Moyle Cl ME8 ...33 D4
Mozart Ct ME4 ...9 E3
Muddy Bush Cnr CT3 ...90 F2
Muir Rd Maidstone ME15 ...75 A2
Ramsgate CT11 ...52 E6
Mulberry Cl
Gillingham ME7 ...33 A4
Ramsgate CT11 ...52 F8
Mulberry Ct
Canterbury CT1 ...87 F8
Hythe CT21 ...176 D3
Littlestone-on-S TN28 ...200 E5
Maidstone ME14 ...75 B5
Mulberry Field CT13 ...72 F1
Mulberry Hill CT4 ...85 D1
Munday Bois Cotts
TN27 ...135 F8
Munday Bois Rd TN27 ...118 E1
Mundella Prim Sch
CT19 ...178 D6
Mungeam Ho ME1 ...9 C4
Munn's La ME9 ...34 E6
Murrain Dr ME15 ...76 A1
Murray Rd ME2 ...9 C8
Murston Inf Sch ME10 ...37 B4
Murston Jun Sch ME10 ...37 B5
Murston Rd ME10 ...37 B4
Murthwaite Ct ME12 ...4 A5
Murton Rd ME13 ...41 E1
Muscovy Rd TN25 ...139 C7
Muscovy Way CT6 ...22 E3
Museum of
Kent Rural Life★ ME14 ...53 D1
Museum St ME14 ...74 F4
Musgrave Cl ME12 ...27 C7
Musgrave Rd ME10 ...36 F6
Musgrove TN23 ...156 A8
Musket La
Eyhorne Street ME17 ...77 B2
Silver Hill ME17 ...77 A2
Mustards Rd ME12 ...6 D2
Mutrix Gdns CT9 ...7 J1
Mutrix Rd CT9 ...28 B8
Mutton La ME13 ...62 A6
Mymms Cl CT5 ...44 C8
Mynn Cres ME14 ...76 A4
Myrtle Cres ME5 ...31 F5
Myrtle Rd **5** CT19 ...178 E6
Mystole La CT4 ...108 C8
Mystole Rd CT4 ...108 A8

Mid – New 227

Napier Rd continued
Dover CT16 ...149 B2
Gillingham ME7 ...10 D4
Napleton Ct CT11 ...52 C6
Napleton Rd
Faversham ME13 ...62 C7
Ramsgate CT11 ...52 C6
Napoleon Wlk ME17 ...101 C5
Napwood Cl ME8 ...33 D6
Nares Rd ME8 ...33 D4
Nargate Cl CT3 ...90 A8
Nargate St CT3 ...90 A8
Narrabeen Rd CT19 ...177 E6
Narrowbush La TN29 ...198 B7
Naseby Ave CT20 ...177 D5
Nash Cl ME5 ...32 C2
Nash Court
Farming World★ ME13 ...63 D4
Nash Court Gdns CT9 ...28 F8
Nash Court Rd CT9 ...28 F8
Nash Gdns CT10 ...30 B4
Nash Hill CT18 ...161 D6
Nash La CT3 ...28 F7
Nash Rd Margate CT9,CT10 ...28 F7
Preston CT3 ...70 D6
Nashenden Farm La ME1 ...31 A8
Nashenden La ME1 ...9 A2
Nasmyth Rd CT7 ...27 A8
Nat's La TN25 ...141 A5
Natal Rd Chatham ME4 ...10 A3
Dover CT16 ...149 C4
Nativity Cl ME10 ...36 E4
Nautilus Cl ME12 ...4 A6
Nautilus Dr ME12 ...4 A6
Naval Terr ME12 ...1 B3
Naylands CT9 ...7 H1
Naylor's Cotts ME7 ...33 B1
Neal's Place Rd CT2 ...66 C3
Neale St ME4 ...9 F2
Neame Rd CT7 ...27 A7
Neames Forstal ME13 ...84 E7
Neason Ct CT19 ...178 F6
Neason Way CT19 ...178 F6
Neath Rd TN29 ...202 A2
Neatscourt Cotts ME12 ...3 C4
Nelson Ave ME12 ...4 D5
Nelson Cl Ashford TN24 ...157 B8
West Minst ME12 ...3 A8
Nelson Cres CT11 ...52 E6
Nelson Ct CT7 ...26 E8
Nelson Ho **8** ME15 ...97 F5
Nelson Park Rd CT15 ...150 E8
Nelson Pl CT10 ...30 B5
Nelson Rd Gillingham ME7 ...10 D4
Whitstable CT5 ...20 D1
Nelson St Deal CT14 ...117 C7
Faversham ME13 ...62 C6
Nelson Terr ME5 ...10 C1
Nelson Wlk ME10 ...36 B5
Neptune Bsns Pk ME2 ...9 F7
Neptune Terr ME12 ...1 E2
Neptune Way ME2 ...9 F7
Nesbit Rd TN29 ...194 F4
Ness Rd TN29 ...203 C6
Ness The CT1 ...88 B5
Nether Ave TN28 ...200 D6
Nethercourt Cir CT12 ...52 A6
Nethercourt Farm Rd
CT11 ...52 B7
Nethercourt Gdns CT11 ...52 B6
Nethercourt Hill CT11 ...52 B6
Nethergong Hill CT3 ...47 D3
Netherhale Farm Rd CT7 ...26 B3
Nethersole Cl CT2 ...67 A4
Nethersole Rd CT4 ...112 F1
Netley Cl ME14 ...75 D4
Nettlefield TN24 ...139 E5
Nettlepole La TN27 ...119 C1
Nevill Gdns CT14 ...117 B1
Neville Cl ME14 ...75 B5
Neville Rd ME4 ...9 C4
New Barns Rd ME14 ...75 A8
New Beverley Ho CT2 ...66 F2
New Bridge **10** CT16 ...166 E7
New Cotts Guston CT15 ...149 C6
Harbledown CT2 ...65 E1
Teynham ME9 ...38 A4
New Covenant Pl ME1 ...9 D4
New Cross St CT9 ...7 I2
New Cut Chatham ME4 ...9 F4
Dean Street ME15 ...96 D7
New Cut Rd
Chilham CT4,ME13 ...85 A3
Maidstone ME14 ...75 D5
New Delhi House **5**
ME15 ...97 E5
New Dover Rd
Canterbury CT1,CT4 ...88 C4
Capel-le-F CT18 ...164 C2
New Forest La CT4 ...85 B3
New Gardens Rd ME9 ...38 C2
New Haine Rd CT12 ...29 A3
New Hall Cl TN29 ...195 C8
New Hall Mus★ TN29 ...195 C8
New House Cl CT1 ...87 E4
New House La CT4 ...87 C2
New La TN29 ...203 C6
New Rd Chatham ME4 ...9 F4
Egerton TN27 ...119 A2
Elham CT4 ...144 F4
Eythorne CT15 ...131 C7
Harbledown CT2 ...65 D3
Herne CT2,CT6 ...45 C4

New Rd *continued*
Hythe CT21 ....176 B1
Hythe, Saltwood CT21 ...176 B4
Langley Heath ME17 ....98 C5
Minster (Sheppey) ME12 ...4 C6
Rochester ME1 ....9 D4
Rough Common CT2 ......66 B3
Sheerness ME12 ....200 C6
New Rectory La TN23 ...156 B4
New Rents 5 TN23 ....139 B2
New Road Ave ME4 ......9 E4
New Road Cotts CT6 ...45 E5
New Road Cty Prim Sch
ME4 ....10 A3
New Road Hill ME5 .....172 F4
New Road Ind Est ME12 ...1 B1
New Romney Pl CT13 ...93 F8
New Romney Sta★
TN28 ....200 C6
New Ruttington La CT1 ...67 A1
New St Ash CT3 ....71 E1
Ashford TN24 ....139 B2
Canterbury,Martyr's Field
CT1 ....87 E7
Canterbury,St Dunstan's
CT2 ....66 E1
Chatham ME4 ....9 E3
Deal CT14 ....117 D7
12 Dover CT16,CT17 ....166 D8
Folkestone CT20 ....178 D5
Herne Bay CT6 ....22 F5
Lydd TN29 ....203 C6
Margate CT9 ....7 I2
Sandwich CT13 ....94 A8
Sheerness ME12 ....1 C1
2 Whitstable CT5 ....20 D2
New Stairs ME4 ....9 F6
New Town Gn TN24 ....156 D8
New Town St
Canterbury CT1 ....67 B2
Chartham CT4 ....86 C5
New Villas ME15 ....96 C7
Newark Ct 1 ME2 ....9 B7
Newark Yd ME7 ....9 B7
Newbridge Ave ME10 ...36 E7
Newbury Ave ME16 ....74 C6
Newbury Cl
Birchington CT7 ....27 B6
Dover CT17 ....165 F7
Folkestone CT20 ....177 D5
Newcastle Hill 5 CT11 ..52 E7
Newchurch La TN26 ...193 A7
Newchurch Rd ME15 ...75 A1
Newcomen Rd ME12 .....1 D2
Newenden Cl
Ashford TN23 ....155 F6
Maidstone ME15 ....75 D6
Newgate Gap CT9 ....8 A3
Newgate Lower Prom CT9 .8 A3
Newgate Prom CT9 ....8 A3
Newham St ME4 ....10 B3
Newhouse Cnr CT3 .....48 E1
Newhouse La ME13 .....83 D7
Newing Cl CT3 ....89 E8
Newington CE Prim Sch
ME9 ....35 B7
Newington Ct CT12 .....29 B1
Newington Ent Ctr ME9 ..35 C8
Newington Ind Est ME9 ..34 F6
Newington Jun
Foundation Sch CT12 ..52 A8
Newington Nursery
& Inf Sch CT12 ....52 B8
Newington Rd
Folkestone,Newington
CT18 ....177 A8
Ramsgate CT12,CT11 ...29 B1
Newington Sta ME9 ....35 B6
Newington Wlk ME15 ...75 C6
Newland Green La
TN27 ....135 D8
Newland Rd ME12 ....2 F7
Newlands Ashford TN23 ..155 D6
St Mary's Bay TN29 ...194 F3
Whitfield CT16 ....149 B6
Newlands Ave ME10 .....36 B5
Newlands Dr CT14 .....134 B8
Newlands Farm Cotts
ME13 ....104 C4
Newlands Ho CT11 ......29 E2
Newlands La CT12 ......29 D2
Newlands Prim Sch CT11 .29 E1
Newlands Rd
Charing TN27 ....119 F5
Ramsgate CT12 ....29 D1
Newlyn Ct 1 ME14 ......75 A4
Newlyn's Mdw CT15 ...147 D1
Newman Dr ME10 ....37 A8
Newman Rd CT13 ....112 C5
Newmans Cl CT10 ....30 A6
Newnham Cl ME4 ....11 C2
Newnham La ME9,ME13 ..81 D7
Newnham Vineyard★
ME9 ....81 C7
Newport Ct CT1 ....88 B6
Newton Cl Chatham ME5 ...32 C2
1 Maidstone ME16 .....74 E3
Newton Rd
Faversham ME13 ....62 D7
Whitstable CT5 ....21 B2
Newtown Rd TN23,TN24 ..156 D7
Nicholas Cl ME16 ......74 A3
Nicholas Dr CT12 ......51 D5
Nicholas Rd TN24 ......139 B6
Nicholls Ave CT10 ......29 F2

Nicklaus Dr ME5 ....31 F3
Nickle Cotts CT4 ....86 A4
Nickleby Cl ME1 ....9 C2
Nickleby Cl TN26 ....170 C6
Nightingale Ave
Hythe CT21 ....187 D8
Whitstable CT5 ....43 B6
Nightingale Cl
Chartham CT4 ....86 C6
Gillingham ME8 ....33 E6
Sevington TN24 ....157 B7
Nightingale La CT15 ...113 C2
Nightingale Pl CT9 ....8 A2
Nightingale Rd
Dover CT16 ....149 C2
Faversham ME13 ....62 C7
Herne CT6 ....45 F7
Nile Rd ME7 ....10 C4
Nine Acres TN24 ....139 C5
Nine Ash La ME13 ......63 D3
Ninn La TN23,TN26 ....138 B2
Nixon Ave CT12 ....29 C1
No Name St 3 CT13 ....73 A1
Noah's Ark Rd CT17 ...166 A8
Noah's Ark Terr CT17 ..166 B8
Noakes Mdw TN23 .....156 A8
Nobel Cl ME9 ....38 C2
Nobel Ct ME13 ....62 C7
Noble Ct CT9 ....28 A8
Noble Gdns CT9 ....28 A8
Nonington CE Prim Sch
CT15 ....113 C5
Nonsuch Cl CT1 ....88 C8
Nore Cl Gillingham ME7 ..10 E1
Sheerness ME12 ....1 D1
Noreen Ave ME12 ....4 A6
Norfolk Cl Chatham ME5 ..32 C3
Gillingham ME8 ....11 D2
Norfolk Dr TN23 ....139 A2
Norfolk Rd Canterbury CT1 .87 E6
Lydden CT9 ....28 D5
Maidstone ME15 ....97 C8
Margate CT9 ....8 B3
Norfolk Sq CT12 ....29 B2
Norfolk St CT5 ....43 D8
Norman Castle★ CT1 ...87 F7
Norman Cl Gillingham ME8 .33 B5
Maidstone ME14 ....75 B6
Norman Rd
Ashford TN23,TN24 ...156 B7
Broadstairs CT10 ......29 A8
Canterbury CT1 ....88 A7
Faversham ME13 ....62 C7
Ramsgate CT11 ....52 B6
St Margaret's at Cliffe
CT15 ....151 B6
Warden ME12 ....6 A6
Westgate-on-S CT8,CT9 ..7 D1
Whitstable CT5 ....43 E8
Norman St 8 CT17 ....166 D8
Norman Tailyour Ho
CT14 ....117 D5
Norreys Rd ME8 ....33 B7
Norrie Rd CT7 ....27 A6
Norrington Mead 3
CT19 ....178 A7
Norrington Rd ME15 ...97 B6
North Ave CT11 ....52 D6
North Barrack Rd CT14 .117 D4
North Borough Jun Sch
ME14 ....75 A6
North Camber Way
CT20 ....150 B1
North Cl CT20 ....177 D4
North Close Bsns Ctr
CT20 ....177 D4
North Court Cl CT3 .....91 A8
North Court La CT14 ...115 A4
North Court Rd CT3 .....91 A8
North Cres ME17 ....96 D4
North Ct Deal CT14 ....117 C7
Maidstone ME15 ....75 A1
Ramsgate CT12 ....29 B2
North Dane Way ME5 ...32 C4
North Downs Cl ME4 ....85 C2
North Eastling Rd ME13 .81 F8
North Exit Rd CT16 ....166 H8
North Foreland Ave CT10 .30 B7
North Foreland Hill CT10 .30 B8
North Foreland Rd CT10 ..30 B7
North Holmes Rd CT1 ...88 B8
North La
Boughton Street ME13 ..84 F8
Canterbury CT2 ....66 F1
Faversham ME13 ....62 C8
7 Folkestone CT20 ...177 E3
North Lea CT14 ....117 C7
North Lockside Rd ME4 ..10 D8
North Lyminge La CT18 .161 C7
North Military Rd CT17 .166 C7
North Pends TN24 .....139 E5
North Pondside Rd ME4 ..10 A8
North Quay ME13 ......40 D1
North Rd Cliffs End CT13 ..51 A1
Dover CT16 ....166 C8
Folkestone CT20 ....177 D4
Gillingham ME4 ....10 B8
Gillingham,Brompton ME4,
ME7 ....10 A7
Hythe CT21 ....176 B2
Kingsdown CT14 ......134 D6
Queenborough ME11 ...2 F5
Sandwich CT13 ....95 A7
North Rd W CT21 ......176 A3
North Return Rd CT16 ..166 G8
North Sch The TN24 ...139 D1
North Side Three Rd
ME4 ....10 C8

North St Ashford TN23 ..139 C2
Ashford TN24 ....139 C3
Deal CT14 ....117 D7
Dover CT17 ....166 B7
Folkestone CT19 ......178 E5
Herne Bay CT6 ....23 A5
New Romney TN28 ....200 A6
Rochester ME2 ....9 B7
Sittingbourne ME10 ...36 F7
Warmlake ME17 ....98 E1
North View Hersden CT3 ..46 F1
Maidstone ME15 ....75 B1
North View Cotts ME15 ..96 C7
North Way
Finglesham CT14 ......116 A7
Maidstone ME14 ....75 B7
Northbourne Ave CT17 .166 B8
Northbourne
CE Prim Sch CT14 ...115 F5
Northbourne Court
Gdns**★ CT14 ....116 B5
Northbourne Park Sch
CT14 ....115 C6
Northbourne Park Sch
(Annexe) CT14 ....115 D6
Northbourne Rd
East Studdal CT15 ....115 E1
Gillingham ME8 ....11 B4
Great Mongeham CT14 ..116 C4
Northbourne Way CT9 ....8 E2
Northbrooke TN24 .....139 C3
Northbrooke La TN24 ...139 C3
Northcliffe Gdns CT10 ...30 A7
Northcote Rd Deal CT14 .117 D5
Kingsdown CT14 ......134 D4
Rochester ME2 ....9 A7
Northdown Ashford TN24 .139 C4
Doddington ME9 ....80 F7
Stockbury ME9 ....56 D8
Northdown Ave CT9 ......8 B2
Northdown Cl ME13 .....63 A3
Northdown Hill CT10,CT9 .29 D7
Northdown Park Rd CT9 ..8 C1
Northdown Prim Sch CT9 ..8 C1
Northdown Rd
Broadstairs CT10 ......29 E6
Margate CT9 ....8 B2
Northdown View ME17 ..100 F6
Northdown Way CT9 ......8 C1
Northdowns Cl CT15 ...132 B6
Northern By-Pass TN27 .120 C8
Northfleet Cl ME14 ......75 C5
Northgate Canterbury CT1 .67 A1
Rochester ME1 ....9 C6
Northleigh Cl ME5 ......97 A6
Northpoint Bsns Est ME2 ..9 D8
Northumberland Ave
Ashford TN24 ....139 D5
Gillingham ME8 ....11 E1
Margate CT9 ....8 C2
Northumberland Ct
Maidstone ME15 ....97 D7
Margate CT9 ....8 C3
Northumberland Rd
ME15 ....97 D8
Northwall Ct CT14 .....117 C7
Northwall Mews CT14 ..117 C7
Northwall Rd CT14 .....117 B8
Northwood Dr ME10 ....36 F1
Northwood Rd
Broadstairs, Ramsgate
CT10,CT12 ....29 C3
Whitstable CT5 ....20 F2
Norton Ave CT6 ....46 A8
Norton Dr CT12 ....50 B6
Norton Gr ME5 ....31 E3
Norton Knatchbull Sch
The TN24 ....139 E2
Norton Rd
Five Wents ME17 ......98 D1
Lynsted ME13,ME9 ....60 E5
Norview Rd CT5 ....43 B7
Norway Dro CT15 ......151 A8
Norway Terr 4 ME14 ...75 A7
Norwood Gdns TN23 ...139 B2
Norwood La TN29 ......193 E7
Norwood Rise ME12 .....4 C7
Norwood St TN23 ......139 B2
Norwood Wlk E ME10 ...36 C5
Norwood Wlk W ME10 ...36 B5
Notley St CT1 ....67 A1
Notley Terr 3 CT1 ......67 A1
Nottingham Ave ME15 ..97 C5
Nottingham Rd CT7 .....26 F5
Nouds La ME9 ....60 D7
Nunnery Fields CT1 .....88 A7
Nunnery Fields Hospl
CT1 ....88 A6
Nunnery Rd CT1 ....87 F7
Nursery Ave
Maidstone ME16 ....74 B6
Maidstone,Bearsted ME14 .76 B3
Nursery Cl Densole CT18 ..163 A7
Ramsgate CT11 ....52 C7
Sheerness ME12 ....1 E1
Whitstable CT5 ....21 C5
Nursery Fields Acol CT7 ..27 B3
Hythe CT21 ....176 A2
Nursery Gdns CT10,CT9 ...8 E1
Nursery La Densole CT18 .163 A7
Sheldwich ME13 ....83 D5
Whitfield CT16 ....148 F7
Nursery Rd ME8 ....33 D8
Nursery Wlk CT17 ......66 E2
Nurserylands CT6 ....22 F5
Nutberry Cl ME9 ....38 D2
Nutfield Cl ME5 ....32 B8

Nutfields ME10 ....37 B3
Nutley Cl TN24 ....139 C1
Nutts Ave ME12 ....6 G2
Nutwood Cl ME14 ......75 E4

O

Oak Ave Eythorne CT15 ..131 D5
Gillingham ME7 ....10 E6
Minster (Sheppey) ME12 ...4 F6
Oak Bglws TN29 ....203 C6
Oak Caer TN25 ....172 F4
Oak Cotts
East Studdal CT15 ....132 E8
Sellindge TN25 ....174 D7
Selling ME13 ....84 D4
Oak Dr
Boughton Street ME13 ..64 A3
Hawkinge CT18 ....163 B5
St Mary's Bay TN29 ...194 F3
Oak Gr CT14 ....114 B2
Oak Hall Pass CT21 ....176 C2
Oak Hill CT13 ....93 B6
Oak Ho 6 ME5 ....31 F4
Oak La Lydd TN29 ......203 B6
Minster (Sheppey) ME12 ...4 F7
Upchurch ME9 ....12 D2
Oak Lodge Rd TN28 ....200 B7
Oak Rd ME10 ....37 C5
Oak Ridge TN26 ....183 F8
Oak St CT14 ....117 D6
Oak Tree Ave ME15 .....97 C5
Oak Tree Gr CT9 ....28 A4
Oak Tree Prim Sch
TN23 ....155 F8
Oak Tree Rd TN23 .....155 F8
Oak Trees Com Sch
ME15 ....97 C7
Oak Wlk CT21 ....176 C2
Oakapple La ME16 ......74 A3
Oakdale Rd CT6 ....23 A4
Oakdene Rd CT12 ......29 C1
Oakenpole TN23 ....138 E1
Oakfield Ct CT12 ....52 B8
Oakfield Rd TN24 ......139 D5
Oakfields ME10 ....36 C3
Oakhurst Cl ME5 ....31 F3
Oakland Cl ME5 ....31 F3
Oakland Ct Cliffs End CT12 .51 C5
Herne Bay CT6 ....22 E5
Oaklands Ashford TN23 .138 F1
Mersham TN25 ....157 E4
Oaklands Ave CT14 .....29 C5
Oaklands Cty Inf
& Jun Sch ME5 ....31 F4
Oaklands Way CT2 .....68 B7
Oakleigh Ho TN23 .....155 E8
Oakleigh La CT4 ....89 B5
Oakleys The CT15 ......130 D5
Oakridge CT10 ....8 G1
Oaks Ave CT14 ....22 D2
Oaks Bsns Village The
ME5 ....32 C1
Oaks Com Inf Sch The
ME10 ....36 D2
Oaks Dene ME5 ....31 F1
Oaks Pk CT6 ....66 B3
Oaks Rd Folkestone CT20 .177 A6
Tenterden TN30 ....179 B8
Oaks The Broadstairs CT10 ..29 F7
Hawkinge CT18 ....163 B3
Hersden CT3 ....46 F1
St Nicholas at Wade CT7 .25 F2
Oaks View CT21 ....187 C8
Oakside Rd CT3 ....112 E5
Oaktree Ho ME10 ......37 B3
Oakum Ct ME4 ....10 B2
Oakvale Cl CT17 ....166 B7
Oakwood CT9 ....29 C8
Oakwood Ct ME16 .....74 D3
Oakwood Dr CT5 ....21 A1
Oakwood Ind Est CT10 ..29 E6
Oakwood Park
Gram Sch ME16 ......74 C3
Oakwood Rd
Maidstone ME16 ....74 D3
Sturry CT2 ....68 A7
Oakwood Terr ME10 ....37 C4
Oakwood Villas CT11 ...29 E1
Oare Marshes
Nature Reserve★ ME13 .40 B6
Oare Marshes NR & Watch
Tower Info Cntr★ ME13 .40 C6
Oare Rd ME13 ....40 C1
Oast Cotts Dargate ME13 .64 D8
Sheldwich ME13 ....83 C8
Oast Ct Margate CT9 ....28 F8
Sittingbourne ME10 ...36 C2
Oast Ho CT4 ....85 C2
Oast Ho The 3 ME8 ...33 F8
Oast La ME13 ....104 E6
Oast Meadow TN24 ....139 F1
Oast Paddock The CT3 ..92 A6
Oast The Canterbury CT1 .88 B6
Staple CT3 ....92 A6
Oasthouse Field TN29 ..192 F4
Oasts The ME14 ....76 C4
Oastview ME8 ....34 A8
Oaten Hill CT1 ....88 A7
Oaten Hill Pl CT1 ....88 A7
Oaze The CT5 ....43 C6
Occupation Rd TN25 ...123 C7
Ocean Cl CT7 ....27 B8
Ocean View
Broadstairs CT10 ......30 A1
Herne Bay CT6 ....23 F6

Ocelot Ct 6 ME4 ....10 B3
Octavia Ct ME5 ....32 B3
Octavian Dr CT21 .....175 A3
Odiham Dr ME16 ....74 C7
Odo Rd CT17 ....166 C8
Officers' Rd ME4 ....10 B8
Officers Terr ME4 ....9 F7
Offley Cl CT9 ....8 C1
Ogilvy Ct CT10 ....29 E7
Okehampton Cl TN24 ..139 F7
Olantigh Ct CT7 ....27 A7
Olantigh Rd TN25 .....123 F3
Olave Rd CT9 ....8 B1
Old Ash Cl TN24 ......139 C5
Old Ashford Rd
Charing TN27 ....120 C7
Lenham ME17 ....101 E5
Old Badgins Rd ME13 ...83 B6
Old Bailey The ME17 ...100 E6
Old Bakery Cl TN29 ....194 F4
Old Bakery Mews ME13 ..63 F4
Old Bakery The ME12 ....3 F5
Old Barn Cl ME7 ....32 F6
Old Billet La ME12 ....5 C6
Old Boundary Rd CT9 ....7 D1
Old Bridge Rd CT5 .....20 E1
Old Carriageway The
ME7 ....32 F4
Old Castle Wlk ME8 ....33 D4
Old Charlton Rd CT16 ..149 D2
Old Chatham Rd
Kit's Coty ME20 ....53 D6
Maidstone ME14 ....53 F1
Old Church Rd CT4 .....86 E1
Old Court Hill CT15,CT3 .113 C6
Old Crossing Rd 1 CT9 .28 B8
Old Dairy Cl 3 CT11 ....52 F7
Old Dover Rd
Barham CT4 ....112 B1
Canterbury CT1 ....88 B6
Capel-le-F CT18 ....164 C1
Old Dr ME15 ....96 F6
Old Dungeness
Lighthouse★ TN29 ....205 F6
Old Farm Cl CT5 ....43 C6
Old Farm Rd CT7 ....26 D7
Old Ferry Rd ME9 ....14 C7
Old Fold CT5 ....44 C8
Old Folkestone Rd
CT17 ....166 A4
Old Forge La ME9 ......56 F3
Old Garden Ct CT4 .....86 E1
Old Gate Rd ME13 .....62 B8
Old Green Rd
Broadstairs CT10 ......29 F7
Margate CT9 ....8 C1
Old Hall Dr CT12 ....51 C5
Old Ham La ME17 .....101 A4
Old High St The CT20 ..178 E5
Old Hockley Rd ME13 ...82 C2
Old Hook Rd ME12 ......4 F2
Old House Rd ME9 .....34 E4
Old Kingsdown Cl CT10 ..29 E3
Old Lain ME17 ....100 F6
Old Lenham Rd ME9 ....80 C4
Old London Rd CT21 ..175 C2
Old Loose Hill ME15 ....96 F4
Old Mead CT19 ....178 A7
Old Mill La ME20 ....53 C3
Old Mill Mews CT19 ...177 F7
Old Mill Rd ME17 ......76 F1
Old Oast Bsns Ctr The
ME20 ....53 A1
Old Orch TN23 ....155 D8
Old Orch The ME8 .....34 A8
Old Park Ave
Canterbury CT1 ....67 C2
Dover CT16 ....149 A3
Old Park Cl CT16 ......149 A4
Old Park Ct CT1 ....67 C2
Old Park Hill CT16 .....149 B4
Old Park Rd CT16 .....149 B2
Old Pattens La ME1 .....9 D2
Old Pond Rd TN23 .....155 F4
Old Priory Sch The CT11 .52 D6
Old Railway Works
(Ind Est) TN24 ....156 D8
Old Rd Chatham ME4 ....9 F4
Elham CT4 ....144 F4
Sarre CT7 ....48 C6
Old Rectory Cl
Hawkinge CT18 ....163 B4
Mersham TN25 ....157 C4
Old Rectory The TN25 ..122 E2
Old Roman Rd CT15 ...133 C2
Old Ruttington La CT1 ...67 A1
Old Saltwood La CT21 ..176 B4
Old Saw Mill The TN26 ..153 E6
Old School Cl
Lenham ME17 ....101 D4
Sturry CT2 ....67 F6
Old School Ct
Egerton TN27 ....118 F3
Folkestone CT20 ....178 E5
Old School Gdns CT9 ....8 A1
Old School Mews CT4 ...86 C2
Old School The TN24 ..156 D8
Old School Yd 2 CT10 ..29 E5
Old Surrenden Manor Rd
TN26 ....154 C5
Old Timber Yard Ind Est
CT11 ....52 A7
Old Tovil Rd ME15 .....75 A2
Old Town Gaol Mus★
CT17 ....166 D8
Old Town Hall Mus★ CT9 ..7 I3
Old Trafford Cl ME16 ...74 B6
Old Tree La ME17 ....97 D3

Old – Phi 229

Old Tree Rd CT3 47 B7
Old Valley Rd CT4 128 F7
Old Vicarage Gdn CT2 67 F6
Old Vicarage Gdns TN25 123 E2
Old Vicarage The CT13 93 C7
Old Way TN26 190 D7
Oldborough Manor Com Sch ME15 97 B6
Oldchurch Ct 3 ME16 74 E3
Oldfield Cl Gillingham ME8 33 D8
Maidstone ME15 75 E1
Oldhawe Hill CT3,CT6 46 D7
Oldhouse La TN29 191 E1
Oldstairs Rd CT14 134 D4
Oliver Cl ME4 10 B2
Oliver Twist Cl ME1 9 B4
Olivers Cotts ME14 76 C4
Olivine Cl Chatham ME5 54 A8
Sittingbourne ME10 36 C7
Olliffe Cl ME5 31 F2
Omer Ave CT9 8 C2
Onslow Rd ME1 9 D3
Ontario Way CT16 149 B3
Opal Gn ME5 32 B2
Orache Dr ME14 75 E5
Orange St CT1 87 F8
Orange Terr ME1 9 D5
Orbit Cl ME5 54 A8
Orbital Pk TN24 156 F6
Orchard Ave CT14 117 B5
Orchard Bank ME17 98 B1
Orchard Bsns Ctr ME16 74 C8
Orchard Cl Canterbury CT2 66 F4
Coxheath ME17 96 C3
Langley Heath ME17 98 E4
Littlebourne CT3 89 F7
Mersham TN25 157 E3
Minster (Thanet) CT12 50 B7
Ramsgate CT12 29 B3
Whitfield CT16 148 F8
Whitstable CT5 20 F3
Wingham CT3 91 A7
Orchard Cotts ME16 96 A8
Orchard Ct
Chillenden CT3 113 F8
Herne Bay CT6 22 F1
Orchard Dr Ashford TN23 138 F4
Littlestone-on-S TN28 200 E6
Maidstone ME14 75 E4
Newington ME9 35 A5
River CT17 148 E3
Wye TN25 123 F1
Orchard Field TN26 153 D4
Orchard Fields CT21 160 E2
Orchard Flats CT1 88 D7
Orchard Gdns CT9 28 A8
Orchard Gr ME12 4 C6
Orchard Hts TN23 138 F5
Orchard Ind Est ME15 97 F3
Orchard La Ashford TN24 139 F6
Challock TN25 105 B2
St Nicholas at Wade CT7 25 F1
Orchard Mews CT14 117 D5
Orchard Pk CT6 23 D4
Orchard Pl
Faversham ME13 62 D7
2 Maidstone ME16 74 E3
Sittingbourne ME10 37 A3
Orchard Rd Eastry CT13 93 B3
Herne Bay CT6 22 F3
Margate CT9 28 A8
St Mary's Bay TN29 195 A5
St Michaels TN30 167 A3
Orchard Residences The CT1 88 A5
Orchard Row CT6 23 A1
Orchard Sch CT1 87 F6
Orchard St Canterbury CT2 66 E1
Gillingham ME8 33 E8
Maidstone ME15 75 A3
Orchard The ME14 76 B4
Orchard Valley CT21 176 A2
Orchard View Ash CT3 71 F1
Tenterden TN30 179 C8
Teynham ME9 38 C3
Orchard Villas
1 Chatham ME4 9 F3
River CT17 148 E4
Orchard Way ME12 5 D1
Orchards The CT4 144 F4
Orchid Cl ME12 4 A4
Orchids The
Etchinghill CT18 161 D4
Mersham TN25 157 E4
Ordnance St ME4 9 E3
Ordnance Terr 9 ME4 9 E4
Orgarswick Ave TN29 195 C7
Orgarswick Way TN29 195 C7
Oriel Rd TN23 138 F4
Orient Pl CT2 66 F1
Orion Rd ME1 31 C7
Orion Way TN24 156 E8
Ormonde Ct CT21 176 C1
Ormonde Rd
11 Folkestone CT20 178 E6
Hythe CT21 176 C1
Ormsby Gn ME8 33 E3
Orr Cl CT18 162 F4
Osborne Gdns CT6 23 D4
Osborne Rd
Ashford TN24 156 F8
Broadstairs CT10 29 F4
Gillingham ME7 10 C5
Kingsdown CT14 134 C6
Osborne Terr CT9 7 J1
Osbourn Ave CT8 27 E8
Oscar Rd CT10 30 B4
Osier Field TN24 139 E7
Osier Rd ME9 38 E3
Osprey Ave ME5 10 E2
Osprey Cl CT5 43 C7
Osprey Ct 2 Dover CT16 149 B2
Sittingbourne ME10 37 A3
Ospringe CE Prim Sch ME13 62 A6
Ospringe Pl ME13 62 B6
Ospringe Rd ME13 62 B7
Ospringe St ME13 62 A6
Ostend Ct ME10 14 F1
Ostlers La CT7 48 D6
Oswald Pl CT17 149 B2
Oswald Rd CT17 149 B2
Otham Cl CT2 67 A4
Otham La ME15 76 C2
Otham St Maidstone ME15 76 C2
Otham ME15 98 B7
Ottawa Cres CT16 149 C3
Ottawa Way CT16 149 B3
Otterbourne Pl ME15 75 E1
Otterden Cl TN23 155 F6
Otterden Rd ME13 81 D3
Otterham Quay La ME8 12 B2
Otteridge Rd ME14 76 A3
Otterpool La CT21,TN25 174 D4
Otway St Chatham ME4 10 A3
Gillingham ME7 10 D6
Otway Terr 1 ME4 10 A3
Out Elmstead La CT4 111 F2
Oval The TN29 186 D1
Overland La CT3 71 A3
Owen Sq CT14 117 B2
Owen's Cl CT21 177 B3
Owens Court Cotts ME13 83 F8
Owens Way ME7 11 A6
Owl's Hatch Rd CT6 22 C1
Owletts Cl ME15 97 D8
Ox La TN30 167 B2
Oxen Lease TN23 155 E8
Oxenden Cnr CT3 23 F1
Oxenden Cres CT3 91 A8
Oxenden Park Dr CT6 22 E4
Oxenden Rd CT20 177 E4
Oxenden St CT6 22 E5
Oxenden Way CT4 128 F8
Oxenturn Rd TN25 140 E8
Oxford Cl 5 CT5 20 D1
Oxford Ct CT1 87 F7
Oxford Mans 4 CT5 20 D1
Oxford Rd Canterbury CT1 87 F7
Gillingham ME7 10 D3
Maidstone ME15 97 D8
Oxford St 6 Margate CT9 7 J1
Whitstable CT5 20 D1
Oxford Terr CT20 178 D4
Oxney Cl CT7 26 F7
Oxney Cotts TN30 190 A4
Oyster Cl Herne Bay CT6 22 B3
Sittingbourne ME10 36 E6

P

Packer Pl ME5 32 A8
Packer's La CT11 52 E7
Pad's Hill ME15 75 A4
Padbrook La CT3 70 D6
Paddock Cl Deal CT14 116 F5
Folkestone CT20 177 F5
Lydd TN29 203 B6
Paddock Rd
Ashford TN23 155 E7
2 Birchington CT7 27 A7
Paddock The
Canterbury CT1 88 B8
Chatham ME4 9 F4
Chilham CT4 85 C2
Dover CT16 166 D8
Paddock View CT5 43 E7
Paddocks The
Broadstairs CT10 29 F7
Gillingham ME7 33 A5
Great Chart TN23 138 C1
Herne Bay CT6 23 F5
Margate CT9 8 C1
Padsole La ME15 75 A4
Padstow Manor 1 ME7 10 C6
Padwell La TN23 155 C8
Paffard Cl CT2 67 F6
Paffard Ct CT2 67 F6
Page Pl CT19 178 D8
Page Rd CT18 162 F3
Paget Row ME7 10 C5
Paget St ME7 10 C5
Pagitt St ME4 9 E3
Paine Ave TN29 203 C6
Painesfield Cl TN29 186 C4
Painter's Forstal Rd ME13 61 E3
Palace Ave ME15 75 A4
Palace Cl CT5 21 B2
Palace Cotts ME9 80 F8
Palace Ct Chatham ME5 10 D2
Hythe CT21 176 C2
Palace Ind Est ME15 97 F4
Palace St 17 CT1 67 A1
Palace Wood Inf Sch ME16 74 C6
Palace Wood Jun Sch ME16 74 C6
Palm Bay Ave CT9 8 D3
Palm Bay Gdns CT9 8 C3
Palm Bay Prim Sch CT9 8 D3
Palm Ct CT9 7 C1
Palm Tree Cl CT15 131 D7
Palm Tree Way CT18 161 B7
Palmar Rd ME16 74 D6
Palmarsh Ave CT21 187 D7
Palmarsh Cres CT21 187 D7
Palmarsh Prim Sch CT21 187 D8
Palmbeach Ave CT21 187 D8
Palmer Cl CT6 46 B8
Palmer Cres CT9 29 C8
Palmer Rd CT3 91 A8
Palmers Cross Hill CT2 66 A1
Palmerston Ave
Broadstairs CT10 30 B3
Deal CT14 117 C2
Palmerston Ct CT14 117 D2
Palmerston Rd
Chatham ME4 9 F1
River CT16 148 F5
Palmerston St 4 CT19 178 D6
Palmerston Wlk ME10 37 C4
Palting Way CT20 178 B4
Pamela Ct ME7 10 D5
Pannell Dr CT18 162 F4
Panteny La ME9 37 E2
Pantheon Gdns TN23 155 F5
Panton Cl ME5 32 C4
Papion Gr ME5 31 E2
Papworth Cl 1 CT19 178 A7
Parade CT1 87 F8
Parade Rd CT20 177 F3
Parade The
Birchington CT7 26 D8
Folkestone CT20 178 E5
Greatstone-on-S TN28, TN29 204 E7
Margate CT9 7 I3
Sevington TN24 156 F5
Sittingbourne ME10 36 F2
Paradise CT11 52 D7
Paradise Cotts ME9 34 E5
Paradise Row CT13 72 F1
Paragon CT11 52 E5
Paragon St CT11 52 D5
Paraker Way CT21 177 B4
Pardoner Cl CT2 87 C7
Pardoners Way CT16 149 A3
Parfitt Way CT16 149 B2
Parham Cl CT1 67 B2
Parham Rd
Canterbury CT1 67 B2
Chatham ME4 9 F2
Paris Cnr TN26 153 F6
Parish Rd Chartham CT4 86 C3
Minster (Sheppey) ME12 4 A5
Park Ave Birchington CT7 27 A6
Broadstairs CT10 29 E2
Deal CT14 117 C5
Dover CT16 149 D1
Gillingham ME7 10 D3
Leysdown-on-S ME12 6 G1
Loose ME17 96 E2
Maidstone ME14 75 B6
Queenborough ME11 3 B4
Sittingbourne ME10 36 E1
Whitstable CT5 20 F3
Park Barn Rd ME17 99 C5
Park Chase CT10 29 E2
Park Cl Hawkinge CT18 163 A4
Margate CT9 8 D1
Park Cotts CT11 29 E2
Park Cres ME4 31 F8
Park Crescent Rd CT9 8 A1
Park Ct ME13 62 E7
Park Dr Hothfield TN26 138 A6
Sittingbourne ME10 36 D1
Park Farm Cl
Shadoxhurst TN26 155 A1
Tyler Hill CT2 66 E6
Park Farm Prim Sch CT19 178 C6
Park Farm Rd CT19 178 C7
Park Gate CT10 29 F2
Park Ho ME14 75 B6
Park La Bethersden TN26 154 C8
Birchington CT7 27 A6
Bishopsbourne CT4 111 C5
Boughton Monchelsea ME17 97 D2
Elham CT4 144 F5
Maidstone ME14 74 F7
Margate CT9 8 A2
Park Lea CT14 117 C5
Park Mall 2 TN24 139 B2
Park Manor ME7 10 B5
Park Mews 6 CT16 166 D8
Park Par TN29 195 C7
Park Pl Ashford TN24 156 F8
Ashford, Willesborough TN23 156 B7
Dover CT16 166 D8
Herne CT6 46 A8
Margate CT9 7 I1
Park Rd Ashford TN24 139 D6
Broadstairs CT10 30 B6
Dover CT16 149 B2
Faversham ME13 62 D7
Folkestone CT19 177 E6
Herne Bay CT6 22 F4
Hythe CT21 176 B1
Littlestone-on-S TN28 200 E5
Margate CT9 8 A2
Preston CT3 70 D7
Queenborough ME11 2 F5
Ramsgate CT11 52 C7
Sheerness ME12 1 E1
Sittingbourne ME10 36 E3
Temple Ewell CT16 148 D5
Westgate-on-S CT7 27 D6
Park Rd N TN24 139 B3
Park St Ashford TN24 139 C2
Deal CT14 117 D6
Dover CT16 166 D8
Lydd TN29 203 C6
Park Terr Throwley ME13 82 D1
Woodnesborough CT13 93 D7
Park Vale TN24 139 D6
Park View
Folkestone CT19 178 E7
Sturry CT2 67 F6
Park View Cl CT3 91 D2
Park View Ct ME15 75 E1
Park View Rise CT15 113 D4
Park View Terr 2 TN30 179 A7
Park Way Coxheath ME17 96 D3
Maidstone ME15 75 B1
Park Way Prim Sch ME15 75 B1
Park Wood Cl TN23 156 B5
Park Wood Forest Wlks★ TN26 181 C4
Park Wood Gn ME8 33 D5
Park Wood Par ME15 97 F5
Park Wood Trad Est ME15 97 F4
Parker Cl Gillingham ME8 33 E5
Hamstreet TN26 183 A7
Parkfield Rd
Folkestone CT19 178 C6
Gillingham ME8 11 F1
Parkland Ct CT10 29 F6
Parkside Com Prim Sch CT1 67 D2
Parkside Ct CT11 52 D7
Parkway The CT7 27 B7
Parkwood Cl CT10 29 F2
Parkwood Inf Sch ME8 33 E5
Parkwood Jun Sch ME8 33 E5
Parkwood Rd CT2 66 C4
Parr Ave ME7 10 D6
Parrs Head Mews ME1 9 C6
Parsonage Chase ME12 3 F5
Parsonage Cotts ME9 58 A5
Parsonage Farm (Rural Heritage Ctr)★ CT4 145 A6
Parsonage Fields CT12 49 C7
Parsonage La
Rochester ME2 9 C8
Sittingbourne ME9 14 A1
Parsonage Rd CT6 23 A3
Parsonage Stocks Rd ME13 82 F5
Parsonage Villas CT15 165 C5
Partridge La ME13 62 D7
Pasley Rd ME4,ME7 10 A7
Pasley Rd E ME7 10 B7
Pasley Rd N ME4 10 B7
Pasley Rd W ME7 10 A7
Pastime Cl ME10 36 E8
Pasture The TN24 139 D6
Patchways TN29 184 E3
Path Field Cotts CT15 164 E5
Patricia Way CT10 29 D3
Patrixbourne Ave ME8 11 C2
Patrixbourne Rd CT4 89 B2
Pattens Gdns ME1 9 E2
Pattens La ME1 9 E1
Pattens Pl ME1 9 D2
Paul's Pl 8 CT16 149 C1
Pavement The TN30 167 B3
Pavilion Cl CT14 117 C8
Pavilion Ct CT20 178 E4
Pavilion Dr ME10 14 F1
Pavilion Mdw CT17 148 E4
Pavilion Rd CT19 178 D6
Pay St CT18 162 F7
Payden St ME17 102 D8
Payers Pk CT20 178 D5
Payne's La ME15 97 B7
Pays La TN25 104 D1
Payton Cl CT9 29 A7
Payton Mews 4 CT1 67 B1
Peacock Mews 7 ME16 74 E4
Peacock Pl ME13 84 A6
Peacock Rise ME5 32 A4
Peafield Wood Rd CT4 127 E4
Peak Dr CT13 93 B3
Pean Court Rd CT5 43 D3
Pean Hill CT5 43 D2
Pear Tree Alley 3 ME10 36 E5
Pear Tree Cl CT10 29 C4
Pear Tree La
Dymchurch TN29 186 D1
Gillingham ME7 32 E7
Maidstone ME15 97 B6
Pear Tree Row ME17 98 B5
Pear Tree Wlk ME9 35 A5
Pearmain Wlk CT1 88 C7
Pearman Cl ME8 12 A1
Pearson's Way CT10 29 E7
Peartree Cotts ME8 34 B8
Peartree Rd CT6 23 C3
Peckham Cl ME2 9 C8
Pedding Hill CT3 71 A1
Pedding La CT3 92 A8
Peel Dr ME10 37 C4
Peel St ME14 75 A6
Peelers Ct CT2 66 F1
Peene Cotts CT18 162 B1
Pegwell Ave CT11 52 A5
Pegwell Bay Ctry Pk★ CT12 51 C2
Pegwell Cl CT11 52 A5
Pegwell Ct CT11 52 B5
Pegwell Rd CT11 52 B5
Pelham Gdns CT20 178 A4
Pelwood Rd TN31 201 A2
Pemberton Ct CT21 177 B3
Pemberton Rd TN24 139 D2
Pemberton Sq 4 ME2 9 C8
Pembroke ME4 10 B8
Pembroke Ave CT9 7 F1
Pembroke Ct
Chatham ME4 10 A4
1 Ramsgate CT11 52 E7
Pembroke Gdns ME8 33 E4
Pembroke Mews TN28 200 C8
Pembroke Rd ME17 96 C3
Pembroke Rise ME4 10 A7
Pembury Ct 6 ME10 36 E4
Pembury Gdns ME16 74 D3
Pembury St ME10 36 E4
Pembury Way ME8 11 E2
Penbury CT14 117 C1
Pencester Ct CT16 166 E8
Pencester Rd CT16 166 D8
Penderel Mews TN30 179 B8
Penenden Ct ME14 75 B7
Penenden Heath Rd ME14 75 C7
Penenden St ME14 75 A6
Penfield La ME9 59 A4
Penfold Cl Chatham ME5 32 B7
Park Wood ME15 97 E5
Penfold Gdns CT15 130 E5
Penfold Hill ME17 99 B8
Penfold Rd CT19 178 F6
Penfold Way ME15 96 F6
Pengelly Pl CT2 66 F2
Penhurst Cl ME14 75 F5
Penlee Point TN24 139 D5
Penn Cl ME10 37 B2
Penn Hill TN23 155 E6
Pennant Rd ME1 31 C7
Pennine Way
Ashford TN24 139 B4
Maidstone ME15 76 A1
Pennington Cl CT2 68 C7
Penny Cress Gdns ME16 74 C3
Penny Cress Rd ME12 4 A4
Penny Pot La CT4 108 B4
Pennypot Ind Est CT21 175 F1
Penrose Ct CT21 176 C1
Penryn Manor 4 ME7 10 C6
Pensand Ho CT21 176 D1
Penshurst Cl
Canterbury CT2 67 A3
Gillingham ME8 11 E2
Penshurst Gdns CT9 8 F2
Penshurst Rd CT11 52 F7
Penshurst Rise ME13 62 B8
Penstocks The ME15 74 D2
Pent Vale Cl CT19 178 A6
Pent Valley Sch CT19 177 F7
Pepy's Way ME2 9 A8
Pepys Ave ME12 1 C2
Percival Terr CT17 166 B7
Percy Ave CT10 8 F2
Percy Rd Broadstairs CT10 29 F5
Margate CT9 8 A3
Ramsgate CT11 52 D8
Peregrine Cl CT21 187 D8
Peregrine Dr ME10 37 A2
Peri Ct CT1 87 E6
Perie Row 9 ME7 10 A6
Perimeter Rd CT16 166 G8
Periwinkle Cl ME10 36 E5
Periwinkle Ct 4 ME10 36 E5
Perkins Ave CT9 28 F8
Perries Mead CT19 178 B7
Perry Court Rudolf Steiner Sch CT4 108 E7
Perry La CT3 70 C3
Perry St Chatham ME4 9 E3
Maidstone ME14 74 F6
Perryfield St ME14 74 F6
Perth Gdns ME10 36 C4
Perth Way CT16 149 C3
Pested Bars Rd ME17 97 D5
Pested La TN25 105 C4
Petchell Mews 11 CT1 67 B2
Peter St Deal CT14 117 D7
Dover CT16 166 C8
Folkestone CT20 178 E5
Petfield Cl ME12 4 C6
Petham Gn ME8 11 C2
Petham Prim Sch CT4 109 C3
Petlands ME17 97 D5
Pett Bottom Rd CT4 110 C5
Pett Hill CT4 88 F1
Pett La TN27 120 D7
Pett Lane ME9 57 B7
Pett's Cres CT12 50 B5
Pettfield Hill Rd ME13 82 B1
Pettits Row ME13 62 B7
Pettman Cl CT6 22 F3
Pettman Ct 5 CT10 29 E5
Pettmans Mews CT5 20 C2
Petts La CT3 91 A8
Peverel Dr ME14 76 A5
Peverel Gn ME8 33 D4
Peverell Rd CT16 149 B4
Pharos Dr CT16 149 E1
Pheasant La ME15 97 B8
Pheasant Rd ME4 10 C2
Pheasants' Hall Rd CT4 110 F2
Philip Corby Cl CT9 8 B2
Philipine Village Craft Ctr★ TN29 197 A6
Philippa Ho CT19 178 F6
Phillip Rd CT19 177 E6
Phillippa Ct ME10 36 E8
Phillips Ct ME8 11 B2
Phillips Rd CT7 27 A6

Phoenix Ind Est ME2 . . . . .9 D7
Phoenix Pk ME15 . . . . .97 F4
Phoenix Rd ME5 . . . . .32 B2
Piccadilly The 4 ME5 . . . .10 B3
Pickelden La CT4 . . . . . . .107 F8
Pickering St ME15 . . . . . . .97 B6
Pickhill Oast ME15 . . . . . .179 B4
Pickneybush La TN29 . . . .194 A7
Pickwick Cres ME1 . . . . . . .9 C3
Picton Rd CT11 . . . . .52 C7
Pier Approach Rd ME7 . . .10 D7
Pier Ave Herne Bay CT6 . . .22 E4
  Whitstable CT5 . . . . .21 A2
Pier Rd ME7 . . . . .10 E7
Pier Rd Ind Est ME7 . . . . .10 D7
Pier The CT16 . . . . .148 F8
Pierpoint Rd CT5 . . . . .43 D7
Pierremont Ave CT10 . . . . .30 A4
Pigeon La CT6 . . . . .23 A2
Pigtail Cnr ME12 . . . . .4 E6
Pike CI CT19 . . . . .178 A7
Pike Rd CT14,CT15 . . . . . .114 E4
Pikefields ME8 . . . . .11 C2
Pilckem CI CT1 . . . . .67 D1
Pilgrim Spring CT19 . . . . .178 D8
Pilgrims Ct TN27 . . . . . . .120 C7
Pilgrims La Chilham CT4 . . .85 E1
  Whitstable CT5 . . . . .43 B4
Pilgrims Lakes ME17 . . . .100 E6
Pilgrims Rd CT1 . . . . .88 C7
Pilgrims View ME14 . . . . . .53 E3
Pilgrims Way
  Boughton Aluph TN25 . . . .123 A4
  Boxley ME14 . . . . .54 E3
  Broad Street ME14,ME17 . . .77 C6
  Canterbury CT1 . . . . .88 C7
  Charing TN27 . . . . .120 E8
  Detling ME14 . . . . .55 B1
  Dover CT16 . . . . .149 A3
  Eccles ME20 . . . . .53 B6
  Hollingbourne ME17 . . . . . .77 F3
  Lenham ME17 . . . . .101 B7
  Westwell TN25 . . . . .121 D5
Pilgrims Way Prim Sch
  The CT1 . . . . .88 C7
Pilgrims' Way TN25 . . . . .159 E8
Pilot Rd ME1 . . . . .31 C8
Pilot's Farm Rd CT4 . . . . .110 A4
Pilots Ave CT1 . . . . .117 A4
Pimp's Court Cotts ME15 96 E6
Pimp's Court Farm Ctr
  ME15 . . . . .96 E6
Pimpernel CI ME14 . . . . . .76 B4
Pimpernel Way ME5 . . . . . .31 E4
Pin Hill CT1 . . . . .87 F7
Pine Cotts ME14 . . . . .74 E8
Pine Gr Gillingham ME7 . . .33 A5
  Maidstone ME14 . . . . .75 B6
Pine Ho 5 ME14 . . . . .75 B4
Pine House 3 ME5 . . . . . . .31 F5
Pine Lodge ME16 . . . . .74 C3
Pine Lodge Ct CT14 . . . . .117 B5
Pine PI ME15 . . . . .74 E1
Pine Tree Ave CT2 . . . . . . .66 E2
Pine Tree CI CT8 . . . . .27 B7
Pine Way CT19 . . . . .177 D7
Pine Wlk CT6 . . . . .23 E5
Pineham Rd CT15 . . . . . . .149 D6
Pines Gardens The★
  CT15 . . . . .151 B5
Pines The CT10 . . . . .29 D4
Pineside Rd CT3 . . . . .89 E8
Pinetree CI CT5 . . . . .20 F3
Pinewood CI CT12 . . . . . . .29 C1
Pinewood Dr ME5 . . . . . . .54 D8
Pink's Cnr ME4 . . . . .14 E3
Pinks Cnr CT12 . . . . .50 D8
Pinners Hill CT15,CT3 . . .113 C6
Pinners La CT15 . . . . .113 C5
Pinous Ho ME10 . . . . .36 D5
Pintail Way CT6 . . . . .23 C2
Pioneer Bsns Pk CT11 . . . .52 C8
Pioneer Rd CT16 . . . . . . .149 A3
Pippin Ave CT4 . . . . .111 B8
Pippin CI Coxheath ME17 . .96 B2
  Sittingbourne ME10 . . . . . . .36 D6
Pippin Croft ME7 . . . . .33 A6
Pirbright CI ME5 . . . . .32 D2
Pitstock Rd ME9 . . . . .59 B5
Pitt Rd Langley Heath ME17 99 A2
  Maidstone ME16 . . . . .74 B1
Pittlesden TN30 . . . . .179 A7
Pittlesden PI 1 TN30 . . . .179 A7
Pittock Ho CT14 . . . . .117 B3
Pivington La TN27 . . . . . .119 C2
Pivington Mill Ind Est
  TN27 . . . . .119 C2
Pixwell La CT14 . . . . .116 D3
Place La Hartlip ME9 . . . . . .34 D4
  Woodchurch TN26 . . . . . . .169 B3
Place The CT4 . . . . .112 F1
Plain Cotts CT20 . . . . .178 B4
Plain Rd
  Brabourne Lees TN25 . . . .158 F5
  Folkestone CT20 . . . . .178 B4
Plains Ave ME15 . . . . .75 C1
Plains Of Waterloo
  CT11 . . . . .52 F7
Plaistow Sq ME14 . . . . . . .75 C6
Plantation CI TN26 . . . . . .138 A7
Plantation La ME14 . . . . . .76 A3
Plantation Rd
  Faversham ME13 . . . . .62 C7
  Gillingham ME7 . . . . .11 A6
  Whitstable CT5 . . . . .21 D2

Platt's Heath Prim Sch
  ME17 . . . . .100 F2
Platters The ME8 . . . . .33 C7
Playdell Ct 12 CT20 . . . . .178 D4
Playing Fields CT13 . . . . . .93 E7
Playstool CI ME9 . . . . .35 B6
Playstool Rd ME9 . . . . . . .35 A6
Plaza Ct 7 ME10 . . . . .37 A4
Pleasance Rd N TN29 . . . .204 E5
Pleasance Rd S TN29 . . . .204 F2
Pleasance Road Central
  TN29 . . . . .204 F3
Pleasant Row 10 ME7 . . . .10 A4
Pleasent PI ME12 . . . . .3 E6
Plenty Brook Dr CT6 . . . . .22 F3
Plewis Ho ME7 . . . . .10 E7
Pleydell Cres CT2 . . . . . . .67 F7
Pleydell Gdns CT20 . . . . .178 D4
Plimsoll Ave CT19 . . . . . . .178 E8
Plomley CI ME8 . . . . .33 D4
Plough Cotts ME17 . . . . . .98 C2
Plough Ct CT6 . . . . .23 D2
Plough Hill CT15 . . . . .165 C4
Plough La CT5 . . . . .21 D3
Plough Rd ME12 . . . . .5 C5
Plough Wents Rd ME17 . . .98 B2
Ploughmans Way
  Chatham ME5 . . . . .32 A1
  Gillingham ME8 . . . . .33 E6
Plover CI ME8 . . . . .32 D1
Plover Rd ME12 . . . . .4 A5
Pluckley CE Prim Sch
  TN27 . . . . .136 D7
Pluckley CI ME8 . . . . .11 C3
Pluckley Gdns CT9 . . . . . . .8 E2
Pluckley Rd
  Bethersden TN26 . . . . . . .153 D7
  Biddenden Green TN27 . . .135 B8
  Charing TN27 . . . . .120 B5
  Hothfield TN26,TN27 . . . . .137 B4
Pluckley Sta TN27 . . . . . .136 C3
Plum Tree Gdns TN26 . . . .169 B1
Plum Tree Rd ME9 . . . . . . .56 B8
Plumford Rd ME13 . . . . . . .62 A2
Plumpton Wlk
  5 Canterbury CT1 . . . . . . .67 B1
  6 Maidstone ME15 . . . . . .97 F6
Plumpudding La ME13 . . . .42 E1
Plumstone Rd CT7 . . . . . . .26 F1
Plumtree Gr ME7 . . . . .33 A4
Plumtrees ME16 . . . . .74 A2
Plurenden Manor
  Farm Cotts TN26 . . . . . . .168 E3
Plurenden Rd TN26 . . . . .168 E7
Poachers CI ME5 . . . . .32 C5
Podkin Wood ME5 . . . . . . .53 F8
Poets Cnr CT9 . . . . .7 J1
Poets Wlk CT14 . . . . .117 C1
Poison Cross CT13 . . . . . . .93 B4
Poldark Ct 14 CT11 . . . . . .52 F7
Poles The ME9 . . . . .12 E4
Polhill Dr ME5 . . . . .31 F2
Pollard CI TN23 . . . . .155 F8
Pollard Ct ME7 . . . . .10 C5
Pollard PI CT5 . . . . .43 C6
Polo Way CT5 . . . . .21 D1
Pomfret Ho CT4 . . . . .86 D1
Pomfret Rd CT4 . . . . .86 D1
Pommeus La CT14 . . . . . .133 D7
Poncia Rd TN23 . . . . .156 A7
Pond Cotts Herne Bay CT6 23 D2
  Sittingbourne ME10 . . . . . . .58 D8
Pond Dr ME10 . . . . .37 A2
Pond Farm Rd
  Hollingbourne ME17 . . . . . .56 D1
  Sittingbourne ME9 . . . . . . .35 F1
Pond Hill CT3 . . . . .90 D1
Pond Hill Rd CT20 . . . . . .177 C5
Pond La
  St Margaret's at Cliffe
  CT15 . . . . .150 D7
  Womenswold CT4,CT3 . . . .112 D3
Pondfield TN25 . . . . .139 C8
Ponycart La CT4 . . . . .126 E3
Poorhole La CT10 . . . . .29 B5
Poot La ME9 . . . . .12 E5
Pope House La TN30 . . . . .167 B4
Pope St Godmersham CT4 107 E4
  Maidstone ME16 . . . . .74 C2
Popes La CT2 . . . . .67 F7
Popes Wood ME14 . . . . . . .75 F6
Poplar La TN23 . . . . .138 F3
Poplar Dr Elvington CT15 .114 B2
  Herne Bay CT6 . . . . .22 D2
Poplar Field TN30 . . . . . . .188 D4
Poplar Gr ME14 . . . . .74 C5
Poplar La TN29 . . . . .203 D7
Poplar Rd
  Broadstairs CT10 . . . . .29 E6
  Ramsgate CT11 . . . . .52 D7
  Wittersham TN30 . . . . . . .188 D4
Poplar View ME13 . . . . . . .63 E3
Poplars TN26 . . . . .182 A7
Poplars The
  Ashford TN23 . . . . .156 A7
  Bethersden TN26 . . . . . . .153 E5
  Hersden CT3 . . . . .46 F1
Poppy CI Gillingham ME7 . .10 E5
  Maidstone ME16 . . . . .74 D3
Popsal La CT3 . . . . .91 B6
Porchester CI ME15 . . . . . .97 A6
Port CI Chatham ME5 . . . . .32 B3
  Maidstone ME14 . . . . .76 A5
Port Lympne Wild
  Animal Park★ CT21 . . . .174 D2
Port Rise ME4 . . . . .9 F3
Portal House Sch CT15 .151 A6
Portebello Ct CT14 . . . . . .117 D7

Porter CI ME12 . . . . .4 A6
Porter's La ME13 . . . . .62 B2
Porters Wlk ME17 . . . . .98 E4
Portland Ave ME10 . . . . . . .37 C4
Portland CI
  Ashford TN24 . . . . .139 C7
  Hythe CT21 . . . . .176 B2
Portland Ct
  3 Hythe CT21 . . . . .176 B2
  Ramsgate CT11 . . . . .52 E7
Portland Rd
  Gillingham ME7 . . . . .10 E6
  Hythe CT21 . . . . .176 B2
Portland St 1 ME4 . . . . . . .10 B2
Portland Terr
  Ripple CT14 . . . . .133 D8
  Sheerness ME12 . . . . .1 D2
Portree Mews ME7 . . . . . . .10 E3
Portsdown CI ME16 . . . . . .74 B2
Portway CT5 . . . . .43 C8
Post Barn Rd ME4 . . . . .9 F2
Postley Commercial Ctr
  ME15 . . . . .75 A2
Postley Rd ME15 . . . . .75 A1
Postling TN23 . . . . .138 E1
Postling Rd CT19 . . . . . . .177 E2
Postling Wents CT21 . . . .175 F8
Postmill Dr ME15 . . . . .74 F1
Potten Street Rd CT7 . . . . .25 E3
Potter St CT13 . . . . .73 A1
Potters CI TN24 . . . . .138 E6
Potters Cnr TN24 . . . . . . .138 E6
Pottery Cotts TN25 . . . . . .140 E5
Potyn Ho ME1 . . . . .9 C4
Pouces Cotts CT12 . . . . . . .27 F1
Poulders Gdns CT13 . . . . . .93 E8
Poulders Rd CT13 . . . . .93 E8
Poulsen Ct 8 ME10 . . . . . .37 B4
Poulton CI CT17 . . . . .165 F8
Poulton Close Bsns Pk
  CT17 . . . . .148 E1
Poulton La CT3 . . . . .92 C8
Pound Ct TN23 . . . . .156 A3
Pound Farm Cotts CT18 . .177 A4
Pound Ho TN23 . . . . .156 B8
Pound La Ashford TN23 . .155 F4
  Brabourne Lees TN25 . . . .158 F5
  Canterbury CT1 . . . . .66 F1
  Elham CT4 . . . . .144 F4
  Molash CT4 . . . . .105 F4
Poundhurst Rd TN26 . . . .171 C3
Powell CI ME20 . . . . .53 A3
Powell Cotton Dr CT7 . . . . .27 B6
Powell Inf Sch CT14 . . . . .149 B4
Power Station Rd ME12 . . . .3 E7
Pratling St ME20 . . . . .53 C4
Precincts The CT1 . . . . . . .88 A8
Prentis CI ME10 . . . . .36 E5
Prentis Quay ME10 . . . . . .36 E5
Prescott CI CT15 . . . . .149 E6
Prescott Ho TN28 . . . . . . .200 A4
Prestedge Ave CT11 . . . . .29 C2
Preston Ave
  Faversham ME13 . . . . .62 E6
  Gillingham ME7 . . . . .10 E1
Preston Gr ME13 . . . . .62 D6
Preston Hall Gdns ME12 . . .6 E4
Preston Hill CT3 . . . . .70 B1
Preston La
  Faversham ME13 . . . . .62 D6
  Preston CT3 . . . . .70 B5
Preston Malt Ho ME13 . . . .62 D6
Preston Par CT5 . . . . .42 F7
Preston Pk ME13 . . . . .62 D6
Preston Prim Sch CT3 . . . .70 C6
Preston Rd Manston CT12 . .28 E2
  Stourmouth CT3 . . . . .48 D1
  Wingham CT3 . . . . .70 B3
Preston St ME13 . . . . .62 D7
Pretoria Ho 8 ME15 . . . . .97 E5
Pretoria Rd
  Canterbury CT1 . . . . .88 B8
  Chatham ME4 . . . . .9 F2
  Gillingham ME7 . . . . .10 D3
Price's Ave Margate CT9 . . .8 B2
  Ramsgate CT11 . . . . .52 C6
Prices Ct 5 ME10 . . . . . . .37 B4
Priest & Sow Cnr CT5 . . . .21 B3
Priest Ave CT2 . . . . .87 C7
Priest Fields CT6 . . . . .23 F5
Priest Wlk CT5 . . . . .21 C3
Priestdale Ct ME4 . . . . .9 E3
Priestfield Rd ME7 . . . . . . .10 E5
Priestfield Stad
  (Gillingham FC) ME7 . . . .10 E5
Priestfields ME1 . . . . .9 B3
Primrose Ave ME8 . . . . . . .33 B5
Primrose CI ME4 . . . . .31 E7
Primrose Dr TN23 . . . . . . .156 B4
Primrose Gr ME9 . . . . .58 A6
Primrose Hill CT4 . . . . .86 B7
Primrose Ho 10 ME15 . . . .97 E7
Primrose La ME9 . . . . .58 A6
Primrose PI CT17 . . . . . . .149 B1
Primrose Rd CT17 . . . . . . .149 A1
Primrose Way
  Cliffs End CT12 . . . . .51 C5
  Whitstable CT5 . . . . .21 C1
Prince Andrew Rd CT10 . . .29 E7
Prince Arthur Rd ME7 . . . .10 B6
Prince Charles Ave
  Chatham ME5 . . . . .32 B4
  Minster (Sheppey) ME12 . . .4 C6
  Sittingbourne ME10 . . . . . . .37 C3
Prince Charles Rd
  CT10 . . . . .29 C7
Prince Of Wales Cvn Pk
  CT21 . . . . .187 E8

Prince of Wales Rdbt
  CT17 . . . . .166 D6
Prince Of Wales Terr
  CT14 . . . . .117 D5
Prince William Ct CT14 117 D7
Prince's Ave CT12 . . . . . . .29 E1
Prince's Gdns CT9 . . . . . . .8 C2
Prince's Rd CT11 . . . . .52 E6
Prince's St Margate CT9 . . .7 J2
  7 Ramsgate CT11 . . . . . . .52 E6
  Rochester ME1 . . . . .9 C4
Prince's St CT9 . . . . .8 D3
Princes Ave Chatham ME5 .32 B5
Princes CI CT7 . . . . .26 D7
Princes Cres 10 CT9 . . . . . .7 J2
  Sandwich CT13 . . . . .95 A8
Princes Dr Sandwich CT13 .73 F2
Princes Par TN26 . . . . . . .176 E2
Princes St Deal CT14 . . . .117 D7
  11 Dover CT16 . . . . .166 D7
  Maidstone ME14 . . . . .75 A5
Princes Terr CT21 . . . . . . .175 F1
Princes Way
  Canterbury CT2 . . . . .66 E1
  Detling ME14 . . . . .55 A1
Princess Anne Rd CT10 . . .29 E7
Princess CI CT5 . . . . .21 C3
Princess Margaret Ave
  Margate CT9 . . . . .8 E7
  Ramsgate CT12 . . . . .29 A1
Princess Mary Ave ME4 . . .10 B7
Princess Rd CT5 . . . . .21 C3
Princess St CT19 . . . . . . .178 E6
Prinys Dr ME8 . . . . .33 C4
Prior Rd TN28 . . . . .204 E8
Prior's Lees 9 CT20 . . . . .178 D4
Prioress Rd CT2 . . . . .87 D3
Prioress Wlk CT13 . . . . . .149 A3
Priory CI Broadstairs CT10 .29 F3
  East Farleigh ME15 . . . . . . .96 B8
  New Romney TN28 . . . . . .199 F6
Priory Ct Gillingham ME8 . .11 A2
  Leysdown-on-S ME12 . . . . .6 G2
Priory Fields Sch CT17 . .166 B8
Priory Gate 4 ME14 . . . . .75 A5
Priory Gate Rd CT17 . . . .166 C8
Priory Gdns
  Canterbury CT1 . . . . .88 A6
  Folkestone CT20 . . . . .178 D4
Priory Gr CT17 . . . . .166 C8
Priory Hill CT17 . . . . .166 C8
Priory Ho CT17 . . . . .166 C8
Priory Inf Sch CT17 . . . . . .52 D7
Priory La Herne Bay CT6 . . .23 A3
  Sellindge TN25 . . . . .159 D4
Priory of St Jacob CT1 . . .87 E6
Priory PI ME13 . . . . .40 C1
Priory Rd Aldington TN25 172 C4
  Dover CT16,CT17 . . . . . . .166 D8
  Faversham ME13 . . . . .62 C8
  Gillingham ME8 . . . . .11 A2
  Maidstone ME15 . . . . .75 A3
  Ramsgate CT11 . . . . .52 D6
  Rochester ME2 . . . . .9 A6
Priory Row ME13 . . . . .62 C8
Priory St 10 CT16 . . . . . . .166 D8
Priory Sta CT17 . . . . .166 C8
Priory Station
  Approach Rd CT17 . . . . .166 C7
Priory The TN29 . . . . .203 C6
Priory Way TN30 . . . . .179 C2
Pritchard Ct ME7 . . . . .10 C3
Proctor Wlk CT4 . . . . .162 F4
Progress Est The ME15 . . .98 A4
Promenade
  Birchington CT7 . . . . .26 F8
  Deal CT14 . . . . .117 D3
Promenade The ME12 . . . .6 G2
Prospect Ave ME2 . . . . .9 B8
Prospect CI CT8 . . . . .27 E7
Prospect Cotts
  Boughton Lees TN25 . . . . .122 E3
  Harbledown CT2 . . . . .65 E1
Prospect Ct 17 CT11 . . . . .52 E6
Prospect Gdns CT12 . . . . . .50 B7
Prospect Hill CT6 . . . . .23 A5
Prospect Mews CT21 . . . .176 C2
Prospect PI
  7 Broadstairs CT10 . . . . . .30 B4
  Canterbury CT1 . . . . .88 A7
  Dover CT17 . . . . .149 B1
  Eastling ME13 . . . . .81 E6
  Maidstone ME14 . . . . .74 E3
  St Nicholas at Wade CT7 . . .25 E1
Prospect Rd
  Birchington CT7 . . . . .26 F7
  Broadstairs CT10 . . . . .30 B4
  Folkestone CT20 . . . . .177 D3
  Hythe CT21 . . . . .176 C2
  Minster (Thanet) CT12 . . . .50 B6
Prospect Row
  Chatham ME4 . . . . .10 A3
  Gillingham ME7 . . . . .10 A6
Prospect Terr Elham CT4 .144 F4
  18 Ramsgate CT11 . . . . . . .52 E6
Prospect Way TN25 . . . . .158 E5
Provender La ME13,ME9 . .61 A6
Provender Way ME4 . . . . . .75 E5
Providence La ME1 . . . . . . .9 C5
Providence St TN23 . . . . .156 C8
Puckle La CT1 . . . . .88 A6
Pudding La Ash CT3 . . . . . .71 D1
  Maidstone ME14 . . . . .74 F4
Pudding Rd ME8 . . . . .33 F8
Pullman CI CT12 . . . . .52 C8
Pump La
  Gillingham ME7,ME8 . . . . .11 D3

Pump La continued
  Gillingham,Twydall ME8 . . .11 D2
  1 Gillingham ME7 . . . . . . .11 D2
Purbeck Rd ME4 . . . . .9 C2
Purchas Ct CT2 . . . . .66 C4
Purchase La TN26 . . . . . . .154 E8
Purr Wood CT4 . . . . .107 B2
Purser Way ME7 . . . . .10 C7
Puttney Dr ME10 . . . . .37 A8
Pye Alley La CT5 . . . . .43 C3
Pym Ho TN27 . . . . .120 D7
Pynson's Ind Est CT10 . . . .29 C4
Pyott Mews 3 CT1 . . . . . . .67 E1
Pyrus CI ME5 . . . . .54 A8
Pyson's Rd CT10,CT12 . . . .29 D3
Pyson's Road Ind Est
  CT10 . . . . .29 D3

Q

Quain Ct CT20 . . . . .178 C4
Quantock Dr TN24 . . . . . .139 B4
Quantock Gdns CT12 . . . . .29 B3
Quarries The ME17 . . . . . . .97 C4
Quarrington La TN25 . . . .158 B8
Quarry Cotts TN30 . . . . . .189 C3
Quarry Rd Hythe CT21 . . .176 B3
  Maidstone ME15 . . . . .75 A2
Quarry Sq ME14 . . . . .75 A5
Quarry View TN23 . . . . . .155 D7
Quarry Wlk CT21 . . . . . . .177 A3
Quarry Wood TN25 . . . . . .173 A6
Quay Cotts ME9 . . . . .38 E6
Quay La Faversham ME13 . .62 D8
  Sandwich CT13 . . . . .73 A1
Quay The ME9 . . . . .38 E6
Quayside ME4 . . . . .10 B8
Queen Anne Rd ME14 . . . .75 B4
Queen Bertha Rd CT11 . . .52 E6
Queen Bertha's Ave CT7 . .27 C8
Queen Elizabeth Ave CT9 . .8 D1
Queen Elizabeth Rd
  CT16 . . . . .166 F8
Queen Elizabeth Sq
  ME15 . . . . .97 D6
Queen Elizabeth the Queen
  Mother Hospl CT9 . . . . . .28 E7
Queen Elizabeth's Sch
  ME13 . . . . .62 D8
Queen Mother Ct The ME1 9 B4
Queen St Ashford TN23 . .139 B2
  Chatham ME4 . . . . .10 A4
  Deal CT14 . . . . .117 D6
  Dover CT16,CT17 . . . . . . .166 D7
  Folkestone CT20 . . . . .178 E5
  Herne Bay CT6 . . . . .22 F5
  Margate CT9 . . . . .7 I2
  Ramsgate CT11 . . . . .52 E6
  Rochester ME1 . . . . .9 C4
Queen Victoria
  Meml Hospl CT6 . . . . . . .23 B4
Queen's Ave
  Birchington CT7 . . . . .26 D7
  Broadstairs CT10 . . . . .30 B6
  Maidstone ME16 . . . . .74 D5
  Margate CT9 . . . . .7 I1
  Ramsgate CT12 . . . . .29 B1
Queen's Ct CT6 . . . . .23 A4
Queen's Gate Rd CT11 . . .52 C8
Queen's Gdns CT16,CT17 166 D8
Queen's Lea CT15 . . . . . .164 E5
Queen's Prom CT9 . . . . . . .8 B3
Queen's Rd Ash CT3 . . . . .71 D2
  Ashford TN24 . . . . .140 A1
  Broadstairs CT10 . . . . .30 B4
  Chatham ME5 . . . . .10 D1
  Faversham ME13 . . . . .62 D7
  Gillingham ME7 . . . . .10 C4
  Littlestone-on-S TN28 . . . .200 D6
  Lydd TN29 . . . . .203 C6
  Maidstone ME16 . . . . .74 C4
  Ramsgate CT11 . . . . .52 F7
  Westgate-on-S CT8 . . . . . . .27 F8
Queen's Rise CT14 . . . . . .133 F5
Queen's Way ME12 . . . . . . .3 A8
Queenborough Dr ME12 . . .4 B7
Queenborough Fst Sch
  ME11 . . . . .3 B5
Queenborough Rd
  Halfway Houses ME12 . . . . .3 C6
  Queenborough ME12 . . . . . .3 C4
Queenborough Sta ME11 . .3 A5
Queendown Ave ME8 . . . . .33 D5
Queendown Rd CT7 . . . . . .28 A3
Queens Ave
  Canterbury CT2 . . . . .66 E1
  Dover CT17 . . . . .166 A7
  Herne Bay CT6 . . . . .23 D5
  Hythe CT21 . . . . .177 B6
Queens Ct Ashford TN24 . .139 C3
  Hythe CT21 . . . . .176 B1
  Margate CT9 . . . . .8 A3
Queens Gdns
  Broadstairs CT10 . . . . .30 B3
  Herne Bay CT6 . . . . .22 F5
Queens Ho ME16 . . . . .74 B5
Queens Mews CT14 . . . . .117 D6
Queens Par
  12 Faversham ME13 . . . . . .62 D7
  Margate CT9 . . . . .8 A3
Queens Rd Ashford TN24 139 C3
  Aylesham CT3 . . . . .112 F5
  Minster (Sheppey) ME12 . . .4 D7
  Whitstable CT5 . . . . .21 A2
Queens The CT14 . . . . . . .117 D5
Queens Way ME14 . . . . . . .55 A1
Queensbridge Dr CT6 . . . .22 C4

Queensdown Rd CT14 . . 134 D4
Queensway
Dymchurch TN29 . . . . 186 E2
Lydd TN29 . . . . 203 C6
Queenswood Rd ME20 . . . 53 D7
Quern Rd CT14 . . . . 117 A2
Quern The ME15 . . . . 74 E1
Querns Pl CT1 . . . . 88 B8
Querns Rd CT1 . . . . 88 C8
Quested Rd CT19 . . . . 177 E6
Quested Way ME17 . . . . 100 C6
Quetta Rd CT12 . . . . 28 F1
Quex Park Mus★ CT7 . . . 27 B5
Quex Rd CT8 . . . . 27 F8
Quex View Rd CT7 . . . . . . 27 A5
Quickstep Cl ME10 . . . . . 36 F8
Quickthorn Cres ME5 . . . . 31 E5
Quince Orch TN26 . . . . . 183 A7
Quinion Cl ME5 . . . . 54 A8
Quinnell St ME8 . . . . 11 E1
Quinton Rd ME10 . . . . 36 C7

R

Rabbit Hole CT4 . . . . 129 A7
Radfall Cnr CT5 . . . . 44 C6
Radfall Gate CT5 . . . . 44 C6
Radfall Hill CT5 . . . . 44 D5
Radfall Rd CT5 . . . . 44 D4
Radfall Ride CT5 . . . . 44 C5
Radleigh Gdns ME1 . . . . . . 9 E1
Radley Cl CT10 . . . . 30 A6
Radnor Bridge Rd CT19, CT20 . . . . 178 E5
Radnor Chambers 13 CT20 . . . . 178 D4
Radnor Cl CT6 . . . . 23 B1
Radnor Cliff CT20 . . . . . . 178 A3
Radnor Cliff Cres CT20 . 178 A3
Radnor Park Ave CT19 . 178 C6
Radnor Park Cres CT19 . 178 C5
Radnor Park Gdns CT19 178 C6
Radnor Park Rd CT19 . . 178 C6
Radnor Pk W CT19 . . . . 178 B6
Radnor St 17 CT19 . . . . 178 E5
Raggatt Pl ME15 . . . . 75 B2
Raglan Pl 10 CT10 . . . . . . 30 B4
Ragstone Hollow TN25 . 173 A6
Ragstone Rd ME15 . . . . . 76 A2
Railway Ave CT5 . . . . 20 E1
Railway Cotts ME9 . . . . . 38 D3
Railway Hill CT4 . . . . . . 128 E8
Railway Rd ME12 . . . . 1 C2
Railway St Chatham ME4 . . . 9 F4
Gillingham ME7 . . . . 10 D6
Railway St Ind Pk ME7 . . 10 D6
Railway Terr Margate CT9 . . 7 H1
Queenborough ME11 . . . . 3 A5
Rainham Cl ME15 . . . . 75 A1
Rainham Mark Gram Sch ME8 . . . . 11 D2
Rainham Rd ME5 . . . . 10 C3
Rainham Sch for Girls ME8 . . . . 33 C8
Rainham Sh Ctr ME8 . . . . 33 F8
Rainham Sta ME8 . . . . 11 F1
Raleigh Cl Ashford TN24 . 157 A8
Chatham ME5 . . . . 32 A6
Raleigh Ct 1 CT11 . . . . . . 52 F8
Raleigh Way ME12 . . . . 3 E6
Ram La TN25,TN27 . . . . . 137 C8
Ramillies Cl ME5 . . . . 32 A6
Ramp A CT16 . . . . 166 H8
Ramp B CT16 . . . . 166 H8
Ramp C CT16 . . . . 166 G8
Rampart Rd CT21 . . . . . . 176 B2
Rampion Cl ME14 . . . . 75 E5
Ramsey Cl CT2 . . . . 66 E1
Ramsey Ho 8 CT1 . . . . 87 F7
Ramsgate Maritime Mus★ CT12 . . . . 52 E6
Ramsgate Model Village★ CT12 . . . . 52 D5
Ramsgate Motor Mus★ CT12 . . . . 52 D5
Ramsgate Rd
Broadstairs CT10 . . . . 30 B4
Broadstairs,Dumpton CT10, CT11 . . . . 29 F2
Margate CT10,CT9 . . . . 29 A6
Sandwich CT13 . . . . 73 A7
Ramsgate Sch The CT12 . 29 A2
Ramsgate Sta CT12 . . . . . 52 C8
Ramstone Cl TN25 . . . . . 158 E5
Rancorn Rd CT9 . . . . 7 G1
Randall Rd ME4 . . . . 9 E1
Randall St ME14 . . . . 74 F6
Randalls Row ME15 . . . . . 96 F5
Randle Way ME9 . . . . 37 E2
Randolph Cl CT1 . . . . 88 A7
Randolph Ct CT9 . . . . 7 C1
Randolph Gdns TN24 . . . 139 E5
Randolph Ho
13 Folkestone CT20 . . . . . 178 E5
Gillingham ME7 . . . . 10 C5
Randolph Rd Dover CT17 149 B1
Gillingham ME7 . . . . 10 C5
Randolph Sq CT9 . . . . 7 J3
Ranelagh Gdns 1 CT10 . . 29 E5
Ranelagh Gr CT10 . . . . 29 E5
Ranelagh Rd Deal CT14 . 117 D5
Sheerness ME12 . . . . 1 D2
Range Rd Eastchurch ME12 . 5 D1
Hythe CT21 . . . . 176 B1
Range Road Ind Est CT21 . . . . 176 B1
Ransley Gn TN26 . . . . . . 183 F8
Ransome Way CT7 . . . . . . 26 F6
Raspberry Hill La ME9 . . . 14 D6
Ratling Rd CT3 . . . . 112 F7
Rattington St CT4 . . . . 86 E2
Ravelin Ho ME12 . . . . 1 D2
Ravenlea Rd CT20 . . . . . 178 A5
Ravens Dane Cl ME15 . . . 76 A1
Ravensbourne Ave CT6 . . 23 B3
Ravenscourt Rd
Deal CT14 . . . . 117 C5
Rough Common CT2 . . . . . . 66 B3
Ravenswood Ave ME2 . . . . 9 B8
Rawdon Rd
Maidstone ME15 . . . . 75 A3
Ramsgate CT11 . . . . 52 C6
Rawling St ME9 . . . . 58 F3
Rayham Rd CT5 . . . . 44 A8
Rayleigh Cl ME16 . . . . 74 D7
Rayleigh Ho 2 ME15 . . . . 97 D8
Raymer Rd ME14 . . . . 75 B8
Raymond Ave CT1 . . . . 88 A6
Raymond Fuller Way TN24 . . . . 139 E4
Raymoor Ave TN29 . . . . . 195 A4
Rayners Hill ME17 . . . . . 102 C5
Reach Cl CT15 . . . . 150 F5
Reach Meadow CT15 . . . 151 A6
Reach Rd Lympne CT21 . 174 D2
St Margaret's at Cliffe CT15 . . . . 150 F5
Reachfields CT21 . . . . . . 176 A1
Reading Cl CT14 . . . . 117 B1
Reading House 4 ME15 . 97 F5
Reading Rd CT17 . . . . . . 165 F7
Reading St
Broadstairs CT10 . . . . 29 F8
Tenterden TN30 . . . . 180 C2
Reading Street Rd CT10, CT9 . . . . 29 E8
Readscroft Rd ME8 . . . . . 33 D5
Rebecca Ct 6 CT9 . . . . 8 B2
Recreation Cl ME14 . . . . . 75 B6
Recreation Ground Rd TN30 . . . . 179 B7
Recreation Way ME10 . . . . 14 F1
Rectory Bglws TN26 . . . . 169 F8
Rectory Cl TN26 . . . . 169 A2
Rectory Gdns CT5 . . . . 21 D2
Rectory Grange ME1 . . . . . 9 C2
Rectory La Barham CT4 . 112 A2
Harrietsham ME17 . . . . . . 100 E5
Hythe CT21 . . . . 176 B5
Lyminge CT18 . . . . 161 C6
Maidstone ME16 . . . . 74 A1
Rectory Rd
Broadstairs CT10 . . . . 30 B5
Deal CT14 . . . . 116 F4
Sittingbourne ME10 . . . . 37 B3
St Mary in the Marsh TN29 194 B4
Rectory Way TN24 . . . . . 139 C5
Rectory Wlk TN26 . . . . . 183 A7
Reculver Ave CT7 . . . . 26 E8
Reculver CE Prim Sch CT6 . . . . 24 A4
Reculver Cl CT6 . . . . 23 F5
Reculver Ctry Pk★ CT6 . . 24 B6
Reculver Dr CT6 . . . . 23 E5
Reculver La CT6 . . . . 24 B6
Reculver Rd CT6 . . . . 23 D5
Reculver Wlk ME15 . . . . . . 97 F7
Reculvers Rd CT8 . . . . 27 F7
Red Lion Ct 6 CT21 . . . . 176 B2
Red Lion La 5 CT5 . . . . . . 20 D2
Red Lion Sq 7 CT21 . . . . 176 B2
Red Rd CT2 . . . . 64 D5
Red Robin Cotts ME9 . . . . 35 B6
Red Tree Orch TN23 . . . . 155 E7
Redan Pl ME12 . . . . 1 E2
Redberry Rd TN23 . . . . . . 156 B5
Redbridge Cl ME5 . . . . 32 C4
Redbrook St TN26 . . . . . 168 D5
Redbrooks Way CT21 . . . 175 F2
Redcliffe La ME14 . . . . 75 B7
Redcot La CT2 . . . . 68 B7
Redfern Ave ME7 . . . . 10 E5
Redgates CT6 . . . . 23 A5
Redhill Rd CT8 . . . . 27 E8
Redhouse La CT4 . . . . . . 109 D6
Redhouse Wall CT14 . . . . . 95 B1
Redington TN24 . . . . 139 C3
Redland Shaw ME4 . . . . 9 E1
Redlands Ct CT17 . . . . . . 148 E4
Redmill Cl CT20 . . . . 177 E5
Redoubt Way TN29 . . . . 187 B4
Redruth Manor 3 ME7 . . . 10 C6
Redsells Cl ME15 . . . . 76 A1
Redsull Ave CT14 . . . . . . 117 A3
Redvers Cotts CT16 . . . . 148 E5
Redvers Rd ME4 . . . . 10 A2
Redwing Rd ME5 . . . . 32 B7
Redwood Cl
Canterbury CT2 . . . . 66 E2
Chatham ME5 . . . . 32 B2
Redyear Cotts TN24 . . . . 140 A1
Redyear Ct TN24 . . . . 140 A1
Reed Ave CT1 . . . . 67 D3
Reed Cres TN23 . . . . 156 C3
Reedland Cres ME13 . . . . . 62 C8
Reedmace Cl TN23 . . . . . 155 D8
Reeds Cl CT6 . . . . 23 C4
Reeves Alley 1 CT5 . . . . . 20 D1
Reeves Pas 7 ME13 . . . . . 62 C7
Reeves Way CT5 . . . . 21 C2
Reform Rd ME4 . . . . 10 B2
Regency Cl
Gillingham ME8 . . . . 33 C3
Sheerness ME12 . . . . 1 B3
Whitstable CT5 . . . . 43 F7
Regency Ct ME10 . . . . 36 D4
Regency Pl CT1 . . . . 67 B2
Regency Villas CT4 . . . . . 129 C5
Regent Dr ME15 . . . . 97 A8
Regent Rd ME7 . . . . 10 C4
Regent St CT5 . . . . 20 D2
Regents Pl TN23 . . . . 139 B2
Regents Wlk CT6 . . . . 23 D5
Reginald Rd ME16 . . . . 74 E3
Regis Cres ME10 . . . . 36 F7
Regis Manor Com Prim Sch ME10 . . . 36 E7
Regulbium Roman Fort & Reculver Towers★ CT6 . 24 D7
Reinden Gr ME15 . . . . 75 F1
Remston Mews 12 CT1 . . . 67 B2
Renault Cl CT6 . . . . 22 A4
Rendezvous St CT20 . . . 178 D5
Rendezvous The CT9 . . . . . . 7 I3
Renown Rd ME5 . . . . 32 C2
Rentain Rd CT4 . . . . 86 D2
Repton Cl CT10 . . . . 29 F6
Repton Manor Rd TN23 139 A3
Repton Way ME5 . . . . 31 F4
Reservoir Rd CT5 . . . . 20 E2
Resolution Cl ME5 . . . . . . 32 A6
Rest Harrow ME13 . . . . 83 C5
Restharrow Rd ME14 . . . . 75 E4
Retreat The
Birchington CT7 . . . . 27 B8
Doddington ME9 . . . . 80 D7
Ramsgate CT12 . . . . 52 B8
Rettendon Dr ME10 . . . . . 36 F8
Revenge Rd ME5 . . . . 54 C8
Reynolds Cl CT6 . . . . 23 B4
Reynolds La CT3 . . . . 24 D3
Rhee Wall TN26 . . . . 190 D7
Rheims Ct CT2 . . . . 66 D1
Rheims Way CT1,CT2 . . . . 87 E8
Rhodaus Cl CT1 . . . . 87 F7
Rhodaus Ho CT1 . . . . 87 F7
Rhodaus Town CT1 . . . . . . 87 F7
Rhode St ME4 . . . . 10 A4
Rhodes Gdns CT10 . . . . . . 30 A6
Rhodes Ho 5 ME5 . . . . 10 C2
Rhodewood Cl ME15 . . . . . 76 A1
Richard Ct 7 CT9 . . . . 8 B2
Richard St Chatham ME4 . . . 9 F4
Rochester ME1 . . . . 9 C3
Richardson Way CT12 . . . 51 D5
Richborough Castle & Mus★ CT13 . . . . 72 E5
Richborough Rd CT8 . . . . 27 F7
Richbourgh Rd CT13 . . . . 72 E3
Richdore Rd CT4 . . . . . . 125 C6
Richmond Ave CT9 . . . . 8 B1
Richmond Cl ME5 . . . . 32 B4
Richmond Ct CT16 . . . . . 149 D1
Richmond Cty Inf Sch ME7 . . . . 10 C6
Richmond Dr
Herne Bay CT6 . . . . 23 E5
New Romney TN28 . . . . . . 200 C8
Sittingbourne ME10 . . . . 36 E7
Richmond First Sch ME12 . 1 E2
Richmond Gdns CT2 . . . . 66 C2
Richmond Rd
Gillingham ME7 . . . . 10 C7
Ramsgate CT11 . . . . 52 D6
Whitstable CT5 . . . . 21 B1
Richmond St
Folkestone CT19 . . . . 177 D6
Herne Bay CT6 . . . . 22 F5
Sheerness ME12 . . . . 1 E2
Richmond Way ME15 . . . . 97 A8
Riddles Rd ME10,ME9 . . . . 36 C3
Ridge Meadow Cty Prim Sch ME5 . . . . . . 31 F6
Ridge The TN24 . . . . 139 E6
Ridgeway Lympne CT21 . . 175 A3
Whitstable CT5 . . . . 21 C1
Ridgeway Cliff CT6 . . . . . . 22 C5
Ridgeway Rd CT6 . . . . 46 A7
Ridgeway Terr TN25 . . . . 158 C5
Ridgeway The
Boughton Street ME13 . . . . 64 A3
Broadstairs CT10 . . . . 29 F3
Chatham ME4 . . . . 31 E7
Gillingham ME7 . . . . 10 C7
Margate CT9 . . . . 8 B1
River CT17 . . . . 148 E2
Smeeth TN25 . . . . 158 B5
Ridgeway Wlk CT6 . . . . . . 46 A7
Ridgway ME16 . . . . 74 B2
Ridham Ave ME10 . . . . 15 A1
Riding Hill TN24 . . . . 139 C6
Ridings The
7 Canterbury CT1 . . . . 67 B1
Margate CT9 . . . . 8 F3
Whitstable CT5 . . . . 21 D1
Ridlands CT1 . . . . 88 A5
Ridley Cl CT6 . . . . 46 A8
Ridley Rd ME1 . . . . 9 B4
Rigden Rd TN23 . . . . 156 B7
Rigden's Ct 7 ME10 . . . . . 36 E5
Rigshill Rd ME13 . . . . . . 103 B6
Riley Ave CT6 . . . . 21 F4
Ring Wall CT14 . . . . 94 E2
Ringlestone Cres ME14 . . . 74 F8
Ringlestone Rd ME17 . . . . 78 D4
Ringold Ave CT12 . . . . 52 A8
Ringsloe Ct CT7 . . . . 26 D8
Ringwood Cl
Canterbury CT2 . . . . 66 E3
Gillingham ME8 . . . . 33 D8
Ringwood Rd ME15 . . . . . 97 C8
Ringwould Rd
Kingsdown CT14 . . . . 134 B5
Ringwould Rd *continued*
Ringwould CT14,CT15 . . . 133 D4
Ripley Rd TN24 . . . . 157 A8
Ripon Cl ME8 . . . . 11 D3
Ripper's Cross TN26 . . . 137 D4
Ripple Cross CT14 . . . . . 133 F6
Ripple Rd CT14 . . . . 133 F7
Ripple Sch The CT14 . . . 133 D8
Ripple Vale Sch CT14 . . . 133 E8
Risborough La CT19, CT20 . . . . 177 D5
Risborough Way CT20 . . 177 E6
Risdon Cl CT2 . . . . 67 F6
Rise The Ashford TN23 . . . 155 E7
Borden ME9 . . . . 36 B2
Gillingham,Brompton ME4 . . 10 A7
Gillingham,Hempstead ME7 . 33 A3
Halfway Houses ME12 . . . . . . 3 C5
Kingsdown CT14 . . . . 134 D5
Rochester ME1 . . . . 9 D3
St Margaret's at Cliffe CT15 . . . . 151 B6
Rising Rd TN23 . . . . 139 A1
River Bank Cl 8 ME15 . . . 75 B4
River Cl ME15 . . . . 96 A7
River Ct Chartham CT4 . . . . 86 D3
River CT17 . . . . 148 F2
River Dale CT17 . . . . 148 F3
River Dr CT17 . . . . 148 F2
River Mdw CT17 . . . . 148 F3
River Prim Sch CT17 . . . 148 E3
River St 6 Gillingham ME7 10 A6
River CT17 . . . . 148 E3
River View Gillingham ME8 11 D3
Maidstone ME15 . . . . 74 F2
Rushenden ME11 . . . . 2 F3
Sturry CT2 . . . . 67 F7
River View Cl 6 ME4 . . . . . 9 F3
Riverdale Rd CT1 . . . . 67 B2
Riverhead Cl
Maidstone ME16 . . . . 74 D6
Margate CT9 . . . . 8 B1
Sittingbourne ME10 . . . . . . 36 C3
Rivers Rd ME9 . . . . 38 D2
Rivers Wlk ME17 . . . . 101 C5
Riversdale Rd
Ashford TN23 . . . . 156 C8
Ramsgate CT12 . . . . 29 B1
Riverside CT4 . . . . 86 C3
Riverside Bsns Pk TN24 139 D2
Riverside Cl Bridge CT4 . . 89 A1
Kingsnorth TN23 . . . . 156 A4
Riverside Ct 3 CT2 . . . . . . 66 F1
Riverside Ctry Pk★ ME7 . 11 D5
Riverside Ind Est CT21 . 175 B1
Riverside Mews CT4 . . . . . 89 A1
Riverside Rd CT13 . . . . . . 51 A1
Riverside Ret Pk CT1 . . . . 87 D6
Riverside Sch TN23 . . . . 138 F1
Riverview TN23 . . . . 138 E1
Riviera Ct 6 CT20 . . . . . 177 E3
Riviera Rd CT20 . . . . 178 A3
Riviera The CT20 . . . . . . 177 F3
Roach St ME2 . . . . 9 A7
Road of Remembrance CT20 . . . . 178 D4
Robert Napier Sch The ME7 . . . . 10 E3
Robert St CT14 . . . . 117 D7
Roberts Cl ME10 . . . . 36 D7
Roberts Rd
Gillingham ME8 . . . . 33 E8
Greatstone-on-S TN28 . . . 200 E1
Whitstable CT5 . . . . 42 F6
Robeshaw ME9 . . . . 58 E2
Robin Ct ME1 . . . . 9 D4
Robin Hood La
Chatham ME5 . . . . 31 D1
Lydd TN29 . . . . 203 C5
Robin Hood Lane (Lower) ME5 . . . . 31 F2
Robin Hood Lane (Upper) ME5 . . . . 31 E1
Robin House 5 ME16 . . . . 74 E4
Robin La TN29 . . . . 203 C6
Robin's Cl CT21 . . . . 187 C8
Robina Ct CT9 . . . . 8 D3
Robins Ave ME17 . . . . . . 101 C5
Robins Cl ME17 . . . . 101 C4
Robins Ct ME14 . . . . 75 B7
Robson's Yd CT17 . . . . . 166 C8
Robus Cl CT18 . . . . 161 C7
Robus Terr CT18 . . . . 161 C7
Robyn Cotts TN26 . . . . . 167 E8
Rochester Airport ME1, ME5 . . . . 31 C6
Rochester Ave
Canterbury CT1 . . . . 88 B7
Rochester ME1 . . . . 9 C4
Rochester Castle★ ME1 . . . 9 C6
Rochester Cath★ ME1 . . . 9 C6
Rochester Ct ME2 . . . . 9 E8
Rochester Gate ME1 . . . . . 9 D5
Rochester Gram Sch for Girls ME1 . . . . 9 C2
Rochester Ho 1 ME15 . . . 97 D7
Rochester Mathematical Sch The ME1 . . . . 9 C1
Rochester Rd
Burham ME1 . . . . 53 A8
Chatham ME1,ME5 . . . . 31 C4
Pratling Street ME20 . . . . . 53 B4
Rochester St ME4 . . . . 9 E3
Rochester Sta ME1 . . . . 9 D5
Rock Ave ME7 . . . . 10 C3
Rock Hill Rd TN27 . . . . . 118 E2
Rock Rd Maidstone ME14 . 75 A6
Sittingbourne ME10 . . . . 36 E4
Rockingham Pl CT6 . . . . . . 23 B2
Rockstone Way CT12 . . . . . 29 A1
Rocky Bourne Rd TN25 . 172 D5
Rocky Hill ME16 . . . . 74 E4
Rocky Hill Terr 2 ME16 . . 74 E4
Rodmer Cl ME12 . . . . 4 C8
Rodmersham Gn ME9 . . . . 59 B7
Rodmersham Sch ME9 . . . 59 B7
Rodney St CT11 . . . . 52 D6
Roebuck Rd
Faversham ME13 . . . . 62 A7
Rochester ME1 . . . . 9 C5
Roentgen Ho ME10 . . . . . . 36 D5
Roethorne Gdns TN30 . . 179 B8
Roffen Rd ME1 . . . . 9 C2
Rogersmead TN30 . . . . . . 179 A7
Rokesley Rd CT16 . . . . . . 149 B5
Rolfe La TN28 . . . . 200 B7
Roll's Ave ME12 . . . . 5 C1
Rolvenden Ave ME8 . . . . . 11 C3
Rolvenden Dr ME10 . . . . . 36 B5
Roly Eckhoff Ho CT16 . . . 149 B3
Roman Cl Chatham ME5 . . . 31 D1
Deal CT14 . . . . 117 B6
Roman Hts ME14 . . . . 75 C6
Roman Rd
East Studdal CT15 . . . . . . 132 C5
Faversham ME13 . . . . 62 C7
Ramsgate CT12 . . . . 29 C2
Whitfield CT15 . . . . 149 D8
Roman Sq ME10 . . . . 36 F3
Roman Way
Elvington CT15 . . . . 114 B2
Folkestone CT19 . . . . 177 C6
Kingsnorth TN23 . . . . 156 C4
St Margaret's at Cliffe CT15 . . . . 150 F5
Romany Ct ME5 . . . . 10 D1
Romany Rd ME8 . . . . 11 C2
Romden Rd
Biddenden Green TN27 . . . 135 D1
Biddenden Green,Haffenden Quarter TN27 . . . . 152 B8
Rome House Cnr TN28 . 200 A6
Rome Rd TN28 . . . . 200 A6
Rome Terr ME4 . . . . 9 F4
Romilly Gdns CT12 . . . . . . 29 C2
Romney Ave CT20 . . . . . . 177 F5
Romney Cl
4 Birchington CT7 . . . . 27 A7
Maidstone ME14 . . . . 76 A3
Romney Ct ME10 . . . . 36 E5
Romney Marsh Rd TN23, TN24 . . . . 156 B6
Romney Pl ME15 . . . . 75 A4
Romney Rd
Ashford TN24 . . . . 139 E1
Chatham ME5 . . . . 32 B5
Hamstreet TN26 . . . . 183 A7
New Romney TN29 . . . . . . 199 E3
Romney Sands Holiday Village★ TN28 . . . . 204 D8
Romney Sands Sta★ TN28 . . . . 204 E8
Romney Way CT21 . . . . . 175 F1
Romney, Hythe & Dymchurch Rly★ CT21 176 A2
Romsey Cl TN24 . . . . 140 A2
Romulus Gdns TN23 . . . . 155 F4
Ronalds Ct 6 ME10 . . . . . . 37 A4
Rook La ME9 . . . . 35 F6
Rookery Cl Ashford TN24 139 D7
Bredgar ME9 . . . . 58 A6
Rookston Cnr CT3 . . . . 48 D1
Roonagh Ct ME10 . . . . 36 E2
Roosevelt Ave ME5 . . . . . . 32 A8
Roosevelt Rd CT16 . . . . . 149 B3
Rope Walk Mews CT13 . . . 93 F8
Rope Wlk ME4 . . . . 9 F5
Ropemakers Ct ME4 . . . . . 10 A1
Roper Cl Canterbury CT2 . . 66 E1
Gillingham ME8 . . . . 33 C3
Roper Rd Canterbury CT2 . 66 E1
Teynham ME9 . . . . 38 D3
Rose Acre Rd CT3 . . . . 89 F7
Rose Cotts Hythe CT21 . . 176 B4
Lenham Heath ME17 . . . . . 119 B8
Rose Ct ME17 . . . . 96 D1
Rose Gdns Birchington CT7 26 F6
Eythorne CT15 . . . . 131 D7
Herne Bay CT6 . . . . 23 C4
Minster (Thanet) CT12 . . . . 50 B6
Rose Hill
9 Ramsgate CT11 . . . . 52 E6
Wittersham TN30 . . . . 189 B5
Rose La
Bishopsbourne CT4 . . . . . . 111 C6
Canterbury CT1 . . . . 87 F8
Lenham Heath ME17 . . . . . 119 B8
Rose St Rochester ME1 . . . . 9 D3
Sheerness ME12 . . . . 1 C2
Rose Street Sch ME12 . . . . 1 C2
Rose Terr ME13 . . . . 62 D5
Rose Wlk CT18 . . . . 163 A4
Rose Yd ME14 . . . . 75 A4
Roseacre Cl CT2 . . . . 66 E1
Roseacre Ct CT9 . . . . 8 E2
Roseacre Gdns ME14 . . . . 76 A3
Roseacre Jun Sch ME14 . 76 A4
Roseacre La ME14 . . . . . . 76 A4
Rosebery Ave
Herne Bay CT6 . . . . 23 E5
Ramsgate CT11 . . . . 29 F1
Rosebery Cl ME10 . . . . 37 D4

Rosebery Rd Chatham ME4 ...9 E2
Gillingham ME7 ...10 D7
Rosedale Rd CT9 ...8 A1
Roseholme ME16 ...74 D2
Roselands CT14 ...117 C1
Roselands Gdns CT2 ...66 D2
Roselawn Gdns 3 CT9 ...28 B8
Roselea Ave CT6 ...22 F3
Roseleigh Ave ME16 ...74 C5
Roseleigh Rd ME10 ...36 D2
Rosemary Ave
Broadstairs CT10 ...30 A3
Halfway Houses ME12 ...3 D6
Rosemary Cl 4 ME5 ...31 F4
Rosemary Cnr TN29 ...197 D8
Rosemary Ct ME1 ...9 D4
Rosemary Gdns
Broadstairs CT10 ...29 F2
Whitstable CT5 ...44 A8
Rosemary La 16 CT1 ...87 F8
Rosemary Rd ME15 ...76 A3
Rosemount Cl ME15 ...96 F4
Rosetower Ct CT10 ...29 F8
Rosiers Ct 1 CT2 ...66 E1
Ross Gdns CT2 ...66 B3
Ross St ME1 ...9 D4
Ross Way CT20 ...177 E5
Rossendale Ct 10 CT20 ...178 E6
Rossendale Gdns 8
CT20 ...178 E6
Rossendale Rd CT20 ...178 E6
Rossetti Ct CT7 ...26 F7
Rossetti Rd CT7 ...26 F8
Rossland Rd CT12 ...52 A8
Rosslyn Gn ME16 ...74 B5
Rothbrook Dr TN24 ...139 C7
Rother Vale ME5 ...32 C3
Rothley Cl TN30 ...179 B8
Rothsay Ct CT11 ...29 F1
Rough Common Rd CT2 ...66 B3
Round Wood Cl ME5 ...32 A1
Roundel Cl ME9 ...38 D2
Roundel The ME10 ...36 F2
Roundwell ME14 ...76 D3
Rover Rd ME5 ...32 B2
Row The Ash CT3 ...71 E5
Elham CT4 ...144 F5
Ruckinge TN26 ...183 F8
Rowan Cl Ashford TN23 ...138 E2
Staple CT3 ...92 A6
Sturry CT2 ...67 F6
Rowan Ct CT10 ...30 A5
Rowan Ho 4 ME5 ...31 F5
Rowan Lea ME5 ...10 B1
Rowan Wlk ME4 ...9 E3
Rowans The ME12 ...4 B7
Rowbrocke Cl ME8 ...33 D3
Rowe Cl CT9 ...28 F7
Rowena Rd CT8 ...7 C1
Rowetts Way ME12 ...5 D3
Rowland Ave ME7 ...10 E2
Rowland Cl ME7 ...10 E1
Rowland Cres CT6 ...23 E5
Rowland Dr CT6 ...22 C2
Roxburgh Rd CT8 ...7 D1
Royal Ave CT5 ...43 C5
Royal Cinque Ports
Golf Links CT13,CT14 ...95 B4
Royal Cl CT10 ...29 F4
Royal Cres Margate CT9 ...7 H2
Ramsgate CT11 ...52 D5
Royal Eagle Cl ME2 ...9 E7
Royal Engineers Mus*
ME7 ...10 B6
Royal Engineers' Rd
ME14 ...74 F7
Royal Espl Margate CT9 ...7 F1
Ramsgate CT11 ...52 C5
Royal Military Ave
CT20 ...177 D5
Royal Military Rd
Aldington TN25 ...173 D1
Hythe CT21 ...175 D1
Royal Mus* CT1 ...87 F8
Royal Par CT11 ...52 E6
Royal Rd Ramsgate CT11 ...52 D6
Sheerness ME12 ...1 D2
Royal Sch
for Deaf Children CT9 ...7 J2
Royal Sovereign Ave
ME4 ...10 B7
Royal Star Arc 5 ME14 ...74 F4
Royal Victoria Hospl
CT19 ...178 C6
Royal Victoria Pl 5
CT16 ...166 D8
Royds Rd TN24 ...156 D6
Royston Gdns CT15 ...150 F6
Royston Rd ME15 ...76 A3
Roystons Cl ME8 ...11 F2
Royton Ave ME17 ...101 D5
Rubery Dro CT3 ...72 C7
Ruckinge Cnr TN26 ...183 F8
Ruckinge Rd TN26 ...183 A7
Ruckinge Way ME8 ...11 C3
Rudge Cl ME5 ...32 C4
Rugby Cl Broadstairs CT10 ...29 F5
Chatham ME5 ...31 F4
Rugby Gdns TN23 ...156 C8
Rugby Rd CT17 ...166 A6
Ruins Barn Rd ME10,ME9 ...58 D6
Rule Ct ME12 ...3 B8
Rumfields Rd CT10 ...29 D4
Rumstead La ME17,ME9 ...56 D4
Rumstead Rd ME9 ...56 E4
Rumwood Ct ME17 ...98 B5
Runcie Ho 6 CT1 ...87 F7
Runcie Pl CT2 ...66 D1
Runham La ME17 ...100 E3
Running Horse Rndbt
The ME14 ...53 E1
Runnymede Gdns ME15 ...97 A8
Runnymede Mews ME13 ...62 C7
Rush Cl Chatham ME5 ...32 A3
Dymchurch TN29 ...195 B6
Rusham Rd CT3 ...70 C1
Rushenden Ct ME11 ...2 F3
Rushenden Rd ME11 ...3 A4
Rushmead Cl CT2 ...66 D2
Rushmead Dr ME15 ...97 A7
Russel Dr CT5 ...21 D3
Russell Cl ME10 ...36 C3
Russell Ct ME4 ...10 B3
Russell Pl ME13 ...40 B3
Russell Rd
1 Folkestone CT19 ...178 D6
Kit's Coty ME20 ...53 D7
Russell St Dover CT16 ...166 E7
Sheerness ME12 ...1 C2
Russells Ave ME8 ...34 A8
Russet Ave ME13 ...62 E5
Russet Ct ME17 ...96 C3
Russet Rd CT1 ...88 C8
Russets The
Maidstone ME16 ...74 B5
Whitstable CT5 ...21 D1
Ruth House ME16 ...74 E5
Rutherford Coll CT2 ...66 E4
Rutherford Rd TN24 ...139 B5
Rutland Ave CT9 ...8 C2
Rutland Cl CT1 ...88 D7
Rutland Gdns
Birchington CT7 ...26 F7
Margate CT9 ...8 C2
Rutland Ho 3 CT9 ...8 B2
Rutland Pl ME8 ...33 C3
Rutland Rd CT16 ...149 B3
Rutland Way ME15 ...97 E8
Ryan Dr ME15 ...76 A2
Rycaut Cl ME8 ...33 D3
Rydal Ave CT11 ...52 B7
Ryde Cl ME5 ...32 B8
Ryde St CT2 ...66 E1
Ryder's Ave CT8 ...27 D8
Rye Ct TN23 ...155 D7
Rye Rd Brookland TN29 ...197 D8
Wittersham TN30 ...189 A2
Rye Wlk CT6 ...23 C2
Ryecault Cl 4 ME16 ...74 E3
Ryegrass Cl ME5 ...32 C6
Ryland Ct 4 CT20 ...178 E5
Ryland Pl 5 CT20 ...178 E5
Rylands Rd TN24 ...139 D5
Rype Cl TN29 ...203 C5
Ryswick Mews TN28 ...200 C8

S

Sabre Ct ME7 ...11 A1
Sackett's Gap CT9 ...8 C3
Sacketts Hill CT10 ...29 C6
Sackville Cl TN26 ...138 A7
Sackville Cres TN23 ...139 A2
Saddler's Wall La TN29 ...191 B1
Saddlers Cl ME14 ...75 E5
Saddlers Hill CT3 ...91 D2
Saddlers Mews CT5 ...21 D1
Saddlers Way TN23 ...156 B5
Saddleton Gr CT5 ...43 D8
Saddleton Rd CT5 ...43 D8
Sadlers Cl ME5 ...31 D2
Saffron Way
1 Chatham ME5 ...31 F5
Sittingbourne ME10 ...36 F7
Saffron's Pl 12 CT20 ...178 E5
Sage Rd ME1 ...9 B3
Sailfield Ct ME4 ...9 F7
Sailmakers Ct 5 ME4 ...10 B2
St Agnes Gdns ME12 ...1 D1
St Alban's Rd CT3 ...46 E1
St Albans Cl ME7 ...10 E7
St Alphege CE Inf Sch
CT5 ...20 D1
St Alphege Cl CT5 ...43 B7
St Alphege La 8 CT1 ...66 F1
St Alphege Rd 4 CT16 ...149 C1
St Ambrose Gn TN25 ...123 E2
St Andrew Rd ME7 ...10 D7
St Andrew Terr CT17 ...149 A2
St Andrew's Cl
Maidstone ME16 ...74 A2
Whitstable CT5 ...43 E7
St Andrew's Gdns CT15 ...130 E5
St Andrew's Lees CT13 ...94 A8
St Andrew's Rd
Deal CT14 ...117 C6
Littlestone-on-S TN28 ...200 E6
Maidstone ME16 ...74 A3
Ramsgate CT11 ...52 F8
St Andrews CT19 ...178 E5
St Andrews Cl
Canterbury CT1 ...87 E7
Folkestone CT19 ...178 B7
Herne Bay CT6 ...23 A4
Margate CT9 ...28 F7
St Andrews Gdns CT17 ...149 B2
St Andrews Way CT14 ...115 A3
St Angela's Sch CT8 ...27 D7
St Ann's Rd
Dymchurch TN29 ...195 B7
Faversham ME13 ...62 B7
St Anne Ct ME16 ...74 E4
St Anne's Ct
1 Dover CT16 ...149 B2
Herne Bay CT6 ...22 E5
St Anne's Dr CT6 ...22 D4
St Anne's Gdns CT9 ...28 F8
St Anne's Rd
Ashford TN23 ...155 F7
Whitstable CT5 ...20 F2
St Anselm's Catholic Sch
CT1 ...88 C5
St Anthony's Sch CT9 ...8 C1
St Anthony's Way CT9 ...8 C1
St Augustine of Canterbury
RC Prim Sch ME8 ...33 D3
St Augustine's Abbey
CT11 ...52 D5
St Augustine's Abbey
(rems of) CT1 ...88 A8
St Augustine's Ave CT9 ...28 F8
St Augustine's Cres CT5 ...21 D3
St Augustine's Ct CT1 ...88 B8
St Augustine's Pk CT11 ...52 C6
St Augustine's
RC Prim Sch CT21 ...176 E2
St Augustine's Rd
Canterbury CT1 ...88 B7
Deal CT14 ...116 F4
Ramsgate CT11 ...52 D5
St Augustines Bsns Pk
CT5 ...21 E3
St Barnabas Cl
Ashford TN23 ...155 F7
Gillingham ME7 ...10 D3
Maidstone ME16 ...74 C8
St Bart's Rd CT13 ...93 F8
St Bartholemews Cl 4
CT17 ...166 C8
St Bartholomew's Hospl
ME1 ...9 E4
St Bartholomew's Hospl
CT13 ...94 A7
St Bartholomew's La 4
ME1 ...9 E4
St Bartholomew's Sch
ME10 ...36 F7
St Bartholomew's Terr 2
ME1 ...9 E4
St Benedict's Lawn CT11 ...52 D5
St Benedicts
RC Prim Sch ME5 ...32 C2
St Benet's Rd CT8 ...27 E7
St Benets Ct TN30 ...179 B8
St Benets Way TN30 ...179 B8
St Catherine's Dr ME13 ...62 D6
St Catherine's Gr CT12 ...28 D1
St Catherine's Hospl
ME1 ...9 D4
St Catherines TN29 ...199 A7
St Catherines Ct CT11 ...29 F1
St Christopher Cl CT9 ...29 D8
St Christopher's Sch CT1 ...88 B6
St Christophers Gn CT10 ...29 F5
St Clare Rd CT14 ...117 C1
St Clement's Ct CT6 ...23 A3
St Clement's Ho ME1 ...9 D5
St Clement's Rd CT8 ...7 C1
St Clements 8 CT13 ...73 A1
St Clements Cl ME12 ...6 D2
St Clements Ct CT10 ...29 E6
St Clements Rd ME12 ...6 E3
St Cosmus Cl TN25 ...105 B1
St Crispin's Com Prim
Inf Sch CT8 ...27 E7
St Crispin's Rd CT8 ...27 E7
St David's Cl
Birchington CT7 ...27 B8
Whitstable CT5 ...43 E8
St David's Rd Deal CT14 ...117 C6
Ramsgate CT11 ...29 F1
St Davids Ave CT17 ...166 A5
St Denys Rd CT18 ...163 B5
St Dunstan's Cl CT2 ...66 E1
St Dunstan's Rd CT9 ...8 A2
St Dunstan's St CT2 ...66 E1
St Dunstan's Terr CT2 ...66 E1
St Dunstans Ct 4 CT2 ...66 E1
St Eanswythe Way 19
CT20 ...178 D5
St Eanswythe's
CE Prim Sch CT20 ...178 D4
St Edmund's RC Sch
CT16 ...149 D2
St Edmund's Rd CT14 ...116 E4
St Edmund's Sch CT2 ...66 C3
St Edmunds Rd CT1 ...87 F8
St Edmunds Way ME8 ...12 B1
St Edward's RC Prim Sch
ME12 ...1 C2
St Ethelbert's RC Prim Sch
CT11 ...52 F8
St Faith's La ME14 ...76 B4
St Faith's St ME14 ...74 F4
St Faiths Sch CT3 ...71 C1
St Francis Cl Deal CT14 ...116 F4
Maidstone ME14 ...75 B7
Margate CT9 ...29 D8
St Francis RC Prim Sch
ME14 ...75 B7
St Francis Rd CT19 ...177 F6
St Francis Sch ME14 ...75 B7
St Francis' RC Sch
ME14 ...75 A5
St Gabriel's Ct 12 CT20 ...178 E6
St George's Ave
Herne Bay CT6 ...22 D4
Sheerness ME12 ...1 C1
St George's Bsns Ctr
TN23 ...138 F2
St George's CE
Foundation Sch CT10 ...29 C5
St George's CE Mid Sch
ME12 ...4 E6
St George's Cl CT5 ...43 E7
St George's Ct ME12 ...3 B8
St George's Lees CT13 ...94 A8
St George's Pass CT14 ...117 D6
St George's Pl
Canterbury CT1 ...88 A8
Hythe CT21 ...187 D8
St George's Rd
Broadstairs CT10 ...30 A4
Deal CT14 ...117 D6
Folkestone CT19 ...177 F6
Gillingham ME7 ...10 C6
Ramsgate CT11 ...52 F8
Sandwich CT13 ...94 A8
St George's Sq
3 Ashford TN24 ...139 B2
Maidstone ME16 ...74 E3
St George's St CT1 ...88 A8
St George's Terr CT6 ...22 E5
St Georges Ave ME12 ...5 D2
St Georges Bsns Pk
ME10 ...37 B4
St Georges Cres CT17 ...166 B5
St Georges Ct CT17 ...149 A2
St Georges La CT1 ...88 A8
St Georges Pl
Sandwich CT13 ...94 B8
St Margaret's at Cliffe
CT15 ...150 F6
St Georges St CT1 ...88 A8
St Giles Cl CT17 ...166 B5
St Giles Rd CT17 ...166 B5
St Giles Wlk CT17 ...166 B5
St Gregory's 9 CT1 ...67 A1
St Gregory's Cl CT14 ...116 F4
St Gregory's
RC Prim Sch CT9 ...28 E8
St Gregory's Rd CT1 ...67 B1
St Helen's Rd ME12 ...1 E1
St Helier's Cl ME16 ...74 B2
St Hilda Rd CT19 ...177 E6
St Hilda's Rd CT21 ...176 B1
St Jacob's Pl CT1 ...87 D6
St James Cl ME12 ...6 E4
St James La 5 CT16 ...166 E7
St James Rd CT14 ...134 D5
St James St CT16 ...166 E7
St James' Ave
Broadstairs CT10 ...29 E5
Ramsgate CT12 ...29 B1
St James' Gdns CT5 ...43 D8
St James' Park Rd CT9 ...28 A8
St James's Terr CT7 ...27 B8
St Jean's Rd CT8 ...27 E7
St John Bsns Ctr The 10
CT9 ...7 J1
St John Fisher
Catholic Sch ME4 ...9 E3
St John Fisher
RC Lower Sch ME4 ...9 F2
St John's Ave
Ramsgate CT12 ...29 A1
Sittingbourne ME10 ...37 B3
St John's CE Inf Sch ME4 ...9 E3
St John's CE Prim Sch
ME14 ...75 E4
St John's Church Rd
CT19 ...178 C6
St John's Cl CT18 ...163 A7
St John's Commandery
(rems of)* CT15 ...146 E4
St John's Cotts 11 CT13 ...72 F1
St John's Ct TN24 ...157 A6
St John's Hospl 6 CT1 ...67 A1
St John's La
Ashford TN23,TN24 ...139 C2
Canterbury CT1 ...87 F8
St John's Pl CT1 ...67 A1
St John's Rd Dover CT17 ...166 C7
Faversham ME13 ...62 D7
Gillingham ME7 ...10 C3
Margate CT9 ...7 J2
New Romney TN28 ...200 A6
Whitstable CT5 ...21 D3
St John's St
Folkestone CT20 ...178 D5
7 Margate CT9 ...7 J2
St John's Way CT18 ...163 A7
St Johns Cres CT2 ...66 D6
St Johns Rd
Elvington CT15 ...114 B2
Hythe CT21 ...176 A3
St Johns Way ME1 ...9 A2
St Joseph's RC Prim Sch
Aylesham CT3 ...113 A5
Broadstairs CT10 ...29 F5
St Julien Ave CT1 ...67 D1
St Katherine Rd ME12 ...3 E7
St Laurence Ave ME16 ...74 C8
St Laurence Cl ME9 ...37 D2
St Laurence Ct CT11 ...52 C7
St Laurence In Thanet
CE Jun Sch CT12 ...52 B8
St Lawrence Ave CT11 ...52 B5
St Lawrence Cl CT1 ...88 B6
St Lawrence Coll CT11 ...52 D8
St Lawrence Coll
(Jun Sch) CT11 ...52 E8
St Lawrence Ct TN28 ...200 A6
St Lawrence Forstal CT1 ...88 B6
St Lawrence Gd (Kent
Cty Cricket Club) CT1 ...88 B6
St Lawrence Ind Est
CT11 ...52 B7
St Lawrence Rd CT1 ...88 B6
St Leonard's Rd CT14 ...117 B4
St Leonards Ave ME4 ...9 F2
St Leonards Ct CT21 ...176 B1
St Leonards Rd
Hythe CT21 ...176 B1
Maidstone ME16 ...74 C8
St Louis Gr CT6 ...22 C4
St Luke's Ave
Maidstone ME14 ...75 B5
Ramsgate CT11 ...52 E8
St Luke's Cl CT8 ...27 E8
St Luke's Rd
Maidstone ME14 ...75 B5
Ramsgate CT11 ...52 E8
St Luke's Wlk CT18 ...162 F4
St Lukes Cl CT5 ...43 E7
St Lukes Ct TN23 ...155 F7
St Magnus Cl CT7 ...27 A8
St Magnus Ct CT8 ...27 A8
St Margaret's at Troy Town
CE Prim Sch ME1 ...9 C4
St Margaret's Banks ME1 ...9 D5
St Margaret's CE Jun Sch
ME8 ...33 E8
St Margaret's Cl CT5 ...43 A6
St Margaret's Inf Sch
ME8 ...33 E8
St Margaret's Mews ME1 ...9 C5
St Margaret's Rd
St Margaret's at Cliffe
CT15 ...151 A5
Westgate-on-S CT8 ...27 E7
St Margaret's St
Canterbury CT1 ...87 F8
Rochester ME1 ...9 C5
St Margaret's-at-Cliffe
Prim Sch CT15 ...151 A6
St Margarets Cl ME16 ...74 B2
St Margarets Ct 1
CT20 ...178 B5
St Margarets Dr
Deal CT14 ...134 B8
Gillingham ME8 ...33 C5
St Margarets Rd CT7 ...27 F3
St Mark's Cl CT20 ...177 D5
St Marks Cl CT5 ...43 E8
St Marks Ho ME7 ...10 C5
St Martin's CE Prim Sch
CT18 ...177 B5
St Martin's Cl
Detling ME14 ...55 A1
Dover CT17 ...166 B5
St Martin's Hill CT1 ...88 C8
St Martin's Hospl CT1 ...88 D8
St Martin's Pl CT1 ...88 B8
St Martin's Rd
Canterbury CT1 ...67 B1
Deal CT14 ...116 F4
Guston CT15 ...149 E4
St Martin's Sch CT17 ...166 A7
St Martin's Terr CT1 ...88 B8
St Martin's View CT6 ...46 A8
St Martins Ave CT1 ...88 B8
St Martins Cl
Canterbury CT1 ...88 B8
Newington ME9 ...35 C7
St Martins Ct CT1 ...88 B8
St Martins Rd
Folkestone CT20 ...177 D6
New Romney TN28 ...200 B6
St Mary Ct 13 ME13 ...62 D7
St Mary of Charity
CE Inf Sch ME13 ...62 D7
St Mary of Charity
CE Jun Sch ME13 ...62 D7
St Mary's Ave Margate CT9 ...8 D1
Margate CT9 ...29 D8
St Mary's CE Prim Sch
Ashford TN23 ...139 A3
Chilham CT4 ...107 B8
Dover CT16 ...166 E8
Folkestone CT19 ...178 F6
St Mary's Church* CT6 ...24 C7
St Mary's Cl Eastry CT13 ...93 C2
Hamstreet TN26 ...183 A8
Nonington CT15 ...113 C5
Woodnesborough CT13 ...93 B6
St Mary's Ct 17 CT1 ...87 F8
St Mary's Cty Prim Sch
ME2 ...9 B7
St Mary's Gdns
Gillingham ME4 ...10 B7
St Mary's Bay TN29 ...195 A5
Upstreet CT3 ...47 E3
St Mary's Gr
Tilmanstone CT14 ...115 A4
Whitstable CT5 ...42 F7
St Mary's Mdw CT3 ...91 A8
St Mary's Pl ME9 ...35 C7
St Mary's RC Prim Sch
Deal CT14 ...116 F3
Gillingham ME7 ...10 D6
Whitstable CT5 ...20 F2
St Mary's Rd
5 Broadstairs CT10 ...30 B4
Deal CT14 ...117 C1
Elham CT4 ...144 F4
Faversham ME13 ...62 D7
Gillingham ME7 ...10 C6
Minster (Thanet) CT12 ...50 B6
Patrixbourne CT4 ...89 B3
Rochester ME2 ...9 B7
St Mary in the Marsh
TN28,TN29 ...194 C5
West Hythe CT21 ...175 B1
St Mary's Row ME12 ...4 A6
St Mary's St CT1 ...87 F8

St Mary's Terr **2** CT20 ..178 E5
St Mary's View ME9 .....35 C7
St Mary's Westbrook Sch
 CT20 ....178 A5
St Marys Cl CT18 ......161 D3
St Marys Dr CT18 ......161 D3
St Marys Gn TN24 ......139 E7
St Marys Mews TN24 ..156 F8
St Matthew's CE Inf Sch
 ME1 ....9 A2
St Matthew's Cl ME9 ....35 C7
St Matthews Dr ME1 .....9 A2
St Mawes CT9 ....7 C1
St Michael's Alley **11**
 CT11 ....52 E6
St Michael's CE Jun Sch
 ME16 ....74 E3
St Michael's CE Prim Sch
 Maidstone ME16 ......74 E3
 St Michaels ME30 ....167 A3
St Michael's Cl
 Chatham ME4 ....9 F3
 5 Sittingbourne ME10 ..36 F4
St Michael's Ct
 6 Folkestone CT20 ..178 E5
 5 Rochester ME2 ......9 B8
St Michael's Pl CT11 ....66 E2
St Michael's RC Prim Sch
 ME4 ....9 F3
St Michael's Rd
 Canterbury CT2 ......66 E2
 Maidstone ME16 ......74 D3
 Sittingbourne ME10 ...37 A4
St Michael's St CT20 ...178 E5
St Michael's Terr TN30 ..167 B3
St Michael's Wlk CT18 ..162 F4
St Michaels Ave CT9 ....29 D8
St Michaels Cl
 Canterbury CT2 ......66 A1
 Pratling Street ME20 ..53 C3
St Mildred's Ave
 Birchington CT7 ....26 E8
 Broadstairs CT10 .....30 A4
 Ramsgate CT11 ....52 B5
St Mildred's Ct **4** TN30 ..179 A7
St Mildred's Gdns CT8,CT9 **7** D1
St Mildred's Prim Inf Sch
 CT10 ....30 A4
St Mildred's Rd
 Margate CT9 ....8 A2
 Minster (Thanet) CT12 ..50 B5
 Ramsgate CT11 ....52 C6
 Westgate-on-S CT8 .....7 C1
St Mildreds Ct
 Canterbury CT1 ......87 E8
 Deal CT14 ....117 C1
St Mildreds Pl CT1 ......87 E7
St Monicas CT17 ....166 C7
St Monicas Rd CT14 ....134 D6
St Nicholas at Wade
 CE Prim Sch CT7 ......25 E2
St Nicholas
 CE Cty Inf Sch ME2 ....9 A7
St Nicholas CE Prim Sch
 Kingsdown CT14 .....134 C5
 New Romney TN28 ...200 B7
St Nicholas Cl Deal CT14 116 F4
 Sturry CT2 ....67 F1
St Nicholas Cnr CT7 ....25 F1
St Nicholas Hospl CT2 ..66 C1
St Nicholas Rd
 Canterbury CT1 ......87 D6
 Faversham ME13 ......62 A7
 Hythe CT21 ....176 A2
 Littlestone-on-S TN28 ..200 E6
St Nicholas Rdbt CT7 ...26 B2
St Nicholas Sch CT1 ....87 F6
St Nicholas Terr **1**
 CT21 ....176 B2
St Nicholas Vineyard★
 CT3 ....71 D1
St Patrick's Cl Deal CT14 117 C6
 Whitstable CT5 ....43 E7
St Patrick's Rd
 Deal CT14 ....117 C6
 Ramsgate CT11 ....52 F1
St Patricks Rd CT17 ....166 A4
St Paul's Ave ME13 .....62 A7
St Paul's Ct CT20 .....177 E4
St Paul's Rd CT9 ....8 A3
St Paul's St **2** ME10 ...36 E5
St Paul's Way CT20 ....177 E4
St Pauls Cres ME13 ....64 A3
St Pauls Inf Sch ME14 ..75 A7
St Pauls Rd ME13 ......64 A3
St Pauls Terr CT1 ......88 A8
St Peter St ME1 ....9 D4
St Peter's Bridge ME14 ..74 F4
St Peter's CE Prim Sch
 Aylesford ME20 ....53 A3
 Folkestone CT19 ....178 E5
St Peter's Cl ME12 ......3 D6
St Peter's Ct
 Broadstairs CT10 .....29 F5
 Faversham ME13 ......62 A7
St Peter's Cty Inf Sch
 ME1 ....9 C3
St Peter's Footpath
 Margate CT9 ....29 A8
 Margate CT9 ....7 J1
St Peter's Gr CT1 ......87 F8
St Peter's in Thanet
 CE Jun Sch CT19 .....29 F7
St Peter's La CT1 ....66 F1
St Peter's Meth Prim Sch
 CT1 ....87 F8
St Peter's Park Rd CT10 .29 F5
St Peter's Path ME1 .....9 D5

St Peter's Pl CT1,CT2 ....87 F8
St Peter's RC Prim Sch
 Sittingbourne ME10 ...36 E4
 Sittingbourne,Fernleigh
 ME10 ....36 D2
St Peter's Rd
 Boughton Street ME13 ..64 A3
 Broadstairs CT10 .....29 F5
 Margate CT10,CT9 ....29 A7
 Whitstable CT5 ....20 D2
St Peter's St
 Canterbury CT1,CT2 ...87 F8
 Sandwich CT13 ....73 A1
St Peter's Way TN26 ..170 A8
St Peter's-in-Thanet
 CE Jun Sch CT19 .....29 E5
St Peters Cotts **17** CT5 ..20 D2
St Peters Pl ME9 ....60 A6
St Peters St ME16 ......74 F4
St Philip Howard
 RC Prim Sch CT6 .....22 E5
St Philip's Ave ME15 ....75 B2
St Radigund's
 Com Prim Sch CT17 ..149 A1
St Radigund's Ct CT17 ..149 A1
St Radigund's Pl CT1 ....67 A1
St Radigund's Rd CT17 ..149 A1
St Radigunds St **22** CT1 ..67 A1
St Richard's
 RC Prim Sch CT16 ...149 A1
St Richard's Rd CT14 ...116 F3
St Richard's Wlk CT17 ..166 A4
St Ronan's Cl ME15 .....97 C7
St Saviour's Cl ME13 ....62 E7
St Saviour's Hospl CT21 176 F2
St Saviours CE Jun Sch
 CT8 ....27 E8
St Saviours Cl CT19 ...178 D7
St Saviours Ct CT8 .....27 E8
St Saviours Rd ME15 ...97 D6
St Simon of England
 RC Prim Sch TN23 ...156 A8
St Simon Stock Sch
 ME16 ....74 C4
St Stephen's Cl
 Canterbury CT2 ......66 F1
 Sittingbourne ME9 ....35 C7
St Stephen's Ct CT2 ....66 F2
St Stephen's Fields CT2 .66 F1
St Stephen's Gn CT2 ....66 F1
St Stephen's Hill CT2 ...66 E4
St Stephen's Inf Sch CT2 66 F3
St Stephen's Jun Sch
 CT2 ....66 F3
St Stephen's Lodge CT2 .66 F2
St Stephen's Manor
 CT10 ....30 B7
St Stephen's Rd CT2 ....66 F2
St Stephen's Sq ME15 ..74 C4
St Stephen's Way CT20 .177 F4
St Stephen's Wlk TN23 ..155 F7
St Stephens Mews ME1 .31 E8
St Swithin's Rd CT5 .....21 B3
St Teresa's RC Prim Sch
 TN24 ....139 B4
St Theresa's Cl TN24 ...139 B3
St Thomas Hill CT2 .....66 D3
St Thomas More
 RC Prim Sch ME5 .....32 A1
St Thomas of Canterbury
 Prim Sch ME8 ....11 B2
St Thomas Sch ME10 ...37 C3
St Thomas' Cross TN26 .170 E3
St Thomas' RC Prim Sch
 CT1 ....67 A1
St Thomas's Hospl CT13 .72 F1
St Vincent Rd CT15 ....150 F7
St Vincent's Cl
 Littlebourne CT3 ......68 F1
 Whitstable CT5 ....43 E7
St Welcume's Way
 ME17 ....100 E6
St William of Perth
 RC Prim Sch ME1 ......9 B2
St William's Way ME1 ....9 D2
St Winifred Rd CT19 ...177 F6
Salbris Cl TN29 ....195 D8
Salem St ME15 ....75 A3
Salisbury Ave
 Broadstairs CT10 .....29 F5
 Gillingham ME8 ......33 D8
 Ramsgate CT11 ....52 F8
Salisbury Cl ME10 ......37 C4
Salisbury Ho **5** ME15 ...97 D7
Salisbury Rd
 Canterbury CT2 ......66 E2
 Chatham ME4 ....10 A3
 Deal CT14 ....117 B2
 Dover CT16 ....149 D1
 Folkestone CT19 ....177 E7
 Herne Bay CT6 ....23 C5
 Kit's Coty ME20 ......53 D7
 Maidstone ME14 ......75 A6
 St Margaret's at Cliffe
 CT15 ....151 B6
 Whitstable CT5 ....43 D8
Sally Port ME7 ....10 A6
Sally Port Gdns ME7 ....10 B6
Salmestone Grange★
 CT9 ....28 E8
Salmestone Prim Sch
 CT9 ....28 E8
Salmestone Rd CT9 .....28 D8
Salmestone Rise CT9 ...28 E8
Salmon Cres ME12 ......3 F6
Salt Marsh La **15** CT5 ...20 D2
Salt's Ave ME15 ....96 F3
Salt's Dr CT10 ....29 E5

Salter Collection Mus★
 CT14 ....117 D5
Salter's La TN29 ......197 C8
Salters La ME13 ....62 D4
Salthouse Cl TN29 ....197 D8
Saltings The
 Littlestone-on-S TN28 ..200 E5
 10 Whitstable CT5 ....20 D2
Salts Cl CT5 ....20 D1
Salts La ME15 ....97 A4
Saltwood CE Prim Sch
 CT21 ....176 B4
Saltwood Gdns CT9 .....8 E2
Saltwood Rd ME15 .....74 F1
Samara Cl ME5 ....32 A1
Samian Cres CT19 .....177 C6
Samphire Cl ME14 .....75 E4
Samphire Ct CT5 ......166 E8
Samphire Hoe Ctry pk★
 CT15 ....165 E2
Samuel Mews TN29 ...203 D7
San Remo CT9 ....7 C1
Sancroft Ave CT2 ......66 C1
Sanctuary Cl
 Broadstairs CT10 .....29 F2
 River CT17 ....148 D4
Sanctuary Rd ME8 ......11 A3
Sand Ct ME12 ....6 G2
Sand End CT5 ....43 C6
Sandalwood Dr CT7 ....25 F1
Sandbach Ho CT9 ....8 B3
Sandbanks Rd ME13 ...41 C2
Sandbourne Dr ME14 ...53 F1
Sanders Ct ME12 ....4 A5
Sandford Rd ME10 .....36 B5
Sandgate Ct ME8 ......33 F4
Sandgate Espl CT20,
 CT21 ....177 D2
Sandgate High St CT20 .177 A4
Sandgate Hill CT20 ....178 A4
Sandgate Prim Sch
 CT20 ....177 F4
Sandgate Rd CT20 ....178 C4
Sandhurst Cl
 Canterbury CT2 ......67 A4
 Gillingham ME8 ......11 C3
Sandhurst Rd CT9 ....8 F2
Sandilands TN24 ......139 E2
Sandle's Rd CT17 ......26 F7
Sandling Cl TN23 .....155 F6
Sandling Ct ME14 ......75 B7
Sandling La ME14 ......75 A8
Sandling Prim Sch ME14 75 B8
Sandling Rd Hythe CT21 .175 F6
 Maidstone ME14 ......74 F7
 Maidstone,Ringleston
 ME14 ....74 F7
Sandling Sta CT21 .....175 F6
Sandown Cl CT14 ....95 D1
Sandown Cotts
 Margate CT9 ....8 A3
 Teynham ME9 ....38 E1
Sandown Ct CT14 .....117 C7
Sandown Dr
 Gillingham ME8 ......33 D7
 Herne Bay CT6 ....22 D4
Sandown Lees CT13 ....94 D8
Sandown Rd Deal CT14 .117 D8
 Sandwich CT13 ....94 B8
Sandown Sch CT14 ....117 C7
Sandpiper Ct
 3 Birchington CT7 ....26 F8
 Margate CT9 ....7 I3
Sandpiper Rd
 Chatham ME5 ....32 D2
 Whitstable CT5 ....43 B7
Sandpit Hill CT3 ....47 C4
Sandringham Ho ME1 ....9 B4
Sandringham Rd ME8 ...33 E3
Sandstone Ct CT20 ....178 A3
Sandstone Dr ME10 ....36 E8
Sandstone Rise ME5 ...54 C8
Sandway Rd ME17 ....100 F4
Sandwich Bay
 Bird Obsy★ CT13 .....94 E7
Sandwich Cl CT20 .....177 F5
Sandwich Ind Est CT13 .73 B1
Sandwich Inf Sch CT13 .72 F1
Sandwich Jun Sch CT13 .93 F7
Sandwich Rd Ash CT3 ..71 C1
 Ash,Each End CT3 .....72 A2
 Cliffs End CT13 ....51 D4
 Eastry CT13 ....93 C3
 Eythorne CT15 ....131 C8
 Nonington CT15,CT3 ..113 F6
 Sandwich CT13 ....93 D7
 Tilmanstone CT14 ....115 B2
 Whitfield CT15,CT16 ..149 A7
 Woodnesborough CT13,
 CT14 ....93 D5
Sandwich Sta CT13 ....94 A8
Sandwich Tech Sch CT13 93 F6
Sandwood Rd
 Ramsgate CT10 ....29 F1
 Whitstable CT5 ....43 F8
Sandy Cnr TN26 ......154 F5
Sandy Dell ME7 ....33 A3
Sandy La Ashford TN24 .140 B1
 Daniel's Water TN26 ..154 E6
 Hythe CT20,CT21 ....177 B3
 Maidstone,Harbourland
 ME14 ....75 C8
 Maidstone,Penenden Heath
 ME14 ....75 C7
 Maidstone,Ware Street
 ME14 ....76 A5
 Tenterden TN30 .....179 A7
Sandy Mount ME14 .....76 B5

Sandy Pl TN25 ....158 D5
Sandyhurst La TN25 ...139 B8
Sanger Cl CT9 ....7 I1
Sangro Pl CT1 ....67 D1
Sanora Way ME10 ......36 C7
Santon La CT3 ....70 E8
Sanspareil Ave ME12 ....4 A6
Sappers Wlk ME7 ......10 C5
Saracen Cl ME13 ....11 A1
Saracen Fields ME5 ....54 C8
Sarafand Ho ME1 ....9 B4
Sarah Gdns CT9 ....29 D8
Sark Ct ME7 ....195 C8
Sarre Ct CT7 ....48 D6
Sarre Pl CT13 ....93 F8
Sarre Mill★ CT7 ....48 D7
Sarsen Hts ME5 ....31 F1
Satis Ave ME10 ....36 E7
Satmar La CT15,CT18 ..164 E4
Satmore La CT18 .....164 C4
Saunders La CT3 ....71 F1
Saunders St
 7 Chatham ME4 ....9 F3
 Gillingham ME7 ......10 C6
Saunders Way TN31 ...201 A2
Savage Rd ME5 ....32 B3
Savernake Dr CT6 ......23 B2
Saw Lodge Field TN23 .156 C4
Sawpit Rd ME9 ....59 B2
Sawyers Ct ME4 ....10 B2
Saxon Ave ME12 ....4 B6
Saxon Cl CT21 ....176 E2
Saxon Rd Bridge CT4 ..89 A1
 Faversham ME13 .....62 C7
 Ramsgate CT11 ......52 B6
 Westgate-on-S CT8 ....7 C1
Saxon Shore CT5 ......43 C8
Saxon St **9** CT17 ....166 D8
Saxons Cl CT14 ....117 C8
Saxons Dr ME14 ....75 B7
Saxton St ME7 ....10 C5
Sayer Rd TN27 ....120 C8
Sayers La **6** TN30 ...179 A7
Scanlons Bridge Rd
 CT21 ....176 A2
Scarborough Dr ME12 ...4 C8
Scarlett Cl ME5 ....32 C5
Sceales Dr CT12 ......51 D6
Sceptre Way CT5 ......43 B7
School Ave ME7 ....10 C4
School Cl The CT7 ......7 C1
School Hill CT4 ......107 B8
School La
 Bekesbourne CT4 .....89 C4
 Blean CT2 ....66 A6
 Borden ME9 ....35 F4
 Boughton Street ME13 .63 F3
 Folkestone,Newington
 CT18 ....177 A7
 Fordwich CT2 ....68 A4
 Goodnestone CT3 ....91 D2
 Herne Bay CT6 ....23 B1
 Hoath CT3 ....46 E6
 Ickham CT3 ....90 C8
 Iwade ME9 ....14 C4
 Lower Halstow ME9 ..13 B2
 Lower Hardres CT4 ..110 B6
 Maidstone ME15 .....75 E1
 Newington ME9 ......35 B7
 Platt's Heath ME17 ..100 F2
 Ramsgate CT11 ......52 E7
 Sittingbourne ME9 ...37 D2
 Stalisfield Green ME13 .103 D6
 Staple CT3 ....92 A6
 Stourmouth CT3 .....48 E2
 Wingham CT3 ....91 A7
School Rd
 Appledore TN26 .....181 C1
 Ash CT3 ....71 C2
 Bethersden TN26 ....153 D4
 Charing TN27 ....120 C8
 Densole CT18 ....162 E7
 Faversham ME13 .....62 C6
 Hothfield TN26 ......138 A7
 Hythe CT21 ....176 B4
 Sandwich CT13 ....72 F1
 Tilmanstone CT14 ...114 F4
School View ME9 ......58 C8
Schrieber Mews ME7 ...10 D5
Scimitar Cl ME7 ....11 A1
Scocles Cotts ME12 .....4 C5
Scocles Rd ME12 ....4 C5
Scoggers Hill ME13 ....85 A7
Scot's La TN25 ....159 F8
Scotby Ave ME5 ....32 B4
Scotchmen Cl ME12 .....3 A2
Scott Ave ME8 ....12 A1
Scott St ME14 ....74 F6
Scott's Terr ME1 ....9 F3
Scotteswood Ave ME4 ...9 F2
Scotton St CT3 ....123 F2
Scragged Oak Rd
 Detling ME14 ....55 C5
 Hollingbourne ME17 ..56 C1
Scraps Hill ME9 ....37 F4
Scrapsgate Rd ME12 ....4 A7
Scrubbs La ME16 ......74 D4
Sea App ME12 ....6 E4
Sea Rd Hythe CT21 ...177 A2
 Kingsdown CT14 ....134 C6
 Westgate-on-S CT7,CT8 ..7 C1
Sea St Herne Bay CT6 ..22 C3
 St Margaret's at Cliffe
 CT15 ....151 A6
 Whitstable CT5 ....20 D2
Sea View Ave CT7 .....26 E8

Sea View Cl CT18 .....164 B1
Sea View Cotts ME9 ...13 B3
Sea View Gdns ME12 ....6 E3
Sea View Hts CT7 .....26 D8
Sea View Rd
 Birchington CT7 ......26 E8
 Broadstairs CT10 .....30 A6
 Cliffs End CT12 ......51 D6
 Herne Bay CT6 ....23 C5
 St Margaret's at Cliffe
 CT15 ....150 F4
Sea View Sq CT6 ......22 F5
Sea View Terr
 Folkestone CT20 ....177 D3
 Margate CT9 ....7 G2
 Minster (Sheppey) ME12 ..5 A5
Sea Wall
 Dymchurch TN29 ....195 D8
 Whitstable CT5 ....20 D2
Seabourne Cl TN29 ...195 B6
Seabourne Way TN29 ..195 B7
Seabrook CE Prim Sch
 CT21 ....177 B2
Seabrook Ct CT21 ....177 B3
Seabrook Gdns CT21 ..177 B2
Seabrook Gr CT21 ....177 A2
Seabrook Rd CT21 ....176 B2
Seabrook Vale CT21 ...177 B4
Seacroft Rd CT10 ......30 A4
Seadown Cl CT21 .....177 A4
Seafield Rd
 Broadstairs CT10 .....30 A4
 Ramsgate CT11 ......52 C6
 Whitstable CT5 ....21 B3
Seaford Ct ME1 ....9 B5
Seagar Rd ME13 ......40 B1
Seager Rd ME12 ....1 F2
Seagrave Cres CT19 ...178 F6
Sealand Ct ME1 ....9 B5
Seamark Cl CT12 ......49 D2
Seamark Rd CT12,CT7 ..26 E2
Seapoint Rd CT10 ......30 B3
Seasalter Beach CT5 ...43 A7
Seasalter Cl ME12 ......6 E4
Seasalter Cross CT5 ...43 A6
Seasalter La CT5 ......43 A5
Seasalter Rd CT5,ME13 ..41 E3
Seaside Ave ME12 ......4 C8
Seathorpe Ave ME12 ....4 C8
Seaths Cnr CT3 ....91 A7
Seaton Ave CT21 .....176 B3
Seaton Cotts TN25 ...122 E3
Seaton Rd Gillingham ME7 ..10 E3
 Wickhambreaux CT3 ..69 D2
Seaview Ave ME1 ....6 H1
Seaview Cotts **6** CT10 ..30 B4
Seaview Ct CT10 ......30 B3
Seaview Ho CT19 .....178 D8
Seaview Hts TN29 ....195 C7
Seaview Rd
 Gillingham ME7 ......10 C4
 Greatstone-on-S TN28 ..200 E1
Seaville Dr CT6 ....23 E5
Seaway Cotts CT5 .....20 C1
Seaway Cres TN29 ....194 F4
Seaway Gdns TN29 ...194 F4
Seaway Rd TN29 .....195 A4
Second Ave
 Broadstairs CT10 ......8 G2
 Chatham ME4 ....10 C1
 Eastchurch ME12 .....5 F5
 Gillingham ME7 ......10 E3
 Margate CT9 ....8 F3
 Rushenden ME11 ......2 F3
 Sheerness ME12 ......1 C1
Secretan Rd ME1 ....9 B1
Sedge Cres ME5 ....31 E4
Sedley Cl ME8 ....33 C3
Seeshill Cl CT5 ....43 E8
Segrave Rd CT19 .....178 F5
Selbey Cl CT6 ....23 C4
Selborne Rd CT19 .....29 B8
Selbourne Rd ME7 .....10 D7
Selbourne Wlk ME15 ...97 F6
Selby Rd ME15 ....97 F4
Selkirk Rd CT16 ......149 B3
Sellindge Prim Sch
 TN25 ....159 C1
Selling CE Prim Sch
 ME13 ....84 B6
Selling Ct ME13 ....84 C5
Selling Rd Chilham CT4 ..85 B3
 Faversham ME13 .....62 F3
 Selling ME13 ....84 E6
Selling Sta ME13 ......84 E7
Sellinge Gn ME8 ......11 C3
Selsea Ave CT6 ....22 D4
Selstead Cl ME8 ......11 C2
Selsted CE Prim Sch
 CT15 ....146 C6
Selway Ct CT14 ......117 B3
Selwood Cl ME12 ......3 E6
Selwyn Ct CT10 ....29 C5
Selwyn Dr CT10 ....29 F5
Semaphore Rd CT7 ....26 F8
Semple Cl CT12 ....50 C7
Semple Gdns ME4 ......9 F3
Senacre La ME15 ......97 E6
Senacre Sq ME15 .....97 E6
Senacre Tech Coll ME15 .97 D6
Senacre Wood Prim Sch
 ME15 ....97 F7
Sene Pk CT21 ....176 D3
Senlac Cl CT11 ....52 B6
Serene Ct **12** CT10 ....30 B4

Serene Pl [9] CT10 ......30 B4
Sessions House Sq ME14 74 F5
Setford Rd ME5 ....32 C6
Setterfield Ho CT21 ...176 D2
Setterfield Rd CT9 ......7 J1
Settington Ave ME5 ....10 C1
Sevastopol Pl CT1 .....67 D1
Seven Stones Dr CT10 ..30 A1
Sevenacre Rd ME13 ....62 C8
Sevenscore Farm Cotts
  CT12 ....51 A5
Severn Rd ME5 ....32 C5
Sevington La TN24 ....157 A7
Sevington Pk ME15 ....96 F6
Sewell Cl CT7 ....27 A6
Sexburga Dr ME12 ......4 B8
Sextant Pk ME2 ....9 E6
Seymour Ave
  Westgate-on-S CT9 ....7 D1
  Whitstable CT5 ....20 E1
Seymour Cl CT6 ....23 B1
Seymour Pl CT1 ....87 E7
Seymour Rd
  [1] Chatham ME5 ......10 B3
  Gillingham ME8 ......12 C1
St Margaret's at Cliffe
  CT15 ....150 F8
Shackleton Cl ME5 ....32 B6
Shadoxhurst Rd TN26 .169 C7
Shaftesbury Ave CT19 .177 E7
Shaftesbury Ct CT14 ..117 D2
Shaftesbury Dr ME16 ..74 C4
Shaftesbury Rd
  Canterbury CT2 ....66 F3
  hersden CT3 ....46 E1
  Whitstable CT5 ....20 D1
Shaftsbury St CT11 ....52 F7
Shah Pl CT11 ....52 D7
Shakespeare Ct CT17 .166 B7
Shakespeare Pas CT9 ...7 H2
Shakespeare Rd
  Birchington CT7 ......27 A8
  Dover CT17 ....166 B6
  Gillingham ME7 ......10 C3
  Margate CT9 ....7 J1
  Sittingbourne ME10 ...37 A4
Shakespeare Terr [8]
  CT20 ....178 C4
Shalder Ho ME7 ....10 D7
Shalloak Rd CT2 ......67 D6
Shallows Rd CT10 .....29 D6
Shalmsford Ct CT4 ....86 C2
Shalmsford Rd CT4 ....85 E2
Shalmsford St CT4 ....86 B2
Shamel Bsns Ctr ME2 ...9 C7
Shamley Rd ME5 ......32 C2
Shamrock Ave CT5 ....43 B7
Shanklin Cl ME5 ......32 C8
Shapland Cl CT6 ......23 C3
Share & Coulter Rd CT5 .21 D1
Sharon Cres ME5 ......31 F4
Sharps Gn ME8 ....11 D5
Sharsted Hill ME9 .....81 C8
Sharsted Way
  Gillingham ME7 ......33 A3
  Maidstone ME14 ......76 B5
Shatterlocks Inf Sch
  CT16 ....149 B2
Shaw Cross TN24 .....139 D5
Shawdon Ave CT13 ....95 A7
Shaws Way ME1 ....9 C3
Shawstead Rd ME7,ME7 .32 D5
Sheal's Cres ME15 ....75 A2
Sheals Ct ME15 ....75 A2
Shear Way TN29 .....186 C5
Shearers Cl ME14 .....75 E4
Shearwater ME16 .....74 B5
Shearwater Ave CT5 ...43 C7
Shearwater Ct ME12 ....3 B8
Shearwater Ho TN29 .195 A3
Shearway Rd CT19 ...177 F8
Sheepfold La TN25 ...156 C4
Sheerness Harbour Est
  ME12 ....1 B3
Sheerness Heritage Ctr
  Mus★ ME12 ....1 D2
Sheerness-on-Sea
  (Terminus)ME12 ......1 C2
Sheerstone ME9 ....14 D4
Sheerwater Rd CT3 ....70 F5
Sheerways ME13 ......62 A6
Sheet Glass Rd ME11 ...3 A3
Shelden Dr ME8 ....33 F8
Shelden Bsns Ctr ME2 ..9 D8
Sheldon Cl CT3 ......113 A6
Sheldwich Cl TN23 ...156 A6
Sheldwich Prim Sch
  ME13 ....83 C6
Shell Grotto★ CT9 .....7 J2
Shell Ness
  Nature Reserve★ ME12 .19 E4
Shellbeach Rd ME12 ...19 D6
Shelley Ave CT1 ......67 C2
Shelley Rd ME16 .....74 C2
Shellness Rd ME12 ....19 D7
Shellons St CT20 ....178 D5
Shelvin La CT4 ......129 C3
Shenley Gr ME14 .....53 F2
Shepherd Dr TN24 ....10 D7
Shepherd's Close Rd CT4 89 E1
Shepherd's Cross CT5 .132 B1
Shepherds Gate ME7 ..32 F5
Shepherds Gate Dr ME14 75 E6
Shepherds Way
  Langley Heath ME17 ...98 E4

Shepherds Way continued
  Whitstable CT5 ....44 C8
Shepherds Well Sta
  CT15 ....130 D5
Shepherds Wlk
  Hythe CT21 ....175 E1
  Whitstable CT5 ....44 C8
Shepherdsgate CT2 ....66 F1
Shepherdsgate Dr CT6 .46 A8
Shepperton Cl ME5 ....32 C4
Sheppey Cl [3] CT7 ....27 A7
Sheppey Coll ME12 .....1 C3
Sheppey Com Hospl ME12 4 C7
Sheppey Cotts ME12 ....1 E2
Sheppey Rd ME15 .....97 A7
Sheppey St ME12 ......1 B2
Sheppey Terr ME12 ....4 F5
Sheppey View CT5 ....43 C6
Sheppey Way Iwade ME9 14 F6
  Queenborough ME12,ME9 .3 D2
  Sittingbourne ME9 ....36 B7
Shepway TN24 ....139 E5
Shepway Cl CT19 ....178 D6
Shepway Cross CT21 .175 B3
Shepway Ct ME15 .....97 C8
Shepway Inf Sch ME15 .97 E8
Shepway Jun Sch ME15 .97 E8
Sheraton Ct ME5 ......31 F1
Sherbourne Dr ME16 ..74 B2
Sheridan Cl Chatham ME5 32 C7
  Maidstone ME14 ......74 E8
Sheridan Rd CT16 ....149 B3
Sheriff Dr ME5 ....32 A2
Sheringham Cl ME16 ..74 D7
Sheringham Ho [5] ME15 97 D8
Sherman Cl ME7 ......11 B1
Shernold Sch ME16 ...74 D5
Shernolds ME15 ......97 B7
Sheron Cl CT14 ......117 A5
Sherriffs Court La CT12 49 E6
Sherwood Ave ME5 ...32 A2
Sherwood Cl
  Ashford TN24 ....139 D7
  Faversham ME13 .....40 B1
  Herne Bay CT6 ....23 C2
  Whitstable CT5 ....43 C6
Sherwood Ct CT8 ......7 C1
Sherwood Dr CT5 .....43 C6
Sherwood Gdns CT11 ..29 E1
Sherwood Rd CT7 .....26 F5
Shillingheld Cl ME14 ..75 F5
Ship Cl TN29 ....195 C8
Ship La ME1 ....9 E4
Ship St CT19 ....178 D6
Shipland Hos TN27 ...136 D8
Shipley Ct ME14 ......75 A4
Shipley Mill CL TN23 .156 C4
Shipman Ave 87 C8
Shipmans Way CT16 .149 A3
Shipwrights Ave ME4 ..10 B2
Shipwrights Lee CT5 ..20 C2
Shipyard Area ME13 ...40 D1
Shire La ME13 ....103 C6
Shireway Cl CT19 ....178 A7
Shirley Ave Chatham ME5 31 D5
  Ramsgate CT11 ....29 E1
Shirley Ct ME15 ......97 E5
Shirley Way ME15 .....76 A3
Shoebury Terr ME12 ...5 A5
Sholden Bank CT14 ..116 E4
Sholden CE Prim Sch
  CT14 ....116 F5
Sholden New Rd CT14 116 F6
Shooter's Hill [5] CT17 149 C1
Shooters Hill CT15 ..131 C8
Shore Cl Birchington CT7 .26 D8
  Herne Bay CT6 ....22 B3
Shorefields ME8 ......12 B2
Shoregate La ME9 ....12 F6
Shoreham La TN30 ...167 A3
Shoreham Wlk ME15 ..97 F7
Shoreland Ct ME1 .....9 B5
Shorncliffe Cres CT20 177 C5
Shorncliffe Ind Est
  CT20 ....177 D4
Shorncliffe Rd CT20 .177 F5
Short La Alkham CT15 .147 D1
  Snargate TN29 ......191 D6
Short St [3] Chatham ME4 10 B3
  Chillenden CT3 ......114 A8
  [5] Sandwich CT13 ...73 A1
  Sheerness ME12 ......1 C2
Short's Prospect ME12 17 C8
Shortlands ME8 ......97 F5
Shortlands Rd ME10 ..37 B4
Shorts Way ME1 ....9 A3
Shotfield Cl CT13 .....70 C6
Shottendane Rd CT9,CT8 28 C7
Shottenden Rd
  Gillingham ME7 ......10 D7
  Shottenden CT4,ME13 105 D8
Shrimpton Cl CT4 .....85 B3
Shropshire Terr [1] ME15 97 E7
Shrub Hill Rd CT5 ....44 D7
Shrubbery The
  Barham CT4 ....111 F1
  Deal CT14 ....117 C1
Shrubcote TN30 .....179 C7
Shrubsole Ave ME12 ...1 D1
Shrubsole Dr ME14 ...53 F3
Shuart La CT7 ....25 F4
Shurland Ave
  Leysdown-on-S ME12 ...6 H1
  Minster (Sheppey) ME12 .4 B6
  Sittingbourne ME10 ..36 F1
Shuttle Rd CT10 ......30 B5
Sibert's Cl CT15 .....130 F5

Sibertswold
  CE Prim Sch CT15 ...130 E4
Sidings The
  Dymchurch TN29 .....195 B7
  Lyminge CT18 ....161 C7
Sidney Rd Gillingham ME7 .10 C7
  Rochester ME1 ....9 A2
Sidney St
  Folkestone CT19 ....178 E7
  Maidstone ME16 .....74 C2
Silchester Ct ME14 ...75 C7
Silvanus Ho CT11 .....52 D7
Silver Ave CT7 ....27 B6
Silver Bank ME5 .....32 A6
Silver Birch Gr TN23 .156 B4
Silver Birches
  Chatham ME5 ....32 A3
  Ruckinge TN26 ......171 A4
  Sheerness ME12 ......1 H1
Silver Hill Chatham ME4 ..9 F3
  Rochester ME1 ....9 A2
  Tenterden TN30 .....167 B1
Silver Hill Gdns
  Ashford TN24 ....140 A1
  [4] Chatham ME4 .....9 F3
Silver Hill Rd TN24 ..140 A1
Silver St Deal CT14 ..117 D7
  Silver Street ME9 ....57 F5
Silver Tree ME5 ......32 B1
Silverdale ME16 ......74 A2
Silverdale Ave ME12 ...4 A6
Silverdale Dr
  Gillingham ME8 ......33 F7
  Herne Bay CT6 ....23 D2
Silverdale Gr ME10 ...36 D3
Silverdale Rd CT11 ...52 A5
Silverlands Rd CT18 .161 C7
Silvers The CT10 .....29 C4
Silverspot Cl ME8 ....33 F7
Silverweed Rd ME5 ...31 F4
Simmonds La ME15 ...98 B6
Simmonds Rd CT1 ....87 E7
Simon Ave CT9 ....8 D2
Simon Langton
  Girls Gram Sch CT1 ..88 C5
Simon Langton Sch
  for Boys CT4 ....88 C5
Simon's Ave TN23 ...155 F7
Simone Weil Ave TN24 139 B4
Simpson Rd ME10 ....36 C5
Sinclair Cl ME8 ......33 E5
Singapore Dr ME7 ....10 B5
Singer Ave CT6 ......22 B4
Singledge Ave CT16 .148 F6
Singledge La CT15 ...131 C2
Singleton Cl CT12 ....50 B6
Singleton Ctr The TN23 155 D8
Singleton Hill TN23 .155 D8
Singleton Rd TN23 ..138 C1
Sion Hill CT11 ....52 E6
Sir Evelyn Rd ME1 ....9 B1
Sir John Hawkins Way
  ME4 ....9 F4
Sir John Moore Ave
  CT21 ....176 B2
Sir John Moore Ct [5]
  CT20 ....177 E3
Sir Roger Manwood's
  Sch CT13 ....94 B8
Sir Thomas Longley Rd
  ME2 ....9 E6
Siskin Cl Ashford TN25 .139 B7
  Hawkinge CT18 ......162 F4
Sissinghurst Dr ME16 .74 B4
Sittingbourne & Kemsley
  Light Rly★ ME10 .....37 A7
Sittingbourne Com Coll
  The ME10 ....37 C2
Sittingbourne Rd
  Maidstone,Detling ME14 75 E8
  Maidstone,Penenden Heath
  ME14 ....75 B6
Sittingbourne Sta ME10 36 F4
Six Fields Path TN30 .179 A7
Sixth Ave ME12 ....6 A5
Skeete Rd CT18 .....160 E7
Skene Cl ME8 ....12 A1
Skinner Rd TN29 ....203 C6
Skinner St Chatham ME4 ..9 F3
  Gillingham ME7 ......10 C5
Skinner Street Prim Sch
  ME7 ....10 C6
Skinner's Alley [3] CT5 20 D1
Skinner's Way ME17 ..98 E4
Skinners Cl ME20 .....53 A6
Skye Cl ME15 ....97 A7
Skylark Way TN23 ...156 D3
Slade Cl ME5 ....32 B2
Slade Rd ME17 ......102 D8
Slades Cl CT5 ....44 C8
Slatin Rd ME2 ....9 B8
Sleigh Rd CT2 ....67 F6
Slicketts Hill ME4 ....10 A4
Slip La CT15 ....147 C2
Slipway Rd ME12 ......1 A3
Sloe La CT10,CT9 .....29 B6
Slough Rd ME9 ......59 A3
Smack Alley ME13 ....62 D8
Small Hythe Cl ME15 .76 B2
Small Hythe Rd TN30 179 C3
Smallhythe Place (Mus)
  TN30 ....188 C8
Smallhythe Rd TN30 .179 A6
Smarden Prim Sch
  TN27 ....135 A1
Smarden Rd TN27 ...136 B6
Smarden Wlk ME8 ....12 B1

Smarts Cotts ME14 ....76 C4
Smeed Cl [4] ME10 ....37 B4
Smeed-Dean Ctr The
  ME10 ....37 A4
Smeeth Com Prim Sch
  TN25 ....158 D5
Smith Rd ME5 ....32 B3
Smith St ME2 ....9 A6
Smiths Orch ME9 .....57 F5
Smithy Dr TN23 .....156 C4
Smuggler's Way CT7 ..27 A8
Snakes Hill CT3 ......91 A5
Snargate La TN29 ...191 C5
Snargate St CT17 ...166 D7
Snell Gdns CT6 ......22 B2
Snipe Cl TN25 ......139 C2
Snow Ho ME7 ....10 E7
Snowball Rd TN23 ..156 B4
Snowdon Ave ME14 ..75 B5
Snowdon Cl ME5 .....32 B7
Snowdon Par ME14 ..75 C5
Snowdown Caravan Site
  CT15 ....113 A4
Snowdown Ct CT3 ...112 F5
Snowdown Sta CT15 113 B3
Snowdrop Cl CT19 ..178 C8
Sobraon Way CT1 ....67 D1
Sole Street Cotts CT4 125 B7
Solent Gdns ME5 .....32 B8
Soleshill Rd CT4 .....84 E1
Solihull Cotts CT12 ..49 E6
Solomon Ho CT14 ...117 B3
Solomon Cl ME8 .....12 A1
Solomons La ME13 ...62 D7
Solomons Rd ME4 .....9 F4
Somerfield Barn Ct
  TN25 ....174 C8
Somerfield Cl ME16 ..74 D5
Somerfield Hospl The
  ME16 ....74 E5
Somerfield La ME16 ..74 D4
Somerfield Rd ME16 ..74 D4
Somerset Cl Chatham ME5 32 C8
  Deal CT14 ....117 B3
  Ramsgate CT12 ......29 B2
Somerset Rd
  Ashford TN24 ....139 B3
  Canterbury CT1 ......88 D8
  Deal CT14 ....117 C3
  Folkestone CT19 ....177 E6
  Maidstone ME15 .....97 C8
Somme Ct CT1 ....67 D1
Sommerville Cl ME13 .62 E7
Somner Cl CT2 ....66 D1
Somner Wlk ME15 ....97 F4
Sondes Cl CT6 ....23 A2
Sondes Rd CT14 ....117 D5
Sorrell Rd ME5 ......31 F4
Sotherton TN24 ....156 E7
Souberg Cl CT14 ....117 C8
South Ave
  Aylesham CT15 .....113 A3
  Gillingham ME8 ......11 B2
  Sittingbourne ME10 ..37 A3
South Bank of Swale
  Nature Reserve★ ME13 41 A6
South Barham Rd CT4 128 C6
South Borough
  Prim Sch ME15 ......75 A2
South Brooks Rd TN29 202 F2
South Bush La ME8 ...34 B4
South Camber Way
  CT16 ....150 B1
South Canterbury Rd
  CT1 ....88 A6
South Cl CT1 ....88 A8
South Cliff Par CT10 ..30 B1
South Court Dr CT3 ...91 A7
South Cres CT17 .....96 C4
South Ct Deal CT14 ..117 D6
  Ramsgate CT12 ......29 B2
South Deal Prim Sch
  CT14 ....117 B4
South Eastern Rd
  Ramsgate CT11 ......52 F7
  Rochester ME2 ....9 C7
South Exit Rd CT16 .166 C8
South Goodwin Ct CT14 117 D4
South Green La ME9 ..56 F6
South Kent Coll
  Ashford TN23 ....156 A8
  Dover CT16 ....166 C8
  Folkestone CT20 ....178 B5
South Kent Coll of Tech
  TN23 ....139 C1
South Lea TN23 .....156 A3
South Lodge CT5 .....20 E3
South Lodge Cl CT5 ..20 E3
South Military Rd CT17 166 C5
South Motto TN23 ..156 B5
South Park Bsns Village
  ME15 ....75 A1
South Park Rd ME15 ..75 C1
South Pondside Rd ME4 10 A8
South Quay ME11 ....40 D1
South Rd Dover CT17 166 B8
  Faversham ME13 .....62 C7
  Gillingham ME4 ......10 B7
  Gillingham,Brompton ME4,
  ME7 ....10 A7
  Herne Bay CT6 ....23 A5

South Rd continued
  Hythe CT21 ....176 D1
  Kingsdown CT14 ....134 D5
  Sandwich CT13 ....73 A8
South Side Three Rd
  ME4 ....10 C8
South St
  Boughton Street ME13 .84 F8
  Canterbury CT1 ......67 C2
  Deal CT14 ....117 D6
  Lydd TN29 ....203 C6
  Queenborough ME11 ...2 F5
  Whitstable CT5 ....44 A7
South Stour Ave TN23 156 C8
South Street Crossing
  CT5 ....44 A7
South Street Rd ME9 .56 C7
South View CT3 ......46 F1
South View Gdns ME12 .1 D1
South View Rd CT5 ...43 D6
South Wall CT14 ....117 B7
Southall Cl CT12 .....50 C7
Southbourne TN23 ..155 E5
Southbourne Gr ME5 .32 A4
Southbourne Rd CT19 178 E5
Southdown Rd ME12 ..3 E6
Southenay La TN25 ..159 C4
Southern Way CT19 .178 E6
Southernwood Rise
  CT20 ....177 F4
Southfields ME1 ......9 C3
Southgate Rd TN30 .179 C7
Southill Rd ME4 ......9 F3
Southland's
  Comm Comp Sch TN28 200 B7
Southlees La ME9 ....56 F3
Southmead Cl CT19 .178 A6
Southover Ct [2] CT20 177 E3
Southsea Ave ME12 ...4 C8
Southsea Dr CT6 .....22 D4
Southstone Ct CT21 .176 C1
Southwall Rd CT14 ..117 B6
Southward Gdns CT11 52 B7
Southwold Pl CT8 ....27 E7
Southwood Rd
  Ramsgate CT11 ......52 C6
  Whitstable CT5 ....21 B2
Sovereign Bvd
  Gillingham ME7 ......10 F2
  Gillingham,Twydall ME8 ..11 A2
Sovereigns The ME16 .74 D4
Sowell St CT10 ......29 F5
Spade La ME9 ....34 C6
Spanton Cres CT21 ..176 A3
Sparrow Castle [3] CT9 ..7 J1
Speakman Ct CT1 ....52 C6
Spearhead Rd ME14 ..74 F7
Spearpoint Cnr TN24 139 F5
Spectrum Bsns Ctr ME2 .9 B7
Spectrum Bsns Est ME15 97 F4
Speedwell Ave ME5 ..31 F4
Speedwell Cl
  Gillingham ME7 ......10 E5
  Maidstone ME14 .....75 E5
Speke Rd CT10 ......29 E6
Spekes Rd ME7 ......33 B6
Spelders Hill TN25 ..141 B4
Speldhurst Cl TN23 .155 E5
Speldhurst Ct ME16 ..74 D4
Speldhurst Gdns CT9 ..8 F3
Spence Cl CT18 .....163 A4
Spencer Cl ME5 ......32 A5
Spencer Flats ME5 ...32 B8
Spencer Ho [3] CT20 .177 F5
Spencer Rd CT7 ......27 A8
Spencer Sq CT11 .....52 D6
Spencer St [9] CT11 ..52 D6
Spencer Way ME15 ...97 E7
Spenlow Dr ME5 .....54 A8
Spenser Rd CT6 ......22 F4
Spicer Cl CT21 ......176 C1
Spicer Homes ME10 ..36 F2
Spicer's Pl CT3 ......69 C2
Spiers The ME7 ......11 C5
Spillett Cl ME13 .....62 B6
Spillway The CT5 .....74 D2
Spindle Glade ME14 ..75 C5
Spindlewood Cl ME5 .32 B3
Spinnaker Cl [4] ME1 ..9 C1
Spinnens Acre Jun Sch
  ME5 ....32 C1
Spinney La CT3 .....112 E4
Spinney The
  Ashford TN23 ....138 E3
  Chatham ME5 ....32 B1
  Maidstone ME15 .....75 B2
  Margate CT9 ....8 E1
  River CT17 ....148 E2
Spire Ave CT5 ....44 A8
Spires The Canterbury CT2 66 F2
  Maidstone ME16 .....74 D4
Spitalfield La TN28 ..199 F6
Spitfire & Hurricane
  Memls Mus★ CT12 ...28 A2
Spitfire Cl ME5 ......32 B6
Split Ho CT17 ....149 A1
Split La CT4 ....127 A5
Sportsfield ME14 .....75 B5
Spot La ME15 ....76 A2
Spratling La CT12 ....28 F1
Spratling St CT12 ....28 E1
Sprig The ME14 ......76 A4
Spring Farm Rd TN29 192 C5
Spring Grove Sch TN25 123 C2
Spring Ho CT21 .....176 C2
Spring Hollow TN29 .195 A4
Spring La Canterbury CT1 88 C7

Spring La *continued*
Fordwich CT2 ....68 A4
Hythe CT21 ....177 A4
Spring Terr 15 CT20 ..178 D5
Spring Vale ME16 ......74 E4
Spring Wlk CT5 ....43 C7
Springett Way ME17 ..96 D3
Springfield Ave
Maidstone ME14 ......74 F4
St Michaels TN30 ....167 C2
Springfield Cl CT11 ...29 E2
Springfield Pass CT21 .176 B2
Springfield Rd
Dover CT16 ....149 B2
Gillingham ME7 ......10 E6
Margate CT9 ....8 E3
Sittingbourne ME10 ..36 D5
Springfield Terr 7 ME4 ..9 F4
Springfield Way CT21 ..177 B3
Springhead Rd ME13 ...40 D1
Springside Terr CT18 ..161 C6
Springvale Gillingham ME8 33 C6
Iwade ME9 ....14 D4
Springwood Cl
Ashford TN23 ....138 E3
Maidstone ME16 ......74 A3
Springwood Ct TN28 ..200 B6
Springwood Dr TN23 ..138 E3
Springwood Rd ME16 ..74 A3
Sprotlands Ave TN24 ..139 F1
Sprothill Cl ME10 ......36 E6
Spurgeons Cotts ME17 ..96 E2
Spurway ME14 ....76 A4
Square Hill ME15 ......75 B4
Square Hill Rd ME15 ..75 B4
Square The
Birchington CT7 ......27 A7
Chilham CT4 ....107 B8
Elham CT4 ....144 F4
Lenham ME17 ....101 D5
Selling ME13 ....84 A6
Sittingbourne ME10 ..14 F1
Squeeze Gut Alley 8
CT5 ....20 D2
Squire Ave CT2 ....87 C8
Squires Cl ME12 ....5 E3
Squires Way CT16 .....149 A3
St Malo Ct 9 CT20 ....178 C4
Stable Cl ME5 ....32 C5
Stable Ct Chilham CT4 ..107 B7
Faversham ME13 ......62 D6
Stable Mews CT18 .....161 D4
Stablemead CT19 ......178 A7
Stace Cl TN30 ....179 C8
Staceys St ME14 ....74 F5
Stade The CT19 ......178 E5
Stadium Way ME10 .....37 C6
Stadler Cl ME16 ......74 D7
Staffa Rd ME15 ....97 A7
Stafford Cl TN23 .....138 F2
Stafford St ME7 ....10 C5
Staffordshire St 8 CT11 52 E7
Stag Rd ME5 ....32 B5
Stagshaw Cl ME15 .....75 A2
Staines Hill CT2 ....68 B7
Staines Pl CT10 ....30 B5
Stalham Ct ME7 ....33 B4
Stalin Ave ME5 ....32 B8
Stalisfield Rd
Charing TN27 ....103 E3
Stalisfield Green ME13,
TN27 ....103 C5
Throwley ME13 ......82 C6
Stampers The ME15 ....74 D2
Stanbury Cres CT19 ...178 F4
Stancomb Ave CT11 ....52 C5
Standard Ave CT6 ......22 A4
Standen Cl ME8 ....33 E4
Standen La CT18 ......163 E5
Staner Ct CT12 ....52 A8
Staner Hill CT12 ......51 F8
Stanford Dr ME16 .....74 C3
Stanhope Ave ME10 ....37 A3
Stanhope Cl ME14 .....74 E7
Stanhope Rd
Ashford TN23 ....155 F7
Ashford, Stanhope TN23 155 E6
Deal CT14 ....117 D6
Dover CT16 ....149 C2
Rochester ME2 ......9 A7
Stanhope Sq TN23 ....155 F6
Stanley Ave
Minster (Sheppey) ME12 4 C1
Queenborough ME11 ..3 A4
Stanley Cl TN29 ......187 B4
Stanley Gdns CT6 .....22 F3
Stanley Pl
Broadstairs CT10 ....30 A4
Ramsgate CT11 ......52 E7
Stanley Rd
Broadstairs CT10 ....30 A6
Chatham ME5 ....32 C6
Deal CT14 ....117 D5
Folkestone CT19 ....177 E6
Gillingham ME7 .....10 C6
Herne Bay CT6 ......22 F4
Margate CT9 ....8 A3
Ramsgate CT11 .....52 D8
Whitstable CT5 .....43 D7
Stanmore Ct CT1 ......88 B7
Stansfeld Ave CT18 ...163 A4
Stansted Ct ME16 .....74 D7
Staple Cl ME10 ....36 E5
Staple Rd CT3 ....91 C6
Staple St ME13 ....63 F5
Staple Vineyard CT3 ..91 F5
Staplehurst Ave CT10 ..30 A2

Staplehurst Gdns CT9 ...8 E2
Staplehurst Rd
Gillingham ME8 ......11 B3
Sittingbourne ME10 ..36 D5
Staplers Ct ME14 ......75 B8
Staplestreet Rd ME13 ..64 A4
Star Hill ME1 ....9 D5
Star La Folkestone CT19 177 D7
Gillingham ME7 ......33 A7
Margate CT9 ....29 A5
Star Mill Ct ME5 ......10 D2
Star Mill La ME5 ......10 D2
Star Rd TN24 ....139 D2
Starle Cl CT1 ....67 B1
Starnes Ct 5 ME14 ....75 A5
Starvation Cnr 1 CT5 ..20 D2
Starveacre La ME8 .....36 B1
Station App Adisham CT3 112 E8
Birchington CT7 ......26 F7
Maidstone ME16 ......74 F3
Martin Mill CT15 ....133 C2
Minster (Thanet) CT12 50 C5
New Romney TN28 ...200 C6
Station Approach Rd
CT11 ....52 D8
Station Cotts ME13 .....84 E7
Station Dr CT14 ......117 A1
Station Mews Elham CT4 144 F4
Tenterden TN30 ......179 A7
Station Rd Adisham CT3 ..90 E1
Ashford TN23 ....139 C2
Birchington CT7 .....27 A7
Bridge CT4 ....88 F2
Charing TN27 ....120 C7
Chartham CT4 ....86 D3
Deal CT14 ....117 B1
Dymchurch TN29 ....195 B7
East Farleigh ME15 ..96 A4
Faversham ME13 .....62 D6
Folkestone CT19 ....177 F5
Gillingham ME8 .....12 A2
Harrietsham ME17 ..100 D6
Herne Bay CT6 ......22 E4
Hythe CT21 ....176 D3
Lydd TN29 ....203 D6
Lyminge CT18 ......161 C6
Maidstone ME14 .....74 F5
Margate CT9 ....9 H2
Martin Mill CT15 ...133 D1
Minster (Thanet) CT12 50 C5
New Romney TN28 ..200 C6
Newington ME9 .....35 B6
Patrixbourne CT4 ....89 C4
Pluckley TN27 ....136 C5
Rochester ME2 ......9 C7
Shepherdswell CT15 130 D5
Smeeth TN25 ....158 B3
St Margaret's at Cliffe
CT15 ....150 E8
Tenterden TN30 ....179 A7
Teynham ME9 ....38 D2
Westgate-on-S CT8 ..7 D1
Whitstable CT5 .....20 E2
Station Rd E CT1 ......87 F7
Station Rd W CT2 ......66 F1
Station Row ME9 ......38 D3
Station St ME10 ....36 F4
Station Terr TN28 ....200 C6
Stede Hill ME17 ....78 F3
Steed Cl CT6 ....46 B8
Steeds Cl TN23 ......156 A1
Steeds La TN23,TN26 ..156 B1
Steele St ME9 ....9 A8
Steerforth Cl ME1 .....9 C2
Stella Maris
RC Prim Sch CT19 ..178 C6
Stelling Minnis
CE Prim Sch CT4 ...126 F6
Stembrook CT16 ......166 D8
Stembrook Ct 4 CT16 166 D7
Stempe Cl CT18 ......163 B3
Step Style ME10 ......37 B2
Stephen Cl CT10 ......30 A4
Stephen Ct 2 CT20 ...178 D5
Stephen's Cl CT9 ......28 B7
Stephens Cl
Faversham ME13 .....62 B8
Ramsgate CT11 .....52 C8
Stephenson Rd CT2 ....66 F3
Steps Hill Rd ME9 .....56 D6
Sterling Ave ME16 ....74 C5
Sterling Cl CT10 ......29 E5
Sterling Rd
Queenborough ME11 ..3 A5
Sittingbourne ME10 ..36 D1
Stevens Cl TN27 ......118 F3
Stevenson Cl ME15 ....74 F3
Stickfast La ME9 ......14 A1
Stiles Cl Folkestone CT19 178 A7
Minster (Sheppey) ME12 ..4 A6
Rochester ME1 ......9 A3
Stirling Cl Gillingham ME8 33 E4
Rochester ME1 ......9 A3
Stirling Way CT12 .....29 A2
Stirling Rd TN24 .....156 D7
Stisted Way TN27 ....118 F3
Stock La TN25 ....158 A4
Stockbury Dr ME16 ....74 D7
Stockbury Gdns CT9 ...8 E2
Stockdale Gdns CT14 ..117 C4
Stocker's Hill ME13 ...63 C4
Stockers Brow ME9 ....59 A7
Stockers Hill ME10,ME9 59 A7
Stockett La ME15 ......96 D6
Stockham Ct CT19 ....177 E7
Stocks Rd TN30 ......188 F3
Stocks The ME13 ......83 C6
Stockton Cl ME14 ......75 B8
Stockwood Chase CT2 ..66 A2

Stoddart Rd CT19 ....177 E6
Stodmarsh National
Nature Reserve★ CT3 ..69 D8
Stodmarsh Rd CT3 .....68 C3
Stombers La CT18 ....163 C6
Stonar Cl Ramsgate CT11 29 E1
Sandwich CT13 ......73 A1
Stone Abbage TN27 ...136 D4
Stone Barn Ave CT7 ...27 A6
Stone Bay Sch CT10 ...30 B6
Stone Cnr TN30 ......189 A6
Stone Cross Lees CT13 93 F7
Stone Gdns CT10 ......30 B5
Stone Gn TN30 ....189 F4
Stone Hill TN25 ......159 A2
Stone Hill Rd TN27 ...118 F2
Stone Ho CT10 ....30 B7
Stone House Mews CT10 30 B7
Stone Rd CT10 ....30 B5
Stone St Faversham ME13 62 C7
Lympne CT21 ....175 A4
Stanford TN25 ......160 C3
Stelling Minnis CT4 ..126 D4
Westenhanger TN25,CT21 175 B6
Stoneacre★ CT15 ......98 B7
Stoneacre Cl ME8 .....33 D5
Stoneacre Ct ME15 ....75 A1
Stoneacre La ME15 ....98 B7
Stonebridge TN25 ....141 A5
Stonebridge Cotts TN23 156 B8
Stonebridge Green Rd
TN27 ....119 A4
Stonebridge Way ME13 62 B7
Stonecross Lea ME5 ...10 C1
Stonedane Ct ME13 ....62 C8
Stonegate TN25 ......123 E2
Stonehall Rd CT15 ....147 F8
Stoneheap Rd CT14,
CT15 ....115 E1
Stonestile Farm Rd
TN27 ....103 A3
Stoney Bank ME7 .....10 F1
Stoney Rd ME13 ......64 B3
Stony La ME1 ....31 C5
Stonyway La CT15 ....165 C5
Stopford Rd ME7 ......10 D4
Storehouse Wharf ME1 ..1 A3
Stour Cl Ashford TN23 ..138 E1
Chartham CT4 ....86 D2
Stour Cres CT1 ....67 D3
Stour Ct 7 Canterbury CT1 87 F8
Sandwich CT13 ......72 F1
Stour Rd CT4 ....86 D2
Stour St CT1 ....87 F8
Stour Valley Cl CT3 ...47 D3
Stourmouth Rd CT3 ....70 C8
Stourside Studios 4 CT1 66 F1
Stowting CE Prim Sch
TN25 ....160 B8
Stowting Hill TN25 ...143 A1
Straight La TN29 .....191 F1
Strakers Hill CT15 ....132 D8
Strand Approach Rd ME7 10 E2
Strand Rdbt The ME7 ..10 E2
Strand St CT13 ....72 F1
Strand The CT14 .....117 A4
Stranger's Cl CT1 .....87 C6
Stranger's La CT1 .....87 C6
Strangford Pl CT3 .....23 B2
Strangford Rd CT5 ....20 F2
Strasbourg St CT9 .....29 A6
Stratford Ave ME8 ....33 D8
Stratford La 2 ME8 ....33 F8
Straw Mill Hill ME15 ..74 E1
Stream Wlk CT5 ....20 D2
Street End CT1 ....71 E1
Street End Rd ME5 ....10 B1
Street The Acol CT7 ...27 B3
Adisham CT3 ....112 C8
Appledore TN26 .....190 D8
Ash CT3 ....71 D1
Ashford TN24 ......157 B8
Ashford, Kennington TN24 139 F1
Barham CT4 ....111 F1
Bethersden TN26 ....153 D5
Bishopsbourne CT4 ..111 C4
Borden ME9 ....36 B2
Bossingham CT4 ....127 A7
Boughton Street ME13 64 C3
Boxley ME14 ....54 C3
Brabourne TN25 ....159 C8
Bredgar ME9 ....58 A5
Bredhurst ME7 .....33 B1
Brook TN25 ....141 B6
Chilham CT4 ....107 B8
Deal CT14 ....116 F6
Denton CT4 ....129 B3
Detling ME14 ......55 A1
Doddington ME9 ....80 E7
East Langdon CT15 ..133 A1
Eastling ME13 .....81 E6
Egerton TN27 ......118 F3
Eythorne CT15 .....131 D7
Finglesham CT14 ...116 B8
Folkestone,Newington
CT18 ....177 A7
Godmersham CT4 ..107 B2
Goodnestone CT3 ...91 D2
Great Chart TN23 ..138 C1
Guston CT15 ....149 E6
Hamstreet TN26 ...183 A7
Hartlip ME9 ....34 D5
Hastingleigh TN25 .142 B6
Hawkinge CT18 ....163 B5
Hothfield TN26 ....138 A4
Ickham CT3 ....69 C2
Iwade ME9 ....14 E4

Street The *continued*
Kingston CT4 ....111 D3
Lower Halstow ME9 ..13 B3
Lympne CT21 ......174 F2
Lynsted ME9 ....60 A6
Maidstone ME14 ....76 C4
Martin Mill CT15 ...133 D3
Mersham TN25 .....157 E4
Newnham ME9 .....81 C8
Nonington CT15 ...113 D1
Northbourne CT14 .116 A5
Oare ME13 ....40 B2
Patrixbourne CT4 ..89 B3
Petham CT4 ....109 B3
Postling CT21 ......160 F2
Preston CT3 ....70 C6
Shadoxhurst TN26 .170 A8
Sittingbourne ME9 ..37 E3
St Nicholas at Wade CT7 25 F2
Staple CT3 ....91 F6
Stone in Oxney TN30 190 A5
Stourmouth CT3 ....48 E1
Upchurch ME9 .....12 F4
West Hougham CT15 164 F5
Wickhambreaux CT3 69 C1
Wittersham TN30 ...188 D3
Womenswold CT4 ..112 D2
Woodnesborough CT13 93 C7
Wormshill ME9 .....79 A7
Worth CT14 ....94 B5
Streete Court Rd CT8 ..27 F8
Streete Ct CT8 ....27 F8
Streetfield CT6 ....46 B8
Streetfield Rd ME8 ....11 F1
Stringer Dr CT7 ....27 A6
Strode Cres ME12 .....1 D2
Strode Park Rd CT6 ....23 A2
Strond St CT17 ......166 D6
Strouts Rd TN23 .....155 D7
Strover St ME7 ....10 C7
Stuart Cl CT1 ....75 C6
Stuart Ct Canterbury CT1 88 A6
Dover CT17 ....166 C8
Stuart Ho CT14 ......117 A5
Stuart Rd
Folkestone CT19 ....178 E6
Gillingham ME7 ....10 D3
Studds Cotts CT6 ......22 A3
Studfall Cl CT21 .....187 D8
Studio Cl TN24 ......139 E6
Stumble La TN23 ....156 B1
Stuppington Court Farm
CT1 ....87 E4
Stuppington La CT1 ...87 F5
Sturdee Ave ME7 .....10 F1
Sturdy Cl CT21 ......176 D2
Sturges Rd TN24 ....139 B3
Sturla Rd ME4 ....10 A3
Sturmer Cl CT1 ......88 C7
Sturry CE Prim Sch CT2 68 A7
Sturry Court Mews CT2 67 F5
Sturry Hill CT2 ....67 F6
Sturry Rd CT1,CT2 ...67 C3
Sturry Sta CT2 ....67 F5
Sturry Way ME8 ......11 C2
Style Cl ME8 ....33 E4
Sudbury Pl CT8 ....27 E7
Suffolk Ave
Gillingham ME8 .....11 F1
Westgate-on-S CT8 ..27 D7
Suffolk Dr TN23 .....139 A2
Suffolk Gdns CT17 ...165 F7
Suffolk Rd Canterbury CT1 88 D8
Maidstone ME15 ....97 D8
Suffolk St CT5 ....43 D8
Sugarloaf Wlk CT19 ..178 D8
Sultan Rd ME5 ....32 C2
Summer Cl Hythe CT21 175 F2
Tenterden TN30 ....167 C1
Summer Ct CT2 ....66 C1
Summer Hill CT2 .....66 C1
Summer Hill Pk TN24 157 C7
Summer La CT2 ....66 E6
Summer Leeze TN24 ..156 E8
Summer Leeze Gdns
TN24 ....156 E8
Summer Rd CT7 ....25 C1
Summerfield Ave CT5 ..20 F1
Summerfield Farm
Pottery★ CT13 .....92 C4
Summerfield Rd CT9 ..8 E2
Summerhill TN23 .....155 E6
Summerville Ave ME12 ..4 A5
Sumpter Way ME13 ...61 F7
Sun La Hythe CT21 ...176 C2
St Nicholas at Wade CT7 25 F2
Sun St CT1 ....87 E8
Sun Terr ME5 ....32 B4
Sun Valley Way CT15 .131 C8
Sunbeam Ave CT6 ....21 F4
Sunderland Cl ME1 ....9 A3
Sunderland Dr ME8 ...34 A8
Sunderland Ho 3 ME7 ..10 C7
Sundew Gr CT11 ......52 E8
Sundridge Cl CT2 .....67 A4
Sundridge Dr ME5 ....32 A4
Sunningdale Ave 4
CT19 ....178 A7
Sunningdale Cl ME8 ...33 D6
Sunningdale Ct ME15 ..75 B4
Sunningdale Dr ME8 ...33 D6
Sunningdale Wlk CT6 ..22 D1
Sunny Bank Hythe CT21 175 F2
Sittingbourne ME10 ..37 B5
Sunny Cnr CT17 ......166 B5
Sunnyfields Cl ME8 ....33 E8
Sunnyfields Dr ME12 ..3 C6

Sunnyhill Rd CT6 ......22 C4
Sunnymead CT2 ....66 D7
Sunnymead Ave ME7 ..10 E5
Sunnyside Doddington ME9 80 E7
Littlestone-on-S TN28 ..200 D6
Lydd TN29 ....203 B6
Sunnyside Ave ME12 ..4 A6
Sunnyside Cl CT11 ....16 D1
Sunnyside Cotts CT14 117 C6
Sunnyside Gdns CT13 ..93 E8
Sunnyside Rd CT20 ...177 D3
Sunray Ave CT5 ....43 B7
Sunset Cl Eastchurch ME12 ..5 F6
Whitstable CT5 .....43 C6
Sunshine Ct 1 ME8 ....33 F8
Superabbey Est ME20 ..53 B2
Surf Cres ME12 ....5 F6
Surrenden TN27 ......136 F7
Surrenden Rd CT19 ...177 F6
Surrey Gdns CT7 ......26 F7
Surrey Rd Canterbury CT1 88 D7
Maidstone ME15 ....97 C8
Margate CT9 ....8 B3
Susan's Hill TN26 ....168 E3
Sussex Ave Ashford TN24 139 E3
Canterbury CT1 ....88 D7
Margate CT9 ....7 J1
Sussex Cl CT6 ....22 B4
Sussex Dr ME5 ....32 A4
Sussex Gdns
Birchington CT7 ....26 F7
Herne Bay CT6 .....22 B4
Westgate-on-S CT8 ..7 D1
Sussex Mansions CT8 ..7 D1
Sussex Rd
Folkestone CT19 ....178 D6
Maidstone ME15 ....97 D8
New Romney TN28 .200 A6
Sussex St CT11 ....52 E7
Sussex Wlk CT1 ....88 D7
Sutherland Cl CT21 ...176 A2
Sutherland Dr CT7 ....27 B6
Sutherland Gdns ME8 ..3 A8
Sutherland Rd CT14 ..117 C6
Sutton Cl
Folkestone CT19 ....178 A7
Gillingham ME8 .....34 A8
Sutton Cotts ME13 ....84 C3
Sutton La
Ringwould CT14 ....133 F5
Ripple CT14 ....133 C8
Sutton Rd Hersden CT3 ..46 E1
Langley Heath ME17 .98 C5
Maidstone ME15 ....97 D6
Sutton St ME14 ......76 D4
Suttons The TN31 ....201 A1
Swadelands Cl ME17 ..101 C5
Swadelands Sch ME17 ..101 C5
Swain Rd Gillingham ME8 33 B6
St Michaels TN30 ...167 D3
Swakeley Wlk CT5 .....21 D3
Swale Ave Rushenden ME11 ..2 F1
Sheerness ME12 .....1 C1
Swale Cl CT6 ....23 A3
Swale Sta ME9 ....15 A7
Swale View ME13 .....64 B6
Swalecliffe Ave CT6 ...22 B4
Swalecliffe
Com Prim Sch CT5 ..21 B2
Swalecliffe Court Dr CT5 21 D3
Swalecliffe Rd CT5 ....21 B2
Swallow Ave CT5 ......43 B6
Swallow Cl CT9 ....28 C8
Swallow Ct CT6 ....45 F7
Swallow House 4 ME16 74 E4
Swallow Rise ME5 ....32 A5
Swallowfield TN24 ...156 E7
Swamp Rd TN29 .....199 B4
Swan Apartments 12
ME15 ....97 E5
Swan Cl ME10 ....37 B4
Swan Cotts TN30 ....188 D3
Swan Gn TN25 ....159 D1
Swan La TN25 ....159 E2
Swan St TN30 ....188 C3
Swanfield Rd CT5 .....43 D8
Swanstree Ave ME10 ..37 B2
Swanton La
Canterbury CT3 .....68 D2
River,Lydden CT15 ..147 C6
Swanton Mill★ TN25 .157 B2
Swarling Hill Rd CT4 ..109 C2
Swaynes Way CT13 ...93 B2
Sweechbridge Rd CT6 ..23 F3
Sweechgate CT2 ......67 E7
Sweetbriar La CT15 ..114 B2
Sweetlove Pl CT3 .....91 A8
Sweyn Rd CT9 ....8 A3
Swift Cres ME5 ....32 C6
Swift House 6 ME16 ..74 E4
Swinburne Ave CT10 ..30 A3
Swinford Gdns CT9 ....29 C8
Swingate Cl ME5 .....32 B2
Swingate Inf Sch ME5 ..32 C1
Sycamore Ave CT3 ...112 E5
Sycamore Cl
Broadstairs CT10 ....29 C4
Chartham CT4 ......86 F1
Dymchurch TN29 ...195 C8
Herne Bay CT6 .....23 C5
Hythe CT21 ....175 E1
Lydd TN29 ....203 D7
Margate CT9 ....28 C4
Sycamore Cres ME16 ..74 C5
Sycamore Dr CT14 ...117 B4

Sycamore Gdns TN29 ..195 C8
Sycamore Grange CT11 ..29 F1
Sycamores The CT3 .....68 E8
Sydcot Dr CT14 ....117 D8
Sydenham Rd CT14 .....117 D7
Sydenham St CT5 ....20 D2
Sydney Ave ME10 ....36 C4
Sydney Cooper CT2 ....66 B2
Sydney Rd Chatham ME4 ..10 A3
  Deal CT14 ....117 A1
  Ramsgate CT11 ....52 F8
  Whitstable CT5 ....43 E8
Sydney St TN23 ....156 C8
Sylewood Cl ME1 ....31 B8
Sylvan Glade ME5 ....54 A8
Sylvan Rd ME8 ....33 C8
Symmonds Dr ME10 .....37 A6
Symons Ave ME4 ....10 A2
Syndale Pl 1 CT11 ......52 F7

T

Tabret Cl TN24 ....139 D6
Tadburn Gn ME5 ....32 B4
Taddington Wood La
  ME5 ....31 E2
Taddy Gdns CT9 ....29 C8
Tadley Ct Chatham ME1 ..31 C8
  Gillingham ME7 ....10 F6
Tadworth Rd TN24 .....139 D5
Tail Race The ME15 ....74 E2
Taillour Cl ME10 ....36 F7
Talavera Rd CT1 ....88 D8
Talbot Ave CT6 ....22 B3
Talbot Rd Maidstone ME16 74 C6
  Margate CT9 ....8 B2
Tall Trees CT17 ....99 D2
Tally Ho Rd TN26 ......155 C2
Tamarind Cl ME7 ....33 A4
Tamarisk ME12 ....19 E5
Tame La CT21,TN29 ....185 F6
Tamley La TN25 ....142 B6
Tams Gdns ME12 ....4 D6
Tangier Cl CT15 ....149 E3
Tanglewood Cl ME8 .....33 C6
Tangmere Cl ME7 ....10 F5
Tanker Hill ME8 ....33 D6
Tankerton Cir CT5 ......20 F3
Tankerton Ct CT5 ....21 B3
Tankerton Mews CT5 ...20 E3
Tankerton Rd CT5 ......20 F3
Tanner's Hill CT21 ....176 C3
Tanner's Hill Gdns CT21 176 C3
Tanners St ME13 ....62 C7
Tannery Ct 6 ME10 .....36 E5
Tannery La Ashford TN23 139 C2
  10 Sandwich CT13 ......72 F1
Tapleys Hill CT4 ......110 B5
Target Bsns Ctr ME15 ...97 F4
Target Firs CT16 ......148 D5
Tariff Reform Cotts
  ME13 ....62 D5
Tarragon Rd ME16 ......74 B3
Tartane La TN29 ....195 C8
Tasker Cl ME15 ....76 B3
Tassell's Wlk CT5 ......21 D3
Taswell Cl CT16 ......166 E8
Taswell Rd ME8 ....12 A1
Taswell St CT16 ......166 E8
Tatler Cl ME5 ....32 D2
Tatsfield Cl ME8 ....11 A2
Taunton Cl ME15 ....97 F6
Taverners Rd ME8 ....33 E7
Tavistock Cl Chatham ME5 31 F1
  Gillingham ME8 ....33 E7
  Sittingbourne ME10 ....36 D4
Tavistock Rd CT11 ......29 E1
Tay Cl ME5 ....32 B5
Taylor Cl ME17 ....100 D6
Taylor Rd
  Folkestone CT19 ......177 E6
  Lydd-on-S TN29 ....204 E6
  Minster (Thanet) CT12 ..50 B6
Taylor's La ME2 ....9 B7
Taylors TN29 ....194 F3
Taylors Hill CT4 ......107 B8
Taylors La TN29 ......194 F3
Taylors Yd TN25 ......123 E2
Taywood Cl TN24 ......139 F1
Teasaucer Hill ME15 ...96 F8
Teasel Cl ME14 ....75 F4
Teasel Rd ME5 ....31 F4
Teddars Leas Rd CT18 .161 E4
Tedder Ave ME5 ....32 A7
Teddington Cl CT1 .....67 B2
Teelin Cl TN29 ....195 A4
Telegraph Rd CT14 ....117 B3
Telford Cl
  Folkestone CT19 ......178 E6
  Herne Bay CT6 ....22 C2
Telford Ho 1 ME14 .....75 A6
Telford St CT6 ....22 E5
Telham Ave CT12 ....52 B8
Temeraire Hts CT20 ...177 C3
Temeraire Manor 2
  ME7 ....10 A6
Templar Rd CT16 ......148 D5
Templar St CT17 ......166 C8
Temple Cl Ashford TN23 .139 E6
  Temple Ewell CT16 ....148 D6
Temple Ct CT2 ....66 D1
Temple Ewell CE Prim Sch
  CT16 ....148 D5

Temple Gdns
  Rochester ME2 ....9 A6
  Sittingbourne ME10 ....37 B3
Temple Manor* ME2 .....9 A6
Temple Mews 10 CT1 ...87 F8
Temple Side CT16 .....148 D6
Temple Way CT14 ....94 A4
Templeman Liby CT2 ...66 E4
Ten Acre Way ME8 ......12 B1
Ten Perch Rd CT1 ......87 D6
Tennyson Ave CT1 ......67 D3
Tennyson Gdns CT3 ...112 F6
Tennyson Pl CT19 .....178 E7
Tennyson Rd
  Ashford TN23 ....156 A6
  Gillingham ME7 ....10 C3
Tenterden & District
  Mus* TN30 ....179 A7
Tenterden CE Jun Sch
  TN30 ....179 B7
Tenterden Dr CT2 ....67 A4
Tenterden Inf Sch TN30 179 B7
Tenterden Rd
  Appledore TN26 ....181 B1
  Chatham ME5 ....32 B5
  Tenterden Sta* TN30 .179 A8
Tenterden Vineyard*
  TN30 ....179 C1
Terence Cl ME4 ....10 A2
Terminus Dr CT6 ....23 D5
Terminus Rd ME16 ......74 A2
Terrace Cotts CT4 ....127 A6
Terrace Rd
  Elvington CT15 ....114 B1
  Maidstone ME16 ....74 E3
  Sittingbourne ME10 ...37 B3
Terrace The
  Canterbury CT2 ....66 F3
  Faversham ME13 ....62 A7
  Pluckley TN26 ....120 A1
  Rochester ME1 ....9 C5
  Shepherdswell CT15 ..130 D5
Terry's La CT5 ....20 D2
Teynham Cl CT9 ....8 F2
Teynham Dr CT5 ....20 F2
Teynham Gn ME8 ....11 A4
Teynham Parochial
  CE Prim Sch ME9 .....38 C2
Teynham Rd CT5 ....20 F2
Teynham St ME9 ....38 F4
Teynham Sta ME9 ......38 D3
Thames Ave
  Gillingham ME8 ....33 E8
  Sheerness ME12 ....1 C1
Thames Ct ME12 ....6 G2
Thames View Inf Sch
  ME8 ....11 D2
Thames View Jun Sch
  ME8 ....11 D2
Thanet Cl CT10 ....30 B5
Thanet Coll
  Broadstairs CT10 ......30 A3
  Margate CT9 ....7 I2
Thanet Enterprise Ctr
  CT10 ....29 D7
Thanet Gdns CT19 ....178 F6
Thanet House 7 ME15 ..97 F5
Thanet Place Gdns CT10 30 B6
Thanet Rd
  Broadstairs CT10 ......30 B4
  Margate CT9 ....7 J2
  Ramsgate CT11 ....52 F7
  Westgate-on-S CT8 ....27 D8
Thanet Reach Bsns Pk
  CT10 ....29 C4
Thanet Terr TN26 .....138 A6
Thanet View
  Eythorne CT15 ....131 B8
  St Nicholas at Wade CT7 .25 F2
Thanet Way
  Boughton Street ME13 ..63 D6
  Herne Bay CT3,CT6,CT7 ..23 C3
  Whitstable CT5 ....21 C2
  Yorklets CT5,ME13 ....42 E2
Thanington Ct Farm CT1 87 C6
Thanington Rd CT1 .....87 C6
Thatchers The ME16 ....74 B5
Theatre Sq 7 TN30 ...179 A7
Theatre St CT21 ......176 C2
Theodore Pl ME7 ....10 C5
Theresa Rd CT21 ......176 B1
Third Ave Chatham ME5 .10 C1
  Eastchurch ME12 ......5 F6
  Gillingham ME7 ....10 F4
  Margate CT9 ....8 B3
Thirlemere Cl ME16 ....74 D8
Thirlmere TN24 ....139 D6
Thirlmere Ave CT11 ....52 A7
Thirlmere Cl ME7 ......11 A5
Thirlmere Gdns CT3 ..112 F6
Thirsk House 6 ME15 ..97 F6
Thistle Hill Way
  Minster (Sheppey) ME12 ..4 A4
  Minster (Sheppey) ME12 ..4 C5
Thistle Wlk ME10 ......37 B5
Thistlebank ME5 ....32 A3
Thistledown ME14 .....74 A6
Thistledown Cl ME7 ....33 A4
Thomas Aveling Sch The
  ME1 ....31 C8
Thomas Ct 9 ME10 .....37 B4
Thomas Rd
  Faversham ME13 ......62 D7
  Sittingbourne ME10 ....37 B4
Thomas St ME1 ....9 C3
Thompson Cl Deal CT14 .134 B8

Thompson Cl continued
  Folkestone CT19 ......178 B7
  Gillingham ME8 ....34 A8
Thomson Rd TN25 .....139 B5
Thorn Cl ME5 ....31 D1
Thorn Est The TN27 ...136 B6
Thorn Gdns CT11 ....29 E1
Thorn Hill Rd ME12 .....6 D4
Thorn La CT4 ....126 C2
Thorn Wlk ME10 ....37 C5
Thornbridge Rd CT14 ..117 B2
Thorndale ME5 ....31 D4
Thorndale Cl ME5 ......31 D4
Thornden Cl CT6 ....22 B2
Thornden Ct CT2 ....66 C4
Thornden Wood Rd
  Herne Bay CT6 ....22 B1
  Whitstable CT6 ....44 E4
Thorndike Cl ME4 ......31 F8
Thorndike Rd TN29 ...186 C4
Thorne Hill CT12 ......51 A6
Thorne Rd CT12 ....50 B6
Thorney Croft Cl ME17 .99 D2
Thorneycroft Rd ME13 103 D3
Thornham Rd ME8 ......11 C3
Thornhill Pl ME14 .....75 A6
Thornhurst CT6 ....23 D4
Thornlea TN23 ....138 E2
Thornton Cl TN24 .....140 A1
Thornton La CT13,CT14 114 A1
Thornton's La 7 CT16 .166 E7
Thorold Rd ME5 ....10 B3
Thorpe Wlk ME8 ....33 D3
Thrale Way ME8 ....33 E4
Thread La ME13 ....64 B4
Three Acres Site CT19 .178 B8
Three King's Yd CT13 ..73 A1
Threshers Dr ME14 .....75 E5
Throwley Dr CT6 ....22 C4
Throwley Rd ME13 .....82 D5
Thrupp Paddock CT10 ..8 G1
Thrush Cl ME5 ....32 B7
Thruxted La CT4 ....86 B1
Thundersland Rd CT6 ..23 B4
Thurlow Ave CT6 ....23 C5
Thurnham CE Inf Sch
  ME14 ....76 A4
Thurnham La ME14 .....76 C7
Thurston Pk CT5 ....20 E1
Thurstone Ct ME14 ....74 F6
Tiber Cl CT19 ....177 C6
Tichborne Cl ME16 .....74 C6
Tickham La ME9 ....60 C5
Tideway The ME1 ....31 C8
Tilbury Rd ME8 ....12 A2
Tilden Cl TN26 ....167 D7
Tilden Ct TN26 ....167 E7
Tilden Gill Rd TN30 ..179 C7
Tile Fields ME17 ....77 D2
Tile Kiln Hill CT2 ....66 B5
Tile Kiln La CT19 ....177 F7
Tile Kiln Rd TN24 ...139 C7
Tile Lodge Cotts TN27 119 E8
Tile Lodge Rd TN27 ..119 E8
Tillard Cl CT4 ....109 B3
Tillery La TN29 ......198 A3
Timber Tops ME5 ......54 D8
Timberbank ME5 ....32 A6
Timball Tower Mus*
  CT14 ....117 D5
Timperley Cl CT14 ....117 B6
Tina Gdns CT10 ....30 A6
Tinbridge Pk ME13 ....63 A5
Tinker's Alley ME4 ....9 F7
Tintagel Manor 6 ME7 .10 C6
Tintern Rd ME16 ....74 D7
Titchfield Cl 5 ME15 .97 F5
Titchfield Rd ME15 ....97 F6
Tithe Barn La TN23 ...155 D8
Tithe Yd ME17 ....101 D5
Tivoli Brooks CT9 .....7 I1
Tivoli Park Ave CT9 ...7 H1
Tivoli Rd CT9 ....28 E8
Tobruk Way ME5 ....31 F6
Toby Rd TN29 ....204 E6
Todd Cres ME10 ....37 A8
Toddington Cres ME5 .31 D1
Toke Cl TN23 ....138 C1
Tolgate La ME2 ....9 B7
Tolgate Way ME14 ....53 E4
Toll Gate CT14 ......117 A4
Toll La TN27 ....120 E7
Tollemache Cl CT12 ...27 F2
Tollgate Cl CT5 ....43 C8
Tolsford Cl
  Etchinghill CT18 ....161 D3
  Folkestone CT19 ....177 D6
Tomay Cotts CT6 ......24 A3
Tomlin Dr CT9 ....29 C8
Tonbridge Cl ME16 ....74 D3
Tonbridge Rd ME16 ...74 C3
Tonford La Canterbury CT1 87 B6
  Harbledown CT2 ....87 A7
Tong Rd ME10 ....37 B4
Tonge Rd ME10 ....37 C4
Tontine St CT20 ......178 E5
Tookey Rd TN28 ......200 B6
Top Rd TN30 ....189 E3
Topaz Dr ME10 ....36 C6
Tormore Mews CT14 ..117 A4
Tormore Pk CT14 ....117 A4
Toronto Cl 6 CT16 ...149 B3
Toronto Rd ME7 ......10 E4
Torrington Cotts CT12 ..30 D7
Torrington Rd TN23 ..156 C8
Tothill St CT12 ......50 C7
Tournay Rd TN23 .....155 F8
Tourney Cl CT21 .....174 F3

Tourney Rd TN29 .....203 C5
Tourtel Rd CT1 ....67 A1
Tovil Gn ME15 ....74 E2
Tovil Green Bsns Pk
  ME15 ....74 E1
Tovil Hill ME15 ....74 E2
Tovil Rd ME15 ....74 F2
Tovil, St Stephen's
  CE Inf Sch ME15 .....74 E2
Tower Bglws CT7 ......27 A8
Tower Cl 4 CT20 .....177 E3
Tower Est TN29 ......186 E2
Tower Gdns Hythe CT21 176 C1
  Maidstone ME14 ....76 B4
Tower Hamlets Rd
  CT17 ....166 C8
Tower Hamlets St 1
  CT17 ....166 C8
Tower Hill Dover CT17 .166 C8
  Whitstable CT5 ....20 E3
Tower La ME14 ....76 B4
Tower Par CT5 ....20 E2
Tower Rd CT5 ....20 E2
Tower St CT17 ....166 C8
Tower Way 1 CT1 ......87 F8
Towers Sch The TN24 .139 D8
Towers The TN27 .....103 E1
Towers View TN24 ...139 C7
Town La CT4 ....86 C6
Town Rd CT4 ....109 C5
Town Wlk CT20 ......178 D4
Townley St CT11 ......52 D6
Townsend Farm Rd
  CT15 ....150 F6
Townsend Terr CT17 .166 B5
Townwall St CT16 ....166 E7
Toy Mus* CT5 ....20 E3
Tracies The ME9 ......35 C6
Trafalgar Par ME12 ...4 B6
Trafalgar Rd CT7 .....27 F3
Trafalgar St ME7 .....10 C5
Tram Rd The CT20 ...178 E5
Tramways ME5 ....10 C2
Transom Ho 3 ME1 ....9 C1
Trapfield Cl ME14 .....76 C4
Trapfield La ME14 .....76 C4
Trapham Rd ME16 ....74 D5
Travers Gdns ME9 ....57 F5
Travers Rd CT14 .....117 A5
Travertine Rd ME5 ...32 B1
Treasury View CT3 ...90 C8
Trefoil The ME9,ME13 .60 E6
Trefor Jones Ct CT16 149 B2
Trelawn Cres ME5 ....32 B2
Trenley Cl CT3 ....67 F1
Trent Rd ME5 ....32 B5
Trenton Cl ME16 ......74 B7
Trevale Rd ME1 ....9 B1
Trevino Dr ME5 ....31 F2
Trevor Dr ME5 ....74 C5
Tribune Cl ME12 ....3 B8
Tribune Dr ME10 ......36 F6
Trident Cl ME2 ....9 E7
Trigg's Row ME9 ......38 D2
Trimworth Rd CT19 ..177 F6
Trinity Cres CT20 ...178 B4
Trinity Ct Aylesford ME20 53 A3
  Margate CT9 ....7 J3
Trinity Gdns CT20 ...178 C4
Trinity Hill CT9 ......7 J3
Trinity Homes CT14 ..117 C1
Trinity Pl Deal CT14 .117 A4
  Ramsgate CT11 ....52 F7
Trinity Rd Ashford TN24 139 F7
  Folkestone CT20 ....178 B4
  Gillingham ME7 ....10 C6
  Sheerness ME12 ....1 D2
  Sittingbourne ME10 ...36 F7
Trinity Sq
  Broadstairs CT10 .....29 F7
  Margate CT9 ....7 J3
Trinity Trad Est ME10 36 F6
Tritton Cl TN24 .....139 F7
Tritton Fields TN24 .139 F7
Tritton Gdns TN29 ..186 D1
Tritton La TN28 .....200 B6
Troodos Hill ME14 ...74 F8
Trotts Hall Gdns ME10 .36 F3
Trotwood Cl ME5 .....54 A8
Troubridge Cl TN24 .157 B7
Troughton Mews CT9 ..7 H1
Trove Ct 5 CT11 ......52 F7
Troy Town La TN25 ..141 B5
Troys Mead ME17 .....77 D2
Trueman Cl CT2 ....66 A7
Trumpet Ho TN23 ....156 B8
Truro Cl ME8 ....11 D3
Truro Rd CT11 ....52 F7
Tudor Ave
  Dymchurch TN29 .....186 D1
  Maidstone ME14 ....75 B6
Tudor Byway TN24 ...139 D6
Tudor Cl CT7 ....27 B8
Tudor End TN24 ......139 D5
Tudor Gr ME8 ....33 F8
Tudor Ho Deal CT14 .117 A5
  Tudor Ho* Margate CT9 ..7 J2
Tudor Rd Ashford TN24 139 D5
  Canterbury CT1 ....87 E7
  Folkestone CT19 ....177 D6
Tufa Cl ME5 ....32 B1
Tufton Rd Ashford TN24 139 D2
  Gillingham ME8 ....11 F1
  Hothfield TN26 ......138 A7
Tufton St Ashford TN23 139 B2
  Maidstone ME14 ....75 A4
Tufton Wlk 9 TN23 ..139 B2
Tunbury Ave ME5 .....31 F1

Tunbury Ave S ME5 .....31 F1
Tunbury Cty Prim Sch
  ME5 ....31 F1
Tunis Ct CT1 ....67 D1
Tunis Row CT10 ....30 B5
Tunstall CE Prim Sch
  ME9 ....58 C8
Tunstall Rd
  Canterbury CT2 ....67 A4
  Sittingbourne ME10,ME9 .58 D8
Tupman Cl ME1 ....9 B4
Turgis Cl ME17 ....98 E4
Turketel Rd CT20 ....178 A4
Turmine Ct ME12 ....4 A5
Turnagain La 3 CT1 ...87 F8
Turnden Gdns CT9 .....8 E2
Turner Cl ME10 ....37 A7
Turner Ct
  5 Folkestone CT20 ..177 F5
  Margate CT9 ....8 A2
Turner St CT11 ....52 E7
Turners Ave TN30 ....179 B8
Turners Cl ME12 ....1 D1
Turnpike Cl CT21 ....176 A2
Turnpike Hill CT21 ..176 A3
Turnstone Cl ME9 .....14 E4
Turnstone Ct TN29 ..195 A3
Turnstone Rd ME5 ....32 C1
Tuscan Dr ME5 ....32 C1
Tweed Terr CT21 .....176 A1
Twelve Acres TN24 ..156 F8
Twiss Ave CT21 ......176 D2
Twiss Gr CT21 ....176 D2
Twiss Rd CT21 ....176 D2
Twisden Ent Ctr ME8 ..11 C4
Twydall Gn ME8 ....11 B3
Twydall Inf Sch ME8 ..11 B2
Twydall Jun Sch ME8 ..11 B2
Twydall La ME8 ....11 B2
Twyford Cl ME8 ....12 A2
Twyford Ct ME14 ......75 D6
Twyne Cl CT2 ....68 A6
Tydeman Rd ME15 .....75 F2
Tydeman's Ave CT5 ..21 C1
Tyland Barn Wildlife
  Conservation Ctr*
  ME14 ....53 E3
Tyland La ME14 ......53 F3
Tyler Cl CT2 ....66 F3
Tyler Dr ME8 ....33 E4
Tyler Hill Rd CT2 ....66 C6
Tyler Way CT5 ....21 E3
Tyndale Pk CT6 ....23 B5
Tyne Cl ME5 ....32 C5
Tyrwhitt-Drake Mus
  of Carriages* ME15 ..75 A3
Tysoe Ct ME15 ....4 A5
Tyson Ave CT9 ....7 E1
Tyson Rd CT19 ....178 E7

U

Uden Rd TN29 ....187 B4
Uffington Ct CT3 ......91 A2
Ufton Cl ME15 ....75 E1
Ufton La ME10 ....36 E3
Ulcombe Gdns CT2 ....67 A3
Ulcombe Hill ME17 ....99 F1
Ulcombe Rd ME17 .....98 E3
Ulley Rd TN24 ....139 D7
Ullswater Gdns CT3 ..112 F6
Ullswater Ho 5 ME15 ..97 E7
Ulster Rd CT9 ....28 F8
Undercliff CT20 .....177 E3
Undercliffe Rd CT14 .134 D5
Underdown Ave ME4 ...9 F1
Underdown La CT6 .....22 F2
Underdown Rd
  Dover CT17 ....166 B7
  Herne Bay CT6 ....22 F5
Underhill Cotts CT18 177 B8
Underhill Rd CT20 ...177 B5
Underwood CT18 .....163 C6
Underwood Cl
  Ashford TN24 ....139 D6
  Canterbury CT4 ....88 B5
  Maidstone ME15 ......74 F2
Underwood Ct CT1 ....88 B6
Unicorn Cotts CT4 ....89 B5
Unicumes La ME16 ....74 C2
Union Cres CT9 ....7 J2
Union Pk ME15 ....97 F4
Union Pl
  4 Canterbury CT1 ....67 A1
  Chatham ME4 ....10 A4
Union Rd Bridge CT4 ..88 F1
  Deal CT14 ....117 D6
  Minster (Sheppey) ME12 ..4 C7
  Ramsgate CT11 ....52 F8
Union Row CT9 ....7 J2
Union Sq 3 CT10 .....30 B4
Union St Canterbury CT1 67 A1
  Chatham ME4 ....10 A3
  Dover CT17 ....166 D6
  Faversham ME13 ......62 C7
  Maidstone ME14 ......75 A5
  9 Ramsgate CT11 .....52 E7
  Rochester ME1 ....9 C5
  Sheerness ME12 ....1 B2
Unity Pl 2 CT11 ......52 F7
Unity St Sheerness ME12 ..1 C2
  Sittingbourne ME10 ..36 E3
Univ of Greenwich ME4 .10 B8
Univ of Kent
  at Canterbury CT2 ....66 D4
University Rd CT2 .....66 D3
Unwin Cl ME20 ....53 A3

Upbury Manor High Sch
ME7 . . . . .10 B4
Upbury Way ME4 . . . . . .10 A4
Upchurch Wlk CT9 . . . . . .8 E2
Updown Way CT4 . . . . . .86 F1
Uphill CT18 . . . . .163 B4
Uplands CT2 . . . . .66 F4
Uplands Way ME12 . . . . . .3 C5
Uplees Cotts ME13 . . . . .39 F5
Uplees Rd ME13 . . . . . . .40 A3
Upnor Ho ME15 . . . . . . .97 E8
Upnor Rd ME2 . . . . .9 D8
Upper Approach Rd
CT10 . . . . .30 A3
Upper Brents ME13 . . . . .62 D8
Upper Bridge St
Canterbury CT1 . . . . . . .88 A8
Wye TN25 . . . . .123 F2
Upper Britton Pl ME7 . . . .10 B5
Upper Chantry La CT1 . . .88 A7
Upper Corniche CT20 . . .177 C3
Upper Dane Ct CT9 . . . . . .8 B1
Upper Dane Rd CT9 . . . . . .8 B1
Upper Denmark Rd
TN23 . . . . .156 B8
Upper Dumpton Park Rd
CT11 . . . . .52 E8
Upper East Rd ME4 . . . . .10 B4
Upper Fant Rd ME16 . . . .74 D2
Upper Field Rd ME10 . . . .37 B5
Upper Free Down CT6 . . .23 B2
Upper Gore La CT13 . . . . .93 A2
Upper Gr CT9 . . . . .7 J2
Upper Hunton Hill ME15 .96 A3
Upper Luton Rd ME5 . . . .10 C2
Upper Malthouse Hill
CT21 . . . . .176 B2
Upper Maltings Pl CT7 . .26 F7
Upper Rd
Dover CT15,CT16 . . . . .150 C2
Dover,Eastern Docks
CT16 . . . . .166 H8
Maidstone ME15 . . . . . .75 B2
Upper St
Hollingbourne ME17 . . . .77 E3
Kingsdown CT14 . . . . . .134 D5
Leeds ME17 . . . . .98 F5
Tilmanstone CT14 . . . . .115 A3
Upper St Ann's Rd ME13 .62 B6
Upper Stone St ME15 . . .75 A3
Upper Strand St CT13 . . .73 A1
Upper Tickham Cotts
ME9 . . . . .60 D6
Upper Vicarage Rd
TN24 . . . . .139 D7
Upstreet CT18 . . . . .161 D3
Upton Cl CT19 . . . . .178 A7
Upton Jun Sch CT10 . . . .29 F4
Upton Rd CT10 . . . . .29 F5
Urquhart Cl ME5 . . . . . .32 A5
Ursuline Dr CT8 . . . . . . .27 D7

V

Vale Cotts ME9 . . . . .57 A8
Vale Dr ME5 . . . . .31 E6
Vale Pl CT11 . . . . .52 D6
Vale Rd Broadstairs CT10 .29 F4
Loose ME15 . . . . .96 A4
Ramsgate CT11 . . . . . . .52 D6
Ripple CT14,CT15 . . . . .133 B8
Whitstable CT5 . . . . .43 D8
Vale Sq CT11 . . . . .52 D6
Vale The CT10 . . . . .30 A4
Vale View Com Sch
CT17 . . . . .166 B7
Vale View Rd
Aylesham CT3 . . . . .112 E5
Dover CT17 . . . . .166 B7
Valebrook Cl CT20 . . . . .177 C5
Valence Ho ME15 . . . . . .97 C7
Valenciennes Rd ME10 . .36 E3
Valentine Cl ME7 . . . . . . .11 A1
Valentine Rd ME15 . . . . .97 E7
Valerian Cl ME5 . . . . . . .31 E4
Valestone Cl CT21 . . . . .177 B4
Valetta Way ME1 . . . . . . .9 B4
Valiant Rd ME5 . . . . .32 C2
Valkyrie Ave CT5 . . . . . . .43 C7
Vallance The ME9 . . . . . .60 A6
Valley Cotts
Alkham CT15 . . . . .147 C1
Stalisfield Green ME13 . .103 D8
Valley Dr ME15 . . . . .96 F6
Valley Park Com Sch
ME14 . . . . .75 C4
Valley Rd Barham CT4 . .111 E2
Canterbury CT1 . . . . . . .87 E6
Folkestone CT20 . . . . . .177 E4
Gillingham ME7 . . . . . . .10 E4
Lydden CT9 . . . . .28 E4
River CT17 . . . . .148 E3
Valley Rise ME5 . . . . . . .31 F1
Valley The ME17 . . . . . . .96 D3
Valley View CT15 . . . . . .131 C8
Valley View Rd ME1 . . . . .9 B1
Valley Wlk CT21 . . . . . . .177 B3
Vancouver Dr ME8 . . . . .11 C1
Vancouver Rd CT10 . . . .149 C3
Vange Cottage Mews ME1 .9 B4
Vanity La ME17 . . . . .96 D1
Vanity Rd ME12 . . . . .6 F2
Varne Ct CT10 . . . . .177 F3
Varne Lodge CT20 . . . . .177 F3
Varne Mews TN28 . . . . .200 E4
Varne Pl CT19 . . . . .178 F5
Varne Rd CT19 . . . . .178 F5

Vaughan Dr ME10 . . . . . .36 F8
Vauxhall Ave
Canterbury CT1 . . . . . . .67 C3
Herne Bay CT6 . . . . .22 A3
Vauxhall Cres CT1 . . . . . .67 C3
Vauxhall Industrial Rd
CT1 . . . . .67 D4
Vauxhall Rd CT1,CT2 . . .67 C4
Vectis Dr ME10 . . . . .36 F8
Ventnor Cl ME5 . . . . .32 C8
Ventnor La CT9 . . . . .7 J2
Venture Ct TN29 . . . . . .186 D1
Vere Rd CT10 . . . . .30 A4
Vereth Rd CT11 . . . . .52 D6
Vernon Holme (Kent Coll
Inf & Jun Sch) CT2 . . . . .66 A1
Vernon Pl Canterbury CT1 .88 A7
Deal CT14 . . . . .117 C8
Verwood Cl CT2 . . . . . . .66 E2
Vesper Ct TN27 . . . . . . .135 A1
Vestey Ct CT8 . . . . .7 C1
Viaduct Cl CT12 . . . . . . .52 C8
Viaduct Terr TN26 . . . . .182 F7
Viaduct The CT17 . . . . . .166 B5
Viburnum Cl TN23 . . . . .138 E2
Vicarage Cl ME20 . . . . . .53 A3
Vicarage Cres CT9 . . . . . .7 J1
Vicarage Ct ME9 . . . . . . .35 B7
Vicarage Gdn CT12 . . . . .49 C7
Vicarage Gdns CT3 . . . . .91 A7
Vicarage Hill CT4 . . . . . .109 B4
Vicarage La
Ashford TN23 . . . . .139 C2
Blean CT2 . . . . .66 A6
Deal CT14 . . . . .116 F5
East Farleigh ME15 . . . . .96 B6
Elham CT4 . . . . .144 F4
Faversham ME13 . . . . . .62 A4
Lower Halstow ME9 . . . . .13 C3
Nonington CT15 . . . . . .113 C5
Sandwich CT13 . . . . . . .72 F1
Selling ME13 . . . . .84 C6
St Margaret's at Cliffe
CT15 . . . . .150 F6
Tilmanstone CT14 . . . . .115 A3
Vicarage Pl CT9 . . . . .7 J1
Vicarage Rd
Folkestone CT20 . . . . . .177 F3
Gillingham ME7 . . . . . . .10 C5
Minster (Sheppey) ME12 . .4 D7
Rochester ME2 . . . . .9 B8
Sittingbourne ME10 . . . .36 E6
Vicarage St
Broadstairs CT10 . . . . . .29 C5
Faversham ME13 . . . . . .62 D8
Vicary Way ME16 . . . . . .74 D5
Vickers Cl CT18 . . . . . . .163 A4
Victor Ave CT8 . . . . .8 D2
Victoria Ave
Broadstairs CT10 . . . . . .29 E8
Hythe CT21 . . . . .176 B2
Margate CT9 . . . . .8 B1
St Margaret's at Cliffe
CT15 . . . . .151 B6
Westgate-on-S CT8 . . . . .27 F8
Victoria Cres
Ashford TN23 . . . . .139 B1
Dover CT16 . . . . .166 D8
Victoria Ct Hythe CT21 . .176 C1
Maidstone ME16 . . . . . .74 E3
Victoria Dr CT6 . . . . .22 C5
Victoria Gr
Folkestone CT20 . . . . . .178 D5
Hythe CT21 . . . . .177 B2
Victoria Ho CT1 . . . . .20 D2
Victoria Hospl CT14 . . . .117 B5
Victoria Par
Broadstairs CT10 . . . . . .30 B4
Ramsgate CT11 . . . . . . .52 F7
Victoria Pk Dover CT16 . .166 E8
Herne Bay CT6 . . . . .23 A5
Victoria Pl
Faversham ME13 . . . . . .62 C7
Hythe CT21 . . . . .176 C1
Victoria Rd Ashford TN23 .139 B1
Broadstairs CT10 . . . . . .29 E6
Canterbury CT1 . . . . . . .87 E7
Capel-le-F CT18 . . . . . .164 B2
Chatham,Luton ME4 . . . .10 B2
Chatham,Walderslade ME5 .31 E3
Deal CT14 . . . . .117 D5
Folkestone CT19 . . . . . .178 C5
Hythe CT21 . . . . .176 C1
Kingsdown CT14 . . . . . .134 C4
Littlestone-on-S TN28 . .200 E5
Lydden CT9 . . . . .28 D4
Margate CT9 . . . . .7 J2
Ramsgate CT11 . . . . . . .52 F7
Sittingbourne ME10 . . . .36 D4
Victoria Rd W TN28 . . . .200 D5
Victoria Road Prim Sch
TN23 . . . . .139 B1
Victoria Row CT1 . . . . . .67 A1
Victoria St Dover CT17 . .149 B1
Gillingham ME7 . . . . . . .10 D6
Maidstone ME16 . . . . . .74 E3
New Romney TN28 . . . .200 A6
Rochester ME2 . . . . .9 B7
Rochester,Troy Town ME1 . .9 D5
Sheerness ME12 . . . . . . .1 D1
Whitstable CT5 . . . . .20 D2
Victoria Terr Hythe CT21 .177 B2
Minster (Sheppey) ME12 . .5 A5
Rochester ME1 . . . . .9 A2
Sittingbourne ME10 . . . .36 D4
Victory Manor ME7 . . . . .10 A6
Victory Pk ME2 . . . . .9 E7

Victory Rd CT15 . . . . . . .133 F1
Victory St ME12 . . . . .1 C2
Vidal Manor ME7 . . . . . . .10 A6
Viewlands ME5 . . . . .10 C3
Vigo Terr ME9 . . . . .38 B1
Viking Cl CT7 . . . . .26 D8
Viking Ct Broadstairs CT10 .30 B3
Canterbury CT2 . . . . . . .66 F2
Viking Prim Sch CT12 . . . .8 A2
Viking Ship CT12 . . . . . . .51 E5
Village View ME5 . . . . . .10 C3
Village Way TN26 . . . . . .183 A7
Villas The CT3 . . . . .47 A1
Villiers Cl CT17 . . . . .166 C7
Villiers Ho CT10 . . . . .30 B7
Villiers Rd CT1 . . . . .67 D1
Vincent Cl
Broadstairs CT10 . . . . . .29 C3
Folkestone CT20 . . . . . .177 E5
Vincent Ct ME12 . . . . .1 D1
Vincent Gdns ME12 . . . . . .1 D1
Vincent Pl TN24 . . . . . . .139 F4
Vincent Rd
Kit's Coty ME20 . . . . . . .53 C7
Lydden CT9 . . . . .28 C4
Sittingbourne ME10 . . . .37 C3
Vine Cl CT11 . . . . .29 E2
Vine End CT11 . . . . .29 E2
Vine Lands TN29 . . . . . .203 B6
Vine Lo CT11 . . . . .29 E2
Vineries The ME7 . . . . . .10 E5
Viners Cl ME11 . . . . .36 F1
Vines La ME1 . . . . .9 C5
Viney's Gdns CT15 . . . . .167 C1
Vineyard Cres ME8 . . . . .12 B1
Vinson Cl ME13 . . . . .41 D1
Vinten Cl CT6 . . . . .46 B8
Vinters Rd ME14 . . . . . . .75 B4
Vintners Way ME14 . . . . .75 E4
Violet Ave CT12 . . . . .29 C2
Violet Cl ME5 . . . . .54 A8
Virginia Rd
Gillingham ME7 . . . . . . .10 C7
Whitstable CT5 . . . . .44 A8
Vixen Cl ME5 . . . . .32 C6
Vlissingen Dr CT14 . . . . .117 C8
Volante Dr ME10 . . . . . . .36 E7
Vulcan Cl Chatham ME5 . .32 B7
Whitstable CT5 . . . . .43 C7

W

Wacher Cl CT2 . . . . .66 F2
Waddenhall Farm CT4 . .126 B6
Waddington Dr CT1 . . . .163 A4
Waddle Cnr TN30 . . . . . .189 D3
Wades Cl TN29 . . . . .194 B4
Wadham Pl ME10 . . . . . .37 B2
Waghorn St ME4 . . . . . . .10 B2
Wagoners Cl ME14 . . . . .75 E4
Wain Ct ME12 . . . . .4 A5
Wainwright Ct CT10 . . . . .30 B6
Wainwright Pl TN24 . . . .156 D8
Wake Rd ME1 . . . . .31 C8
Wakefield Way CT21 . . . .176 B1
Wakefield Wlk CT21 . . . .176 D1
Wakehurst Cl ME17 . . . . .96 B3
Wakeley Jun Sch ME8 . . .12 A1
Wakeley Rd ME8 . . . . . . .12 A1
Wakeleys Cotts ME8 . . . .34 B8
Walcheren Cl CT14 . . . . .117 C8
Waldens The ME17 . . . . .99 E2
Waldershare Ave CT3 . . . .95 A7
Waldershare Rd CT15 . . .132 A5
Walderslade Ctr ME5 . . . .32 A3
Walderslade Girls Sch
ME5 . . . . .31 F5
Walderslade Prim Sch
ME5 . . . . .32 A3
Walderslade Rd ME5 . . . .31 F5
Walderslade Woods ME5 .53 F8
Waldron Dr ME15 . . . . . .96 F6
Waldron Rd CT10 . . . . . .30 B2
Walk The ME17 . . . . .99 E2
Walker La CT7 . . . . .26 D8
Walkers Outland (RSPB
Reserve) TN29 . . . . . . .204 B1
Wall Rd TN24 . . . . .139 B3
Wall The ME10 . . . . .36 E5
Wallace Mews CT19 . . . .178 D7
Wallace Rd ME1 . . . . .31 E8
Wallace Way CT10 . . . . . .29 E4
Wallbridge La ME8,ME9 . .12 D3
Waller Rd TN28 . . . . . . .204 E7
Wallers Rd ME13 . . . . . . .62 A7
Wallis Ave ME15 . . . . . . .97 E5
Wallis Rd TN24 . . . . .139 D2
Wallwood Rd CT11 . . . . . .52 F8
Walmer Castle CT14 . . . .117 D1
Walmer Castle Rd CT14 .117 C1
Walmer Ct ME14 . . . . . . .75 A5
Walmer Gdns
Cliffs End CT12 . . . . .51 D5
Deal CT14 . . . . .117 A2
Sittingbourne ME10 . . . .36 D5
Walmer Rd CT5 . . . . .43 E8
Walmer Sch CT14 . . . . . .117 B2
Walmer Sta CT14 . . . . . .117 A1
Walmer Way Deal CT14 . .117 A2
Folkestone CT20 . . . . . .177 F5
Walmsley Ho CT14 . . . . .178 E6
Walmsley Rd CT10 . . . . . .29 E5
Walner Gdns TN28 . . . . .200 B7
Walner La TN28 . . . . . . .200 B7
Walnut Cl Ashford TN24 .139 D6
Chatham ME5 . . . . .32 B8
Walnut Ridge TN25 . . . .173 A6

Walnut Tree Ave ME15 . . .97 A5
Walnut Tree Cl CT7 . . . . .27 A7
Walnut Tree Cotts ME13 .84 E8
Walnut Tree Dr ME10 . . . .36 D4
Walnut Tree La
Maidstone ME15 . . . . . .97 A5
Westbere CT2 . . . . .68 D7
Walpole Rd CT9 . . . . .7 J3
Walsby Dr ME10 . . . . . . .37 A8
Walseley Terr TN29 . . . .203 C5
Walsham Rd ME5 . . . . . .31 F1
Walshaw House ME14 . . .75 A6
Walsingham Cl ME8 . . . . .33 D3
Walsingham House
ME14 . . . . .75 A6
Waltham Cl
Ashford TN24 . . . . .140 A2
Margate CT9 . . . . .8 E2
Waltham Rd
Gillingham ME8 . . . . . . .11 C3
Waltham CT4 . . . . .108 F1
Walton Gdns CT19 . . . . .178 D7
Walton Manor Cl CT19 . .178 D7
Walton Rd CT19 . . . . . . .178 D6
Waltons The CT19 . . . . .178 C8
Wanden La TN27 . . . . . .135 C8
Wanstall Ct CT7 . . . . .27 A7
Wansted House Sch CT9 . .8 A3
Wantsum Cl CT6 . . . . . . .23 F5
Wantsum Mews CT13 . . .72 F2
Wantsum Way CT7 . . . . . .25 E3
Wantsume Lees CT13 . . .72 E2
Warblers Cl ME2 . . . . .9 A7
Warden Bay Rd ME12 . . .6 B3
Warden Cl ME16 . . . . . . .74 C4
Warden Ct CT17 . . . . . . .149 C1
Warden House Mews
CT14 . . . . .117 A4
Warden House Prim Sch
CT14 . . . . .117 A5
Warden Point Way CT5 . .43 C6
Warden Rd Rochester ME1 .9 C2
Warden ME12 . . . . .6 B5
Warden Terr ME12 . . . . . .5 A6
Warden View Gdns ME12 . .6 D1
Warden Way ME12 . . . . . .6 B5
Wardour Cl CT10 . . . . . . .30 B4
Wards Hill Rd ME12 . . . . .4 B8
Wardwell La ME9 . . . . . .13 C1
Ware St ME14 . . . . .76 A5
Warehorne Rd TN26 . . . .183 A7
Warlingham Cl ME8 . . . . .12 A1
Warmlake ME17 . . . . . . .98 F1
Warmlake Est ME17 . . . .98 E1
Warmlake Rd ME17 . . . . .98 C1
Warner St ME4 . . . . .9 F3
Warnford Gdns ME15 . . .97 A8
Warre Ave CT11 . . . . .52 C5
Warren Cl
Folkestone CT19 . . . . . .178 F6
Sittingbourne ME10 . . . .37 B2
Warren Dr CT10 . . . . .29 E5
Warren Dr The CT8 . . . . .27 D7
Warren Hos TN27 . . . . . .119 E8
Warren Hts CT13 . . . . . . .72 F1
Warren La Ashford TN24 .139 A4
Hartlip ME9 . . . . .34 C3
River,Lydden CT15 . . . . .147 D6
Warren Lo CT1 . . . . .87 B6
Warren Rd
Folkestone CT19 . . . . . .178 F6
Kit's Coty ME20 . . . . . . .53 D7
Littlestone-on-S TN28 . .200 D6
Warren Ret Pk TN24 . . . .139 B4
Warren St
Stalisfield Green TN27 . .103 A3
Warren Street ME17 . . . .102 D7
Warren The
Brabourne Lees TN25 . . .158 E5
Selling ME13 . . . . .84 E7
Whitstable CT5 . . . . .43 C6
Warren View TN23 . . . . .138 F4
Warren Way CT19 . . . . . .178 F6
Warren Wood Cty Prim Sch
& Language Unit ME1 . .31 C8
Warren Wood Rd ME1 . . .31 C8
Warten Rd CT11 . . . . .29 F1
Warwick Cres ME10 . . . .36 C5
Warwick Dr CT11 . . . . . . .52 B5
Warwick Pl ME16 . . . . . .74 E3
Warwick Rd
Ashford TN24 . . . . .139 E5
Canterbury CT1 . . . . . . .88 C8
Deal CT14 . . . . .117 D2
Margate CT9 . . . . .8 B2
Whitstable CT5 . . . . .20 D2
Washford Farm Rd
TN23 . . . . .155 E5
Washington Cl TN23 . . . .149 B3
Washington St TN29 . . . .198 C6
Wass Dro CT3 . . . . .71 B7
Wat Tyler Way ME15 . . . .75 A4
Watchester Ave CT11 . . . .52 C5
Watchester Ct CT12 . . . . .50 B5
Watchmans Terr
ME5 . . . . .10 C2
Water Farm CT4 . . . . . . .144 F4
Water La Bayfield ME13 . .61 F4
Canterbury CT1 . . . . . . .87 F8
Faversham ME13 . . . . . .62 C7
Harrietsham ME17 . . . . .100 B5
Kingswood ME17 . . . . . .99 F3
Maidstone ME15 . . . . . .75 A4
Maidstone,Bearsted ME14 .76 E6
Sturry CT2 . . . . .67 F5
Water Mdws CT2 . . . . . . .67 F4
Water St CT14 . . . . .117 D1
Waterbrook Ave TN24 . . .157 A4

Upb – Wel **237**

Watercress La
Ashford TN23 . . . . .155 F8
Wingham CT3 . . . . .90 F6
Waterditch La ME17,
TN27 . . . . .102 E5
Waterfall Rd TN26 . . . . .138 B6
Waterham Rd ME13 . . . . .42 C1
Waterlock Cotts CT3 . . . .91 A7
Waterloo Cres CT16,
CT17 . . . . .166 E7
Waterloo Hill ME12 . . . . . .4 D6
Waterloo Mansions
CT16,CT17 . . . . .166 E7
Waterloo Mus CT10 . . . . .30 B5
Waterloo Pl CT11 . . . . . . .52 F7
Waterloo Rd
Folkestone CT20 . . . . . .177 D5
Gillingham ME7 . . . . . . .10 C4
Sittingbourne ME10 . . . .36 D5
Whitstable CT5 . . . . .20 D2
Waterloo St ME15 . . . . . .75 A3
Waterloo Terr ME12 . . . . .5 A5
Waterlow Rd ME14 . . . . .75 A6
Waterman Ho TN23 . . . .156 B8
Watermead CT12 . . . . . .155 F7
Watermeadow Cl ME7 . . .32 F6
Watermill Cl
Maidstone ME16 . . . . . .74 B5
Rochester ME2 . . . . .9 C8
Waters Edge ME15 . . . . .74 F2
Waters Pl ME7 . . . . .33 A6
Watersend CT16 . . . . . . .148 D5
Waterside TN24 . . . . . . .139 F1
Waterside Ct
Hythe CT21 . . . . .176 B2
Rochester ME2 . . . . .9 E6
Waterside Dr CT8 . . . . . . .7 D1
Waterside La CT16 . . . . . .10 F7
Waterside View ME12 . . . .6 E4
Watersmead CT16 . . . . . .148 C5
Waterstone Pl ME13 . . . .62 A6
Waterworks Hill CT15 . . .133 B3
Waterworks La CT15 . . . .133 B3
Watery La CT4 . . . . .109 C5
Watkin Rd CT19 . . . . . . .178 C6
Watling Ave ME5 . . . . . . .10 D2
Watling Pl ME10 . . . . . . .37 A3
Watling St Canterbury CT1 .87 F8
Chatham ME5 . . . . .10 D2
Watson Ave ME5 . . . . . . .31 D5
Watsons Cl TN25 . . . . . .139 C8
Watsons Hill ME10 . . . . . .36 E5
Wattle Cnr TN30 . . . . . . .189 D3
Watts Cotts TN24 . . . . . .139 D7
Watts Yd CT13 . . . . .72 F1
Watts' Ave ME1 . . . . .9 C4
Watts' St ME4 . . . . .9 E3
Wauchope Rd CT5 . . . . . .42 F6
Wave Crest CT5 . . . . .20 C1
Waverley Ave ME12 . . . . .4 B7
Waverley Cl Chatham ME5 .32 D2
Coxheath ME17 . . . . . . .96 C3
Waverley Rd CT9 . . . . . . .28 C8
Way Farm Cotts CT12 . . .50 E7
Way Hill CT12 . . . . .50 E7
Wayborough Hill CT12 . . .50 D7
Wayfield Cty Prim Sch
ME5 . . . . .32 A7
Wayfield Rd ME5 . . . . . . .32 A7
Wayne Cl CT10 . . . . .29 E5
Wayside TN30 . . . . .167 B2
Wayside Ave TN30 . . . . .167 B3
Wayside Flats TN30 . . . .167 B2
Weald Cl ME15 . . . . .97 C6
Weald Ct ME10 . . . . .36 D2
Weald The TN24 . . . . . . .139 C3
Wealden Ave TN30 . . . . .167 B1
Wealden Ct ME5 . . . . . . .10 B3
Wealden Forest Pk
CT2,CT6 . . . . .45 D4
Wealdhurst Pk CT10 . . . .29 D5
Wear Bay Cres CT19 . . . .178 F6
Wear Bay Rd CT19 . . . . .178 F5
Weatherall Cl ME13 . . . . .64 B2
Weatherly Cl ME1 . . . . . . .9 C4
Weatherly Dr CT10 . . . . .29 F2
Weavering Cotts ME14 . .75 E3
Weavering St ME14 . . . . .75 F4
Weavers The ME16 . . . . .74 B5
Weavers Way
Ashford TN23 . . . . .155 E2
Dover CT16 . . . . .149 A3
Webb Cl CT19 . . . . .178 A7
Webster Rd ME8 . . . . . . .11 F1
Webster Way CT18 . . . . .163 B4
Weddington La CT3 . . . . .71 E2
Wedgewood Cl ME16 . . . .74 B5
Wedgewood Dr ME5 . . . .32 A7
Weeds Wood Rd ME5 . . . .31 F4
Week St ME14 . . . . .75 A4
Weekes St ME11 . . . . .3 A5
Weigall Pl CT11 . . . . .52 C7
Weighbridge Way CT16 . .166 H8
Welcombe Ct ME8 . . . . . .33 D8
Well Cl CT2 . . . . .68 A6
Well La Bayfield ME13 . . .61 B3
Fordwich CT2,CT3 . . . . .68 A3
St Margaret's at Cliffe
CT15 . . . . .150 F6
Well Rd Lyminge CT18 . .161 C6
Maidstone ME14 . . . . . .75 A5
Queenborough ME11 . . . .3 A5
Rushenden ME11 . . . . . . .2 F3
Well St ME15,ME17 . . . . .96 E4
Well Winch Rd ME10 . . . .36 D5

Weller Ave ME1 ....9 D2
Wellesley Ave CT14 ...117 C3
Wellesley Cl
  Broadstairs CT10 ....29 E3
  Westgate-on-S CT8 ......27 E7
Wellesley Rd
  Ashford TN23 ....139 C2
  Dover CT16 ....166 E2
  Margate CT9 ....8 B1
  Sheerness ME12 ....1 C2
  Westgate-on-S CT8 ......27 E7
Wellesley Terr CT13 ....94 A8
Wellesley Villas TN24 ..139 C3
Wellfield Rd CT20 .....178 A5
Wellington Cl CT8 ....7 C1
Wellington Cres CT11 ..52 F6
Wellington Ct CT14 ...117 D3
Wellington Gdns
  2 Dover CT16 ....149 B3
  Margate CT9 ....7 J3
Wellington House **6**
  ME15 ....97 E5
Wellington Par
  Kingsdown CT14 ....134 E6
  Kingsdown,Hawkshill
  CT14 ....134 D7
Wellington Pl
  Folkestone CT20 ....177 D3
  Maidstone ME14 ....74 C1
Wellington Rd
  Deal CT14 ....117 D5
  Folkestone CT20 ....177 D5
  Gillingham ME7 ....10 C4
  Lydden CT9 ....28 D4
  Sittingbourne ME10 .....36 B5
  Temple Ewell CT16 ....148 D5
  Westgate-on-S CT8 ......27 E7
Wellington St CT5 .....43 D5
Wellington Terr CT20 ..177 D3
Wellis Gdns CT9 ....7 G1
Wells Ave CT1 ....88 B7
Wells Cl
  New Romney TN28 .....200 C6
  Tenterden TN30 ....179 B8
Wells Ho ME10 ....37 B4
Wells Rd CT19 ....177 F6
Wells Way ME13 ....40 B1
Welsdene Rd CT9 ....28 B8
Welson Rd CT20 ....178 A5
Wemmick Cl ME1 ....31 D7
Wemyss Ct **13** CT1 .....67 B2
Wemyss Ho **14** CT1 ....67 B2
Wemyss Way CT1 ....67 C1
Wenderton La CT3 ......70 A2
Wenham's La TN29 ....192 E2
Wents Wood ME14 ......75 F5
Wentworth Ave CT9 .....7 E1
Wentworth Cl CT18 ...161 C6
Wentworth Dr
  Gillingham ME8 ....33 E7
  Ramsgate CT12 ....29 A1
  Sittingbourne ME10 .....36 C5
Wentworth Gdns CT6 ...22 D2
Wentworth Ho ME10 ....36 C5
Wesley Terr CT18 .....161 C7
West Beach CT5 ....20 C1
West Borough Prim Sch
  ME16 ....74 B3
West Cliff CT5 ....20 D1
West Cliff Arc **8** CT11 ..52 E6
West Cliff Ave CT10 ....30 B3
West Cliff Ct CT10 .....30 B3
West Cliff Dr CT6 ......22 B4
West Cliff Gdns
  Folkestone CT20 ....178 D4
  Herne Bay CT6 ....22 B4
West Cliff Prom CT11 ..52 D5
West Cliff Rd
  Broadstairs CT10 ....30 B3
  Ramsgate CT11 ....52 B5
West Cliff Terr CT11 ...52 B5
West Ct ME15 ....75 A1
West Dr ME5 ....31 D5
West Dumpton La CT11 ..29 E1
West End TN26 ....168 F3
West End Cotts ME9 ....80 D7
West Hill Rd CT6 ....22 C5
West Hythe Rd CT21 ..187 A8
West La Sheerness ME12 ..1 B2
  Sittingbourne ME10 .....37 A4
West Lane Trad Est
  ME10 ....37 A4
West Lawn Gdns CT20 .177 D3
West Lea CT14 ....117 C7
West Minster Prim Sch
  ME12 ....3 B8
West Norman Rd CT16 .166 E8
West Par CT21 ....176 B1
West Park Ave CT9 ......8 D1
West Park Farm North
  Ret Pk CT19 ....178 B8
West Park Rd ME15 ....75 B2
West Pas ME12 ....1 B2
West Pl TN29 ....197 D8
West Ramp CT16 ......166 G8
West Rd Folkestone CT20 177 C4
  Gillingham ME4 ....10 A7
  Sandwich CT13 ....51 A1
West Ridge ME10 ....36 D3
West Rise CT12 ....29 B1
West Side CT15 ....133 A1
West St Ashford TN23 ..139 B2
  Deal CT14 ....117 D6
  Dover CT17 ....166 C8

West St continued
  Faversham ME13 ....62 C7
  Gillingham ME7 ....10 D6
  Harrietsham ME17 .....100 C6
  Hothfield TN26 ....137 F7
  Lenham ME17 ....79 E1
  New Romney TN28 .....200 A6
  Queenborough ME11 .....2 F5
  Sheerness ME12 ....1 B2
  Sittingbourne ME10 .....36 E4
  Woodside Green ME17 ..101 E8
West Street Cotts CT14 ..94 A1
West Terr CT20 ....178 D4
West View CT19 ....178 D8
West View Cl CT6 ......22 C2
West Wlk ME16 ....74 B3
West Wood Rd ME9 .....56 B8
Westbere La CT2 ....68 B7
Westbourne TN23 ......155 D6
Westbourne Gdns CT20 .178 B4
Westbourne St ME10 ...36 E4
Westbrook Ave CT9 ......7 F1
Westbrook Cotts CT9 ....7 G1
Westbrook Gdns CT9 ....7 G1
Westbrook La CT6 ......22 B3
Westbrook Prom CT9 ....7 G2
Westbrook Rd CT9 ......7 G2
Westbrook Wlk **8** ME13 .62 C7
Westbrooke Cl ME4 .....10 A2
Westbury Cres CT17 ...166 B6
Westbury Hts CT17 ....166 B6
Westbury Rd Dover CT17 166 B6
  Westgate-on-S CT8 ......27 E8
Westcliff Dr ME12 ......4 D8
Westcliff Ho **4** CT20 ...178 D4
Westcliff Rd CT9 ....7 G1
Westcourt La CT15 ....130 C5
Westcourt Rd ME7 .....10 A6
Westdean Cl CT17 .....148 E2
Westenhanger Sta
  TN25 ....175 B7
Westerham Cl
  Broadstairs CT9 ....8 F1
  Canterbury CT2 ....67 A4
  Gillingham ME8 ....11 B3
Westerham Rd ME10 ...36 C3
Westerhill Rd ME17 ....96 C1
Westerhout Cl CT14 ...117 C8
Western Ave
  Ashford TN23 ....139 A3
  Bridge CT4 ....89 A1
  Gillingham ME4 ....10 A8
  Halfway Houses ME12 ....3 D6
  Herne Bay CT6 ....22 E4
Western Cl CT17 ......166 C6
Western Espl
  Broadstairs CT10 ....30 B2
  Herne Bay CT6 ....22 C5
Western Gdns TN24 ...156 E8
Western Heights Rdbt
  CT17 ....166 C5
Western Ho CT14 .....117 C7
Western Link ME13 .....62 A8
Western Rd Deal CT14 ..117 C7
  Maidstone ME16 ....74 C2
  Margate CT9 ....29 C8
Western Service Rd
  CT16 ....166 G8
Western Undercliff CT11 .52 C5
Westfield CT2 ....66 A6
Westfield Bsns Ctr ME2 ..9 C7
Westfield Cotts ME9 ...13 A2
Westfield La CT18 ....161 C3
Westfield Rd
  Birchington CT7 ....27 A7
  Margate CT9 ....28 C8
Westfield Sole Rd ME5,
  ME15 ....54 D8
Westfields TN27 ......136 B8
Westgate Ave CT7 .....28 A4
Westgate Bay CT8,CT9 7 C1
Westgate Cl CT2 ....66 C1
Westgate Court Ave CT2 .66 D1
Westgate Garden Flats
  CT2 ....87 E8
Westgate Gr CT2 ......66 F1
Westgate Hall Rd **5** CT1 .66 F1
Westgate Rd ME13 .....62 E7
Westgate Terr CT5 .....20 E2
Westgate-on-Sea Sta
  CT8 ....27 E8
Westland Way CT18 ...163 B3
Westlands Ave ME10 ...36 B4
Westlands Rd CT6 .....22 C3
Westlands Sch The ME10 36 B4
Westlea Cl CT20 ......178 A3
Westleigh Rd CT8 ......27 D8
Westmarsh Cl ME15 ....97 F7
Westmarsh Dr CT9 ......8 C2
Westmeads Com Inf Sch
  CT5 ....20 E2
Westmeads Rd CT5 ....20 E2
Westminster Rd CT1 ...67 C4
Westminster Wlk CT12 .29 C1
Westmoors TN23 ......155 E6
Westmoreland Dr ME9 .13 C3
Westmorland Cl ME15 .97 E7
Westmorland Gn ME15 .97 E7
Westmorland Rd ME15 .97 E7
Westmount Ave ME4 ....9 F3
Westmount Ho **4** CT9 ...9 B2
Weston Rd ME2 ....9 A8
Westonville Ave CT9 ....7 F1
Westover Gdns CT10 ...29 E7
Westover Rd CT10 .....29 E6
Westree Ct **7** ME16 ...74 E3
Westree Rd ME16 ......74 E3

Westway ME17 ....96 C3
Westwell La
  Charing TN25,TN27 ....120 F5
  Potters Corner TN24,TN25 138 E7
  Westwell TN25,TN26 ...121 B4
Westwood Ind Est CT9 ..29 A6
Westwood Pl ME13 .....62 D5
Westwood Rd
  Broadstairs CT10 ....29 C4
  Maidstone ME15 ....97 A7
Westwood Ret Pk CT9 ..29 A5
Wetheral Dr ME5 ....32 B4
Wey Cl ME5 ....32 C5
Wey St TN26 ....183 D3
Weybridge Cl ME5 .....32 C4
Weyburn Dr CT12 ....29 A1
Weyhill Cl ME14 ....75 C6
Weymouth Cl CT19 ....177 D7
Weymouth Rd CT19 ...177 D6
Weymouth Terr CT19 ..177 D7
Wharf Rd Gillingham ME7 .10 C7
  Maidstone ME15 ....74 E2
Wharfedale Rd CT9 .....8 A1
Wharton Gdns TN24 ..156 E8
Whatman Cl ME14 .....75 C6
Whatmer Cl CT2 ....68 A6
Wheatcroft Cl ME10 ....37 B4
Wheatcroft Br ME8 ....33 F7
Wheatear Way ME5 ....32 B7
Wheatfields Chatham ME5 32 D2
  Maidstone ME14 ....75 D4
Wheatley Rd
  Ramsgate CT12 ....29 C1
  Whitstable CT5 ....20 E2
Wheatsheaf Cl
  Boughton Street ME13 ..64 A3
  Maidstone ME15 ....97 B8
Wheatsheaf Gdns ME12 ..1 C1
Wheatsheaf La CT15 ..133 B2
Wheeler St ME14 ......75 A5
Wheelers The ME8 .....33 B6
Wheelwrights The
  ME17 ....100 D6
Wheelwrights Way CT13 .93 B2
Wheler Rd TN27 ......120 C8
Whewell Terr **1** CT20 .178 E5
Whiffen's Ave ME4 ......9 F5
Whiffen's Ave W ME4 ....9 F5
Whigham Cl TN23 .....155 D7
Whimbrel Cl ME10 .....36 F8
Whimbrel Wlk ME5 ....32 C5
Whinfell Ave CT11 .....51 F7
Whinless Rd CT17 ....166 A8
Whiston Ave TN26 ....153 C4
Whitby Rd CT10 ......177 D6
Whitchurch Cl ME16 ...74 E4
Whitcombe Cl ME5 .....32 C2
White Acre Dr CT14 ..134 B8
White Cliffs **11** CT20 ...178 D4
White Cliffs Bsns Ctr
  CT16 ....149 A6
White Cliffs Bsns Pk
  CT16 ....149 B6
White Ct CT20 ....177 E3
White Hart Mansions CT9 .7 J3
White Hill
  Boughton Aluph TN25 ..123 B6
  Challock TN25 ....105 E1
White Hill Cl CT4 .....110 A8
White Hill Rd ME9,ME14 .33 D1
White Horse Hill CT18 .163 C3
White Horse La
  6 Canterbury CT1 ....87 F8
  Otham ME15 ....98 A6
  Rhodes Minnis CT4 ....144 A3
White House Farm Ct
  CT15 ....113 E5
White Marsh Ct CT5 ...20 E2
White Mill Mus★ CT13 .72 E2
White Post ME17 ....78 B5
White Post Gdns CT3 ..71 E1
White Rd ME4 ....10 A2
White Rock Ct ME16 ...74 E3
White Rock Pl **5** ME16 .74 E3
White Wood Rd CT13 ..93 B1
Whiteacre La CT4 .....125 E4
Whitebeam Dr ME17 ...96 B3
Whitecliff Way CT19 ..178 F6
Whitefriars Mdw CT13 ..94 A8
Whitefriars Way **13** CT13 72 F1
Whitegate Ct ME8 .....33 D5
Whitehall TN29 ....197 E8
Whitehall Bridge Rd CT2 87 E8
Whitehall Cl CT2 ......87 E8
Whitehall Dr ME17 .....99 D3
Whitehall Gdns CT2 ...66 E1
Whitehall Rd
  Broad Street ME14 .....77 A6
  Canterbury CT2 ....87 E8
  Canterbury,Harbledown
  CT2 ....87 D7
  Ramsgate CT12 ....29 C1
  Sittingbourne ME10 .....36 E2
Whitehall Way TN25 ..159 D1
Whiteheads La ME14 ...76 A4
Whitehorse Hill ME5 ...10 B3
Whitehouse Cres ME1 ..53 A8
Whitehouse Dro CT13,
  CT3 ....72 D7
Whitelocks Cl CT4 ....111 D3
Whitenbrook CT21 ....177 A3
Whiteness Gn CT10 .....8 F1
Whiteness Rd CT10 .....8 G1
Whites Hill CT14 .....115 B2
Whitewall Ctr ME2 ......9 D8
Whitewall Rd ME2 ......9 D8
Whitewall Way ME2 .....9 D7
Whiteway Rd ME11,ME12 ..2 F6

Whitfield Rd TN23 ....156 B8
Whitfield Ave
  Broadstairs CT10 ....29 E7
  Dover CT16 ....149 B2
Whitfield Cotts TN23 ..156 B8
Whitfield Ct CT16 ....149 A6
Whitfield Hill River CT16 148 E4
  Temple Ewell CT16 ....148 F4
  Whitfield CT16 ....148 F5
Whitfield Rdbt CT16 ..149 A6
Whitfield Sch & Aspen
  Specl Unit CT16 ......149 A7
Whitgift Ct CT2 ....66 D1
Whiting Cres ME13 ....62 A8
Whiting Ho TN29 .....203 C5
Whitmore St ME16 .....74 D2
Whitstable & Seasalter
  Endowed CE Jun Sch
  CT5 ....20 D1
Whitstable & Tankerton
  Hospl CT5 ....21 A2
Whitstable & Tankerton
  Sta CT5 ....20 E1
Whitstable Jun Sch CT5 20 D1
Whitstable Mus & Art
  Gallery★ CT5 ....20 D1
Whitstable Rd
  Canterbury CT2 ....66 D2
  Faversham ME13 ....62 E7
  Faversham, Goodnestone
  ME13 ....63 B6
  Herne Bay CT5,CT6 .....21 F3
  Herne Bay, Studd Hill CT6 .22 B3
  Rough Common CT2 ....66 B4
Whittaker St ME1 ......10 A4
Whittington Terr CT15 .130 C5
Whybornes Chase ME12 ..4 C7
Whyman Ave ME4 ......10 A1
Whytecliffs CT10 ......30 A2
Wichling Cl CT2 ....67 A3
Wick La CT4 ....129 E7
Wicken House ME16 ...74 E4
Wicken La TN25,TN27 .120 E6
Wickenden Cres TN24 .157 A8
Wickets The TN24 ....156 F7
Wickham Ave CT11 ....52 G8
Wickham Cl ME9 ....35 B6
Wickham Court La CT3 .69 B3
Wickham La CT3 ....69 B1
Wickham Mill CT3 .....69 C2
Wickham Pl ME17 .....101 D5
Wickham Rd CT3 ......69 B2
Wickham St ME1 ....9 D3
Wickham Terr ME11 .....2 F5
Wickhambreaux
  CE Prim Sch CT3 ......69 C2
Widgeon Wlk CT18 ....163 B3
Widred Rd CT17 ......166 C8
Wierton La ME17 ....97 F1
Wife Of Bath Hill CT2 ..87 C8
Wigmore Cotts CT3 ...131 C8
Wigmore La CT15 ....131 C8
Wigmore Rd
  Gillingham,Park Wood ME8 .33 B4
  Gillingham,Wigmore ME8 .33 B5
Wigmore Wood CT15 ..33 B4
Wigwam Paddocks CT7 .27 A8
Wihtred Rd ME9 ....37 D2
Wilberforce Rd
  Coxheath ME17 ....96 D3
  Folkestone CT20 ....177 E3
Wilbrough Rd CT7 ......27 A7
Wilcox Cl CT3 ....112 D5
Wild Air CT7 ....26 F8
Wilderness Hill CT9 .....8 A2
Wildfell Cl CT4 ....54 C8
Wildish Rd ME13 ......62 A8
Wildman Cl ME8 ....33 D3
Wildwood Cl ME17 .....99 E2
Wildwood Glade ME7 ..33 B4
Wildwood Rd CT2 .....67 F6
Wildwood Wildlife Pk★
  CT2,CT6 ....45 D4
Wiles Ave TN28 ......200 B6
Wiles Ho TN28 ....200 B6
Wilfred Rd CT11 ....52 C8
Wilgate Green Rd ME13 .82 F6
Wilkes Rd CT10 ....29 E4
Wilkie Rd CT7 ....27 A8
Wilks Cl ME8 ....12 B2
Will Adams Ct **9** ME7 ..10 C6
Will Adams Rdbt ME8 ...10 F2
Will Adams Way ME8 ...10 F1
Willement Rd ME13 ....62 B7
Willesborough Ct TN24 .140 A2
Willesborough Ind Pk
  TN24 ....140 A1
Willesborough Inf
  & Jun Sch TN24 ......157 A8
Willesborough Rd TN24 139 F4
Willesborough Windmill★
  TN24 ....140 A1
Willetts Hill CT12 ......49 D7
William Ave
  Folkestone CT19 ......178 B7
  Margate CT9 ....29 C8
William Gibbs Ct **14**
  ME13 ....62 D7
William Harvey Hospl
  The TN24 ....140 C1
William Judge Cl TN30 .179 D7
William Pitt Ave CT14 ..117 B6
William Pitt Cl CT21 ..176 D2
William Rd TN23 ......156 B8
William Rigby Dr ME12 ..3 E7
William St
  Faversham ME13 ....62 D7
  Gillingham ME8 ....12 A1

William St continued
  Herne Bay CT6 ....22 F5
  Sittingbourne ME10 ....36 E4
  Whitstable CT5 ....20 D2
Williamson Rd TN29 ..204 E5
Willingdon TN23 ......155 E5
Willingdon Pl CT14 ...117 C1
Willingdon Rd CT16 ..149 A5
Willington Gn ME15 ...97 E7
Willington St ME15 ....75 F2
Willis Ct ME12 ....3 F5
Willis Ho ME1 ....9 C4
Willop Cl TN29 ....186 F3
Willop Way TN29 .....186 F3
Willoughby Ct **14** CT1 ..87 F8
Willow Ave
  Broadstairs CT10 ....29 D4
  Faversham ME13 ....62 A7
Willow Cl Canterbury CT2 .67 A2
  Hythe CT21 ....175 E1
  Margate CT9 ....8 C2
Willow Ct
  Broadstairs CT10 ....30 A5
  Folkestone CT20 ....177 E4
  Maidstone ME15 ....97 A6
Willow Dr
  Hamstreet TN26 ....183 A7
  St Mary's Bay TN29 ...194 F3
Willow Ho Sheerness ME12 .1 C2
  Sittingbourne ME10 .....37 B3
Willow House **2** ME5 ..31 F5
Willow Rd
  Great Mongeham CT14 .116 C3
  Whitstable CT5 ....43 C5
Willow Rise ME15 .....75 F1
Willow Tree Cl
  Ashford TN24 ....139 F1
  Herne Bay CT6 ....23 D5
Willow Tree Farm
  Cvn Pk CT21 ....187 D8
Willow Way
  Maidstone ME15 ....75 B3
  Margate CT9 ....28 C8
  Whitstable CT5 ....44 C8
Willow Waye CT15 ....131 D7
Willowbank CT5 ......194 F3
Willowbank Ct **12** ME15 .75 B4
Willowby Gdns ME8 ...33 E4
Willows CT2 ....66 C4
Willows The
  Ashford TN24 ....139 D6
  Gillingham ME8 ....11 E2
  Newington ME9 ....35 B6
  Sheerness ME12 ....1 I1
  Sittingbourne ME10 ....14 F1
Willson's Rd CT11 .....52 D6
Wilmecote Ct ME8 .....33 D8
Wilmington Way ME8 ..11 B2
Wilmott Pl CT13 ....93 B2
Wilson Ave Chatham ME1 .31 E7
  Deal CT14 ....116 F4
Wilson Cl Ashford TN24 .140 A1
  Maidstone ME15 ....97 E7
Wilsons La ME15 ......96 A5
Wiltie Ct CT19 ....178 C5
Wiltie Gdns CT19 ....178 C5
Wilton Cl CT14 ......117 C5
Wilton Rd
  Folkestone CT19 ......178 B6
  Margate CT9 ....28 F1
Wilton Terr ME10 ......36 B5
Wiltshire Cl ME5 ......32 C8
Wiltshire Way **4** ME15 .97 E7
Wimborne Pl CT12 .....52 B8
Wimbourne Dr ME8 ....33 B7
Win Pine Ho CT21 ....176 A1
Winant Way TN16 ....149 B3
Wincheap CT1 ....87 E7
Wincheap Foundation
  Prim Sch CT1 ....87 E6
Wincheap Gn **4** CT1 ...87 F7
Wincheap Ind Est CT1 ..87 D7
Winchelsea Ct CT17 ..166 C7
Winchelsea Rd
  Chatham ME5 ....32 B5
  Dover CT17 ....166 B7
Winchelsea St CT17 ..166 B7
Winchelsea Terr CT17 .166 B6
Winchester Ave ME5 ...31 F4
Winchester Gdns CT1 ..88 A6
Winchester Ho **4** ME15 .97 D7
Winchester Pl **9** ME14 .75 A5
Winchester Way ME8 ...34 A8
Wind Hill TN27 ....119 E7
Wind Hill La TN27 ....119 E7
Windermere ME13 .....62 E6
Windermere Ave CT11 .52 A7
Windermere Ct TN24 .139 C4
Windermere Dr ME8 ...33 D7
Windermere Gdns CT3 .112 F6
Windermere Gr ME10 ..36 D3
Windermere Ho **4** ME15 .97 E7
Winding Hill ME13 .....83 F6
Windmill Ave CT12 ....29 B3
Windmill Cl
  Ashford TN24 ....140 A1
  Bridge CT4 ....89 A1
  Canterbury CT1 ....88 C8
  Herne Bay CT6 ....23 A2
Windmill Ct
  Boughton Monchelsea
  ME17 ....97 B3
  Whitstable ME10 ....43 C7
Windmill Hill ME17 ...100 B1
Windmill Hts ME17 ....76 B4
Windmill Manor ME7 ..10 C4
Windmill Par CT11 .....52 C6
Windmill Quay Rd ME12 ..4 E2

Windmill Rd
Canterbury CT1 ....88 C8
Gillingham ME7 ....10 C4
Herne Bay CT6 ....23 A2
Sittingbourne ME10 ....36 D6
Whitstable CT5 ....43 D7
Windmill Rise ME12 .....4 E6
Windmill Row ME17 ...98 D2
Windmill St CT21 ....176 B1
Windmill View CT9 ....29 A8
Windmill Wlk CT12 ...29 B1
Windsor Ave Chatham ME4 .9 F2
Margate CT9 ....8 B1
Windsor Cl
Broadstairs CT10 ......29 E5
Maidstone ME14 ....75 B6
Windsor Ct Deal CT14 ..117 C2
Margate CT9 ....8 B1
Windsor Dr ME10 ....36 D2
Windsor Gdns
Herne Bay CT6 ....22 B3
Warden ME12 ....6 D4
Windsor Ho Deal CT14 ..117 A5
6 Dover CT17 ....166 D7
Whitstable CT5 ....20 D1
Windsor Mews
9 Margate CT9 ....7 J2
New Romney TN28 .....200 C8
Windsor Rd
Canterbury CT1 ....87 C6
Cliffs End CT12 ....51 D7
Gillingham ME7 ....10 D5
Windward Rd ME1 .....9 C1
Windyridge ME7 .....10 E1
Winehouse La CT18 ..164 D3
Wineycock ME9 ......81 C8
Winford Mews ME1 ....9 A2
Wing Ho ME12 ....6 H1
Wing Rd ME12 ....6 H1
Wingate Ct 7 ME10 ...36 E4
Wingate Rd CT19 ....178 E2
Wingham Bird Pk★ CT3 .70 C1
Wingham Cl
Gillingham ME8 ....11 C3
Maidstone ME15 ....97 F7
Wingham Prim Sch CT3 .91 A7
Wingham Rd CT3 ......90 D8
Wingham Well La CT3 ..90 F5
Wingrove Dr
Maidstone ME14 ......75 E5
Rochester ME2 ....9 C7
Wingrove Hill CT17 ...148 E2
Wings Ct CT10 ....30 B5
Winifred Ave CT13 ....29 C2
Winifred Rd ME15 ....75 F3
Winkle Cl CT6 ....22 B3
Winnipeg Cl CT16 ...149 C3
Winstanley Cres CT11 .52 D8
Winstanley Rd ME12 ...1 D2
Winston Cl CT1 ......88 C7
Winston Ct CT7 ......27 A8
Winston Gdns CT6 ....23 D4
Winston Ho 4 CT20 ..177 F5
Winter Dr CT18 .....163 B5
Winterage La CT18 ...162 C7
Winterstoke Cres CT11 .52 G8
Winterstoke Way CT11 .52 F8
Winton Way TN29 ....195 A5
Wirrals The ME5 .....32 A4
Wises La ME10,ME9 ...36 A4
Wish The TN26 ......181 F6
Wissenden La TN26 ..153 B6
Wisteria Ho 11 ME15 ..97 E7
Withersdane Cotts
TN25 ....124 A2

Witley Wlk CT16 .....149 B7
Wittersham CE Prim Sch
TN30 ....188 D2
Wittersham Cl ME5 ...32 B5
Wittersham Rd
Stone in Oxney TN30 ...189 C3
Wittersham TN30 ......188 C5
Wivenhoe TN23 ......155 E5
Wivenhoe Cl ME8 .....12 A2
Wolfe Ct CT14 ......117 D3
Wolfe Rd ME16 ....74 D7
Wollaston Cl ME8 ....33 D3
Wollaston Rd CT14 ..117 D4
Wolseley Ave CT6 ....22 A4
Wolseley Pl 4 TN24 ..139 B3
Wood Ave CT19 ......178 E7
Wood Cottage La CT19 .177 D7
Wood Hill CT2 ....66 E6
Wood La TN23 ....156 C3
Wood Rd CT21 ......176 B1
Wood St Dover CT16 ..166 D8
Gillingham ME7 ....10 A6
Lynsted ME9 ....59 F8
Sheerness ME12 ....1 D2
Wood View CT3 ......46 E5
Wood Yd CT14 ......117 D6
Woodberry Dr ME10 ..37 C3
Woodberry Flats CT10 .30 A3
Woodbridge Dr ME15 ..74 F1
Woodbrook TN27 ....120 D7
Woodbury La TN30 ...179 A7
Woodbury Rd ME5 ....31 F1
Woodchurch CE Prim Sch
TN26 ....169 A2
Woodchurch Cl ME9 ..11 C2
Woodchurch Cres ME8 .11 C2
Woodchurch House ME8 11 C2
Woodchurch Rd
Appledore TN26 ......181 C4
Margate CT7,CT9 ....28 A5
Shadoxhurst TN26 .....155 A1
Tenterden TN30 ......179 D8
Westgate-on-S CT7 ....27 F3
Woodchurch Windmill
(dis)★ TN26 ....169 A3
Woodcock Gdns CT18 .163 A4
Woodcote CT5 ....21 D1
Woodcourt Cl ME10 ..36 E2
Woodcut ME14 ....75 A8
Woodfield Ave CT19 ..177 E7
Woodfield Cl CT17 ...177 E7
Woodford Ave CT11,CT12 .29 D1
Woodford Ct CT7 .....27 A7
Woodford Rd ME16 ...74 B2
Woodgate CT4 ....110 E3
Woodgate Cl ME13 ...62 C8
Woodgate Ct ME13 ...84 E7
Woodgate La ME9 .....35 C2
Woodhall Terr ME11 ...3 A5
Woodhurst ME5 ....31 D4
Woodland Ave
Aylesham CT3 ....112 E5
Birchington CT7 ......27 B6
Woodland Cl CT17 ...148 E2
Woodland Cotts CT18 .161 B7
Woodland Dr ME12 .....4 D7
Woodland Rd
Herne Bay CT6 ....22 B2
Lyminge CT18 ....160 E8
Woodland View TN30 .188 E4
Woodland Way
Broadstairs CT10 ......8 G1
Canterbury CT2 ....66 D4
Dymchurch TN29 ......187 A5

Woodland Way *continued*
Maidstone ME14 ......75 B7
Woodnesborough CT13 ..93 C6
Woodlands Blean CT2 ..65 F7
Chatham ME5 ....32 A2
Coxheath ME17 ....96 B3
Hernhill ME13 ....64 C7
Woodlands Cl ME14 ...75 B7
Woodlands Dr CT21 ..177 A4
Woodlands Prim Sch
ME7 ....10 F4
Woodlands Rd
Adisham CT3 ....112 C8
Ashford TN24 ....139 F2
Gillingham ME7 ......10 F4
Sittingbourne ME10 ...37 B3
Woodlawn St CT5 .....20 D2
Woodlea TN24 ....139 C3
Woodman Ave CT5 ....21 E3
Woodnesborough La
CT13 ....93 B3
Woodnesborough Rd
CT13 ....93 E7
Woodpecker Dr ME9 ..14 E4
Woodpecker Glade ME8 .33 D6
Woodrow Chase CT6 ..23 A1
Woodruff Cl ME8 .....12 D4
Woods Hill CT4 .....125 C5
Woods Ley CT3 ....71 D2
Woodshale Cotts ME9 ..14 D1
Woodside Ashford TN23 .155 E6
Boughton Street ME13 ..64 B2
Gillingham ME8 ....33 C6
Woodside Ave CT4 ....86 D2
Woodside Cl CT16 ...148 E4
Woodside Gdns ME10 ..36 D2
Woodside Rd
Maidstone ME15 ......97 C7
Sturry CT2 ....67 F7
Woodstock Rd
Deal CT14 ....117 C4
Rochester ME2 ....9 A7
Sittingbourne ME10 ...36 E1
Woodstock Way TN24 .139 C6
Woodvale Ave CT5 ....44 C8
Woodville Cl CT1 .....87 D6
Woodville Rd
Maidstone ME15 ......75 A2
Ramsgate CT12 ....29 C1
Woolaston Cl ME15 ...74 F1
Woolbrook Cl ME8 ....12 B2
Woolcomber St CT16 .166 E7
Wooldeys Rd ME8 ....11 F2
Woolett Rd ME10 ....36 C5
Woollets Cl CT6 .....22 C3
Woollett St ME14 ....75 A5
Woolley Rd ME15 ....97 F7
Woolmer Dr TN24 ...157 A7
Woolpack Hill TN25 .158 D5
Woolreeds Rd TN23 ..156 A7
Woolwich Cl ME5 ....32 A7
Wootton Cl CT4 .....109 A4
Wootton Dr CT4 ....109 A4
Wootton Gn ME8 .....11 D3
Wootton La CT15,CT4 .146 C7
Wopsle Cl ME1 ......31 D7
Worcester Cl
Faversham ME13 ....62 E6
Minster (Sheppey) ME12 .4 C6
Worcester Dr ME10 ..36 D6
Worcester Gr CT10 ..29 F6
Worcester La CT3 ....88 E7
Worcester Rd ME15 ..97 D7
Wordsworth Cl ME5 ..32 C7
Wordsworth Gdns CT3 .112 F6

Wordsworth Rd ME14 ..75 B7
Workhouse La ME15 ..96 C5
Workhouse Rd
Kingswood ME17 ....99 A1
Throwley ME13 ....82 F1
World's End ME9 .....60 E7
Wormdale Hill ME9 ...35 B3
Wormdale Rd ME9 ....35 B4
Worsfold Ct ME15 ....75 A1
Worth La CT20 ......177 E3
Worth Prim Sch CT14 .94 B5
Worthgate Pl 2 CT1 ..87 F7
Worthington St 11 CT16,
CT17 ....166 D8
Wotton Cl ME15 .....97 E5
Wotton Rd TN23 ....156 B6
Wotton Trad Est TN23 .156 B6
Wraightsfield Ave TN29 195 D8
Wraik Hill CT5 ....43 C5
Wrangleden Cl ME15 ..97 E5
Wrangleden Rd ME15 ..97 E5
Wreight Ct ME13 .....40 B1
Wren Ind Est ME15 ...97 F4
Wren Way ME5 ....32 B6
Wrens Ct ME9 ....58 A8
Wrens Rd ME9 ....58 A7
Wrentham Ave CT6 ...22 B2
Wright Cl ME8 ......11 C2
Wright's Way ME12 ...17 C8
Wrights Cl TN30 .....11 A8
Wrotham Ave 19 CT10 ..30 B4
Wrotham Rd CT10 ....30 B4
Wyatt Ho 1 ME2 ......9 A7
Wyatt Pl ME2 ....9 A7
Wyatt St ME14 ....75 A4
Wych Elm Way CT21 .187 E8
Wycherley Cres CT16 .149 B4
Wye Coll (Univ
of London) TN25 .....123 F2
Wye Downs National
Nature Reserve★ TN25 141 D7
Wye Gdns CT9 ....8 F2
Wye Rd TN25 ....122 F3
Wye Sta TN25 ....123 D2
Wye Valley Agricultural
Mus★ TN25 ....141 B5
Wyke Manor Rd ME14 .75 A4
Wykeham Cl ME11 .....2 F3
Wykeham Cotts ME17 ..96 F2
Wykeham Gr ME17 ....99 A7
Wykeham Rd ME10 ...37 B4
Wykeham St ME2 .....9 B8
Wyles Rd ME4 ....9 E2
Wyles St ME7 ....10 C7
Wyllie Ct ME10 ......36 E7
Wynd The TN27 .....103 D1
Wyndam Rd ME4 ......9 E2
Wyndham Ave CT9 .....8 B2
Wyndham Rd CT10 ...166 B8
Wynn Ellis Ho CT5 ...20 E3
Wynn Rd CT5 ....21 A2
Wytchlings The ME17 ..99 D2
Wytherling Cl ME14 ..75 F5
Wyvern Cl ME10 .....36 E7
Wyvern Way TN24 ...139 E3
Wyvill Cl ME8 ....33 D7

Y

Yard The CT4 ....111 F1
Yardhurst Gdns CT9 ...8 F3
Yardley Ho CT10 ....30 B7
Yarrow Cl CT10 ......30 A3
Yarrow Ct ME14 .....75 F5

Yarrow Rd ME5 ......31 F4
Yates Cl TN31 ......201 A2
Yaugher La ME9 .....34 C3
Yeates Dr ME10 .....37 A8
Yellow Sands ME12 ...19 E5
Yelsted ME9 ....34 A1
Yelsted La Chatham ME14 .54 D7
Yelsted Rd ME9 .....56 A7
Yeoman Ct ME14 ....76 B3
Yeoman Dr ME7 .....10 F1
Yeoman Gdns TN24 ..157 B8
Yeoman Ho ME1 ....9 D4
Yeoman La ME14 ....76 B4
Yeoman Pk ME15 ....76 A2
Yeoman Way ME15 ...76 A2
Yeomans Sq TN23 ...155 D8
Yevele Cl ME11 ....3 A5
Yew Cl TN23 ....138 E2
Yew Tree Cl
Broadstairs CT10 .....29 D4
Chatham ME5 ....32 D1
Deal CT14 ....117 A4
Stanford TN25 ....160 B1
Yew Tree Cotts ME14 ..53 F1
Yew Tree Farm CT3 ..114 A8
Yew Tree Gdns
Birchington CT7 ......27 A7
Fordwich CT2 ....68 A4
Yew Tree Mews CT14 .117 A3
Yew Tree Pl ME7 .....33 B1
Yew Tree Rd TN29 ...194 F3
Yewhedges ME13 ....81 E4
Yewtree Cross CT18 .161 C8
Yoakes La TN29 .....192 F1
Yoakley Sq CT9 ......28 F8
Yoke Cl ME2 ....9 B8
York & Albany Cl CT14 .117 B1
York Ave
17 Broadstairs CT10 ...30 B4
Chatham ME5 ....31 F3
Gillingham ME7 ......10 C4
York Cl CT6 ....22 D4
York Hill ME5 ....10 C2
York Ho 10 CT17 ....166 D7
York Mews CT19 ....177 E2
York Rd Ashford TN24 .139 D5
Canterbury CT1 ....87 E7
Deal CT14 ....117 D4
Herne Bay CT6 ....22 D5
Maidstone ME15 ......75 C2
Rochester ME1 ....9 C3
York St Broadstairs CT10 .30 B4
Dover CT16,CT17 .....166 D7
Ramsgate CT12 ....52 E6
York Street Rdbt CT16,
CT17 ....166 D7
York Terr CT7 ....27 B7
Young Cl CT14 .....117 B6
Young's Pl CT15 ....164 F5
Ypres Ct CT1 ....67 D1
Ypres Dr ME10 ......14 F1

Z

Zarena Ct 8 CT20 ...177 F3
Zealand Rd CT1 ......87 F6
Zetland Ave ME7 ....10 E2
Zillah Gdns ME8 .....33 C6
Zion Pl CT9 ....7 J3

Street Atlases from Philip's

Philip's publish an extensive range of regional and local street atlases which are ideal for motoring, business and leisure use. They are widely used by the emergency services and local authorities throughout Britain.

Key features include:

◆ Superb county-wide mapping at an extra-large scale of 3½ inches to 1 mile, or 2½ inches to 1 mile in pocket editions

◆ Complete urban and rural coverage, detailing every named street in town and country

◆ Each atlas available in two handy sizes – standard spiral and pocket paperback

'The mapping is very clear... great in scope and value'
★★★★ BEST BUY   AUTO EXPRESS

1 Anglesey, Conwy and Gwynedd
2 Bedfordshire
3 Berkshire
4 Birmingham and West Midlands
5 Bristol and Bath
6 Buckinghamshire
7 Cambridgeshire
8 Cardiff, Swansea and The Valleys
9 Cheshire
10 Cornwall
11 Cumbria
12 Denbighshire, Flintshire and Wrexham
13 Derbyshire
14 Devon
15 Dorset
16 County Durham and Teesside
17 Edinburgh and East Central Scotland
18 Essex
19 North Essex
20 South Essex
21 Fife and Tayside
22 Glasgow and West Central Scotland
23 Gloucestershire
24 North Hampshire
25 South Hampshire
26 Herefordshire and Monmouthshire
27 Hertfordshire
28 East Kent
29 West Kent
30 Lancashire
31 Leicestershire and Rutland
32 Lincolnshire
33 London
34 Greater Manchester
35 Merseyside
36 Norfolk
37 Northamptonshire
38 Nottinghamshire
39 Oxfordshire
40 Shropshire
41 Somerset
42 Staffordshire
43 Suffolk
44 Surrey
45 East Sussex
46 West Sussex
47 Tyne and Wear and Northumberland
48 Warwickshire
49 Wiltshire and Swindon
50 Worcestershire
51 East Yorkshire and Northern Lincolnshire
52 North Yorkshire
53 South Yorkshire
54 West Yorkshire

How to order

The Philip's range of street atlases is available from good retailers or directly from the publisher by phoning 01903 828503

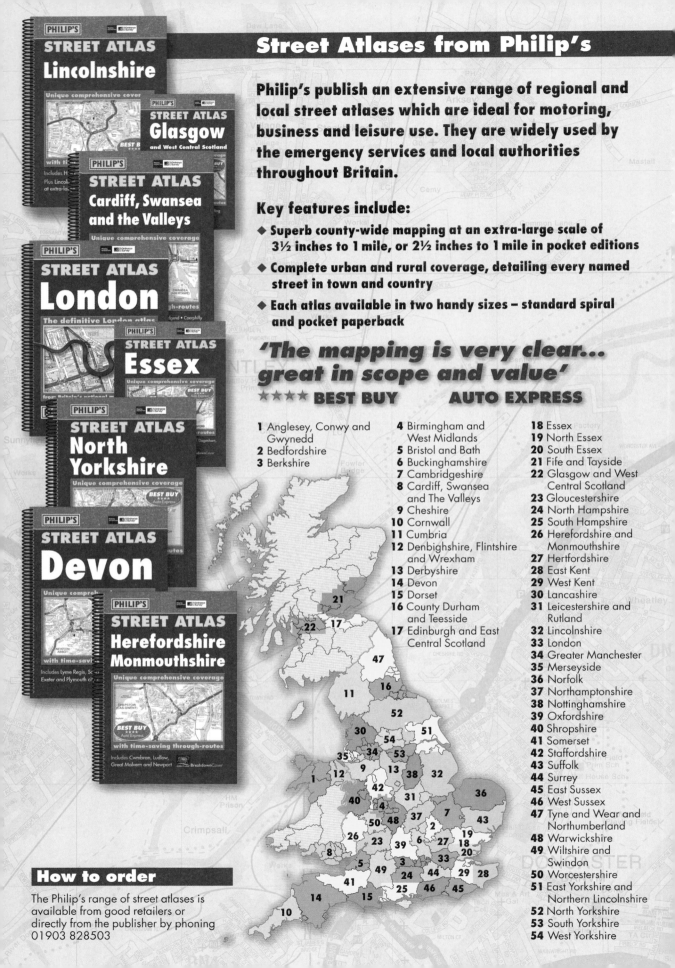